PRAISE FOR

THE MARSHALL PLAN

"Brilliant . . . Mr. Steil's is by far the best study yet, because it is so wise and so balanced in its judgments. . . . The maturity and surety of Mr. Steil's book is nowhere more in evidence than in his final chapter. . . . The book has an invaluable 'Cast of Characters,' a daunting bibliography and a huge 74 pages of notes. It's quite a tribute that it all reads so well."

—Paul Kennedy, *The Wall Street Journal*

"Trenchant and timely . . . Steil has written an ambitious, deeply researched narrative that not only delineates the interlocking gears of international politics and economics in early post-war Europe but also introduces a large cast of statesmen, spies and economists that perhaps only Dickens could have corralled with ease. . . . The book builds intellectual excitement as the characters act and react to one another. . . . Steil's focus on the debate over the future of Europe's economy provides a fresh perspective on the coming Cold War."

—*The New York Times Book Review*

"*The Marshall Plan* is elegant in style and impressive in insights. Steil, director of international economics at the Council on Foreign Relations, has an enviable gift for presenting complex economic and geopolitical issues in crisp, readable prose."

—*Financial Times*

"Big, serious, and thoroughly intelligent . . . Steil embeds [the Marshall Plan] in a sharp and critical political history of the first years of the cold war itself. In his final chapters, he looks far beyond the period of the Marshall Plan and discusses parallels and contrasts with the twenty-first century scene."

—Neal Ascherson, *The New York Review of Books*

"This is a gripping, complex, and critically important story that is told with clarity and precision. The book is superbly documented and reflects an extraordinary level of research."

—Terry Hartle, The Christian Science Monitor

"It may be hard to imagine someone hurrying home to curl up with a work of political history, but Benn Steil's fascinating new book, *The Marshall Plan: Dawn of the Cold War* (Simon & Schuster, four stars out of four), could change that."

—USA Today

"Even readers who consider themselves well-versed on what became the Marshall Plan will be gripped by the details in Benn Steil's retelling of just how Mr. Truman's idea became reality. . . . Mr. Steil, an economist for the Council on Foreign Relations, is at his narrative best in recounting how the program was put together."

—The Washington Times

"An excellent new book . . . Steil's account picks its way through [the] arguments and counter-arguments with a quiet skill . . . Steil's mastery of both the sources and the narrative is exemplary."

—The Telegraph

"Steil has a gift for historical narrative."

—The Washington Free Beacon

"Steil's superb narrative combines diplomatic, economic and political history with descriptions of such episodes as the Berlin Airlift, along with vivid portraits of the diverse primary personalities. . . . Compelling, authoritative and lucid . . . This dramatic and engaging account of one of the most complex but enduring achievements of American foreign policy deserves a wide readership."

—*BookPage*

"A fresh perspective on the Marshall Plan . . . Though scholars have covered the subject many times before, general readers will do well to choose this lively, astute account. . . . Steil writes a vivid, opinionated narrative full of colorful characters, dramatic scenarios, villains, and genuine heroes, and the good guys won. It will be the definitive account for years to come."

—*Kirkus Reviews* (starred review)

"Benn Steil has made clarifying complex subjects a specialty: first with his well-received *The Battle of Bretton Woods*, and now with this comprehensive history of the Marshall Plan. Drawing on an equally keen grasp of diplomacy, economics, and grand strategy, Steil sets a new standard for our understanding, not just of the Cold War, but also of the post–Cold War era, in which the future of Europe and the role of the United States in it are once again at stake. An outstanding—and certainly timely—accomplishment."

—John Lewis Gaddis, Robert A. Lovett
Professor of Military and Naval History, Yale University

THE

MARSHALL PLAN

DAWN OF THE COLD WAR

BENN STEIL

SIMON & SCHUSTER PAPERBACKS

NEW YORK   LONDON   TORONTO   SYDNEY   NEW DELHI

A Council on Foreign Relations Book

Simon & Schuster Paperbacks
An Imprint of Simon & Schuster, Inc.
1230 Avenue of the Americas
New York, NY 10020

First Simon & Schuster trade paperback edition February 2019

SIMON & SCHUSTER PAPERBACKS and colophon are registered trademarks of Simon & Schuster, Inc.

For information about special discounts for bulk purchases, please contact
Simon & Schuster Special Sales at 1-866-506-1949 or business@simonandschuster.com.

The Simon & Schuster Speakers Bureau can bring authors to your live event.
For more information or to book an event, contact the Simon & Schuster Speakers Bureau
at 1-866-248-3049 or visit our website at www.simonspeakers.com.

Interior design by Ruth Lee-Mui

Manufactured in the United States of America

10   9   8   7   6   5   4   3   2   1

Library of Congress Cataloging-in-Publication Data is available.

ISBN 978-1-5011-0237-0
ISBN 978-1-5011-0238-7 (pbk)
ISBN 978-1-5011-0239-4 (ebook)

The Council on Foreign Relations (CFR) is an independent, nonpartisan membership organization,
think tank, and publisher dedicated to being a resource for its members, government officials, business
executives, journalists, educators and students, civic and religious leaders, and other interested citizens in
order to help them better understand the world and the foreign policy choices facing the United States and
other countries. Founded in 1921, CFR carries out its mission by maintaining a diverse membership, with
special programs to promote interest and develop expertise in the next generation of foreign policy leaders;
convening meetings at its headquarters in New York and in Washington, DC, and other cities where senior
government officials, members of Congress, global leaders, and prominent thinkers come together with
CFR members to discuss and debate major international issues; supporting a Studies Program that fosters
independent research, enabling CFR scholars to produce articles, reports, and books and hold roundtables
that analyze foreign policy issues and make concrete policy recommendations; publishing *Foreign Affairs*,
the preeminent journal on international affairs and U.S. foreign policy; sponsoring Independent Task
Forces that produce reports with both findings and policy prescriptions on the most important foreign
policy topics; and providing up-to-date information and analysis about world events and American foreign
policy on its website, www.cfr.org.

The Council on Foreign Relations takes no institutional positions on policy issues and has no affiliation
with the U.S. government. All views expressed in its publications and on its website are the sole
responsibility of the author or authors.

For my precious

MOM *and* DAD,

and

GLORIA, ETHAN, *and* OWEN

CONTENTS

FOREWORD

IN 1944, FRANKLIN D. ROOSEVELT SET OUT TO FORGE A NEW, COOPERATIVE postwar order. In it, the Soviet Union would, he believed, become a major power with its own peculiar interests. Yet it would be shepherded by a new United Nations and International Monetary Fund into collaboration with an agenda conducive to American security and prosperity—an agenda founded on free trade and respect for the independence of weaker neighbors.

Not long after Roosevelt's death in April 1945, however, it became clear that Joseph Stalin had an agenda all his own, and that he was not going to play by American rules. Just before New Year's Day 1946, at the deadline for ratification of the IMF agreement, he pulled out. He had, in fact, never intended to adapt Soviet policies to the requirements of membership. He had simply sought two benefits from cooperation in creating the new body. The first was a return by others to a monetary system that would boost the value of Soviet gold stocks. He got that, with no need to participate. The second was more unconditional U.S. financial aid for his country, as it had received during the war.

When it became clear that none was forthcoming, he lost interest. As for the United Nations, the United States granted his priority demand: a veto on the Security Council. With it, he saw Soviet membership as no bar to extending his frontiers—which he set out to do in 1946.

Meanwhile, America's natural allies in western Europe looked to be teetering on the edge of economic, social, and political collapse. The U.N. and IMF, which had been founded to maintain peace and stability rather than manufacture it, were powerless to reverse this slide. In 1947, therefore, President Harry S. Truman's State Department, now under the leadership of General George C. Marshall, disowned FDR's "One World" vision. Under formidable time constraints, they set out to formulate a new economic and security architecture appropriate to a Europe divided into Two Worlds: a capitalist and a communist one.

This book situates the Marshall Plan more directly at the center of the emerging Cold War than earlier accounts, highlighting the seriousness with which Stalin treated the threat it represented to his new, hard-won buffer zone in central and eastern Europe. The Soviet leader's blueprint for postwar Europe assumed the Americans would withdraw, leaving behind a weak, pastoralized Germany, ongoing reparations from which would fund Soviet reconstruction and development. The Marshall Plan, however, promised a continuing energetic U.S. presence, underwritten by a reindustrialized capitalist western Germany at the heart of an integrated, capitalist western Europe. Many of the most dramatic episodes of the early Cold War, such as the Prague coup and the Berlin blockade, were driven by Stalin's determination to undermine the Marshall Plan and American influence in Europe broadly. On the flip side, Washington's support for a new transatlantic military alliance represented a reluctant acknowledgment that economic security would not take hold in western Europe without physical security.

Institutions that were outgrowths of the Marshall Plan, in particular the European Union and NATO, remain important elements of the postwar liberal international order—even as they are subjected to more critical scrutiny than at any time since their founding. In showing how the Plan evolved, I have brought to bear new material from American, Russian, German, and Czech sources that I hope will make an important story even more resonant. And given the enduring passion for creating new "Marshall Plans" to solve the world's problems, the story of the old, original one is, I believe, a story well worth telling.

THE MARSHALL PLAN

American, British, and Soviet leaders gather at Potsdam to discuss the future of Germany and postwar Europe, July 17, 1945. Foreground: British Foreign Secretary Anthony Eden (*left*) and Permanent Undersecretary of State for Foreign Affairs Alexander Cadogan (*right*). Background: Soviet leader Joseph Stalin (*center*) and Foreign Minister Vyacheslav Molotov (*left*).

ONE

PROLOGUE

THE GREATEST ACT OF GEORGE WASHINGTON'S PRESIDENCY WAS HIS
leaving of it. Having defeated the world's most powerful nation in war, the
celebrated general could have led his country like a European monarch—till
his death. Yet determined to set the United States apart from the political
order of the mother continent, he refused to serve a third four-year term. In
a farewell address on September 19, 1796, he urged his countrymen "to steer
clear of permanent alliances with any portion of the foreign world," above all
Europe. "Europe," he said, "has a set of primary interests which to us have . . .
a very remote relation. Hence she must be engaged in frequent controver-
sies . . . foreign to our concerns." It was therefore "unwise . . . to implicate ourselves" in the "combinations and collisions of her friendships or enmities."[1]
Generations of American statesmen would recall his warning with reverence
and, at times, foreboding.

Yet a century and a half later, in 1945, the reflections of America's first
president seemed idyllic. The United States had just fought two world wars in

the space of thirty years, at a cost of 522,000 American lives, both of which had been started four thousand miles from its shores. When Germany surrendered on May 7, 3,077,000 American troops were in Europe.

After the First World War ended in 1918, there took root in the United States a deep-seated popular desire to disengage from Europe—to re-embrace Washington's injunction. This sentiment has been called, simply, "isolationism," but it encompassed many strains. In the 1930s it included pacifists, pro-Communists, and pro-Fascists; it included those sympathetic to Germany and those who believed French and British resistance hopeless. In 1939, less than 3 percent of the American public supported the United States entering the latest European conflagration on the side of France and Britain; 30 percent were against even trading with any warring country.[2] A series of Neutrality Acts, enacted to keep the United States from becoming entangled with warring nations on either side, channeled such sentiment. Legislation in 1935 instituted an embargo on trading in arms and other war materials. The following year Congress added a ban on loans or credits to belligerents, reflecting the findings of the so-called Nye Committee, which held that bankers had pushed the nation into the previous European catastrophe.

It took a devastating Japanese attack on the U.S. Pacific Fleet at Pearl Harbor in December 1941 to rupture this powerful inertia. The United States returned to war, both in Asia and in Europe, this time with the conviction in the White House that structures had to be put in place to prevent future conflict. There would be a United Nations with a muscular Security Council to prevent military aggression, and an International Monetary Fund (IMF) and International Trade Organization (ITO) to prevent what Treasury Secretary Henry Morgenthau called "economic aggression." Pressure would be placed on the country's ally of choice, Great Britain, to dismantle its imperial institutions, which were a moral and practical affront to this vision. Awkward accommodations would be made to its new and much stronger ally of necessity, the Soviet Union, to secure its cooperation. In concert with a liberated China, President Franklin D. Roosevelt's "Four Policemen" would oversee their respective quadrants of the globe, a stratagem that uncomfortably blended Wilsonian internationalism with Monroevian spheres of influence.

Roosevelt had publicly declared his hopes for "a peace loving" Soviet

Union "shattered" after its brutal and unprovoked invasion of Finland in November 1939, motivated partly by Stalin's fear that Germany or Britain might use the country as a base to attack Leningrad. FDR condemned Stalin's government as "a dictatorship as absolute as any other in the world."[3] Yet he remained acutely aware that George Washington's apprehensions on European entanglement had never left his nation's psyche. Certain that the American public would not tolerate a lengthy European occupation, Roosevelt was determined to withdraw troops from Europe quickly after Germany's surrender—within two years. This priority drove his steadfast efforts to cooperate with Stalin, despite his harboring none of the romantic illusions about Communist authoritarianism held by some in his administration. But it also explains the constant tension between the White House and the State Department, including diplomatic staff in Moscow, who found the president's unwillingness to confront the Kremlin an ominous sign for the postwar landscape—one in which Stalin would be free to impose his will on Soviet-occupied territories.

British prime minister Winston Churchill shared these fears, particularly as regards Poland—a country he saw as a barrier to Soviet westward expansion, much as Stalin saw it as a barrier to Western encroachment.[4] But FDR never bought into Churchill's vision of Britain and America marching forward shoulder to shoulder into the postwar era. "The President shared a widespread American suspicion of the British Empire as it had once been," noted Foreign Secretary Anthony Eden. And he had "no fear that other powers," besides the United States, "might fill that role" after the war.[5] Yet by 1947, such fear would concentrate minds in the State Department and Pentagon.

The Big Three wartime conference at Yalta in February 1945 was Roosevelt's last face-to-face meeting with Stalin, a final chance to reconcile clashing interests over the shape of postwar Europe before the advancement of Soviet, American, and British troops settled matters on the ground. Washington and Moscow having nothing more in common than a soon-to-be-vanquished Nazi enemy (with whom Stalin connived from 1939 to 1941), the prospect for genuine agreement seemed remote. Conscious that a war-weary American public constrained his military and political leverage, the president had to rely on charms more than arms to persuade Stalin to permit genuine political independence in the East. Yet determined to secure Soviet membership in the new United Nations and entry into the war against Japan, he was willing to trade away much in Europe—not least Polish democracy and war reparations from the Western occupation zones of Germany—to get them. And what wiles he used in his cajoling were largely undermined by the ubiquity of Soviet listening devices in the American residence and directional microphones outside it.[6] Given later Soviet behavior in the U.N. and imminent U.S. nuclear arms developments, Roosevelt would overpay for Stalin's concessions.

Stalin also relied on charm, to evade commitments on territory the Red Army would soon control. "Don't worry," he told his alarmed foreign minister, Vyacheslav Molotov, after reading an American draft of the Declaration of Liberated Europe. "We can deal with it in our own way later. The point is the correlation of forces."[7] As for relations with the United States, which was bound to interpret the Yalta agreements differently, he was equally unconcerned. "The best friendships," he offered, "are those founded on misunderstandings."[8]

Indeed, "there was hope, as we left Yalta," State Department Sovietologist Charles (Chip) Bohlen recalled, "of genuine cooperation with the Soviet Union on political questions after the war."[9] A "spirit of Yalta," the press declared, was guiding the wartime allies.[10] Yet problems under the surface bubbled up almost immediately. In late March 1945, furious at Moscow's undermining of Polish independence and treatment of American prisoners of war (which was not terrible by Soviet standards) in territory liberated by the Red Army, Roosevelt banged his wheelchair: "We can't do business with Stalin. He has broken every one of his promises he made at Yalta."[11] By 1947, in both the United States and much of Europe, Yalta would become "a synonym for betrayal of freedom and the appeasement of world communism."[12] There would be consequences.

ROOSEVELT'S SUDDEN DEATH IN APRIL 1945 SHOCKED AND DISTRESSED Stalin. Instinctively suspicious, he suspected foul play. His intelligence reports told him anti-Soviet hard-liners were gaining ground in Washington.[13]

Yet the president's passing brought to power a man unprepared for the job, possessed of no desire or capacity to refashion the postwar foreign and security policy blueprint passed down to him.

"Who the hell is Harry Truman?" asked FDR's incredulous chief of staff, Admiral William Leahy, nine months earlier, after learning that the 1944 Democratic convention had chosen him as the president's running mate.[14] Upon ascending to the White House, Truman refused even to discuss Churchill's pleadings that General George Patton advance on Berlin to create bargaining leverage with Stalin—so committed was he to staying on the cooperative path laid out by Roosevelt.

The diplomatic demeanor of the two presidents, however, was very different. Though FDR had privately been no less critical of Soviet behavior than Truman,[15] and Truman no less desirous of good relations with Moscow than FDR, Truman rarely masked his frustrations the way FDR did. In his first meeting with Molotov in Washington on April 23, the new president gave the Russian a tongue-lashing over the creeping Sovietization of Poland. When the latter protested that he had "never been talked to" that way "in [his] life," Truman doubled down: "Carry out your agreements," he recalled responding, "and you won't get talked to like that."[16]

Molotov took Truman's tone as clear evidence that American policy had taken a hard right turn. Stalin, for his part, had always expected the worst from Truman. As a senator in 1941, Truman had, just after Hitler invaded the Soviet Union, casually told a *New York Times* reporter that "if we see that Germany is winning we ought to help Russia, and if Russia is winning we ought to help Germany, and that way let them kill as many as possible."[17] Indeed, for every American who would die in the war thirteen Germans and *seventy Russians* would perish. And once the war was won, at enormous cost to the Soviet military, civilian population, and infrastructure, Truman as president would infuriate Stalin by terminating Lend-Lease matériel assistance. In talks with Truman's liaison Harry Hopkins, Stalin condemned the aid cut as a "brutal" act against an ally. Truman repented of the bungle and resumed supply flows, but Stalin took his behavior as a sure sign of hostile intent.

Yet in early July 1945, still navigating foreign affairs without a compass, Truman was confident he would soon set matters straight with Stalin, face-to-face.

The president boarded the USS *Augusta*, en route to Europe for the third and final of the Big Three wartime conferences, in a decidedly optimistic frame of mind. He was determined to bring Europe "ninety years of peace." The Russians have "always been our friends," he wrote in his diary on July 7. "And I can't see any reason why they shouldn't always be."[18]

Two weeks with Stalin and Molotov, however, changed his perspective. "You never saw such pig-headed people as the Russians," he would write to his mother on July 31. "I hope I never have to hold another conference with them."[19]

What had gone wrong?

When the president arrived in Potsdam, Germany, he and his new secretary of state, James (Jimmy) Byrnes, were determined to put disputes over Polish independence behind them[20] and to forge agreement with Stalin on more pressing matters. They remained committed to pushing forward with Roosevelt's priorities at Yalta: early Soviet entry into the war against Japan, and participation in the new United Nations. Yet they could no longer indulge Henry Morgenthau's vision of a pastoralized postwar Germany—the "Morgenthau Plan"—the way FDR had. With Germany's surrender in May, the priority was now to stabilize it—not to uproot its industry and watch it descend into starvation and unrest. Germany needed food. Europe needed coal. Coal needed to be mined and moved. This meant repairing Germany's industrial apparatus and transport links. Economic castration no longer seemed such a bright idea.

Stalin had little problem giving Truman a commitment to declare war on Japan by mid-August: it would give the Soviet Union a basis for recuperating territorial losses from the disastrous 1904–05 Russo-Japanese War. Pledging that the Soviet Union would join the United Nations (which it did in October), with veto power in the Security Council, also gave him negotiating leverage over unfinished matters in the postwar settlement. But Truman's German agenda collided head-on with his own.

At Yalta, Stalin had demanded $20 billion in German war reparations, half of which for Russia. Roosevelt had neither blanched nor acceded, preferring not to commit to a figure. Byrnes, however, took a harder line. Determined not to repeat the mistakes of the post–World War I settlement, through which the United States inadvertently ended up giving Germany the funds with which it paid the French and British, he insisted that reparations from current production in the Allied (western-occupied) zones could only be paid to Russia *after* covering the cost of keeping Germans and their coal industry alive. Stalin, uninterested in how Germans subsisted or mined coal, dismissed Byrnes' formulation. This stalemate crossed all major issues, infuriating Truman.

Yet on July 31, just after Truman had penned the angry letter to his mother, Byrnes, an accomplished political bargainer, triumphantly sold Stalin on a "package deal, take it or leave it."[21] However morally abhorrent Truman found the terms, he agreed to let Stalin take German territory for Poland and offered conditional recognition for Soviet-backed regimes in Romania, Hungary, and Bulgaria. In return, Stalin agreed to depart without a guaranteed dollar figure for reparations—with the caveat that the Allied zones would deliver 15 percent of their "usable and complete" capital equipment to the Soviet zone in return for East German food, coal, and other natural resources.[22]

Relieved he had managed to preserve the cooperative relationship Roosevelt had established with Stalin, Truman was still unnerved by the price. During the difficult negotiations on Germany, Stalin kept referring to dividing "everything" according to whether it was to the east or the west of the Soviet-Allied occupation line. Truman suspected he was not just speaking of Germany. Did Stalin mean "a line running from the Baltic to the Adriatic?" he asked the Soviet leader. Indeed, Stalin confirmed matter-of-factly, adding that Finland and eastern Austria should also be within the Soviet zone.[23] Truman had never imagined himself coming to Potsdam to carve Europe into spheres of influence, but faced with the alternative of returning home empty-handed he raised no objections.

The new British prime minister, Clement Attlee, called the Potsdam agreement "an important milestone."[24] But millstone might have been more accurate. Despite the agreement, Stalin and Truman would continue to appeal to Yalta in claiming the other was failing to meet his commitments. Moscow would insist that the Allied zones of Germany owed far greater reparations, Washington that the economy of the eastern zone was being improperly Sovietized. The institutions set up to draft peace treaties with the former enemy countries and to oversee the German occupation—the Council of Foreign Ministers and the Allied Control Council—would soon begin to collapse under the weight of unresolvable differences over Germany. In 1947 these would spill over onto the rest of the continent, with Truman convinced that the Russians were bent on sabotaging democracy in the West, and Stalin that the Americans were using economic stratagems to undermine pro-Soviet governments in the East.

❖

ROOSEVELT HAD LARGELY BEEN HIS OWN SECRETARY OF STATE. HIS RELA-tions with the longtime official holder of the position, Cordell Hull, had deteriorated to the point of open hostility by the time the latter resigned in November 1944. To the extent that others had power over foreign policy, it tended be in the economic sphere—about which FDR cared little. Henry Morgenthau, his old Hyde Park neighbor who, with little knowledge of economics or foreign affairs, had run the Treasury since 1934, used his platform and access to great effect. Not having policy ideas of his own so much as instincts, Morgenthau relied on his ambitious, obliquitous deputy, Harry Dexter White, to give them form and substance.

White, one of the most enigmatic American political figures of the twentieth century, boosted Treasury's global influence through his mastery of the forty-four-nation Bretton Woods Conference, which created the IMF in 1944, and the war-aid terms imposed on the penurious British. Yet like Henry Wallace—who would tap him as a future treasury secretary during his 1948 presidential campaign—White was also a great admirer of the Soviet Union and its economic system. He would, over the course of twelve years in Washington, to a much greater degree than Wallace, use his position to aid Moscow materially and with secret intelligence.[25] He would also give substance to the so-called Morgenthau Plan to deindustrialize postwar Germany—effectively to render the country pastoral and infirm. Together with the dismantling of Britain's empire under Washington's approving gaze, the Morgenthau Plan became a pillar of Stalin's expectations that he would be able to control a buffer of central and eastern European nations without interference from an indifferent United States and a weak and divided western Europe.

Yet Truman, who considered Morgenthau a "blockhead," and opposed his meddling in German affairs, forced him to resign before leaving for Europe in July. This marginalized White, who would die of a heart attack three years later, right after defending himself against espionage charges (many later substantiated) before the House Un-American Affairs Committee.[26] Treasury would become a backwater under Truman, while the State Department would not only regain full authority over traditional foreign affairs but come to arrogate power over foreign economic policy as well. By the time General George C. Marshall became secretary of state in January 1947, men of a very different political and intellectual disposition—such as Dean Acheson, George Kennan, Will Clayton, General Lucius Clay, and Republican senator Arthur Vandenberg—were in position to reshape policy on many fronts, to enormous consequence.

After Potsdam, Truman would continue to reach out to Stalin periodically for political purposes, to show the war-weary American electorate he was dedicated to peace, but the new president was far more inclined than FDR to let his foreign-policy team craft and conduct policy. Direct presidential contact with foreign leaders diminished; the control of cable contact was returned to the State Department.[27] And the diplomats and experts were less willing to ignore Russian history and behavior. "Never . . . did I consider the Soviet Union a fit ally or associate," Kennan would later reflect.[28]

Of course, hard political substance, and not just personnel changes, poisoned relations between Moscow and Washington in 1945, and it is far from clear that Roosevelt would have been more able or willing than Truman to assuage Stalin. Not least on the list of matters that troubled the Soviet leader at Potsdam was Truman's oblique revelation of America's powerful new weapon. Though Stalin had been well informed about the atom bomb project through his American spy network, the demonstration of its destructive power in Japan two weeks later still staggered him. Whatever the president's true disposition toward his country, Stalin knew the United States now had the capacity to devastate it in an instant.

"Hiroshima has shaken the world," Stalin told his weapons team. "The balance has been broken. Build the bomb—it will remove a great danger from us."[29]

Stalin was convinced the Americans would try to use their atomic monopoly "to force us to accept their plans on questions affecting Europe and the world." But "that is not going to happen," he told Andrei Gromyko, his ambassador in Washington.[30] All future meetings of the Council of Foreign Ministers, through which the Soviet Union, the United States, Britain, and France had pledged to coordinate postwar policy in Europe, would be poisoned by these fears and suspicions. Stalin directed Molotov to reject concessions to the West on the political organization of the new Soviet "satellites," as he himself called them, in southeast Europe. Most importantly for the future of the continent, Stalin refused all Western proposals for occupied Germany that involved Soviet troop withdrawals in the east.[31] And at the end of 1945, just at the deadline for forty-four nations to ratify the Bretton Woods agreement, the Soviets announced that they were staying out. This struck a major blow to FDR's "One World" vision.

In the course of four weeks in early 1946, Stalin, Kennan, and Churchill would issue what would become rallying cries of the "Cold War"—a term George Orwell had coined in 1945 to describe the dystopian "permanent state" of hostility emerging between the United States and the Soviet Union.[32] On February 9, Stalin gave an address at the Bolshoi Theater condemning world capitalism and its political face, imperialism, as the engines of world war. Two weeks later, Kennan sent his famous "Long Telegram" from Moscow, arguing that the Soviet Communist government was inherently expansionist, "impervious to logic of reason," and responsive only to "the logic of force." And two weeks after that, Churchill gave his historic "iron curtain" speech in Fulton, Missouri, warning of the dangers of "communist fifth columns" operating in western and southern Europe. All three circulated widely in the capitals of North America and Europe, helping to solidify the growing sense that conflict between East and West was inevitable. The only question was the form it would take.

For Stalin, 1946 was a year of probing. The Soviet empire's western flank was now strong, with its forces occupying or looming over all of eastern and central Europe. But its southern flank was still vulnerable—as it had been during the Crimean War of 1853–56 and two world wars. Turkey and Iran loomed as potential U.S.-backed adversaries. With Britain headed toward bankruptcy, and imperial retrenchment looking inevitable, this might be a window to secure borders, acquire oil reserves, dominate critical parts of the Mediterranean and Middle East, and transform his empire into a maritime power. What he needed to know was how far the United States would go to stop him.

⁕⁕⁕

THE MID-1940S REPRESENTED THE APEX OF TWENTIETH-CENTURY AMERI-can economic diplomacy. The 1944 Bretton Woods initiative championed by FDR's Treasury was grounded in the belief, born of the Depression and World War II, that economic instability led to currency wars, trade wars, and ultimately military wars. Using the tools of the new science of macroeconomics, Treasury believed, governments could end the plague of economic slumps and thereby sustain a cooperative global ban on competitive devaluations—a monetary form of "economic aggression." But the scheme took as its starting point political stability, something lacking in the chaotic aftermath of the war.

In response to the rising threat of a new security vacuum in Europe, Truman's State Department effectively mothballed the newly born IMF, dismissing disdainfully the assumptions Morgenthau and White had made to justify their faith in it—that Soviet cooperation would continue into the postwar period; that Germany's economic collapse could be safely, and indeed profitably, managed; that the British empire could be peaceably dismantled; and that modest balance-of-payments credit support was sufficient to reestablish global trade. These had been based on "misconceptions of the state of the world around us," future secretary of state Dean Acheson reflected, "both in anticipating postwar conditions and in recognizing what they actually were when we came face to face with them. . . . Only slowly did it dawn upon us that the whole world structure and order that we had inherited from the nineteenth century was gone and that the struggle to replace it would be directed from two bitterly opposed and ideologically irreconcilable power centers."[33]

Bohlen concurred. "The United States is confronted with a condition in the world which is at direct variance with the assumptions upon which, during and directly after the war, major United States policies were predicated," he wrote for a meeting of top State and War Department officials in August 1947. "Instead of unity among the great powers on the major issues of world reconstruction—both political and economic—after the war, there is complete disunity between the Soviet Union and the satellites on one side and the rest of the world on the other. There are, in short, two worlds instead of one."

To be sure, economics as a tool of diplomacy would become *more* rather than less important under Truman than under Roosevelt. But it was now to focus on "the drawing together and consolidation of the non-Soviet world," in Bohlen's words, and not to rely "on the non-existent thesis of one world." It was no longer "advisable for this Government to continue to press for long-range objectives," he concluded, "however desirable in themselves, which do not immediately and directly bear upon the solution of Western European problems." Further initiatives, Bohlen concluded, "should be consciously limited to Western Europe, based on the concept of the economic unity of Europe west of the Stettin-Trieste line" marking the border with what was now Soviet Europe.[34]

Indeed, many of Truman's top advisers had by 1947 come to see western European unity and recovery as the only viable alternative to a major new American military engagement in Europe. "The greatest danger to the security of the United States," warned the new Central Intelligence Agency, "is the possibility of economic collapse in western Europe and the consequent accession to power of communist elements."[35] Secretary of the Army Kenneth Royall insisted he would need 160,000 additional troops and a $2.25 billion (20 percent) boost to the military budget if Congress voted down a European aid plan.[36] Former ambassador to Moscow Joseph Davies worried that the resulting "armaments race [with Russia] would probably bankrupt us."[37]

Importantly, the character of the new economic thinking was radically different from that under FDR. Rather than lending Europe reconstruction funds and wishing it well, a new integrated western European entity would be constructed using American blueprints, cash, and—ultimately, contrary to all early intentions—security guarantees. This effort—the Marshall Plan, as it would come to be known—would entangle the United States in European affairs in precisely the manner George Washington had warned against.

This is the story of how and why it happened, what it achieved, and the legacy effects we continue to live with today.

Communist demonstration in front of the Propylaea building of the University of Athens at the start of the Greek civil war, 1944.

TWO

CRISIS

"BLESSED ARE THE DEAD," READ THE GRAFFITI ON THE WALLS OF THE Reichstag, or what was left of it, "FOR THEIR HANDS DO NOT FREEZE."

It was February 1947; nineteen thousand Berliners had been treated for frostbite in the past three months. Not that they hadn't been prepared for winter. They had begun in the autumn of 1946, just before the ground froze, digging thousands of graves for those who would die of cold and starvation before spring.[1]

Europe in the war's early aftermath was "a rubble heap, a charnel house," Churchill said, "a breeding ground of pestilence and hate."[2] Canals were blocked, rivers frozen, bridges fallen, roads cratered, rail lines mangled, factories gutted. In Germany, once the workshop of Europe, Russian looters finished the job Allied bombs had not. Farmers grew only what they could eat, assuming they could grow anything at all. In a civilization built on an intricate division of labor across town and country, this meant widespread hunger, malnutrition, and death.

The New York Times called Europe "The New Dark Continent"—a place "which no American can hope to understand." Much of it was still lawless, violent, even savage. The British military governor in Hanover, Germany, described daily scenes of "looting, fighting, rape, [and] murder." War reporter Leonard Mosley documented surreal scenes of "screaming people" pillaging "a store for door knobs . . . kick[ing] and scratch[ing] and beat[ing] with iron bars those who had more doorknobs than themselves." And this "in a city where half the doors no longer existed."[3]

The European war had been to an unprecedented degree, in historian Tony Judt's words, "a civilian experience," with over 36 million war-related deaths.[4] In many ways, its formal end simply shifted the perpetrator and victim groups. During the war, organized brutality had been directed not merely at enemies from abroad but at Fascists and collaborators at home. Now, in countries such as Yugoslavia, Italy, and Greece, those who had carried out the violence were in charge. Thousands of partisans remained armed, refusing to trust civil authorities that continued to rely on functionaries tied to discredited regimes.

In Italy, as many as twenty thousand suspected collaborators were murdered in the months following the Fascist defeat in April 1945. In Yugoslavia, partisans killed some seventy thousand accused collaborationists, civilians as well as soldiers. In Poland, thirty thousand would die in conflict over the new Communist regime between the end of the war and 1948. In France, some ten thousand were killed in extrajudicial reprisals. An estimated twenty thousand women suspected of collaboration—that is, sleeping with the enemy—were subjected to public degradation and violence. Mass trials, purges, expropriations, expulsions, and executions were used in eastern Europe—typically instigated by the Soviet occupation authorities—to eliminate political elements on the right; in Greece they were used to undermine the left. On a single day, May 19, 1945, the Czechoslovak Extraordinary Peoples' Courts handed out over twenty thousand sentences (7 percent of which were for life or the death penalty) to "traitors, collaborators and fascist elements." By 1948, Romania would imprison nearly a quarter million for political crimes, roughly 2 percent of the population. Up to 200,000 were arrested and deported from Hungary to the Soviet Union. Most wound up in the Gulag.

Ethnic minorities—notably Jews, who as "capitalists" or "communists" were held responsible for deprivations befalling communities in central and eastern Europe—were subjected to brutal mass attacks and expulsions. The most infamous postwar pogrom took place at Kielce, in south-central Poland, in July 1946, when false reports of a Jew abducting a Catholic boy triggered a massacre of forty-two Jews in a single day. Over 63,000 Jews flooded into Germany from Poland in the three months that followed; seventy thousand left for Palestine. Ethnic Germans fled the country, under Soviet direction, in the most prodigious numbers: roughly seven million (on top of three million from Czechoslovakia). By the end of 1947 there were virtually no ethnic minorities left in Poland.[5] (Perversely, the new Soviet occupation thus made Poland more "Polish" than before the war.)

In all, some twelve million ethnic Germans left eastern and central Europe for the occupied zones of Germany, which were struggling to sustain the local population. Seven million foreigners had been forced to work in the country during the war, over a fifth of the country's labor force, and many of these were now also on the march—part of the horrific mass movement of homeless humanity crisscrossing the devastated continent.

After the First World War, borders had moved while people remained largely in place. This time was different, with borders mostly stable while people moved (Poland being the major exception, where border movements led to at least 1.2 million being evicted from their homes). At the end of the Second World War, fifty million Europeans were homeless, half of whom in the western part of the Nazi-ravaged Soviet Union. In Germany, 40 percent of prewar housing was destroyed.[6] All told, Stalin and Hitler forcibly displaced some thirty million between 1939 and 1943. Many were now being shunted "back home." Non-Soviet Russians and Ukrainian partisans, for example, were herded across the Soviet border by British and American troops, meeting their fate (typically work camps or death) at the hands of waiting NKVD security forces.[7]

Local economies of sorts continued to function, but often only in their most Hobbesian form. During the war, the right to property had dissolved, with occupiers and resisters taking and distributing, retaking and redistributing, in the cause of war, justice, or opportunity. In the process, trust in authority and one's fellows had been shattered. "Belgians and French and Dutch had been brought up in the war to believe that their patriotic duty was to cheat, to lie, to run a black market," future Belgian prime minister Paul-Henri Spaak reflected decades later. "These habits became ingrained after five years."[8] Liberation, which, like invasion, had generally been carried out by foreigners, had not meant a return to "legitimate" local rule. The Nazis, after all, had run France with just 1,500 German functionaries. They had relied mainly on willing French collaborators. Now there was no right to anything, no common sense of justice to appeal to; only brute physical control over property.

"It [was] hardly an exaggeration," the head of United Nations relief in western Germany wrote, "to say that every man, woman and child in Western Europe is engaged to a greater or lesser degree in illegal trading of one kind or another. . . . [I]t is hardly possible to support existence without doing so." U.S. assistant secretary of war John J. McCloy memoed Truman in April 1945 that Germany was on the verge of "complete economic, social, and political collapse"—a collapse "unparalleled in history unless one goes back to the collapse of the Roman Empire."[9]

Money had become part of the problem, having in parts of central and eastern Europe lost all meaning. In Hungary, inflation in 1946 rose to a peak of about 160,000 percent *per day*.[10] Buying and selling with money was like setting one's watch to a crazed clock. As a result, commercial exchange broke down, and production for exchange along with it. The human effect of this breakdown was dire. Average daily calorie consumption in the British occupation zone of Germany plummeted by a third between mid-1946 and early 1947, from 1,500 to 1,050.[11] In major urban centers such as Vienna and Budapest it had fallen to as low as 800.[12] "We are threatened," said French economics minister André Philip, "with total economic and financial catastrophe."[13]

U.S. State Department officials who would rise to public prominence in the coming months had been in Europe late in the war, and in its early aftermath. What they saw and heard disturbed them. In December 1944, fifty-one-year-old assistant secretary of state Dean Acheson wrote from Greece, where a thousand villages had been obliterated,[14] of the potential for a continent-wide bloodbath if Europe were not somehow rehabilitated quickly. "The peoples of the liberated countries . . . are the most combustible material in the world," he memoed to Roosevelt special assistant Harry Hopkins. "They are violent and restless." Failure to put them to productive work would mean "agitation and unrest," to be followed by "arbitrary and absolutist controls" and ultimately "the overthrow of governments."[15] More than fifty thousand Greeks would die in the renewed civil war that would erupt in 1946, one that would have dramatic and enduring effects much further afield. Acheson's immediate concern in 1944 was, of course, winning the war with Hitler, but he also returned to Washington convinced that economic stabilization was vital to preventing another calamitous European conflagration.

In September 1945, forty-one-year-old diplomat George Kennan had, since June the previous year, been on his second tour of duty in Moscow, this time as the number two ("counselor") to Ambassador W. Averell Harriman. Making his way by train between Moscow and Helsinki, four months after the formal end of the European fighting, he was moved to capture the eerie images in his diary. Vyborg, a modern and vibrant Finnish port city before the war, was at its end empty, rotting Soviet war booty. At the remains of its train station on his way back to Moscow, Kennan noted "rays of early morning sunshine [catching] the gutted shells of apartment buildings, flood[ing] them momentarily with a chill, pale gleam." The train pulled away, clacking "slowly through a devastated and deserted country . . . houses, doorless and windowless . . . sinking gradually back into the new vegetation around them," which "still concealed tens of thousands of live land mines."[16]

In such a world, people wanted change. Economic change came in different forms, ranging from industrial planning in France to nationalization in Britain to outright seizure of farms and enterprises in Hungary and much of the Soviet-controlled East.[17] Many thought that the disasters of authoritarianism in Europe were the products of the laissez-faire brutality, inefficiency, and inequity in the interwar years. "Nobody in Europe," wrote British historian A. J. P. Taylor in 1945, any longer "believes in the American way of life—that is, private enterprise."[18]

People also wanted political change. Communist parties throughout Europe were promising a radical alternative to capitalism. History seemed to be on their side. The Soviet Union was victorious in war, and now far and away the most powerful country on the continent. Communists received 19 percent of the vote in Italy, 24 percent in Finland (where Communist Mauno Pekkala became prime minister), and 26 percent in France in 1945–46. And although no national elections in Germany would take place before 1949 (in the west), Communists took up to 14 percent in some regional contests. Together with the Socialists, the total left-wing vote was 39 percent in Italy and 47 percent in France. In Italy, many thought the revolutionary left was destined to take control of the country. The merging of the left parties in the Soviet zone of Germany seemed a template for wider Europe.[19]

Back in Washington, where belief in the civilizing influences of the market had been far less shaken by the war than in Europe, officials were worried by developments. The State Department view, represented by its decidedly anti-statist under secretary of state for economic affairs, Will Clayton, was that the new postwar European approach was doubly misguided, entrenching failed interventionist doctrines nationally while erecting barriers to cooperation and trade internationally. The sweeping 1946 Monnet Plan for industrial modernization in France, for example, cohered only in a context in which French access to German raw materials and markets could be assured. Europe as a series of national economic silos would, in Clayton's view, never regain its former vitality. The American aid that was being extended—over $13 billion between 1945 and 1947 ($161 billion in today's money)—could therefore provide only *relief* and not *recovery*. Or in the perspective of New York Democratic congressman Emanuel Celler, it was simply "promot[ing] too damned much Socialism."[20]

Meanwhile, the mood in the American heartland was set against the idea that American troops or treasure had any further useful role to play in Europe. The "popular attitude toward foreign policy," Acheson observed, could be summed up as "bring the boys home" and "don't be a Santa Claus."[21] Europe could choose to prosper or perish as it wished. President Truman had himself jumped on the homefront-first bandwagon following the Japanese surrender in August 1945, canceling Lend-Lease aid abroad and proclaiming a sweeping twenty-one-point progressive economic reform program at home.

In Britain, too, there was an urge to turn the page. The country could not quite decide, though, whether to go forward or back. Winston Churchill, who had just led his nation through to victory in war, was unceremoniously booted from office while representing it at the final Big Three wartime conference at Potsdam in July 1945. Clement Attlee's Labour Party swept to power on a platform of creating full employment, a National Health Service, and a cradle-to-grave welfare state. "Let us face the future" was the theme of the victorious campaign. Yet the belief remained, even within the Labour leadership, that the country's strength lay in its past—in (a reformed) empire. "I know that if the British Empire fell," Foreign Minister Ernest Bevin told the House of Commons in February 1946, "it would be a disaster. I know, further, it would mean that the standard of life of our constituents would fall considerably."[22] But what a difference a year would make.

⁜

BRITAIN'S NATIONAL DEBT HAVING QUADRUPLED DURING THE WAR, THE strain of policing occupied Europe and restless far-flung colonies had, by 1947, become an intolerable financial burden. "We are, I am afraid," Chancellor Hugh Dalton wrote to Attlee on January 20, "drifting in a state of semi-animation, towards the rapids."[23] Over the course of a dramatic few weeks between January 27 and February 20, one pillar after another of British imperial power came crashing down—Burma, Palestine, Greece, India. The driving force was a desperate lack of dollars and gold, which the war had rendered the only acceptable means of international payment.

The Communist insurgency in Greece had the most immediate ramifications for Britain's relations with both the United States and Russia. "I am very doubtful indeed about this policy of propping up . . . weak states in the Eastern Mediterranean against Russia," Dalton put to Attlee in November 1946, "even with American aid." It was time, he concluded by February 1947, to "put an end to our endless dribble of British taxpayers' money to the Greeks."[24]

To make matters worse, the weather over Britain turned violent in mid-January 1947. Temperatures plummeted and, on the 23rd, snow began to fall incessantly: it did not stop for seven weeks. Blizzards hammered the country. For three weeks in February, temperatures did not rise above freezing; high winds amplified the chill. Travel all but stopped, as roads and rail lines disappeared under feet of snow. Already near-destitute men and women lost their jobs. The Royal Air Force parachuted food and supplies into isolated farms and

villages. Fuel and power supplies collapsed; water pipes burst. Homes went un-
heated. People venturing out risked their lives. Death rates among older Britons
soared.[25]

Now, against the background of a collapsing economy, with over half of
British industry at a standstill, the government decided to prioritize conservation of Britain's inadequate dollar reserves, which were running down at an
alarming rate. In 1945, Washington had demanded that the string and glue
holding debt-ridden Britain's empire together—imperial trade preference
and an inconvertible pound sterling—had to go as a condition for $3.75 bil-
lion in loan assistance. But with convertibility now looming on July 15, 1947,
guaranteeing a run on Britain's meager dollar stash by its eager colonies and
dominions, the British government could do little more than hunker down in
London. The imperial mind-set had been slow to adapt, but the crisis could no
longer be postponed. It fell to Britain's ambassador in Washington, Lord Inverchapel (Archibald Clark Kerr), to hand off the crumbling edifice of empire to
its main creditor.

Inverchapel, his private secretary told Dean Acheson on February 21, 1947,
wished to deliver to the new secretary of state "a blue piece of paper"—diplomatic parlance for a message of great importance. George Marshall having left
that morning to speak at a bicentennial celebration at Princeton, the embassy
allowed Acheson to breach protocol by reviewing a facsimile of the documents,
holding back the "ribbon copy" to present to the general on Monday. The rev-
elations, Acheson recalled, "were shockers."

In six weeks' time, Inverchapel said, Britain would begin withdrawing its
forty thousand troops from Greece. It would further cut off aid to both Greece
and Turkey, which was costing half a billion dollars a year ($5.4 billion in to-
day's money). The United States would need to take over the security and financial burden, immediately.[26]

The British pullout, Acheson understood, was the final act of the Pax
Britannica—the global order that had defined the nineteenth century. Since
Greece was the last barrier to Soviet domination of the Aegean and the Adri-
atic, the responsibility was now on Washington to prop it up.

The following day, Marshall delivered his speech at Princeton. Though
he had prepared it before learning of the British decision, it foreshadowed his

reaction to it. "I think we must agree," he told his young audience, "that the negative course of action followed by the United States after the First World War did not achieve order or security, and that it had a direct bearing upon the recent war and its endless tragedies":

> There were people in those days who understood the lessons of history, who knew well what should be done in order to minimize the danger of another world disaster, but their combined voice was a feeble one and their proposals were ignored. . . .
>
> You should have an understanding of what course of action has created power and security and of the mistakes which have undermined the power and security of many nations, and above all, a clear understanding of the institutions upon which human liberty and individual freedom have depended. . . .
>
> You should fully understand the special position that the United States now occupies in the world, geographically, financially, militarily, and scientifically, and the implications involved. The development of a sense of responsibility for world order and security, the development of a sense of overwhelming importance of this country's acts, and failures to act, in relation to world order and security—these, in my opinion, are great musts for your generation.[27]

❖

STANDING BEFORE A LARGE MAP OF THE NEWLY EXPANDED SOVIET UNION shortly after the German surrender in May 1945, Stalin nodded with approval. The vast buffer in Soviet-occupied eastern Europe would now protect his empire against future Napoleons and Hitlers. He took the pipe from his mouth, waving it under the base of the Caucasus. This time he shook his head and frowned.[28]

"I don't like our border here." This was where the Soviet republics of Georgia, Armenia, and Azerbaijan met the hostile powers of Turkey and Iran.[29]

So in June, Molotov summoned the Turkish ambassador. Uncompromisingly, he laid out for the stunned diplomat new Soviet claims to the Kars-Ardahan regions of eastern Turkey, encompassing some 6,500 square miles and 300,000 people. The Soviet republics of Georgia and Armenia would soon press additional claims.[30] *Pravda* published arguments from Soviet strategists asserting their unquestionable legitimacy.[31]

In an attempt to extend his Caucasus border and force oil concessions from Tehran, Stalin also began organizing an armed separatist movement in northern Iran—using Soviet troops that had occupied the country under the wartime Anglo-Russian-Iranian Treaty of 1942. When the Iranian government sent forces to quell the rebellion, the Soviets barred the way. On March 1, 1946, Moscow announced that it would keep its troops in the country beyond the March 2 deadline for withdrawal specified in the treaty. Privately urged on by Washington, Iran appealed to the new United Nations Security Council, making it the object of the first major superpower confrontation in the body. In April, Truman signaled his intention to defend Iranian sovereignty by transporting the body of Mehmet Münir Ertegün, the deceased former Turkish ambassador to Washington, home on the mightiest battleship in the American fleet—the USS *Missouri*. Anxious to end the bad publicity, and unwilling to risk an armed confrontation, Stalin retreated. He withdrew the last of his troops from Iran in May.[32]

In August, however, he probed again, this time demanding that Ankara accept joint control of the strategic Turkish Straits and Dardanelles, including provision for Soviet military bases. The ultimatum was a blatant contravention of Turkey's sovereign rights in the waterways under the Montreux Convention of 1936.[33] At Yalta, Roosevelt and Churchill had agreed, off the record, to Stalin's demand to review the convention; he now took this assent as license to ignore it.

"What would Britain do if Spain or Egypt [could] close the Suez Canal?" Stalin had asked Churchill rhetorically in October 1944. "Or what would the United States Government say if some South American Republic [could] close the Panama Canal?" It was equally "impossible for Russia to remain subject to Turkey, who could close the Straits and hamper Russian imports and exports and even her defence."[34] These were waterways used by the French and British to lay siege to Sevastopol during the Crimean War. The Germans controlled them during two world wars. A Soviet military presence would provide Stalin's largely landlocked empire with both security and unrestricted access to a global maritime route.

Back in Washington, Acheson watched Stalin's actions with alarm. The eastern Mediterranean marked the intersection of his fears of British retrenchment and Soviet advance. The president, he was relieved to see, grasped the threat. Briefing him in the Oval Office, surrounded by top military brass, the under secretary was awed to see Truman take "a great big map" from his desk drawer and deliver "a ten-minute lecture on the strategic importance" of the region.

Truman had a passion for maps. Maps adorned his old Senate office, which he had used to follow the war. After moving into the White House, he was a regular visitor to the highly secure Map Room, where movements of ships and armies were constantly updated with colored pins. Using them as props, he impressed many under him, such as Acheson and chief of staff to the commander in chief Admiral William Leahy, with his autodidact's knowledge of geography and military history.

With no hesitation, Truman told Acheson to inform the Soviet chargé d'affaires (an ambassadorial subordinate) of his full support for Turkish rights in the Straits and his intention to take any act of aggression to the Security Council. He backed it up by ordering a flotilla of military ships to the Mediterranean and, secretly, authorized plans for strategic air force operations in the region. Stalin, after his intelligence agents confirmed that Truman was prepared to fight for Turkey, dropped his demands on Ankara in late October 1946.[35] The map meeting would be seminal in the political bonding between Truman and Acheson.

In spite of Britain's weakening position and Stalin's provocations in 1946, Washington was caught unprepared by Britain's retrenchment in 1947. Stuck in a nineteenth-century diplomatic and military posture, the United States had neither a policy nor the immediate capacity for deterring a determined aggressor in a traditional British theater of imperial control. General Walter Bedell Smith, the newly appointed ambassador in Moscow, thought Turkey had "little hope of independent survival unless it [were] assured of solid long-term American and British support."[36] British retreat, now, was tantamount to "open[ing] three continents to Soviet penetration."[37]

Reinstalled in Washington teaching Grand Strategy at the National War College, Kennan feared the Soviets would underestimate U.S. determination to

prevent their further encroachment in the region, believing it raised the odds
of war. Acheson, who unlike Kennan held no theory of Soviet conduct, was
alarmed by the brute cartography of it. To his mind, the Kremlin's efforts to
establish naval bases in the Turkish Straits presaged domination of an enfeebled
Turkey, to be followed by penetration into Greece and "the whole Near and
Middle East." The region would then be "cut off from the Western world," encouraging the Russians to push on into India, from which British lines of passage would be cut. China would follow.

Two years prior, FDR's State Department had been critical of Britain's military support for the brutal Greek royalists in their fight against Communist
rebels. But the geopolitical landscape had since changed. Greece, American
ambassador Lincoln MacVeagh reported, was in complete political, economic,
and social disarray; armed Communist bands, he warned, would take over if
the government collapsed. Mark Ethridge, the U.S. delegate to a U.N. commission investigating Greek border disputes, reported that the "Soviets feel that
Greece is [a] ripe plum [waiting] to fall into their hands in a few weeks."[38]

When London had been urging a coalition against the Soviet threat on the
European continent, Washington was uninterested. Now that Washington was
warming to the idea, London hadn't the means to participate. Acheson, who
had fought pitched battles with the FDR Treasury over its efforts to unravel
the British empire financially, now scrambled to deal with the consequences of
its success. It was a crisis, he believed, "in some ways more formidable than the
one described in the first chapter of Genesis."[39]

❖

DEAN GOODERHAM ACHESON, SON OF AN EPISCOPAL BISHOP, HAD BEEN
born for this moment—a moment his political memoir would term "the Creation." His abiding admiration for the Pax Britannica had, until this point, been
a nostalgic one—one that made him an awkward bystander at times during two
tours with the FDR administration. At Treasury in the early 1930s, he could
not abide the president's willful destruction of the gold standard, an inheri-
tance from the last century; at State in the early 1940s, he condemned efforts to
encourage Britain's imperial liquidation. Britain had, until Pearl Harbor, stood
alone against Hitler, and its collaboration, he believed, would be needed to

restore order after his defeat. Now that the ruinous effects of British insolvency were clear, Acheson became consumed with a sense of mission. As convinced of the need to resist Soviet expansion as he had been of the need to roll back Nazi expansion before it, he set out to initiate a new American order to carry out the resistance. He hoped that this time the United States would not have to resort to arms.

Acheson was no reflexive cold warrior. He sought détente over confrontation. In 1944 he supported extending debt forgiveness and reconstruction aid to Moscow.[40] In November 1945 he gave a speech to the Soviet-American Friendship Society, before thousands at Madison Square Garden in New York, proclaiming that "we understand and agree with [the Soviet Union] that to have friendly governments along her borders is essential both for the security of the Soviet Union and the peace of the world."[41] In a January 1946 address he called it "absolutely unthinkable that we should fight Russia."[42] The press needled him as "Red Dean."[43]

But he had also been deeply distrustful of the Soviet leadership since its crushing of Polish independence in 1945—a distrust that turned to alarmed wariness after Stalin's belligerent February 1946 "election" speech at the Bolshoi Theater, on the eve of the first postwar balloting for the Supreme Soviet, in which he painted a dark landscape of inevitable conflict with the capitalist West. Acheson thought Secretary of State Jimmy Byrnes too naively compromising in his dealings with him.[44] The media began to take note of the shift in his posture. "When the facts seemed to him to merit a change," as they did in the case of the Soviet Union, wrote James Reston of *The New York Times*, Acheson "switched with the facts."[45]

When in January 1947 Marshall asked Acheson to stay on as his under secretary, and de facto chief of staff, he accepted with the proviso that he would return to private life on June 30—hardly sufficient time to erect a new postwar diplomatic architecture. But the dangerous breach in Western defenses left by Britain's retrenchment left him in no doubt of his responsibility for doing so now. Eloquent and possessed of a lawyerly love of logic and detail, Acheson was an ideal complement to Marshall. Their relationship would become much like that between Alexander Hamilton and George Washington—never close, but each essential to the other's success.[46]

George Frost Kennan, too, was no instinctual cold warrior. Six feet tall, thin, balding, with engaging blue eyes and a smile "chilling or charming as its owner decrees,"[47] an eclectic, emotional, even melancholic intellectual, Kennan had what at times seemed an all-consuming empathy for Russia. Fascinated by foreign peoples generally, or more specifically those living outside the United States (where he favored old-stock Protestants such as himself), Kennan— whose great-uncle of the same name had traveled Russia and written popular books on Siberian life and tsarist authoritarianism[48]—had a powerful affinity for Russians. "It gave me an indescribable sort of satisfaction," he said after returning to Moscow in 1944, "to feel myself back again in the midst of these people—with their tremendous pulsating warmth and vitality. I sometimes feel that I would rather be sent to Siberia among them . . . than to live on Park Avenue among our own stuffy folk."[49]

Deeper still was Kennan's love for the Russia of literary renderings—of Tolstoy, Dostoyevsky, and Chekhov (of whom he was writing a biography, never finished). His facility with the language, buoyed as it was by his literary engagement with it, astonished Russians—even Stalin himself.

Kennan's warm sentiments for the country and its culture, however, did not extend to its leadership. He abominated it. Like Acheson, he was unnerved by Moscow's brutal subjugation of "liberated" Poland after 1945, as he was by the massacre of thousands of Polish officers at Katyn five years prior. He saw these as harbingers of wider aggression to come.

Kennan had had two postings to the embassy in Moscow, the first from 1933, right after FDR normalized relations with the Communist government, to 1937, and the second from 1944 to 1946. On May 9, 1945, he watched the city's frenzied celebration of the war's end from the embassy's balcony. Terrified of being swept away by the surging mass of revelers, he, as deputy chief of mission with Ambassador Harriman away, felt he had no choice but to engage them, lest silence be interpreted as official indifference or hostility. Walking downstairs and stepping out onto the pedestal of one of the building's large columns, he summoned his courage. "Congratulations on the day of victory!" he shouted in Russian. "All honor to the Soviet allies!" The crowd roared. Kennan, heart pounding, dashed back inside.

Harriman, the former banker—pragmatic, peremptory, businesslike, monolingual; Kennan's temperamental and intellectual opposite—had great regard for his deputy's insights, but was put off by his impractical tendency to ruminate. Kennan, he said, was "a man who understood Russia but didn't understand the United States."[50] Bohlen seemed to agree, urging his friend to reacquaint himself with his native land by automobile after returning from Moscow in May 1946.[51]

Kennan certainly did not understand his government, or more specifically what he considered its absurd belief that it could conclude a Grand Alliance with Moscow to preside over a peaceful postwar world. In early 1946 he set out to disabuse Washington of its notions in the most famous and influential diplomatic cable in history—what has come to be known as the Long Telegram.

Byrnes had asked for Kennan's analysis of Stalin's notorious election speech. What he got back on February 22 was a 5,326-word cable,[52] well exceeding the department's length limits, written in a singular style mixing high prose with telegrammatic abbreviation, expounding on the forces driving the behavior of Soviet rulers.

Kennan argued that the natural neuroses and insecurities of Russian autocrats were born of a geographic vulnerability to outside predators, and found their ultimate political pretext in Marxist dogma:

> In this dogma, with its basic altruism of purpose, they found justification for their instinctive fear of [the] outside world, for the dictatorship without which they did not know how to rule, for cruelties they did not dare not to inflict, for sacrifice they felt bound to demand. In the name of Marxism they sacrificed every single ethical value in their methods and tactics. Today they cannot dispense with it. It is [the] fig leaf of their moral and intellectual respectability. Without it they would stand before history, at best, as only the last of that long succession of cruel and wasteful Russian rulers who have relentlessly forced [the] country on to ever new heights of military power in order to guarantee [the] external security of their internally weak regimes.

The implications for American policy were stark: "We have here," he wrote, "a political force committed fanatically to the belief that with [the] US there can be no permanent *modus vivendi*, that it is desirable and necessary that the internal harmony of our society be disrupted, our traditional way of life be destroyed, the international authority of our state be broken, if Soviet power is to be secure." Negotiations with them were ultimately fruitless. Soviet leaders, he argued, were "impervious to logic of reason." They were, however, "highly sensitive to logic of force."[53]

As the content of the cable flowed through the Washington foreign policy apparatus the effect was rapid, widespread, and consequential. "The year 1946," Acheson would later write, "was for the most part a year of learning that minds in the Kremlin worked very much as George F. Kennan had predicted they would."[54]

The rhetorical quality of the cable should not be underestimated. Kennan's prose had, in Acheson's words, "a sort of sad lyrical beauty about it which drugs the mind."[55] Even if the Russia his cable purported to explain had been fictional, its sheer logical eloquence, not typically seen in such a medium, would have ensured an impact. It offered a sense of epiphany, of a great and important mystery being unraveled. It gave justification to inchoate animus. And the message seemed clear, devoid of the usual messy diplomatic caveats: Russia was implacably hostile to American interests, and had to be confronted whenever and wherever those interests were challenged. Even those, like future secretary of defense James Forrestal, who had been convinced that Marxism was driving Russian expansionism, rather than being co-opted to justify it (as Kennan was arguing), embraced this message.[56]

Kennan would sharpen and expand upon it in an article he was now, in the spring of 1947, honing for the establishment journal *Foreign Affairs*—an article he would naively publish anonymously under the pseudonym "X," but which would make its easily identifiable author famous. The piece would argue that "the main element of any United States policy toward the Soviet Union must be that of a long-term patient but firm and vigilant containment of Russian expansive tendencies." Such "containment" would have to be conducted through "the adroit and vigilant application of counter-force at a series of constantly shifting geographical and political points."[57]

On the basis of the telegram and the article, Henry Kissinger would later credit Kennan with coming "as close to authoring the diplomatic doctrine of his era as any diplomat in our history."[58] But what did "containment" mean? When translating the article for Stalin, certain Soviet analysts wanted it hardened to "strangulation." Though they were overruled, Stalin still interpreted containment as "extremely hostile to the USSR."[59] Given the context painted of an implacable foe, together with the reference to "force," the article appeared to be pointing to armed confrontation. Indeed, Kennan's War College lectures in the fall would highlight the benefit in negotiations of "quiet but effective augmentations of our military and air strength." Soviet leaders, he said, "are not gamblers when faced with the reality of military force."[60]

But Kennan was never that simple. In two of the most important paragraphs of his cable, he insisted that a robust diplomatic offensive against Moscow needed to encompass what Harvard's Joseph Nye would today term "soft power"[61]—being able to influence the behavior of others who might otherwise fall under Soviet influence. "We must," Kennan said, "put forward for other nations a much more positive and constructive picture of [the] sort of world we would like to see than we have put forward in [the] past." Europeans, he wrote, were "tired and frightened by experiences of [the] past." They were seeking "security," to be understood in the widest sense: encompassing domestic order, material well-being, and freedom from foreign threat. "We should," he went on, "be better able than [the] Russians to give them this." But if the United States failed to act, if it retreated into the old isolationism, the "Russians certainly will" act to fill the gap. Americans must never, however, Kennan emphasized, behave like Russians. "[W]e must have [the] courage and self-confidence to cling to our own methods and conceptions of human society."

It is no leap to read into these passages, however vague, a call for the United States to bolster free and independent European nations through material, as well as military, assistance: a prescription that lay ready for the first hard evidence of the malady. In early 1947, it was at hand.

Kennan argued that Moscow would exploit all "timely and promising" opportunities to expand its power. Initially, it would focus on "neighboring points . . . of immediate strategic necessity, such as Northern Iran [and] Turkey."[62] The State Department, special assistant Joseph Jones[63] explained, now saw these countries, together with Greece, as a single "barrier" to Russia "breaking through . . . into the Middle East, South Asia, and North Africa." And given that "every Communist party in the world" was, Bohlen asserted, "the subservient instrument of Moscow Policy, the installation of a Communist regime in Athens would have meant extension of Soviet control in the eastern Mediterranean."[64] The upshot, Jones said, was that "everyone in the executive branch" now recognized what "British abdication from the Middle East" meant: that "if Russian expansion was to be checked, the United States [would have to] move into the defaulted position in the Middle East."[65]

Such a move could not be undertaken without reckoning with its consequences. Soviet foreign minister Molotov had been blunt in condemning British political, economic, and military support for the royalists in Greece as unacceptable interference in that country's internal affairs and a threat to international peace and security. He had typically been more restrained in leveling charges against the United States, but any overt move by the Truman administration to take over the British role in Greece with financial and military aid would, at least many in Washington believed, elicit a harsh reaction from the Kremlin.[66] Confining the boundaries of a confrontation to Greece seemed, therefore, a virtual impossibility at this point, whatever the two sides might wish for. Thus would begin what Jones was famously to call "The Fifteen Weeks"[67]—America's monumental, breakneck transformation into a political superpower, filling the breach left by Britain's imperial implosion.

❖

ACHESON'S STAFF FOLLOWED ORDERS TO "WORK LIKE HELL" OVER THE weekend of February 22–23, preparing reports on the political, military, and financial situations in Greece and Turkey and position papers laying out the case for U.S. aid. Following a businesslike tête-à-tête between Inverchapel and Marshall on Monday morning, the 24th, Acheson finally sat down with his new boss.

The unflappable sixty-six-year-old general had found Inverchapel's news "unpleasant . . . but not wholly unexpected."[68] Unafflicted by Acheson's Anglocentrism, Marshall would certainly have recoiled from his deputy's biblical analogies. The final collapse of the British empire was, to him, a well-signaled event with regrettable but manageable consequences.

He probed the practicalities. How long could the British be induced to keep troops in Greece? What forces would be necessary to replace them? How would the administration get an effective government going? What would it cost and over what timetable? Acheson had no answers. Needing to prepare for a critical conference on Germany with his Soviet, British, and French counterparts next month in Moscow, Marshall directed Acheson to find them.

Matters proceeded at breakneck speed. Following a lunch meeting with Truman and Marshall, War Secretary Robert Patterson and Navy Secretary James Forrestal agreed with Acheson on the central elements of the recommendations they would prepare for the president: that it was vital to the security of the United States that Greece and Turkey be strengthened so as to safeguard their independence, that only the United States could do this, and that Congress would need to provide the necessary authority and funds.[69]

On February 25, Acheson met with State's top political, economic, legal, and information officers to hash out alternate courses of action and an initial draft of the department's "Position and Recommendations" paper. Perspectives differed over the prudence of challenging the Soviets so directly at that juncture. Whereas "some were elated over the possibility that the United States might at last stand out boldly against Soviet expansion," others were concerned about doing so when American "military strength was at a low ebb."[70] The exchange was robust, if unnervingly compressed given the enormity of the commitments being proposed. Acheson let the discussion range until it was time to deliver his summation, at which point he issued the inevitable directive: devise a plan for immediate financial and military aid to Greece and Turkey.

Russia specialist Loy Henderson and the Near Eastern Affairs staff worked into the night drafting the final version of the recommendations, which Patterson and Forrestal approved the following day. But the backing came only after an intense discussion of whether similar aid was needed for South Korea, China, and other vulnerable countries and territories; Army chief of staff General Dwight Eisenhower wanted the study to be expanded with a view to making a wider appropriation request. Though the group rejected a wider request as impractical, given the obstacles of time and Congress, the question of the geographic boundaries of the commitment to containing Communism would not go away. Indeed, it would come to trouble Kennan and others who saw great dangers in the president issuing blanket guarantees to protect the globe from communists.

Truman had his report that afternoon. Convinced since Potsdam that the Communist police state was as great a threat as the Nazi one,[71] he signed off.

❖

FOR THE STATE DEPARTMENT, THE MILITARY, AND THE PRESIDENT TO CO-alesce, in peacetime, so rapidly around such a far-reaching, potentially open-ended, American commitment abroad was unprecedented. "The consciousness that a chapter in world history had come to an end," Jones observed, "was so real and ever-present as to seem almost tangible" to all involved.[72] Yet the initiative still faced an enormous hurdle in the form of the Republican-controlled legislature. Truman, an accidental and politically isolated Democratic president, knew he needed to get them on board immediately; the White House telephoned invitations to the House and Senate leadership for a meeting at ten the following morning.

Eight congressmen, four Republican and four Democrat, joined Truman, Marshall, and Acheson at the White House on February 27: Senate Foreign Relations Committee chairman Arthur Vandenberg (R-MI), Styles Bridges (R-NH), Tom Connally (D-TX), and Alben Barkley (D-KY) represented the Senate; Speaker Joseph Martin (R-MA), Minority Leader Sam Rayburn (D-TX), Charles Eaton (R-NJ), and Sol Bloom (D-NY) represented the House.[73] Acheson eyed the scene around the circular table with foreboding. "I knew we were met at Armageddon," he reflected later, continuing to pile on the biblical references.

Truman invited his new secretary of state to explain why the group had been assembled at such hasty notice. Marshall, as was his practice in such settings, read from a prepared script.

He "flubbed" it—at least according to Acheson. In Jones' word, Marshall was "cryptic." He "conveyed the . . . impression that aid should be extended to Greece on grounds of loyalty and humanitarianism and to Turkey to strengthen Britain's position in the Middle East," rather than to resist Soviet expansion. The congressional majority, committed as it was to cutting foreign aid and taxes, was in no mood for suggestions that it do the opposite without strong cause. Their leaders demanded to know why the United States should be "pulling British chestnuts out of the fire" and "how much [it was all] going to cost."[74]

When delivering unwelcome news, style is never separable from substance. Skepticism brooks no charity toward inept messengers. Marshall, a dry speaker even in the most friendly of settings, had an aversion to tub-thumping rhetoric. Yet Jones' account is still curiously at odds with what Marshall actually said— which was that the country was "faced with the first crisis of a series which might extend Soviet domination to Europe, the Middle East, and Asia." The words, at least, could hardly have been starker. But Jones was close to Acheson, whose portentously titled memoirs *Present at the Creation* declared: "This was my crisis. For a week I had nurtured it."[75] Part of him may simply have wanted to reclaim it as his own.

"Is this a private fight," Acheson whispered to Marshall as the congressmen grumbled, "or can anyone get into it?" Marshall turned to Truman, asking him to give Acheson the floor. Truman agreed.

Acheson was conscious of having one chance to reset the discussion. Failure to persuade the visitors would be fatal for the funding request. With a litigator's skill, a preacher's conviction, and a politician's feel for his moment in history, he laid out a narrative focused on the clear and present communist threat.

Senators Vandenberg and Connally, Acheson recalled to the group, had traveled with Secretary Byrnes from conference to conference in Europe, trying with tenacious goodwill to negotiate peace settlements.[76] The Soviet Union, meanwhile, he said, busied itself encircling Germany, Turkey, Iran, and Greece, probing for opportunities to destabilize them. With the British pullback, Greece was, Acheson warned, at imminent risk of collapse. Unhindered by any organized resistance, the Soviets would take control, after which it was only a matter of time before Turkey succumbed. From Turkey, he said, the eastern Mediterranean and Middle East would be open to them, after which penetration of South Asia and Africa was inevitable. All the while, Soviet-backed communist movements would continue to undermine Hungary, Austria, France, and Italy.

Aiding Greece, Acheson insisted, had nothing to do with British chestnuts; Britain was finished. Its financial position was untenable. Only two great powers remained in the world: the United States and the Soviet Union—a polarization of global power unparalleled since the time of Rome and Carthage. The ideological chasm between the two was unbridgeable; democracy and individual liberty were antithetic to dictatorship and absolute conformity. The Soviet Union, which already spanned huge swaths of two continents, was determined to expand its control to two thirds of the world's surface and three fourths of its people. Aiding Greece and Turkey, therefore, was not about helping the British. It was not about humanitarianism. It was about supporting free peoples against communist aggression and subversion, in the service of preserving America's national security. The choice, therefore, was whether to act with determination or lose by default.

A pregnant silence followed. It was Vandenberg who broke it.

He was, he said, "greatly impressed, even shaken" by developments in the Mediterranean. Greece and Turkey, though, however serious their situations, were only part of a much bigger problem the United States needed to face. It was essential, therefore, that any request for funds and authority to act be accompanied by "a message to Congress, and an explanation to the American people," about the "grim facts of the larger situation." Greece, he would clarify to a colleague six days later, "cannot be isolated by itself. On the contrary, it is probably symbolic of the world-wide ideological clash between Eastern communism and Western democracy; and it may easily be the thing which requires us to make some very fateful and far-reaching decisions."[77]

According to Henderson, who was present at the meeting with the congressional leaders, Vandenberg added that the president would have to "scare the hell out of the country." But if he would have a go, the senator would back him. "And I believe that most members will do the same."[78] Truman pledged to set out his aid request for Greece and Turkey against the broader background and in the frankest terms.[79] "It was Vandenberg's 'condition,'" Jones concluded, "that made it possible, even necessary, to launch the global policy that broke through the remaining barriers of American isolationism."[80]

News of the secret morning meeting spread, as of course did speculation as to its agenda and meaning. The administration now had to get out in front of the story. Acheson arranged for an off-the-record briefing with twenty newspaper correspondents that evening.[81]

In *The New York Times*, Reston hit all the notes Acheson needed Congress and the public to hear. Greece was at serious risk of falling to the Kremlin-backed

Communist insurgency. This was a critical point in terms of American policy toward Britain, an ally in grave financial circumstances, and the Soviet Union, expansion of whose power and influence the administration was committed to checking—a policy of "stern containment." Reston noted that there was "no enthusiasm on Capitol Hill for additional foreign loans" and "little willingness to think through the broader implications of the British economic crisis on our foreign policy." Importantly, however, he concluded that "few leading members of the majority [Republican] party seem eager to take the responsibility for the consequences of rejecting the President's request" for funds and authority.[82] Such wariness could help soften the opposition the administration would face.

The next morning, February 28, Acheson assembled his key departmental officers in the secretary's conference room, explaining with "unusual gravity" the historic decisions that had been made over the preceding days and laying out the work ahead. They would have to craft a presidential message explaining the "global struggle between freedom and totalitarianism." It would have to stress, he said, in words that would have made Kennan shudder, the "protection of Democracy everywhere in the world."

There were, however, clear tensions in Acheson's framing of the mission. On the one hand, staff were told to proceed "vigorously without any regard to the effect that the Greece-Turkey program, or any public statement of it, might have on the Moscow Conference or upon [the Secretary's] personal position there." On the other, they were instructed "not to be belligerent or provocative"; the policy was not to be "directed against any country or even movement."[83] The latter might work as a statement of principle, but not of practical fact. The administration was only backing massive aid to Greece and Turkey because of the presumed intentions of one country: the Soviet Union. These tensions over how broadly Moscow would be confronted, and through what means, would bedevil two fateful initiatives that would emerge in the coming weeks and months: one a "Doctrine" to be named for the president, and another a "Plan" to be named for the secretary of state.

⁜

EACH PROPOSED SENTENCE OF THE PRESIDENT'S MESSAGE TO CONGRESS was scrutinized from every angle: diplomatic, political, and stylistic. Numerous

State Department and White House staff were involved. Truman himself criticized an early draft as too wordy and technical. The Missourian being a straight speaker, there was little room to hide ambiguities behind rhetorical flourish. "I wanted no hedging," Truman insisted. "It had to be clear and free of hesitation and double-talk."[84] Difficult and consequential decisions would, therefore, have to be made about what was said and what was not.

"If F.D.R. were alive I think I know what he'd do," observed Acheson, a man who was "without affection" for the former president. "He would make a statement of global policy but confine his request for money right now to Greece and Turkey." Jones revised accordingly. The president would ask for $400 million ($4.32 billion in today's money) to aid the two countries, and those two countries alone, through the first half of 1948.

In the end, the speech would be far more Greece than Turkey—strikingly more, given the greater strategic importance of the latter. Turkey's location made it vital to the defense of the eastern Mediterranean and the security of nations on three continents. Military assistance to Ankara was considered imperative in private discussions between the executive branch and congressional leaders. Yet there was great reluctance to have the president highlighting this publicly. Turkey had not suffered the war destruction that Greece had, and was not in the midst of a domestic uprising. There was therefore an element of raw power diplomacy to Turkish aid that, it was feared, would alienate the American public. Turkey, moreover, unlike Greece, shared a border with the Soviet Union. Though the Soviet Union would, most strikingly, not be mentioned in the address, the State Department still feared that Moscow would make propaganda out of an American military-aid initiative in Turkey that appeared to threaten it with Western "encirclement." Turkey, one witness before the House Committee on Foreign Affairs observed wryly, "was slipped into the oven with Greece because that seemed to be the surest way to cook a tough bird."[85]

Treatment of Great Britain was also cautious. The inability of Britain to continue aid to Greece and Turkey would be cited in each case as a reason why American aid was necessary; yet no suggestion would be made that the United States was stepping directly into the breaches of a collapsing empire. FDR had been too forthright in highlighting the evils of empire for his accidental successor to appear to be creating one.

The speech was anything but cautious, however, in pushing the boundaries of what Congress had previously considered prudent foreign economic policy. When bankrupt Britain had been holding the fort alone against Nazi Germany in 1941, Congress still demanded economic "consideration" for Lend-Lease aid—which was merely in the form of loans, and not grants. When in 1945 Morgenthau and White fought to justify the Bretton Woods monetary and financial agreements before Congress, they were again touting only loans, and not grants, to revive the collapsed international trading system. That vision would be challenged by the new International Bank for Reconstruction and Development (IBRD), whose 1946/47 annual report observed, understatedly, that "the problem [of recovery] is deeper and more difficult than was envisioned at Bretton Woods."[86]

Even just a few days before the president's address, Truman had delivered a major speech on foreign economic policy at Baylor University that, having been written largely before the Greek and Turkish crisis, went little beyond calling for reciprocal agreements to boost trade. Will Clayton, who had drafted much of it, wanted the president to stress the need for "bolder [economic] measures than have ever been seriously advanced before," but was overruled.[87] Nowhere in the Baylor speech was there a suggestion that the United States might need to intervene, on its own, in the internal economic affairs of other nations—to provide hundreds of millions of dollars in assistance and to direct their use. Or that doing so might be necessary to their survival as independent nations, and even essential to American national security itself.

It was a calculated political gamble for the president to take such a message to Congress. To be sure, the groundwork had been laid in advance through meetings with congressional leaders and briefings to the press. Vandenberg would himself urge Marshall to tell Stalin in Moscow that the United States would use "economic intervention" to block Soviet expansion.[88] Still, when Truman assembled his cabinet on March 7 to review the crisis and the program he planned to put before Congress, the support they gave him was tempered by deep skepticism that a majority could be brought to assent. The Senate, after all, had just voted three days earlier to cut the president's budget for the coming fiscal year by $4.5 billion, and the House fifteen days earlier by $6 billion.[89] And as Truman himself noted, the commitment he was asking them to make had no fixed borders or timeline: "It means," he observed gravely, that "the United States is going into European politics," with no clear plan to get out.[90]

Thus was the ground being laid for a radical change in aid policy, one that would place it in the service of front-line foreign policy. Previous large-scale assistance for war-victim relief had been channeled through the United Nations Relief and Rehabilitation Administration (UNRRA). Founded in 1943, UNRRA was mainly financed by the United States, but outside of its direct control. UNRRA's criteria for support were "non-political."

American support for UNRRA activities, however, had been steadily eroding, and was dealt a blow by two incidents in August 1946 in which U.S. C-47 transport planes were shot down while inadvertently passing over Yugoslav territory on their way from Austria to Italy. In the first incident, on August 9, there were no fatalities, but officials in Belgrade initially denied U.S. consular access to the seven Americans. In the second, on the 19th, all five crew members were killed.

Secretary of State Jimmy Byrnes was enraged. He directed Clayton to take whatever action necessary to stop further UNRRA shipments to Yugoslavia, 73 percent of whose relief assistance from the organization was being funded by the United States. He further demanded that "when UNRRA expired, any new appropriations by Congress for foreign relief should be allocated by the United States and should go to those countries who would not denounce us for granting them the relief they asked for."[91] This reflected not only his personal views, but the reality that UNRRA was now deeply unpopular in Congress. He suggested that it was countries like Greece and Turkey that should get American aid, rather than those "who either from helplessness or otherwise are opposed to our principles."[92] Half a year later, a new secretary of state would have aid to these two states at the center of his department's agenda.

The president's speech would therefore mark a radical break from FDR's vision of a United States acting on the world stage through the new United Nations. It would instead mark the first time a U.S. administration would justify a muscular course of unilateral action outside the U.N., even though it would claim to do so in support of the organization's ends.[93] It would also signal, Acheson said privately, that "we were entering an adversary relationship" with the Soviet Union.[94]

❖

IRONICALLY, THE MAN WHOSE IDEAS ON THE IMPORTANCE OF CONTAIN-
ing Russia were most influential in framing the president's message was also the
most critical high-level voice over both its content and tone. But George Kennan would make a career out of repeatedly testing his powers of persuasion and
then recoiling from the consequences.

Kennan backed economic aid to Greece, but, believing the Soviet threat
remote, wanted to keep military aid to a minimum. He opposed any aid what-
soever to Turkey, which was successfully, he believed, resisting Soviet pressures
on its own. (He would temper this view three weeks later; by the summer he
would be backing covert operations in both countries.[95]) Even though the
speech would not mention the Soviet Union, Kennan thought it dangerously
confrontational. The emphasis on the irreconcilability of two "way[s] of life,"
one free and one relying on "terror and repression," combined with an un-
bounded American commitment to aid free peoples "resisting attempted subjugation" might, he feared, even provoke the Russians to launch a war.

Others, however, such as Forrestal, a hawk's hawk, felt that the United
States had to make a show of power in Greece and Turkey to deter the Soviets from pressing forward elsewhere. White House counsel and speechwriter
Clark Clifford agreed, and wanted the message strengthened; it was time for
"the opening gun" in the effort to awaken the American public to the dimensions of the Soviet threat.[96] He did the final touch-ups to the president's address
together with his aide George Elsey, who had coauthored a dark and ominous
100,000-word analysis of "American Relations with the Soviet Union" the
September prior. The Clifford-Elsey report, as it became known, had featured
a call for the United States to "support and assist democratic countries which
are in any way menaced or endangered by the U.S.S.R." Truman had ordered all
copies to be locked away at the time. "It would blow the roof off the Kremlin,"
he said. But for such elements of the report, the time had come.

The resulting speech, in Marshall's view, was "too much rhetoric," or in
Bohlen's reckoning "too much flamboyant anti-Communism." In Acheson's
view, though, it was sometimes necessary, when dealing with Congress, to
make arguments "clearer than the truth."

The White House insisted the Senate would never approve such a sweeping new policy without a spotlight on the communist threat.[97] Truman thought the first State Department draft "too much like an investment prospectus." He wanted "no hedge in this speech": It was to be "America's answer to the surge of Communist tyranny." The president himself rewrote the words "I believe it *should* be the policy of the United States" as "I believe it *must* be the policy . . . ," making a doctrine out of a statement of belief.[98]

Kennan's apparent split with Elsey went much deeper than just concern over the speech's tone. He never bought into Acheson's "rotten apple" theory—that one bad apple, Greece, could spoil the barrel. But many of Acheson's colleagues echoed him. When revolution is successful in one country, Ambassador MacVeagh argued, "it is the doctrine of international communism to breed [it] into the next country. . . . Greece and Turkey are a strategic line. If [the communists] break that down, the whole Near East falls." What Acheson described as rot spreading from apple to apple would later be captured by the image of falling dominoes, each knocking the next into the subsequent. Dominoes would become the metaphor of choice for Truman's successor, Eisenhower, in reference to Indochina in 1954.

Why were images of rotting apples and falling dominoes, typically offered with no reference to the politics, culture, topography, or indeed any specifics of the actual countries in question, as compelling as they were to those making the decisions? One answer lies in the rise of the discipline of geopolitics, as practiced through the analysis of maps and the spatial relations between their objects. Briton Halford Mackinder, arguably its founding father, had died only the day before the cabinet meeting approving Truman's speech proposal, on March 6. Mackinder, a man who "thought in metaphors,"[99] had undergone several major political conversions in his career, all driven largely by epiphanies triggered by the study of maps. The focal point of his final one was the supposed strategic centrality of the vast Eurasian "Heartland," which was dominated by Russia. "Who rules East Europe," he famously wrote in 1919, "commands the Heartland: Who rules the Heartland commands the World-Island: Who rules the World-Island commands the World."[100] The contiguous Heartland surface mass looms threateningly large on a map, particularly when the map is centered on it and distorted by an oval presentation (see Map 1).[101]

In 1943, Mackinder wrote an influential piece in *Foreign Affairs*, applying spatial analysis, arguing that "if the Soviet Union emerges from the war as conqueror of Germany, she must rank as the greatest land power on the globe."[102] The phenomenon of "cartohypnosis" was excoriated by some analysts at the time, but its influence would only grow during the Cold War.[103]

Truman had no difficulty accepting Acheson's and MacVeagh's postulates that the Caucasus and eastern Mediterranean were gateways to rapid Soviet world domination. Kennan, however, was deeply disturbed by what he saw as a turn toward naive and simplistic geostrategic thinking in the White House. He thought MacVeagh's thesis was nonsense; the Middle East, with its "patriarchal" system, was not amenable to Soviet control. Many countries—even China, he stressed—could "fall prey to totalitarian domination without any tragic consequences for world peace."[104] The father, witting or otherwise, of what was to become a doctrine of containing Soviet expansion, Kennan was nonetheless critical of what he saw as a dangerous American impulse "to see universal formulae or doctrines in which to clothe and justify particular actions."[105] But it was too late to try to change the president's thinking.

Truman would tell his daughter, Margaret, that he had been "worn to a frazzle" by "this terrible decision" to make the speech.[106] "I knew that George Washington's spirit would be invoked against me," he later reflected. Permanent entanglement in foreign rivalries was not something an American president undertook lightly. "But I was convinced that the policy I was about to proclaim was indeed as much required by the conditions of my day as was Washington's by the situation in his era."[107]

❖

SOMBERLY CLAD IN DARK SUIT AND DARK TIE, TRUMAN STRODE INTO THE packed House chamber just after 1 p.m. on March 12, 1947. Acheson sat in the front row, "perfectly tailored . . . stiff and straight as if at a memorial service, hands folded in his lap."[108] The mood was palpably solemn as Truman opened a black folder and began his address. (See Appendix A for the full text.)[109]

Speaking for nineteen minutes—clearly, slowly, with a measured forcefulness—he laid out a sweeping new doctrine of American global engagement. Each principle was introduced with a biblically inspired "I believe," a contrivance of Clifford and Elsey's to connect the president to his upbringing in Missouri.[110]

"I believe it must be the policy of the United States to support free peoples who are resisting attempted subjugation by armed minorities or by outside pressures," Truman declared. This support should come, first and foremost, in the form of "economic and financial aid," this being "essential to economic stability and orderly political processes." The assertion greatly elevated the role of economic intervention in the American diplomatic arsenal.

Truman juxtaposed the $400 million he was requesting to support Greece and Turkey with the $341 *billion* ($3.69 trillion in today's money) the United States had spent fighting World War II, declaring the former to be "an investment in world freedom and world peace." Though left unsaid, the implication was that a vastly more costly war could result if Congress rejected the assistance. The belief that massive economic assistance could achieve American objectives while obviating a costly military buildup would become the greatest misperception behind the storied aid initiative to come.

The backdrop of domino theory was unmistakable. "It is necessary only to glance at a map," Truman said, "to realize that the survival and integrity of the Greek nation are of grave importance in a much wider situation:

> If Greece should fall under the control of an armed minority, the effect upon its neighbor, Turkey, would be immediate and serious. Confusion and disorder might well spread throughout the entire Middle East. Moreover, the disappearance of Greece as an independent state would have a profound effect upon those countries in Europe whose peoples are struggling against great difficulties to maintain their freedoms and their independence while they repair the damages of war.

Greece and Turkey were not isolated centers of conflict; they were the front lines of a wider struggle to determine the political map of the postwar world.

This was, Truman concluded, "a serious course upon which we embark," one which he would "not recommend . . . except that the alternative is much more serious." For "If we falter in our leadership," he warned, "we may endanger the peace of the world—and we shall surely endanger the welfare of our nation." For this reason, he was "confident that the Congress [would] face these responsibilities squarely."

The chamber—members of both parties—rose in applause. Many, however, were visibly discomforted.[111]

Truman nodded left, nodded right. A sober Acheson knew that much work remained to create an actionable program out of the speech. The reaction in the hall, he concluded dispassionately, had been "a tribute to a brave man rather than unanimous acceptance of his policy."[112] The speech would live on to become "probably the most controversial that has been made by a president in the twentieth century."[113] It would be credited with stirring American intervention in Greece and Turkey, just as it would be blamed for McCarthyism and, later, Vietnam.

❖

"THE EPOCH OF ISOLATION AND OCCASIONAL INTERVENTION IS ENDED," declared *The New York Times*. "It is being replaced by an epoch of American responsibility[114]. . . . President Truman [has] called for action which will launch the United States on a new and positive foreign policy of world-wide responsibility for the maintenance of peace and order."[115]

"President Truman's latest address to Congress was, beyond question, one of the most momentous [congressional addresses] ever made by an American Chief Executive," enthused Barnet Nover of *The Washington Post*.[116]

"President Truman's message . . . is a corollary of the Monroe Doctrine," opined William Philip Simms in the *Washington Daily News*. "[T]he implications of the 'Truman Doctrine' are as grave as any the people of the United States ever were called upon to face."[117]

"The decision that Congress, acting for the American people, must [now] make is whether we will join issue with the already undeclared ideological war, by actively assisting those countries menaced by Russian communism," The *Augusta Chronicle* concluded, "or whether we shall continue a feeble diplomacy, based on appeasement and half-hearted opposition, while the totalitarian ideology of Russia nibbles away at the freedom of the peoples of the world."[118]

Despite the president's speech containing a single reference to communists (Greek ones),[119] and no references to the Soviet Union, the American press had judged the speech consequential, even if oblique as to the precise target of the call to action. "Congress," *The New York Times* wrote, "stepped into its new task" after the speech "somewhat bewildered."[120] Senator Vandenberg, however, highlighted the broad message just after leaving the House chamber: "The plain truth is that Soviet-American relationships are at the core of this whole problem. . . . The president's message faces facts," he declared, "and so must Congress."[121]

Across the ocean, the Soviet journal *New Times* criticized American aid to the "fascist" Greek and Turkish regimes, as well as Washington's aspirations to "world hegemony," but did not treat the speech as new policy. New York Soviet consul Yakov Lomakin reported to Deputy Foreign Minister Andrei Vyshinsky that "70–80% of the American people are opposed to granting aid to Greece and Turkey" because they feared it "could lead to war between the Soviet Union and the United States."[122]

The reaction of the Soviet leadership to the speech was critical, but not alarmist. Ambassador to Washington Nikolai Novikov told Molotov that the speech showed the United States would support "reactionary regimes" in Europe, while trying to undermine the progressive ones that had been established in the East. Molotov responded that "the President is trying to intimidate us, to turn as at a stroke into obedient little boys. But we don't give a damn."[123] He still believed that the Americans had no choice but to cooperate on the real issue that divided them: Germany. A Communist Party Central Committee analysis was even more confident, proclaiming that Truman's speech had been directed as much at London as it was Moscow. "[I]t signifies Britain's expulsion from its sphere of influence in the Mediterranean and the Near East."[124]

The Truman Doctrine, as Molotov and Stalin saw it, was a regional policy, directed at an area that was simply not a Soviet priority. There would be a time and a place to challenge it; just not now. In his encounter with Marshall in Moscow the following month, Stalin would not even mention the matter.

For its part, the State Department had misapprehended the position of Greece in the hierarchy of Soviet geopolitical objectives, conflating an ally's failings (Britain's) with an opponent's strategy. It had judged Greece a vacuum in the collapsing British imperium into which Stalin would pour arms, funds, and troops if the United States did not declare its immediate intention to do the same with greater alacrity. Yet the Soviet leader had accepted that Greece was of little strategic importance to Moscow relative to other Balkan states, and had no designs on the country at this point.[125]

Stalin had in fact remained allegiant to the infamous October 1944 "percentages" agreement scribbled by Churchill, according to which Britain would maintain "90%" influence in postwar Greece in return for predominant Soviet influence in most of the Balkans and eastern Europe. Shortly after the deal, former foreign minister Maxim Litvinov wrote a strategy memorandum assigning all of the Balkans to the Soviet "security sphere," with the explicit exception of Greece and Turkey.[126] When French leader Charles de Gaulle asked Stalin about Greece shortly after, he replied, "Ask Churchill."[127]

Despite ample scope for strategic interpretation conducive to his interests, Stalin, in Churchill's words, "adhered strictly and faithfully to [the] agreement.... [D]uring all the long weeks of fighting the Communists in the streets of Athens, not one word of reproach came from *Pravda* or *Izvestiia*." Stalin "let his people be beaten up in Greece for the sake of his larger plans": establishing control in "his" parts of the continent, particularly Poland and Yugoslavia, with a minimum of force and treasure. When Molotov in February 1945 proposed an amendment to the draft Yalta declaration calling for "support [to] be given to the political leaders" of countries who were resisting the Nazis, clearly intended to legitimate Soviet backing for communist fighters in the East and the Balkans, Stalin reassured a worried Churchill: "[T]he prime minister," he said, "need have no anxiety that Mr. Molotov's amendment was designed to apply to Greece." In April, following Roosevelt's death, Stalin emphasized to Churchill and Truman that he recognized "how important . . . Greece [is] to the security of Great Britain," and therefore did not "interfere" there. He expected a similar appreciation for Soviet security interests in Poland.[128]

Stalin might, of course, have considered his part of the Balkan deal moot after the British abdication in Greece. But all evidence says otherwise. Molotov, in a January 1945 note for his staff, drew a distinction between the government of Poland, which was a "big deal" for Moscow and no business of the West, and those of "Belgium, France, Greece" and other states in the Western orbit, where "no one asked" what Moscow thought.[129] And in handwritten comments on a Vyshinsky memo the following month, he referred to Greece, where Moscow had "not interfered," as "the *Anglo-American* zone of military action," and not just a British protectorate.[130]

Picking his points of conflict with care, Stalin had also never been persuaded of the Greek rebels' capabilities, and had decided early on they were not worth the costs and risks of Soviet support. In January 1945 he had told Yugoslav leaders that the Greek Communists "believed mistakenly that the Red Army would reach to the Aegean Sea. . . . We cannot send our troops to Greece. The [Greek Communists] made a stupid error."[131] He would repeatedly castigate Yugoslav prime minister Josip Broz Tito for aiding them in a lost cause. He did not want his allies doing anything that would attract American air and naval power into the Mediterranean and threaten his interests in eastern and central Europe.

Truman's speech changed little in this regard. In early 1948, Stalin would once again scold Yugoslav diplomats for their country's continued assistance to the Greek guerrillas. The conflict "had no chance of success at all," he told them. "What, do you think, that . . . the United States, the most powerful state in the world, will permit you to break their line of communication in the Mediterranean? Nonsense!"[132] By the summer of 1949 the communist insurgency would be defeated.

As for Turkey, Stalin had been chastened by Truman's tough response to his threats the previous summer. "It was good that we backed down in time," Molotov later reflected. "Otherwise it would have led to a joint [British-American] aggression against us."[133]

But if the State Department was over-alarmist about Greece and Turkey, it underestimated Stalin's willingness to challenge British and American prerogatives elsewhere in Europe. It failed to see that the counterpart to Soviet forbearance in the Mediterranean was a dogmatic insistence on its political and economic rights in Germany and nations further east. Thus the State Department's analysis was off the mark not so much in its emphasis on an irreconcilability of American and Soviet interests as in its understanding of where those interests actually lay.

ON CAPITOL HILL, TRUMAN WAS UNABLE TO BASK IN APPLAUSE FOR LONG. Resistance to the new Truman Doctrine emerged from both sides of the aisle.

The criticisms were numerous and weighty. The Greek government was corrupt. The Turks failed to fight on our side during the war. Economic aid might be fine, but military aid was dangerous. It would end hopes of rapprochement with the Russians. It was bailing out the British empire. The cost was exorbitant. It was warlike. It was power politics. It committed America to supporting reactionary governments. And if Greece, why not China? Where would it end? Former FDR vice president Henry Wallace was relentless in opposition. Truman, he said, was plunging the country into a "reckless adventure." He was "betraying the great tradition of America" by committing it to a policy of "ruthless imperialism."[134]

Perhaps the one focus of opposition to the speech that caught the White House genuinely by surprise was the president's bypassing of the new United Nations. Opinion polls a week after the speech found that the public preferred, by a margin of more than two to one, to see the Greek problem handed over to the U.N. The U.N. thereby became a rallying cry for both the pro-Soviet left and the isolationist right.

Vandenberg was now on the defensive. Though he stressed that the U.N. had neither the funds for relief nor the authority to provide military assistance, he threw out some banal proposals for the U.N. to investigate violations of Greek sovereignty and to conclude military-support agreements with member states. He later called it "a colossal blunder" of the administration to ignore the U.N.[135]

Columnist and author Walter Lippmann, a virtual "minister without portfolio" in Washington,[136] thought the U.N. kerfuffle only part of a wider error the administration had made in talking only with the British government before announcing its proposed action; it should have brought in "the French, the Chinese, and the Russians" themselves. In any case, it needed now to explain its intentions before the Security Council, "not waiting until Gromyko attacks them"—referring to the Soviet U.N. ambassador. What would happen, Lippmann asked, if a Communist-led government came to power somewhere by elections and called upon Moscow for aid? "What under the 'Truman Doctrine' do we do if the Soviet government says there is an emergency, that it has been invited to intervene, [and] that the UN is not in a position to extend the kind of help required?"[137] The president needed to preempt such action by involving the U.N., not simply declaring its impotence and thereby inviting the Soviets to do the same.

Acheson accused Lippmann of "sabotaging" U.S. foreign policy. But he acknowledged privately that he should have advised Truman first to seek U.N. protection for Greece and Turkey. The inevitable Soviet veto would have given the administration helpful political cover. The damage done, however, he and Vandenberg hammered out an amendment to the Greece-Turkey aid bill that situated the U.S. initiative in the context of U.N. purposes and actions, and laid out conditions under which U.S. assistance would be subsumed by the body. To flatter the senator into supporting the bill, the administration named it the "Vandenberg Amendment." Acheson, who knew the Soviets would never allow the U.N. to take charge, considered it "a cheap price to pay for Vandenberg's patronage."[138]

U.S. ambassador to the U.N. Warren Austin went before the body on March 28, 1947, to explain American actions in Greece and their complementarity with U.N. initiatives under way. Gromyko, not surprisingly, blasted U.S. preemption of the Security Council and interference in Greek and Turkish internal affairs.

His challenge didn't hurt matters; quite the opposite. Though both Republicans and liberal Democrats had grave reservations about Truman's initiative, the political consequences of appearing soft on communism overwhelmed most congressmen. Even Lippmann came out in favor of the $400 million aid bill, which was approved by a vote of 67 to 23 in the Senate on April 22 and by a similar margin of 287 to 107 in the House on May 9.[139] The president signed it into law on May 22.

WILLIAM LOCKHART CLAYTON WAS AN UNLIKELY STRATEGIC COLLABOrator for professional intellectuals such as Dean Acheson and George Kennan. His formal education in the South was minimal. He left school at age fifteen to work as a secretary to a St. Louis cotton merchant. A boy of great raw intellect and stubborn independence, he took the hardscrabble road to creating the largest cotton brokerage in the world. A 1936 *Time* magazine cover article gave him the sobriquet "King Cotton."

A tall, direct but mannerly, angularly good-looking teetotaler, "a polished cowboy [with] bushy white sideburns,"[140] Clayton was drawn into politics after the market crash of 1929, determined to help halt the country's slide toward protectionism. He blasted the 1930 Republican Smoot-Hawley tariffs as "the greatest crime of the century." Having no party affinity, let alone affiliation, he only warmed to the new FDR administration after the president named his close friend, and passionate free trader, Cordell Hull as secretary of state in 1933. He considered Roosevelt's interventionist domestic economic policies radical and misguided, yet acceded when the president asked him to run raw materials purchasing through the Reconstruction Finance Corporation in 1940. Though his wife, Sue, a passionate New Dealer, had pushed him into government, she would thereafter work diligently to get him back out. Despite never being accepted by the left of the Democratic Party, and despite offering to resign five times, Clayton advanced through a series of posts focused on procurement, finance, and foreign economic policy before becoming Truman's under secretary of state for economic affairs in 1946.[141]

Now, ill and secluded at his ranch near Tucson, the sixty-seven-year-old Clayton crystallized his thoughts on the growing European crisis. The result was a memorandum dated March 5 that further galvanized Acheson.

The memo's coverage was sweeping, its prose unadorned, its tone grave. The fall of Britain, the rise of Russia, the collapse of Greece—all these imminent threats, Clayton wrote, had worrisome implications for the Middle East, France, Africa, and American hopes of preventing a "third world war."

Clayton, like Acheson, was concerned by the uncontrolled collapse of the British empire. "The reins of world leadership," Clayton wrote, "will be picked up either by the United States or by Russia. If by Russia," he warned, "there will almost certainly be war in the next decade or so, with the odds against us." Russia, he said, was "boring from within" to undermine weak governments in Europe and beyond. The United States needed urgently to bolster them, but lacked the capacity to take the necessary sustained action because the war-weary American public simply did not fathom the grave danger posed by an unchecked Russia. Marshall's imminent trip to Moscow, Clayton predicted, would yield nothing: "The odds are heavily against any constructive results there."

What was needed, Clayton said, was that the president himself "shock" the American people with "the truth and the whole truth." The "integrity and independence" of many nations, vital to long-term American security interests, was under assault. The new United Nations was ill-equipped to deal with this threat, as it came not in the form of traditional external military aggression but a much less visible, though equally insidious, undermining of legitimate national political institutions from the inside.

Though the United States did "not wish to interfere in the domestic affairs of any country," Clayton insisted, it had no choice but to tie financial aid to reforms that would ensure it was "permanently beneficial." The new IBRD had ostensibly been created to provide aid to war-torn nations but, like the United Nations, it was unsuited to the current challenge. The fundamentally political character of the crises made intervention by international bodies untenable.

Clayton would have no patience with objections that would be raised against U.S. aid—that it was unaffordable and would lead to renewed military conflict. He insisted that "World War III" was inevitable if the United States *failed* to involve itself "in the affairs of foreign countries" at this critical moment, and that anchoring today's fragile peace would be far less costly than fighting such a war.[142]

On the same day, Acheson delivered a short memo to Secretary of War Patterson on "the Greek and Turkish problem," stressing that it was only "part of a much larger problem growing out of the change in Great Britain's strength"—a delicate way of referring to the global political vacuum created by the collapse of the British empire. The president, Acheson noted, had on February 26 approved in principle Patterson's call for immediate aid to Greece and Turkey. Acheson now wanted to go further, urging a study of "situations elsewhere in the world which may require analogous financial, technical, and military aid on our part."[143]

With Clayton's and Acheson's memos, the stage was being set for a muscular diplomatic offensive to prevent the Kremlin from expanding its influence be-yond the parts of eastern and central Europe it currently occupied. Simultane-ously, however, the secretary of state would be flying to Moscow with the aim of salvaging cooperation in the country of greatest strategic significance to both the United States and the Soviet Union: Germany.

Council of Foreign Ministers meeting in Moscow, March 1947. From left: British Foreign Secretary Ernest Bevin, U.S. Secretary of State George Marshall, Soviet Foreign Minister Vyacheslav Molotov, and French Foreign Minister Georges Bidault.

THREE

RUPTURE

MARCH 9, 1947: MARSHALL'S C-54 ARRIVED IN MOSCOW FROM BERLIN ON A brisk, snowy afternoon. In preparation for the secretary's motorcade, the Soviets had decked out the area around the embassy, creating "a virtual Potemkin village" to showcase the nation's heroic economic recovery. The avenues gleamed, the garbage having been shunted into nearby alleys. The decision for Marshall to stay at Spaso House, the embassy residence, was wise, or fortunate; the refurbished Moskva Hotel, where his staff stayed, was bugged.[1]

George Catlett Marshall was the first American general given the five-star rank, and the first career soldier appointed secretary of state. Formal to the point of brusqueness, he called all colleagues by their last name and expected all to do likewise with him. "Only my wife calls me George," he corrected Truman. He treated interlocutors with decorum, and demanded the same of them, including the man he had flown to Moscow to see. When at a boozy dinner Molotov asked whether soldiers turning statesmen in America meant that "the troops [were] goose-stepping," Marshall looked away. "Please tell Mr. Molotov that I'm not sure I understand the purport of his remark," he told his translator, Bohlen, "but if it is what I think it is please tell him I do not like it."

Appointed Army chief of staff in 1939, Marshall had his maiden diplomatic encounter with the Soviet foreign minister. Molotov had come to Washington in May 1942 demanding more Lend-Lease aid and an immediate second front in the European war. Roosevelt brought in Marshall, his chief military strategist, to set out the terms under which it could be launched. Marshall was characteristically direct. Given the rate of ship loss inflicted by German bombers, he explained, the United States did not have the naval capacity to send supplies through Murmansk *and* to invade western Europe. So "what do you want," he asked in summation, "the second front or Murmansk? It isn't possible to provide both." He then berated the translator for abbreviating his remarks.

Though Stalin typically punished such impertinence from his own officials, he was, it later emerged, impressed with the general's straightforward manner. Marshall was also direct with his own president, who was anxious to assure Molotov of an August start date for the main Anglo-American invasion. Marshall warned against it, rightly predicting that the British would not be ready.[2] The invasion would not come for another two years.

At the war's end, Marshall was serving a new Democratic president, one who was stumbling to shape relations with the two new great powers: the Soviet Union and China. Marshall's retirement on November 26, 1945, lasted all of six days before Truman was on the phone asking him to go to China to broker peace between Chiang Kai-shek's corrupt Kuomintang Nationalists and Mao Tse-tung's brutal, anti-American Communists. He accepted, turning down as much as half a million dollars to write his memoirs.[3] In China Marshall got his first bitter taste of diplomacy between irreconcilable rivals.[4] In parallel, over in Europe, Secretary of State Jimmy Byrnes was getting nowhere in discussions with Molotov over peace treaties with the defeated Axis nations. Citing health issues, but laboring under strained relations with the president, Byrnes agreed to stay on only until the end of the year. Truman, through General Eisenhower, told Marshall he wished him to take Byrnes' place.

"My answer is in the affirmative," Marshall responded, military style, "if that continues to be [the president's] desire. My personal reaction is something else."[5]

Despite his failure to buttress the "liberals" in each of the warring Chinese camps, and to achieve any breakthrough in the negotiations, Marshall remained a hero at home. On January 8, 1947, the GOP-controlled Senate Foreign Relations Committee confirmed him unanimously. The Senate did the same. The whole process took under an hour. The media pressed the new secretary of state on his presidential ambitions. Marshall insisted, truthfully, that he would never run for office.[6]

Though he considered himself a failed diplomat at that point—"I tried to please everyone, [so] that by the time I left [China] nobody trusted me"[7]— Marshall had learned a lesson abroad. His biggest failure was not one of persuasion, which was never likely to succeed, but neglecting to set out an alternative strategy. He would not repeat this mistake with Molotov.

Vyacheslav Skryabin derived his revolutionary name from the Russian word *molot*, or hammer. As a communist, Molotov was, from a young age, a true believer. He embraced the tenets of Marxist theory, from its characterization of history as a series of struggles between the proletariat and its exploiters to its promise of revolutionary victory over the forces of global capitalism. He first met Stalin, ten years his senior, when he was twenty-two, in 1912; both were at the time working to create the new party newspaper, *Pravda*. After the overthrow of Tsar Nicholas in March 1917, Stalin supported collaboration with the democratic provisional government; Molotov, more doctrinaire, did not. But both rallied around Lenin in the run-up to the Bolshevik coup in November. The Russian civil war that followed, in which millions were killed or starved to death, was a defining event for all three men. Persuasion as a tactic was of little use in such a conflict; physical and psychological coercion became the methods of choice. The three became vessels of "conspiracy, self-righteousness, cruelty, single-mindedness, and contempt for written rules and compromises."[8]

All future conflicts, both internal and external, would be seen through the lens of deadly struggle. Ends would get blurred along the way; global communism would remain the ultimate end, but more proximate ones, notably physical and political survival, would command their energies. Ideology nonetheless remained the basis for confidence that capitalism needed merely to be outlasted. Internal contradictions assured its collapse.

In 1921, at Lenin's suggestion, Molotov became the Party Central Committee's secretary, a position in which he established his permanent professional persona. Though known to be an affectionate family man, in affairs of state he was ruthlessly efficient—and efficiently ruthless. Severe with staff, he carried out tasks in any way necessary. Obsequious toward those in charge, he threatened no one above him. Lenin supposedly called him the "best filing clerk in Russia"; Trotsky called him "mediocrity incarnate." When Stalin was appointed party general secretary in 1922, Molotov became his loyal subordinate. He would continue to play this role in different posts through to his present one, to which he ascended in 1939 when Stalin removed the Jewish Litvinov to smooth transactions with Hitler.

That Molotov, though well-educated, spoke only Russian and knew little of the world were of no consequence.[9] He followed his *vozhd*, his leader, unquestioningly, authorizing the political murder of thousands with icy insouciance. "Haste ruled the day," he later reflected on the process. "Could one go into all the details?"[10] Within the party he was known as "Iron Ass," a reference to his ability to master even petty details, as well as to outlast opponents through boundless stubbornness and stamina. Foreign counterparts came to know these skills, and to hate as well as admire his performances. Byrnes called him a "lineal descendant" of Job, a man of "unlimited patience." In any negotiation, he "will win your reluctant admiration for the resourcefulness he exhibits in his delaying tactics. He will sit through it all imperturbably, stroking his mustache or spinning his pince-nez glasses as he waits for a translation and smoking Russian cigarettes in what seems to be an endless chain."[11] "Observing in action all the great world statesmen of our century," remarked John Foster Dulles, representing the Republican majority in Marshall's delegation, "I never came across diplomatic skills at as high a level as those of Molotov."[12] French foreign minister Georges Bidault spoke of Molotov's "untiring capacity for repeating himself."[13] Churchill remarked that he had "never seen a human being who more perfectly represented the modern conception of a robot." Yet "in the conduct of foreign affairs, Sully, Talleyrand, and Metternich," the greatest diplomats of all time, "would welcome him to their company."[14]

Molotov may have been the more accomplished negotiator, but Marshall had at least one advantage. Unlike in China, he had come to Russia with a fallback position—a plan, or at least the outlines of one, to cut loose the tethers of Yalta and move forward on matters of vital U.S. interest unilaterally. Truman's speech was still two days away, but, together with Clayton's and Acheson's memos, it would establish a framework for using financial, technical, and military aid to bolster allies against Soviet trespass. Molotov, in contrast, had no Plan B. A western Germany beyond Soviet control was, at this point, still unthinkable.

❖

THE ENCOUNTER BETWEEN MARSHALL AND MOLOTOV BEGAN IN THE ORnate main hall of the Aviation Industry Building on March 10. The British and French foreign ministers, Ernest Bevin and Georges Bidault, represented the other two occupying powers in the Berlin-based Allied Control Council (ACC) governing Germany. Though spiritually aligned with Marshall, the Briton and the Frenchman each had his own national interest to protect in charting Germany's future. The Soviet foreign minister was ready for opportunities to exploit divisions in the Western camp.

Ambassador Novikov set the scene: "Molotov, . . . Marshall, . . . Bidault, . . . Bevin and their assistants [sat] solemnly at a huge, round table, with their advisers sitting behind them with fat folders, ready to assist their chiefs at any moment."[15] Molotov, observed Colonel Marshall (Pat) Carter, the secretary of state's liaison officer, sat "chin in hand," occasionally nodding slowly with no discernible meaning. He was "completely poker-faced." The tortoise-shelled Bevin, cigarette dangling loosely from his mouth, resembled "a cross between Santa Claus and a Welsh coalman." Bidault, in contrast, was the "smoothy type," effecting an air of ennui, wishing "to look bigger than he is." The self-taught Bevin couldn't pronounce his name, alternating between "Biddle" and "Bidet."[16]

For his part, Bidault, who had not met Marshall previously, observed that the general was "unaffected" yet "quite cautious," never "strik[ing] up rash poses or speak[ing] off the cuff." He read from notes. He "did not pretend to be infallible," but was firm "once he had made up his mind" on an issue—"nothing could [make] him change it, not even the President of the United States in person." Weeks of interacting with Marshall would leave an indelible impact on France's top diplomat. Deeply patriotic, an active French resistance fighter during the war, Bidault was never shy about criticizing the United States; yet he would echo Truman in calling Marshall "the greatest American alive."[17]

Certainly too American for Molotov. In his characteristic guileless and un-adorned style, Marshall stressed the importance of reviving German political life. The ACC, he said, was making no progress; the various states of the country needed to adopt constitutional guarantees of rights to association, speech, and movement. "We will never democratize Germany," Marshall concluded, "by the mere negative process of depriving the Nazis of their positions and influence." The interjection, Ambassador Smith observed, "was probably the most forthright statement on the rights of man ever made in Russia." This was enough to explain its failure to engage Molotov, who saw German democratization as a hostile act to undermine Soviet rights.

The Soviet Union, Molotov put back laconically, was not interested in "the generalities of democracy."[18] Within the joint economic region the Americans and the British had established in the western part of the country, known as Bizonia, they were, he complained, merely rebuilding the old capitalist cartels and trusts that had helped bring about the war. Back in November, War Secretary Patterson had told a reporter that "Russia will be so impressed by the success [of Bizonia] that [it] will fall into line and join us";[19] the opposite was the case.

The exchange exposed the widening chasm between Washington and Moscow. Whereas the Americans appealed to hope, fear drove the Soviets. Marshall spoke of a stable, pacific, independent Germany as an aspiration, one that could be met with goodwill and cooperation among the victorious wartime allies. Molotov spoke of Germany as a looming mortal threat, one that could only be eliminated through Soviet power over the country's economic and political structures.

The danger for both sides lay in the fact that the United States would not disengage from Europe until its aspirations were met; this in turn would heighten Soviet mistrust of American intentions, encouraging Moscow to tighten its grip on eastern Europe and foment resistance to non-Communist parties in the West. Realists such as Churchill and Byrnes had tried to head off such a spiral of conflict by groping toward a division of the continent into spheres of influence—a classic European concept to which Kennan had become a late convert. Yet unbridgeable differences over Germany were making a broader mutual accommodation impossible.[20]

Molotov returned again and again to the issue of reparations, which he insisted were Moscow's right based on agreements made, though never officially recorded, during the wartime conferences. The Soviet Union wanted $10 billion ($108 billion in today's money) out of current German production. But Marshall was immovable. "We cannot accept a unified Germany," he explained, "under a procedure which in effect would mean that the American people would pay reparations to an ally." Western Germany had to be able to feed itself before it took care of others. The United States was financing reparations, since it was filling the gap between what western Germany needed to survive and what it was capable of producing for consumption and trade. Failure to revive western Germany would mean an unacceptable never-ending drain on the U.S. Treasury.

For the Soviet Union, a revived industrial western Germany under American protection meant, in the long run, a renewed threat of invasion. Stalin, as an autocrat, was by nature and by circumstance paranoid; but paranoids have enemies. And Germany, which had just wiped out over a tenth of the Soviet population and a quarter of its capital assets, would always be one.[21] Germany's revival also meant a denial of the resources Moscow needed, and expected, to rebuild its own shattered infrastructure. Molotov rejected the logic of Marshall's arguments about deficits in the western zones: these, he insisted, could be controlled just by cutting back German consumption. Germany was a rich country: its living standards simply had to fall until the needs of its victims were met.

More resources would need to be extracted from the east of Germany if less were extracted from the west, which created economic and political problems for Moscow. "America, England, and France were helping West Germany," Molotov later recalled, and "bit by bit we were creating . . . our Germany." But "what would these people think of us if we had pulled everything out of the country? . . . After all, we were taking from the Germans who wanted to work with us. It had to be done very carefully."[22]

⊹

REPARATIONS HAD BEEN A SOURCE OF CONTENTION AMONG THE WARtime allies going back to Yalta. In February 1945, Roosevelt accepted the logic of reparations and agreed to $20 billion ($268 billion in today's money)—half of which for Russia—as a basis for further discussion; but he would make no commitments. Churchill, however, opposed reparations that large, recalling the bitter experience with such claims after World War I.

"If you want a horse to pull your wagon," the PM told Stalin, "you have to give him some hay." Twenty billion dollars was roughly equivalent to Germany's prewar gross exports. Starved Germans with no equipment would be in no position to produce on such a scale. But Stalin waved him off. Feeding the horse could be dangerous, he said. It might must just "turn around and kick you."[23]

Despite the differences with Churchill, Roosevelt's sympathetic bent settled the matter for the Soviets. "We assess [Yalta] as a highly positive fact, particularly . . . on the issue of reparations," the Commissariat of Foreign Affairs informed Soviet diplomats immediately following the Crimean conference.[24] When FDR died in April, however, Truman brought in his own hard-nosed reparations negotiator, Edwin Pauley. The Texas oilman transformed the tenor of the discussions from moral to commercial. Attitudes toward Russian claims hardened, particularly as reports came in from Europe of Russian troops stripping bare German factories, railroad equipment, and the like—a third of the country's capital equipment—and shipping the useful portions back to Russia.[25]

By the time of the Potsdam Conference in July 1945, U.S. experts had also persuaded the administration that repeating the German reparations experience of the 1920s would be a political and economic disaster. This time, reparations debt had to be calculated only after first allowing for a reasonable German standard of living.

The Big Three agreed that it should not be better than that of the neighbors Germany had brutalized. But this formulation only led to haggling. Britain, whose occupation zone was the most industrialized, pushed for high ceilings on German production. More output would afford Britain more tradable goods to pay for food imports. The bitter and fearful French, in contrast, demanded even stricter caps than the Russians. Paris also wanted to place the Ruhr under international control and annex the Saar as a means of arrogating Germany's economic might and defanging its military. It had pressed the same course after World War I to underwrite German reparations and French border security.[26]

The Russians, for their part, believed the Americans had the lessons of the 1920s entirely wrong. The mistake made after World War I was allowing the Germans to escape obligations to their victims. "Everybody [in Russia] would say that reparations come first and imports after because we have suffered so much," insisted Ivan Maisky, Russia's diplomatic éminence grise. "If there is a conflict between reparations and imports, then imports must give way."

Will Clayton rejected this stance point-blank. "The American people will not again," he put back, "as they did after [the] last war, finance Germany." Byrnes echoed him categorically: "Not a dollar will be paid on reparations until imports are paid for."[27] Ambassador Harriman insisted that the United States follow a "policy of taking care of Western Allies and other areas under our responsibility first, allocating to Russia what may be left."[28]

In theory, Washington and Moscow were to avoid conflict in Germany through implementation of agreed provisions for handling its economic affairs. The Potsdam protocol called for treating Germany, though divided into four zones of occupation, as a single economic unit. Common policies were to be set for production, pricing, currency, transportation, and the like, but with due allowance for "varying local conditions." Import and export programs were to be devised for the entire country, with essential commodities to be distributed equitably across the zones. The Allied Control Council was to determine a level of industry in the country that could support a base standard of living no higher than the European average, excluding Britain and the Soviet Union. So-called excess industrial capacity would then be dismantled and distributed as reparations.[29] The Soviets, who had wanted a simple, firm, hard-dollar commitment on reparations, signed on to the arrangement only because it was the best they could get from the Americans in exchange for an agreement on Polish border changes.[30]

In practice, the protocol proved unworkable. "The Potsdam Agreement was incomplete, unrealistic, and ambiguous," in the verdict of U.K. Treasury economist Alec Cairncross. "The clauses governing reparations," in particular, "proved to be contradictory and obscure." Since the unanimity required for action in the ACC was generally impossible to achieve, it was inevitable that each of the four powers would end up doing what it wanted in its own zone. And the fact that each power would lay first claim to reparations in its own zone was, as Treasury's Wilfred Eady presciently observed in July 1945, "a decisive step towards the separation of Germany into a Western Area and an Eastern Area under Russia."[31]

❖

THE REPARATIONS STANDOFF WITHIN THE ACC TURNED BITTER IN MAY 1946. The Soviets, who had been receiving 10 percent of reparations from the western zones, were failing to meet reciprocal obligations to deliver food and raw materials from the eastern zones. Soviet General Georgy Zhukov insisted that food supplies were insufficient to permit shipments to the West. Moscow further decided that moving industrial plants from Germany to the Soviet Union, a form of reparations approved by the western powers, was too costly and time-consuming. It began taking reparations from current production instead.

In effect, the Soviets chose to "have the golden eggs laid by the goose [rather] than the goose itself."[32] To this end, they transformed two hundred enterprises in their zone, representing over a quarter of its productive capacity, into Soviet-controlled corporations in which they granted themselves a majority stake. The output was then shipped to the Soviet Union for internal use or reexport.[33] This arrangement made "economic unity" in Germany, to which the three powers had committed at Potsdam, a practical impossibility.

The British and Americans took the position that no occupying power could claim reparations from current production in its zone before Germany *as a whole* was self-supporting. British military governor Sir Brian Robertson argued that the so-called first-charge principle had to be applied: exports needed to be sufficient to pay for imports *before* reparations were paid. But his Soviet counterpart, Vasily Sokolovsky, retorted that the principle had no bearing on reparations, as exports were a matter to be managed on a *zonal* basis. American deputy military governor Lucius Clay rejected this interpretation, insisting that only a common trade policy could satisfy the requirement of economic unity.

Sokolovsky shrewdly shifted the blame to the French governor, Pierre Koenig (whom Clay dismissed as an "absolute out-and-out Gaullist" nationalist[34]), by asking him whether his government were ready to establish a central administrative apparatus to bring unity about. Koenig responded as the Russian expected: *non*. So whereas the French claimed to support the Anglo-American stance on German economic unity, the absence of any machinery to implement it made the issue moot.[35]

The hard-driving General Clay, known unaffectionately in the State Department as "the Kaiser," declared an impasse. Acting on his own initiative, he now made one of the most fateful decisions of the early Cold War. He banned further reparations deliveries from the American zone, and ordered an end to the dismantling of German factories for such purposes. The British and French followed soon after, having little choice given the American refusal to partici-pate further in the four-power administrative machinery to value plants for reparations.[36]

"The Potsdam agreement must be implemented as a whole and not in part," Clay wrote by way of explanation to General Oliver Echols at the War Depart-ment. "Germany must be treated as an economic unit; indigenous resources must be used first to meet essential German requirements and second to pro-duce exports that can finance essential imports."[37] Whereas Clay was determined to create a self-sustaining Germany with a base standard of living, from which it might advance without limit, the Soviets were determined to hold down Germa-ny's industrial capacity and ensure a continuous flow of reparations—irrespec-tive of the effect on the local population. They would thereafter maintain that Washington had destroyed Potsdam by reneging on its reparations and policy-coordination commitments. Washington would retort that Moscow was at fault for failing to fulfill its commitments on German economic unity.

✥

A FEW WEEKS AFTER CLAY'S SUSPENSION OF REPARATIONS, IN JUNE 1946, former Soviet foreign minister Maxim Litvinov agreed to an interview with American correspondent Richard Hottelet in Moscow. His remarks were so candid that Hottelet decided to report them to the U.S. embassy rather than air them. The Soviet Union, Litvinov said, was withdrawing into the "outmoded concept of geographical security," for which Germany was now of the essence. It had become the world's "greatest problem." And since "each side," East and West, "wants a unified Germany under its control," it would "obviously [have to] be broken up into two parts." There was no other solution.[38]

Yet Clay had not intended to precipitate anything of the sort. His relations with Zhukov and Sokolovsky were warm, and he displayed persistent (Kennan would insist naive) faith that differences with Moscow could and would be over-come. Grilled by reporters in Berlin as to whether his action had been directed at the Russians, he shook his head no: "Not to the Russians. It's to everybody."[39]

"Everybody" was Clay's euphemism for the French and the Russians, possibly more so the former.[40] Walt Rostow, on a State Department mission in Berlin, cabled Washington that "Whether correct or not it is the Berlin [State Department] view that Clay's hold-up of reparations is designed rather more to get the French obstruction cleared up than to show up Russian intentions."[41] Clay's correspondence indeed shows clear and enduring frustration with the French for undermining four-power cooperation on reparations and trade. "The Russians are tough horse-traders," Clay would tell a *New Republic* journalist in early 1947, "but we are negotiating with them on a basis of reasonable give and take. . . . The French, with their demand for the Saar and the internationalization of the Ruhr, are far more intransigent."[42] But if his intention was to shake the French rather than anger the Russians, he failed.

Having not been party to the Potsdam accords, the French felt nothing but bitter resentment over their exclusion. Concerned mainly with annexing territory and stripping the remainder for reparations, the French sought to run their occupation zone in splendid isolation. Clay wrote an angry thirty-page memo in April 1946 stressing the grave economic and political consequences of bowing to French demands in Germany. Amputating the heavily industrialized Ruhr region, with its thirteen million inhabitants, would reduce the rest of the country to "a pastoral economy" dependent on American aid. The resulting unemployment and unrest would fuel "Communism and totalitarianism," thereby undermining the aim of democratizing the country and obliging the United States to increase its armed presence.

The State Department argued that failure to accommodate French concerns would fuel communism *in France*. French Communists would use the specter of German military revival to stir popular fear and anger toward Washington. Clay, for his part, was disgusted by French security arguments for severing off the Ruhr, insisting they were based on "a prehistoric concept of warfare" that should have been buried with "the overrunning of the Maginot Line."[43] When it came to France, Clay and the State Department could agree on little beyond the belief that the other's policies would aid communism.

The State Department's disposition would largely prevail. The French unilaterally declared a customs barrier between the Saar and Germany in December 1946, integrating it economically with France—a first step toward annexation.

An angry Clay was dissuaded from resigning only by Byrnes' sheepish pledges of sympathy with his opposition to the move.[44] Yet it had been Byrnes himself who had declared in Stuttgart in September that "The United States does not feel that it can deny to France, which has been invaded three times by Germany in 70 years, its claim to the Saar territory."[45] When it came to Germany, the State Department treated the French as a mere benign tumor and the Soviets, increasingly, a malignant one.

�֎

OVER THE COURSE OF 1946, THE LOGICAL FABRIC OF STATE DEPARTMENT policy toward postwar Europe was being stretched taut. On the one side, there was the first-charge policy on German imports, such as food, which required that they be paid for before reparations were made. Since France and other liberated countries expected reparations, this policy required maximizing German export revenue by selling its output, such as coal, at market prices. The larger the German trade surplus, the more money available for reparations. On the other side, however, it was also policy to put the recovery of the liberated countries ahead of Germany's. This policy, in contrast to the first-charge policy, encouraged the United States to *underprice* German exports so as to keep down import costs for its allies.

Underpricing won out, resulting in a substantial German trade deficit that had to be covered by the War Department's budget, fueling tensions with the State Department. The American taxpayer ultimately bore the cost, as it had in the 1920s: financing German recovery by handing to others the means by which Germany could otherwise finance itself. And "in the mind of the public," Clay complained to State, the spending in Germany amounted to "feeding the enemy."[46]

The most logical way to address the problem would have been to increase German industrial production. But doing so would have contravened U.S. occupation policy, which held that production should be restricted to prevent Germany reemerging as a military power. By the summer of 1946, the administration saw that this policy could only protect Europe from Germany by turning it into a permanent ward of the U.S. military, which it considered unacceptable. It therefore shifted policy toward Germany in a direction Clay had been urging since April—one that would alter American relations with both western Europe and the Soviet Union.

The State Department set out to merge the American, British, and French occupation zones of Germany (see Map 2). The American zone, Kennan noted, "had never been economically self-supporting in modern times."[47] It contained less than a fifth of German manufacturing capacity for domestic production and industrial exports.[48] And so on July 30, Byrnes secured Bevin's agreement to fuse the industrialized British zone with the more pastoral American one. This would give the United States a direct share in control over the Ruhr, a region critical to the future political as well as economic landscape of Europe. For the British, who were spending $80 million a year to support their occupation—$50 million more than they were extracting in reparations, even as they imposed bread rationing at home—the arrangement promised to slow the drain on their dwindling foreign exchange reserves.

In September 1946, having made no progress in advancing interzone cooperation with either the French or the Russians, Byrnes announced in Stuttgart that the Americans would no longer hold German recovery hostage to the "failure of the Allied Control Council" to carry out the Potsdam provisions on economic unity. "Zonal barriers," he said, "should be completely obliterated so far as the economic life and activity in Germany are concerned."[49]

The Anglo-American bizone came into effect on New Year's Day 1947. In advocating for the fusion, Clay believed that "if the Russians . . . saw that we were successful [in generating] immediate and rapid recovery . . . they would want to become part of it."[50] Yet Stalin saw in Bizonia the embryo of a capitalist, American-dominated West German state over which he would have no control. He would therefore oppose it bitterly. It is ironic that Clay, who at the time of Marshall's meetings with Molotov was the most powerful advocate of cooperation with Moscow, was also, through his role in suspending reparations and creating Bizonia, the man most responsible for the rupture in U.S.-Soviet relations.

❖

NOW, HERE IN MOSCOW IN MARCH 1947, MARSHALL WAS TRYING TO CONvince Molotov that if Germany could produce more, then everyone, including Russia, would benefit. Molotov could not see it this way.

His view should not have surprised Marshall. After all, FDR and Morgen-thau had bludgeoned Churchill into accepting precisely the *opposite* logic a mere two and a half years prior at a military conference in Quebec—that Germany needed to be stripped of productive capacity to prevent a third world war. Uncomfortably for Marshall, Paris, too, continued to see a revived Germany as an intolerable danger, a stance he disparaged as "outmoded and unrealistic."[51]

Bidault, personally, agreed with Marshall. "To keep the German enemy of 1945 helpless and in perpetual subjection was what we had tried to do in 1918," he observed, "and failed."[52] He and his government were also allied with the United States over the desirability of a decentralized Germany, which would mitigate the country's threat to French security. But his government was also committed to securing reparations and placing the industrialized Ruhr under international control—a position that allied it with Moscow.[53]

Particularly given that a third of the French government was Communist, the Soviets expected cooperation from Bidault. French ambassador General Georges Catroux had met privately with Molotov in Moscow on February 19, 1947, stressing the importance of "the Soviet Union and France . . . work[ing] out a common position" on reparations from current production "prior to the Council of Ministers" meeting.[54] But the anti-communist Bidault considered it "madness" to allow the Soviets, who were "already draining the resources of Germany's Eastern Zone . . . to despoil the rest of it as well."[55] As for internationalization of the Ruhr, he felt he could no longer "go on defending it" once it became clear that "Russia [would] use it as an argument for getting even further into Germany."

Refusing to break with Marshall on Germany, Bidault incurred Russian wrath. Molotov retracted his support for French annexation of the Saar, leaving the proud, urbane Bidault isolated and humiliated. The Russian pointedly excluded him in a dinner toast to his American and British counterparts, before mischievously correcting himself by announcing that "no one should be forgotten."[56] Bidault hit back, toasting "those of us here who love freedom."[57]

Divisions within the western camp were still useful in giving Molotov another angle to press his case for reparations: Moscow, he said, might accept a revival of the Ruhr, contra France, if a portion of its production were allocated to the Soviet Union. Was Molotov hinting that a deal could be done on terms that did not load the bill onto Washington? Contrary to notions that Marshall was by this time locked into a policy of containment that precluded compromise, he worked the cables to persuade Truman to give him room to trade vague language on reparations for Russian cooperation on German economic unification. This seemed to be the diplomatic breakthrough Clay had been hoping for.[58]

Among Marshall's team, however, Bohlen, Smith, and Dulles opposed him. In Washington, Acheson did, too; it was "a mistake to believe that you can, at any time, sit down with the Russians and solve questions," he told the Senate Foreign Relations Committee. None of them believed Stalin would follow through on economic unification. A deal would therefore just make European recovery hostage to further Soviet diplomatic maneuvering.

At Acheson's urging, Truman initially denied Marshall the "elbow room" he sought on reparations, but the secretary of state pushed back. Truman revised his response to "no objection," with the proviso that Marshall stick by his proposed conditions—that reparations from current production would not result in a German trade deficit or divert coal or other raw materials from vital uses.

On April 1, Marshall made his boldest attempt to satisfy Molotov, presenting the new American reparations proposal. Unexpectedly, however, he now found himself undercut by his closest ally, Bevin. The British government being under far greater financial strain from occupation than Marshall's, Bevin wanted Molotov to affirm the British understanding of what "economic unification" would mean if the Soviets committed to it: free movement of goods and people across the occupation zones, and Soviet acknowledgment of shared responsibility for British costs—to date and in the future. For good measure, he argued that reparations from current production might, in any case, be precluded by Potsdam. An exasperated Marshall pressed for a simple agreement on principles, with details to be worked out by experts, but Molotov would neither rebuff him outright nor commit to any terms.[59]

The wrangles with Molotov had become a psychological endurance test for Marshall—an endless sequence of ponderous, pointless verbal jousts. Marshall sat through the mind-numbing translations stiff, erect, arms folded, peering over tortoiseshell reading glasses perched at the end of his nose. Molotov refused even to cut into the dead time by submitting speeches for translation in advance. Padding out the sessions with barren drone seemed to suit his purposes.

Day after day, week after week, Marshall's grim diplomatic war of attrition with Molotov ground on. In his downtime, Marshall read Harold Nicolson's *Congress of Vienna* for inspiration, yet whatever the issue—German and Austrian peace treaties, occupation force levels, reparations, the German border with Poland—progress seemed forever beyond reach. Still, the Russians continued to lay out elaborate banquets, excursions to the Bolshoi, every manner of trapping to suggest that agreement could be—would be—reached, if only the foreign guests would see fit to reciprocate in substance what they could not in hospitality.

This was not to be. After enduring forty-four fruitless four-hour sessions with Molotov over five weeks, Marshall requested an audience with Stalin himself.

❖

ON THE NIGHT OF APRIL 15, 1947, ACCOMPANIED BY SMITH AND BOHLEN, who would act as translator, Marshall made his way to the Kremlin through what appeared to Smith to be the most heavily policed street on earth. Ushered through a series of antechambers, the Americans arrived in a wood-paneled conference room where the Generalissimo, in his mustard-colored military uniform, stood waiting. Molotov, Novikov, and a translator were present. Portraits of Russian Napoleonic war heroes stared down from the walls.

Bolshevism, Kennan had argued, was just the standard under which the latest Russian autocrats marched. Peter the Great had fathered the strategy of dominating neighbors by "protecting" them. Catherine the Great pushed the empire to the south and west. Czar Alexander I, who witnessed his capital's desecration by Napoleon's army, insisted that eastern Europe was to be treated as Russia's buffer against the West. Sergei Sazonov, Russia's foreign minister at the outbreak of World War I, determined that they needed to be turned into client states.[60] Many of them, however, particularly Poland, Hungary, and Romania, had remained hostile to Russia and its interests during the interwar period. Hitler's aggression had therefore driven home to Stalin how much remained to be done.

It was 10 p.m. Stalin welcomed Marshall, complimenting him for having aged much better than he had. He, Stalin—at sixty-eight, two years older than Marshall—was now, in contrast, "just an old man." Bohlen agreed. He was surprised to see how the Soviet leader had aged.[61] Five foot five, pock-faced, with a coarse, streaked mustache, yellowed teeth matching his eyes, his physical figure seemed to betray his legend.

Iosif Vissarionovich Dzhugashvili took the revolutionary name Stalin, or "man of steel," in his early thirties, around 1910, after a decade in and out of prison and labor camps for crimes ranging from organizing mass strikes and bank robbery to racketeering and murder.[62] Having in his teens excelled at a Tblisi theological seminary, publishing Georgian-language poetry in his spare time, he might have gone in a different direction had his mother, cut off financially by his violent, drunkard father, been able to continue paying his tuition.

By that time, however, he had already become attracted to forbidden "revolutionary" literature—such as the novels of Victor Hugo, the possession of which got him punished—and Marxist periodicals such as Kvali ("The Furrow"). Still, he had to find employment following his expulsion from the seminary in 1899 for skipping an exam. After a spell of student tutoring, he took a job as an "evaluator-observer" in the Tiflis Observatory, which afforded him the time to cultivate his radical and anti-tsarist passions. He was dismissed in 1901 following a police raid on the facility, in which several of his colleagues were arrested for possessing illegal literature, and would thereafter finance himself entirely through criminal and political activity.

Around that period, he became acquainted with the writings of Vladimir Ilyich Lenin, eight years his elder. Joining the Bolshevik faction of Lenin's Social Democratic Labor Party in 1903, the young revolutionary met Lenin in 1905. Recognizing his talents and energy, Lenin co-opted Dzhugashvili into serving on the breakaway Bolshevik Party Central Committee in 1912 and designated him to write an important doctrinal piece on managing nationalities within the Russian empire. Having no language or scholarly skills, the author relied on Bolshevik publicist Nikolai Bukharin to complete the assignment in 1913.[63]

It was from his position as secretary general of the party's Central Committee, which Stalin assumed in 1922, two years before Lenin's death, that he began to consolidate power, marginalizing and later killing rivals, such as

Bukharin and Trotsky, as well as myriad potential and imagined rivals. Mass purges, show trials, and labor camps became central to his efforts to establish himself as an unassailable dictator in the 1930s, providing a man with paranoid tendencies ever greater cause to fear lurking enemies.

Stalin's systematic murder of thousands of his own military and intelligence corps in the 1930s and 1940s, a centerpiece of his perpetual "strategy" to eliminate opposition and subversion, would have doomed the Soviet Union had it not been for its capacity to produce weapons and absorb casualties. His nonaggression pact with Hitler in 1939 freed him to annex eastern Poland (then including western Belorussia and Ukraine), Estonia, Latvia, Lithuania, and parts of Romania while leaving Soviet borders unprotected, yet nearly caused his own country's annihilation after Germany invaded in 1941.

After the war, Stalin's efforts to extend Soviet power were guided by a crude, unwavering, and empirically false Marxian belief in the inevitability of capitalist intramural conflict and collapse. Confident that time was on his side, however, he was also pragmatic and patient.

As a diplomat, he excelled. Lurking beneath his "unpretentious facade," Kennan observed after meeting him in 1945, were great "depths of calculation, ambition, love of power, jealousy, cruelty, and sly vindictiveness" as well as "diabolical skill as a tactician."[64] Attlee said of Stalin that he "reminded me of the Renaissance despots—no principles, any methods." Of his style, there was "no flowery language—always Yes or No, though you could only count on him if it was No."[65]

Stalin adapted his demeanor to his opponents' capacity for resisting his will. With Moscow's eastern European "allies," he was typically condescending, offensive, and brutally direct. Tito's lieutenant Milovan Djilas, who in 1962 published *Conversations with Stalin*, referred to him as "a monster, who, while adhering to abstract, absolute and fundamentally utopian ideas, in practice had no criterion but success—and this meant violence, and physical and spiritual extermination."[66] With Churchill, he needled and flattered as he saw fit. With Roosevelt, he was almost invariably charming, even when unwilling to concede substance, owing to the paucity of issues on which he could afford a rupture with Washington.

Part of Stalin's negotiating prowess owed to his choice of deputy. As Smith put it, Stalin cultivated the myth that there were "two schools of thought [in] the Politburo, [a] conciliatory one headed by Stalin and [a] tough one by Molotov. . . . This [was] one of [the] oldest gags on [the] Soviet confusion-propaganda circuit."[67] Molotov so infuriated his counterparts with his sullen stubbornness that they were almost grateful to have their demands denied less unpleasantly by his boss. "Molotov was almost always the same, with hardly a shade of variety, regardless of what or who was under consideration," Djilas observed[68]—nothing like the temperamentally dexterous Stalin. "Hooded, calm, never raising his voice, [Stalin] avoided the repeated negatives of Molotov which were so exasperating to listen to," observed Anthony Eden, reflecting on Yalta. "By more subtle methods he got what he wanted without having to be so obdurate." Stalin was, for Eden, the best negotiator he ever encountered.[69]

❖

GEORGE MARSHALL, NEVER AT EASE WITH SMALL TALK, BRIEFLY RETURNED Stalin's pleasantries, recalling "with great interest" their previous meeting at the Tehran Conference in 1943, where "amphibious and cross-river operations" had been discussed.

"Yes," Stalin interjected, "the second front."[70]

Marshall had wished to remind Stalin of the two countries' recent historic collaboration, but the "second front" held different meanings for the two men. From Stalin's perspective, it had been deliberately, devastatingly, and unforgivably late. America and Britain, he believed, delayed launching it for years in order that Germany and the Soviet Union might first grind each other into rubble and impotence. Stalin, of course, had also used this tactic—letting Germans slaughter the Warsaw Poles in August 1944.

Marshall steered the meeting toward business.

He would, he advised Stalin, speak frankly—not as a diplomat, but as he had been trained, as a soldier. He explained that he was "very concerned," even "somewhat depressed at the extent and depth of misunderstandings and differences . . . revealed at this conference." The Soviet Union, he said, had been held in high esteem among the American people at the end of the war. But since that time, the Soviet government had not kept faith with agreements and was hindering progress on new ones.

The American Lend-Lease arrangement with the Soviet Union, Marshall reminded Stalin, "had been the most generous of all," and the unwillingness of the Soviets to settle their obligations—such as the return of merchant ships and war vessels—was having "a very bad effect on the United States Congress and on public opinion." Now, here in Moscow, an atmosphere of "suspicion and distrust [was making] agreement virtually impossible."[71]

Marshall was indeed speaking frankly; even brutally, as he later termed it.

Impassive, Stalin puffed a cigarette; looking down, to the side, occasionally into Marshall's eyes as he listened to the American and his translator. A red pen in his right hand throughout, he doodled wolves' heads on a notepad, in plain sight of his guests—a practice he was known to have cultivated some time ago for the purpose of disconcerting them. Harriman had experienced it in his first audience with him at the beginning of the war.[72]

Marshall turned to the main issue dividing Washington and Moscow: Germany. They were not making progress on any of the central matters: demilitarization, reparations, or the country's future economic and political architecture.

Germany had brought the Soviet Union and the United States together in a common cause, from 1941 to 1945, but now that it was caged between the eastern and western halves of the continent, each under the effective control of their respective militaries, it served only to magnify the consequences of their clashing ideologies and geostrategic interests. Little of substance, or even of clear meaning, regarding Germany's future had been decided among FDR, Churchill, and Stalin at Yalta two years prior, in spite—or because—of it being by far the most consequential issue the three governments would have to resolve. Stalin had at the time been content to wait; he expected "the correlation of forces" to move in his favor, as they did when the Red Army beat Eisenhower to Berlin.

Now, here in Moscow, Marshall said, there was a misconception that the United States "intended to dismember Germany." But his government "did not have any such intention"; it "in fact desired the opposite." It wanted the country unified economically, allowing the more industrial west to exchange goods freely with the agricultural east. But it also believed that a powerful central German government "would constitute a real danger for the peace of the world."[73] Marshall further believed, yet did not say, that the main source of this danger was the Kremlin-controlled KPD (Kommunistische Partei Deutschlands) German Communist Party, which had held power in the east since forcibly absorbing and dismantling the SPD Social Democratic Party in 1946.

Marshall now directed his frustration at his interlocutor for the past six weeks. "Mr. Molotov," he said, "had charged that the British-American bi-zonal arrangement was in violation of Potsdam." But it "was as plain as this table that the United States and Great Britain had been forced to take this action in defense of their own taxpayers, by reason of the failure to establish economic unity in Germany."

As for reparations, Marshall continued, Molotov was exaggerating what the United States had received from the American zone, while refusing himself even to provide any figures as to what the Soviet Union had received. The two delegations had, further, reached "an impasse on the demilitarization treaty."

There was also the wider context, Marshall added: Europe. "We are," he said, "frankly determined to do what we can to assist those countries which are suffering from economic deterioration." If "unchecked, [this] might lead to economic collapse and the consequent elimination of any chance of democratic survival."[74]

Trying to close on a positive note, Marshall reiterated his "desire to rebuild the basis of cooperation that had existed during the war." He had, he said, "come to Generalissimo Stalin with that hope, feeling that if they cleared away some of the suspicion it would be a good beginning for the restoration of that understanding."[75]

Stalin nodded. Marshall, he said, was "quite right, that only on the basis of frankness and sincerity could cooperation and friendship be developed."

"As to lend lease," he confessed, "there was occasional sloppiness in the operation of the Soviet Government." It was "very busy here because [we] suffered such great losses in the war. . . . This might be the reason for the delays." But "there was another side to the lend lease question," he told Marshall: "namely the credits which had been linked to lend lease."

Two years ago, Stalin explained, in response to Ambassador Harriman's question regarding what orders the Soviet government was prepared to place in the United States, and what credits it needed to settle them, his government had submitted a memorandum requesting three to six billion dollars. Six billion, Stalin said, had been "long promised." Now, after two years had passed, "no reply [had yet] been received." This was, he suggested pointedly, "possibly due to sloppiness on the part of the United States."

Novikov was stunned. Six billion? "I only knew of a promise of a one billion dollar loan," he later recorded. And "I was not the only one struck by Stalin's bitter reproach." Marshall was whispering in Smith's ear as Stalin spoke; Smith scribbled furiously. He reached across the table and handed Novikov a note.

"Mr. Novikov!" it read, "you know too well that it's not so. Six billion have never been promised. Please, explain it to Mr. Stalin." Novikov translated and handed the message to Molotov. "Without moving a brow," Molotov "put the sheet into a folder." He "did not say a word" to Stalin, whose "strange memory lapse . . . haunted me," Novikov noted. "[W]hat I saw was an elderly, very elderly, tired man, who, likely, was carrying his great burden of responsibility with great difficulty."[76] Stalin would correct himself, but only to the extent of conceding that "one year" had passed rather than two.

Stalin moved on to Germany. "The [Council of Foreign Ministers]," he said, "had no authorization to repeal . . . the agreements entered into by the three governments." He looked at Bohlen.

"Mr. Bohlen must remember those conversations" at Yalta, where he translated for FDR, when "all the Americans, including President Roosevelt, [Secretary of State Edward] Stettinius and Hopkins had said they thought [the Soviet demand for $10 billion in reparations] was very small." And spread "over twenty years this would not be hard for the Germans." But "now there was apparently a different point of view," that despite the Soviet Union having removed "barely two billion dollars" worth of assets no more reparations would be permitted— not even from current production. "This the Soviet Union could not accept." The Soviet people, Stalin said, had suffered terribly at the hands of the Germans. He had "no pity, sympathy, or love for them." Reparations were right and necessary.

As for "the subject of German unity," the Soviet Union "stood like the British and Americans for economic unity." But that was not enough, Stalin said; economic unity was not "feasible without political unity."

"[We] are against a *strong* centralized German government," Stalin clarified;

we want only one that "should stand above and not below the *Länder* [state] governments." But "[we] must not repeat the same mistakes as Napoleon, who set up scattered German governments." He thereby gained "a tactical advantage from a temporarily weakened Germany," but strengthened the hand of "German militarists" who dreamed of reuniting Germany. "Napoleon's action in effect gave birth to Bismarck and the Franco-Prussian war."

If these errors were now repeated, the Soviet Union risked "losing control of the instrument of German unity and handing it over to the militarists and chauvinists." The German people would then soon follow another dangerous and bellicose leader down the path of reconsolidation.[77]

✤

HOWEVER INCOHERENT ITS ELEMENTS, THE CONTOURS OF SOVIET POLICY toward Germany had been largely settled for a year now. Stalin had no inclination to reopen it. In May 1946, thirty-eight top Soviet officials, including General Georgy Zhukov and Deputy Foreign Minister Solomon Lozovsky, had submitted their conclusions on Byrnes' proposal for German demilitarization and great-power security guarantees in Europe. They were unequivocal: Moscow must reject it. The United States, they argued, was trying to drive the Soviet Union out of Germany to secure its "economic domination of that country" and "to preserve [its] military potential [in Europe] as a necessary base for carrying out their aggressive aims in the future." Stalin concluded that Washington was reneging on Roosevelt's Tehran commitment to withdraw U.S. troops within two years of the war's end, seeking instead Soviet "sanction for the U.S. playing the same role in European affairs as the U.S.S.R." And once Soviet troops were out of Germany, Zhukov warned, the Americans would "demand a withdrawal . . . from Poland"—a critical military corridor with Germany—"and ultimately from the Balkans." Within a few years, there will be "a German-Anglo-American war against the USSR."[78]

In this light, Marshall's calls to rebuild Germany and to end reparations were two sides of the same coin. America intended to take over Germany, rearm it, and turn it against Russia. Marshall might as well have been pushing on a closed door from the inside; Stalin would oppose any plan that precluded Soviet control over the western half of Germany. "All of Germany must be ours," Stalin told Bulgarian and Yugoslav leaders in 1946. "That is, Soviet, Communist."[79] Stalin kept talking to Marshall only because he wanted Washington "to shoulder the responsibility for Germany's division," if such could not be avoided.[80]

Yet Stalin had, in fact, supported dismembering Germany before he opposed it. Stalin was, in 1941, the first of the Allied leaders to press for it, wanting Germany, according to a Molotov cable to Maisky in London, "divided into a series of more or less independent states so as to provide a guarantee for the peace of European states in the future"—a message that Maisky relayed to a skeptical Eden. At Yalta Stalin had with him specific proposals from his advisers for a division of the country into four, five, and seven states, but pressed only for the word "dismemberment" to be added to the German surrender formula. With American support, the Soviets prevailed over British concerns that it would rouse German nationalism and resolve to fight.

After Yalta, however, Stalin did an about-face. Fearing that the absence of a central authority in Germany might hinder his ability to extract reparations from the industrialized west of the country, he ordered his delegation to the March 1945 meeting of Allied foreign service officials in London to take the line that dismemberment was only to be a last resort, if Germany could not be brought into line through other means. Thereafter, he and Molotov would publicly blame the Americans and the British for championing it.[81]

In the final months of the war, meanwhile, Stalin groomed Walter Ulbricht and his KPD Communist Party to organize the Soviet occupation zone in Germany. The diminutive, Lenin-bearded fifty-one-year-old Ulbricht had risen through the Communist hierarchy in the 1920s, fleeing Germany in 1933 and settling in Moscow, via Paris and Prague, in 1938. There, he avoided the fate of so many less adroit Communist Party members and activists by backing Stalin's every move, from show trials to the Nazi-Soviet Pact. Politburo member Lavrentiy Beria, master of the Soviet internal-security system, called him "the greatest idiot" he had ever seen, but Stalin found him a most useful one after the war's end.[82]

Thanks to the treachery of British MI6 intelligence agent Kim Philby, the Soviets were also able to identify, and then capture or murder, most of eastern Germany's Catholic wartime anti-Nazi—and anti-Communist—resistance leaders.[83] So Stalin was well prepared for the present stalemate with the

Americans, who had few natural allies in the east. What he was unprepared for was the role his own actions would play in hardening the hostilities between eastern and western Germany, making impossible the progressive unification under Communist leadership that he was now seeking.

While telling Ulbricht in early 1946 that he wanted Germany to be "democratic," allowing approved non-Communist parties to participate, he also demanded a "purge of the state administration, public ownership of enterprises . . . expropriation of big landowners" and obedience to directives from Moscow.[84] In April he forced a merger of the KPD and the Social Democratic SPD into the KPD-dominated Socialist Unity Party (Sozialistische Einheitspartei Deutschlands—SED). This only increased anti-Russian anger in Germany, where Berliners referred to Communists as "SEDisten"—Sadists.[85]

Facing a huge anti-Communist electoral turnout on October 20 of that year, particularly in Soviet-occupied East Berlin, Stalin now stiffened his opposition to Washington's federalization proposals, which would have strengthened local control and weakened his own. And in the wake of the crushing defeat—the SED finishing third, with under 20 percent of the vote—he became ruthlessly pragmatic. To the shock and dismay of SED leaders who met with him in January 1947, he pressed them to abandon their "policy of elimination . . . in order to avoid a scenario in which all former fascists are pushed into the adversarial camp."

"The Soviet zone has its own fascists," Stalin said. "Can they not organize their party under a different name?" He did not mean "persuading [them] to the side of the SED; they would not be willing." But just "to not push them all to the Americans."

The SED chairmen were appalled. "Nazis are in administrative positions in the western zones," Otto Grotewohl said, "but such a course of action from us would not be understood to the masses working in the west." Wilhelm Pieck nodded; what Stalin was asking was "impossible."

"Impossible?" Stalin asked. "It seems possible to me."

Pieck was incredulous: the SED had to continue "the struggle . . . against active Nazis," he insisted.

But "what about distinguishing not-very-active Nazis from very-active Nazis?!," Stalin put back.[86] The goal, he explained, was "winning over" the population in the west.[87] To that end, the first task was to get the Allies to agree to a nationwide plebiscite on some carefully worded question related to German unity—one that would assist Communist expansion.[88] "If we succeed in completing this first stage, that will be well and good." And "if we don't, we'll accept the consolidation of German administration in the Soviet zone."[89] The critical matter was ensuring that "the cause of German unity [not] be transferred from our hands to the hands of the bourgeoisie."[90] This suggested Stalin was willing to suffer western Germany remaining under Allied control if it proved necessary to ensuring that the east stayed communist.

As for Washington's policy on Germany, it had, since 1945, lurched just as radically as Moscow's. The Truman administration was now in revolt against the Morgenthau mind-set that had held sway, however tenuously, in Washington a mere two and a half years prior, which viewed a united, industrially revived Germany as a continued threat to Europe. FDR's State Department never supported Morgenthau's plan for deindustrialization and dismemberment, believing it "would provide a ready-made program for nationalistic agitators"; instead it supported only decentralization, or federalization, as a means of containing German nationalism and militarism. Once Truman became president, he condemned Morgenthau's "meddling" and put the State Department back in control of foreign policy.[91]

Europe's economic crisis now made Morgenthau's ideas look reckless. Real gross domestic product (GDP) in Britain was tumbling (down 2.6 percent for the year), while inflation in the United States was soaring (14.4 percent for the year), pushing up British import costs. "Production," concluded a widely circulated report by former president Herbert Hoover, following a European trip in February, was "the one path to recovery in Europe." And "the whole economy of Europe," he insisted, "is interlinked with the German economy." His ally Vandenberg called Germany "the core of the whole European problem."[92]

Despite the massive wartime damage Germany sustained, reflected in the destruction of 40 percent of its housing stock, a remarkable 80 percent of the country's industrial plant capacity remained intact. Germany exited the war with a *greater* functioning machine tool stock than it had on entering it—much of it new (one third of industrial equipment was less than five years old, up from one tenth in 1939). Only raw material shortages and political uncertainty held back its recovery—and Europe's. The United States could, therefore, Hoover concluded, "keep Germany in these economic chains, but it will also keep Europe in rags."[93]

Clay and Dulles agreed with Hoover, although the two disagreed bitterly over how to manage Germany. Clay, who considered Dulles overly indulgent of the French, wanted to maintain the territorial integrity of the country and avoid rupture with the Soviets; Dulles wanted to put the Ruhr under international control and use the resources of the Rhine basin to jump-start a new federated "western Europe."[94] This idea was beginning to capture the imagination of a State Department in search of ways to give substance to the Truman Doctrine. For his part, Stalin naturally opposed German reindustrialization, particularly when its object was to bolster European capitalism.

❖

SIX WEEKS OF TALKS IN MOSCOW HAD NOT EVEN BEGUN TO CLOSE THE gap between Soviet and American visions for Germany. Yet Stalin had one final proposal.

"If our views on this subject cannot be reconciled," he put to Marshall, "there was a way out," a compromise. "Let the German people decide through a plebiscite what they wished."[95]

Marshall recoiled. He knew full well where a "plebiscite" would lead. He had seen the results in Poland, last July, in a baldly manipulated referendum that cleared the way for Communist control. General elections followed in January 1947, in the run-up to which anti-Communist Peasant Party supporters were arrested by the thousands and their candidates stricken from electoral lists. Yet in order to prevail, the Communists still had to resort to mass ballot stuffing. Churchill had fought a lonely last-ditch diplomatic offensive against Stalin at Yalta to preserve an independent Poland as a barricade against Soviet westward expansion. But FDR, more concerned with securing Soviet UN membership and entry into the Pacific war, capitulated to Stalin's insistence on Allied recognition of the Soviet-backed provisional Polish government and toothless Western monitoring of future elections.[96] Now, in Moscow, Marshall was determined to defend another such barricade a few hundred miles to the west, in Germany.

All Marshall and Stalin could agree on was that neither the United States nor the Soviet Union could risk the possibility of Germany becoming an ally of the other. "We must insist on keeping Western Germany free of communistic control," Kennan would later urge.[97] Marshall would call "domination of all Germany by [the] Soviets . . . the greatest threat to the security of all Western Nations."[98]

Thus, after ninety minutes of serial monologue, the two men resolved nothing. Marshall was grim. Yet Stalin remained disconcertingly calm, almost detached.

"It is wrong to give so tragic an interpretation to our present disagreements," he told Marshall. They were, he said, like quarrels between family members. Differences over Germany were, he added, pointedly replacing the familial analogy with a martial one, "only the first skirmishes and brushes of reconnaissance forces."

Agreement might come in time, he assured Marshall. "When people had exhausted themselves in dispute," Stalin said, "they recognized the necessity for compromise. We may agree the next time," he added encouragingly. "Or, if not then, the time after that."[99] His manner suggested what researchers would later identify as signs of hostile diplomatic intent. Unwarranted "positive sentiment" and a "focus on future" possibilities, as opposed to present circumstances, suggest imminent betrayal.[100]

Marshall was now alarmed—not that Stalin continued to disagree with the American position, but that he was content to let disagreement drag on while Germany and Europe convulsed. "The worse, the better"—a phrase famously attributed to the nineteenth-century radical Russian writer Nikolai Chernyshevsky, and later to Lenin—appeared to be the Soviet leader's view.[101] Marshall now saw that Molotov's mulishness could not be explained away by his character. The foreign minister had been carrying out his boss' orders. The Soviets, Marshall concluded, were "not negotiating in good faith." They "were doing everything possible to achieve a complete breakdown in Europe."[102]

"It was the Moscow Conference," said Ambassador Robert Murphy, Clay's political adviser and the top U.S. diplomat in Germany, "which really rang down the Iron Curtain."[103] Skeptical of prospects for cooperation with the Soviets before the conference, Murphy would thereafter see them as wholly untrustworthy and decry anything resembling American appeasement.[104]

Secretary of State George Marshall speaks on the European economic crisis at Harvard University, June 5, 1947.

FOUR

PLAN

THE EUROPEAN RECOVERY PROGRAM, MARSHALL WOULD LATER SAY, "was an outgrowth of [my] disillusionment over the Moscow Conference." He had considered "inaugurating [it] at the conclusion of the conference," but decided that some delay was wise: "I did not want it to appear that the western allies had come to Moscow with a prior agreement to go ahead without Soviet cooperation." There were also "differences with Britain over reparations, etc." which he did not want exposed.[1] He spent his flight home digesting notes on the continent's crumbling economy and sketching out ideas "to prevent the complete breakdown of Western Europe."[2]

Hitler's conquests had shown the dangers posed by a hostile power controlling the industrial resources of western Europe, which were second in importance only to those of the United States.[3] Washington, therefore, to Marshall's mind, now had to act on its own—without Russia or, if necessary, against it.[4] Reporting to Truman on April 27, 1947, the evening following his return to Washington, he insisted there was no time to be lost in fashioning the administration's response.

The next day, Marshall gave a radio broadcast, reciting the "melancholy catalog" of disagreements between Washington and Moscow. "Disintegrating forces," he said, "are becoming evident." Europe could no longer wait for compromise. "The patient is sinking while the doctors deliberate."[5]

Though no course of treatment had been set, the bureaucracy had begun to mobilize while Marshall was away. On April 21, a coordinating committee of State, War, and Navy department staff (SWNCC) weighed in. The output, which Acheson presented to Marshall upon his return, was a grand muddle, giving every impression that it was the product of a committee of disparate interests working in haste—as it was. U.S. economic aims, security needs, geopolitical ambitions, and humanitarian concerns were all heaped into the mix.

"The conclusion is inescapable," the report said, "that, under present programs and policies, the world will not be able to continue to buy United States exports at the 1946–47 rate beyond another 12–18 months." The anticipated "substantial decline in the United States export surplus would have a depressing effect on business activity and employment in the United States."

U.S. gross national product (GNP) had fallen 11.6 percent in 1946, driven by the collapse of government spending after the war. The president's Council of Economic Advisers was now predicting a further small decline in the coming twelve months; a revival of the European economies would be critical to limiting the downturn. Minimizing "the cost and duration of United States economic assistance" to accomplish it would demand coordination of European national recovery programs. It would further "require a substantial increase in trade with Soviet-dominated areas, *provided* such trade can be arranged on terms compatible with the economic and political independence of western-oriented areas."[6]

But this was blather. Trade could not be "required" conditional on it being politically agreeable; either western recovery required eastern trade or it didn't. The United States, the report also offered obliquely, "will probably continue to undertake to alleviate starvation and suffering as such *where this action is consistent with U.S. interests.*" This was a meaningless observation and tepid recommendation rolled into one, concocted both to acknowledge and disparage calls for the administration to play Red Cross.

Most passionate was the urging for the United States "to take care that other nations do not pass under the influence of any potentially hostile nation."

Economic weakness made states prone to "subversive and 'boring from within' tactics or the threat of overwhelming force." Though the Soviet Union is never mentioned by name in this section, "preventing advancement of Communist influence" is highlighted as a primary aim of the president's call to aid Greece and Turkey.

However inadequate was the document as a basis for Marshall to confront an unsympathetic Congress, engage a war-wearied public, and orchestrate an economic metamorphosis among its allies, the SWNCC had put forward all the elements that Marshall would soon have to meld into a plan: supporting European nations that could resist communism, preventing a humanitarian crisis, and confronting a threat to American economic recovery. What was missing was a workable blueprint, articulated such that it could survive the backlash it would generate at home and abroad.

The first major step in creating a blueprint followed in short order. On April 29, just after his radio pronouncement, Marshall summoned Kennan, whom he had met only twice during the war, and directed him to leave his post at the National War College. At Forrestal's urging, Marshall was appointing him head of the new Policy Planning Staff (PPS)—a State Department think tank that would soon come to play a central role in the Cold War. "You can't operate and plan at the same time," Marshall would later offer by way of explanation for the new body.[7]

Forrestal had been calling for American "economic leadership" to rebuild Europe in response to the Communist threat, and it would be Kennan's job to figure out how to exercise it. "I don't want to wait for Congress to beat me over the head," Marshall told him from behind his polished, paper-free desk.[8] Despite the immensity of the assignment, he ordered Kennan to report back within two weeks. No further guidance was offered, beyond a directive to "avoid trivia."[9]

Among the challenges Kennan would face were staff and space, of which he had none. He hastily recruited personnel, among which Walt Rostow and Charles Kindleberger, Clayton protégés who would go on to become great figures in their own right. The group labored around the clock in commandeered conference rooms that, in James Reston's words, had "about as much character as a chewing gum factory."[10]

For Kennan, who felt out of his depth on economic matters, and who feared the reaction the report would engender from critics who knew them far better than he, the experience was "an intellectual agony more intensive than anything I had previously experienced." Constant carping in the press over what Truman should and should not do in Europe only stoked the pressure. At one stressful point, the exhausted new PPS head excused himself from a meeting, left the building, and wept.[11] He knew, however, that succumbing to discord or "pessimistic voices" was not an option. "We had to come up with something," Kennan reflected years later, "and we did."[12]

✤

THE BELIEF THAT ECONOMICS SHOULD OCCUPY A PRIME PLACE IN THE American diplomatic arsenal took root at the turn of the century, with Secretary of State John Hay's enunciation of "Open Door" principles for global trade with China. Hay argued for a free, open market and equal trading opportunity for merchants of all nationalities operating in the country. Such a principle would, he believed, benefit the U.S. economy while preventing disputes among the powers operating in China.[13]

President Woodrow Wilson globalized the principle with the third of his Fourteen Points after World War I, calling for "the removal, so far as possible, of all economic barriers" among nations.[14] American bankers helped stabilize Europe's economy in the 1920s with the discreet support of the Harding and Coolidge administrations.[15] Currency and trade wars in the 1930s stimulated more activist executive branch action: Treasury targeted global monetary reform, and the State Department nondiscriminatory trade, as elements vital to international cooperation and economic stability. Acheson, Harriman, and Clayton all tilted toward the Democratic Party in the 1930s not in support of the New Deal but of Secretary of State Cordell Hull's free trade agenda and in opposition to the GOP slide toward protectionism.

Truman, like FDR, was receptive to the notion that economic intervention could and should be used aggressively, at times as an alternative to military intervention, to secure vital American national interests. The administrations differed, however, in two primary regards.

The first was that FDR allowed the Treasury to take the lead in the crafting of foreign economic policy, which owed more to his friendship with Morgenthau than to any predilection for one bureaucracy over another. Truman chose to lodge such powers in the State Department. Several of his "Wise Men," as they would come to be called, were dissenting voices in the previous administration.[16] Acheson, who had served in both Treasury and State under FDR, had been a determined opponent of Morgenthau's and White's tenacious application of financial leverage over tapped-out Britain. They had, he lamented, "envisage[d] a victory [in war] where both enemies and allies were prostrate—enemies by military action, allies by bankruptcy."[17] Blaming the rise of "totalitarian military states" on the collapse of the nineteenth-century economic order over which Britain had presided, he was now determined to help erect a new American-led one.[18] Kennan, who had been disgusted by what he saw as naive and misguided pro-Soviet sentiment in FDR's Treasury, was eager to help chart Europe's recovery in part by ending hopeless efforts to cooperate with Moscow.

The second difference was over handling of a defeated Germany. FDR backed Morgenthau in his plan to pastoralize the country (though later evading association with it), whereas Truman backed Secretary of War Henry Stimson, an ardent opponent of the plan, in believing that "an economically strong, productive Germany was essential to the future stability of Europe."[19]

Morgenthau had sought to block Germany's reemergence as an economic and military power by dismantling its industry and distributing the pieces among its victims. The German people, he said, could live on "soup kitchens" if necessary. An alarmed Stimson cautioned against "taking mass vengeance," emphasizing that "speed of reconstruction is of great importance if we hope to avoid dangerous convulsions in Europe." Others warned that the Morgenthau Plan would prolong the war, precipitate famine, raise occupation costs, and aid Soviet interests at American expense.

Yet FDR allowed it to form the basis of what became U.S. occupation policy—Joint Chiefs of Staff directive JCS 1067—in September 1944.[20] The directive instructed the American military governor in Germany to take "no steps (a) looking toward the economic rehabilitation of Germany or (b) designed to maintain or strengthen the Germany economy." On the ground in Berlin in the spring of 1945, Clay would find it an enormous source of frustration.

Lewis Douglas, his adviser on occupation financing, fumed that it prevented "the most skilled workers in Europe from producing as much as they can for a continent which is desperately short of everything."

The directive, Douglas said, had been "assembled by economic idiots."[21] Morgenthau, its inspiration, "didn't know shit from apple butter"—in Truman's cruder verdict.[22] Morgenthau was a self-described apple farmer with no background in economics. In appointing his longtime Hyde Park neighbor Treasury secretary in 1934, FDR, quipped Gladys Straus, a prominent New York donor, had managed to find "the only Jew in the world who doesn't know a thing about money."[23] Truman maligned Morgenthau for interfering in German affairs and forced him to resign in July 1945, a few months after stepping into the Oval Office.[24]

The War Department did its best to soften both the letter and the spirit of the directive. With the approval of the Treasury and the State Department, Assistant Secretary McCloy added a provision allowing for "the production or maintenance of goods and services" necessary to prevent epidemics or major civil unrest.[25] Still, Morgenthau, even after leaving office, and his allies kept up the pressure on the War Department to maintain a "hard peace."

Truman faced an additional economic challenge that his predecessor had not had to reckon with in wartime. At the end of the conflict, there was a conviction in Washington, particularly conspicuous in Congress, that dangers lay in simply calibrating military resources to the degree of threat perception. Unrestrained military spending was, in this view, the handmaiden of high inflation, perpetual budget deficits, confiscatory taxes, and heavy-handed economic controls. The Russians, many believed, had a plan to force the United States to bankrupt itself through ever-expanding foreign entanglements. This had two important effects.

The first was on military doctrine itself. In geographer Halford Mackinder's terminology, defending the world's "Rimlands" from the threat posed by Russian domination of the "Heartland" could be accomplished, in principle, either by a strategy of a comprehensive "perimeter defense" or a much more limited "strongpoint defense."[26] Kennan, in his soon-to-be-famous *Foreign Affairs* article, "The Sources of Soviet Conduct," implicitly backed the former, calling for the United States "to confront the Russians with unalterable counter-force *at every point* where they show signs of encroaching upon the interests of a peaceful and stable world."[27] Yet this strategy assumed unlimited overdraft facilities to finance it, an assumption at odds with the view that profligacy was itself a danger. Kennan appeared to have largely abandoned this expansive conception of containment by the time his article was published in July, shifting toward an approach that focused on threats that combined "hostility with capability." This change in view brought him closer to the pragmatic Acheson.

The defense of critical points on the map, rather than entire lines, emerged as a tenet of enemy containment largely because of the domestic political requirement of cost containment. Marshall himself came to hold that "concentration" rather than "dispersal of our forces . . . appears to be the wisest course, especially in view of our present limitations."[28] But Kennan could also justify it on the grounds that, in his belief, Stalin had no intention of starting a war with the United States if eastern Europe's subservience could be achieved through other means. Forrestal believed America's atomic monopoly afforded it several "years of opportunity" to "assume risks otherwise unacceptable." These risks could be kept at tolerable levels through low-cost initiatives such as propaganda and psychological warfare.[29]

The second effect is that promotion of economic recovery and rehabilitation in Europe, and later Japan, emerged as a central element of containment on the grounds that it would be far less costly than military readiness and engagement. These ideas had been already been brewing in 1945. At Potsdam, Stimson and McCloy had called for the creation of a "completely coordinated plan to be adopted for the economic rehabilitation of Europe as a whole." Harriman, a Russia hawk after his war years dealing with the Kremlin, had urged massive European reconstruction aid to both FDR and Truman.[30] But by 1947 the ideas were ready to take center stage.

"Our resources are not unlimited," Truman would state six months after ushering in his namesake doctrine. "We must apply them where they can serve most effectively to bring production, freedom, and confidence back to the world." By the summer of 1948, Robert Lovett, who would succeed Acheson, would restate the Truman Doctrine with as much force as Truman had stated it over a year prior. "[T]he line must be drawn somewhere or the United States would find itself in the position of underwriting the security of the whole

world. . . . We lack sufficient . . . resources simultaneously to finance the economic recovery of Europe, to furnish arms and equipment to [the] countries
which request them, and to build up our own military strength."[31] Army Secretary Royall insisted he would need a 20 percent boost to the military budget if
Congress voted down a European aid plan.[32]

Forrestal characterized American priorities in Europe as "economic stability,
political stability and military stability . . . in about that order." He even bluntly
stated that the government was "keeping its military expenditures below the
levels which our military leaders must in good conscience estimate as the minimum which would in themselves ensure national security." U.S. defense expenditures had fallen from $83 billion in fiscal year 1945 to $42.7 billion in 1946 and
$12.8 billion in 1947. Over that period, the armed forces of the United States
had shrunk from 12 million to 1.6 million personnel. Military parsimony was
allowing the government "to increase [its] expenditures to assist in European recovery." It was, he concluded, "a calculated risk" that would offer "a prospect of
eventually achieving national security."[33] For his part, Truman thought it was only
common sense to "spend twenty or thirty billion dollars to keep the peace" over
the coming four years than to spend multiples of that annually fighting a war.[34]

What made economic and financial aid such a radical alternative to a military buildup, however, was that the former had never been tried on such an
enormous scale, and in such a critical diplomatic confrontation. The administration knew from experience how to prepare for, fight, and win wars, but it
was basing its new economic strategy on informed supposition and conviction.
Who could say what it took to resuscitate economies in war-ravaged countries
run by weak and embattled governments?

Kennan, however, always emphasized that what the United States needed
above all was a *psychological* advantage over the Soviet Union in the countries
it targeted for assistance. Economic aid, he felt, was at least as much intended
to revive a sense of purpose and self-reliance in recipient nations as it was to
improve material conditions.

Though administration policy would be resolute in opposing communism
it would not seek to impose an American orientation in return for assistance.
But opposing communism could still be read as a hypocritical denial of choice.
Acheson rationalized it: "I remember when it was accepted doctrine to say in

the United States, 'We don't care if another country wants to be communist, that is all right, that is an internal matter, that is a matter for them to decide.' It was only as we had more and more experience with communism that we learned it was not a doctrine which people picked up and looked over and either adopted or rejected. . . . They were being coerced." Foreign coercion, however, did not imply that the United States itself needed to coerce. The conviction was widespread within the State Department that the ability of countries to resist Soviet pressure depended on their being "independent and self-confident centers of power" in their own right, and not wards of Washington.[35]

How, though, would the United States deal with governments that were communist but unallied with Moscow? This question would take on importance in the matter of Tito and communist Yugoslavia in 1948. Acheson would assert that it was in the "obvious interest" of the United States that " 'Titoism' [be] an erosive and disintegrating force in [the] Sov[iet] sphere." The administration's East European chiefs of mission would conclude that "any and all movements within world communism which tend to weaken and disrupt the Kremlin's control within the communist world represent forces which are operating in the interests of the West and therefore should be encouraged and assisted." These statements made clear that it was Soviet influence, rather than communism as such, that the United States would oppose through the use of economic and political levers.[36]

⁂

ACHESON'S MOST PUBLIC ROLE IN DEFINING THE TRUMAN DOCTRINE came at the behest of the president. On April 7, 1947, Truman asked the under secretary for a "favor." He had some time ago agreed, as a gesture to his wife's friends in Mississippi, to speak on foreign affairs at the Delta State Teachers College. But with the state's senior senator, Democrat Theodore Bilbo, fighting for reinstatement in the face of corruption charges, the president hoped to stay out of heated local politics. Marshall was unavailable as a substitute; Acheson was the hosts' third choice.

Cleveland, Mississippi, may not have been a hub for major foreign policy addresses, but Churchill had shown the year prior, in Fulton, Missouri, that locality was no barrier to being heard nationally—or indeed, globally. Acheson was anxious for a forum in which he could, invoking Clayton's word, help to "shock" the country into recognizing the economic crisis unfolding in Europe and America's self-interest in reversing it. Deputizing for the president on May 8 was as good an opportunity as he was ever going to get.[37]

Before leaving Washington, Acheson briefed British newsmen Leonard Miall, Malcolm Muggeridge, and René MacColl over lunch, off the record, on the significance of what they would hear in Mississippi. His aim was to confront the growing fear in Britain and western Europe that the United States had become misguidedly transfixed on the continent's southeast, blinded by the more overt military and political aspects of the conflicts there. Henry Wallace's campaign against the Truman Doctrine was making this task harder and more urgent. Acheson needed to reassert the president's broader message.

It had been Acheson's idea for Truman's congressional address to be global in scope but for his aid request to be limited to two countries: Greece and Turkey. Yet the drawbacks of this approach were by this time evident. "The President's Doctrine of March 12 had been broad enough *in conception* to contain the floodwaters," Jones noted, "but the specific project of aid to Greece and Turkey had sandbagged only a tributary to the main stream, which was now out of banks." France, Italy, and Britain were themselves falling into dire circumstances. Reconstruction was "grinding to a halt."[38] Food was no longer reaching the cities from the country; factories were scrounging for vital raw materials. Gold and dollars with which to import essentials such as fuel were nearly evaporated. Strikes were spreading. Inflation was mounting. And as the Moscow foreign ministers conference slogged on through April, it became clear that the Soviets were going to be part of the problem, and not the solution.

The starched patrician Acheson was not the natural envoy to send out into the cotton fields and cattle pastures of Mississippi, yet he took to his assigned role ably. As he ambled out onto the hot, crowded college basketball court, listeners overflowing onto the grass outside, the under secretary removed his coat, rolled up his sleeves, and, using only notes he had scribbled onto the backs of his speech pages, looked directly into the sea of faces around him as he spoke. This contrivance lent his address the desired impromptu air, though he had memorized and barely deviated from the prepared text, conscious as he was of having a much wider audience.

Acheson began by tying the rapidly deteriorating economic situation in Europe to "elementals" that were well understood "in this rich agricultural region" of the American heartland. "[H]ow short," he said, "is the distance from food and fuel to peace or to anarchy." With "factories destroyed, fields impoverished and without fertilizer or machinery to get them back in shape, transportation systems wrecked, populations scattered and on the borderline of starvation, and long-established business and trading connections disrupted," Europe was in danger. And "the lack of a peace settlement"—particularly as regards Germany, the great "workshop of Europe"—was holding back vital reconstruction. With Europe short on material and monetary resources to import even the most basic provisions essential to survival and rebuilding, American assistance efforts had been "only in part suggested by humanitarianism." They were "a matter of national self-interest. For . . . until the various countries of the world get on their feet and become self-supporting there can be no political or economic stability in the world and no lasting peace or prosperity for any of us." Hopeless and hungry people, Acheson warned, "often resort to desperate measures." The United States government therefore needed the authority and resources to act forcefully and expeditiously.

Acheson spelled out how large the gap would be in the coming years between Europe's basic needs and its capacity to pay in dollars or gold. He then shepherded his listeners to the inevitable conclusion that they would have to accept more goods from abroad, and to make sacrifices in consumption at home, to ensure that the country could supply Europeans with items necessary "to maintain their physical strength and . . . carry on essential measures of reconstruction."

Furthermore, the United States needed to take "whatever action is possible immediately, even without full Four Power agreement, to effect a larger measure of European, including German, recovery." This was code for saying that Soviet objections would not impede American action. "European recovery," he insisted, "cannot await 'compromise through exhaustion,' " and recovery could not take hold "until the various parts of Europe's economy are working together in a harmonious whole." A "coordinated European economy" was therefore "a fundamental objective of our foreign policy."

Using American economic might to support "human dignity, human freedom, and democratic institutions," he said in closing, is "necessary if we are to preserve our freedoms and our own democratic institutions. It is necessary for our national security. And it is our duty and our privilege as human beings."[39]

The applause from the assembled was "standing, generous, and polite," though it is doubtful that many understood the importance the administration vested in the speech.[40] Truman later referred to it as "the prologue to the Marshall Plan." Indeed, Acheson developed several of its essential elements here for the first time. In particular, the idea that Europe, or at least the western part of it, needed to work as "a harmonious whole" was consequential. To that point, reconstruction efforts, such as they were, were uncoordinated and almost entirely national in scope. Acheson's emphasis on German industrial recovery was also a stark repudiation of the Morgenthau Plan.[41]

Soon after the speech, the *Times'* James Reston, one of Acheson's favored newsmen, asked the under secretary to clarify whether his speech represented "new policy" or just "kite flying." Acheson told him confidently to "ask the president"—which he did.

"Yes," Truman responded. The under secretary spoke for him.

❖

ALARMED BY ACHESON'S SPEECH, VANDENBERG DEMANDED TO SEE MARshall and the president. How could Acheson, he asked, call for a massive new foreign aid progam?

Marshall assured him that no new request for aid money would be forthcoming during the current session of Congress. But he wasn't going to lie. An aid bill would be coming his way in due course.

This was not what the senator wanted to hear. He spoke regularly of "bipartisan foreign policy" as something precious and fragile,[42] and he expected the president to do his part to keep it alive. "Harry," he said to Truman, "I want you to understand from now on that I'm not going to help you with crash landings unless I'm in on the takeoff." The two former Senate colleagues, who had never been close, would thereafter form a powerful political bond. Without it, the coming historic repositioning of U.S. foreign policy would not have been possible.

Born forty-seven days apart in 1884, sixty-three-year-old Vandenberg and Truman came from similar modest Midwestern backgrounds. Both saw their fathers' finances ruined at a young age, obliging them to work hard to keep their families fed. They were smart and loved words, but in different ways—Truman reading them, Vandenberg writing and speaking them. Truman boasted of reading all three thousand books in the local library by the age of fourteen. Vandenberg was vice president of his high school literary society, winning the silver prize in the Michigan State Oratorical Contest.[43] Truman took no interest in writing or reciting.

Their political careers followed different paths. Vandenberg, always passionate about foreign affairs, was a full-throated isolationist through the 1930s, right up until December 1941. He supported the Neutrality Acts prior to the war and opposed Lend-Lease aid to Britain after it broke out. "We have tossed Washington's Farewell Address into the discard," he wrote in March 1941, after the aid bill passed the Senate. "We have thrown ourselves squarely into the power politics and the power wars of Europe, Asia and Africa. We have taken the first step upon a course from which we can never hereafter retreat."[44] But everything changed in December. "My convictions regarding international cooperation and collective security for peace," he later wrote, "took firm form on the afternoon of the Pearl Harbor attack. That day ended isolationism for any realist."[45]

Truman, in contrast, never experienced an epiphany in worldview. His passion in the Senate was rooting out domestic corruption. Having been a compromise candidate for the vice presidency, he was hurled onto the front lines of foreign affairs after FDR's death, just months after reluctantly assuming the job. But he was a quick learner. And though legend would label him decisive, it is perhaps more accurate to say he did not second-guess himself *after* deciding.[46] He hated the job of president, but carried it out without regret or doubling back.

Vandenberg had coveted the presidency for years. FDR introduced him to Britain's King George VI in 1939 saying, unsmilingly, "Here's a chap who thinks he's going to succeed me in the White House; but he isn't." Though he had enormous policy differences with FDR, particularly over what he saw as the president's coddling of the belligerent Soviet government, Vandenberg still admired him as a "gallant soul" and "a superb example of personal courage."[47] Truman had no more in common with Vandenberg temperamentally than did FDR, yet there was a complementarity—an absence of clashing egos—that allowed them to work together with ease. The country would be fortunate in the pairing.

❖

KENNAN PRODUCED AN IMPORTANT MEMO FOR ACHESON ON MAY 16, 1947, a dry run for the Policy Planning Staff paper (PPS/1) requested by Marshall. He began by paying obeisance to the "high quality and value" of the SWNCC work on European recovery, before delicately indicating that he would be making suggestions "which will affect the assumptions and points of departure on which the [SWNCC] is proceeding." Kennan then laid out the principles on which his staff was working, creating a shining contrast with the verbose jumble emanating from the SWNCC.

A four- to five-year "schedule of American aid," Kennan said, would supplement "a program of intramural economic collaboration among the western European countries." (Walter Lippmann, when visiting Kennan at the War College in April, had suggested inviting the Europeans to draw up such a plan, and this may have had some influence on Kennan's thinking.)[48] Notably, no mention was made, in contrast to the SWNCC report, of any "requirement" for trade with eastern Europe; participation would merely be left open for "states within the Russian orbit," which would first have to "guarantee that their participation will be constructive." As for the Western countries, no aid could be forthcoming without "guarantees [that] preclude communist sabotage or misuse." Western Europe as an organized political and economic construct was here taking shape, its boundaries marked by willingness and ability to participate in an American-led recovery program, its outlook marked by resistance to Communism.

Foreshadowing the emergence of a new West German state, Kennan said that occupation policies in Germany would have to be altered to ensure that the western zone made "the maximum contribution to the economic restoration of western Europe." The French, he argued, would have to be forced to accept a revitalized Germany and the British to accept an integrated western

Europe. Outside of such a new construct, Britain "would appear to have no future," and the United States would have to consider "abandoning her strategically and politically."[49] This refrain would be replayed by American observers of Britain's testy relationship with the European continent repeatedly over the coming decades.

Equally notable was Kennan's insistence that the administration "be careful not to talk in terms of loans when there is no plausible prospect of repayment." Assistance needed to take the form of "outright grants." This was a further slap at Morgenthau's legacy: loans to bankrupt Britain to tide it through a postwar transition, and loans to Allied nations through a new IMF to restart global trade—loans that in theory cost America nothing, and in practice achieved nothing. It was time for the U.S. government, in Kennan's rendering, to level with the American heartland, speaking frankly about the requirements for peace and prosperity. It would need to articulate what forms of engagement were required and what it would cost.

Yet "a concrete outline for the Marshall Plan" only took shape, Acheson later reflected, with the return of Will Clayton from a six-week desolation tour of western Europe on May 19. While Kennan was laboring away on PPS/1, Clayton was organizing his own thoughts for Marshall. "Will was genuinely alarmed that Europe was on the brink of disaster," recounted Paul Nitze, then a forty-year-old deputy director of the Department's Office of International Trade Policy.[50] Clayton now communicated his diagnosis to Acheson in a consequential memo dated May 27. Acheson contrasted it with Kennan's report, which "dwell[ed] more on difficulties and dangers . . . than on the imperative need for action." Action was Clayton's preoccupation. Acheson, who considered Clayton "one of the most powerful and persuasive advocates" he ever dealt with in government, sent the memo "on at once to the General."[51] It would have "a powerful impact both upon the content of [Marshall's forthcoming] speech and probably upon his decision to make it."[52]

Even more so in recitation than in writing, Clayton was able to impart to his audience a sense of urgency. His stories of fearful peasants, workers, and merchants hoarding to avoid hunger were vivid and compelling in a way that numbers, dire as they were, failed to capture.

Parisians were starving. But why? Clayton explained that it was not that farmers could not grow enough, or that they could not deliver what they grew; farmers would simply not supply cities with food as long as the latter could produce nothing to offer in return. Money was losing acceptability as a voucher for tomorrow's goods; inflation was destroying its value.

"It is now obvious," Clayton wrote, "that we grossly underestimated the destruction to the European economy by the war. We understood the physical destruction," but failed to understand how "economic dislocation[,] nationalization of industries, drastic land reform, severance of long-standing commercial ties, [and] disappearance of private commercial firms through death or loss of capital" would destroy the productive apparatus. Capitalism, Clayton was sure, was the source of Europe's former economic strength, and reviving it was essential to preventing "social and political disintegration."[53]

Large-scale aid, Clayton said, was necessary "to save Europe from starvation and chaos." He estimated the need at $18–21 billion ($227 billion in today's money), spread over three years; Nitze estimated $25 billion ($270 billion today) over five years. But aid was not enough. Clayton, again like Kennan, wanted a reconstruction plan to be drawn up by "the principal European nations"—the U.K., France, and Italy. Yet whereas Kennan envisioned the United States providing only "friendly" assistance in its drafting, Clayton envisioned a more assertive American role. In Acheson's words, Clayton wanted the plan merely to "appear to come" from Europe. He would, further, brook no outside interference. Other countries might pitch in with "surplus food and raw materials," but this was not to be "another UNRRA." The United States, he said, "*must run this show*."[54]

Clayton insisted that the plan "should be based on a European economic federation on the order of the Belgium-Netherlands-Luxembourg Customs Union." Europe, he insisted, "cannot recover . . . if her economy continues to be divided into many small watertight compartments." Clayton was no theoretician, but the theory of customs unions—the idea that maximizing output required free movement of the various factors of production—was in vogue, and would have appealed to his free market instincts. Customs unions were multistate free trade zones with common external tariffs. Economists at the time argued that the rise of the United States to industrial supremacy in the early twentieth century had been assisted by the fact that it operated as such a union among its semiautonomous states, allowing the country to take advantage of economies of scale and specialization according to comparative advantage. Europe, Clayton believed, needed to follow that model to catch up.

Clayton further believed that the Bretton Woods vision of a stable global trading and payments system could not be realized without political action to restore a balance, or "equilibrium," in world trade. Yet such equilibrium had not been seen since 1914, when it fell victim to the catastrophe of World War I and the collapse of the classical gold standard. Now, in the wake of a second world war, Europe could not export enough to pay for essential imports from the United States. Creating a United States of Europe, so the new thinking went, was the innovation necessary to restore equilibrium.

Prominent Republicans, such as future secretary of state John Foster Dulles, shared this belief. Truman himself laid out a vision of it shortly after assuming the presidency in the spring of 1945. Pointing Stimson to a map, he explained that the challenge of securing a postwar settlement "was to help unify Europe by linking the breadbasket [of the east] with the industrial centers [of the northwest] through a flow of free trade."[55] Stimson agreed, believing further that German economic integration, and reintegration with wider Europe, had to be a critical component of this vision.[56] Equally important, failure to act upon these convictions would mean that Europe would remain dependent on U.S. aid.

"The old approach," Reston wrote in the *Times*, "was to deal with the shattered economies of the several nations one at a time, lending now to Britain, then to France, then to Italy, etc." But this had failed. Recovery in May 1947 seemed as far off as it did after Germany's surrender two years earlier. "The new approach is based on the growing conviction that the problems of all these countries are interrelated and that Europe cannot recover by shoring up, one at a time, the various national economies."[57] Over in London, *The Economist* cheered the new approach: "let the United States knock heads together and impose an agreement," it said; "there are plenty of Europeans who would welcome American dictation, if it were for a good cause."[58]

❖

ON MAY 23, ACHESON RECEIVED PPS/1, IN FULFILLMENT OF MARSHALL'S directive—a "general orientation" plan for aid to western Europe. It read as if the prose were Kennan's. And as with every paper written under his direction, it was.

Kennan began almost defensively, with a statement of what the plan was not. "Communist activities" were not "the root of the difficulties of western Europe," he wrote. Rather, "the present crisis" was a product of "the disruptive effect of the war on the economic, political, and social structure of Europe and . . . a profound exhaustion of physical plant and spiritual vigor. This situation has been aggravated . . . by the division of the continent into east and west."

But this division was, of course, a product of the Soviet occupation of the eastern continent and the installation of Communist-led governments. And "further communist successes would create serious danger to American security," Kennan wrote. Yet American aid had to be directed "not to the combatting of communism as such but to the restoration of the economic health and vigor of European society." It was "economic maladjustment which makes European society vulnerable to exploitation by any and all totalitarian movements," a vulnerability "which Russian communism is now exploiting."

The concision of the prose created the risk that readers would perceive, wrongly, that the PPS was downplaying the Soviet-backed communist threat in Europe. But Kennan was anxious to frame communism as just another brand of totalitarianism, which the American public already understood to be a threat. "[T]he United States approach to world problems," he said, must not appear to be "a defensive reaction to communist pressure." This appearance had colored the media's interpretation of the Truman Doctrine, which had become shorthand for "a blank check to give economic and military aid to any area in the world where the communists show signs of being successful." Partly to "correct this misunderstanding," the Europeans themselves would need to draw up the economic program.

There was, finally, the critical question of how to define the program's borders. To exclude the East was to invite blame for creating the iron curtain; to include it was to invite Soviet sabotage. The solution, Kennan argued, was to advance the project as a "general European (not just western European)" one, but in a manner ensuring that "the Russian satellite countries would either exclude themselves by unwillingness to accept the proposed conditions or agree to abandon the exclusive orientation of their economies." Either way the satellites chose, the United States would win diplomatically.

Kennan's objective for American economic intervention was clear: ensuring western Europe's ability to resist communist subversion. But as for the form that intervention would take, he was groping blindly. He was no economist, and had no aptitude for playing one. The two suggestions he lobbed out meekly were to find a way to move Rhineland coal to areas of need and to provide immediate unspecified assistance to Italy. His critical insight was that there was a psychological precondition for Europe's revival, and that bold American action was necessary to create it. Yet no further could he go without others who would be essential to transforming Marshall's message into a plan.

✤

KENNAN PROVIDED THE STRATEGIC LOGIC BEHIND A EUROPEAN RECOVery program. Clayton offered the vision of an integrated western Europe that could carry it out. The third major influence on the program's development was not even present in Washington; his views were never solicited, and he would remain an outsider at every point in the process.

Lucius Dubignon Clay was born in Marietta, Georgia, in 1898, one year later than he claimed in order to qualify for West Point.[59] His father, a three-term senator, passed down to him a knack for navigating obstacles in Washington. Being of a more monocratic bent, however, the younger Clay resisted the many calls to follow his father's path into electoral politics. In his graduating class of 137, Clay came first in history, first in English, and 128th in conduct. "If we lived in an earlier age, he would have been a baron or a duke," observed a Washington colleague. "He would be a benevolent one, but he'd be an autocrat nonetheless."[60]

Like the others in the top quarter of his class, he was assigned to the Army Corps of Engineers in 1918. Though he persisted in seeking out combat opportunities, he would rise to the rank of brigadier general in 1942—at age forty-three, the youngest ever—without seeing battle. In his various civil and military engineering posts in the United States, Latin America, and Asia, he developed an unrivaled reputation for bringing order, discipline, focus, and accountability to the most complex logistical tasks. In March of 1942, Marshall appointed him director of matériel in the War Department, where he managed the Army's prodigious procurement activities and administered Allied military aid. There he became known as a formidable master of bureaucratic bottlenecks. He was, according to one colleague, "forceful, persuasive, and bright as hell."[61]

In October 1944, Clay transferred to Europe to manage logistics for General Eisenhower. But the stint was brief. Byrnes, then director of the Office of War Mobilization, called him back in November to take over management of war production. The personal bonds he established with Eisenhower and Byrnes would remain strong in the years to come. Yet he lasted less than five months in that job before FDR, acting on the force of a remarkable consensus among his advisers, tapped him to be deputy military governor of Germany on March 31, 1945. In practice, he would run the American zone of the country.

With Germany in physical, financial, and moral ruin, it was a daunting assignment. His prior experience had given him "as much familiarity with an entire economy of a nation as anyone could have." Yet knowing little of the German nation and nothing of the language, he tried to beg out of it. Once he understood the matter was settled, however, he focused on clearing away constraints on his ability to run the country. Enlisting Byrnes' support, he ensured that he would report to Eisenhower, and not to a bureaucracy in Washington. The official order confirming his new position came down on April 17, five days after FDR's death.

Press coverage of Clay's appointment was enthusiastic, though in part for the wrong reason. *The Washington Post* thought that the task "call[ed] for authoritarianism," which Clay would muster unashamedly. The *New York Herald Tribune* concurred, suggesting that meant "life will be hard for the German[s]."[62] Yet Clay would press his authority to make it otherwise. He was determined to create a well-fed citizenry that could rebuild the country and, in the shortest possible order, govern it effectively and responsibly. In this effort, he would find himself confronting his government's official policy head-on.

Clay's appointment had been vigorously supported by Treasury Secretary Morgenthau, yet the two could not have disagreed on occupation policy more completely. Clay was not given the occupation directive, JCS 1067, until he boarded the plane for Paris, and did not read the Morgenthau Plan upon which it was based until arriving at Eisenhower's headquarters in Reims.[63] But Clay quickly "realized that the cost to the United States was going to be terrific unless we could get this thing moving again—which we were not permitted to do if we literally followed our instructions." He also thought the directive "too vindictive . . . to have long suited the American people."[64] His issues with it were more than technical; they were moral and strategic.

Clay's unvarnished views on Germany were summarized in a memo he wrote to Marshall on May 2, 1947—six weeks after he formally became military governor.[65] Germany, Clay said, was bankrupt. It avoided starvation only through Washington's disease-and-unrest appropriations, and had no prospect of supporting itself without the means to pay for imports. Its coffers were empty, its debts unmanageable, its credit nonexistent. And Allied policy blocked all avenues to profitable export.[66] Without change, the country would become an intolerable drain on American resources and political energies.

Clay had fought to get the occupation directive repealed and replaced in the spring of 1945, but "got nowhere." He would repeatedly exploit its disease-and-unrest loophole, which gave him the authority to deviate from its harsh approach, but there were limits to how far even he could bend a policy without breaking it. He was convinced that the directive's requirement that he bust up "large" agricultural estates, which were small by American standards, was economic madness; but he did it. "If we hadn't had 1067, I am sure that our original approach would have been quite different," he reflected years later. "We would have been instructed from the very beginning to assist in getting the Germans back on their feet." Making them "citizens of the world again" sooner would have helped "to get Europe back on its feet again" sooner and at less cost.[67] In a March 1946 cable to Washington, Clay put the issue in the context of containing communism. "There is no choice between becoming a Communist on 1500 calories and a believer in democracy on 1000 calories," he wrote. "It is my sincere belief that our proposed ration allowance in Germany will not only defeat our objectives in middle Europe but will pave the road to a Communist Germany."[68]

Clay's thinking had notable influence on Marshall in the wake of his fruitless efforts in Moscow to engage Stalin in a new cooperative approach to Germany. The directive be damned, Marshall instructed Clay to put Bizonia on a self-sustaining basis.

The U.S. and U.K. would take the first steps toward localizing administrative power in Germany on May 23, 1947, when they formally agreed to German participation on a new Bizonal Economic Council, a precursor to a West German government. The moral and economic albatross of JCS 1067, which now seemed purposeless in light of America's atomic monopoly, would be replaced in July by JCS 1779, which made the creation of a self-supporting German economy a primary goal of American occupation policy. The United States would thereafter be committed to West German economic unification and (limited) self-government. By October, even the denazification program was to be handed over to Germans.

Abandoning denazification was more a matter of necessity than enlightenment: the United States and Britain could no longer afford Germany as an enemy. As Noel Annan, a British intelligence officer in Germany, put it, "it is odious to find oneself in alliance with a people who had been willing to go along with Hitler to keep Communism at bay. But the best hope for the West was to encourage the Germans themselves to create a Western democratic state."[69]

They provided such encouragement not merely by alleviating physical deprivations, but by permitting an indigenous German culture of sorts to begin reviving in the bombed-out cities. "In the midst of the most desolate metropolis in the world," Vienna-born Jewish novelist and journalist Hilde Spiel wrote of Berlin, "among grey and bleached skeletons of houses, theatres of a splendour such as a Londoner might seek in vain . . . are rising again." Much had changed since 1945, when the Americans lured Germans into theaters with promises of cowboy films, only to show them shocking footage of concentration camp liberations instead.

The German and Austrian literary exile communities in the United States and Britain, many of whose prominent members were Jewish or married to Jews, were split over whether they should welcome the transformation. Perhaps the earliest sophisticated treatments of the moral question of German national war guilt to emerge from this community were Thomas Mann's *Doctor Faustus*, published in October 1947, and Carl Zuckmayer's *The Devil's General*, a play that opened to controversy and popular acclaim in Frankfurt in November.[70]

The Bizonia authorities could not begin physically reviving Germany, however, without cooperation from Germany's neighbors. "Germany could not raise enough food to be self-supporting," Clay stressed. And it could not "export without having its revenues from these exports confiscated by the country buying those products, since all of them held unpaid German securities."[71] Its neighbors would not extend it trade credit or, in the case of France, even consent to the country controlling its own strategic industrial and commodity resources. This is where the wider European context became critical. German recovery would have to be embedded in a European recovery, with American grants substituting for German reparations.

Contrary to Kennan, and the State Department broadly, Clay held Paris and not Moscow primarily responsible for the breakdown in four-power cooperation over Germany. He considered Kennan dogmatic and dangerous in his writings on Stalin's government. The two disparaged each other's intellectual temperament, accusing the other of holding ignorant misapprehensions about the nature of the Soviet government. Clay thought Kennan remote and highbrow, dismissing him as "all theory." The latter recalled a meeting between the two in Berlin, in the spring of 1946, in which he was "upbraided by the general over what he considered to be our anti-Soviet views" at the State Department.[72] For his part, Kennan thought Clay blinkered and naive to Stalin's agenda, chiding him for having been suckered by "Zhukov's personality."[73]

Perhaps, but Clay was not dogmatic or ideological in his desire to find a modus operandi with Moscow. He was no Russophile, and insisted on dealing with Stalin from a position of strength. "I don't think we would have had a Cold War if we'd kept a strong army in Europe in 1945," he would reflect decades later.[74] His prime concern was always restoring the German economy, and he was willing to pursue it with or without Soviet cooperation.[75]

Clay's initial influence on Marshall's European recovery ideas was modest. Marshall would unveil them without even mentioning a role for Germany. As for Clay himself, Marshall saw him not as part of his team but as a commander suffering from "localitis"—an affliction blinding him to the world beyond his own theater of responsibility.[76] Clay saw the problem through the other end of the scope: State was, in his words, "interested in Germany's relations with other countries [and] not in Germany itself."[77]

But it was also true that to wean Europe off American aid and dollar dependence there was no alternative but to reconstitute Germany's industrial capacity. Before the war, nearly 60 percent of all German imports came from, and 75 percent of all German exports went to, other European countries. "[U]ntil there is a revival of Western Germany's capacity to produce and consume at reasonable levels," a later joint U.S.-U.K. military governors report would argue, "there is little chance of restoring the Western European standard of living to pre-war levels."[78]

Clay's contribution to a European recovery program would lay in push-ing a revivified Germany from its periphery into its core. He accomplished this through dogged persistence over time, chipping away at State's inclination to keep the French calm even when it meant keeping Germany down.

※

MARSHALL ASSEMBLED HIS ADVISERS—ACHESON, CLAYTON, KENNAN, Bohlen, and Ben Cohen—on May 27 to review the PPS work. The general, breviloquent and somber, opened the discussion by stating that the adminis-tration would not "sit back and do nothing" while Europe faltered.[79] Now, what should they do? He stayed silent while each of them had his say.

Clayton painted a grim portrait of a continent in collapse. Bohlen talked of the need to begin laying the ground for West European economic federation. As for Russia, he said, Kennan had it right. The proposal needed to embrace the whole of Europe, not divide it. Division would be Stalin's job.

"Are we safe," Marshall put back to them, "in addressing this to all of Eu-rope? What if Russia reacts affirmatively and decides to come in?"[80]

This question was the heart of the matter for him. "Many people in Europe were very timid about opposing the Soviet Union," he reflected years later, "and I feared that if we started our plan by throwing the Soviets out it would scare these people and perhaps keep some of the European countries out of the pro-gram."[81] Appearing to pick a fight with Moscow would have been a particular problem for France and Italy, where Communist parties were strong and a con-stant threat to the stability of their weak governments.

Kennan was keenly aware of the risk that the Soviet Union might "accept" the administration's plan. The Russians, after all, had cooperated on Bretton Woods for years, but merely as leverage to extract cheap U.S. credits. Stalin only stiff-armed the accords right at the ratification deadline, at the end of 1945, when it was clear that nothing—despite the energetic efforts of Harry Dex-ter White, his influential source and advocate at Treasury—was forthcoming. Soviet cooperation with an American plan for Europe, Kennan knew, would signal only their interest in the dollars and intelligence-gathering opportuni-ties it might afford, allowing them at the same time to work to undermine the recovery the plan was meant to germinate. Such a scenario assumed, of course, that Congress would even allow an aid scheme to go forward that the Soviets could steer and profit from. But courting Moscow's embrace was, to Kennan, a necessary, calculated risk.

Even assuming that the communist movement could be beaten back in western Europe, as Kennan was convinced it would, the reality would still be grim—an East-West economic and political rupture. The only question would then be whether the winds of popular judgment would waft blame toward Washington or Moscow. Kennan was determined that it be Moscow. This objective required that the administration, in his words, "play it straight," or at least appear to. It had to force Stalin to react.

Stalin could not opt in without giving up his reparations claims on Germany and opening the country's financial accounts to foreign scrutiny, both of which seemed unlikely. Still, "if Russia accepted, we should welcome it," Kennan told Marshall. The United States could then treat Russia not as a beneficiary, but as prospective donor—a supplier of free food and raw materials to western Europe. Stalin would then walk away.

Stalin could not, however, decline an American aid offer without either loosening his grip on eastern Europe, much of which would embrace the plan, or tightening it by denying its new governments the right to choose. The latter option would come at the cost of revealing his true aims before the world: not to liberate the territories he occupied, but to subjugate and exploit them. "We [would] put Russia over the barrel," Kennan said. "Either it must decline or else enter into an arrangement that would mean an ending of the Iron Curtain."[82]

Marshall, who made decisions firmly but deliberately, refused to be drawn further at that point. Conscious that any proposal for funding a massive aid program faced the prospect of a devastating congressional defeat, he warned the men against any leaks before excusing them.

❖

THE NEXT AFTERNOON, MAY 28, CARL HUMELSINE, DIRECTOR OF STATE'S Executive Secretariat, brought Marshall a stack of papers to sign and reminded him of open issues on which he needed to decide. One was whether he still wished to attend commencement ceremonies at Harvard on June 5. He had turned down invitations to take an honorary degree the past two years, but this

year had provisionally agreed. Now Marshall hesitated, reckoning he would
have to speechify for his honor. What about that speech on aid to Europe they
had been kicking around?, Humelsine suggested.

Marshall summoned Acheson on May 29: was Harvard the right forum
at which to say something on Europe? No, Acheson said: commencement
speeches usually get poor news coverage; the speech "might fall flat"—a curious reaction from a man who had just given the speech of his life at a Mississippi teachers college.

Marshall agreed the address might not make the front pages. But that
would not be a bad thing. Let the ideas germinate. The timing was good, the
venue was right. He ordered his acceptance cabled to Harvard.

He wrote to Colonel Carter the next day asking him to have draft text prepared. "It is of tremendous importance that our people understand the situation in Europe," he explained, "particularly the dominant character of economic
factors." It should emphasize that this was "an extremely critical period through
which we are passing," and that "irritation and passion should have no part" in
the policy response. It should be broad but concise: the whole "talk" should be
"less than ten minute[s]."[83]

Marshall made no mention of Russia. Carter, however, had been on his
plane back from Moscow, and knew that the meetings with Molotov and Stalin
were impelling his boss. He asked Marshall's trusted translator, Bohlen, to take
the lead in drafting the text.

Bohlen lacked Kennan's skills as a strategic thinker. Yet despite being a
wealthy blueblood, who took the name "Chipper" (later Chip) from his fellows in Harvard's Porcellian Club, he was easygoing and bonded with people
naturally.[84] His direct language suited Marshall's style. Closeting himself for
two days, he condensed and sharpened Kennan's and Clayton's ideas, adapting
them as best he could to his master's voice. The draft then went to Clayton and
Acheson for edits before going to the secretary early the following week.[85]

Marshall recounts also directing Kennan to draft something independently. The two texts were, in the end, "quite apart," he judged, and he "cut
out" segments of one and the other and blended them with his own thoughts.[86]
Marshall wrote and rewrote even as he flew to Boston on June 4.

Truman was aware of the department's efforts to craft a European aid plan but would, remarkably, not see so much as a draft before the text was made public later that day. Marshall would years hence call this an oversight on his part.[87] In any case, Truman kept some distance from the beginning. "Anything going up [to Capitol Hill] bearing my name will quiver a couple of times, turn belly up and die," he told Clark Clifford, who wanted to call it the Truman Plan. "I've decided to give the whole thing to General Marshall. The worst Republican on the Hill can vote for it if we name it after the General."[88]

Given the deliberate lack of fanfare surrounding the speech, pursuant to Marshall's orders, the American press took little notice of the text. But since Marshall was going to invite Europe to take the initiative, Acheson made sure that the British press would.

As he had done before his Mississippi speech, Acheson met Miall, Muggeridge, and MacColl for lunch shortly before the speech. The three British correspondents had by this time virtually assumed the status of the under secretary's foreign press office. Accounts of the timing and content of their discussions differ. Miall said he and his colleagues had invited Acheson on June 2, with the latter never mentioning Marshall's speech. Jones said that Acheson had invited them on June 4, and had specifically told them of Marshall's speech. Acheson said he talked about the speech on June 5. What is clear, however, is that Acheson told them Marshall was inviting Europe to present Washington with a compelling, cooperative request for aid. He asked the men to telephone or cable Marshall's text to London and to make sure it got into Bevin's hands without delay: "it will not matter what hour of the night it is; wake Ernie up."[89]

❖

ON THE MORNING OF THE COMMENCEMENT EXERCISES, JUNE 5, MIALL phoned his editor at the BBC in London, Tony Wigan, telling him that the text of Marshall's imminent speech was "extremely important." Wigan suggested they could broadcast it, but Miall argued against—"his voice is so poor." Miall said he would read the words himself; he was afraid Britons would miss the message if the transmission were left to Marshall.

Indeed, the Harvard audience of fifteen thousand hearing Marshall that afternoon, delivering the speech in his characteristic unemotional, clipped, bright-voweled voice, must have been at least as conscious of the limitations of the orator as they were of the importance of the oration.[90] Acheson called the speech "short, simple, and altogether brilliant,"[91] but only the first two would have been apparent to most listeners.

Setting reading glasses on his nose, Marshall began with the undirected observation that "the world situation is very serious." But "the problem," he said, "is one of such enormous complexity that the very mass of facts presented to the public . . . make it exceedingly difficult for the man in the street to reach a clear appraisement of the situation." Furthermore, being remote from the troubled areas, "it is hard for [Americans] to comprehend the plight and consequent reactions of the long-suffering peoples, and the effect of those reactions on their governments."

This served as Marshall's jumping-off point for introducing Clayton's thoughts on why the vast "visible destruction of factories, mines, and railroads," as terrible as it was, was so much less serious than what was not visible: "the dislocation of the entire fabric of the European economy."

"Long-standing commercial ties, private institutions, banks, insurance companies and shipping companies," Marshall said, had "disappeared, through loss of capital, absorption through nationalization or by simple destruction." People were losing confidence in their national currencies. In consequence, "the division of labor [which] is the basis of modern civilization . . . is threatened with breakdown." Fields are being withdrawn from cultivation, creating shortages of food in towns and cities. Governments, in consequence, are being forced to spend their scarce foreign money on vital necessities from abroad, exhausting funds "urgently needed for reconstruction." Europe's needs "for the next three or four years" vastly exceed her ability to pay, and without "substantial additional help" she faces "economic, social, and political deterioration of a very grave character.

"The remedy," Marshall said, "lies in breaking the vicious circle and restoring the confidence" (a more prosaic rendering of Kennan's "spiritual vigor") "of the European people in the economic future of their own countries and of Europe as a whole." Here, Marshall was adumbrating Clayton's idea that revival would require not just national recovery but advances toward "European economic federation." Given the obvious "consequences to the economy of the United States" of the failure to break this circle, Marshall said, again channeling

Clayton, it was only "logical that the United States should do whatever it is able to do to assist" in this crisis.

Then, in a now famous line whose inspiration was Kennan's but whose dramatic rendering was Bohlen's, Marshall stated: "Our policy is directed not against any country or doctrine but against hunger, poverty, desperation and chaos." The phrase had been crafted so as to mark the Soviets, if they rejected the plan, as "partisans of hunger, poverty, and chaos."[92] Marshall continued: "Its purpose should be the revival of a working economy in the world so as to permit the emergence of political and social conditions in which free institutions can exist." That is, the policy was not directed *against* the only country it could have been directed against, the Soviet Union, but *toward* the advancement internationally of the "free institutions" which that country opposed as a matter of ideology.

Then, in Marshall's first statement to elicit a reaction from the assembled, he said:

> Any government that is willing to assist in the task of recovery will find full cooperation, I am sure, on the part of the United States Government. Any government which maneuvers to block the recovery of other countries cannot expect help from us.

Vigorous applause drowned Marshall out, forcing him to restart his subsequent sentence:

> Furthermore [applause] . . . Furthermore, governments, political parties or groups which seek to perpetuate human misery in order to profit therefrom politically or otherwise will encounter the opposition of the United States.

Again, applause.

Marshall's audience had not been moved to respond to his rendering of the varieties or causes of Europe's suffering. Nor had they been so moved by his calls for American action to ameliorate it. But they had been stirred by his allusions to Soviet obstructionism.

Marshall's final statements of substance were those bringing forth the admonitions of both Kennan and Clayton, highlighted for the British journalists by Acheson, that the initiative must now come from "the countries of Europe" acting in concert:

> It would be neither fitting nor efficacious for this Government to under-
> take to draw up unilaterally a program designed to place Europe on its feet
> economically. This is the business of the Europeans. . . . The role of this
> country should consist of friendly aid in the drafting of a European program
> and of later support of such a program so far as it may be practical for us to
> do so. The program should be a joint one, agreed to by a number, if not all
> European nations.

At this point, Marshall had only the haziest of templates for what a success-ful program should look like. He would describe it shortly after his speech only as being "somewhat along [the] lines [of the] Monnet Plan but on [a] much larger scale"[93] In ad-libbed words, he ended by emphasizing his belief that "the whole world of the future hangs on a proper judgment" as to what "must be done" by the United States to bring about Europe's recovery, concluding only that the judgment had to be rendered without "passion," "prejudice," or "the emotion of the moment."

The speech was more understated than Truman's had been, and certainly less bellicose. The American press, now conditioned to the "give 'em hell, Harry" approach to serious initiatives, hardly took notice. The next day's flac-cid *New York Times* headline on the speech said it all: "Marshall Pleads for Eu-ropean Unity." (The full text of Marshall's speech is provided in Appendix B.)

Over in London, though, the speech had scored a bull's-eye on Acheson's target. Bevin, who had listened to Miall's reading on the BBC, said it was "like a lifeline to a sinking man. It seemed to bring hope where there was none." He cabled the State Department to inform them he was "taking the initiative" and heading off to Paris to get Bidault on board.[94] "I may do Bevin an injustice," Marshall later commented, "but I had the impression at the time that part of his initiative stemmed from an ambition to be the European leader for the plan." As for Bidault, he was "certain this accounts for most of [his] contributions."[95]

Bidault insisted that the French and British governments engage the Sovi-ets on Marshall's initiative. He and Socialist prime minister Paul Ramadier were anxious not to afford the French Communists opportunity to claim they were American stooges, stoking conflict with Moscow. Like Kennan, though, he was determined not to let Moscow delay or obstruct progress.[96] Stalin would have to choose between partnership or isolation.

Eleanor Roosevelt, the most influential and accomplished first lady in American history, had been disappointed with Truman's speech in March. But Marshall's speech elated her. This was the right way, she believed, to confront Soviet expansionism without a war of ideologies.[97] Having been a passionate supporter of the Morgenthau Plan for pastoralizing Germany, she did not yet grasp how at odds Morgenthau and Marshall would soon be. No doubt Marshall—given the widespread revulsion toward Germany—was not anxious to highlight this.

Stalin, too, liked the Morgenthau Plan, but in contrast to Mrs. Roosevelt found Marshall's speech far more menacing than Truman's. As Kennan had anticipated, the initiative took the Soviet leader by surprise. At the time, Stalin had, unlike Marshall, not yet concluded that cooperation—or his version of it—was at an end. To the contrary, while Marshall's program was taking shape Stalin was still talking optimistically, both to American visitors and the Russian public, about progress on "the German problem." A May 16 editorial in a hardline anti-Western journal highlighted "the value of the Moscow conference [in] clear[ing] the way—given good will on all sides—to the necessary, if exacting, work of reconciling the different points of view and arriving at agreed decisions."[98] Stalin would not have disseminated such a message had he thought negotiations over Germany were at an end.

Stalin further believed that cooperation should be pushed forward more broadly. Talks over Korea, where two years earlier the Americans had taken the Japanese surrender in the south and the Soviets in the north, were making progress. In May, Stalin instructed his delegates to reach an agreement with the Americans over forming an interim government if sufficient representation could be secured for "leftist" South Korean groups.[99]

But the Marshall Plan was about to change everything.

Soviet Foreign Minister Vyacheslav Molotov (*center*) speaking with French Foreign Minister Georges Bidault (*right*) through an interpreter, Paris, 1946 or 1947.

FIVE

TRAP

MOLOTOV PORED OVER THE RUSSIAN TRANSLATION OF MARSHALL'S speech, underlining phrases suggesting American intent:

"very serious situation"

"bodes no good for the world"

"clear to everyone what effects this could have on the economy of the United States"

"must do everything within its power so as to assist in the return of normal economic conditions"

And most importantly:

"[governments] which seek to perpetuate human misery in order to profit therefrom politically or otherwise will encounter the opposition of the United States"

He added margin scribbles on the structure of the plan, noting in particular Marshall's insistence that aid would be limited to supporting a progam Europeans would develop in concert.[1]

Molotov was looking for evidence, certain it was there, of impending American economic crisis and imperialist animus. Determined to avoid a trap, he was also alert to the opportunity for setting one. Ambassador Novikov was as well. Five thousand miles away in a hostile foreign capital, however, he was doubtless conscious of the need to demonstrate his fealty to the Kremlin through a muscular display of vigilance. In a cable to Molotov from Washington on June 9, 1947, he asserted that Marshall's plan contained menacing "outlines of a Western European bloc" that was "directed against us."[2] But that did not mean that Moscow should reject it—to the contrary. He surmised that the State Department did not want Soviet participation: Moscow should therefore participate in order to undermine its aims.

This was Marshall's fear. Had Kennan miscalculated, then, in betting that Moscow would recoil from their overture? At this point, it seemed so.

On June 18, Bevin and Bidault met with Jefferson Caffery, the American ambassador to Paris. They presented him with an advance copy of an invitation they intended to deliver to the Soviet chargé that evening, inviting Molotov to three-way talks in Paris over Marshall's proposal during the week of June 23. Caffery reported to Marshall that the two had told him, separately, that they hoped the Soviets would "refuse to cooperate."[3]

The Kremlin followed public and private reports on the meetings among the western allies in Paris, combing for signs of duplicity. Molotov's aides warned him of evidence "to conceal from the Soviet Union the already-reached agreement on a number of issues," such as the establishment of a new European Economic Commission "related to the implementation of the Marshall Plan." The Americans were trying to bribe France "toward the Anglo-Saxons," in particular to force the Soviet Union "to accept serious concessions on the resolution of the German problem." Furthermore, plans were in place "to represent the USSR as an enemy of the reconstruction and stabilization of Europe" if it rejected the terms of the Plan. Moscow would then be "the party guilty of the division of Europe into two adversarial blocs." For Paris, this would "justify France's transition into the camp of the Anglo-Saxons."[4]

Molotov was not about to let the western schemers off easily. "At first I agreed to participate," he reflected years later, referring not just to the talks but to the Marshall Plan itself. Three days later, the Politburo Central Committee ratified his decision to join the talks. He cabled his acceptance on June 23.

Molotov also instructed the Soviet ambassadors in Warsaw, Prague, and Belgrade to direct their host governments to "ensure their own participation in the elaboration of the economic measures under consideration and make their own claims."[5] The governments in Warsaw and Prague each responded to Molotov's cable with enthusiasm, beyond what was required or prudent.[6]

The Polish ambassador to Moscow replied immediately, saying his "government is very interested in the current discussion of the aid plan [and] ready to participate in the exchange of opinions on this question." He emphasized that "the stabilization of Poland is imperative to the conditions of stabilizing Europe."[7] Czechoslovak foreign minister Jan Masaryk, son of the country's post–World War I founder, unaffiliated with any party in the coalition government, was overjoyed upon learning by radio of Molotov's decision to attend the conference.[8] "Czechoslovakia is ready to cooperate completely," he cabled, "in the cause of creating the prerequisites for the provision of the American assistance [and] to propose Czech projects at an appropriate time."[9] National Socialist trade minister Hubert Ripka called Molotov's unexpected move "a good omen."[10] The Yugoslav government affirmed its readiness "to take part in the preliminary negotiations" provided that the initiative "is based on the principles of the United Nations Charter."[11]

Yet Molotov never intended to let them negotiate terms. Suggesting the confrontational stance he would take on behalf of the eastern bloc, the Soviet press termed the American plan "the Marshall Doctrine." It was, Pravda said, part of Washington's "campaign against the forces of world democracy and progress." Its aim was the "quick formation of a notorious western bloc under the unconditional and absolute leadership of American imperialism."[12] It was a "plan for political pressures with dollars and a program for interference in the internal affairs of other states."[13]

On June 24, Molotov gave Stalin a draft of the instructions he intended to deliver to the Soviet delegation in advance of the talks. It suggests he intended to bargain hard over terms, but not to strangle the initiative. Stalin scribbled edits that show the same intent, but a more emollient tone.

"Before consideration of any concrete proposals related to American aid to Europe," Molotov wrote, "the Soviet delegation must contest any terms of aid that may lead to infringement upon the sovereignty of European countries or their economic enslavement." Stalin crossed out the words "their economic enslavement," writing in the more anodyne "disruption of their economic independence." The edits suggest he did not want to poison the well prematurely.

Molotov delimited how far the Soviet delegation could go to reach agreement with the French and British. He insisted that they must block any plan that would "strengthen the pre-war relations between economically separate European countries"—a condition that undermined the American objective of integrating Europe.

Molotov also outlined terms related to Germany. Its resources, he said, could not be utilized for "stabilization of the European economy" without first reaching agreement on the country's "economic unity" and its "reparation obligations." Stalin's edits suggest a harder line here. Changing "economic unity" to "political and economic unity,"[14] he would have had in mind Marshall's resistance to a strong German central government—resistance that served to keep the country's larger and more industrialized western territory under American control. Stalin would not abide a plan that abetted this.

Also on June 24, Novikov cabled Molotov expressing deeper concerns than he had previously. "[T]he 'Marshall Plan,'" he said, makes it appear "as if the United States has decided to give the European states themselves the initiative in establishing a program of economic reconstruction for Europe." Its content, however, would be largely dictated by Washington. "It is to this end that [Clayton's present] talks in London are directed." Washington's aim, Novikov explained, was the "subordination of the European countries to American capital and the creation of anti-Soviet groupings."[15]

Stalin's economic adviser, the Hungarian-born Evgeny Varga,[16] also wrote to Molotov, arguing that Marshall's scheme aimed to forestall America's "imminent economic crisis, the approach of which no one in the USA denies." Washington must, "in its own interest," he explained, "grant much greater credits than it has done heretofore—just to rid itself of surplus goods at home." Though it "knows in advance that part of those credits will never be repaid," it hoped thereby to forge a "bloc of bourgeois countries under U.S. domination."[17] Still, Varga, like Novikov, backed Molotov's participation in Paris, no doubt in part because the Central Committee had already done so.

Over in London that day, as Novikov had noted, Clayton was meeting with Bevin. The two discussed how American aid could be used to undermine Soviet influence in Europe—even in the East. The Marshall Plan was, Bevin enthused, "the quickest way to break down the iron curtain." Russia, he wagered, could "not hold its satellites against the attraction of fundamental help toward economic revival in Europe."[18]

❖

ON JUNE 26, MOLOTOV'S PLANE SET DOWN ON A BAKING TARMAC AT PARIS' Le Bourget Airport. The city was in the midst of an oppressive heat wave, a mirror-image of the bitter cold that had destroyed millions of acres of winter wheat earlier that year. The size of Molotov's entourage, eighty-nine-strong, suggested he intended either to engage seriously or to rouse the French Communists if he were disappointed.[19] Despite being booted from the French government by a center coalition in May, the Communists had more parliamentary seats than any other party; and with 90 percent of the public saying things were going "badly or rather badly" in France, they were still a political force.[20]

Arriving in the early evening at the Quai d'Orsay, home of the French Foreign Ministry since 1853, Molotov wasted little time before probing Bidault for conspiratorial intent. What, he asked, had Paris and London learned from Washington about Marshall's initiative? "Perhaps the two ministers prepared whatever is required," Molotov suggested obliquely.

"[We] did not prepare anything," Bidault protested. "The English government, of course, has its own proposals, and the French government prepared a bit of something from its side as well."

"[Then] the time," Molotov observed, "was not spent in vain after all."

No, Bidault agreed. "The time was, of course, not lost," he said, mirroring the Russian's gentle sarcasm, "because Mr. Molotov was invited."[21]

Molotov knew from British ambassador Sir Maurice Peterson in Moscow that Bevin had brought economic experts to Paris to discuss the plan with Bidault over a week ago.[22] Bidault's protestations confirmed for him that he was walking into a stitch-up.

The official business began the following day, June 27. The three delegations assembled in the elegant but intimate Salon des Perroquets, named for the ancient tapestries on the wall. Exercising his prerogative as host, Bidault rose to deliver the formal opening statement.

A founding figure of the Christian Democrat MRP party, forty-seven-year-old Georges Bidault was uniquely positioned to navigate France through the delicate shoals of joining an American-led alliance. The Communists to his left would never have crossed Moscow; the Gaullists to his right would never have trusted Washington. De Gaulle himself, Bidault later observed, "never said a word about the Marshall Plan, but accused the Americans of being opportunists, ignoramuses and exploiters." Whatever "legitimate grudges against the Americans" the French people might harbor, however, nothing, to Bidault's mind, could "do justice to General Marshall and to the generosity of the American people."[23] He would not let the present opportunity slip.

Hailing Marshall's speech for its acuity in identifying "the nature and origins" of Europe's economic plight, Bidault wasted no time highlighting for Molotov what would be the insurmountable block to Russian cooperation: that to "enlist the interest of the greatest creditor nation of the world," Europe's aid request would "have to follow a coherent programme" drawn up in "concert" based on its combined "balance sheet." To this end, a steering committee of participating governments should be established, he said, with the aim of completing a comprehensive report by the first of September. This was, in Bidault's rendering, to be no reprisal of wartime Lend-Lease, under which the Soviets simply submitted demands to Washington for expeditious fulfillment.

Bidault's tone was confident, his reasoning clear and fluid—until he turned to "the problem of Germany." It was here that he sounded less like a statesman in control of his brief and more like a spokesman awaiting one. Germany's reconstruction, he said, "raises precisely all the questions upon which it has so far been impossible to reach an agreement," such as "the level of German industry, reparations, the regime for the Ruhr, etc. It is true, this presents a difficulty which cannot be denied." Indeed, Bidault's own government was in a muddle on these matters. The September report should, he concluded, be "drawn up . . . without prejudice to our decisions as regards the final statute of Germany."[24]

Molotov responded with the official Soviet opening statement the following day, June 28. The contrast to Bidault's gloss was stark. Concurring only that "reconstruction [and] the subsequent economic development of the countries of Europe" would be "facilitated" if the United States "could provide these countries with the economic assistance which they need," he framed Marshall's proposal as an American response to an American problem. "[I]t is to the interest of the United States . . . to make use of the possibilities of their credit to enlarge their foreign markets, especially in view of the approaching crisis"—that being the inevitable and imminent crisis of capitalism. The Soviet government had nonetheless accepted the Franco-British invitation to discuss the proposal, "notwithstanding the fact that the planning which is the basis of the socialist economy of the Soviet Union excludes the danger of the crises and economic troubles which are the theme of the American Minister's speech."

As for the "plan of work drawn up by the French government, and supported by the British government," however, Molotov's government had "serious doubts."

"It seemed perfectly clear that questions of internal economy were a matter concerning the sovereignty of the peoples themselves." France had "her own economic plan," as did Britain. "The Soviet people," for their part, were at present "engaged in the successful execution of their STALIN Plan, a five-year plan [that] ensures a steady increase in the material and cultural prosperity of the Soviet people." For "the countries of Europe [to] decide for themselves what American aid they require" was, therefore, all well and good; each country knew its needs and interests. But "attempts made from without to intervene in the economic life of various countries have not had nor can have any positive effects." Thus "the [present] attempts made to force the Conference to proceed to perfect a general economic programme for the European nations—which would inevitably involve the intervention of certain states—could not serve as a basis for collaboration."

Through a strategy of imposing bilateral trade agreements on eastern European countries, Moscow had, since the war, redirected trade patterns in the region toward the Soviet Union. This was integral to its ambition of creating a permanent security zone between itself and Germany. Anglo-French support for an American plan to reintegrate the eastern economies with those of the West therefore represented a threat to Soviet economic and political control over this zone.

As for "the problem of Germany," Molotov continued, it "is a problem quite apart." The various unresolved questions should not be discussed in Paris, but should remain the exclusive purview of the Council of Foreign Ministers.[25]

The floor was now Bevin's. In spite of Molotov's disparaging of the French and British plans, which confirmed Bevin's beliefs about Moscow's unwillingness to cooperate, he was determined to test the limits of his diplomatic powers before conceding what would be a risky breakdown in Anglo-Soviet relations.

The son of a farm laborer's widow, father unknown, the sixty-six-year-old Bevin began life the unlikeliest of prospects to become his country's chief diplomat. "He murdered the King's English," observed Clay, who marveled at witnessing him address George VI as plain "King."[26] Presented once with draft text intended to bear his name, he shook his head no: "It's just not me," he said. "You won't mind if I take it away and de-grammaticize it?"[27]

Orphaned at the age of eight, a school dropout at eleven, Bevin toiled in hard manual labor jobs until in 1911, at age thirty, becoming a full-time union officer. He rose steadily through the ranks, working to create what would by the late 1930s become the world's largest trade union: the Transport and General Workers' Union. It was his role as general secretary that led Churchill to invite him, in 1940, to become minister of labour in the wartime coalition government. Bevin became one of the Tory prime minister's most trusted Labour Party figures. He played a vital role in mobilizing British industry and the workforce to supply the mammoth war effort.

With the upset Labour general election victory in July 1945, incoming prime minister Clement Attlee, to the approval of outgoing foreign secretary Anthony Eden and King George, added to the surprise by bypassing Hugh Dalton to name Bevin foreign secretary. The former union leader quickly put his stamp on the job, inspiring loyalty in the Foreign Office both for his integrity and his firm hold on diplomatic power.

Still, many supporters and detractors alike viewed him as "long-winded, vain, vindictive, profoundly suspicious, and prejudiced." He had issues with "Jews, Germans, Roman Catholics, and intellectuals of all kinds, groups that, when taken together, comprised a large proportion of those with whom he had to deal." Truman considered Bevin a "boor." Soviet diplomat Andrei Gromyko concurred.[28] Acheson, however, who knew him far better, saw him in a much more affectionate light. "Ernie [was] solid, squared away to the world," Acheson said. He had "curious flashes of temper and anger." But "if after testing you a little bit he decided he was your friend, he was, and that stood through thick and thin."[29]

John Maynard Keynes, Britain's storied economist, had in 1944 warned of an impending "Financial Dunkirk."[30] After the cessation of American war aid, Britain would be unable to sustain its imperial commitments or meet its welfare state ambitions at home. Bevin would be obliged to preside over the former, though much of his diplomacy would be geared toward persuading his own countrymen that he was not. "[I] do not accept the view . . . that we have ceased to be a Great Power," he intoned before the House of Commons on May 16, 1947. Yet ten days prior he had told colleagues that he would have to "bluff his way through in foreign policy, given the financial weakness of this country." And he warned British miners, his political base, that his ability to carry out an independent foreign policy was dependent on their willingness to provide him with more coal.[31]

Bevin resented American dollar diplomacy, in particular the linking of desperately needed financial assistance to London's submission on political matters central to British sovereignty. The American loan agreement, signed in December 1945 after nearly four months of difficult and often humiliating negotiations in Washington, required Britain to accept American air and naval bases on British and Commonwealth territory. Bevin's decision to support the

manufacture of British nuclear weapons was driven not by a German or Soviet threat, but by his belief that the country "could not afford to acquiesce in
an American monopoly of the new development."[32] Britain, as Bevin saw his
country, was "the last bastion of social democracy," standing against both "the
red tooth and claw of American capitalism and the Communist dictatorship of
Soviet Russia."

It was the Soviets, however, whom Bevin knew to be the greater threat to
British interests. No one, he told a group of left-wing critics in June 1946, had
done more to defend the Russian Revolution than he. Yet what he got in return
was Russian "Communists [trying] to break up the [trade] Union that I built."
The Soviets were not to be trusted. Their stranglehold over eastern Europe,
"clos[ing] the door and prevent[ing] entry or any contact with those peoples
for trade or anything else," could not be abided. Their territorial ambitions
cut "across . . . the throat of the British Commonwealth."[33] With Bevin at the
helm, British foreign policy was certainly more overtly hostile to Moscow than
it would have been had the more accommodationist Attlee been able to run it
himself.[34]

Still, Bevin was no Kennan. He had no theory on the sources of Soviet
conduct, and was willing, at times seemingly eager, to suspend disbelief, to
probe for hidden good intentions. Bevin at times ascribed the unbending, even
brutal, nature of Russian negotiating behavior to inexperience and isolation. In
November–December 1946 he had been part of the New York meeting of the
Council of Foreign Ministers that forged agreement on peace treaties with Italy,
Finland, Hungary, Bulgaria, and Romania, drawing optimistic inferences from
the experience. "I think we are learning how to cooperate," Molotov had said on
the boat back to Europe, and Bevin liked to cite this remark in evidence. Even
after the March–April 1947 foreign ministers meeting in Moscow, from which
Marshall had returned to Washington wearing a shroud of gloom, Bevin was
optimistic that slow progress was being made.[35]

Here in Paris, now, Bevin's response to Molotov was unfailingly gracious.
He ensured the Russian that he, Bevin, "should not wish to be a party" to any
project that would "interfere with the sovereignty of participating Governments." Yet still it was necessary, he insisted, "that we should undertake work in
collaboration . . . and that our demands should be co-ordinated." For Molotov,

sovereignty and coordination were incompatible conditions from which to approach American aid. Yet Bevin maintained, however implausibly, that "Mr. Molotov's remarks provide the basis on which we can approach the problem from similar points of view."[36]

Following a second meeting with Bidault and Bevin on June 29, Molotov sent a coded cable to Moscow highlighting his effort to impress upon Bidault the gulf that existed between the Soviet and French visions for shaping Marshall's still hazy initiative. "The difference," Molotov reported having told Bidault, is "that the Soviet project limits the tasks . . . to the discussion of the issues which are directly related to the American economic assistance to Europe, whereas the French project envisages also the design of economic programs which encompass both the domestic economies of European countries and . . . economic relations between them."[37] This had been Molotov's oblique way of telling Bidault that Moscow would be happy to submit an assistance request, as part of a package of such national requests, but that it had no intention of subjecting its resources or requirements to external evaluation, or to participate in any form of coordination underwritten by Washington. Neither would it allow its satellites to do so.

❖

MOLOTOV'S SUSPICIONS OF HIS COUNTERPARTS' INTENTIONS WERE SOON confirmed. The Kremlin was receiving a constant flow of intelligence from highly placed British sources—among whom Guy Burgess at the Foreign Office in London and Donald Maclean at the British embassy in Washington. Maclean, who had access to all of the embassy's classified cable traffic, was reporting—according to Pavel Sudoplatov, the spymaster who had overseen Trotsky's assassination—that "the goal of the Marshall Plan was to ensure American economic domination of Europe."[38]

On the night of June 29, a brown-jacketed *Feldjäger* special messenger raced through the streets of Moscow. Arriving at the Kremlin gates, he handed the guard an envelope marked "Very Urgent." A few minutes later, Stalin, sitting in his dimly lit office, opened it and removed the intelligence report, growing increasingly "indignant" as he read. He quickly wrote out text, and directed his secretary, Alexander Poskrebyshev, to call Politburo members and request their approval. Once the last "yes" vote was secured in the early hours of June 30, Poskrebyshev told Vyshinsky to encipher the cable and send it to Paris.

The message directed Molotov to obstruct Marshall's plan from being implemented in eastern Europe. Clayton and Bevin, the cable explained, had agreed that the Marshall Plan was not to be focused on providing *assistance* of the sort that had been carried out by UNRRA, but rather exclusively on the long-term economic *reconstruction* of Europe. It was to be implemented outside the United Nations framework, for the reason that German industrial revival was considered essential to rehabilitation of the continent—and Germany was not a member of the U.N. Most importantly, the cable stated, "Britain and America will oppose payment of reparations to the Soviet Union from current production."

At the time, reparations were the Soviet Union's only source of foreign capital—capital that was vital to modernizing its chemical and machine tool industries. At Yalta and Potsdam, Stalin believed he had secured Roosevelt's and Churchill's consent to a five-year flow of German industrial machinery and goods. Yet the Kremlin's British moles now indicated that the United States and Great Britain would end this arrangement in favor of an American-controlled reconstruction scheme, partially financed by Germany.

The Marshall Plan was, therefore, according to Sudoplatov, "totally unacceptable because it would obstruct our consolidation of control in Eastern Europe. It meant that Communist parties already established in Romania, Bulgaria, Poland, Czechoslovakia, and Hungary would be deprived of economic levers of power." Constructing a network of puppet regimes across eastern Europe depended on Moscow's ability to strip Germany bare, funneling its resources through local Communist parties into building a new command economy throughout the vast territories it occupied. It is no wonder that Molotov was cautioned to "object to any discussion . . . of the utilization of German economic resources to meet the requirements of European countries [or] of economic assistance to Germany from the USA."[39] Anything to do with Germany needed to be handled "through the [Allied] Control Council, where we have the right to 'veto.'"[40]

AT THE JUNE 30 MEETING, MOLOTOV HAD BEEN RAISING "RELATIVELY minor questions [and] objections" when an assistant handed him Vyshinsky's decoded cable. "It seems," Acheson recalled from accounts of the meeting, "that Molotov has a bump on his forehead which swells when he is under emotional strain." As Molotov read the telegram, "he turned pale and the bump on his forehead swelled. After that, his attitude suddenly changed and he became much more harsh."[41]

Molotov told Bidault and Bevin that "the German issue" and "the drafting of an all-around program for the European countries" were not proper subjects for their present conference.[42] Reading from the telegram, he retreaded his arguments of the prior three days.

"In effect," Bevin said, smiling disbelievingly, "what you are asking the United States Government to do is to give us a blank check. If I were to go to Moscow with a blank check and ask you to sign it I wonder how far I would get with your end." Bidault nodded in agreement. The inevitable split between Moscow and the London-Paris axis had arrived.

Shortly after adjourning, the Soviet delegation, in a departure from their previous insistence on keeping the discussions secret, bared its objections to the French proposal in a public statement distributed to the TASS news agency.[43] That evening, Molotov cabled back to Stalin that "Britain and France [were] now in dire straits [and that] their only hope was the United States, which demands that [they] set up some kind of European body to facilitate interference in the economic and political affairs" of Europe. "Britain and—and to some extent—France count on using this body to promote their own interests."[44]

Bidault's frustrations boiled over on July 1. He began by calling it "grave" that "on the eve of a decision" the three delegations might "not reach an understanding." He drew attention to the "fundamental differences" between the Soviet and French positions. First, the Soviets proposed "to establish only a list of needs in American credits" that would be received by a European Committee for transmission to the United States. France believed this was entirely insufficient. "[Mr. Marshall's] text is perfectly clear," Bidault stressed; "if there is no European mutual aid, there is no American aid." Second, "Mr. Molotov fears that [such] a general economic plan may result in an interference in the internal affairs of European States, and be an infringement of their sovereignty." This was, however, something that "the French Delegation has never foreseen, or considered, or admitted." Sovereignty was to remain sacrosanct.[45]

Bidault and Molotov were by this time talking past each other. "Sovereignty" in the context of the Marshall Plan was, for Bidault, European governments making autonomous decisions regarding what adjustments in their economic structures they were willing to make in order to satisfy, with as little wastage of scarce resources as possible, the combined needs of their people. And such adjustments were essential to securing American aid, which was itself essential to ensuring that Europe had adequate provisions to allow them to be implemented without further hardship. For Molotov the requirement for mutual adjustment was an imposition from without, and therefore a fundamental interference with sovereignty. And if the Americans were determined to usurp sovereign powers as the price for their assistance, then Europeans simply had to reject it.

Molotov reported home that no "joint decisions on the substance of the issue in question" were likely, as the Soviet "stand differs in its essence from the Anglo-French position."[46] At this point, however, he was still willing to engage with his French and British counterparts, believing that their differences with the United States would doom Marshall's scheme.

But "I changed my mind," Molotov later recalled. Western tensions, he decided, would be greater with Moscow out of the picture. So "I sent a second memorandum," this time saying he wanted to reject the Plan.[47] Tito deputy Djilas remembers things differently. In Paris for a congress of the French Communist Party, he was invited to lunch at the Soviet embassy. With jazz playing in the background—best for thwarting listening devices, the Russians explained—Molotov said he had been ordered to oppose the Plan by the Politburo.[48] In any case, it was to be a fateful decision.

On July 2, at the fifth and final meeting, "Molotov adopted a completely uncompromising attitude," Bevin recorded. The Russian laced into the latest French proposal for an "all-embracing European programme" to be elaborated by "a new organization, standing above the European countries," demanding their "obedient behaviour," and "intervening in [their] internal affairs." One day Poland will be told: "produce more coal!" The next, Czechoslovakia will be told to buy machines abroad and grow more crops. They were to "lose their former economic and national independence, to the advantage of certain strong powers," as a mere "pretext" for securing some undetermined American aid.

"The Soviet government," Molotov pronounced, "cannot, of course, take this course."

Bevin turned to Bob Dixon, his private secretary, whispering: "This really is the birth of the Western bloc."[49]

Molotov plowed on. As for Germany, it was unacceptable that its "resources should be used for any purpose rather than reparations." Germany could not be the beneficiary of an Allied reconstruction scheme. Yet in the next breath he blasted the western powers for harming the country through "federalization." Molotov insisted that only "the genuine restoration of Germany as a united democratic State" could ensure that "the needs of the German people" were met.

"The Franco-British proposal," he concluded, would "lead to nothing good." It would "split Europe into two groups of States and will create new difficulties in the mutual relations between them. In this event American credits will serve not the economic restoration of Europe" but rather the exploitation of weaker countries by "certain strong Powers striving for domination."

"The Soviet Government," he ended ominously, "considers it necessary to warn the Governments of Britain and France of the consequences of such action."[50]

Bidault was furious. "[Mr. Molotov] concludes by warning my country, [but] I, for my part, would like to warn the Soviet delegation against any action which might lead to the separation of Europe into two groups." The sovereignty and independence of all European nations, he insisted, would be fully respected. What was being asked of them was nothing more than "national statistics," freely and independently provided, that would "be brought together and compared so as to determine resources and needs"—to create a European "balance sheet."

Mr. Molotov had noted "that American aid is uncertain," he said. But it would "be even more so if the data of the problem are not respected, and if, of course, Europe does not speak up and say . . . what she can do for herself, and what we all lack."

Regarding Mr. Molotov's protestations that Poland could be ordered to produce more coal, or Czechoslovakia less machinery, this claim was, Bidault insisted, nonsense. "[I]t is *in* independence and *for* independence that their collaboration is sought."

As for the objection that France was proposing "a decisive place" for the United States in the "restoration of the economic life of the European countries," Bidault explained that "decisive" did not mean "principal." At Waterloo, he noted, "the decisive role," as opposed to the principal role, "was played by a few thousand men who arrived at the last moment." Likewise, with the Marshall Plan it was each European nation, "and all of us together," that would play the principal role. Yet in the coming months the American role would indeed be decisive, in that "they are the few thousand men who will decide the battle and the victory over misery."[51]

For Molotov, such clarification was sterile pedantry. The Soviet Union was not about to collaborate in a new European "battle" in which the American role was to be decisive. If the United States wished to provide assistance for the recovery of the European nations—which was, after all, of vital and pressing interest to the survival of American capitalism—such a proposal would receive Soviet consideration. Yet there could be no American meddling in the sovereign internal affairs of these nations, as the French and British advocated.

Bevin joined in, condemning Molotov's statement as "a travesty of the facts." British policy, he insisted, "was to cooperate with all and dominate none." And "with regard to the division of Europe, nobody had striven more than I," he added, "for the unity of Europe" and that of Germany. As for the "grave consequences" with which Molotov threatened Britain, "such threats had [never] and would not cause us to hesitate to pursue what we considered to be our duty." He pledged, like Bidault, to take Marshall's proposal forward.[52]

Molotov stood, announcing that the Soviet Union was withdrawing from discussions. The Marshall Plan, he said, was "nothing but a vicious American scheme for using dollars to buy its way" into European affairs.[53] His delegation followed him out of the hall.

※

MOLOTOV "COULD HAVE KILLED THE MARSHALL PLAN BY JOINING IT,"
Harriman later reflected, disbelievingly.[54] "Bevin did a superb job of getting
Molotov out of Paris—by careful maneuvering. . . . [H]e had the courage to
invite Molotov and the bluntness to get rid of him."[55] But falling into the trap
confirmed the Russian as "essentially a dull fellow." [56]

Bidault agreed. "I could never figure out why Molotov had acted like
that. . . . [I]f he had continued to side with us, he could not have lost anything . . .
but he [chose] the only way to lose for sure."[57]

"Sometimes the communists do strange things," Byrnes told Bidault. "If
Molotov had stayed in Paris, he [could] have referred to the Potsdam accords
in order to demand 50 percent of all available financial assets. This would have
embarrassed the United States as much as France. Then Molotov would have
demanded aid for Yugoslavia, Poland, etc. . . . It is difficult to believe that this
would have been acceptable to Congress. In deciding to act otherwise, [Mos-
cow] has greatly aided the United States."[58]

For Paul Hoffman, Republican founder of an influential business leaders
forum who would soon play a vital role in taking the Marshall Plan from idea
to program, "the Molotov walkout" was a watershed. It made it "transparently
clear that Russia was not interested in European reconstruction, but in chaos."[59]

Of course, Molotov was not the decision maker; Stalin was. Kennan had
applied keen insights into the systematic defects in the Soviet leader's psychology, pulling off a maneuver worthy of Clausewitz. The Soviets and their satellites could have bled Marshall's offer to death with demands and grievances
over terms. Instead, Stalin allowed himself to be goaded into rejecting it, casting
the Soviet Union as an enemy of recovery.

"We were fortunate in our opponents," concluded a relieved Acheson.[60]
"Uncle Joe helped us again," Harriman added.[61]

❖

ALWAYS FINELY ATTIRED, AT HOME IN HIGH SOCIETY, DEAN ACHESON LIVED
a lifestyle government service could not finance. A return to his law practice being
the only alternative to austerity, he stepped down, as scheduled, on July 1, 1947.

Fifty-one-year-old banker and former Stimson deputy Robert Lovett
succeeded him. Lovett would oversee progress of the Marshall Plan through

its most critical period. Thin, bald, with high, sharp cheekbones, Lovett operated on a constant, high-intensity nervous energy. Born to wealth, with an accent to match, he was nonetheless dubious of diplomats and Washington elites, preferring the company of artists, writers, even enlisted men. Reserved, cautious, humorous, profane, and practical, he was an implementer and not an innovator. He had little time for the egos around the administration, men like General Clay. As Marshall would spend much of the remainder of his tenure traveling abroad and recuperating from medical interventions, Lovett would drive deliberations on the substance of the Marshall Plan forward. Though a friend of Acheson's from their days at Yale, he took a more skeptical view of an expansive role for the United States in global affairs. The United States should not, he felt, aim to fill Britain's former role. The country had first to build up its resources, and to focus them on countering the immediate threat: Soviet aggression.[62]

On July 3, Bidault and Bevin issued a joint communiqué from Paris announcing the invitation of twenty-two European countries to cooperate in devising a collective plan for European recovery.[63] The assemblage, it said, would begin work on July 12 and complete it by September 1, after which it would submit the agreed blueprint and request for economic assistance to the United States. Bidault sent a copy of the formal invitation to the Soviet ambassador in Paris, assuring him that his country would still be welcome to participate were his government to change its decision.

Bidault's deputies, however, privately offered a different statement of his views. "The Soviets," they told Ambassador Caffery, "have forced Europe to band together to save itself." The Kremlin is hoping to exploit the "chaos [that] will follow" economic collapse and "take over the Western European countries with their well-organized Communist Parties." Yet its "desire to sabotage European reconstruction will be as clearly revealed as is our determination to . . . save ourselves and to profit from the splendid initiative taken by Secretary Marshall."[64]

On July 4, American Independence Day, French prime minister Paul Ramadier called for, and won, a vote of confidence over the government's support for the Marshall Plan.[65] Meanwhile, matters between Washington and Moscow were rapidly deteriorating. With Stalin now convinced the United

States was using the Marshall Plan to keep its military in Europe, the breakdown in relations reverberated around the globe. Negotiations between the USSR and the United States over the formation of an interim Korean government collapsed.[66]

That same day, the Communist Party of the Soviet Union (CPSU) cabled seven East European Communist Party leaders telling them that whereas the Soviet Union had rejected the Marshall Plan "it would be better" for their governments "not to refuse to participate in [the upcoming Paris] meeting, and instead to send their delegations to show the unacceptability of the Anglo-French plan and to prevent its unanimous adoption." Their delegations should "then leave the meeting, potentially with more delegates from other countries."[67] Molotov reinforced the message in telegrams to his embassies on July 5 and 6.[68] On the 7th, the Central Committee cabled Tito praising his "firmness on the issue of the American enslaving loans," but telling him "it would be better . . . to take part" before walking out.[69]

This position, however, was not to be Moscow's last word. As eager expressions of interest came forward from Czechoslovakia and Poland, the Kremlin did an about-face.[70]

"At first we decided . . . to propose to all the socialist countries to participate," Molotov explained years later, "but we quickly realized that was wrong." The problem was that "we still could not count on them," singling out the Czechs for particular suspicion.[71]

Satellite participation in the Marshall Plan was a possibility Moscow could not abide. It would restore East-West trade links that had been superseded by bilateral ones imposed by Moscow after the war. It was only a matter of time before American political influence set in among them. From this point on, then, the Soviet Union would rely on unilateral action to protect its interests.[72]

For Marshall, the epiphany that U.S.-Soviet cooperation had outlived its usefulness came on April 15, 1947, during his meeting in Moscow with Stalin. For Stalin, it would not come for another three months, with the imminent threat of the Marshall Plan incorporating Germany and the East. If one wants to set a firm birthdate for the Cold War, therefore, a strong case can be made for July 7, 1947—the day that Molotov ordered further cables to be dispatched to the satellites, rescinding his previous day's instructions for them to send delegations to Paris. It was only at this point that both sides, the United States and the Soviet Union, became irrevocably committed to securing their respective spheres of influence—politically, economically, and militarily—without mutual consultation. Europe, which had previously been divided into allies, former enemies, and neutrals, was now divided between Marshall states and the Soviet bloc (see Maps 3 and 4).[73]

Problems, Molotov told the eastern states, had emerged. Britain and France "do not [now] intend to carry out changes in their plan for economic recovery in Europe without [adverse] considerations for the sovereignty and economic independence of small countries." European recovery, moreover, was being used as a pretext for creating an anti-Soviet "Western bloc," which was to "include Germany." The governments were now, therefore, advised not to participate, although each could "present its own grounds for refusal."[74]

Most of the eastern states understood the nonnegotiability of the new instructions, and rejected or backed out of the Paris initiative immediately. The Romanian government explained that the Franco-British proposal would lead "inescapably [to] a breach of independence [and] a meddling in the domestic affairs" of European countries. Moreover, "any plan for economic stabilization of Europe may reach its goals only [by] cooperation with the USSR."[75] Yugoslavia, which had been prepared to follow earlier instructions to "send [a] delegation . . . and give a good fight to America and its satellites" before walking out,[76] now denounced it. Foreign minister Stanoje Simić said the Franco-British outline "would allow certain powers to interfere with the economic and political sovereignty of other countries" and free Germany from obligations to compensate its victims.[77] In an interview, Tito accused the United States of "disingenuous intents" and trying to "isolate" his country through "some kind of economic blockade."[78]

The Poles, who had been planning to send cabinet ministers to highlight their seriousness, "wavered initially"—in Stalin's words. So the Kremlin made matters clearer. On July 8, Radio Moscow announced, to the great surprise of Poland's Communist president, Bolesław Bierut, that Poland and Romania would refuse to take part.[79] A "very agitated" Bierut summoned the Soviet ambassador at 6 p.m., "calling the attention of the Soviet government to the fact that the Polish government [had] not taken any decision in this matter," and that "such communications [put] the leadership of the Polish Workers Party in a very difficult situation in respect of their partners in the democratic [i.e., eastern] bloc."[80] It was to no avail.

On Wednesday, July 9, Polish foreign minister Zygmunt Modzelewski informed the American ambassador in Warsaw, Stanton Griffis, in a manner "extremely apologetic and at least apparently regretful," that Poland would not send a delegation to Paris, reversing the indications he had given two days prior. Relaying what were presumably talking points from Moscow, he said that Poland would have "little or nothing to say" at the conference, as the "plan was already substantially [fixed] in form," and that rehabilitation of "the aggressor nation," Germany, was wrongly being given priority over assistance to its victims. The idea of European integration as a Trojan horse for German hegemony would become a staple of Communist diplomatic doctrine.[81]

Griffis surmised that between Monday and Wednesday, Modzelewski, "if not the entire Polish Cabinet, had . . . been overruled by higher authority."[82] This development came as a grave disappointment to Ramadier, who considered Poland "indispensable" to European economic unity, particularly given the importance of its coal production. "To wish to have Europe stop this side of [the] Vistula," he told Caffery, "would be equivalent to having [the] United States stop at [the] Mississippi."[83] In a sign that brewing Cold War politics were now infusing the Bretton Woods institutions, the World Bank halted consideration of a loan to Poland after its decision not to go to Paris. The Bank's American president, John J. McCloy, said Poland's action raised the question of its independence from Russia and its ability to guarantee repayment of a loan.[84]

The only holdout at this point was, as Molotov had feared, the Czechs.

❖

IN SOME REGARDS, CZECHOSLOVAKIA MIGHT HAVE BEEN EXPECTED TO REquire the least encouragement to follow orders. Unlike Poland, there were no Soviet troops in the country, yet the coalition National Front government had been largely obedient to Moscow, to which it was bound by preferential trading agreements. Communists had won 38 percent of the vote in the last elections, in May 1946, making them the largest party in the government.[85] The country had been abandoned by the West to Hitler at Munich, in 1938; in 1945, the Americans ceded the liberation of Prague to the Soviet army. Stalin's portrait was ubiquitous on the city's billboards. He was, whatever his imperfections, the closest thing the country had to a guarantee against another German invasion.

Yet Czechoslovakia had also received over $200 million ($2.3 billion in today's money) in much needed American financial assistance since the war's end. Now, presented with the manna of Marshall aid, Masaryk was once again overcome by an excess of enthusiasm. "The Czech government," he told Soviet, British, and French officials on July 1, "has authorized me to let you know that Czechoslovakia with one voice welcomes the opportunity that the offer outlines."[86]

To be sure, Masaryk had not yet gone rogue. He had, in fact, on July 2—the day Molotov stormed out of the Paris meetings with Bevin and Bidault, and two days before the invitations to the coming meetings had gone out—asked for and received permission from the Soviet chargé in Prague, Mikhail Bodrov, before advising the cabinet to accept the anticipated invitation.[87] Yet this was clearly not the tone of a man whom the Kremlin could count on to storm out of a capitalist aid conference.

The Czech cabinet held a heated and inconclusive debate over whether to retract the government's acceptance. Communist prime minister Klement Gottwald informed Bodrov of the stalemate: "the government will not support us" in pulling out of the conference. "The British and French have [already] been informed of their decision," Communist Ministry of Foreign Affairs state secretary Vladimír Clementis added by way of explanation. "[I]t has been carried by the press. [Ambassador Jindřich] Nosek in Paris has received instructions to the effect that he is entrusted with the task of attending the conference."[88]

In Moscow, Stalin did not take the news well. A Czech delegation was scheduled to arrive for trade treaty talks in a few days. The Marshall Plan would now be the main agenda.[89]

THE CZECHS ARRIVED AT THE KREMLIN ON JULY 9. THAT EVENING, Gottwald was summoned to meet privately with Stalin, Communist to

Communist. His fellow delegation members waited nervously in a drawing room for hours, not knowing where he was. When he emerged, he tried to reassure them: "Everything is alright," he said. He had "come to an agreement with Stalin. We're to see him [all together later] this evening."[90]

Meeting privately with Masaryk and Prokop Drtina, the National Socialist justice minister, however, Gottwald's tone turned severe:

> Now we're in a pretty pickle because of your policy towards the West! Never before have I seen [Stalin] so beside himself. He reproached me bitterly for having accepted the invitation to participate in the Paris Conference. He doesn't understand how we could have done it. He insists that we acted exactly as if we were preparing to turn our backs on the Soviets. I thought we were wrong in approving that decision without first referring it to Moscow, but you people were in such a terrible hurry! Now we're in a fine mess! Stalin is furious, and I think he has a right to be. You'll see for yourselves tonight. Stalin wants us to go and see him at 11 p.m.

At eleven, the Generalissimo ushered them in. Masaryk was taken aback: contrary to Gottwald's warning, he found Stalin's tone one of "benevolence" and "calm."

It was Gottwald, and not Stalin, who steered the discussion onto the business of Paris. He offered that his government "had decided from the beginning to recall its representatives in case of need." No definitive position had ever been taken, he explained:

> We now find ourselves confronted with a new situation, since we are the only Slavic State and only State of eastern Europe which has accepted the invitation to go to Paris. Is it not natural, therefore, that the Czechoslovak Government should wish to know the point of view of the U.S.S.R.?

Masaryk now understood why Stalin was being so "friendly, almost jovial." They had been set up. "The game was clear: [Stalin] had come to an understanding with Gottwald; the interview with us was nothing but a formality."

Stalin explained that he had been obliged to change his stance on Czech participation in Paris. The Soviet government had, after some investigation, determined that "the Great Powers [were] attempting to form a Western bloc and isolate the Soviet Union." France, "which has no program for a revival of her [own] economy," and Britain, which "is also in dire financial straits," could not be the ones "trying to put together a program for the economic revival of Europe." The instigator and "main creditor" behind it was, of course, "the USA, because neither France nor England has a kopeck." Participation in such an American scheme would obviously "endanger [Czech] political and economic sovereignty." Even going to Paris would "show that you want to cooperate in an action aimed at isolating the Soviet Union."

Masaryk still hoped the Soviet leader could see reason. Sixty to 80 percent of Czechoslovakia's raw materials came from the West, he explained to Stalin. It was impossible for his government to ignore this fact. Drtina added that the importance of western trade to his country was much greater than that of other Slavic states.

Stalin waved them off. Czechoslovakia's trade balance with the West was an adverse one, he said. Since its exports were not substantial enough to pay for its imports, it had to pay the difference in foreign exchange. This was a bad deal.

But this was "a crushing argument *in favour* of our adherence to the Plan," observed an ill and exasperated Ripka after reading the transcript in Prague. It was the very reason why Czechoslovakia needed the American credits.

Stalin continued: "[B]y your participation in Paris . . . you let yourselves be used as a tool against the USSR. Neither the Soviet Union nor its government would tolerate it."

"Everyone knows what that kind of warning means in Stalin's mouth," Ripka commented, "especially when it is addressed to a small neighbouring country."[91]

Back in 1945, Stalin had told Czechoslovakia's Socialist president Edvard Beneš that "the Soviet Union will not interfere in the internal affairs of its allies." But he had prefaced this by saying that he "wants nothing more than to have allies who are always prepared to resist the German danger."[92] And an ally who accepted Marshall aid was *assisting* the German danger. It was therefore not an ally.

Masaryk now got the message, or at least part of it. There would be no Marshall aid for his country. Yet he still hoped to present to the world the image of an independent Czechoslovakia.

The Soviet government, Masaryk pleaded to Stalin, "should help us in our delicate situation. We do not have any great illusions, [but] perhaps the matter could be fixed in such a manner that one would go to the Conference on one day and leave it on the next?"

No, Stalin said. Czech participation would be "a break in the front; a success for the Western Great Powers. Switzerland and Sweden are still wavering. Your acceptance would certainly also affect their decision."

Drtina tried a different tack. If the Czechs could not take American help, then surely, he put to Stalin, the Soviets could do more for them? Drtina pleaded with him to take "into account the fear which our population has, that namely the detachment from the West should not result in general impoverishment. That would not only have serious economic consequences, but also political ones." Marshal Stalin should also consider the "downward turn" in Czech trade with the Soviet Union. He hoped the ongoing negotiations between the two governments would "improve this state of affairs."

"[I]n our present situation," Masaryk summed up, "we need a kind of consolation prize, a gesture of the Soviet side."

"Your situation is better than that of France or England," Stalin put back. But "the USSR is prepared to help you in your economic affairs." It would buy more Czech industrial equipment—drilling pipes, electric motors, and the like. "Our harvest is good this year. . . . The agricultural plan has been fulfilled, indeed exceeded. We can help our friends: Bulgaria, Poland, and also you."

This offer—to barter food for machine parts—Stalin presented as self-evident generosity. He reiterated, however, that the Czech government needed first to reverse its decision on the conference.

"You could announce to Paris," Stalin suggested, that it had "become evident that the acceptance of the invitation could be interpreted as a stroke against the USSR, in particular since none of the Slav or other East European states accepted the invitation." In closing he added, for good measure: "I believe that the sooner you do that, the better."[93]

With that, the Czechs were dismissed.

MASARYK WAS HORRIFIED. THE SOVIETS, HE CONCLUDED, SOUNDING LIT-
tle different from Marshall after his Moscow meetings, "do not want Europe
to recover economically; they are afraid of the success of the reconstruction
of western Europe. . . . As I listened to Stalin I had more and more clearly the
feeling that he is counting on war. Everything they do is done with one aim in
view: war."[94]

Prior to Marshall's speech, Stalin had wielded an iron fist at home but had
been willing to tolerate, to varying degrees, a measure of political independence, including non-Communist participation, in the nations just beyond Soviet borders. This tolerance was finished. Governments were now with Stalin
or against him. Poland, Hungary, Romania, and Bulgaria, as well as Czechoslovakia, would all be brought to heel.

Gottwald cabled the government in Prague with an account of the meeting. A Czech informant for the American embassy quickly passed on a copy to
the U.S. ambassador, Laurence Steinhardt, who forwarded it on to Marshall
with instructions to the State Department to "take every precaution" to prevent
it becoming known that the text had come from the embassy.[95]

Returning to Prague, Gottwald convened the cabinet on July 10, two days
before the Paris conference, for a final full day of contentious discussions. The
Soviets, anxious for the Czechs to make the right decision, were spreading the
message that the Marshall Plan was not about helping Europe but rebuilding
Germany. Masaryk, Ripka, and the non-Communists were anguished, but
aware that Stalin would extinguish the embers of Czech democracy if the government did not reverse itself.[96] The real battle in the cabinet, therefore, was
over the wording of the statement, which Communist vice premier Viliam
Široký was sent out to read publicly at 9 p.m. It left little doubt as to the source
of the reversal:

An exceptional meeting of the government took place on July 10th that
focused on the participation of Czechoslovakia at the Paris conference. It
was found out that many countries rejected the invitation, especially all
Slav states and other central and western European countries. Countries

that Czechoslovakia remains in close economic and political relations with based on contractual obligations will not participate in the Paris conference. In this situation, the Czechoslovakian participation would be interpreted as an act against the Soviet Union and other allies. Hence, the government has decided not to participate in the conference.

Clementis informed the British and French ambassadors a half hour later.[97]

Economist Ladislav Feierabend, minister of finance in the London-based government-in-exile during the war, was appalled. "Why didn't the democratic members of Gottwald's government resign?" he asked incredulously. This would have produced a "government crisis" that would either have affirmed the original decision to go to Paris or resulted in new elections. "And if that had happened, and Gottwald had managed to establish a new government with a parliamentary majority, Czechoslovakia would have been in a different situation."[98]

Social Democrat food minister Václav Majer said later that the humiliating about-face had "smashed the illusion of Czechoslovak independence to smithereens."[99] Ripka reported that Prague residents were calling it "another Munich."[100]

"I went to Moscow as the foreign minister of an independent sovereign state," a bitter Masaryk would tell a former British diplomat, and "I returned as a lackey of the Soviet Government."[101]

Masaryk and his fellow democrats, however, too often wanted to have it both ways. Steinhardt singled out Masaryk as an example of Czechs who "indulge in double-talk [and] place bets on both sides."[102] Upon signing the alliance agreement with Moscow in December 1943, Masaryk, as a representative of the government-in-exile, had declared that his country's "relations with other neighbors will be from the angle of our Soviet agreement." Beneš had told Molotov that "In questions of the organization of Central Europe, we will do nothing without your consent."[103] Fears of having no one to protect their country from Germany underlay this servility.

Now, National Socialist Party chairman Petr Zenkl, who had insisted that the government had "acted correctly when [it] accepted the invitation to the Paris conference," was unapologetically pragmatic: "Our situation . . . changed at the moment when the delegation . . . was notified of the Soviet opinion toward the Marshall plan. The political perspective trumped the economic one. We remain a faithful ally, and accept both the advantages and disadvantages of this alliance."[104] Drtina had "secretly hoped the government in Prague could possibly express opposition to the overt political pressure that Stalin had put us under. . . . However, it is questionable whether it would have been wise to" accept the Paris invitation. "Czechoslovakia was in no danger in case of a break-up with the Americans; however I could not be sure of what would happen in the case of a break-up with the Soviets."[105] The country's "most important guarantee of security [rested] in close cooperation with the U.S.S.R." Minister of Posts František Hála insisted the government "had to adapt politically" to the Kremlin's position "because we have no guarantee from any other state against attack."[106]

Given Czechoslovakia's geographic position, its politicians were sensitive to the security dimensions of the Marshall aid invitation. But, as Washington would soon learn, they were not uniquely so. Even nations to the west would come to demand military protection, against Germany *and* Russia, as a condition for accepting American integration demands that would reduce their self-sufficiency and increase their economic vulnerability.

From his base in Moscow, Ambassador Smith was concerned about the implications of the Czech volte-face for the Marshall Plan broadly. "The Czechoslovak reversal on the Paris Conference, on Soviet orders," Smith cabled to Marshall on July 11, "is nothing less than a declaration of war by the Soviet Union on the immediate issue of the control of Europe."

"The lines are drawn," he concluded. "Our response is awaited. I do not need to point out . . . the repercussions of a failure to meet the Soviet challenge, in terms not only of the control of Europe, but of the impact which such a failure would have in the Middle and Far East and throughout the colonial world."[107] The dominoes were arrayed, as Smith saw it, from western Europe to the ends of the earth. Washington now had to act to keep them upright.

Kennan, for his part, was buoyed by developments. The "Russians [have been] smoked out in their relations with satellite countries," he memoed Marshall. "Maximum strain [has been] placed on those relations." Furthermore, western Communist parties were struggling to justify opposition to the plan. "Events of the past weeks," therefore, had delivered "the greatest blow to European Communism since termination of hostilities."[108]

But the Marshall Plan had not yet united the West. It had, through very different means, only united the East.

With British Foreign Minister Ernest Bevin presiding, delegates to the historic sixteen-nation Conference of European Economic Co-operation work at a plenary session to complete their Marshall Plan aid request, Paris, c. September 1947.

SIX

UNITY

JULY 12, 1947: JUST BEFORE 11 A.M., FOREIGN AND TRADE MINISTERS OF SIX-teen nations—Austria, Belgium, Denmark, France, Greece, Iceland, Ireland, Italy, Luxembourg, the Netherlands, Norway, Portugal, Sweden, Switzerland, Turkey, and the United Kingdom—entered the Grande salle à manger at No. 37 Quai d'Orsay.[1] Above each of the nine doors the sculptor Combettes had carved two ethereal children holding a medallion crowned with acanthus leaves and fleurons, traditional European symbols of great power. Above them, the cartouches in the great ceiling's four corners bore France's imperial symbol.[2] Here, in this magnificent hall consecrated to the glories of the French empire, Europe's top diplomats assembled to plea for aid from a former British colony.

They unanimously elected the British foreign minister as conference chair-man—the price he demanded for agreeing to French hosting.[3] Brusque and un-sentimental, Bevin told the gathered that the conference was only "a piece of *ad hoc* machinery to grapple with a special problem." It was not a time for theater or dreaming. "Effective and quick action is required."[4] His cohost, Bidault, in grandiloquent contrast, intoned that "The hour [had] come to construct a Europe." The two representatives of noncommunist Europe thereby highlighted the tensions inherent in American hopes for the gathering: it was to produce, on the one hand, a practical plan with immediate tangible results, and on the other a blueprint for far-reaching and unprecedented cooperation. This difference in emphasis between the two visions—Europe as practical necessity, and Europe as supranational aspiration—would continue to mark the British and French approaches.

The conference set up a Committee of European Economic Co-operation (CEEC) to perform the actual work, to be chaired by Britain's Sir Oliver Franks—an Oxford philosophy don and wartime permanent secretary in the Ministry of Supply.[5] It also created a powerful executive committee, comprising the U.K., France, Italy, Norway, and the Benelux customs union (comprising Belgium, the Netherlands, and Luxembourg), as well as four technical committees (with further subcommittees) covering food and agriculture, fuel and power, iron and steel, and transport. There would be only six weeks for them to forge a plan for a new West European economy that, before Marshall's speech the month prior, few of them had ever imagined.

Notwithstanding the message of unity in the CEEC's name, aimed to appeal to its American benefactor, its member states formed an unlikely cast of collaborators. Some were at the center of empires, some were Lilliputians; some were rich, some poor; some dirigiste, some laissez-faire. Two were longstanding neutrals, another was occupied by two of the others. Some were European in focus, others oriented outwardly. What bound them together was a need for dollars, and a determination to make as few concessions as possible to American aspirations that undermined their sovereignty.

Eight eastern states had, under Moscow's instructions, declined to attend the conference: Albania, Bulgaria, Czechoslovakia, Finland, Hungary, Poland, Romania, and Yugoslavia.[6] Spain was also conspicuous in its absence, having been excluded from the invitation owing to bitter opposition to the Franco dictatorship among Europe's political left. Whether Spain's inclusion might have ended the country's isolation from western Europe much sooner would become a matter of debate for years. Europe's most important economy was, of course, also unrepresented, having not yet been permitted by the occupying powers to create a government to represent it. Western Germany would, how-ever, be an object of intense discussion over the coming weeks.

The day the conference opened, Clay cabled Washington from Berlin, say-ing that an important agreement had been reached with Britain to boost indus-trial output in the German bizone.[7] When Bidault was told, he was adamant that the news be kept quiet. Its announcement at the conference, he warned Caffery, would doom it. "There would," he said, then "be no Europe."[8]

Whether "the German problem" was one of its neighbors' security, which was the French position, or their prosperity, the Benelux position, seemed un-resolvable. France was determined to keep German industrial output down in the service of buttressing national defense, the Benelux to rev it up in the ser-vice of boosting trade. In this clash, the Benelux seemed to have the powerful support of the United States.

With the Soviets out of the picture, though, the main political hurdle was France. The State Department needed, therefore, in Kennan's words, to "place squarely before the French the choice between a rise in German production or no European recovery financed by the U.S."[9] Caffery, in mocking reference to the Morgenthau Plan, cabled Marshall on July 20 that France had still "not abandoned outwardly" its "'pastoral'" approach to the "German problem," and was insisting on "'pulling [out Germany's] heavy industrial teeth.'"[10]

Within the administration, however, the battles over the role of Germany in the recovery plan were no less heated than those between France and the State Department. With the War Department demanding more German output, and France refusing to countenance any plan premised on it, the State Department had to mediate between two vital competing American objectives: creating a Germany that could stand on its feet economically, and securing French coop-eration in the creation of an integrated western Europe.

The result was an acrimonious three-way transatlantic standoff among two cabinet departments and France. Clay insisted that the United States could not "place Germany in a vacuum while we solve world problems as if it did not exist."[11] (Clay's tendency, in Marshall's eyes, was to do the reverse.) "Two years have convinced me that we cannot have a common German policy with the French," he said bitterly.[12] Bidault vowed that he would accept no plan that gave "priority to the reconstruction of Germany over the reconstruction of

France."[13] Both Clay and Bidault threatened to resign: Clay if the French were allowed to influence German production, and Bidault if the State Department refused to renounce plans to boost it.

Clay was telling Marshall he needed to break with the French agenda to save Germany and Europe: "we must proceed vigorously with revival of the German economy . . . if we are to save Germany from chaos and communism, and . . . a communistic Germany is almost certain to result in a communistic Europe." Bidault was telling him he needed to break with the German agenda to save France and Europe. The "French government will continue to insist that this will result," Clay said disparagingly, "and no one can prove otherwise except by the test."[14]

Will Clayton argued that France's interests should be divided into "legitimate" and "illegitimate," with the latter being "ignored completely." He defined legitimate interests as "military security" and "decreas[ing] the economic dependency of France on Germany."[15] But such logical quarantining was useless: any French objection to American action in Germany could be shoehorned into one or both of these formulations. French obstruction therefore constrained the Marshall strategy for reviving Germany.

❖

THE CENTRAL PLANK OF FRANCE'S POSTWAR RECONSTRUCTION POLICY was the Monnet Plan, a five-year economic modernization program premised on a massive increase in steel production that would turn the country into an industrial and export powerhouse—at Germany's expense. This program doubled as a security policy, since a Germany that could not produce steel could not field an army threatening to France. "With the aim of military security," explained a French foreign office official to his American counterpart in 1946, "we prefer to increase French steel production and output to the detriment of the Ruhr."[16] Yet to put the plan into action would require huge imports of German coal and coke, and thus dependence on unlikely German collaboration in its own deindustrialization. The Monnet Plan therefore relied on French control of the German Ruhr area, Rhineland, and Saarland, or at least a measure of such control through schemes aimed at "internationalizing" them.

Here, French interests clashed with those of the Benelux, which saw a robust German recovery as essential for generating the industrial and consumer demand for its exports. The three nations therefore demanded immediate action to boost Germany's coal and industrial output and an end to misguided Allied meddling in German internal economic policy. Italy, equally export-dependent and lacking France's security concerns, backed them. Norway did as well, albeit with protections for its fish and ships.

Caffery was unperturbed by the French position. In spite of relentless Communist propaganda against the Marshall Plan, eight times as many French believed their government was right to participate in the American aid discussions (64 percent) as believed it was wrong (8 percent).[17] Caffery told Marshall that the French would remain publicly wedded to "a modified version of the Morgenthau Plan," but would compromise in the end. Bidault, he said, had hinted as much on several occasions. He merely warned Caffery "not [to] force [France] to do so at the point of a gun."[18] It would only boost the Communists.

This was Caffery at his best, playing the long game, shunning flashy diplomacy or bullying. Guarded, measured, he liked to keep matters the way he kept his swept-back iron-gray hair: undisturbed. With French policy headed in the right direction, he was determined to give Bidault space to maneuver and to keep pride and egos at bay. Asked by a reporter to describe his approach to diplomacy, Caffery said "Getting things done. That's about all it amounts to."[19]

Over at the State Department, Office of European Affairs official H. Freeman Matthews concluded it was time to "force Clay to . . . view our operations and policies in Germany in light of our over-all interests in Europe."[20] Clayton assistant James Stillwell blasted Clay for his obsession with German "economic self-sufficiency ideas," when the "main objective of our occupation policy [must be] to direct the German economy so it will be able to play its rightful share in the Marshall Plan."[21] Lovett appealed to the top War Department officials "to keep in mind the concept of Western Europe rather than the individual countries." As for "the three Western zones of Germany," they "should be regarded not as part of Germany but as part of Western Europe."[22]

Marshall tried to contain the War Department revolt by agreeing, on July 28, to a seven-point written understanding with Truman's new secretary of war, Kenneth Royall, prohibiting any third country—that is, France—from participating in bizonal decisions on German industry. But after heading to Berlin to brief Clay on the "treaty" with State, Royall fueled the crisis by disclaiming publicly the existence of any "agreement by the War Department to consult with France" over plans "to raise the level of industry in Western Germany."[23] An enraged Bidault accused the State Department of duplicity. As Lovett in Washington then tried, unsuccessfully, to calm French ambassador Henri Bonnet by suggesting (falsely) that Royall was misquoted, Clayton tried to keep the Paris talks in a holding pattern.[24]

Marshall determined he had to change course to save the talks. Consultations with the French over Germany, he told Royall at a cabinet meeting on August 8, would begin in London immediately. The "treaty" with Clay was null and void.

In Berlin, Ambassador Murphy feared the fallout of a Clay resignation. "He may feel obliged to make certain public statements of his views and disagreements," he warned Marshall.[25] And no one at State wanted a loose cannon like Clay rolling around the deck in a diplomatic storm. But Marshall would have been happy to replace Clay with Bedell Smith, a close friend and State Department man. Moving Smith would put the administration's German policy where it belonged, subordinate to America's interests in Europe as a whole.[26] Royall promised Marshall "to give [Clay] orders and drop further discussions."[27]

Clay backed off the resignation threat, but still had to be coaxed to London for critical talks with the French and British on Germany. He objected in principle to accepting any French say over German production levels, and in protocol at being subordinate to the dapper Douglas—his former financial adviser on Germany, now ambassador in London. "Whenever we go into a conference on Germany," lamented a State Department official, "we first have to negotiate a treaty with General Clay."[28]

On August 14, Clayton and his colleagues reached a breakthrough agreement with the French and the British to create an "International Board composed of representatives of the UK, U.S., France, Benelux and Germany with power to allocate Ruhr output of coal, coke and steel between German internal consumption and exports." This vague new American commitment to internationalizing the Ruhr would acquire greater significance in the coming years, as French policy groped for means of accommodating German reconstruction in a manner consistent with French concerns.

The first important offshoot would be the Schuman Plan of 1950: the French foreign minister's scheme, devised by Monnet, for French and West German steel and coal production to be placed under a single authority. This would form the basis of a wider European effort in 1952, with the addition of Italy and Benelux, in the form of the European Coal and Steel Community, and the European Economic Community (the "Common Market") in 1958. The price France paid for the American concession on the Ruhr was a secret pledge, first, not to object to revised bizone output levels when these were made public after the Paris talks, and, second, to negotiate over the merger of their occupation zone with the bizone. The latter would begin only after the scheduled November Council of Foreign Ministers (CFM) meeting in London, allowing the Western Allies to frame it as a response to unreasonable Soviet conditions for a quadripartite unification of Germany.[29]

Clay returned to Berlin, and Bidault to Paris—each man satisfied. After a few false starts, Marshall had maneuvered masterfully.

❖

THE BENELUX COLLABORATION ON GRAND DISPLAY AT THE CONFERENCE had for some time been viewed with suspicion, at times hostility, in France. At Bretton Woods three years earlier, future prime minister Pierre Mendès-France insisted on a French IMF quota higher than the combined Benelux quota, just in case the latter were to create a political union and outvote them.[30] And now, here in Paris, the Benelux were fighting to keep the Americans from financing the Monnet Plan. They opposed the French using Marshall funds that would allow France to modernize its industrial plants at the expense of Benelux exports, which were manufactured with older capital stock.[31]

The Benelux also took a keen interest in currency reform, which they saw as central to their export interests. The Benelux delegate on the Executive Committee, Dutchman H. M. H. Hirschfeld, complained about the refusal of the U.S.-U.K. Joint Export-Import Agency of Military Government in Germany to allow greater German trade with the rest of Europe, which owed to fear of accumulating soft currencies. He provocatively accused the British and Americans of creating a "currency curtain" around the country. Benelux support for a European payments union was driven in particular by Belgium's concern that its export growth was being stymied through the stultifying web of bilateral arrangements that had come to control European trade since the 1930s. These aimed at balancing trade between all pairs of nations, as any deficits had to be compensated by scarce gold or dollars. Since Belgium—which had been liberated early, in 1944, and became a supplier to its devastated neighbors—was running current account surpluses with the rest of Europe, its trading partners were unwilling to take more of its exports. Belgium therefore wanted dollar aid directed not to supporting its neighbors' industrial strategies but to supporting their credit lines to prod them to import more.

Other delegations were, however, hostile to this aim. The British Labour government saw no merit in altering its economic program to accommodate more imports from Belgium, and objected to dollar aid being used to finance French policies that were producing runaway inflation (50 percent that year)[32] and large trade deficits. The U.K. interest "lies not so much in tight and rather artificial obligations of convertibility to a group—arbitrarily chosen from the economic point of view—of countries inside the Marshall Europe," pronounced a committee led by Treasury official Sir Richard (Otto) Clarke, "but in expanding the international use of sterling throughout the world as a whole."[33] The State Department opposed this view, but shared British concerns about financing French monetary imprudence. It was moreover, at this point in time at least, unwilling to ask Congress to support a European payments scheme whose alleged need would indict the new American-made IMF as a failure.[34] The Norwegians thought the Belgian scheme nonsense, arguing that it would take many years before most European currencies could be made convertible again.[35] This would turn out to be factually correct, though logically flawed.

By August 1, the embryo of a European payments union was taking shape, with participating countries agreeing in principle to eliminate exchange controls among themselves for goods and services transactions. The aim was to make their respective currencies fully convertible within the union at fixed, "realistic" exchange rates and, ultimately, to make net accruals of the currencies convertible into gold or dollars. An enthusiastic Dutch delegate went further, suggesting to Clayton that the program being developed in Paris might "prove to be a powerful catalytic agent in welding the western European economies into [an economic and political] unit."[36] The conference agreed to establish a committee on payments to continue study of the issue after its conclusion and, though few if any could have anticipated it at the time, its deliberations would ultimately lead to the creation of a successful European Payments Union in 1950. In spite of most European currencies remaining inconvertible until 1958, the EPU would come to play a critical role in reviving intra-European trade.

Italy's obsession at the conference was labor migration—specifically, the desire to export Italians as a means of reducing its legions of underemployed. But France had agreements with Italy to allow limited migration, and had no desire to go further. Britain had its own imperial arrangements for labor importation and, as in so many other areas, was uninterested in Europeanizing the matter.[37] The delegates could therefore agree on nothing more than a follow-up labor conference in January, to be held in Rome. Little progress would be made there either.

Britain brought to the conference a different set of problems. In spite of the leading roles played there by Bevin and Franks, its government was ambivalent about the enterprise. Churchill's legendary devotion to the empire notwithstanding, he was supportive of initiatives to create a "United States of Europe."[38] Yet a British inter-ministerial committee on the Paris talks observed that Britain was "not economically part of Europe." Europe accounted for only a quarter of British trade. Under the country's long-standing policy of imperial preference, it traded twice as much with the Commonwealth as it did with Europe—and moreover did so in its own currency. "The recovery of continental Europe," the committee concluded, "would not itself solve our problem; we depend on the rest of the world getting dollars."[39]

For Britain, being compelled to abandon its position at the center of an empire, even a fraying one, in favor of becoming a mere spoke in a European wheel, meant dishonor, disruption, and a drain on dollar reserves. At a time when nationalization of industry, rather than promoting competition within and across borders, was central to the Labour government's plans for reviving output and lowering unemployment, dismantling trade barriers with Britain's neighbors seemed misguided. But for Marshall, the British were demanding the impossible, wanting to "benefit fully from a European program . . . while at the same time maintaining the position of not being wholly a European country."[40]

⁜

GETTING EUROPEANS TO COOPERATE WAS PROVING MORE DIFFICULT
than the Americans had anticipated. The six-foot-three Will Clayton, assigned
the task of keeping the conference on track, did his best to stay unseen—
traveling from capital to capital using aliases in hotels, and walking miles
between meetings. But as Washington's "ambassador to Europe," as *The New
York Times* called him,[41] his presence was keenly felt wherever he went.

It was not, however, always welcomed. In London, feelings were still raw
over his role in the 1945 negotiations setting the terms of American postwar financial assistance, during which he demanded a hard deadline for ending trade
discrimination and the monetary paraphernalia supporting it. He tangled, at
times roughly, not only with Franks in Paris but Sir Stafford Cripps, the Board
of Trade president, in Geneva, where parallel talks were under way on creating
an International Trade Organization (ITO). Cripps took an unyielding stand
over Clayton's familiar demands for an end to imperial trade preference.

Clayton's mission in Europe was much less well known in his own country,
where half those polled had still not even heard of the Marshall Plan. Those who
had, had little idea what it was. It seemed like a sort of "flying saucer," one State
Department official wrote. "Nobody knows what it looks like, how big it is, in
what direction it is moving, or whether it really exists." Whatever it was, half of
those polled also said they would be unwilling to pay more taxes to support it.[42]

To produce a "European" plan, the CEEC needed data: lots of it. Lengthy
questionnaires were distributed for completion in each national capital, within
two weeks, covering all aspects of the country's economic and financial affairs,
going back to 1929 and projecting forward to the end of 1951. As national income accounting barely existed in most of the world at this point, the exercise
was at times little more than educated guesswork.

Or less, in some cases. After a long day of deliberations, British delegate
Eric Roll, preparing to head off to bed at 2 a.m., saw lights on in the Greek
offices. An official there was filling out his country's questionnaire. "But this
is not for you," Roll remonstrated him; it needs to be completed in Athens.
"You don't think anybody in Athens will know anything about this," the Greek
snorted. "I will just invent the figures myself."[43]

His nonchalance owed only partially to his country's legendary fiscal and bureaucratic deficiencies. Greece, as well as Turkey, resented having its aid tied to an American-dictated European integration agenda in which no one envisioned that it would have a role. It was not an enthusiastic participant.

The State Department intended for the various national policies, plans, and requirements to be subjected to vigorous mutual scrutiny, eliminating inaccuracy, duplication, and ineffectiveness. But this was not to be. Each nation guarded its prerogatives, and refrained from probing too deeply into its neighbors' affairs, for fear of having the favor returned. Washington behaved little differently. The Americans running Germany approached the task of providing projections to Paris in the same way as the other governments, conceding to the conference no authority to change their policies.

Upon learning of the existence of the questionnaires, the Soviets were determined to get hold of them. "The answers to [the] questions will provide important information for the American industrial and financial monopolies," the head of the Soviet foreign affairs ministry's economic department, Vladimir Gerashchenko, wrote to Vyshinsky in a "Secret" memo dated August 13. These entities were "interested in occupying such positions in the economy of these countries from which it would be possible to impose their programs of economic development, hinder them from selling their goods, and thus position their economies at the mercy of U.S. interests." The explanation neatly highlighted the blending of ideological fixation and pragmatism underlying Soviet diplomatic analysis. To give the USSR "the opportunity to judge the state of the economies of Western Europe more fully," Gerashchenko concluded, "it should be entrusted to comrade Bogomolov[44] [in Paris] to try to get the questionnaires already filled out by countries." Vyshinsky underlined these words in blue pencil.[45]

Though the State Department took pains in official and public communications to stress European ownership of the planning venture, back-channel communications, for which Clayton was the point man, were vital in shaping expectations in Paris and London of what the United States would ultimately support. Clayton insisted that any request must have three critical components to have a chance of succeeding in Washington: an explanation for "the man in the street" as to why European recovery was not progressing "in spite of large sums already made available" (about $10 billion); a three- to four-year production program to rectify this failure; and a rough blueprint for "a type of European economic federation" that would "be designed to eliminate the small watertight compartments into which Europe's pre-war and present economy is divided."[46]

The French hosts had their own ideas about what the Marshall Plan should be. Monnet pleaded for some form of "stabilization fund" to support "massive imports of consumers' goods," French shortages of which could not be alleviated owing to inflation and "disorder" in public finances. Clayton acknowledged the reality of the consumer goods problem, but insisted that inflation control required "budget balancing." Hervé Alphand, director-general of economic and financial affairs at the Foreign Office, sought assurance that accommodation would be made under the International Trade Organization charter for the web of bilateral arrangements that European nations were using to balance their trade. Clayton made clear that such would be frowned upon in Washington, not least by himself, but that a customs union along the lines of that operated by the Benelux since 1944 would be most welcomed.[47]

A zealous believer that free and nondiscriminatory trade made for prosperous and peaceful peoples, Clayton saw the creation of a West European customs union as an essential step in the creation of a democratic federation that could resist the Sovietization that had befallen the East. His idea of free trade, however, did not come naturally to the intended beneficiaries. When Spaak, the Belgian PM, pressed him as to how the increased production resulting from the plan would be allocated among the participating states, a polite but exasperated Clayton told him that distribution would always "best be effected by elimination of trade barriers and adherence to principles of multilateralism,"[48] and not by horse-trading.

Progress proved painful. The French and Italians were enthusiastic supporters of a customs union, though only as a commitment in principle, with details to be worked out later. The British were willing to see the concept studied, but only as a way to talk it to death. They threw up insuperable barriers to their own participation, arguing that it infringed economic sovereignty, was incompatible with Commonwealth commitments, and interfered with the special U.K.-U.S. bilateral relationship (existence of which the State Department did not recognize). The Benelux were unwilling to move forward without the British as a counterweight to the French and Italians, while the Scandinavians were ready to move forward, but only amongst themselves.

Franks said that the delegates were also "honestly perplexed" as to how the Americans expected them to produce a program of reducing intra-European trade barriers that did not violate the draft ITO charter. Clayton assured them it would be adapted to accommodate a European plan providing for a steady reduction of tariff barriers, culminating in a zero-tariff customs union.[49]

Clayton's persistence on this issue exasperated his colleagues at State, who saw his efforts as a fruitless personal crusade that would hinder achievement of far more urgent and practical goals. "We are all in agreement with you on the point that a customs union is a desirable long-run objective," Lovett cabled him in Geneva. But "to attempt to work it out now would bog Europe down in details and distract from the main effort."[50]

⁜

CLAYTON, CAFFERY, AND DOUGLAS WERE MARSHALL'S BOOTS-ON-THE-ground in Paris, working to break down the statist mind-set among the Europeans. Lovett, Nitze, and the "planners" on the new State Department Recovery Committee in Washington, in contrast, cared most about getting a shovel-ready plan requiring no leaps of faith from skeptical congressmen. Meeting with Clayton and Caffery in Paris from August 4–6, Nitze nonetheless found common ground on the need to intensify American involvement.

The three were angered by reports that "a number of countries" represented in the CEEC, or interests within them, were buying into the Communist line that they were doing the United States a favor by participating in the Marshall Plan—helping it to "ward off a depression." This idea needed to be scotched, and American expectations set out in no uncertain terms. A timetable for tariff reduction, and eventual elimination, among the participating countries should, they decided, be made mandatory. Delegations should be told the quid pro quo they would provide in return for American aid: meeting targets for production, currency stabilization, and other structural reforms. Failure to reach output quotas for commodities and food would mean a cutoff of aid. Britain should be directed not only to boost its coal output but "to eliminate much of her housing program," which was an intolerable "drain on steel and labor resources."[51] This came perilously close to Molotov's charge that the Marshall Plan was, indeed, an American scheme to control Europe's economies.

The Europeans, hoping they could satisfy their benefactor with concessions to style rather than substance, had in late July considered hiring an American public relations firm to polish the presentation for Yankee tastes. Clayton shot down the idea, telling them such advice could be obtained from the State Department "on a 'within the family' basis."[52]

Marshall, though, was alert to the political dangers of offering too much familial advice. Do not, he cabled on August 11, "make suggestions . . . in [a] manner allowing us to be maneuvered into [a] position where . . . they would regard us as being committed." Congress, he said, would react against being approached "on a crisis basis," as they feel they were with Greece and Turkey. They would want some say on the terms.[53]

Clayton was convinced Marshall was overreacting. "We are in no sense committed" to anything, he cabled Lovett the next day. "I have been saying just these things over and over to" the delegations.[54] Spaak and others, however, would push "wholly unworkable and unacceptable" schemes unless the State Department steered them. John Hickerson, deputy director of the Office of European Affairs, reminded Marshall of his Harvard speech, where he pledged "friendly aid in the drafting of a European program." American guidance was vital to ensure that the German economy ceases to be "a financial burden to the United States," and that the production plans of the participating countries are based on the requirements of *all* of them, collectively.[55]

Lovett, responding for Marshall, returned the frustration in a long August 14 cable, telling Clayton that it was the *Europeans* who were going off the track laid out in the secretary's Harvard speech. This argument conceded, without acknowledging it, that the Europeans needed steering from Washington. The cable laid stress on the *substance*, rather than the desirability of the steering. Lovett said he would not accept "an itemized bill summing up prospective deficits against a background of present policies." The Europeans had to "adjust themselves to certain basic changes . . . in their international position." They had to "imagine [an] economic future without any outside support," one in which they were obliged to sustain themselves only "by the most strenuous individual and collective effort." Only then would they be entitled "to define the gaps" which American aid might fill. Still, he did not want Clayton threatening to withhold aid if specific policies were not adopted or production targets not met. This could backfire if it worsened political tensions in these countries.[56]

Kennan stressed the importance of U.S. drafting assistance on the grounds of timing: it was a matter of vital national interest that Congress act on an aid program before the end of the year. France had, in July, banned all dollar purchases other than for food and fuel. Britain and Italy were expected to follow suit with severe import restrictions. One country after another would then cut imports to offset falling exports. If the United States did not create a trend "in the opposite direction," it might "find [itself] confronted with something far more serious than the present European situation."[57] Another depression could befall the world, creating further opportunity for Soviet adventurism.

Clayton agreed. He worried that progress on the report's drafting might still come to naught without interim funds from Washington. On August 6, he suggested to Marshall that a special session of Congress might be needed to effect this. Britain, France, and Italy were, he said, in "critical" condition. They were running short of food. Without aid this year, they might "so deteriorate economically, socially, [and] politically" that U.S. "objectives in Western Europe and elsewhere may become unattainable."[58]

Britain, having made its currency convertible on July 15 in accordance with the 1945 American loan agreement, was losing roughly $100 million a week, and would run out of dollars and gold within months. An imminent devaluation of the pound seemed certain, obliging Britain to slash imports and abandon yet more of its imperial commitments. The country's position, Kennan said, was dire. It was still over a year away from achieving a level balance of payments, and it had no means of financing the gap. This meant "serious vacuums" in global security, some of which "we might have to fill" before Stalin did. This "could cost far more" than boosting aid to Britain now.[59]

And so policies that the United States considered fundamental just a few years prior were abandoned that summer. German pastoralization was out; industrial resurrection was in. Denazification was slotted for "early termination," even if it meant "further amnesties." Allied control would be simplified, "with more responsibility [handed to] the German people." The IMF, designed by FDR's Treasury to provide tough love to foreign debtors, while protecting America against their devaluation habits, would be prodded to bail out Britain with a quick $320 million ($3.46 billion in today's money). Even Clayton's cherished currency convertibility and nondiscrimination in trade were up for grabs, at least temporarily. He and his colleagues agreed to ignore British commitments to both enshrined in the 1945 loan agreement.[60] Preventing the country's collapse now took priority.

⁜

BY MID-AUGUST, IT WAS BECOMING CLEAR THAT THE CEEC WAS, FROM THE State Department's perspective, failing. Instead of producing a plan for an integrated western European economy that would be self-sustaining by 1952, it was preparing to add up the dollar deficit estimates of sixteen countries, based on the standard of living each "expected" after 1951, and to submit the cumulative bill to Washington for payment. Without even mentioning a dollar value, Franks acknowledged to Clayton and Caffery that the anticipated requirements "exceeded any possible availability" and would have to be scaled down "on a global basis." The committee lacked the power to order cuts to specific country estimates.[61]

Franks' defeatism set off alarms in Washington. The cracks in State Department unity over the essentials of a recovery program now widened into deep fissures. On August 22, a "Meeting on Marshall 'Plan'" was convened, attended by Kennan, Bohlen, Kindleberger, and others, to agree on how to brief Lovett. The group singled out Clayton for fault. Whereas the headstrong Texan was "generally aware of departmental thinking with regard to the 'Plan,'" the group agreed, he held "fundamental divergent views on some aspects." These included his "aversion to continuing European machinery to implement" it, which Clayton saw as statist, and his insistence on "a Customs Union for Europe," which his home-front colleagues saw as an indulgent personal obsession bogging down the talks. It was also a distraction from State Department priorities: a rapid recovery in European output, and a program that could mobilize Congress. The meeting decided that if Clayton could not be brought "in line with the clarified position" by cable, Kennan should be sent to Paris to set him straight.

Though it was true that little progress was being made on the customs

union, it was scapegoating Clayton to suggest this was at fault for lack of progress elsewhere. The group, not incidentally, also decided that more assertive
"friendly aid" would be necessary to compel the Europeans to cooperate more
and demand less, which was a position that Clayton had been pressing for some
time. This meant intrusive American "screening" of the CEEC committee reports, which would in turn necessitate an "appreciable" extension of the September 1 target date for the final report's submission.[62]

Parallel criticisms were also hurled at Clayton from elsewhere in the department over his handling of the ITO negotiations, where he was seen as being
overly purist and insufficiently sensitive to the administration's larger foreign
policy aims. In Clayton's view, the Marshall Plan made the ITO talks "more
important than ever because without [a] sound permanent program of reciprocal multilateral trade, no temporary emergency program could possibly have
any permanent worthwhile results."[63] Clayton, trade official Winthrop Brown
reflected critically years later, "wanted to get total elimination of all [trade] preferences," particularly those operated by Britain among its colonies and dominions. "We civil servants knew it wouldn't be possible [but] he was very hard to
convince."[64]

On August 24, Lovett sent a memo to Marshall headed "Paris talks on unified economic plan," concluding that there was none. With a week to go before
it was due, the conference had thus far, Lovett explained, produced only sixteen
separate "shopping lists"—and expensive ones at that.[65] At a price tag now estimated to be over $29 billion—or nearly 12 percent of that year's U.S. GDP, and
84 percent of that year's federal spending—the combined prospective request
amounted to more than twice the total aid disbursed everywhere, in grants and
loans, by the United States since the end of the war. It was also nearly twice the
$16 billion that Clayton saw as the maximum feasible.

The Paris delegates were consciously, in Kennan's view, taking a Molotov
approach, refusing concessions on economic sovereignty.[66] And just as a family living apart leads a costlier existence than one living under a common roof,
each of the sixteen nations was inflating its recovery bill by assuming a need
for self-sufficiency, wastefully duplicating production capacity. In this regard,
France and Britain, the driving forces behind the conference, were also turning
out to be its biggest headaches.

Though the name of Jean Monnet is indelibly attached to the idea of European federation, at this stage he was well behind Clayton.[67] France stood committed to Monnet's namesake plan for national recovery and development, which had as its centerpiece the replacement of German industrial and export dominance in Europe with its own. Britain, for its part, was wedded to an imperial, rather than European, trade and payments policy. Neither was buying into the Marshall vision of a unified west European economy—one that aimed at maximizing collective rather than national output, and which did so in the shortest time possible.

Washington was no mere wounded bystander in this collision of national agendas. Far from being developed in a domestic political vacuum, the Monnet Plan was a response to rational French distrust of American postwar planning. French commitments to multilateralism at Bretton Woods notwithstanding, driven as they were more by a desire for American dollars than a predilection for American trade theories, French officials feared that prewar trading patterns would be reestablished, to the enduring disadvantage of French industry, if they did not support homegrown champions.

Replacing German manufactures with French manufactures did double duty as a security policy. "The surest guarantee for the maintenance of peace," Alphand wrote earlier that year, "will always consist in the limitation of German steel potential." But the American rejection at Potsdam of the Soviet proposal for international control of the Ruhr had convinced Alphand, rightly, that the Americans would place a much higher priority on European economic revival than on French reconstruction and defense needs. Thus was it made the fulcrum of French policy that revived German raw material production be directed to French rather than German industrial needs.

De Gaulle's choice of the technocratic Monnet to lead the Commissariat Général au Plan obscured the political nature of its work, but its detailed production targets for coal, electricity, steel, cement, agriculture, and railways were, even for him, fig leaves. "The individual figures in the plan," Monnet said, "were all inaccurate and meant nothing."[68] Still, it was left to Bidault to sell to Clayton the idea that France, supplied with coal and coke extracted from an Allied-administered Germany, could meet all of western Europe's steel requirements.

As for Britain, Attlee's government had been watching its dollar reserves plummet at a rate of $176 million a week since July 15, the day on which the country committed monetary suicide in accordance with the terms of the 1945 American loan agreement. The world had been queuing up for the occasion for some time, ready to convert piles of excess sterling into dollars at a bargain price. In such circumstances, multilateralizing European trade and payments was, understandably, the last item on London's agenda. Introducing new import restrictions and exchange controls, in stark contrast, had climbed to the top.[69] Bitterness toward America's global economic agenda was palpable. It was not surprising that the conference shunted off Clayton priorities, such as currency convertibility and customs unions, to "special committees" that would report back only after the conference had been adjourned.

"The British have turned out to be our problem children now," Truman wrote to his sister in August. "They've decided to go bankrupt and if they do that, it will end our prosperity and probably the world's too. Then Uncle Joe Stalin can have his way."[70] The contrast to FDR's attitude two years earlier could not have been more stark. "I had no idea that England was broke," he remarked to Morgenthau after a briefing on British finances in August 1944. "I will go over there and make a couple of talks and take over the British Empire."[71] Truman was not quite taking over the empire, but the United States was reaping the consequences of its liquidation.

Over in Geneva, relations between Cripps and Clayton went from bad to worse. The former now declared it "politically impossible" for his government to take substantial action on eliminating its preferential trade arrangements, in spite of the latter conceding belatedly that sterling could remain inconvertible indefinitely. In a memo to Lovett, an angry Clayton recommended that the administration conclude a multilateral agreement without Britain if Cripps' "callous disregard" of British commitments persisted.[72] "What we must have," Clayton ally Clair Wilcox insisted, "is a front-page headline that says 'Empire Preference System Broken in Geneva.'" Marshall aid and tariff cuts, he argued, were "bargaining weapons that we may never possess again."[73]

Truman, with Marshall's and Lovett's support, rejected this approach, fearing that a public rift between London and Washington would be exploited by Labour left-wingers and the Kremlin, resulting in new security problems in

Greece and Italy while undermining congressional aid support.[74] "An open breach with the U.K.," the U.S. economic affairs counselor in London, Harry Hawkins, cabled Clayton, "will hurt the Marshall plan more than [Britain's] failure . . . to give substantial elimination of preferences."[75] Thus what was seen by the Clayton camp in Geneva as a "weapon" to extract trade concessions from the British—Marshall aid—was seen back in Washington as precious leverage to be preserved for facing down the Soviets.

❖

ON AUGUST 24, LOVETT SENT ANOTHER CABLE, TO CAFFERY AND CLAYTON, stating that the European program, in its current form, failed to meet the department's requirement that its economy be made self-sufficient in the shortest possible period of time. This needed to be accomplished, first and foremost, through mutual aid and cooperation. He directed that the "friendly aid" approach be upgraded, in essence, to one of determined parental guidance.[76] Clayton left Geneva to join Caffery and Douglas in Paris; Kennan and Lovett special assistant Lieutenant Colonel Charles Bonesteel flew in from Washington.

Meeting officially with the conference Executive Committee for the very first time, on August 31, Clayton declared the results to date "disappointing," and warned that if its present program were submitted to Washington it might "prejudice the success of the entire Marshall program." From the American perspective, he explained, the program's highest objective was "the speediest possible reactivation of the European economic machine" and "its restoration to a self-supporting basis." In the interim, the "essential consumption requirements of the people" would be met by the United States.

This formulation would, in spite of the mind-numbing details that would come to define the Marshall program, be the deal in a nutshell—that the United States would underwrite a basic standard of living in the participating countries to afford them the space to liberalize and integrate their economies. In essence, the State Department was tendering the largest foreign aid program in history as a social shock absorber for the largest structural adjustment program in history.

Clayton told the committee that the $29.2 billion request it was contemplating was far too large. It had no prospect of finding political backing in Washington. Given that the aim of the Marshall program was a self-supporting western Europe, the fact that the conference anticipated a continued need for assistance at the end of the period that was as great as its present need reflected, Clayton said, "the unsatisfactory nature of the methods by which [the gap] was calculated and the assumptions on which it was based."

Now, for the first time since the conference began, the State Department laid down terms for the program. It would have to result in "a workable European economy independent of special, outside aid" within four years. It would need to demonstrate progress over that period in achieving production targets on "items essential to European recovery, especially food and coal." It would have to focus on rapid "reactivation of the most efficient existing productive facilities," and finance any desired new "long run development projects" only with funds sourced "outside this program," such as through the new IBRD.

A European plan would, Clayton continued, further require unanimous commitment to "the progressive reduction and eventual elimination of barriers to trade within the area, in accordance with the principles of the ITO Charter." It would also involve participants "mutually undertak[ing] . . . to stabilize their currencies. . . and restore confidence in their monetary systems."

Noteworthy was the absence of any mention of the role that adjustable exchange rates might play in facilitating a rebalancing of either European or transatlantic trade. The emphasis was entirely on "maintain[ing] proper rates of exchange." As at Bretton Woods, the Americans were determined to avoid mass competitive devaluations against the dollar, such as those in the 1930s. But even the IMF, whose American blueprint was hostile to devaluation, had just concluded in its Annual Report that "the maintenance of present parities may . . . impose an unduly contractionist influence . . . and adversely affect the flow of world trade."[77]

Finally, Clayton explained, a European plan would necessitate the establishment of a new "multilateral organization" to monitor progress and ensure compliance with these conditions. This last condition was one which Clayton would be only too eager to water down, having been forced onto the list by the "planners" in Washington.

Franks pushed back. It was unrealistic, he argued, to expect the European economy to recover sufficiently by 1952 such that it would not require further external assistance. As regards the U.K. specifically, recovery could not occur without three conditions being met: a return to "complete convertibility of currencies," such that "export receipts from one part of the world could be transferred to other areas to meet dollar needs"; new markets opening up for export surpluses; and a rise in the prices of exports relative to those of imports (that is, an improvement in the terms of trade). Alphand said that Europe's "viability" depended on its ability to meet production and export targets, which was highly uncertain, and would probably require the establishment of trade relationships with eastern Europe

The Norwegians, backed by the Swedes, voiced strong objection to the requirement for a new aid-recipient body to oversee performance, arguing that oversight could be done by existing organizations such as the U.N. Economic and Social Commission for Europe (ESCE). Norwegian journalist, and future U.N. ambassador, Hans Engen had told the Soviet embassy back in July that the governing Workers' Party only supported the Paris talks because Norway needed foreign exchange and feared, as a small country, the terms Washington would demand in bilateral talks.[78] Kennan, not surprisingly, put the Scandinavian position down to their being "pathologically timorous about the Russians,"[79] whom they did not want to provoke through participation in a grouping established by Washington. Six of the ESCE's seventeen seats were controlled by the Soviet Union and its satellites.[80]

The Americans gave no ground. Kennan put back that if "a balanced position" in western Europe were unlikely by 1952 then a "reconsideration" of the entire exercise would be necessary. Franks' "expectation that deficits will persist," he said, was "based on a higher standard of living than Europe's productivity [would] support." The message was that Britain needed to bring its consumption into line with its production capacity rather than its aspirations. This meant greater austerity in Britain, and not greater demands on the United States. As for Alphand's conditions, most of them related to "objectives the attainment of which primarily depends on the Europeans themselves." They were not the responsibility of the United States. As regards the Scandinavian objection, he insisted that there had to be a direct correspondence between those monitoring the joint enterprise and those participating in it. No existing "international organization [was] in a position to perform this work."

Clayton pointed out that both the "national requirements and production goals" laid down by the conference had failed to take account of what western Europe *as a whole* could support. As regards steel, for example, the conference was assuming that each of the sixteen countries would produce at its maximum capacity, despite the fact that insufficient coal and coke would be available to accomplish this. The group needed, therefore, to go back and identify the most efficient plants from those available among them, "without regard to national boundaries," to maximize output from scarce inputs.

Clayton's demand represented precisely the sort of sovereign intrusion that the committee had deliberately avoided. Franks defended the group's work by highlighting instances in which country reports had been amended under peer pressure, but pointedly reminded Clayton that the conference's terms of reference specified that participant countries would suffer "no diminution of sovereignty."[81] A big gap thus remained between the American federalist vision for western Europe and Franco-British commitments to national planning. Still, the two sides agreed to plow on with a revised deadline of September 15.

❖

THE TENSE, THREE-HOUR EXCHANGE HAD AN AIR OF UNREALITY ABOUT it. The Americans were demanding of weak and embattled European governments a level of political boldness and planning precision that Kennan, at least, knew to be ridiculous. "This conference," he wrote in a ruminative and frank memo following the meeting, dated September 4, "reflects, in short, all the weakness, the escapism, the paralysis of a region caught by war in the midst of serious problems of long-term adjustment, and sadly torn by hardship, confusion and outside pressure. . . . We must not look to the people in Paris to accomplish the impossible." The conference could not and would not, he said, meet Clayton's demands.

Kennan had been posturing in his chiding of Franks over British inability to commit to "viability" by 1952. Kennan in fact saw Britain's circumstances as not merely dire, but near-hopeless—"tragic to a point that challenges description," he called them. "[A]s a body politic, Britain is seriously sick."[82] A secret

State Department report to two House committees, written at the same time, said the country was "in grave financial crisis," and "no longer an 'equal' member of the Big Three."[83]

For decades, the British Labour Party had pined for the opportunity to usher in its grand socialist vision for national revival, but had now come to power at a time when it was unrealizable. The country's traditional markets had disappeared. The national psyche had failed to adjust. Clayton had admonished Franks to lower his expectations for the British standard of living in the coming years, but Kennan believed that Britain would face "genuine hunger by winter" without immediate American assistance, well before Congress would be able to act on any elaborate, multiyear plan. As for France, its wheat crop was the smallest in 132 years, its dollar reserves nearly exhausted.

The conference was also dancing around the critical issue of Germany's future. The United States was as much at fault here as anyone. While rapping European knuckles over failure to subject national policies to multinational scrutiny, Washington had thus far refused to subject its German plans to the requirements of the European plan being forged in Paris.

Politically, it could not have been otherwise. "French inhibitions and fear of communist criticism would alone have prevented that," Kennan said. As Bidault had warned, France had "180 Communists" in its National Assembly "who say [that] the Marshall Plan means Germany first." If they were not shown otherwise, the French "government will not survive." But the end result was that all the parties in the room were "inhibited . . . by the consciousness of what seem to them Herculean differences among the great powers over Germany and by the consequent feeling that the necessary center of any real European planning is beyond the effective scope of their activity."[84] That is, planning the creation of a West European economy without knowing whether Germany was all-in, all-out, or something in between was a charade.

Kennan called for a clean break with the department policy of mere "friendly aid" in the drafting of a recovery plan. Two things now had to happen. First, State should take the best report that can emerge from the conference as no more than a "basis for further discussion." They would subject it to executive branch scrutiny, and then "decide unilaterally what [to] present to Congress." Essentially, State "would just *tell* [the Europeans] what they would get." Second, "without solicitation from the Europeans," State should initi-ate immediate financial and material assistance where it was necessary. Call it " 'Food and Fuel for Europe' or some such slogan." An emergency "short-term aid program," administered by State, he wrote, "would buy us time in which to deal deliberately and carefully with the long-term program." Without such im-mediate aid, the result, certainly in Britain, will be "a catastrophe."[85]

A lesser writer might never have budged his bureaucracy from its settled plans and benchmarks, but Kennan had an ability to persuade readers that they were glimpsing hidden truths—truths that did not diminish them by highlight-ing errors in their thinking, but truths that the writer himself experiences in the telling, with his readers, giving them intellectual cover to adapt their views. And so whereas Kennan did not demolish Marshall Plan shibboleths on his own, he made the demolition easier. Over the next several days, Marshall and Lovett sent cables to Europe calling for concessions to British political obsta-cles;[86] a bending of policy in Germany to the needs of a European program;[87] acceptance of an imperfect Paris report "as a basis for further discussion";[88] and creation of an emergency "interim assistance program as a first element in the Marshall plan."[89]

Lovett told Clayton and Caffery to push the conference to produce its final report—this time, a report "correct at least as to major policy lines"—by Sep-tember 21. But the Europeans chafed at what Bevin called the "clumsy Ameri-can intervention." It gave "the impression . . . that the work of the conference has been unsatisfactory and is now having to be done again under American pressure." Delaying the ministers' receipt of the committee's report beyond the once extended deadline of September 15 would cause public "dismay" over a seemingly failed conference. Bidault called the intervention "intolerable." The Americans, he said, needed to make "concrete offers of substantial assistance [before] they [could] legitimately expect to discuss terms and conditions."[90]

Franks and his fellow Executive Committee members stressed that American pressure for yet deeper changes to the Paris request would be seen as a threat to "national sovereignty"—one that could be extremely dangerous politically, given the fear engendered by Soviet threats against the conferees (such as withholding coal from the Scandinavians). He warned that the State Department's integration agenda smacked of "dirigisme," as it suggested that some "control agency would plan and regulate the basic economic activity of the individual countries." The CEEC could go no further down this route without changing the conference's "terms of reference" and possibly losing some of its participants.

The report, Franks warned, would ultimately fall "short of US essentials in some cases." The committee was willing to accept that certain "adjustments" might be made to the report after being "mutually review[ed]" in Washington, but was unwilling to indicate publicly that the report was in any way only "tentative or preliminary," as this would have serious negative "political repercussions in Europe." It could be a "first" report, but not merely a "temporary" one, subject to correction from Washington.[91]

Entering the endgame, the embedded American negotiating troika of Clayton, Caffery, and Douglas maneuvered adroitly, shrinking the gap between Paris and Washington by playing the Congress card with the delegates and the socialism card with Lovett. The Europeans, unwilling to face down Congress with so much money at stake, agreed to sugarcoat the report's preamble with paeans to flexibility, cooperation, and self-reliance. As for Lovett, the troika prodded him to drop his long-standing demands for a powerful supranational oversight organization, arguing that it promoted "international cartels" and "a planned economy." It would, they argued, be "more prudent and much wiser" just to get the Europeans to commit to "reduc[ing] trade barriers," among themselves and with the United States, and to fix "appropriate exchange rates."[92] At the eleventh hour, the deal was done.

⁜

THE TWENTY-THREE-NATION GENERAL AGREEMENT ON TARIFFS AND trade (GATT) would be completed in Geneva a few weeks later, after which Clayton would write his sixth and final letter resigning from the State Department. He was disappointed that Britain's imperial preferences remained largely intact; Marshall had prevailed in this regard to save the Paris talks. Still, Truman would rightly hail the conclusion of the GATT as "a landmark in the history of international economic relations."[93]

Praise for Clayton's efforts was effusive. "This vast project [the GATT], which makes all previous international economic accords look puny," wrote *The New York Times* on October 15, "is the realization of Mr. Clayton's dream:

that a group of like-minded democratic nations could deliberately reverse the historical trend toward the strangulation of world trade. It is a big step that nobody but Mr. Clayton and a few of his colleagues thought would ever be taken." Relentless but humble, Clayton was seen as "both the symbol of and dynamic force behind the most constructive aspects of American international economic policy."[94] Tributes in the British and French press were also warm in spite of—in some cases because of—Clayton's relentless pressure on European governments to cooperate more and nationalize less. "A champion of liberalism," *Le Monde* called Clayton. "Our diplomats . . . will deplore the absence of one of the Americans who knew best European affairs."[95]

❖

A CHEF'S SALAD OF QUESTIONABLE DATA AND PROJECTIONS, OVER WHICH the oil and vinegar of European and American prose was poured, the two-volume 690-page Paris report submitted by Bevin to Marshall on September 22 was hardly what the State Department had hoped to receive. It made no substantive breakthroughs on Germany or economic integration. It provided no satisfactory roadmap to European self-sufficiency, either in terms of timing or cost to the United States. It envisioned a trade deficit with the dollar area at $19.3 billion over the coming four years, or roughly 20 percent more than what the department considered the largest digestible request. Yet it deemed aid at that level *still* insufficient to free the recipients of dependency on external support.

The report left Clayton's vision of economic federation at just that, a vision. It offered nice words regarding his cherished customs union, padded out with perfunctory descriptions of efforts within the Benelux and Scandinavia to operate little ones. But it concluded that a broader-scale effort would require "complex technical negotiations and adjustments" over many years. Without naming Britain, it also called attention to her "special problems" in cooperating with such an effort.

Prior to the conference, nothing as bold as Clayton's customs union had been contemplated in Europe. Though the concept would become "orthodox" by the 1960s, Dutch delegate Ernst van der Beugel explained years later, in 1947 it belonged "to a very imaginative set of far-reaching ideas." It had wormed its way onto the agenda owing to the impression, which Clayton did much to create, that it would "catch American opinion and imagination." Yet even taking "full account . . . of the boldness of such a step at that time," van der Beugel concluded, one could not "escape the conclusion that a great opportunity was lost."[96] The European Economic Community would not create a customs union until 1968.[97]

The report's appendix on Germany was, in the acid words of historian Alan Milward, "a splendid compilation of all possible conflicting views, sometimes in the same sentences."[98] The German economy, the committee concluded, "must be fitted into the European economy so that it may contribute to a general improvement in the standard of living." Yet it must also "not be allowed to develop to the detriment of other European countries as it has in the past."[99] Not surprisingly, no formula was put forth by which Germany might be developed to the benefit of all and the detriment of none.

This would not be possible unless and until the country was re-rooted in a different political and security context, the creation of which was beyond the powers of the conference. Yet the decision to incorporate western Germany into the plan, however hazily, affirmed its political status as an integral part of an emerging western bloc. Such a bloc had begun to cohere at the conference. "A group of international-minded men," van der Beugel observed, "was formed on many administrative levels." The conference served as "the primary school for many . . . who would play a major role on the post-war European scene, with additional loyalties to a broader entity than their own government."[100]

Their report, notwithstanding its conspicuous failings, also served its most critical immediate political purposes. The Europeans paid obeisance to the American vision of economic federation. They acknowledged the importance of each nation carrying out the necessary measures to "create or maintain its own internal financial stability." They committed to specific production targets, such as increases in output for coal, electricity, refined fuel, and steel ranging from 33 to 250 percent of prewar levels. They rejected a "shopping-list" approach to requesting American aid, emphasizing that the countries involved would address, individually and collectively, the current state of "maladjustment" in their economies. They pledged to seek private and IBRD financing, and not to rely wholly on the United States. They committed themselves to

"the establishment of a joint organisation to review the progress made in carrying out the recovery programme." And they expressed their willingness "to deal
with any amendments which appear desirable" through publication of "supplementary reports."[101]

London-based German writer Sebastian Haffner (*né* Raimund Pretzel)
observed that the Paris conference had been "the first [since the war's end]
held, not only without Russia, but in defiance of Russia, and under a barrage
of hostile Russian propaganda. It was the first uniting friend, foe, and neutral
of the late war. . . . And it was the first completely successful postwar conference"[102]—one that set the stage for the next great challenge: advancing the
Marshall Plan through a skeptical United States Congress.

❖

OVER IN MOSCOW, THE FOREIGN DEPARTMENT OF THE CENTRAL COM-
mittee of the Communist Party was preparing its own analysis of the Marshall
Plan, one that would form the basis of Moscow's coming public assault on it.

Their *spravka*, or "reference," explained that the Truman Doctrine had
been intended not only to support the "monarchic-fascist clique" in Greece,
and the Nazi accomplices in Turkey, but to buttress "reactionary" regimes in
China, Iran, France, and Italy. Its openly aggressive tone, however, had been "a
clumsy move," one that came under instant attack in America itself. Even Walter
Lippmann, "one of the more zealous defenders of American imperialism,"
pronounced it "the wrong method for achieving the right aims." Marshall's
initiative in June was, therefore, a hasty political corrective, dressing up the
Truman Doctrine as generosity.

Though received by "the ruling circles of England and France . . . as a 'Gift
from Heaven,'" the Marshall Plan, the Central Committee explained, in fact
"presents the European people with a reckless lie [that] cover[s] up the true
aims of American imperialist 'philanthropic' ideas." Soviet rejection of the
ruse, however, had done "a great service" by "exposing [its] true nature [and]
help[ing] in the refusal of eight governments of central and southern Europe"
to participate.

The aims of the Plan, the Central Committee went on, were fourfold. The
first was "to bypass the UN" and destroy "the principle of unity among the

great powers." Together with the Truman Doctrine, it gave America a free hand
to do as it chose in Europe and beyond. The second was "to prevent or hinder
the onset of an overproduction crisis in the USA as well as to exert economic
dominance over the entire world." One method would be the "seizure of European markets." The third aim was to staunch the "crisis" in England, "one of the
causes of which was the disturbance brought on by the conditions on the first
post-war [American] loan."

The fourth aim was the most "dangerous and far-reaching." It was to "re-
order the whole of Europe to [America's] advantage." The key to this was the
"restoration of German imperialism"—a policy "directed against the USSR . . .
the European people, and the German people." The Americans were "obstructing the payment of German reparations to the Soviet Union and to other European countries that suffered from the German aggression," blocking "the rise
of democratic movements in Germany," and "striving for the division" of the
country. This contrasted with actions in the Soviet zone, where "a deep process
of democratization is taking place through the reconstruction of the economy
and everyday life."[103]

As for Marshall himself, he had during the war been "an adherent to Roosevelt's foreign policy"—a military general who acted "in counterbalance to the
reactionary politicians." But "after the war, he joined more reactionary imperialist circles." Following the March meetings in Moscow, he "pervert[ed] the
meaning of Soviet proposals on the various questions of the German problem."
His "Marshall Plan" was now "regarded by the democratic public of the entire
world as an expression of the openly expansionist politics of American financial
capital, directed at the creation of a West European bloc under the auspices of
the United States, for the rebirth of the German economy as a military-eco-
nomic base for the USA."[104] ("Marshall Plan" was almost always in quotation
marks, and referred to by the word *zateiia*—here meaning "trick" or "freak.")[105]

"The governments of England and France," the report continued, have
"acted as the initiators of the 'Marshall Plan.' At the Paris conference," which
they organized, "sixteen European governments gathered with haste, hoping to
receive American dollars." But President Truman appeared to be in no rush to
get Congress to provide those dollars. "[T]he more important part of the 'Marshall Plan'" was clearly "to achieve the stabilization of the industrial capacity of

Western Germany as the economic and political center of the Western bloc." For that task, promises of "American dollars are being used to put pressure on European governments in order to achieve more concessions from them relating to Germany."[106]

Germany being the heart of the Marshall Plan, in the Kremlin's analysis, Stalin could be expected to oppose it there hardest. And indeed, sage American analysts would in the coming months sound the alarm over the obvious point of Allied vulnerability in the country: the isolated and indefensible enclave of West Berlin (see Map 2).

Herter Committee congressmen on a fact-finding mission to Europe stand with farmers in southern Italy, September 1947. Representative Richard M. Nixon (R-CA) is third from right.

SEVEN

PERSUASION

EVEN AFTER THE APRIL STALEMATE WITH MARSHALL IN MOSCOW, STALIN expected the Americans to keep talking about Germany and to avoid provocations. The Marshall Plan knocked him off balance. Convinced Washington was now determined to encircle the Soviet Union with hostile capitalist regimes, pushing as far eastward as it could, he shifted to a more aggressive strategy.

On September 18, 1947, Andrei Vyshinsky delivered an angry ninety-two-minute indictment of the Marshall Plan before the United Nations General Assembly. The Polish-descended Soviet representative, the star prosecutor of the late 1930s Moscow show trials, "made up with his zeal for his unworthy origins"—in Bidault's words.[1] Jabbing his finger into the podium repeatedly, Vyshinsky condemned the Plan as "an attempt [by the United States] to split Europe into two camps and . . . to complete the formation of a bloc of several European countries hostile to the interests of Eastern Europe and . . . the Soviet Union." Its "intention is to make use of Western Germany and German heavy industry as one of the most important bases for American expansion in Europe, in disregard of the national interests of the countries which suffered from German aggression." These facts, he said, showed "the utter incompatibility of this policy . . . with the fundamental principles of the United Nations."[2]

The purpose of Vyshinsky's "smear campaign," Ambassador Smith told Marshall, was to "discredit our motives and falsify our intentions." The Soviets want to "sabotage economic recovery" by discouraging smaller governments from accepting "American 'imperialist aid'" and Congress from authorizing it—for "fear [that] war and general unrest" would render it useless.[3] But what truly bothered the State Department, James Reston observed, was not so much embroidered Russian charges of imperialist interventionism but the feeling that the United States was intervening "just enough to be blamed for it and not enough to be effective at it." The department still held up political nonintervention as a quasi-religious principle, yet had not figured out "how to intervene economically without intervening politically."[4]

Central to Stalin's new offensive strategy was the creation of an institution—the Communist Information Bureau, or "Cominform"—to coordinate action among Europe's Communist parties and to reinforce Soviet control in the East. To bring it to life, the Kremlin convened a six-day conference of nine such parties in the scenic Polish mountain village of Szklarska Poręba—home of the first winter games of the International Workers Olympiad two decades prior.[5] Only the Soviet delegation to the conference, to be chaired by CPSU Central Committee secretary Andrei Zhdanov, was told in advance about the new organization, or that the gathering's main objective was to mobilize "the struggle against attempts by American imperialism to enslave economically the countries of Europe"—otherwise known as the Marshall Plan.[6]

The event opened on September 22 with the delegations delivering reports on the political situation in their respective countries. Zhdanov intended these to bring out the sharp divide opening between the Communists of the East and those of the West. Hungarian József Révai decried threats to their new "people's democracy" from the forces of "Anglo-American imperialism." Czech Rudolf Slánský reported that President Beneš "is interfering in government affairs" to assist "the reactionary forces." Yet whereas "the Anglo-Americans are acting through Beneš [and] Masaryk," he told those gathered, the Communists still "retained the upper hand" on "major foreign policy questions" such as "posture toward the Marshall Plan." The easterners, echoing Moscow's wishes, called for an abandonment of the wartime strategy of cooperating with "non-fascist" political parties. Reactionary agents now needed to be "purged" by whatever means necessary.

The western Communists, represented only by France and Italy, had thus far resisted abandoning electoral politics or adopting extralegal means of seizing power, despite having been booted from government by their coalition partners in May.[7] These were temporary setbacks, as they saw it. The key to taking power was persuading their respective publics that they were "nationalist first and Communist second."[8] As *Life* magazine said of Italian Communist leader Palmiro Togliatti, he "has won many Catholics by playing down Marx and playing up the corruption and red tape of the government."[9]

The Kremlin, however, was growing impatient with their passivity. "Many think that the French Communists coordinate their activities" with Moscow, Zhdanov wrote to their leader, the brawny ex-miner Maurice Thorez, in June, but "your steps [to cooperate with other parties] were a total surprise to us." (Given the sensitive nature of Zhdanov's message, Molotov ordered it destroyed once Thorez had read it.) The Central Committee in Moscow also documented its frustrations with the Frenchman. "Despite the concessions in foreign policy that France has exhibited in the face of the Anglo-Saxon bloc [and] the clear contradiction of this foreign policy with French national interests, the [French] Communist party does not see it as necessary to expose it before the masses." It noted further that Thorez had repeatedly failed to give "the working class of France . . . a clear representation of the threat . . . posed by the sweeping offensive against democratic powers, internationally as well as domestically, led by the Anglo-American and French reactionaries."[10]

Zhdanov cabled Stalin from the conference. French delegation head Jacques Duclos, the only one present not to speak Russian,[11] was making an "extremely unfavorable impression" with his tales of the "unprincipled swinging of [his] party from one parliamentary coalition to another." Stalin ordered Duclos whipped into line.

"While you are fighting to stay in the Government," Zhdanov spat out at the

Frenchman, in front of the packed hall, "they throw you out!" Then he turned on Italian delegate Luigi Longo. "[They] carried out a coup against [you], the biggest party in the nation! And you leave the field without battle!"[12] Under the Russian's approving glances, Yugoslav delegates Edvard Kardelj and Milovan Djilas bludgeoned the westerners with condescending lectures on revolutionary tactics. Belgrade would be rewarded for such exemplary "leftism" by being named Cominform's home base.

Duclos and Longo thus became the whipping boys for Stalin's frustration at his own failed strategy of "cooperation" with the West. At Szklarska Poręba, he terrorized them into line. Both issued sheepish, apologetic addresses, duly condemning American imperialism and the Marshall Plan.[13] Their parties thereafter stayed on message, even through the notorious political show trials of the 1950s. But this fidelity came only at the cost of undermining their political credibility at home, a blind spot for Stalin when dealing with Communists in western democracies.[14]

The gathering's main event was Zhdanov's own address, a lengthy polemic titled "On the International Situation." In it, he assumed the mantle of communism's Kennan, pronouncing on the sources, and implications, of American conduct.

What Zhdanov lacked in originality and eloquence, the brutish fifty-one-year-old made up for in ideological correctness and personal loyalty to the *vozhd*.[15] The latter, in return, treated him with a curious mixture of affection and contempt. Despite successfully urging his daughter, Svetlana, to marry Zhdanov's son, Stalin had no compunctions about berating the boy's father in front of her, even as Zhdanov recuperated from heart failure. "Look at him, sitting there like Jesus Christ!" Stalin would say of his pale, sweating guest at the dinner table a few weeks after the conference; it's "as if nothing were of any concern to him."[16] Zhdanov would die of a coronary the following August.

In Poland, however, he was still very much alive, and making the speech of his life. "America," he told the assembled, had "departed from Roosevelt's old course and [was] transitioning . . . for the preparation of new military undertakings." The world had become divided into two hostile and irreconcilable camps—the "democratic" camp led by the Soviet Union, and the "imperialist" camp led by the United States. For the former, the "motives of aggression and exploitation are utterly alien." For the latter, in contrast, aggression and exploitation were essential to forestall the crisis of monopoly capitalism.

The Marshall Plan, Zhdanov explained, was a necessary reaction to "the unfavorable reception which the Truman doctrine was met with" owing to its "frankly imperialistic character." But it was merely "a more carefully veiled attempt to carry through the same expansionist policy." Its essence is "a scheme to create a bloc of states bound . . . to the United States, and to grant American credits to European countries as recompense for their renunciation of . . . independence." Moreover, the United States intended "to render aid . . . not to the impoverished victor countries, America's allies in the fight against Germany, but to the German capitalists . . . making the countries which are in need of coal and iron dependent on the restored economic might of Germany." That recipients would be reduced to the status of vassal states was clear in American demands that, as a condition for the credits France was granted in May, "Communists [had to] be eliminated from the French government."

Of course, the Soviet Union had been invited to discuss the Marshall initiative in Paris. But the purpose was "to mask the hostile nature of the proposals with respect to the USSR, [as] it was well known beforehand that the USSR would refuse . . . the terms proposed by Marshall." If the Soviet Union had "consent[ed] to take part in the talks, it would [have been] easier to lure the countries of East and South-East Europe into the trap." But "the USSR will bend every effort in order that this plan be doomed to failure."[17]

With competent propaganda of any sort, important elements of truth help sustain the narrative logic, even under the weight of passages built on overwrought adjectives or falsehood. Zhdanov's speech was no exception. The Truman Doctrine *was*, even within the State Department, seen as overly bellicose in tone, and the Marshall Plan had been aimed partly at casting it in a gentler light. There *was* indeed concern in the United States that Europe's incapacity to produce and to purchase would harm American economic interests. There *was* a determination to bury the Morgenthau Plan and to revive German industry, for the purpose, among others, of alleviating burdens on the United States. The State Department *did* want to get and keep Communists out of government in western Europe, and wanted Europe to adopt market- and trade-friendly policies. It *did* lure Molotov to Paris under false pretenses, knowing that Soviet "cooperation" would doom the plan. And it *did* hope, though without great expectations, to pry loose some eastern countries from Moscow's grip. Stalin did not have to deduce all this; his spies in London and Washington informed him.

The speech's final task was to lay the groundwork for the new anti-Marshall Cominform. This was not as easy as it might have seemed. The sixty-five-member Communist International, or Comintern, had been abolished in 1943,[18] as Zhdanov acknowledged, because of charges "that Moscow was interfering in the internal affairs of other states, and that the Communist Parties in the various countries were acting not in the interests of their nations, but on orders from outside." These were, he emphasized, "slanderous allegation[s] of the enemies of Communism and the labour movement." But Stalin himself had assured Tito in June of 1946 that he had no intention of resurrecting the Comintern and issuing diktats to foreign Communist parties from Moscow. A reversal of this pledge required a compelling pretext.

It was clear from "experience," Zhdanov said, that "mutual isolation of the Communist Parties is wrong, harmful and, in point of fact, unnatural." Given "that the majority of the leaders of the Socialist parties [were] acting as agents of United States imperialist circles," he concluded, "the Communists must be the leaders in enlisting all anti-fascist . . . elements in the struggle against the new American expansionist plans for the enslavement of Europe."[19] This was his coded call for the Communist parties to renounce coalition politics and to seize power by more aggressive means.

Prior to the summer of 1947, when the Marshall Plan progressed from speech to program, Stalin had never been dogmatic about the forms of socialism pursued by countries within the Soviet sphere. Bulgaria,[20] Czechoslovakia,[21] Hungary,[22] Poland,[23] and Romania[24] all had coalition governments of sorts. His demand had merely been fealty to Moscow on foreign policy. As Kennan himself had written in 1944, "it [was] a matter of indifference to Moscow whether a given area is 'communistic or not. . . . [T]he main thing is that it should be amenable to Moscow influence, and if possible to Moscow authority."[25] But the Czechs and Poles had swooned before the vapors of American aid. Even in front of Zhdanov at Szklarska Poręba, Polish delegate Władysław Gomułka had the temerity to praise his own country's "peaceful road of social change" and to oppose the Soviet demand that Cominform states unanimously endorse collectivization of agriculture. Hard-line Polish delegation adviser Jakub Berman had to talk him out of voting against the new body itself, and soon after had Gomułka censured by the Polish Politburo.[26] Stalin would no longer tolerate such impertinence and bourgeois deviationism among European Communists; they were threatening to undermine his hard-won military victories. Throughout the East, the remaining elements of non-Communist political participation would, by the end of 1948, be fully co-opted or crushed.

Demonstrating that his aim was securing personal obedience, rather than ideological purity, Stalin even turned on the most ardent and spirited of Europe's Marxist dictatorships, Tito's Yugoslavia. In February of 1948 he blasted its "reckless independent actions" in the Balkans, which threatened to make Yugoslavia into a southeastern suzerain, or worse—one that would undermine Moscow's authority in the wider East.[27] Yet Tito refused to back down on his territorial claims or support for the Greek Communists: "We are not a pawn on a chessboard," he declared in March.[28] The second Cominform gathering in Bucharest, in June, would condemn "Titoism" as a heresy.

Stalin refrained, however, from sending the Red Army to bring Belgrade into line. "I'm absolutely sure that if the Soviet Union had a common border with Yugoslavia," reflected his successor, Nikita Khrushchev, years later, "Stalin would have intervened militarily. As it was, though, he would have had to go through Bulgaria, and Stalin knew we weren't strong enough to get away with that. . . . [T]he American imperialists would have actively supported the Yugoslavs—not out of sympathy with the Yugoslav form of socialism, but in order to split and demoralize the socialist camp."[29] The Cominform would meet for a final time, in Hungary, in November 1949. Khrushchev would abolish it in 1956.

As for the West, the creation of the Cominform "seems to foreshadow a fundamental change in Communist tactics in France and Italy," Reston opined in *The New York Times* on October 12, 1947.[30] He was right. Three years earlier,

Stalin had warned Thorez not to undermine de Gaulle (who resigned as head of the provisional government in January 1946); but times had changed, with the Americans now on the offensive. On his return from the Polish debacle, Duclos reported Moscow's new orders to the French Politburo. Zhdanov, he explained to his comrades, now "insisted on the need to destabilize the government. . . . The only objective is to destroy the capitalist economy. . . . In the future, the Kremlin will be completely indifferent to whether or not Communists are in or out of government, but all parties must fight against economic aid from the United States."[31] In fact, the Cominform, which reminded the French and Italian publics of the reviled Comintern, made it all the more difficult for their Communist parties to claim independence from Moscow—which was necessary to attract votes.

The new Central Intelligence Agency (CIA) concluded in a secret November 7 memorandum to the president that the Soviets had abandoned hopes for western Communist parties to attain power by the ballot box. "The post-war opportunity to win Western Europe by political action," Moscow believed, "has now been lost." It was therefore turning to "revolutionary activity in the pre-war style" in order "to defeat the European recovery program."[32]

Moscow, Caffery cabled Marshall, "is convinced that the Marshall Plan [will] serve to promote the formation of a western European bloc [to] serve as a dangerous jump-off place for attacking Soviet Russia." It therefore needed "bold action to neutralize capitalist assistance to France and Italy and to prevent establishment . . . of prosperous regimes . . . under American influence."[33] He said that French prime minister Ramadier was "deeply disturbed" by the situation. His government had been "progressively orienting its policy toward the US and [had] continued to oppose heavy Communist pressure to re-enter the government." It did so "counting largely on the Marshall Plan and interim aid." He urgently needed "a clearer indication that interim aid will be forthcoming"; otherwise "the government will probably collapse" in short order.[34] Italy, American ambassador James Dunn cabled Marshall from Rome, was also "on the verge of a dollar crisis. . . . [P]olitical upheaval [could not] be held off for long. . . . While the Marshall Plan is still a light of hope on the dismal road Italy walks, it is a dim and distant one for the weary traveller."[35]

A gathering of fifty thousand Communist supporters in Paris in October

1947 heard Thorez denounce the Marshall Plan as a "terrible menace" to
French independence. American aid, he said, was nothing more than the "return of stolen goods."[36] In November, Communist-controlled French unions
launched a wave of violent strikes, shutting down docks, coal mines, metal-
works, and auto factories. Industrial production came to a standstill. Garbage
lay uncollected, mail undelivered. By the end of November, over one million
(perhaps as many as two million) workers would walk off their jobs.[37] When
in early December, John Foster Dulles visited Paris to assess the situation, his
train had to be rerouted after the tracks were blown up. Communist-controlled
media denounced capitalism and American imperialism for plunging France
into crisis. And to show Washington that its Marshall Plan would be useless,
union leaders ordered workers to destroy machinery and loot equipment before walking off the job.

Sabotage hit at a strategic weakness in U.S. aid conditionality—that recipient governments would have to meet production targets before further
tranches would be disbursed. The Communists aimed at leaving behind no
productive apparatus for American capital to revive. An angry Minister of the
Interior Édouard Depreux told the National Assembly that the Communist
riots in Marseilles had the same instigators as those in Italy. Without naming
the Soviet Union, he declared that France would not permit "foreigners to stage
violent political battles on her territory."

The new confrontational tactics set back recovery in both countries. Feeling more dependent on Washington than ever, their governments, however,
tacked to the right. Following de Gaulle's speech condemning Soviet dictatorship on October 5, which the State Department judged a "spectacular success,"
the general's Rally of the French People (RPF) party stunned both the Communists and Socialists with a victory in municipal elections two weeks later.[38]
"The course of events in western Europe is demonstrating . . . that highly developed countries cannot be captured by Communist propaganda and infiltration," said Walter Lippmann, whose collection of essays critiquing Kennan, *The
Cold War*, had just been released in book form.[39] "They do not react to hunger,
inflation, and the paralysis of government by turning to the Communist Party.
They turn to the right, not to the left."[40]

On November 18, Thorez met with Stalin in Moscow. The Soviet leader warned him not to wage "the struggle against the Marshall Plan . . . too crudely." Don't let the Socialists paint the Communists as being against American aid, Stalin directed. Insist only that you are against "the enslaving conditions." It was lamentable, of course, he added, that the Soviet Union had not liberated Paris, instead of the capitalists; Thorez agreed, saying that "the French people would have enthusiastically received the Red Army." Stalin assured him, however, that Moscow could still supply the French Communists with arms "if it becomes necessary."[41]

Meanwhile in Paris, de Gaulle fretted privately over a collapse in the franc. Paris was on edge with talk of yet another world war.[42]

The following day, November 19, Socialist prime minister Paul Ramadier—under intense pressure from a mass strike by 700,000 longshoremen, coal miners, and metalworkers—resigned. Seventy-four-year-old former PM Léon Blum, frail since his two-year Nazi incarceration, failed to muster a majority in the National Assembly to replace Ramadier. President Vincent Auriol, confiding to his diary that the country "was on the edge of the abyss,"[43] turned to ascetic MRP (Christian Democrat) finance minister Robert Schuman. On a pledge to "defend the Republic," Schuman secured the necessary majority on the 24th.[44] Born in Luxembourg, educated in then-German Alsace, excused from German military service in World War I on health grounds, Schuman had only become "French" at the age of thirty-two. He would go on to become a celebrated architect of the European Community and the transatlantic alliance.

In Italy, Communist union bosses fulminated against the Marshall Plan. Togliatti—leader of the 2.25-million-member Communist Party, and a target of U.S. Office of Strategic Services (OSS) bugging operations[45]—denounced Christian Democrat prime minister Alcide De Gasperi's "sell out to foreigners." He called on Italians to "liquidate this government of reaction!" Rioters graffitied Rome's ancient walls with party slogans; they defaced Vatican buildings with hammers and sickles. They clashed with *carabinieri* in towns throughout the south. Dozens died in November skirmishes; scores more were seriously injured.[46]

But the violence only "made most Italians more keenly aware that their political future depends to a considerable degree on the Marshall Plan," in the words of *New York Times* Rome reporter Arnaldo Cortesi. De Gasperi appealed to Washington to speed aid. At home, his party pressed the message that the Italian Communists were tools of Soviet foreign policy. The country's only hope for a better future, they insisted, was help from the United States.

"Far from believing in the danger of an American hegemony over Europe," said Foreign Minister Count Carlo Sforza, "I sometimes fear that the United States, tired of so many paltry accusations and insinuations, may end by returning to isolationism and turn her back upon Europe. That would be an intellectual and moral disaster for the United States, but it would be an even graver disaster for the whole of Europe, even for that part that is beyond the so-called 'iron curtain.'"

The political symbolism of the Marshall Plan had, by this point, become so enormous, so much greater than the actual sums involved, that "the outlook would be infinitely brighter for communism [if the Plan were defeated] than if it had never been proposed at all," Cortesi observed.[47] Yet watching the violence unfold, *New York Times* reporter Harold Hinton lamented that there seemed to be "more confidence in the [Marshall] program's success in the Kremlin than exists in certain segments of the United States economic and political life."

✥

AS THE ADMINISTRATION BEGAN ITS AUTUMN OFFENSIVE TO BREAK down homegrown resistance to the Marshall Plan, the priority became sharpening the message. Yes, Europe was in humanitarian crisis, but that would not do. Too many saw aid as a bottomless sinkhole that would drain resources vital to American defense. Yes, boosting Germany's industrial production would create resources to lessen America's financial burden, but it would also help it rearm and threaten its neighbors again. Yes, Britain's empire was imploding more rapidly and violently than had been anticipated. But hadn't America fought two world wars to put an end to Europe's iniquitous imperial impulses? The spotlight, Marshall knew, had to be on Soviet Communism— the threat it represented to the independence of European nations, and in turn to America's own way of life.

Following Germany's surrender in May 1945, Stimson and McCloy had tried to persuade Truman to rebuild German industry. A jolt went through the room when Stimson said that unchecked economic chaos was "likely to be followed by political revolution and Communist infiltration." McCloy recalled that "people sat up and listened when the Soviet threat was mentioned."[48] If you wanted meaningful economic intervention in Europe, McCloy then understood, it was not enough to argue that it would make things better; you needed to emphasize that the alternative was communism.

In July 1946, Congress passed a controversial $3.75 billion postwar loan to Britain ($46 billion in today's money); it did so not on the basis of warm feelings toward a democratic ally, nor even on the belief that aid could do much economic good. Rather it was, in Republican congressman Christian Herter's words, to counter "impending Russian troubles." Or, as Democratic house speaker Sam Rayburn put it, to prevent "England and all the rest [being] pushed toward an ideology I despise."[49]

The State Department now applied what it had learned from such episodes. On September 29, 1947, its new Advisory Steering Committee on European Recovery Program laid out the new political focus in the starkest possible political terms:

> There is reason to believe that the totalitarian [i.e., Communist] forces have decided to engage in, and have already begun, a militant and concerted effort to subvert democratic governments before [a] recovery program can get under way. They are hoping that the food and financial situation in Europe this winter will produce economic conditions sufficiently serious that they can be aggravated by aggressive communist actions to a point where the position of democratic governments in France and Italy can be made untenable and communist regimes installed.[50]

Indeed, West European governments were already issuing rationing directives for the winter, aimed at controlling consumption of scarce commodities such as heating oil. Just one day earlier, the Swedish government decreed that, under anticipated winter conditions, people were forbidden from heating their homes beyond 50° F.[51]

The committee's memo went on:

From the viewpoint of the vital interests of the United States, the principal issue in Europe today is whether or not it will be totalitarian. If the virus of totalitarianism spreads much farther, it will be almost impossible to prevent its engulfing all western Europe. This would mean communist totalitarianism almost everywhere on the continent with the iron curtain moving to the Atlantic.

In the event of a totalitarian Europe, our foreign policy would have to be completely re-oriented and a great part of what we have fought for and accomplished in the past would be lost. The change in the power relationships involved would force us to adopt drastic domestic measures and would inevitably require great and burdensome sacrifices on the part of our citizens. The maintenance of a much larger military establishment would undoubtedly be required. The sacrifices would not be simply material. With a totalitarian Europe which would have no regard for individual freedom, our spiritual loss would be incalculable.[52]

Yet as Europe deteriorated—a pitiful wheat crop, violent strikes, falling dollar reserves—the sense of urgency impelling the administration still found little counterpart in Congress. Truman therefore invited legislators of both parties to the White House on September 29 to frame the case for immediate action.

"We'll either have to provide a program of interim aid relief until the Marshall program gets going, or the governments of France and Italy will fall—Austria too," the president told his reluctant guests, "and for all practical purposes Europe will be Communist." This is as grim a picture of Europe's future as Truman had painted since his call for Greek and Turkish military aid in March. "The Marshall Plan," he went on, "goes out the window" once those governments collapse, "and it's a question of how long we could stand up in such a situation. This is serious. I can't overemphasize how serious."

Rayburn took Truman at his word, but had no wish to be a profile in courage. "I had hoped very much, Mr. President, there would be no special session of Congress," he said. "Can't something be worked out [without Congress]? Can't you find the money in the government agencies?"

No, Truman said, "Congress has got to act." Without a special session,

Truman knew, Republicans would duck responsibility and attack the White House for partisan gain.

"Then the plan had better be well worked out," Rayburn said resignedly, "right down to the details . . . so that we get right to it the minute Congress meets."

Republicans, however, were less ready to buy in. "Mr. President, you must realize there is a growing resistance to these programs," house majority leader Charles Halleck objected. "I have been out in the hustings, and I know. The people don't like it," he said. "They can see very well that for all of the money we have appropriated and spent, billions of dollars, they are worse off over there than before," said New Hampshire senator Styles Bridges.[53]

Conservative opposition to the Plan was widespread. Many questioned the Plan's economic premises. New York representative John Taber said he had seen no "underfed people" in his European travels. Their problem was that they were simply "not working as hard or as vigorously as they should. We in the United States," he said, "got where we are because we worked harder."[54] Nevada senator George Malone attacked the Plan as a "World-wide WPA scheme," referring to Roosevelt's Works Progress Administration, the largest New Deal agency. There was, he said, "no call for the United States to finance socialism all over Europe."[55] New York representative Jacob Javits, who acknowledged that Europe "desperately needed" aid, warned that "the threat of the continent going Communist must not scare the United States into doing something unwise or uneconomic."[56] Ohio representative George H. Bender assailed "the Truman Administration's reckless policy of foreign expenditures," which the president, he said, justified by creating "synthetic" crises.[57] Michigan senator Homer Ferguson argued that loans should be extended only to companies operating in Europe, rather than their governments, as aid to governments only served to undermine free enterprise.[58] This was no way, he said, "to develop democracy or fight communism."[59] Others demanded that any new foreign aid be tied to domestic demands: "No tax relief, no European relief!" insisted Ohio representative Clarence Brown.[60]

Warnings about Europe's political weakness did, however, find purchase with some on the right. "We've got to stop Communism," House Foreign Affairs Committee chairman Charles Eaton told Truman, "and I'm ready to work with Senator Vandenberg."[61] But Truman's challenge was to convince many more Republicans that the Marshall Plan was the answer to communism, rather than being communism itself.

The first major breakthrough actually came from Capitol Hill initiatives of which the White House had been skeptical. Between August and November 1947, more than two hundred congressmen went to Europe on fact-finding tours—what *The Washington Post* called "the greatest legislative exploration in history."[62] The most famous of these missions was undertaken by the eighteen-member "Herter Committee." Organized by internationalist Massachusetts Republican representative Christian Herter, the group split into subcommittees that spent forty-five days traversing the continent (save Yugoslavia, Albania, and the Soviet Union), meeting with public officials and private citizens. Determined that the trip would be no junket, Herter ordered members to bring no evening clothes or wives.

Echoing the attitude that Keynes had found so offensive when pleading for American postwar financial assistance in 1945,[63] one committee member told *The New York Times* that he and his colleagues had "tried to look at Europe in about the way a banker would look at a bankrupt corporation trying to get a loan." From the European side, the American visitors were, in the words of historian Theodore White, received with "a mixture of tongue-tied dread and hushed servility."[64] Yet in spite of ample opportunity for mutual incomprehension, the group returned home, accompanied by seventeen trunks of documents, with a near-consensus on the need for immediate, large-scale, multiyear American economic aid. "I became a convert on this trip," Wisconsin Republican Lawrence H. Smith proclaimed on the floor of the House.[65] This was a pleasant shock to the White House, which had been "afraid the traveling Congressmen would merely gather information to support their own prejudices."[66]

What moved the congressmen was not just the hardship they witnessed but their understanding of the forces exploiting it. "The Marshall Plan," *New York Times* correspondent William White wrote, "appears to draw its greatest strength not from any special feeling that other peoples should be helped for their own sake, but only as a demonstration against the spread of communism."[67] Communist "overlords," South Dakota Republican Karl Mundt said, were disrupting economic activity "so as to produce chaos and put an end to freedom." We must, he said, "turn the Red tide." Herter himself cited the danger posed by Communist-controlled labor unions in western Europe. Freshman California Republican Richard Nixon, assigned to tour Italy, wrote that "the great difficulty [here] is not so much the physical destruction of the war, but the fact that the Communists have chosen this country as the scene of one of their most clever and well-financed operations against the forces of democracy." Alabama Democrat Pete Jarman, who traveled in eastern Europe, spoke of the "feeling of strangulation that one has behind the iron curtain." We in the United States, he concluded, had to recognize "the absolute necessity of our doing whatever is necessary to prevent [communism's] spread."[68]

The committee's final 883-page report, which would not be released in full until May 1948, highlighted the anti-Communist basis of its support for the Marshall Plan: "To the degree that a country is faced with the constant disorders and the sense of hopelessness and insecurity caused by Communist activities," it said, "it becomes more difficult to solve the problem of its economic reconstruction. On the other hand, a state of economic crisis and stagnation is the best breeding ground for the successful continuation of such activities. Thus a vicious circle is formed, a circle which the European recovery program must break in order to succeed."[69]

Vandenberg's strategy to build legislative support for the Plan was to weaken its links to the State Department. Just after Marshall's Harvard speech in June, he urged the president to appoint bipartisan committees to pronounce on the advisability and domestic impact of a large-scale foreign aid program. Truman appointed three of them, the first headed by Commerce Secretary (and former ambassador to Moscow) Averell Harriman, the second by Secretary of the Interior Julius Krug, and the third by Council of Economic Advisers chairman Edwin Nourse.[70] All three of their reports would form part of a Top Secret Soviet report on the Marshall Plan prepared for Gerashchenko in December.[71]

The most important of these committees was Harriman's, the President's Committee on Foreign Aid. A former banker and son of a railroad magnate, Harriman's business bona fides balanced off his Democratic politics and ensured Vandenberg's support. Though a multimillionaire, Harriman was "famed for his battered old hats and rumpled overcoats." Embarrassed friends noted that "the cuffs of his trousers are so frayed that strings of material trail after him along the sidewalk." Asked to explain his choice of party, he would offer that "trickle-through theory is terrible. . . . Besides that, I think being a Democrat is great fun."[72]

With Vandenberg's cooperation, Truman selected the committee members to repel attacks from the left and the right and to provide political cover for waverers. The chosen included Republican Studebaker automobile company president Paul Hoffman, former General Electric chairman Owen Young, American Federation of Labor (AFL) secretary-treasurer George Meany, and former Wisconsin senator Robert La Follette, Jr. La Follette—a former isolationist, Progressive-New-Dealer-turned-Republican—was the most colorful of the group. British philosopher-diplomat Isaiah Berlin branded him "peculiar . . . confused . . . Nationalist . . . unpredictable . . . radical in internal issues and obscurantist in foreign affairs."[73]

Although the nineteen notables had been handpicked to back the principle and practicality of aid, their deliberations did not go smoothly. Heated arguments flared over whether the U.S. economy could support a program of the size the administration was demanding, with the matter of steel resources touching off the "hottest fight."[74] There were also political and ideological melees, the most consequential of which was over whether aid should be conditioned on recipient countries pursuing market-friendly policies. Hoffman skillfully hammered out compromise language pledging belief in "the American system of free enterprise" while abjuring pressure on others to adopt it.

What coherence the group's economic approach achieved owed much to Harriman's choice of executive secretary, Yale economist Richard Bissell, Jr., who would later go on to a colorful career at the CIA. Bissell's analysis was largely of an early Keynesian variety, arguing, for example, that the program would generate inflationary effects in both Europe and the United States that would have to be offset by fiscal and administrative measures—as opposed to the monetary measures that would be orthodox today. But his conclusion, which the group signed off on, backed the report's finding that a major foreign aid program could be managed without imposing undue hardship on the American people. It was a classic product of "New Deal synthesis" thinking:

that supranational planning and scientific fiscal management could be combined with market forces to solve a complex economic problem with political roots.[75] Science did not entirely drive the report's findings, however. Later asked whether it had been a certainty that the group would reach its positive conclusion, Bissell replied: "The honest answer is affirmative to that."[76]

On November 6, Vandenberg, who had been following the committee's progress while working with his fellow senators, called Bissell and told him he wanted the report immediately—by the following morning. Marshall would be testifying on interim and long-term aid before his Senate Committee on Foreign Relations on November 10, and the president would be addressing a special session of Congress on the 17th—the first such address since 1939, at the start of the war in Europe. Vandenberg needed the Harriman Committee's weight behind the initiative to set the stage.

It was outlandish enough to expect Bissell to complete the report in such haste, but impossible to expect that the committee could read, debate, edit, and approve it overnight. So Bissell and Harriman both did the outlandish. Bissell wrote and rewrote until 4 a.m., at which point he stopped typing to get it to the printers. "How he did it," Hoffman said, "I still don't know." As for Harriman, he made sure that each committee member read and signed off on his own particular section, but on nineteen separate phone calls told them just to "make a minority objection" after the report's publication if they took issue with anything else. "An introvert, naturally shy, and lacking oratorical powers," Harriman was nothing if not tenaciously persuasive when he set out to convince a man (or charm a woman).[77]

After the first copies rolled off the press just after dawn, Bissell couriered one to the White House. At 10 a.m. he distributed dozens to the major news outlets.[78] The 286-page tome placed its rhetorical emphasis right where Vandenberg needed it: on the necessity for western Europe to take primary responsibility for righting itself. The self-help motif played to Republican desires to be seen as champions of free enterprise and personal initiative, not collaborators in their undoing. While praising the thrust of the European report from Paris, Harriman's group also hit helpfully on some of the State Department's own objections to it. They argued that the Paris effort did not sufficiently emphasize the primacy of reviving consumption goods production over capital development and housing programs, that it overestimated the availability of certain commodities from the United States, and that it underestimated the financial assistance that could be secured privately and from the new International (World) Bank. Yet they also insisted that it was a "strategic and political" imperative for the United States to plug the region's inevitable trade deficits over the coming few years.

It was, the Harriman report said, "the Communist tactic" to exploit "misery and chaos" to undermine democracy, and such disorder was likely in the absence of immediate and significant American assistance. It set the total requirement for the full four-year period of the program at $12–$17 billion, emphasizing that the allocation of this aid would have to differ somewhat from the Paris blueprint—in particular, in funneling more of it to Germany, recovery of whose coal industry was vital to the entire region. Here, the State Department got useful political cover for its ongoing effort to persuade the French of the need to accept German industrial revival. Harriman also played to Republican distrust of the State Department. The report, like that of the Herter Committee, called for an independent agency to be established—one that would have "the closest possible relations" with Congress.[79]

Supplemented by the Krug and Nourse reports, both of which backed a European aid plan, the Harriman report became Truman's and Marshall's intellectual armor in jousting with Republican opponents. Truman invoked all three reports in his December 19 "Special Address to Congress on the Marshall Plan," concluding, on the grounds of their authority, that the Plan was "proper, wise, and necessary."[80] Harriman's report also became "the bible of those who defended the [Plan] in Congress," not least Vandenberg. [81] It was, in Hoffman's words, "of monumental importance" in shaping private and congressional opinion.[82] New York Times columnist Felix Belair called it "exhaustive and eloquent," even while criticizing it for paying insufficient attention to the sacrifices the American public would be forced to bear.[83] After falling 11.6 percent in 1946, U.S. GNP would fall a further 1.1 percent in 1947.

A month after the report was released, nearly two thirds of Americans had now heard of the Marshall Plan, up from just under half two months prior.[84] At least as important, 56 percent had a favorable impression, and only 17 percent an unfavorable one. The poll numbers gave skeptical congressmen leeway to consider legislation without having to posture against the president.

⁕

WITHOUT THE HARRIMAN AND HERTER COMMITTEES' BIPARTISAN SUP-port for the Marshall Plan, "the program couldn't have gotten Congressional approval," Hoffman reflected years later. But it was far from sufficient. Even the open-minded still had reservations.

"I raise the question," Rep. Lawrence Smith said before the House Committee on Foreign Affairs on November 14, "and it is a sincere one—can we expect from these nations any more in the future than we have [gotten] in the past so long as we give and give?"[85] Overcoming such doubts took more than congressional fact-finding tours and committee reports; it required shaping voter opinion. Given how little hard public knowledge there was of the Marshall Plan, this required a massive, carefully orchestrated public relations campaign—"a Marshall Plan to sell the Marshall Plan."[86]

Impetus for the most important such effort came from wartime secretary of war Henry Stimson, a Republican, in the form of an article in the October issue of *Foreign Affairs*. Having won the war at enormous cost, Stimson argued, the United States could not now afford to lose the peace. "Only two years ago we triumphantly ended the greatest war in history," Stimson wrote. "Most of us then looked forward eagerly to the relative relaxation of peace. Reluctantly we have now come to understand that victory and peace are not synonymous. . . . Close on the heels of victory has loomed a new world crisis."

That crisis was being created by "the tide of Soviet expansion," which, in the absence of firm and immediate American action to counter it, would "roll into the empty places left by war." Those most immediately threatened are "the nations by whose citizens our land was settled and in whose tradition our civilization is rooted." The United States had both a moral and selfish interest in confronting this threat. "The reconstruction of western Europe," he wrote, "is a task from which Americans can decide to stand apart only if they wish to desert every principle by which they claim to live." A "prompt and large-scale program" was required; "the penalty of delay [was] to increase the size of the job and multiply difficulties." And whereas he did not "expect the Russians to make war," the United States needed to prepare for one. "Our military strength must be maintained as a standing discouragement to aggression."[87]

In broad strokes, much as Marshall had used in June at Harvard, Stimson laid out the case for a European recovery program, while also adumbrating what would the following year become more explicit calls for a Western military alliance to protect America's investment in Europe's recovery and political stabilization. The article became a rallying cry for the most important of the many private initiatives set up to advocate for passage of a massive European assistance program: the Committee for the Marshall Plan to Aid European Recovery (often called the "Marshall Plan Committee"). Stimson became its national chairman.

Stimson's successor as secretary of war, Robert Patterson, became chairman of the executive committee. In addition to former top government officials, most importantly Acheson and Clayton, some three hundred notables from business, labor, agriculture, religion, and academia became active members. Acheson in particular was ubiquitous, appearing on radio, at luncheon talks, and at evening functions around the country. The group formed a lobbying organization, created a speakers bureau, and employed a news agency to spread their message. It shaped the details of the aid bill legislation, prepared material for witnesses at congressional hearings, and drew critical public attention to legislative restrictions and amendments it deemed objectionable.[88]

Many other private groups worked in support of the initiative, such as the nonprofit National Planning Association and Committee for Economic Development, both of which focused on how the Marshall Plan should be administered. Think tanks such as the Council on Foreign Relations and the Brookings Institution produced papers and convened meetings.[89] Frequently, there were fewer than six degrees of separation among the leaders of these initiatives. Of the nineteen luminaries on the executive committee of the Marshall Plan Committee, eight were CFR members. Allen Dulles, brother of John Foster Dulles, was president of CFR. Acheson, who joined CFR in December 1947, was also on the Brookings board of directors. Though some were Democrats and some Republicans, they were like-minded internationalists who associated with internationalist-minded institutions.

Myriad business, labor, agriculture, veteran, and religious organizations weighed in, in the main highly supportive. Industry groups representing specific sectors, such as tobacco growers and flour dealers, were naturally enthusiastic at the prospect of having their commodities distributed abroad with government dollars. But the communist argument that the Marshall Plan was about forcing American exports on Europe to forestall a domestic depression found little support in the behavior of industry groups. The leadership of the National Foreign Trade Council (NFTC), the Committee for Economic Development (CED), the U.S. Chamber of Commerce, and the National Association of Manufacturers (NAM) all backed the administration's aims of boosting intra-European trade, stabilizing finances, and closing the "dollar gap"[90]—western Europe's balance of payments deficits with the dollar area—that the new IMF was unable to address.

Union leaders were also enthusiastic. "The ultimate price of a refusal to put the Marshall plan into effect is war," declared AFL secretary-treasurer George Meany, "a war in which America would be practically alone."[91] The AFL and the Congress of Industrial Organizations (CIO), which also supported the Plan, counted over ten million American workers as members.

Iowa farmers organized their own mission to Europe to "find out what kind of food Europe needs, the cost to ship it over and how we can get England in a position whereby she can trade with us."[92] The annual convention of the 3.2-million-member American Legion voted unanimously to endorse the Plan, as it did a second resolution calling for the Communist Party to be outlawed.[93] Speaking on behalf of the World Assembly of the World Council of Churches, the Rev. Dr. Stewart Herman, Jr., declared the Marshall Plan to be "nearer to being Christian than anything offered to Europe by a single government or by a group of governments for more than a generation."[94] The Right Rev. Charles Gilbert, Episcopal Bishop of the New York Diocese, called it "a plan that would bring new life and hope to the vast multitudes of God's despairing children." It should, he said, have the support of Christians everywhere.[95]

The Truman administration organized grassroots campaigns to build awareness of the program and to explain to Americans how they could help. "The way Mother can have an effective hand in accomplishing this important

part of the United States foreign policy," Agriculture under secretary Norris
Dodd told the Women's National Democratic Club, "is to buy closely, figure
out ways to make tasteful meals from the less choice but nonetheless nutritious
foods, and put left-overs into tempting dishes instead of into the garbage can."[96]
Marshall, speaking at the National Garden Conference, called on Americans to
plant twenty million "freedom gardens" to supplement the aid program. Never
in history, he said, had it been more important to raise as much food as possible.
"And I don't speak from a desk in the State Department," he added. "I ordered
my seeds and settings ten days ago."[97]

Spontaneous public initiatives sprang up to supplement the Marshall Plan.
Responding to a suggestion from syndicated columnist Drew Pearson for a
"Friendship Train" to travel the country collecting goods and food for Europe,
restaurants, schools, and private societies such as the Kiwanis Club donated
tons' worth. Greeted by banners and parades as it passed through cities and
towns—its 214 boxcars painted with slogans such as *Vive la France!* and *Viva
l'Italia!*—the train arrived in New York on November 18.[98] Following more
fanfare, the supplies were then shipped to Europe on donated commercial
liner space. The first shipments arrived one month later, on December 17, in
Le Havre, France, at docks decorated in Stars and Stripes and the *Tricolore*.[99]
Dockworkers donating their time unloaded them, one week after they had been
on strike against American imperialism.[100]

As the belief took hold among the American public that the epic European
aid initiative would soon become reality, grand new applications of its thinking began to emerge. In December, a group of economists from the American
South, in collaboration with experts from various government departments,
prepared a report for the House Agriculture Committee arguing that the South
needed its own "Marshall Plan" to address endemic underdevelopment, rooted
in a rutted agrarian economic system. It suggested that "the staggering sum of
approximately 13.4 billion dollars [$145 billion in today's money] is required
for [technological] investment in the South during the next 20 years," much of
which would need to be federally funded.[101] In February 1948, the American
Society for the Prevention of Cruelty to Animals even demanded a Marshall
Plan for Europe's pets and strays.[102] No problem of deprivation and suffering, it
seemed, was too big, or too small, for a Marshall Plan.

IF THE SPIRIT OF YALTA DIED IN PARIS IN JULY 1947, IT LOOKED SET TO BE buried in London in November. The four-power meeting had been on the calendar since April,[103] but differences over Germany had hardened so much, and were of such consequence, that there seemed little left for the two sides to do but posture. Though the administration's position was "not [to] admit having established a political structure" for western Germany, Ambassador Robert Murphy argued in October that they had to be ready to move forward with one after the conference broke down—as he expected it to do.[104] The United States would inevitably be accused of splitting Germany, but that could not stand in the way.

Marshall told the cabinet on November 6 that the Soviets would use "various ruses . . . to try to get us out of western Germany under arrangements which would leave that country defenseless against communist penetration," but that the United States had to ensure the opposite: that Germany become "better integrated into Western Europe."[105]

Over in Moscow, Molotov prepped for the conference with a memorandum from Andrei Smirnov, head of the Foreign Ministry's most important European department. Smirnov chronicled shifts in the western stance on Germany over the past eighteen months. Molotov, blue pencil in hand, underlined passages suggesting Allied guilt.

The western position had "fundamentally changed." In 1946, they wanted a settlement "quickly built on the basis of the Potsdam decisions." By "the beginning of 1947," however, they were seeking "a substitute for the peace settlement"—one that "relieved the German government . . . of the responsibility of carrying out the conditions." Then, after the Moscow Council of Foreign Ministers conference in March, there was "further deviation from the Potsdam decisions"—efforts aimed at "a separate resolution of the German problem," without the Soviet Union. The American position now "stood in complete opposition to that which Byrnes defended in . . . 1946."

Molotov thickly underlined "complete opposition," adding in the lower margin: "Is that so?" And later: "Byrnes? What did he say?"

"On May 29," 1947, the memo continued, "the Anglo-American agreement

on the creation of an 'Economic Council' was concluded, closing out the formulation of West Germany into a separate political unit." And "on July 11, the
U.S. government sent General Clay a new directive . . . at odds with the Potsdam decisions and . . . focused mainly on the attraction of West Germany to the
implementation of the Marshall Plan." Then, "from August 22 to 27, negotiations between the representatives of the U.S., UK and France, regarding the industrial production level for the Anglo-American zone of Germany, took place
in London. Also addressed was the management of the Ruhr mines and control
over them. As a result of these negotiations, the British and the Americans have
created a new plan for the zone's level of industrial production, overturning decisions made by the Allied Control Council in March 1946."[106]

Thus armed with a history of Allied betrayal since 1946, Molotov warily
agreed to receive the French ambassador, Georges Catroux, for a discussion of
German matters on November 5. Catroux, Molotov reported to Stalin, said he
wanted to "try to move the Soviet and French position closer together." In particular, he wished to explore what it might take for Moscow to come nearer "to
the French view on international administration of the Ruhr." The Frenchman
stressed that "he was acting on his own initiative, without any sort of orders
from his government."

Clay would have seen Catroux's behavior as predictable Gallic duplicity;
Molotov certainly did, but from the opposing lens. "The meeting with Catroux," he told Stalin, "demonstrated that the Americans and the English are
now trying to use the French to feel out our position on the German question."[107]

Molotov distrusted the British even more deeply than he did the French.
When in London to negotiate an Anglo-Soviet treaty in May 1942, he surrounded himself with bodyguards and slept with a revolver by his bed.[108] Now,
back in London on November 25, 1947, Molotov entered the gilded salon of
Lancaster House in a chary mood.

The fifth meeting of the Council of Foreign Ministers opened precisely
where the Moscow gathering had left off—in acrimony over Germany. Abandoning his usual poker face for an air of impatience, Molotov reprised Moscow's familiar demands for $10 billion in reparations. Marshall, however, had
even less room for maneuver than in March. With Congress watching over his

shoulder, any concession would threaten prospects for aid legislation. With the discussion thus deadlocked from the start, Bevin felt he had nothing to lose in a frank personal appeal. He invited Molotov to his flat on December 2.

"When our government was trying to stamp out your Revolution," Bevin asked him, "who was it that stopped it? It was *I*," he said emphatically:

> *I* called out the transport workers and they refused to load the ships. . . . Now again I am speaking as a friend. . . . You are playing with fire, Mr. Molotov . . . if war comes between you and America in the West, then we shall be on America's side. . . . That would be the end of Russia and of your Revolution. So please stop sticking out your neck in this way and tell me what you are after.

"I want a unified Germany," replied his stony-faced guest.

"Why do you want that?" Bevin retorted. "A unified Germany might pretend to go communist. But, in their hearts, they would be longing for the day when they could revenge their defeat at Stalingrad. You know that as well as I do."[109]

Molotov was immovable. As French diplomat René Massigli characterized it, it was "only by espousing German unity" that the Soviet Union "obtains [the] means of extending its influence throughout Germany."[110]

Actions by both sides on the ground, however, made unity impossible. While invoking Potsdam to demand their rights in western Germany, the Soviets fell back on its exceptions relating to "local variations" in each occupation zone to assert exclusive powers in the East.[111] Operating through the KPD Communist Party, they had radically transformed their zone, seizing landholdings and nationalizing firms. Meanwhile, the British and Americans acknowledged privately that preparations for implementing the Marshall Plan had deepened "the economic split in Germany." Unification was unacceptable, as it would have allowed the Soviets "to siphon out Marshall Plan assistance through reparations claims."[112]

Meeting with Marshall on December 6, Bevin suggested they lay out for Molotov requirements for Germany's political organization in such a way as to provoke him into revealing, for the record, "that the Soviet objective was a Communist-controlled Germany." Then the rupture would be his doing.

Marshall, however, waved him off. Yes, it would be "popular" with the American people just to "break off and tell the Russians to go to the devil," but it was unwise. It was better to assure Molotov "that we were not permanently breaking" with them, that cooperation was possible if "differences on matters of real substance" could be resolved down the road. Marshall was proposing to behave as Stalin had in April, cloaking unwillingness to collaborate further in hollow expressions of hope.

Yet after several further days of fruitless conferencing, Marshall could see no way of winding matters down amicably. He cabled Lovett with a message for the president: "It is plainly evident that Molotov is not only playing for time but . . . endeavoring to reach agreements which really would be an embarrassment to us in the next four to six months."[113] Marshall requested permission to end the talks.

"We are all with you," Truman responded.

The tone of the meetings now hardened toward mutual contempt. On December 12, Molotov charged that the aim of American aid was to "enslave Germany" and to make it "a strategic base against the democratic states of [eastern] Europe." Marshall's team had been waiting for such a tirade, and began scribbling responses to pass on to him. He ignored them all, telling the Russian that his words were self-evidently "not intended to be used as a basis for Council discussion but . . . solely for propaganda purposes." That Molotov would offer them in such a context, he added, "reflected on the dignity of the Government of the Soviet Union."

Molotov grimaced. Clay had never seen him so angry.

Bevin piled on: Molotov's "insults," he said, "would be resented throughout the British Commonwealth." He should have "ended his speech by thanking his colleagues for listening to the end."[114]

On December 15, Marshall told Molotov he was done discussing German reparations. They had reached an impasse; the problem, as ever, was "Soviet obstructionism." No, Molotov shot back, it was Marshall who was subverting the talks "to give the U.S. a free hand to do as it pleased in its zone of Germany."[115] Bidault interjected: It was better, he said, after seventeen sessions in which they had "accomplished practically nothing," to adjourn than to "further aggravate relations." And so they did, with no mention of future meetings.[116]

"The age of Yalta has come to an end," declared the *New York Herald*

Tribune.[117] Clay saw in that moment the ominous beginnings of "a competitive struggle, not with arms but with economic resources, with ideas and with ideals."[118]

❖

OVER THE NEXT THREE DAYS, CLAY AND ROBERTSON MAPPED OUT PLANS to transform the Frankfurt-based Bizonal Economic Council, comprised of West German representatives, into a true provisional government. Clay's enthusiasm showed a stunning change in mind-set; in the spring he had blasted moves to split the country.

Though Clay had earlier argued that compromise with Russia would spread democracy and U.S. influence to eastern Germany,[119] he now argued for a unilateral posture to keep communism out of the West: "We cannot and we must not take the risk of losing western Germany and having all of Germany become a satellite of the USSR. As powerful as we are, it would be almost impossible for us to resist communism in the face of a Russo-German agreement."[120] The United States was "engaged in political warfare," and had "to attack communism and the police state before the German people."[121]

Clay's conversion from dove to hawk had been inevitable in Bohlen's view, only belated. Back in June 1945, Clay had told Bohlen that Stimson had it right: to gain Soviet trust, the United States would have to show trust. Bohlen responded that "within a year, [Clay] would become one of the officials in the American government most opposed to the Soviets."[122] He was off by a year.

Clay's actions in suspending reparations and initiating bizonal fusion had stoked Soviet hostility, which in turn pushed him to end his campaign of opposition against Marshall's go-it-alone strategy. "Our work in London has brought us into a very close relationship with State Department personnel concerned with occupation policy," he reported to Army under secretary William Draper on December 20, 1947, "and there appears to be little real difference in our thinking as to the future."[123]

Marshall, however, seems to have felt otherwise. With no warning to Clay or the War Department, he would announce a few weeks later, on January 8, 1948, that the State Department would assume full control of the German occupation from July 1—a move that had been urged by Lovett and Kennan.

Marshall's intention was to replace Clay with Bedell Smith, one of the secretary of state's few close friends. General Smith, for his part, was anxious to leave Moscow and gain his fourth star by moving to Berlin as military governor.

Clay was surprised to learn of the impending switch from Smith himself, but professed to be happy to return home. When an angry Byrnes learned of the move, however, he successfully maneuvered (without Clay's knowledge) to line up Senate committee leaders and block confirmation. "I don't think General Marshall or General Smith recognized that the appointment as Military Governor required Senate confirmation," Clay reflected years later.[124] He would, over the year after he was supposed to have returned home, face his greatest challenge yet in Berlin.

Murphy had anticipated this challenge back in October. He had warned that any move to refashion the Bizonal Economic Council into a West German government would transform Berlin, 120 miles to the east of the bizone border, into "an island in the heart of the Soviet zone" in which the Russians "could easily make our lives unbearable."[125] Following the collapse of the London CFM, the CIA warned of the "possibility of steps being taken in Berlin by the Soviet authorities to force the other occupying powers to remove from Berlin."[126] Clay acknowledged there might be "difficulties" in the city, but thought he could manage them. This would prove shortsighted.

Marshall was now convinced that "unless Western Germany . . . is effectively associated with Western Europe nations, first through economic arrangements, and ultimately perhaps in some political way there is a real danger that the whole of Germany will be drawn into [the] Eastern orbit."[127] Bevin, too, was sure of the need for action to prevent "the emergence of a Communist controlled Germany." The two endorsed the Clay-Robertson plans on December 18.[128]

The seventy-two-year-old U.S. chief of staff to the commander in chief, Admiral William Leahy, backed the step, but not without deep reservations over where he was sure it would lead. The Soviets, he noted in his diary, "would offer violent objection"; they would use "military power if necessary" to protect their interests. The United States therefore needed to "begin a partial mobilization of forces of defense without any delay."[129] It was becoming clear that the Marshall Plan and mobilization were not alternatives. To the contrary, Washington might need the second to ensure the success of the first.

THE NEXT DAY, DECEMBER 19, THE KREMLIN-BACKED *TÄGLICHE RUND-schau* Berlin daily insisted that quadripartite control in the city could only be justified as long as the country as a whole remained under four-power rule. Three weeks later it declared that the Anglo-American initiative to create a West German state "nullified" western rights in Berlin.[130]

Within western Germany itself, there was growing realization that self-government in the western zones was the best that could be hoped for at this stage. "None of our people will say so openly," said a German official to *The New York Times*, "but they realize that the only hope for rehabilitation is an unhampered program for Western Germany with United States aid. Eastern Germany must be written off and all we can do is feel sorry for the Germans caught behind the Russian-orientation line."[131]

The State Department had no doubt that German public opinion would be important to the success of their efforts to revive western Europe's war-shattered economy. Germans would obviously welcome aid, but their cooperation could not be taken for granted. Most still did not want their country split, and knew that a hostile Russian reaction to the Marshall Plan made such a split more likely. Since the Allies controlled the flow of news within western Germany, the conditions were not present for a free and informed public debate. Nonetheless, western Germans were broadly aware of the American initiative and the Soviet reaction to it.

On July 22, 1947, three weeks after Molotov's walkout in Paris, the newly formed Economic Council (Wirtschaftsrat) of the bizone had issued a public statement praising the Marshall Plan as an effort to "achieve the solidarity of the peoples in economic life." Konrad Adenauer, Christian Democratic Union (CDU) chairman in the British occupation zone, welcomed the plan as Germany's only chance to improve its standing and influence.[132] He would over the next months also come to see it as the touchstone for judging the wisdom of the entirety of the Allies' occupation strategy.

The left-leaning Social Democrats (SPD) had a much more spirited debate over the initiative. British zone SPD chairman Kurt Schumacher had to implore party delegates to ditch slogans condemning "dollar imperialism," and instead to focus on the "100 million Europeans who were going hungry." Marshall, he reminded them, had pledged not to remake Europe solely through "the orthodox and missionary methods peculiar to American capitalism." Schumacher was attracted by what he saw as elements of a planned economy in the initiative. It was, he argued, economic crisis that brought Hitler to power, and the United States was now indispensable in preventing another one.

Schumacher was a passionate advocate of German unification, who, unlike Adenauer, would have accepted German political neutrality as its price. This stance should have tilted him toward Moscow. Yet he initially clung to the hope that the Marshall Plan might provide an impetus to unification: a resolution of the party congress offered that the "irresistible magnetism" of a revitalized bizone economy would serve to bring this about. Moscow's post-Paris condemnation of the Plan rendered this argument implausible, but also served to reinforce Schumacher's support for it on the grounds that the Soviets were now working against German interests.

Only the Wirtschaftsrat's Communist representatives opposed the Marshall Plan on the basis that it would impede reunification. Communist rejection of the Marshall Plan, however, found little support among the West German public. An October 1947 poll in the American zone reported 78 percent in favor of the Plan, with most believing that Washington's primary motivation was preventing Communists from coming to power in western Europe. Underpinning popular support for the Marshall Plan was the belief that it represented a renunciation of the Morgenthau Plan. "Including Germany in the task of European rehabilitation," Stuttgart's *Wirtschaftszeitung* wrote, "means conceding to it the means for the full use of its economic strengths."[133] It meant that the United States would allow no return to the economic and political autarky of the interwar years, which many held to be the source of the country's problems since the 1930s.[134]

Ulbricht, however, remained confident Germans would put unity before all else. "It is imperative to keep in mind," he wrote to Soviet Central Committee AgitProp chief Mikhail Suslov on December 12, "that it was not yet evident to everyone that a defense of German unity also means a battle against bizonal politics and against the Marshall Plan. This is only becoming apparent to many now, in connection with the debates at the London conference."[135]

Across the Atlantic, Walter Lippmann opposed the new American thinking on West German statehood. "[T]he idea has been abandoned by all responsible men that western Germany should be formed as a state and that we should
make a separate peace with it."[136] It would make "deeper and more permanent
the division between east and west," with enormous economic and political
costs.[137] An opponent of Kennan's "containment" ideas, he equally opposed
linking the Marshall Plan to any sort of West European military alliance. It
would only "confirm the most serious charge which the Communists . . . make
against the Marshall Plan."[138] Yet he was also convinced that the development
of massive U.S. airpower supremacy over the Soviet Union was essential to the
success of the Plan. "Since Mr. Molotov intends to keep the Red Army in the
center of Europe," he wrote, "we have no choice but to build up and maintain
an operational striking force capable . . . of delivering a sustained assault at long
range."[139] James Reston also declared U.S. policy "weak," in that "it is not combined with a clear commitment by the United States to use its power against
any future aggressor in Europe."[140]

The view was taking hold that the Marshall Plan was a necessary but not
sufficient response to the stalemate over Germany. A free and self-sustaining
western Europe would have to be defended by a credible American military
posture. "We had better stop kidding ourselves," one official told Reston anonymously. "While we talk about recovery in Washington and London, the Communists are wrecking our recovery plans in France and Italy. We cannot deal
with this problem through economic aid alone."[141] The Marshall Plan needed
a martial plan.

The Wall Street Journal took a different line. It was critical of the economic
assumptions behind the Marshall Plan, and more broadly of the wisdom of
"the planners in Washington." Yet it also believed, as did many of the Plan's
prominent supporters, that the administration's traditional refrain—that the
Plan was a much less costly alternative to war—was ridiculous:

> There is a close relationship between the [Marshall] program and a big
> military budget, but it has never been a choice between the one and the
> other. On the contrary, the more actively we intervene in European affairs,
> the more we jostle that political powderkeg, the more it behooves us to look

to our own defenses. [The Marshall Plan] is no more an alternative to rearmament than was the lend-lease program before the last war, although the
avowed purpose of lend-lease was to keep us out of the fighting.[142]

Given the reality of the Communist threat from without and within, there
was little chance that Marshall Plan countries would follow through on making
themselves economically interdependent, and thereby undermining their self-
sufficiency, unless, in Reston's words, "they have assurance that they will not be
abandoned in the event of aggression." As to Marshall's determination to move
ahead with West German industrial revival and statehood, France "never will
cooperate . . . unless she has the backing of United States power."[143]

For his part, Stalin did not want or anticipate war at this point, but he had
begun preparing for it. Since 1945, the Soviet armed forces had been slashed
from eleven million to under four million, and military spending from 54 percent of the budget to 18 percent. In November 1947, however, the Politburo
ordered a quadrupling of tank production and a tripling of artillery production for 1948. Troop increases would follow a year later, beginning with parachute and transport divisions. The United States was "conducting a cold war,
of nerves, with the aim of blackmail," Stalin's deputy Georgy Malenkov told
Italian Socialist Pietro Nenni, but "the Soviet Union will not allow itself to be
intimidated."[144]

❖

MARSHALL, WHO REFUSED TO USE THE TERM "MARSHALL PLAN," WENT
before Congress to defend it for the first time on November 10, 1947, at a joint
meeting of the Senate Committee on Foreign Relations and the House Committee on Foreign Affairs. Feeling the strain of the campaign, he was putting
the odds of a bill's passage at no better than fifty-fifty.[145] The result was a much
starker East-versus-West framing than he had offered previously.

Marshall's testimony is striking for the brusqueness with which he passes
from asserting the "tremendous gravity" of Europe's economic problems, on
which he had previously tended to linger, to laying down the Cold War basis
for an aid plan. Which countries were in and which were out would, he said,
be determined "roughly [by] the line upon which the Anglo-American armies

coming from the west met those of the Soviet Union coming from the east." These were shades of Churchill's "iron curtain" speech the year prior. No longer was there any pretense that borders created by war were temporary, that the positioning of forces should no longer matter, that Europe could be reconstructed on principles divorced from power. "To the west of that line the nations of the continental European community have been grappling with the vast and difficult problem resulting from the war with their own national traditions, without pressure or menace from the United States," he said. But "developments . . . to the east of that line bear the unmistakable imprint of an alien hand."[146] Marshall, who had recoiled at anticommunist rhetoric in Truman's "doctrine" speech, and carefully avoided it in his own at Harvard, was now dialing it up to win over Congress. Marshall would years later claim that he "did not want to fight [for the plan] on this basis." But "Vandenberg stated we would have to fight this out on an anti-Communist line," and the senator "was our principal adviser on the basis of U.S. political problems."[147]

Truman took the torch on November 17, delivering his first "Special Message to Congress" on the Marshall Plan. "The future of the free nations of Europe hangs in the balance," he said, and "the manner in which we exert our strength . . . will have a decisive effect upon the course of civilization."[148] His much longer address of December 19 painted the consequences of failure to act in stark political terms. He warned of the need to defend freedom and the rule of law in Europe against "those who would use economic distress as a pretext for the establishment of a totalitarian state." If such forces were to gain the upper hand, "it might well compel us to modify our own economic system and to forego, for the sake of our own security, the enjoyment of many of our freedoms and privileges." This is why the United States had "so vital an interest in strengthening the belief of the people of Europe that freedom from fear and want will be achieved under free and democratic governments." It would not be easy, however. "We must not be blind to the fact that the communists have announced determined opposition to any effort to help Europe get back on its feet." He left unspecified which communists these were, but warned, none too subtly, that "attempts by any nation to prevent or sabotage European recovery for selfish ends are clearly contrary to [the] purposes" of the Charter of the new United Nations.[149] This served to rebut charges that

the United States was acting outside the U.N. while asserting that Soviet behavior was undermining it.

❖

FOLLOWING THE PRESIDENT'S DRAMATIC MARCH 1947 ADDRESS, MANY
Republicans had felt they had been maneuvered into supporting Greek and
Turkish aid by the suggestion that rejecting it meant being soft on Soviet aggression. They were determined not to let the White House corner them again.
Vandenberg at the time called for a moratorium on further aid appropriations
in that session of Congress. By November, however, the tone in Washington
had changed. Vandenberg and Marshall were meeting at Blair House, the White
House guest residence, twice a week, on average, with the media unaware of
their coordination. With a year to go until a critical presidential election, even
the leading Republican contender, New York governor Thomas Dewey, issued
a powerful statement of endorsement.[150]

"If, as Bismarck says, history occurs when things happen," *The Washington Post* observed, "the last five months have teemed with history."[151] There
had, Reston observed, been an "astonishing development of American public
opinion" toward the idea of a broad-scale European aid program. "The future
historian," Reston said, was "likely to be more impressed by the advances that
have been made this summer in getting the nations of the West together on a
common task than by anything else."[152] Yet Republican congressmen still demanded to see the situation for themselves, and their visits to Europe did much
to blunt the line that the White House was exaggerating the need for American assistance. The House of Representatives, Reston observed, was now not
just divided into parties, "but into those who went away and those who stayed
home."[153]

In November, the administration named the Marshall Plan the "European
Recovery Program" (ERP), with the word "recovery" intended to highlight the
difference with other aid initiatives since the war's end.[154] The numerous congressional hearings over the ERP that took place between the fall of 1947 and
the spring of 1948 brought out the sweeping breadth of the administration's
aims, all of which had taken form in a matter of months after Britain's imperial
collapse back in February.

Embracing nineteenth-century language that FDR had been determined to banish from diplomatic parlance, Forrestal highlighted the "imbalance" between the world's "two great powers," one that the United States needed to "redress" by rebuilding western Europe. Ambassador Douglas said that the Europeans needed to create "the type of economic federal union that we now have" in the United States, harking back to the replacement of the American Articles of Confederation with the Constitution in 1787.[155] Marshall called European integration "one of the most important considerations in the entire program."[156] John Foster Dulles said it would create a "counterbalance to the Soviet system of police states." West Germany would become part of a "solid front" whose defenses could not be "easily reduced even by Soviet power." Failure to integrate, however, would perpetuate conditions that might lead more desperate European governments to "accept a Soviet-dictated peace."[157]

But Soviet domination in Europe would not be the end of the story. The supplanting of democratic governments by totalitarian ones tied to Moscow, Douglas argued, would lead to state control of strategic economic assets that would imperil the economic security of the United States. This would in turn lead to demands at home for more government control over the American economy, which was "incompatible with the liberty" its citizens had enjoyed since the nation's founding.[158] America's political isolation would, Harriman believed, necessarily lead to soaring defense expenditures and a militarization of society. The threat extended "even to our very form of government."[159] Hoffman argued that Americans could not "expect to isolate our free economy and have it work."[160] A proliferation of "government monopolies" in Europe, said General Electric chairman Philip D. Reed, would require parallel developments in the United States that would destroy "our free enterprise system."[161]

Broadly, then, the administration's case was that it was necessary to reorganize the economies of western Europe in America's image to prevent its subjugation by Moscow, a development that would undermine the economy, security, and political system of the United States. The narrative did not go unchallenged.

Henry Wallace led the attack from the left. Far from reviving the European economy, he said, the ERP would undermine the most positive elements of it, such as nationalization of industry, social welfare expansion, and government controls on trade. The State Department, which he believed to have been captured by monopoly private interests, was determined merely to perpetuate Europe's "semicolonial dependence on the United States." Its program would cleave the continent into rival blocs, slow recovery by severing traditional East-West trade links, and fan international tensions—possibly leading to "World War III."

In the United States, Wallace said, the ERP would boost the profits of agricultural, oil, steel, and shipping "trusts" at the expense of "American workers and farmers and independent businessmen," who would have to contend with the resulting shortages, inflation, union busting, and social service cuts. In its place, Wallace advocated creation of a $50 billion fund, three times as large as the administration was calling for, run by the United Nations, which would finance a European "new deal." The primary beneficiaries would be the victims of Nazi aggression, including the Soviet Union and the east European states. The U.N. would reverse the "Germany first" orientation of the administration's plan.[162]

Ohio Republican senator and presidential candidate Robert Taft, who had been the most formidable congressional opponent of Bretton Woods three years earlier, led the attack on the ERP from the right. But his objections were less sweeping than Wallace's. Taft backed the vision of an integrated western Europe, embracing western Germany, believing that such integration was necessary to keep the United States out of entangling commitments to prop it up. Taft also supported the principle of American economic aid to western Europe, which his ally Herbert Hoover said was necessary to create "a dam against Russian aggression." Taft believed the administration's request—$17 billion ($184 billion in today's money) over four years—to be much too large, however. Aid at such a level would, he believed, create a dangerous dependency on the United States, sapping both private sector and governmental incentives to manage Europe's own resources properly.

Democrats tried to undermine Taft by arguing that he was only aiding the Soviets and their supporters. "Those who oppose the Marshall Plan, I think," said Illinois senator Scott Lucas before an eight-hundred-delegate Women's Patriotic Conference on National Defense, "should suffer some slight embarrassment in finding themselves in agreement with the Communist Party."[163] But this argument failed to sway Taft's fellow Ohioan, Republican representative Frederick Smith, who considered the Plan itself "outright communism."[164]

Free market commentator Henry Hazlitt testified similarly, advocating an aid package roughly half the size of the administration's request, but conditioned on major changes in recipient-country policies. Hazlitt wanted to roll back the tide of nationalization, trade controls, and social welfare expansion that, he argued, would further constrain output, worsen inflation, and increase Europe's "dollar shortage." Let these currencies trade freely at more appropriate exchange rates—or return to the classical gold standard, in which interest rates moved to balance imports and exports—and the "shortage" would disappear. Instead, France was making it worse by forcing exporters to swap 90 percent of their dollar proceeds for francs at an unattractive rate, discouraging production for export.

The Marshall Plan as formulated, Hazlitt believed, was only going to further the assault on private enterprise that was the primary source of Europe's economic woes. Like Wallace and the left, Hazlitt and the right also believed that the Marshall Plan would redound to the detriment of the U.S. economy, which would reel under the shortages and inflation it would trigger. Their remedies for such maladies, however, could not have been more different.[165] In essence, Wallace saw laissez-faire as the Marshall Plan's malevolent lodestar; Hazlitt, cursing the same navigational object, saw socialism.

With the vote approaching on interim aid to France ($328 million), Italy ($227 million), and Austria ($42 million),[166] Taft launched a new series of attacks, thumping Marshall aid as inflationary, fiscally reckless, and conceptually misguided. "The Administration," he said, "can't get away from the New Deal principle that Government spending is a good thing in itself." Fellow Republicans demanded answers: What do we get for our aid? Won't meddling in Europe's affairs feed the Russian narrative? Isn't China more important? And most importantly, what if France and Italy go Communist anyway? If they "fell under Communist control," Lovett told them, he would advise the president to cut off funds. But he hated having to say so publicly. The Communists, he told Marshall, would brandish his words "for propaganda purposes." Yet it was, he was sure, "necessary . . . to stop this line of questioning" before it wrecked the prospects for aid.[167]

Secretary of State George Marshall testifies on the European Recovery Program before the Senate Foreign Relations Committee, January 9, 1948.

EIGHT

SAUSAGE

"LAWS," OBSERVED NINETEENTH-CENTURY POET JOHN GODFREY SAXE, "like sausages, cease to inspire respect in proportion as we know how they are made." As 1947 drew to a close, legislating Marshall aid looked to be a case in point.

With less than a year to go before he would have to face the voters, the president's political advisers were hard at work trying to leverage Europe's crisis to his benefit. There was, White House Counsel Clark Clifford said, "political advantage" in Truman's tough approach to Russia. He was largely "invulnerable to attack" from the right, not least "because of his brilliant appointment of General Marshall," who was seen as "non-partisan and above politics." But Republicans will insist that "everything that is good about American foreign policy is Marshall" and "everything that is bad is Truman." And if "the American people identify Secretary Marshall, and not the President, as our spokesman, [it] is bad politics for 1948." Truman needed to seize control of the narrative.

The real challenge to the president, however, might not come from the right but the left—a third-party run by Henry Wallace that could tip the election to Dewey. The president needed to get "prominent liberals and progressives" on board by pointing out "that the core of the Wallace backing is made up of Communists and the fellow-travelers."[1] At the same time, Clifford assistant George Elsey said, "the non-military side of the Truman Doctrine should be accented."[2] This is where the European Recovery Program came in.

Truman, a veteran of rough political battles, was not averse, in Lippmann's words, to throwing a "partisan monkey wrench" into the ERP campaign.[3] At Clifford's advice, he picked a fight with the Republicans by linking the ERP to domestic policy, hoping to tar them for rising prices.[4] On November 17, 1947, Truman devoted three quarters of his "Special Message to the Congress" on the ERP to economic challenges on the home front.[5] Meeting the country's global obligations, Truman argued, meant getting its own house in order.

Treasury Secretary John Snyder had demanded that the ERP be fully funded. The administration would insist on balanced budgets in every year of the program.[6] But discipline also needed to be applied on prices, which rose 14.4 percent in 1947. High inflation owed partially to overvalued European currencies, which were fueling demand for American goods.[7] Truman did not make this point. Yet in his longer address on the ERP a month later, on December 19, he would argue that price increases in the United States were exacerbating Europe's plight by raising the cost of vital imports.[8]

The president called for sweeping measures to roll back inflation, including price controls, wage ceilings, rationing, export restrictions, credit restriction, and a commodity speculation crackdown. These he had, only a few weeks earlier, referred to as "police state" methods.[9] But Clifford had convinced him to propose something "absolutely unpalatable to the Republican majority" so as to pass the fault for high prices on to them.[10]

Today, a foreign "dollar shortage" and domestic inflation would be considered matters for monetary policy—central banks abroad allowing the exchange value of their currencies to adjust downward, and the Federal Reserve pushing interest rates upward at home. They would not be subjects of presidential speeches calling for dramatic fiscal and regulatory intervention. Inappropriate monetary policies in both the United States and Europe were, in fact, making the problems necessitating European aid, as well as the problems of financing it, worse.

Truman would, in his December speech, defend the Marshall Plan as a means of reducing Europe's trade deficits with the United States, "particularly by increasing European exports." That the administration was, at this point, still wedded to exchange rate "stabilization," however, suggested that the monetary dimensions of the Plan suffered from an unwillingness to confront domestic interests anxious to sustain a competitive—that is, undervalued—dollar. Snyder would in February 1948 call for some, unnamed, countries among the Marshall aid participants to devalue, subject to IMF approval, but he rejected calls from Congress to convene a special international monetary conference for the purpose of coordinating such devaluation.[11] The administration had no appetite for a new "Bretton Woods."

Lippmann chided Truman for tossing rationing and price controls into his November address, accusing him of using an international crisis to bait the Republicans into taking responsibility for the high cost of living. Instead, he said, "powers need to be given to the Federal Reserve System to check the creation of excess bank credit," as Fed chairman Marriner Eccles wanted. This was the only effective way to restrain inflation, as well as the only responsible way politically. It would allow Congress to deal with the Marshall Plan "wisely and dispassionately," rather than as part of a political package designed to help the administration shed blame for the economy.[12]

Truman's tactics infuriated Vandenberg,[13] but, as Clifford had anticipated, most of the senator's colleagues recoiled before his warnings not to allow Communist "wrecking crews" to destroy Europe's recovery. The Senate interim aid bill breezed through by a vote of 83 to 6 on December 1, 1947.[14] The House version passed by voice vote on the 11th.[15] In the resolution process to meld the two bills, a provision was added permitting aid to China, and House language directing the president to cut off aid if a country came to be dominated by the Communist Party or the Soviet Union was made more general and less prescriptive.[16] On December 15, the final bill—authorizing $522 million ($5.65 billion in today's money) in assistance for France, Italy, and Austria, $75 million less than the administration had requested—passed by voice vote in the Senate[17] and 313 to 82 in the House.

Of the eighty-two voting against, seventy were Republicans. Nearly half the no votes (forty) were from just five states: Illinois, Ohio, Michigan, Indiana, and

Truman's home state of Missouri.[18] The administration still had work to do convincing the heartland of the wisdom of the much larger Marshall aid package. On December 19, the president submitted his ERP legislation to Congress, urging ratification by April 1, 1948, when the stopgap funding would be exhausted.[19]

Simultaneous with the aid votes, Truman got what he wanted on domestic policy: trivial legislation, side by side with the interim-aid vote, authorizing only three of his ten "anti-inflation" measures (export controls, transportation controls, and conservation encouragement). These victories allowed him to pose as a hawk on inflation, an issue he cared little about, while painting the GOP Congress as do-nothings. But it came at a cost. Angry Republicans would press hard in the new year for their own domestic agenda, particularly large tax cuts, which would compete with the ERP for scarce resources.[20]

❖

TIME NAMED GEORGE MARSHALL ITS 1947 "MAN OF THE YEAR." BUT THE magazine still expected the congressional debate over his namesake plan to be "long, serious and, at times, vitriolic."[21] For his part, Vandenberg took little comfort from the victory on interim aid, given the sums involved in the main bill to come. "Marshall is certainly going to have a helluva time down here on the Hill when he gets around to his long-range plan," the senator wrote to his wife. And to Lovett: "We're headed for the storm cellar on the Marshall Plan."[22] Even if some bill might eventually satisfy Republicans, it could, Vandenberg knew, be for a much smaller, and very different, plan than the one Marshall was proposing.

With this risk in mind, Vandenberg had begun to look for sweeteners back in the fall—things that Europe might provide to the United States in return for aid. There was precedent for such requests. Congress had demanded "consideration" from Britain in return for Lend-Lease aid in 1941, in spite of Roosevelt insisting that such aid was itself in the American national interest. Vandenberg now pressed the administration to insist on consideration from Europe and its colonies as a requirement for participating in the Marshall program. This would include preferential U.S. access to strategic rare minerals, such as cobalt for aircraft engines and uranium for atomic energy. The Harriman Committee estimated that $253 million ($2.74 billion in today's money) worth of strategic materials could be made available to the United States each year from the six-teen nations and their dependencies. The State Department pledged to work for such promises from Europe.[23]

Other congressmen sought military cooperation and assistance. "[W]e ought to start getting something for our money," insisted Wisconsin Republican senator Alexander Wiley. "I want to know if any effort has been made to obtain strategic bases or materials in return for our generosity."[24] This cut embarrassingly close to Stalin's charge that establishing such bases was, in fact, the purpose of the Marshall Plan. It was also a repudiation of Roosevelt's statement at Yalta that U.S. troops would not remain in Europe for more than two years after the war.[25] But on Capitol Hill, injecting the principle of consideration into the proposal did much, as it had with Lend-Lease, to blunt the charge that the United States was just giving away its resources with no certain payoff.

And so despite the passion with which the right and the left had bludgeoned the administration's proposal in the fall, the pendulum had, by January 1948, swung in the direction of passage. Few voices of consequence were still suggesting that there should not be a recovery program of some sort, or that the United States could afford to ignore Europe's plight at little or no cost to itself. As James Reston summarized the transformation, the United States had "moved away from isolationism [and] moved farther and faster toward world responsibility than any other country in history." The only question was "whether it [had] moved far enough and fast enough to stay up with events."[26]

Helping the administration's effort was growing support from the leadership of business interest groups, who, often in defiance of their more protectionist rank and file, backed the agenda of expanding trade by shrinking the dollar gap. Acceptance of the need for the United States to import more from Europe represented a sea change in outlook, unimaginable after the First World War. The Chamber of Commerce, which had advocated tariff protection for much of its history, now highlighted "the importance of imports to the United States economy." Its president, Earl Shreve, insisted that the United States had to act as a responsible creditor, taking measures to balance trade and extending "Marshall Plan dollars . . . as a stopgap measure to tide [Europe] over temporarily." Such pronouncements reflected a growing belief among business elites that the competitive position of the United States was as secure as it had ever been and that using economic tools to contain Soviet aggression was necessary to sustain it.

Business support, however, was far from universal. The president of the National Industrial Conference Board, Virgil Jordan, denounced the Marshall Plan as "the most insidious and dangerous development of the deliberate Soviet Communist conspiracy to undermine and cripple the economic power of the United States." The "dollar shortage," he said, was "merely a semantic trick." And financial aid "as a means of outbidding Communism [was] an infantile illusion." Many business leaders saw the aid component of the Plan as inflationary. Cotton and textile interests also expressed concern at potential harm to American business, though generally in more moderate language than Jordan.[27]

Valid though Reston's observation was, isolationism had not been abandoned as an aspiration. Congressmen defended support for the Marshall Plan on the grounds that America needed to take responsibility for shaping matters abroad today so that it might be free of the obligation forevermore once the crisis had passed. The flimsy foundation on which such beliefs rested would become manifest as the Cold War progressed from crisis to crisis. Yet they would never pass from the national psyche. They would reemerge in populist tomes over half a century later, with the implosion of communism as a political force.[28]

✦

TWO PRACTICAL QUESTIONS CAME TO DOMINATE LEGISLATIVE DEBATE over the Marshall Plan: who should run it, and how big it should be.

With respect to the program's management, conflict erupted early on over the role of the State Department. For Republicans, the notion of Truman's foreign service bureaucrats remaking European economies was a nonstarter. It meant incompetence, inefficiency, and a reliance on meddling over markets. It would undermine America's economy as well as Europe's. In response, the Herter Committee and others came together around the idea of creating a new independent agency, to be run by prominent individuals with business backgrounds, recruited from outside government. The White House split over the scope for compromise. Treasury supported the idea. State, which had always expected to run the program, was alarmed.

Lovett began searching for common ground back in September 1947, when he appointed a special committee under the chairmanship of Lincoln Gordon, a former director of the Civilian Production Administration's Bureau of Reconversion Priorities, to draft an administrative blueprint for the ERP. Reporting one month later, it called, Solomon-like, for management of the program to be split. An Economic Cooperation Administration (ECA) would be created to handle operational issues, while decisions related to "foreign policy" would remain with the State Department. Kennan feared that "the operation of the ERP administration will make it difficult for this Department itself to conduct any incisive and vigorous policy with relation to Europe,"[29] but Marshall embraced the proposal as the best he was likely to get.

While insisting that the strategic direction of the ERP, being a matter of foreign policy, had to remain with State, Marshall advised the president to call for lodging "direct operational responsibility for this hazardous and temporary undertaking" outside the department.[30] There was, Clifford argued, "an element of political benefit" to Truman in giving ground to Congress. If Republicans wanted a separate body to implement the program, and problems emerged, the president could blame Congress.[31]

Republicans pressed to keep the State Department at arm's length, arguing that its interference would make it impossible to recruit the best brains and managerial talent to run the ECA. Marshall, however, fought to maintain State's strategic oversight. There cannot, he insisted before the Senate Foreign Relations Committee on January 8, 1948, be "two secretaries of state." "The whole procedure of this program certainly directly affects the foreign relations of the United States," he told the House Committee on Foreign Affairs four days later.[32] In the end, splitting responsibility between the State Department, which would set policy, and the ECA, which would control operations, would prove the only politically viable solution.[33]

There remained the matter, however, of who would run the ECA. Truman, determined to avoid any possibility of conflict between State and the ECA, pressed for Acheson or Clayton. Republican majority whip Kenneth Wherry assailed Acheson on the Senate floor for having supported Bretton Woods and the Morgenthau Plan, the latter of which had cost the United States "more than $20 billion." That was now "out of the window and Mr. Acheson is out of the

Government, and I think that is a good thing."[34] Vandenberg insisted on recruit-ing someone "from the outside business world," someone with "particularly persuasive economic credentials unrelated to diplomacy."[35] Clayton, of course, had had a successful career in private business, but his time in two Democratic administrations disqualified him politically. "The overriding Congressional de-sire," Vandenberg told Marshall, is that the ERP administrator come to the job "not via the State Department."[36] This principle did much to conciliate Taft, who praised the final Senate bill as "infinitely more acceptable" than the White House version. Acheson and Clayton were out. Yet the question of who would run the ECA would not be resolved until after the legislative fight ended.

With regard to funding, the administration pushed for $17 billion over four years—at the upper end of the Harriman Committee estimate of what was needed. "Now it does seem to me that we can afford, over a four-year period, to risk 17 billions for peace," Truman said at a January 29 press conference. It was $4 billion less than the 1948 defense budget, but "less than one-fourth of the half-year that was made a rescission under war."[37] It was also $12.2 billion less than what the sixteen European participants had wanted in Paris, and $2.3 billion less than what they ultimately settled on under friendly American guid-ance.

Vandenberg approved Truman's headline figure, but thought it too large for Congress to swallow in one bite. He wanted the funds doled out in tranches that would have to be approved each year. The State Department, however, hated the idea of having to return to Congress annually for a new multibillion-dollar appropriation. Marshall scolded Congress to do the job in full "or don't undertake it at all."[38]

The White House ultimately bowed to political reality, narrowing its re-quest to $6.8 billion for the fifteen months from April 1, 1948, to June 30, 1949—the end of the following fiscal year. Hoover, however, the great rallying figure for the anti-ERP forces, called on Vandenberg to cut the initial appropri-ation to $4 billion.[39] Taft also threatened to press for delay until the next fiscal year, starting July 1. By transforming a fifteen-month program into a twelve-month one, this would cut the price tag by 25 percent, to $5.1 billion.

❖

IT WAS ANOTHER BLEAK WINTER IN EUROPE. BRITAIN'S RESERVES HAD fallen to $2.4 billion ($24 billion in today's money) in dollars, gold, and assorted "unexhausted credits." They were expected to run dry by the summer. "After that, it will just be impossible to buy either the food or the raw materials necessary for Britain to eat and work," said *The Economist*. "The aspect of starvation and mass unemployment is now alarmingly close." [40]

Europeans followed the politics of the Marshall Plan with great interest. Yet public opinion was split as to the main American objective behind the plan. In both France and Britain, one in four thought it was humanitarian; the same proportion thought it was economic self-interest. One in seven believed it was to stop Communism. Italians were more generous: one in three thought the main motive was humanitarian. [41] The Dutch were skeptical: only one in ten believed this. Four times as many believed it was economic self-interest. [42]

European governments, for their part, were sensitive to both the substance and politics of the aid conditions being debated in Washington. The CEEC delegation to Washington, informally known as "the European Group," several times expressed written concern about how the U.S. government might restrict the way in which their countries spend the proceeds of the domestic sale of American aid supplies—what became known as counterpart funds. "All those [in Europe] who . . . have continually opposed the so-called 'Marshall Plan,'" said an October 27, 1947, European Group memo to the State Department, "will seek to show that the existence of these funds is capable of conferring upon the U.S. considerable powers infringing [our] independence." They urged, therefore, that recipient governments, rather than an American agency, be permitted to control the allocation of such funds, in accordance with any agreements reached with the U.S. government. [43]

The Kremlin viewed European enthusiasm for the Marshall Plan with alarm. In a Top Secret memorandum to Stalin on January 26, 1948, Central Committee AgitProp chief Suslov reported on the proceedings of the International Conference of Socialist Parties in Antwerp. "The ruling [democratic] socialist parties" of western Europe, he wrote, "view the Marshall Plan as an almost miraculous rescue," and argued fiercely with their Czech and Polish counterparts against letting "ideological debate [hinder] rapid implementation."

Suslov warned that the Western Socialists had "one specific purpose—to organize opposition to the activities of the Communist Party."[44] A bulletin of the Soviet Military Administration in Germany expressed equal concern about developments in Germany. "Schumacher and his clique, standing at the head of the SPD, are dancing to the American tune."[45]

Another Central Committee report concluded that "the collusion of the Anglo-American imperialists on the Germany questions [that] took place after the breakdown of the London conference . . . on the basis of a refusal to cooperate with the Soviet Union" had led to "a division of Germany," with "West Germany becoming a half-colony dependent on America and serving its imperialist plans." The forces of "German reaction"—that is, the " 'two Christian parties' " (the CDU and CSU)—were now "consolidat[ing] power . . . on the basis of the acceptance of the 'Marshall Plan.' "[46]

A Russian magazine described Marshall as a "belligerent old man" set on destroying the U.N. and starting "a new criminal war. " Truman was likened to Hitler. The TASS news agency and Moscow radio directed a regular stream of vitriol at the Marshall Plan, which was then spread through Communist Party mouthpieces in Bulgaria, Czechoslovakia, Romania, Hungary, Poland, Albania, Yugoslavia, Italy, and elsewhere. The CIA monitored the broadcasts assiduously. State Department, War Department, and Office of Naval Intelligence officials in Europe reported back to Washington on developments in anti-American propaganda, which Voice of America radio transmissions then aimed to counter.

Administration officials, Reston noted, were growing alarmed over what they saw as Washington's incapacitation in the face of a disciplined and relentless Soviet campaign to spread its foreign policy through satellite governments. "[T]he classic doctrine of non-intervention," these officials were concluding, "is a hazardous theory that requires reconsideration in the light of modern politics and ballistics." Conservative congressmen, such as Massachusetts senator Henry Cabot Lodge, Jr., began proposing funds to translate American newspapers for European distribution, buy ad space in European media, and boost VOA range through investment in medium- and long-wave transmission. Though in the early fall there had been insufficient support to get a House bill boosting counter-Soviet VOA activities to the Senate floor, by the new year the atmosphere had changed dramatically. The Senate passed the bill unanimously on January 16, 1948. Truman signed it into law on the 28th.[47]

Over the first quarter of 1948, Congress held frequent hearings into the Marshall Plan. Vandenberg vested enormous importance in them, determined as he was to compel public figures opining on the *idea* of a recovery program to state unequivocally what they actually wanted Congress to *do*. "We won't hesitate to subpoena," Vandenberg said, if they did not volunteer to clarify and defend their views publicly. This was representative democracy at its most robust, with citizens compelled to participate in order to ensure that the decisions taken had the fingerprints of all who were claiming, through the power of the media, to know what the government should do.

Vandenberg proved a master at eliciting the testimony his skeptical colleagues needed to hear. Frequently, he effectively delivered the testimony himself, leaving the witnesses to agree with him enthusiastically.

"As I understand you," he said to Army Secretary Kenneth Royall during his Senate testimony on January 15, "what you were saying is that if it were not for the prospect of organized stabilization as a source of security you envision an alternative situation which would require immediate and measurable appropriations for larger-scale national armaments than have been thus far requested?"

"That is correct, sir," Royall responded.

"Put still more bluntly, is it fair to say that your judgment offers us the choice, in part, between appropriations for economic cooperation on the one hand, or greater appropriations for military purposes in the interests of our ultimate national security?"

"That is my judgment," offered Royall.[48]

One of the many remarkable aspects of the debate was the outsized role of the House, which is normally the junior partner to the Senate in matters of foreign relations. But the central place of money in the Marshall initiative thrust the House, owing to its "power of the purse,"[49] into the position of full partner. In total, the House Foreign Affairs Committee would hear testimony from twenty-five administration spokesmen, and hear or receive testimony from 150

private citizens. The transcripts filled 2,296 pages. The Senate Foreign Relations Committee would hear roughly half as much testimony: nine governmental and eighty-six other witnesses, generating 1,466 pages.[50]

The scope of the questioning was exhaustive: economics, administration,
geopolitics, and military considerations. How much aid should there be? In
grants? In loans? On what time scale? What should be the aims? What strings
should be attached? Who should run the program? How will currencies be
stabilized? How will inflation be controlled? How will trade be revived? How
will Germany be handled? How will the Russians react? How will we deal with
them?

In his House testimony on January 12, Marshall tried to train the spotlight
on Soviet intentions by quoting CPSU Central Committee secretary Andrei
Zhdanov: "As to the USSR, it will bend every effort in order that this plan be
doomed to failure." Four days later, on January 16, the British Foreign Office
revealed a copy of a secret Cominform document entitled "Protocol M," laying
out a scheme to undermine the Marshall Plan through mass worker strikes in
western Germany. The timing could not have been better for the White House,
as the document buttressed Marshall's claims of an "alien hand" working to
undermine European recovery. Moscow, however, attacked the document as
a forgery. Upon conclusion of the American legislative drama, an embarrassed
British intelligence service would declare that it had been.[51]

The theme of war and peace was a constant in the hearings. Ambassador
Douglas, testifying on January 9, echoed Marshall's argument that the alternative to a recovery program was "continued and larger expenditures for national defense."[52] Forrestal, elevated to defense secretary in September 1947,
said the ERP would be "far less expensive than standing isolated and alone in
an unfriendly world."[53] On the 20th he told the House that failed legislation
would mean moving the political frontier "from Europe to somewhere in the
Atlantic Ocean."[54] John Foster Dulles, who would become Dewey's foreign
policy adviser in the coming presidential campaign, told the Senate that if
France were left to go communist, Congress would be hit with a military appropriations request that would make the ERP bill look "like a bag of pea-
nuts."[55]

But Congress still wasn't buying the either-or, aid-or-war, framing. Might the aid plan itself "possibly lead to war?" Rep. Lawrence Smith (R-WI) asked the secretary of state. No, Marshall insisted—to the contrary, it should "avoid the issue." Yet Smith's concern was sound. If Congress backed the ERP, ever greater political and economic differences would come to define the nations that found themselves on opposing sides of the line Marshall referred to in his November testimony. It took no leap of imagination to conclude that the hardening of such differences would, in short order, take on a military dimension, as each side bound together—with its American or Soviet patron—to prevent the other encroaching into its prerogatives.

Some congressmen urged the secretary of state to begin preparing for war. Rep. Chester Merrow (R-NH) suggested to Marshall that the United States was, in "building those countries up" on the western side of his line, making them into "rich prizes for an aggressor." The Soviet Union, he pointed out, had "three times the fighting planes that we have." The United States, he said, needed urgently to "develop an air force that could make our will felt around the world." Otherwise, the time "may come when the 16 nations will be overwhelmed and we can do nothing about it."[56]

Not all the Plan's supporters were singing from Marshall's hymn sheet. Financier-philanthropist Bernard Baruch, testifying on January 19, said that the Marshall Plan was no more than a good start; it had to be accompanied by political and military union in western Europe. The United States and its European allies, he argued, should "mutually guarantee . . . against aggression. By guarantee, I mean a firm promise to go to war in joint defense if any of them are attacked."[57] Such testimony was a distinctly discordant note for an administration anxious to highlight a prospective peace dividend.

Across the Atlantic, however, Bevin echoed Baruch. "I have done and will continue to do all I can to bring the Marshall Plan to fruition," he said. "But essential though it is, progress in the economic field will not in itself suffice to call a halt to the Russian threat."[58] "The time is ripe for the consolidation of western Europe," he declared. "We are entitled to organize kindred souls in the West, just as [the Soviets] have organized kindred souls in the East."[59] As Reston would point out, such an organization would require American military backing.[60]

The price tag for the Marshall Plan was also a major theme of the hearings.

In the debate over cost, Congress was not, strictly speaking, vetting the administration's estimate of the sums needed to generate European recovery so much as scrutinizing the administration's estimate of what Congress was willing to authorize. Yet sums were put forth in testimony as the finished products of a great scientific exercise and defended as if they represented "liberty itself."[61] One administration official boasted to Reston that, to prepare for a presentation before Vandenberg's committee, his statisticians had made forty thousand calculations to back a single conclusion.[62]

Reston's source was most likely the leader of the statisticians, Paul Nitze, who, in Clayton's words, knew "more about the Marshall Plan than perhaps any other individual" in Washington. Using primitive computers borrowed from the Prudential Life Insurance company, Nitze and his staff churned out the mass of calculations and charts that formed the "Brown Books" on recipient countries' finances, production, and needs. Embodying the irony of the capitalist planner, Nitze was the man who determined how much rice, rubber, iron, and the like would be required where and when and what it would all cost.

As the repository of the vast mass of numbers behind the Marshall Plan, he was naturally a man whom its opponents sought to discredit. Rep. John Taber (R-NY) went so far as to solicit, through a secret intermediary, "derogatory information" on him from the FBI. What came back was speculation that his parents were Communists. At hearings on how to appropriate aid, Taber set out to undermine Nitze's aura as a data wizard by insisting on going alphabetically through every country, and then commodity, in his Brown Books and forcing him to justify each figure from memory. He got as far as Austrian commodities beginning with "p," which revealed Nitze's inability to recount supply and demand estimates for pulses. "The man knows nothing!" shouted Taber. During the weeks of hearings, covering forty-three sessions, Nitze lost fifteen pounds from stress and overwork.[63]

Yet on February 21, a major legislative hurdle was cleared. Vandenberg reported the ERP bill out of his committee, unanimously, to the full Senate for a vote. In the course of the hearings, he had forced two key concessions from the White House: enabling independent administration of the program, and eliminating the politically toxic $17 billion four-year price tag.

He slashed this figure to a less challenging $5.3 billion initial one-year appropriation, without brooking any challenge to the White House's full estimate of what was needed.

Meanwhile, over in Europe, events were helping to boost congressional support.

Communist rally in Prague after the party takes power in a coup, February 1948.

NINE

SUBVERSION

DESPITE HAVING A MUTUAL ASSISTANCE TREATY WITH THE USSR, CZECHO-slovakia, which bordered both western Germany and Ukraine, was a weak link in Stalin's defensive perimeter. Its Communists trumpeted pursuit of the country's "own path" to socialism, which explained why they enjoyed greater popular support there than elsewhere in the East. But the United States and Britain had, according to a European Department official of the Soviet Foreign Ministry, worryingly "established their own centers of influence" in the country. "Reactionary forces" had become "more active in the struggle against progressive forces in the country"—that is, the Communists.[1] Given that Czechoslovakia was now one of the main sources of uranium for Moscow's atomic weapons program,[2] Stalin was on alert for signs of trouble.

These signs had been building since the previous summer. On the eve of the Cominform gathering in September 1947, Molotov had complained to Zhdanov about the unreliability of the Czechoslovak armed forces, and ordered him to raise the matter in Szklarska Poręba. Masaryk, meanwhile, continued to lament being prohibited from going to Paris in July. "We know that the United States will not consider us its favorite sons after the rejection of the Marshall Plan," he told the Czech paper *Svobodné Slovo* in October, "but we hope they will not completely forsake us."[3] In December, the Soviet embassy in Prague cabled Moscow about troubling political developments: "Reactionary elements within the country, actively supported by representatives of the West, [believe] that the parties of the right will receive a majority at the forthcoming [May 1948] elections and that the communists will be thrown out of the government." Early in the new year, the National Socialists, the second largest party behind the Communists, expressed public regret about not having joined in the Marshall Plan.[4] Elements in the Communist Party now began agitating for Moscow to intervene. Stalin, who had been careful not to hand the West propaganda opportunities or to provoke anti-Communist underground forces in the East, decided it was now time to make clear to which bloc the country belonged.

This is what Kennan had warned would happen back in November. "As long as communist political power was advancing in Europe, it was advantageous to the Russians to allow to the Czechs the outer appearances of freedom." It would permit the Czechs "to serve as bait for the nations further west." But once the "danger of the political movement proceeding in the other direction" became apparent in Moscow, the Russians would no longer be able to "afford this luxury." Czechoslovakia could stir liberal democratic forces elsewhere in the East. At that point, the Russians will "clamp down completely on Czechoslovakia," even though they "will try to keep their hand well concealed and leave us no grounds for formal protest."[5]

On February 18, 1948, the four Czechoslovak National Socialist ministers—Zenkl, Ripka, Drtina, and Education Minister Jaroslav Stránský—went to see Beneš to express their alarm over the Communist purging of the Interior Ministry. Hard-line minister Václav Nosek was systematically replacing police commissioners with party loyalists, ignoring protests that his actions were illegal.[6] Above all else, Zenkl explained, it was "absolutely necessary to stop the communization of the police" and the distribution of their arms and ammunition. The National Socialists, Populists, and Slovak Democrats would therefore resign their twelve ministerial posts, amounting to half the cabinet, in advance of the Communist union congress on the 22nd. The mass resignation would prevent the Communists from shifting the spotlight from security to nationalization of industry, an issue on which they would gain support from the left-wing Social Democrats. The ministers wanted Beneš to demand the resignation of the remaining cabinet members from Gottwald, paving the way for either a new government that would reverse the security measures or new elections.

Beneš, who had previously said that he "would not stand for non-Communist parties being eaten up one by one as had occurred in other eastern European countries,"[7] buoyed them by agreeing to back new elections. The Communists, he said, would never give way, as they could not win elections without controlling the police. As for the Russians who were orchestrating the crisis, the brutal way they had blocked Marshall aid for the country still angered him. The Bolsheviks "shriek against Western imperialism to distract attention from their own aggressive expansionism," Beneš said. "They are provoking the whole world" with their behavior.[8]

The Soviet deputy foreign minister arrived in Prague unannounced the following day, February 19. Officially, Valerian Zorin was on a mission to inspect Russian grain supplies. Masaryk and Ripka were incredulous. They understood that Zorin's presence was meant to demonstrate Moscow's support for the new Communist security measures.

Zorin, according to Ambassador Steinhardt, was "not a forceful, door-slamming type" like Vyshinsky. But he delivered his boss' messages clearly enough. Meeting with Gottwald, the Russian told him the time had come to "be firmer" and to stop making "concessions to those on the right." The premier had "to be ready for decisive action and for the possibility of breaching the formal stipulations of the constitution and the laws as they stand."

Gottwald, Zorin reported back to Molotov, did not want to move against the president, who had wide popular support. The premier still clung, Zorin lamented, to "the idea of a normal, parliamentary path . . . without any collisions." Yet he was ready to act more forcefully with Moscow's support. Gottwald wanted Soviet troop maneuvers on the country's borders to pressure Beneš. Stalin, however, still acting in accordance with Kennan's script, refused to provide such overt cover. As Washington had neither the will nor the means to resist, there was no need to show his hand: he would rely on the Secret Police he had sent into Prague a few days earlier. Communist minister of information Václav Kopecký, however, declared that the Red Army was massed on the frontiers, ready to intervene against the "reaction." The Soviet embassy remained silent.

On February 20, with no sign that the Communists would abandon their takeover of the police, the twelve non-Communist ministers submitted their resignations. Gottwald rejoiced at the naïveté of their tactic. "I could not believe it would be so easy. . . . I prayed that this stupidity over the resignations would go on and that they would not change their minds." He denounced them publicly as "lackeys of domestic and foreign reaction, traitors to the nation" who could never be part of a new government. They want, he said, to make the country "a paradise for all the spies and saboteurs sent among us from abroad against our Republic and our allies, particularly against the Soviet Union."

Beneš tried to reassure the democrats. "Naturally, I shall not accept your resignation[s]," he told the anxious ministers. "The Communists must give in," he insisted. "I will not compromise." But the president had also been speaking to Gottwald, and his public comments were less clear cut. He told the press he would accept neither "a Cabinet of technicians"—which Gottwald falsely claimed his opponents wanted to impose—nor one without Communists. There was no defense of the democrats, nor any demand that the *entire* cabinet resign.

Meanwhile, the Communists were organizing Bolshevik-style "Committees of Action" around the country and ordering police officials to pledge their "loyal[ty] to the Government of Klement Gottwald" and to "obey all the orders of the Minister of the Interior." Workers were instructed to attend Communist rallies around the country. Those who refused were locked out or beaten. Ripka found the rhythmic ovations at the events terrifyingly similar to those delivered at demonstrations staged by the Nazi occupiers just a few years earlier.

On February 21, Gottwald told Beneš that if he refused to accept the resignations and allow the formation of a Communist government there would be a general strike and workers' militias in the streets. "Then there is also the Soviet Union!" he added pointedly.[9] The next day, Zorin and the entire Soviet embassy staff attended a Communist-organized congress of the Union of Soviet-Czechoslovak Friendship, timed to commemorate the thirtieth anniversary of the Red Army. Gottwald used the occasion to blast "the Western imperialists" who were "trying to revive capitalism" and fuel German "irredentism." It was, he said, necessary to stand with the country's Soviet ally. "The law," he closed, "should strike all those who undermine the basis of our foreign policy." *Pravda* and Radio Moscow backed the Czech Communists unreservedly, which was duly reported in the Czech Communist press. Still, Beneš insisted to the National Socialist ministers that he would "not give way" to a "*coup d'état*" or "second Munich."

But Beneš was ill and infirm, and the pressure around him was growing by the hour. On February 23, Minister of Defense General Ludvík Svoboda declared that the Army "stands today, and will stand tomorrow, beside the U.S.S.R. and its other allies, to guarantee the security of our dear Czechoslovak Republic." The Communist-controlled Interior Ministry occupied the offices of the non-Communist press, instituting measures to prevent them "from disturbing public opinion by lies and provocations." By the 25th, they were taking the same editorial line as Moscow and the Communists.

Gottwald secured the cooperation of rebel members of the non-Communist parties, effectively making them part of his own party, and submitted a new cabinet list to the president. A communiqué declared the commitment of the new "Renovated National Front" to "the purging of the political parties, whose responsible leaders have abandoned the principles of the National Front," and to "tighten[ing] the alliance with the Soviet Union and the other Slav States." Steinhardt cabled Washington, comparing Gottwald's political tactics to those of Hitler.[10] Bohlen had years earlier opined that "a non-Communist Premier with Communist ministers would be like a woman trying to stay half-pregnant,"[11] but Gottwald's action suggested that a Communist premier with non-Communist ministers was also implausible.

At noon on February 25, to the shock of the now former National Socialist ministers, the country learned from the radio that Beneš had accepted their resignations. Telephoning his office, Ripka would be told only that the president had approved Gottwald's cabinet list. Swearing in the new ministers on the 27th, Beneš would explain that he was trying to prevent the crisis escalating. "[T]he people were so divided that everything might end in confusion." The chief of his Chancellery, Jaromír Smutný, later told foreign journalists that the president had "wanted to avoid the danger of a civil war."[12] Beneš would resign a few months later, on June 7. Gottwald would be elected president the following week.

"Ten years ago Czechoslovakia fell under the sword of the hereditary enemy who had threatened her throughout the centuries," Ripka wrote. "In 1948 she was subjected by Soviet Russia, her ally, from whom she had expected aid and protection against the German danger."[13] The Czech democrats had made a grievous miscalculation—both that a postwar Germany would threaten her security and that the Soviet Union would guarantee it.

In the weeks following the coup, there would be mass purges and arrests. These were followed by a rewriting of the constitution and rigged parliamentary elections. Although non-Communists had garnered 62 percent of the vote in the last free elections, in May 1946, Gottwald's power grab took place in a general atmosphere of resigned calm. A prewar Czechoslovak population—with 357,000 Jews and 2.5 million Sudeten Germans, the cosmopolitan commercial and industrial backbone of the country—might have offered more spirited resistance. But the postwar population, now dominated by small farmers and artisans, was more inclined, as they had been during the war, to adapt than to fight.[14]

Masaryk accepted reappointment as foreign minister, explaining to Steinhardt tearfully that he wanted "to soften the impact of Communist ruthlessness . . . and perhaps aid others in leaving the country."[15] But his tenure was brief. In the early morning of March 10, his body was found on the ground below his third-story office in the Foreign Ministry. Steinhardt and Ripka thought it was suicide. Drtina had tried to kill himself in a similar fashion only two weeks prior.[16] A forensic investigation by the Prague police over half a century later, however, concluded what many had believed at the time, that Masaryk had been pushed.[17] An earlier journalist's investigation also concluded that the Soviets and the Czech Communists knew that Masaryk had been planning to flee the country, which threatened to turn him into an embarrassing cause célèbre. They therefore took preventive action.[18] Ripka himself only escaped, to France, by dint of some remarkable good timing and fortune.[19]

Food protest in Vienna, May 14, 1947.

Secretary of State George Marshall before giving his speech on the European economic crisis at Harvard University, June 5, 1947.

Secretary of State George Marshall testifying on the European Recovery Program before the Senate Committee on Foreign Relations, probably on January 8, 1948.

President Truman being briefed in advance of the London Council of Foreign Ministers meeting, November 13, 1947. From left to right: President Truman, Under Secretary of State Robert Lovett, Director of the Policy Planning Staff of the State Department George Kennan, and State Department counselor Charles Bohlen.

Election propaganda in Rome, c. February 1948. The poster on top left says "Help from America—be it coal, food, medicines—helps us help ourselves." Below, a poster for the Italian Anarchists Federation; to the right, a poster for the Italian Republican Party.

Communist demonstration against the Marshall Plan in Berlin. Visible part of the sign on the left reads "Create jobs through trade with the east!" Sign on the right says "Against the Marshall Plan. Creates unemployment, misery."

A large crowd in the Old Square of Prague listens to Communist Czechoslovak Prime Minister Klement Gottwald following the resignation of the coalition government's non-Communist ministers, February 1948.

A U.S. C-47 cargo plane with food and other relief supplies approaches Berlin's Tempel-hof Airport, breaking the Soviet blockade of overland routes into the western sectors, 1948.

Mass anti-communist rally organized by Berlin's democratic socialist parties, 1948.

Marshall Plan aid shipment at the port of Rotterdam, c. early 1949.

Secretary of State Dean Acheson signs the North Atlantic Treaty, NATO's founding act, in Washington on April 4, 1949, a year and a day after President Truman signed the Marshall aid legislation. Standing beside him, from left to right: Vice President Alben Barkley, President Harry Truman, and State Department Treaty Advisor John Foley. In the background, from left to right: British Foreign Minister Ernest Bevin, Norwegian Foreign Minister Halvard Lange, and Luxembourg Foreign Minister Joseph Bech.

KENNAN LATER WROTE THAT MASARYK'S DEATH "DRAMATIZED, AS FEW other things could have, the significance of what had just occurred" in Prague.[20] The Communist Clementis took over as foreign minister. In short order, Washington's carefully assembled intelligence network in the country was dismantled, its leaders executed.[21]

The coup raised the uncomfortable question, "Who lost Czechoslovakia?" As Office of European Affairs director John Hickerson put it to Marshall, the "absence of any sign of friendly external force was undoubtedly a major factor in the limp Czech collapse."[22] Unlike in Poland, it had not been preordained that the country would be swallowed by the Russian Bear. Czechoslovakia had emerged from the war unaligned. Hitler and Stalin had not allocated it in their pact; Stalin and Churchill had not included it in their "percentages" deal; the Allies had not discussed its orientation at Yalta or Potsdam; both the Soviets and the Americans had liberated it. Kennan had thought it inevitable that Moscow, which saw "only vassals and enemies" near its borders, would do whatever was required to make it one of the former. But others disagreed. Hawkish scholar and State Department official Eugene Rostow later reflected that "failure to deter the Communist takeover of Czechoslovakia in 1948 was one of the most serious mistakes of our foreign policy since the war." Allen Dulles, who would become director of the CIA five years later, blamed the calamity on incompetent American diplomacy and intelligence operations.[23]

Whatever cards Washington had to play, diplomatically and militarily, it gave up most of them in 1945. "I believe that Russia wants to and will cooperate" in Czechoslovakia, Roosevelt told Masaryk. Red Army officials, however, made clear to their Czech counterparts that the country would be brought within the Soviet sphere. Beneš was ordered, under the threat of losing Czech territory, to cut ties with the Polish government-in-exile in London, with whom he had braved the war years, and to recognize the Soviet-controlled Lublin Poles.[24] What capacity the U.S. Army had to countervail was circumscribed by the decision of Generals Marshall and Eisenhower to stop its advance fifty miles west of Prague.[25]

The Red Army, which had been 150 miles further from the Czech capital than Patton, marched into Prague on May 9. It was one of its easier victories, but also one of great subsequent historical significance. "We could have liberated Prague," lamented one bitter U.S. embassy official. "After the war we spent a lot of time trying to convince the Czechs that they weren't part of the East Bloc. But no matter what we said the Soviets came to Prague first."[26] The Czech Communists used this to great advantage, proclaiming it as evidence that only the Russians cared about the Prague citizens being brutalized by the Nazis.

In the months that followed, the War Department agitated for a complete withdrawal of U.S. troops from Czechoslovakia. There was, Murphy said from Germany on August 31, no "overriding political necessity" for their presence. Steinhardt was appalled, arguing that it would make the Czechs "feel that they had been morally as well as physically abandoned by the Americans at the very time they were just beginning to show signs of courage in standing up to the Russians." No one knew for sure how many Soviet troops were in the country at the time, but estimates ran from 165,000 to more than twice that.[27] Truman decided to write to Stalin on November 2 proposing a simultaneous American and Soviet withdrawal by December 1. Given that such a deal would tip the military balance of power in the country overwhelmingly to the Soviets, who would have hundreds of thousands of soldiers available near its borders to smother the country as necessary, Stalin agreed.

Beneš was thrilled to see the foreign forces leave his country, assuming naively that it signaled Stalin's commitment to its independence. He as well as Steinhardt also thought, wrongly, that Gottwald and his fellow Communists were Czech patriots—patriots who would be content to take a backseat in government, rather than appeal to Stalin to put them in front and kick the democrats out. By the summer of 1946, however, it had become clear to Beneš and Masaryk that the Communists were taking orders from Moscow, and that keeping the Red Army out was worth more than bringing U.S. aid in. They had seen the fate of the non-Communist London-based Polish government-in-exile, at Moscow's hands.

When at a Paris gathering of foreign ministers in August 1946 Masaryk applauded Vyshinky's condemnation of American loan offers as "economic enslavement," Byrnes and the State Department turned against them. Beneš begged Steinhardt to understand that such regrettable public gestures were the price his country paid for being permitted a measure of domestic democracy.

But with Masaryk's behavior being called out in *The New York Times*, and the Communists, who railed against "dollar imperialism," blocking any progress on compensating Americans for nationalized property, there was no way diplomatically to repair the breach.[28]

When the following summer the Czechs, under orders from Stalin, rejected the Marshall Plan, the State Department wrote them off as a natural part of the Communist East. It did so despite important voices arguing otherwise. The U.S. chargé in Prague, John Bruins, said that "80 percent of Czech people favor western style democracy over Communism," and pleaded for the United States to help "consolidate this pro-western sentiment."[29] Steinhardt pointed out that "nearly 80 percent of [the] country's total foreign trade is still with [the] west."[30] Masaryk begged Washington to understand the "difficult situation caused by [Czechoslovakia's] contiguity to the Soviet sphere."[31] His pleas fell on deaf ears. Division of Central European Affairs chief James (Jimmie) Riddleberger dismissed him as "weak or blind."[32]

This thinking was both self-justifying and self-fulfilling. The State Department relied on it to make the case, to themselves and the rest of the world, that they could not help those who would not help themselves. After all, Kennan, Clayton, and Marshall had attached this fundamental principle to the Marshall Plan. The initiative had to come from Europeans themselves. America could not save nations that had lost the will to fight. This was a convenient rationalization, as it meant that the State Department had not "lost Czechoslovakia." The country, rather, never had what it took to be a Marshall Plan state.

As for the Czechs, abandoned as they were by the West in 1938, they saw the State Department's *froideur* as confirmation that America was still uninterested in them. Many saw its growing support for rapid German recovery as outright hostility toward their interests. Masaryk and his fellow democrats believed they had no alternative but to reach an accommodation with Moscow. That they could not, in the end, do so showed starkly how seriously Stalin took the threat to his eastern security buffer represented by the Marshall Plan; he could not ultimately abide non-Communists having any real power in the country.

"Those goddamn Americans," Ripka said after agreeing to a grain deal with Moscow in December 1947:

It's because of them that I've had to come here to sign on the dotted line. . . .
We told the Americans, and asked for 200,000 or 300,000 tons of wheat.
And these idiots started the usual blackmail. . . . At this point, Gottwald
got in touch with Stalin, [who] immediately promised us the required
wheat. . . . [T]hese idiots in Washington have driven us straight into the
Stalinist camp. . . . The fact that not America but Russia has saved us from
starvation will have a tremendous effect inside Czechoslovakia—even
among the people whose sympathies are with the West rather than with
Moscow.[33]

It is of course far from clear that Washington could have prevented the collapse of democracy in Czechoslovakia. Stalin may well have used force to ensure it, and the United States would have had few attractive options to counter
it. But the converse *is* clear—that democracy could not have survived without
diplomatic and economic assistance from Washington.

When the Communist putsch came in February 1948, Marshall was
unmoved. "[A] seizure of power by the Communist Party in Czechoslovakia would not materially alter . . . the situation which has existed in the last
three years," he wrote to Caffery in Paris on the 24th, the day before Beneš
gave Gottwald the green light to form a new government. "Czechoslovakia has
faithfully followed the Soviet line in the United Nations and elsewhere, and the
establishment of a Communist regime would merely crystallize and confirm
for the future previous Czech policy." Marshall was only "concerned about the
probable repercussions in Western European countries."[34]

In acknowledgment of the role the Marshall Plan had played in Moscow's
toppling of the Czechoslovak government, Washington became more cautious
with aid to avoid giving it a pretext for interference in "border states." Stalin
told a Finnish delegation in 1945 that Soviet policy toward their country was
one of "generosity by calculation."[35] But such forbearance, Washington knew,
would cease once it failed a cost-benefit test. After receiving $35 million in
U.S. Export-Import Bank credits in 1945–46 ($452 million in today's money),
Finland would thenceforth receive only warm indications of American regard
and respect for its "special position." Further large loans, the State Department reasoned, risked provoking Soviet "counter-measures" that would reduce

"Finland's freedom of action and access to the west." Even after the Marshall Plan had been wound down in 1952, the National Security Council would warn of the need to steer clear of any action that could give rise to "drastic Soviet measures inimical to Finnish independence."[36]

In the case of Tito's Communist Yugoslavia, however, which shared no border with the Soviet Union, Washington *ramped up* economic and military assistance, in line with Kennan's urging, to help deepen the rupture with Moscow. The aid at times included a humanitarian component, such as $38 million ($381 million in today's money) for famine relief in 1950 (which was gratefully welcomed by the populace), but was manifestly geostrategic in nature. It would pay off with Tito's abandonment of the Greek Communist insurgents in 1949 and condemnation of North Korean aggression in 1950.[37] And with regard to Germany, Washington would move with renewed urgency to claim the zones under Western occupation as a permanent part of the democratic-capitalist sphere.

President Truman signs the Foreign Assistance Act, implementing the Marshall
Plan, April 3, 1948. In the background, from left to right: Under Secretary of
State Robert Lovett, Senator Arthur Vandenberg (R-MI), Treasury Secretary
John Snyder, Representative Charles Eaton (R-NJ), Senator Tom Connally
(D-TX), Secretary of the Interior Julius Krug, Representative Joseph Martin
(R-MA), Secretary of Agriculture Clinton Anderson, Representative Sol Bloom
(D-NY), Attorney General Tom Clark, and Postmaster General Jesse Donald-
son. (Secretary of State George Marshall was away attending the Ninth Interna-
tional Conference of American States in Bogotá, Colombia.)

TEN

PASSAGE

MARCH 1, 1948: THE PACKED SENATE GALLERY WAS SILENT. IT WAS NEARLY a year since Truman had delivered the speech that became his namesake doctrine, nine months since Marshall gave voice to a plan to define and to dignify it. Kennan cloaked the plan in a diplomatic strategy; Clayton gave it economic principles and resonance. Many others—Acheson, Clay, Bohlen, Lovett, Caffery, Douglas, Harriman in particular—lent it practical and political substance. But the snow-haired, bow-tied, bespectacled sixty-four-year-old Republican senator who took the lectern that day, white handkerchief poking from the pocket of his somber suit, was as essential as any of them in forging the bill necessary to give the plan effect. Former isolationist and steadfast opponent of spendthrift government, Arthur Vandenberg had credibility with the Republican Congress that even the storied General Marshall could not match. He had drafted and typed his nine-thousand-word speech himself, reworking it seven times.[1]

"Mr. President," Vandenberg intoned with the presence of a studied speechmaker, a man *The New York Times* called "unquestionably one of the best orators in the land":[2]

with the unanimous approval of the Senate Foreign Relations Committee, I report the Economic Cooperation Act of 1948 [that is, the Marshall Plan] in its perfected text. This legislation, Mr. President, seeks peace and stability for free men in a free world. It seeks them by economic rather than by military means. It proposes to help our friends to help themselves in the pursuit of sound and successful liberty in the democratic pattern. The quest can mean as much to us as it does to them. It aims to preserve the victory against aggression and dictatorship which we thought we won in World War II. It strives to help stop World War III before it starts. It fights the economic chaos which would precipitate far-flung disintegration. It sustains western civilization. It means to take western Europe completely off the American dole at the end of the adventure. It recognizes the grim truth—whether we like it or not—that American self-interest, national economy, and national security are inseverably linked with these objectives. . . . The iron curtain must not come to the rims of the Atlantic either by aggression or by default.

There is only one voice left in the world, Mr. President, which is competent to hearten the determination of the other nations and other peoples in western Europe to survive in their own choice of their own way of life. It is our voice. . . .

[This bill] is the final product of 8 months of more intensive study by more devoted minds than I have ever known to concentrate upon any one objective in all my 20 years in Congress. It has its foes—some of whom compliment it by their transparent hatreds. But it has its friends—countless, prayerful friends not only at the hearthstones of America, but under many other flags. It is a plan for peace, stability, and freedom. As such, it involves the clear self-interest of the United States. It can be the turning point in history for 100 years to come. If it fails, we will have done our final best. If it succeeds, our children and our children's children will call us blessed. May God grant His benediction upon the ultimate event.[3]

Senators and guests rose in applause.

Polls found that nearly 80 percent of the American public had now heard of the Marshall Plan, up from under 50 percent in November 1947. Of those who had heard of it, favorable opinions outnumbered unfavorable ones by over three to one (57 percent vs. 18 percent).[4] These numbers were both a reflection of Vandenberg's assiduous shepherding of the legislation through the political process and a vindication of the personal risks he, as a presumed presidential candidate, took in adopting Truman's policy as his own. "[B]ut for [Vandenberg's] leadership and coordination in the Senate," Marshall reflected several years later, "the plan would not have succeeded. I feel that he has never received full credit for his monumental efforts on behalf of the European Recovery Program, and that his name should have been associated with it."[5]

❖

MEANWHILE, OVER IN EUROPE OFFICIALS FROM THE UNITED STATES, Britain, France, and the Benelux nations gathered in London for the most consequential conference on the future of Germany since the war's end. Douglas cajoled the French "tactfully" behind the scenes, using hints that their share of Marshall aid might depend on their cooperation in merging Germany's western zones. But events on the ground also helped his case. The French "greatly fear the Russian advance in central Europe," noted a memo to Washington. Little was heard any longer concerning reparations or "hymns of hate for the Germans." There was talk of a Franco-German, "perhaps even Pan-European[,] collaboration for reconstruction [of] the post war world."[6]

On March 5, 1948, the three Allies issued a historic communiqué announcing a plan to coordinate economic policies between the Anglo-American bizone and the French zone, to incorporate western Germany into the Marshall Plan, and to create a West German federal government.[7] The launch of what came to be known as the "London Program" set off alarms in the Kremlin. "[O]n the basis of restored industry in Western Germany and its massive Ruhr military-industrial system," Foreign Ministry official Vladimir Treskov concluded, the Marshall Plan aimed to "create an arsenal and bridgehead for future aggression."[8] Khrushchev would later reflect that the initiatives "represented a direct threat to [Soviet] national security, a challenge to the impregnability of our borders."[9]

"Within the last few weeks," Clay cabled the Army General Staff's director of intelligence, "I have felt a subtle change in Soviet attitude which I cannot define." War might now "come with dramatic suddenness." In Berlin, Murphy reported to Marshall, "the Soviet delegation now seizes upon every question . . . and every statement . . . to launch violent propaganda attacks."[10]

Shown Clay's "bombshell" on March 15, a distressed Kennan was sure the general had overreacted. Events in Prague, and tensions in Berlin, were, he wrote, predictable "defensive reactions on the Soviet side to the initial success of the Marshall Plan." But the consequence was that "a real war scare ensued." The Air Force and Army leadership began planning contingencies for nuclear weapon deployment in Europe and the Mediterranean. For its part, the CIA could only reassure the president that war was "not probable" within the next fifteen to sixty days.[11]

"The seizure of power in Czechoslovakia and the incorporation of Finland within the Soviet military sphere," Lippmann wrote on March 15, "must be regarded . . . as strategic actions, planned by military men, in anticipation of war."[12] Stalin was pressuring Finland to sign a defense pact,[13] the trigger being his realization that the Marshall Plan was an imminent reality that would "consolidate a large part of Europe against Russia."[14] Reston noted that the United States was committing itself "and half of Europe to the Marshall Plan, which has roused the objections of the Soviet Union, but we have not yet organized a security system that will defend our friends on the Continent or restrain the Russians."[15] It made no sense, he said, to ship "a lot of Marshall Plan goods to Europe to be taken over by the Red Army."[16]

Bevin urged Marshall to recognize "the strategic threat involved in the extension of the Russian sphere of influence to the Atlantic." Marshall, who had for months resisted his entreaties to begin creating a western military pact, now told his British counterpart that the United States was "prepared to proceed at once in the joint discussions on the establishment of an Atlantic security system." Though the two kept Paris in the dark over the talks for fear of leaks to Moscow, their worries were misplaced. The latter was already being kept informed by British double agents Donald Maclean and Guy Burgess.[17]

Congress, too, was on edge. "The *coup d'état* in Czechoslovakia," observed World War II OSS official Edward Mead Earle, "changed the whole climate of opinion on the issue of the Marshall Plan."[18] It made Republicans more receptive to aiding Europe, but also more apprehensive about the military implications.

"What has happened in Czechoslovakia and Finland," Vandenberg said, "makes it obvious that time is of the essence."[19] House speaker Joseph Martin proclaimed that "the constant advance of the iron curtain across Europe [has] created a grave crisis in our international relations." The very "fate of civilization is at stake." The United States had therefore to "build up [its] military and naval establishments. . . . We must make ourselves absolutely supreme in the air and under the sea." In such an environment, the Marshall Plan on its own, insisted Georgia Democrat E. E. Cox, would not pass in the House. It would have to be accompanied by military aid to vulnerable U.S. allies. "The money we have sent abroad" thus far, he said, "has been more than cancelled by the zeal of the Communists."[20]

Lippmann laid out more clinically the deficiencies of the Marshall Plan that had been made apparent by the growing Soviet menace. "All the calculations of the [Marshall Plan] are based on the assumption that [France's and Britain's] military effort would remain at a very low level in order not to draw off manpower, capital equipment and imported raw materials," he wrote. "If now they must arm, and that is what the western alliance demands, then the estimates of the [Plan] will have to be reviewed and revised upward."[21]

Lippmann had sympathetic ears in the administration, although they did not want to raise their voice at the time for fear of jeopardizing passage of the ERP. "My interest in the whole Marshall Plan was the security aspect," Harriman would reflect years later, "and some of us felt that you could not have a successful economic development of Europe unless there was a sense of security; that people could not go ahead and make investments for the future without some sense of security."[22]

And indeed, France and Britain, together with the Benelux countries, set themselves on the path to rearmament through the creation of a new Western Union Defence Organization in Brussels on March 17. But the so-called Brussels Pact was mainly backward-looking: it bound its members to "collaborate in measures of mutual assistance in the event of a renewal of German aggression." The concern about Germany was real, but was beginning to fade into the distance just as Russia began looming larger.[23]

Lippmann was emphatic that the Western Union "now expects and requires effective American military support," as promised under the Truman Doctrine, in Lippmann's interpretation, to "any nation which is threatened with Soviet domination." No longer content to call merely for U.S. airpower supremacy, as he had in December, he now insisted that the United States needed "the power to make a tactical defense of the Western Union at the Elbe if possible, at the Rhine at a minimum."[24]

Belgian prime minister Spaak echoed Lippmann, arguing that "defense arrangements which did not include the United States were without practical value." For him to pretend otherwise was to "deceive the Belgian people."[25] Danish foreign minister Gustav Rasmussen anticipated Moscow putting the same pressure on Denmark for a nonaggression pact as it did on Finland. Such pressure might force it to seek a military alliance with Washington. But he was anxious not to have to take the step before the Marshall Plan went into effect, hoping to "avoid [the] implication [that it] had military strings attached."[26]

Bevin endorsed "the construction of a North Atlantic defence system [to] put heart into the whole of Western Europe and . . . encourage them in their resistance to the infiltration tactics." He stressed that it would also reassure the French of their security "in the event of a resurgence of the German menace."[27] The French feared such a resurgence if a united Germany fell under Soviet domination, as Czechoslovakia had.[28] Douglas passed on their concerns to Marshall, indicating that they were more likely to "relax in their attitude regarding German industry and reconstruction," which were vital to the Marshall Plan, if "assured of long-term defensive cooperation against German aggression."[29] Bidault wrote to Marshall that Soviet methods of external pressure "are similar to those used by Hitler in 1938 and 1939." Truman, he said, now had to understand "the gravity and the imminence of the danger" to France and western Europe. "The U.S. has shown admirably generous concern" through the offer of economic aid. "But the moment has now come to extend the collaboration of the Old and the New World to the political and, as quickly as possible, to the military field."[30]

Lovett emphasized that the Marshall Plan was "intended to . . . lessen dangers and possibilities of war," and that airing the issue of a U.S. defense commitment too soon would spook Congress and jeopardize its legislative prospects. Hickerson, a tough-talking Texan who deeply distrusted the Soviets, also felt that "the state of United States defenses severely limits [its] immediate military capabilities." He stressed to Marshall that "the problem at present is less one of defense against overt foreign aggression than against internal fifth-column aggression supported by the threat of external force, on the Czech model."[31] Secretly, however, the Policy Planning Staff and the National Security Council began preparing for possible U.S. military support of the Western Union, including "a *unilateral* assurance by the United States to the nations in [the] Western Union that the United States will consider armed attack by the USSR or its satellites against any one of these nations to constitute armed attack against the United States."[32] The State Department opened secret talks with the British and Canadians in Washington on March 22, examining "the possibilities of a military ERP."[33] Truman would in April approve private talks with congressional leaders on extending the Brussels security pact to North America.[34]

Thus, it seemed, the core of the Marshall bloc was well on its way to becoming militarized, much as Stalin had always said it would. A Soviet Foreign Ministry analysis prepared for Vyshinsky and Molotov concluded that the new Western Union was "the first official military-political allied agreement in the general creation of the 'Western Bloc,' under the leadership of the USA":

> The agreement presents itself as a military alliance, directed first and foremost against the Soviet Union and new democratic countries, and is an instrument of American expansion. In the economic sense this agreement complies with the Marshall Plan and is part of its development. In the political sense this agreement is leading towards the division of Europe.[35]

The American, British, and French governments would maintain that theirs was only a necessary defensive response to clear acts of Soviet aggression. But one thing was clear to both sides: it would not stop here. In the West, a full-scale transatlantic military alliance was in the making.

❖

STALIN DID NOT WANT WAR—ONLY THE THREAT OF IT IN BERLIN, WHICH he believed the Allies could not defend.

On March 9, 1948, Marshal Sokolovsky and his political adviser, Vladimir

Semenov, were summoned to Moscow from Berlin. Foreign ministry official Andrei Smirnov told them that Moscow now needed to "disrupt [Allied] plans to put together a Western bloc including Germany." If the Allies rejected co-operation within the Council of Foreign Ministers, this would mean they had "finally decided against settling the German question on the basis of the Pots-dam decisions." In that case, "the Soviet Government would . . . be obliged to close off completely its occupation zone, introducing the appropriate financial measures [and] organizing frontier defense."[36]

Shortly thereafter, Stalin began authorizing a spiral of measures designed to asphyxiate the western powers in Berlin. Official and impromptu air, train, and auto traffic restrictions into and out of the city, begun without fanfare early in the new year, were ratcheted up. The city's Soviet-controlled press reported that "subversive and terrorist elements" had been exploiting lax transit controls to undermine the eastern zone, requiring that "supplementary regulations" re-lating to western travel into and out of the city be brought into effect from April 1. Within the city itself, a "People's Police" was established, effectively giving the Communist SED party a private militia in the east.[37]

On March 26, SED co-chairman Wilhelm Pieck told Stalin in Moscow that he would be "glad if the [western] Allies left Berlin." This might be the only way for the Communists to avoid defeat in the city's autumn elections. "Let's try with all our might" then, Stalin responded, "and maybe we will drive them out."[38]

On April 17, Semenov cabled Molotov from Berlin confirming implemen-tation of his orders to block transport communications between Berlin and the Western occupation zones. These notably excluded air traffic,[39] likely owing to a fatal encounter two weeks earlier, on April 5, when a Soviet Yak fighter jet "buzzing" a British civilian plane over Berlin collided with it. Both pilots died, along with two Americans and twelve other Britons. Each side blamed the other.[40] Military airpower being a Western strength, Stalin may have preferred to avoid further such incidents for the time being. "Our measures," Semenov reported, had already "dealt a serious blow to the prestige of the Americans and British in Germany."[41] The Soviets could therefore just let the weak Allied "air bridge" supplying West Berlin collapse of its own weight.[42]

Stalin knew that West Berlin was a hostage he could only kill once. Once it was dead, the rest of Allied-occupied Germany would be beyond his reach, absorbed into the new, hostile western bloc. Given that the priority was to stop the London Program going forward, he would need to restrain his impulse to pull the trigger.

✤

AT THIS STAGE OF THE MARSHALL PLAN'S DEVELOPMENT, GEORGE KENNAN began to marginalize himself. He considered Lippman's views on America's obligation to protect its European allies militarily "preposterous."[43] Kennan was alarmed by moves to establish a West German state, even though he had been advocating the country's division since 1945. He opposed a western military alliance, continuing to lay emphasis on economic recovery as the cornerstone of European security. "Give the Marshall Plan a chance," he recalled wanting to tell the Europeans. "The economic field [is one] in which we are strong. . . . Let's not call attention to our [military] weakness by making a big splash about the military situation right now."[44]

These positions raised questions to which Kennan would never offer compelling answers. How would German recovery, which he accepted as necessary for European recovery, proceed without an end to the Soviet veto over reindustrialization and currency reform? How would France and Britain be made to abandon designs for national economic autarky without American guarantees against both German and Soviet aggression? At a minimum, it was becoming apparent that American economic diplomacy would not achieve its ends without a rupture in the Yalta-Potsdam political and security arrangement.

That Kennan was now oddly positioned to the left of old sparring partners like Lippmann and Clay had one of three possible explanations. The first is that they had misunderstood him—that is, the Kennan of the Long Telegram and "Mr. X." This was Kennan's argument now, that containment had never been about setting up military pacts and shutting down diplomacy. But this is not credible. Kennan had in 1947 been forthright in proclaiming the need for Washington to bare its teeth and forgo illusions about the utility of dialogue with Moscow.

The second is that he had converted his old enemies, but that they had overshot in their converts' zeal. This position is more plausible, particularly in regards to Clay—a man who preferred to bulldoze barriers, whether they be

French or Russian, than maneuver around them. The Soviets had, as Kennan had predicted, shown themselves uninterested in reasoned compromise. They were too suspicious of the West. Clay, Lippman, and other critics of "Mr. X" were now adapting to the new facts on the ground.

The third explanation is the most compelling: that Kennan was, in spite of his writings, never comfortable with the military as a tool of peacetime diplomacy. He reveled in highlighting logical failings in others, but recoiled at seeing his own logic acted upon. Kennan now argued that democracies were ill-suited to the use of armed forces "tactically" in peacetime. The effort to do so only elevated the level of belligerent feeling toward the enemy, dangerously, in order to justify itself. "It was I who pressed for 'containment' and for aid to Europe as a form of containment," he wrote in private notes. But "I think I was wrong. Not in my analysis of the Soviet position, but in my assumption that this government has the ability to 'operate' [tactically] in the foreign field."[45] The experts, like himself, invariably got pushed aside by the military and the politicians.

This defeatism was a repudiation of his own War College lectures the previous October.[46] It was also a staggering admission of strategic failure. It suggested that his own ideal form of containment, the Marshall Plan, could not work without a security element, and that the addition of this element would lead inevitably to war. Of this self-doubting Kennan, Lovett would say, "I liked him more as Mr. X."[47]

In any case, the train had departed and could not be called back. Bohlen, too, had opposed a military alliance, though later came to see it as "simply a necessity."[48] Time would tell whether Kennan's dark new fears would be justified. But his career as government sage was in its last lap.

❖

AS THE LEGISLATIVE DRAMA OF THE MARSHALL PLAN HEADED INTO ITS final act, *The New York Times* focused on the stakes for Moscow and Washington. "International communism," correspondent Drew Middleton wrote, was coming off "nearly three years of sweeping success." The Marshall Plan, however, represented "the most effective political and economic opposition it has encountered since Lenin founded his Communist state nearly thirty-one years ago." We were therefore "entering a period of a major Communist offensive" to undermine it. Endorsing the administration's narrative, Middleton said that the plan struck at "the root of Communist influence in Western Europe," which was "political chaos, economic instability and personal insecurity and fear." Only the United States, with its unrivaled economic might, could "wield such a weapon." The Cominform under Zhdanov would undertake to blunt it by instigating "strikes and industrial sabotage," particularly in Italy, backed up by propaganda, bribes, and threats. This is why the Marshall Plan, "if it is to work in some areas," he concluded, "must be bolstered by military backing."[49] This refrain was becoming ominously familiar.

The Senate floor debate from March 3 to 13 took on this dilemma, without resolution. To get the aid bill passed, Vandenberg tried to treat the Marshall Plan narrowly as a "business enterprise" and to defer larger questions regarding the nature of America's political and military relationship with Europe. Others, however, attacked this approach as unworthy or even irresponsible. Minnesota Republican Joseph Ball insisted that the Russian threat was fundamentally military in character, and that an economic program was therefore inadequate on its own. A military program was necessary to "checkmate the onrolling avalanche of Soviet power—naked, completely ruthless power."

Senator Lodge conceded that the Prague coup could never have been prevented through economic aid; but military support was not, he said, a practical alternative, given the strength and proximity of the Red Army. Another approach was needed to deal with the threat of subversion and internal unrest. He left unanswered, however, the question of whether a vote for the ERP implied a willingness to back it up with the threat of force. Arkansas Democrat John McClellan was unsatisfied with this ambiguity, insisting that no one should cast such a vote unless he were also prepared to support a military alliance with western Europe.[50]

On March 8, the Senate unanimously approved an amendment to the legislation, named for California Republican senator William Knowland, which blocked export to the Soviet Union or its satellites of all goods whose supply was inadequate to meet the demands of the ERP. A complete ban on exports of oil, machinery, and industrial goods to Russia had the support of over 70 percent of the public, and was opposed by only 16 percent.[51] The amendment also required that at least half the aid goods be transported on American ships, to the extent that such were available.

Senator Taft could once again read the tea leaves, and maneuvered to embrace the inevitable while remaining the voice of disillusioned conservatives. "If I vote for this bill," he said on March 13, just before the Senate vote, "it will be with the distinct understanding that we are making a one-year commitment. If we don't want to continue this program after the first year there is no commitment, moral, legal, or otherwise."[52] Five minutes past midnight on March 14, the Senate authorized a one-year $5.3 billion appropriation by a vote of 69 to 17. Thirty-one Republicans voted for—Taft among them—and thirteen against.

Hoover also did an about-turn from his January 21 letter to Vandenberg, writing to House speaker Martin that no reductions should be made to the appropriation.[53] On March 17, Truman made his final plea for speedy House ratification of ERP legislation before a joint session of Congress. The CIA having concluded that a Communist victory in Italy would mean the possibility of Soviet "bases in Sicily and southern Italy [that] would pose a direct threat to the security of communications through the Mediterranean," and have a "demoralizing effect throughout Western Europe," Truman was anxious to get a final bill passed before the April 18 poll.[54]

In contrast to his "Truman Doctrine" address one year prior, the president this time had no hesitation in naming the villain of the new Cold War. "Since the close of hostilities, the Soviet Union and its agents," he said, "have destroyed the independence and democratic character of a whole series of nations in Eastern and Central Europe. It is this ruthless course of action, and the clear design to extend it to the remaining free nations of Europe, that have brought about the critical situation in Europe today." Although "prompt passage of [the European Recovery] program is the most telling contribution" Congress could now "make toward peace," it was no longer sufficient. "[S]o long as communism threatens the very existence of democracy," the United States had to be at a much higher state of military preparedness. He called on Congress to enact both universal military training and a restoration of Selective Service—the draft.[55]

With the House vote nearing, tempers flared in the chamber on March 25. Some accused Truman of stirring up another war scare to keep himself in the White House. "It's an election year, brother!" shouted Rep. Clare Hoffman (R-MI). Charles Vursell (R-IL) insisted the money would be better spent "building the strongest air force in the world." Airpower would deter Stalin, whereas the Marshall Plan would merely encourage him to move his forces westward and pilfer American aid. "When he pulled the iron curtain over Czechoslovakia," Vursell said, "he pulled it down over 2 billions of our money and equipment." Now, "if we approve the present bill, we will next be asked to arm Europe. Then will come lend-lease and finally the sending of millions of soldiers with full equipment to fight and die to protect the 16 nations affected by this program."

The practical impact of Vursell's attack on the bill, though, like those of many of his colleagues, was modest. He was still willing to vote for $3 billion (rather than $5.3 billion) in immediate aid, provided there would be no further appropriations.[56] But the latter question would, in any case, be decided by a new Congress. Rather than defeat the Marshall Plan, then, Vursell's argument fed into the growing belief that aid to western Europe could not end with money and goods. It would have to be backed up by a credible, and costly, new American military investment. Indeed, Republicans insisted, over Democratic objections, to having $275 million ($2.75 billion in today's money) in military aid for Greece and Turkey written into the ERP bill, rather than considered separately (as the Senate had, successfully).[57] The Marshall Plan, it now seemed clear, was to be delivered to Europe under military escort.

But military measures, Reston pointed out, raised difficult wider political questions. If it were now clear that Communists, once they were in government, would not hesitate to use illegal means to seize total power, as they were doing in Czechoslovakia, how was the United States to approach the elections in Italy? Could it afford not to intervene to keep the Communists out of the government? If the answer were no, how could it justify supporting democracy through undemocratic means?

Reston had no answers.[58] But some in the State Department did. Steinhardt told Marshall that the lesson of Prague was that the United States needed to engage in "direct internal interference" in vulnerable parts of Europe "for the purpose of organizing the existing anti-Communist forces effectively." He acknowledged that interference was "contrary to conventional diplomacy, but we have an opponent who breaks the rules."[59]

The relationship between the Marshall Plan and democracy was muddied from the start by the inclusion of Greece, which had been the fulcrum of the Truman Doctrine. But the House weakened the link further on March 30, just before voting on its version of the ERP bill. Supported by anti-Soviet hawks at the Defense Department, it passed a resolution endorsing Spain's inclusion. Spanish dictator Francisco Franco commended the House, calling the vote—which succeeded "in spite of the attitude of its president and secretary of state"—a true representation of the feelings of the American people toward his country.

The House "omnibus" bill also contained $900 million ($9 billion in today's money) in military aid for China, Greece, and Turkey, and international emergency child relief, on top of the $5.3 billion for Europe. The State Department strongly opposed the supplemental funds, partially on the grounds that they might delay passage of an ERP bill and partly because of diplomatic concerns. "The inclusion of ERP in a bill which also dealt with military aid," Hickerson wrote to Lovett on March 8, "would inevitably link ERP to potential military action against the Soviet Union or its agents. This would change the whole emphasis of ERP from a program to promote positively European recovery to a program of defense against Soviet aggression." It might in turn deter "certain countries, notably [neutral] Sweden and Switzerland" from participating. "In that case, we would have engineered a break in the front of non-Communist European cooperation."[60]

Still, the omnibus bill passed in the House on March 31 by a vote of 329 to 74. One hundred seventy-one Republicans voted yes, 61 no; 158 Democrats voted yes, 11 no. The additional funding added by the House would make its way into the final reconciled legislation, although funding for Spain would not. Irked by Communist claims that the United States was "a reactionary force, allied to every undemocratic Government in Europe, from Greece to Spain," and that the Marshall Plan was aimed at securing bases for war with the Soviet Union, the administration, with Vandenberg's support, successfully cajoled the House-Senate conference into excluding Spain. Small remaining Senate and House bill differences were quickly resolved, and on April 2 the Economic Cooperation Act (also known as the Foreign Assistance Act) passed by a vote of 318 to 75 in the House and by voice vote in the Senate.[61]

"This measure," the president said proudly upon signing the Marshall Plan into law on April 3, 1948, "is America's answer to the challenge facing the free world." The United States was, he said, in all history "the first great nation to feed and support the conquered." Truman used a dozen pens to sign the bill, giving one to each of the witnesses from Congress and his administration. Marshall, at a hemispheric conference in Bogotá during the ceremonies, cabled a message calling it "an historic step in the foreign policy of this country." Hoffman called it "probably as well conceived a piece of legislation as was ever put on the books in the U.S."[62] Given the enormity of the political task, in both Europe and the United States, of translating Marshall's Harvard speech into an actual legislated program, or even just a down payment on one, it was certainly remarkable that it had been accomplished in a mere ten months.

"Search back as one may through the annals of the United States or any other power," pronounced *The Economist* from London, "there is no record of a comparable act of inspired and generous diplomacy."[63] The Marshall Plan would, Bevin and Bidault said in a joint statement, "give new courage to the free peoples of the world."[64] Attlee called it "an act of unparalleled generosity and statesmanship."[65]

With the critical Italian elections only two weeks away, Togliatti addressed a rally of twenty thousand Italian Communists, denouncing the Marshall Plan and telling the gathered that the Soviets would aid their country. Boos and chants of *Lunga vita agli Stati Uniti!* (Long live the United States!) drowned him out. On April 17, with 94 percent of eligible voters going to the polls, Italians gave De Gasperi's coalition 48.5 percent of the vote and an absolute majority of seats in the Chamber of Deputies. The Socialists and Communists, the latter of whom had been happy to campaign on a choice of "Russia vs. America," saw their combined share drop from 40 percent in 1946 to 31 percent.[66] In Paris, Bidault breathed a sigh of relief.

Back in Washington, Kennan did as well. A Communist victory in Italy, he said, sounding a tad like the domino theorists he disparaged, would have undermined "our whole position in the Mediterranean, and possibly in Western Europe as well." The result had been a clear demonstration of the Marshall Plan's powerful psychological effect—psychology being the element in which he had always lodged the better part of his confidence. The United States had accomplished "four-fifths" of the effect it was after, Kennan later reflected, "before the first supplies arrived" in Europe.[67]

It is notable, however, that Kennan was not content to let the Marshall Plan speak for itself. He saw it much as a coach might see an athlete whose odds of victory could and should be boosted with banned substances. In the case of the Italian elections, that substance was the CIA's first major covert operation. Though its contents are largely unknown, it certainly included a well-funded propaganda blitz to buoy the Christian Democrats and discredit the Communists. Kennan considered it an enormous success—so much so that he now wanted a sustained and systematic covert effort to complement the Marshall program. "Political warfare," Kennan would write in May, "is the logical application of Clausewitz's doctrine in time of peace." More importantly, the Soviets were doing it at a much higher level. Propaganda, support of friendly foreign elements (legal or otherwise), and clandestine operations were no different from economic aid: they all now had to be part of the American diplomatic toolkit.[68]

⁜

VANDENBERG HAD PAID A HIGH POLITICAL PRICE FOR PUSHING A HISTORIC foreign aid package through Congress, forfeiting any chance of winning the Republican nomination. In return, he expected that his man would run the program through the new Economic Cooperation Administration. Clayton and Acheson, the president's men, would not do. At Acheson's urging, Truman accepted Vandenberg's choice: Paul Hoffman.

Like Clayton, the affable, energetic fifty-seven-year-old Hoffman had impeccable industry credentials, as well as firm backing from business leaders. Like Clayton, he also believed that "the real objective" of the Marshall Plan was "to stop the spread of communism."[69] Unlike Clayton, Hoffman was a Republican.

The only hiccup was that Hoffman did not want the job. Truman, however, would not take no for an answer. Nor even maybe. Before Hoffman could confer with his wife and colleagues at Studebaker, Truman announced that he had accepted the post. Hoffman was stunned, but later professed admiration for Truman's method, which he himself had used in the business world. Hoffman was sworn in on April 9. He started his new job—paying $20,000 a year, an 80 percent salary cut—immediately, announcing the first expenditures that day. He quickly became, in Life's words, "the busiest man in Washington," fielding ten thousand job applications on his first day—before he had been given an office.

Harriman Committee economist Richard Bissell became his first hire, taking the title assistant deputy administrator, and would become the main architect of the structure for directing Marshall aid. Shortly after, Hoffman appointed Harriman himself to run the new Office of the Special Representative (OSR) in Paris—the Marshall Plan's headquarters in Europe. Hoffman politely rebuffed the president's recommendations for ECA appointments, insisting there could be no whiff of politics in the staffing. Truman earned Hoffman's enduring regard for respecting the edict. British Treasury official Sir Richard (Otto) Clarke would call Hoffman's staffing of the program "a most elevating spectacle." [70]

Hoffman was equally adamant that funds would be distributed in strict conformity with the law and the aims of the ERP. Some American companies, he would tell his new staff, had "come to consider [the ERP] a bonanza in which everyone can share as an exporter who has anything to sell." But it needed to be "understood that the full recovery program [actually] contemplates a lower rate of exports from this country."[71] This aim contrasted with Soviet caricatures of the program's purpose.

The first Marshall ships, each loaded with thousands of tons of food, fuel, chemicals, equipment, vehicles, and the like, set sail for the sixteen Marshall Plan countries on April 20. There would soon be 150 crossing the Atlantic at any given time. The first to arrive in France—in Bordeaux's harbor, bedecked in Stars and Stripes, on May 10—was greeted with cheers from the dockers and a welcome speech by Ambassador Caffery. Monnet was elated, writing to Schuman that economic recovery was now, finally, possible in France, "thanks to the Marshall credits."[72]

U.S. and French officials were relieved that the Communists had left the ceremonies and unloading unmolested, but they were not silent. They blasted Harriman and his incoming horde of Marshall administrators as "the new occupying power" and "La 5e Colonne américaine en France." In Italy, Togliatti pledged that the country's "2.5 million Communists would wage an all-out fight against the ERP." "The sun rises in the East," proclaimed a banner at a Communist rally in Vienna, "and no Marshall Plan can change or stay it." The Soviets and their Communist allies in Europe condemned the plan as "an instrument of preparation for war."[73] Truman told Canadian prime minister Mackenzie King that the situation was now as serious as in 1939.[74]

Protest against the Soviet blockade of Berlin, September 9, 1948. In the background, the Reichstag.

ELEVEN

SHOWDOWN

GEORGE KENNAN WAS WORRIED. STILL BELIEVING IN THE MARSHALL plan, still believing that containment was working, he was convinced Washington was overreacting to Soviet provocations.

The Czech coup had been predictable—indeed, Kennan had predicted it. So the surge of support it unleashed for a western defense pact was, he felt, setting the stage for a dangerous escalation of tensions. In a Policy Planning Staff paper written during the coup, he suggested that the success of the Marshall Plan might even help bring the Soviets to the table. Shortly after, he gave an off-the-record press briefing in which he opined that a "spectacular retreat of Soviet and Communist influence in Europe may be expected" within six months.[1]

Determined to help it along, Kennan advised a quiet démarche to Moscow in March. Truman approved it late the following month, and Marshall instructed Ambassador Smith in Moscow to approach Molotov with a carefully drafted oral statement. After warning Molotov at length that Moscow would be making "a tragic error" in assuming Washington would not defend its interests,

265

Smith was to tell him that "the door" was nonetheless "always wide open for full discussion and the composing of our differences."[2]

Molotov agreed to receive the "old spy,"[3] as he called the general. Armed with intercepts of French cables from Berlin to Paris, he was aware of Franco-American tensions over the pace of West German unification and suspension of reparations to Moscow.[4] The meeting was thus a golden opportunity to rupture Allied solidarity. Molotov greeted Smith on May 4, 1948, in a manner the latter described as "grave, attentive and courteous."

Chief of staff to Eisenhower during the war, Smith was able, orderly, candid, straight-talking, "all business." He had a harsh, powerful voice, intimidated subordinates, and made little effort to personate a diplomat. Upon learning that Smith would be sent to Moscow in the spring of 1946, Eisenhower remarked that it would "serve those bastards right."[5]

Script in hand, Smith assured Molotov that America's "entire history was [a] refutation of any suspicion of a policy which involved aggressive war." But he stressed his country's concern over Soviet behavior in Czechoslovakia. The Czech government had accepted the ERP conference invitation, and withdrew it "immediately following [the] visit of Masaryk and Gottwald to Moscow." The United States, he said, "did not oppose Communism because of its Marxian ideology, but purely and simply because we had seen repeated instances," as in Prague, "of Communist minorities coming into power by illegal means and against the will of the majority. . . . The US remained convinced that these minority coup d'etat would have been quite impossible without the moral and physical support of the USSR."

"No one," Molotov responded in a May 9 follow-on meeting, had "been able to find any facts to prove these false allegations. Nor can anyone state with authority that the Communists have used illegal means." The fault lay instead, he said, with "rightist circles . . . that wish to induce changes by violence." As for the United States, "it was well-known that the western European and American press were saying openly" that the military alliance and bases it was establishing "were directed against the USSR." And "events in Greece are not the only example of [its] interference in the internal affairs of other states."[6]

The two agreed on nothing, though Smith fulfilled his mission by transmitting the open-door message. Molotov ran the text up to Stalin, who read that part with delight—scribbling "Ha-ha!" in the margins.[7] Here, he saw, was a chance to undermine Truman with American allies and voters. Kennan had been wrong. "Spectacular retreat" was not on Stalin's agenda.

Though Molotov had agreed that the talk with Smith would be private, TASS published the Soviet version of it on May 10.[8] The State Department was caught unprepared.[9] Stalin, it concluded, was trying "to create the impression . . . that the US had been forced to appeal to the USSR for a settlement." This, he hoped, would "undercut US leadership . . . by sowing distrust among our friends who were not consulted in advance."[10] Indeed, two days later an angry Bevin was, thanks to the TASS release, himself subjected to angry questioning in Parliament over what he had known and when he had known it.[11]

But Stalin wasn't finished. "We do not conduct any cold war," he wrote in a rare note to himself that month. "The cold war is being waged by the U.S.A. and its allies."[12] On the propaganda front, he was fighting back.

Stalin had an accomplice in the U.S. presidential race. According to Gromyko's memos to Stalin from Washington,[13] Henry Wallace began telling him of his plans to travel to Moscow sometime before April, using Czechoslovak U.N. ambassador Vladimír Houdek as a secret intermediary. Meeting face-to-face on April 2, Wallace and Gromyko first discussed Stalin's questions about prospective U.S. presidential candidates—including Wallace himself, who would shortly be chosen by the Progressive Party and endorsed by the Communist Party.[14] They then turned to Wallace's agenda.

Wallace wanted "a statement on the major questions of Soviet-American relations" to be delivered "by Generalissimo Stalin, or by Wallace in agreement with Stalin." It should emphasize, similarly to Smith's later message, that "in relations between the USSR and USA there are no . . . differences that could not be resolved peacefully." Such a statement, Wallace said, "would be important from the perspective of influencing general opinion in the USA." He stressed that "the information spread about Czechoslovakia [in Washington] is a lie," but that there was a "necessity of undertaking something from [Moscow's] end with the aim of convincing [the American] public."

Stalin was intrigued. Though "a trip" by Wallace "would do harm," he scribbled in the margins of the transcript, "a statement would be helpful." As for delivery, it would be "better if it's done by Wallace," Stalin wrote, "with Stalin stating he's in solidarity."[15]

On April 27, Gromyko cabled Molotov that he had received, through Houdek, a draft of Wallace's proposed "Open Letter to Premier Stalin." Stalin reviewed it line by line, scribbling "yes" next to the material he agreed with and edits elsewhere.

Headlining a campaign rally before nineteen thousand at Madison Square Garden on May 11, the day after the TASS publication of the Smith-Molotov dialogue, Wallace read out the "letter," complete with Stalin's edits. Disparaging Smith's message for demonstrating "the same self-righteousness which has led to international crisis," he declared that the open-door part nonetheless vindicated his long-standing claim that peace was in reach. To bring it about, however, Washington needed to change its policies. He called for the Marshall Plan to be "converted" into a U.N. effort to create an "economically unified Europe," as opposed to the divided one Truman was creating. He further called for the "re-establishment of a peace-loving German government in charge of a united Germany which is obligated to the strict fulfilment of the Yalta and Potsdam agreements." This was a swipe at American actions in western Germany.[16]

On May 17, Moscow radio broadcast Stalin's effusive reply. *The New York Times* published the translation. Wallace's "important document," Stalin declared, had rectified "the inadequacy of the statement of the United States Government of May 4"—the Smith message—by providing "a concrete program for peaceful settlement of the differences between the USSR and the United States."[17]

Stalin's duplicity blindsided the State Department yet again. "The distorted publication of the Smith-Molotov exchange," U.S. chargé Elbridge Durbrow cabled Marshall from Moscow, "successfully confused Europe." Now, "Stalin's open letter is primarily designed to confuse America, lend the appearance of substance to the vacuity of Wallace's declarations on foreign affairs and thus emasculate American policy."[18] Kennan would later tell Smith that the department "unwittingly ran head on into a neat little arrangement between the Kremlin and some of the people in the Wallace headquarters." Wallace, however, kept his Houdek-Gromyko channel to Stalin a secret, shielding himself from allegations that he was operating as a Soviet agent.

Kennan was "horrified by the ease with which the press [was] taken in by the Russian maneuver." He was also distraught that there had been something so "seriously wrong with my analysis."[19] When he made the prediction that communism would stage a "spectacular retreat," he had failed to foresee how the political tectonics would be shifting in Stalin's favor. In Greece, Communists assassinated Justice Minister Christos Ladas on May 1; the panicked government declared martial law. In China, Mao's Communists were gaining ground on Chiang's Nationalists.[20] And in West Berlin, the Soviets were tightening their chokehold. Soon enough, Stalin reasoned, the Allies would abandon the city or their planned West German state.

❖

THOUGH STALIN AND MOLOTOV WERE TRYING NEGOTIATORS, THE AMERicans would repeatedly mistake their temperaments and tactics for genuine barriers to resolving the standoff in Germany. The problem was not personalities, but the untenable foundation of the Yalta-Potsdam accords: the idea that the other's understanding of joint power in Germany could be changed through persuasion, coercion, or new circumstances. This foundation was now in rubble, owing to the urgency of dealing with the German economy. And at the heart of the conflict over how it should operate was the institution of money.

In the capitalist West, money and banking allowed autonomous individuals to make informed decisions on working, saving, investing, and exchanging. In the communist East, they allowed the state to direct resources without interference. After 1945, the Soviet Union used state direction of money and banks to eliminate private enterprise, stop unwanted spending, and prevent foreign trade from disrupting domestic economic plans (through inconvertible currencies).

In Berlin, now, there was no form of currency or banking regime that would accommodate western-style free enterprise without disrupting Soviet control of the city's economy and that of the eastern zone more widely. Soviet transportation blockages and currency demands were, therefore, two sides of the same coin. Free Allied movement into and out of the city, together with

central bank co-powers, meant uncontrolled commerce, and therefore an uncontrolled communist polity.[21] This was not only unacceptable but a contradiction in terms.

The issue of Germany's postwar currency had emerged as a source of contention as early as 1944, when FDR's treasury secretary, Henry Morgenthau,
unwitting as to the lengths his deputy would go to support Soviet economic
interests, put Harry Dexter White in charge of organizing the German occupation notes. In overruling the director of the Bureau of Engraving and Printing,
Alvin Hall, who opposed Soviet demands for copies of the American currency
plates, White lied in claiming that the Combined Chiefs of Staff had "directed"
that such copies be handed over. The Soviets, who he said had to be "trusted,"
went on to print up over 78 billion occupation marks—eight times what the
Americans did. Notably, the mass of marks injected by the Soviets was almost
identical to the number of reichsmarks put into circulation by the Nazis, while
the smaller number of American marks was consistent with estimates of the
number of reichsmarks that would have kept prices stable.

The Truman administration halted White's generosity in July 1945, making the Soviet marks—fortunately distinguishable by a dash in the serial number—invalid in western Germany. The Soviets, who knew the marks were
worthless, denied their soldiers the possibility to convert them to rubles. Red
Army troops therefore bought what they could with them from American GIs,
typically paying on the order of 10,000 marks for a $4 watch. The lucky watch
seller would then convert the marks to dollars with the U.S. Treasury at the official rate, established by White, of 10 to 1, thereby netting himself a handsome
$996 profit. The total cost to the American taxpayer, in current-dollar terms,
was as high as $6.75 billion.[22]

In 1946, Clay's currency experts called for the creation of a new western
mark, the deutschmark, to replace the old one. A new currency would achieve
maximum psychological effect. Clay proposed to the Allied Control Council
that the notes be printed up under quadripartite control in the American sector of Berlin, and subsequently issued by a new central bank. The Soviets, who
wanted the ability to print and issue notes at will to cover occupation costs, proposed a two-plant solution—with one in Leipzig, in their zone—that would
allow them to evade western oversight.

Wrangling between the two sides went on into 1948. Each suspected the other's intentions for a shared arrangement, and each worried about the cross-zonal impact of the other issuing its own notes. But by March 1948, separate Germanys seemed unavoidable in Washington. West German inflation was running at roughly 10 percent a month: at the official exchange rate, a carton of American cigarettes cost about $2,000, and would rise to $2,300 by June.[23] Royall thought the administration had been patient enough waiting for Soviet cooperation on reform. The time had come to act. "We have tried to maintain an 'open door' to the Soviets in all our actions in Germany," he wrote to Stimson, "but we cannot permit continued stagnation in that country and still hope to revive Western Europe's economy in keeping with the objective of the ERP." Deputy Assistant Secretary of State Frank Wisner wrote to Lovett on March 10, advising that Clay be told that quadripartite currency reform was no longer a U.S. policy objective. This was, he acknowledged, a "definite move toward recognition of the East-West partition of Germany."

Accepting the Army's verdict that the currency stalemate was playing into Soviet hands, Lovett directed Clay to engineer a break-off in talks.[24] Sokolovsky obliged on March 20, storming out of a meeting in choreographed pique. This served both sides' purposes. Sokolovsky issued new orders "strengthening control on the external borders of Greater Berlin,"[25] and State stepped up transition to the deutschmark.

On May 18, the Soviet government approved a plan to counteract western currency reform. In the event the Allies went ahead, the Soviet Military Administration would have its own East German currency at the ready, and would "allow circulation in the entire area of Greater Berlin *exclusively* to the new banknotes of the Soviet occupation zone."[26]

Facing Soviet pressure, Washington struggled to keep its coalition together. Bidault and his prime minister, Schuman, had to maneuver the London Accord through the French Assembly, roughly half of whose members, mainly Gaullists and Communists, opposed an independent West Germany—or even a West German currency.[27] Knowing, as Clay put it, that "the French . . . have no air transport worthy of the name," the Russians ratcheted up road, bridge, and railway blockages with an eye to boosting the "no" vote on June 16. "French non-acceptance," Clay worried, "will be interpreted

[as] unwillingness to face [the] USSR."[28] It was, in the end, a close-run affair. But with the Socialists coming on board at the last moment, the vote was 297–289 in favor of the London Accord and 300–286 for the deutschmark.[29] Allied unity had held, for now.

✤

ON JUNE 26, HILDE SPIEL, THE VIENNA-BORN WRITER WHO HAD SETTLED in London before the war, talked her way onto an American military aircraft from Frankfurt to Berlin. Warned of the risk of hostile Soviet air maneuvers, she was ordered to don a parachute. The plane shook violently as it entered the narrow, turbulent corridor permitted by the Soviets.

Disembarking unsteadily after vomiting, she found a city in a state of high tension. Berliners out scavenging for food returned to crumbling homes with no electricity, the main source having been cut off in the East. The drone of Allied supply planes overhead was relentless. The roars frightened Spiel, reminding her of the Blitz. But, strangely, the enemy was still invisible. At the theater, Russians greeted her as before. She didn't know what to make of it.[30]

A currency war had just broken out, but the effects had yet to sink in. A week earlier, on June 18, Clay, with Robertson and Koenig, the British and French military governors, had given Sokolovsky a mere few hours' notice before publicly declaring the currency changeover in the west of the country (though not Berlin), which would take place on Sunday the 20th. The angry Russian general called the move "illegal" and promised "actions to protect the economy of the Soviet zone."[31]

On June 19, the Soviets announced that "banknotes issued in the Western occupation zones will not be allowed to circulate in the Soviet zone or in 'Greater Berlin,' which is situated in the Soviet zone and is economically a part thereof." Fearing disorder in the Eastern zone, which would be flooded with old reichsmarks declared worthless in the West, Moscow also blocked all interzonal passenger traffic and incoming road traffic, while instituting an inspection regime for inbound trains. Use of the deutschmark in the east was banned.

Refusing to acknowledge the legitimacy of the transport restrictions, Clay, after warning Soviet officials, sent in a train to challenge them. Following a thirty-six-hour standoff, its crew was overpowered and a Soviet locomotive hauled it back to Helmstedt, on the western frontier.

Unable to provision his garrison by ground, Clay began ferrying in supplies by air.[32] As tensions climbed, currency experts from each side argued bitterly over solutions for Berlin. On June 22, the Americans offered a proposal for a new Berlin currency, under four-power administration. The Soviets rejected it. The British offered a compromise, with the Allies accepting the Soviet mark but placing it under four-power control. Western access rights would be restored. The Soviets, however, spurned all notions of combined control or guaranteed access rights. "We give notice to you and to the German population of Berlin," they told the Allies, "that we shall apply . . . sanctions that will ensure that only one currency will circulate in Berlin" as of June 26, "the currency of the Soviet zone."[33] This, Clay concluded, "would have placed Berlin financially completely in Soviet hands."[34] The Allied governors declared the Soviet decree invalid in the west of the city, and threatened to introduce the deutschmark in their sectors if the Soviets went ahead.

The local Berlin city government, the Magistrat, which functioned with limited authority allowed it by the ACC, now found itself in an impossible political situation. Whose orders would it obey? After emotional debate, it ruled that the Soviet order did not apply outside the Soviet sector. But the elected City Council had the final word. On June 23, the Soviets shuttled in hundreds of SED demonstrators in army trucks hours in advance of its 4 p.m. meeting. With raucous commotion in the hall delaying the start for several hours, the members voted to back the Magistrat. As legislators exited the building into the throngs of protesters, Soviet-sector police helped them identify those who had voted with the West. Many were severely beaten.

That same day, the Soviets announced the introduction of their own east mark into Berlin and eastern Germany, effective June 24. Gummed stamps were attached to old reichsmark bills until new bills were ready. On the 24th, Allied officers declared the Soviet initiative null and void in West Berlin and introduced the deutschmark into the city. To keep room for compromise, though, the bills were stamped with a "B" to distinguish them from non-Berlin deutschmarks. This would facilitate withdrawal at a later date.

Sokolovsky announced that the Allied military government had ceased to exist, and began isolating the three western sectors with a full-scale blockade. He suspended all road, rail, and barge traffic to and from the sectors owing to unspecified "technical difficulties." He cut off electricity and food supplies from the east because of "coal shortages" and the need to prevent western currency from circulating illegally. He moved eight Soviet combat divisions into assembly points near the interzonal border. Reports emerged of Russian barrage balloons being placed near Tempelhof airfield in the American sector to disrupt landings.

The French had once again been dragged along against their will. Berlin Commandant General Jean Ganeval warned Clay of "incalculable consequences which will undoubtedly not be confined to Berlin." Bidault thought "the Western powers [would] find it very difficult to stay there for more than a few weeks unless there [were] a radical change in relations with the Soviet authorities." Those authorities were in turn receiving reports from their "leading comrades in [eastern] Germany," indicating that "the Western powers would [soon] be forced to . . . surrender their positions in Berlin to the Soviet Union."

Clay remained defiant. By the end of June, 480 relief flights were landing each day, one plane every three minutes. "I may be the craziest man in the world," he told Berlin's SPD leader Ernst Reuter, "but I'm going to try the experiment of feeding this city by air."[35]

❖

A BLACK MARKET MONEY EXCHANGE SPRANG UP NEAR WEST BERLIN'S zoo train station, by the Tiergarten. East marks, which circulated freely in the west, traded at four or five to one against west marks, which were banned in the east. Newspapers sold in east marks, though their printing was paid for in west marks. Sugar sold in east marks; raisins in west marks. Potatoes were priceless, having not been seen in weeks. Still, most Berliners, 84 percent in one poll, believed the Allies would sustain the city with adequate food. When the Soviets offered to feed West Berliners who registered in the East a mere 2,050 (out of 2.4 million) showed up.[36]

In western Germany broadly, the new Allied currency, combined with price decontrols and other liberalizing reforms overseen by bizonal economics director Ludwig Erhard, had an immediate regenerative effect on business. "Almost overnight, hoarded goods in manufacturing plants began to move to the stores," Clay wrote to Byrnes. "Even fruits and vegetables from the farm once more went on sale in the market place. . . . Germany is going back to work. . . . [T]he people on the street visibly have taken a new hold on life."[37]

Yet at the time the outlook was ominous. There were now two police forces in the city. Two water and sewage systems. Two gas and light systems—though those in the West operated only during daylight.

Hilde Spiel could feel the change that had swept over Berlin since she arrived a few short weeks ago. Russian officials she knew well were now indifferent or hostile. Being no cold warrior herself, she was dismayed by the change. "Between us and the Russians," she lamented in her diary, "it is all over."

The East Berlin *Tägliche Rundschau* newspaper announced that the Soviet Military Administration was now "the only legitimate occupation authority" in the city. Rumors spread rapidly, fueled by radio reports, that the water supply was threatened by a power cutoff to the city sewage plants and that the western powers were evacuating. As Clay and other Allied authorities tried to reassure Berliners, Reuter and fellow city leaders organized mass meetings—one bringing out over eighty thousand—to rally resistance, to call out the Communists for using starvation as a weapon, and to appeal to the Allies for protection and support.[38]

The Soviets, meanwhile, struggled to communicate one message *to* Germany and another *about* Germany to the nations they dominated in the East. In an effort to, on the one hand, undermine the "so-called Marshall plan," the Warsaw Declaration of the East bloc foreign ministers condemned it for placing West German industry into "the fetters of the American . . . capitalist monopolies." One of the centerpieces of this policy, it said, was currency reform, the creation of a new west mark, which by serving the interest of such monopolies created unemployment and misery. Western Germany was being forced into "enslavement," put to the service of "the military-strategic aims" of Washington and London and the emerging western security alliance. In an effort to, on the other hand, justify the Soviet Union's ever-expanding control in eastern Europe, the declaration invoked the specter of German "militarism," which the Anglo-American plan sought to revive and direct eastward.[39] In the end, the

Soviets failed to convince either Germans or their East European victims that they were defending them or their interests.

Soviet and western soldiers and police intermingled in Berlin in an atmosphere of crisis. When Sokolovsky's car was stopped for speeding in the western zone, guns were drawn and angry words exchanged before the two sides backed down. The general returned to his headquarters without further incident. But a mistake on either side could have triggered a violent confrontation that would have been difficult to contain.

An intense, belated debate now raged within the Truman administration over Western vulnerability in Berlin. How far would the Soviets go? Would they starve Berliners? How would they react if ignored or resisted? Was the Allied presence in Berlin still tenable? What were the costs of withdrawing?

"We are in Berlin by right," an emotional Kennan wrote to a friend, "and do not propose to be ridden out by any blackmail." The United States could not abandon Berlin, or "the world would know well enough that we are turning 2,400,000 people over to all the rigors and terrors of totalitarian rule."[40] Others in the administration, however, were unsure it could be avoided, the president included—though he was determined to try.

For his part, Stalin was unwilling to part with Moscow's unassailable right under Potsdam: veto power over the political architecture of Germany—all of it. "The most complete expression of [America's] aggressive interests is the incorporation of West Germany and the Ruhr . . . into the 'Marshall Plan,'" wrote foreign ministry official D. Ignatiev:

In order to preserve the military-industrial potential of the Ruhr and Western Germany as a whole, the Americans presented demands for the cessation of the dismantlement of German factories for reparations. . . . [This was] in violation of all existing quadripartite arrangements of the occupying powers. . . .

"The Marshall Plan" is aimed at the transformation of the Ruhr and the whole of West Germany into the main military-industrial base of American imperialism in Europe and the transformation of Marshallized countries in the areas dependent on this base. . . .

The Anglo-American economic policy in West Germany promotes

German revisionist elements, which are campaigning against the Yalta and Potsdam decisions on the demilitarization of Germany and its obligations for damages caused by German aggression.[41]

"If we were to lose Germany," Molotov told satellite foreign ministers at a gathering in Warsaw on June 24, "we would have lost the war."[42] Two weeks later, as British intelligence would discover, Moscow secretly informed the ministers of its intention to take control of all Berlin.[43]

The emerging showdown between Washington and Moscow, which would spread over the entire globe during the coming half century, for now seemed oddly fixed on a single city in central Europe. Berlin was a geopolitical black hole, one that was set to absorb ever more of the diplomatic energies of the two former war allies.

✥

BY LEGEND, THE "BERLIN AIRLIFT" WAS A BOLD AND DECISIVE RESPONSE to defeat the blockade and prevent humanitarian disaster. Yet *as a strategy* it was neither bold nor decisive; it was neither intended to beat the blockade nor to feed Berliners indefinitely. No one in the Truman administration believed, at the time, that an airlift was more than a short-term expedient to keep options open. Defeating the blockade, it seemed certain, would require a military challenge. As for humanitarian concerns, these were raised primarily by those who believed the Allies needed to *withdraw* from the city. Moscow would then bring in supplies to curb unrest.

Anticipating escalation after the Soviets shut down interzonal travel, the U.S. Army had begun to position supplies for an "air ferry" on June 18, a week before the full blockade began. The first C-47 flights flew in 5.9 tons of supplies to Tempelhof airfield on June 21. British Dakotas landed their first 6.5 tons at Gatow airfield on the 24th. Soon, massively laden planes would be rumbling over the city's tattered roofs in quick succession, landing as often as one every three minutes. The Allies also began hitting back with a "counter-blockade," halting shipments and traffic by rail and barge from western Germany into the eastern part. Allied officials wryly blamed "technical difficulties" of their own. Sokolovsky was, according to American intelligence reports, "greatly shocked" to discover how dependent the East was on coal, steel, machine tools, and industrial commodities from the West.[44]

On July 3, the military governors reassembled in Berlin for a last effort to defuse the crisis on the ground.[45] The atmosphere was heated. "How long do you plan to keep it up?" Clay demanded of Sokolovsky. "Until you stop your plans for a West German government," he replied.[46]

Truman had at first downplayed the crisis, referring to it as the "German currency squabble with Russia." But Sokolovsky's response made clear that the B-mark issue was secondary. As with the Marshall Plan, Stalin's real concern was the political and military agenda that lay behind American economic interventions. Forever traumatized by the Nazi invasion in 1941, he was determined never again to leave his country vulnerable to German military capacity and intentions.

The timing was, however, also inauspicious for compromise. Only a few days earlier, Stalin had expelled Tito's Yugoslavia from the Cominform. This was "a new factor of . . . profound significance [that] has been introduced into the world communist movement by the demonstration that the Kremlin can be successfully defied by one of its own minions," Kennan observed. "By this act, the aura of mystical omnipotence and infallibility which has surrounded the Kremlin power has been broken. The possibility of defection from Moscow, [heretofore] unthinkable, will from now on be present in one form or another."[47] With dangerous division within his own ranks, Stalin could ill-afford to show weakness over Germany.

As for Truman, he told his staff that there was "nothing to negotiate. . . . Russia has never kept any of the agreements she has made."[48] Yet for all his legendary toughness, he was unwilling to confront Stalin at this stage. He pledged only to stay "as long as we could" without armed conflict. Nothing in the history of air logistics, north Europe's weather, or Soviet behavior suggested that anything more was a responsible objective. An incident with Soviet personnel hampering western traffic could escalate into war. He feared an accidental conflict more than a deliberate one, with a "trigger-happy Russian pilot or hotheaded Communist tank commander" setting off a spiral of deadly response and counter-response.

An airlift, however, was "obviously no solution," Bohlen said. Clay initially

saw it provisioning his garrisons only. It could not possibly, he told Pentagon officials, belying his earlier bluster, "supply the German civilian population with adequate coal and food." Bevin took it as given that it would not "be possible to feed
two million Germans" by air. He hoped only that a "big display [of] strength and
determination" would boost German morale. "Such humanitarian action in the
face of the ruthless Soviet policy of starving the Germans [for] political advantage," he believed, "would show the Russians up in . . . world opinion."

Reuter agreed that Berliners would rally behind a show of will, but stressed
that the city had barely a month's supply of food left.[49] It needed 1,300 tons a
day, plus another 2,000 tons of coal, which required a much larger air operation.
In Washington, the consensus was that the Allies had a two-month window to
resolve the standoff. Ganeval thought the situation would be "absolutely hopeless" by the end of July. The Soviets would then have "a knife at our throat."
Army chief of staff Omar Bradley agreed: "We *must* decide now whether we are
willing to fight."[50]

Preparing to settle in for a diplomatic struggle, Truman was anxious to document the sources of Allied legal rights in the city. Yet the mass of diplomatic
files assembled since Yalta offered the most meager basis for such rights. Ambassador Murphy blamed "a defective [wartime] agreement" with the Soviets,
motivated by a naive American "outburst of faith and good will."[51] Faced now
with the possibility of war if Truman were too aggressive, and a calamitous loss
of credibility if he were too weak, impassioned advisers urged the president to
move decisively in different directions.

Clay led the hawkish wing. "I am convinced," he cabled the Army in Washington, "that a determined movement of [armed] convoys . . . would reach Berlin and [would] prevent rather than build up Soviet pressures which could lead
to war." The Russians, he argued, did not want war. Intelligence reports indicated no abnormal troop movements, stockpiling activities, or other military
preparations. They would therefore not likely interfere. The blockade was intended to drive out the B-mark and halt the creation of a West German government, not to starve the population. The latter would, in Murphy's words, only
undermine "Soviet political aims in Germany." "Nevertheless," Clay conceded,
"I realize fully the inherent dangers in this proposal since once committed we
could not withdraw."[52]

An armed convoy was a sound strategy if the Soviets were bluffing, but Clay was not consistently of that view. He had in fact told the French and British that war over Berlin was "inevitable" within eighteen months. If this were so, a convoy was reckless. There were only 6,500 western troops in Berlin, compared with 318,000 Soviet ones in Berlin and the surrounding eastern zone. Lieutenant General Curtis LeMay, commander of U.S. Air Forces in Europe, thought Soviet forces could overrun West Berlin in eight hours. Bevin and Robertson shared Clay's assessment that the Soviets were bluffing, but thought the convoy scheme flawed. Robertson pointed out that the Soviets could simply stretch tanks out across the autobahn to block it. This would oblige Allied forces to shoot their way through, triggering escalation, or retreat.[53] Lovett argued that the Soviets would just cut bridges in front of and behind the convoys, stranding them by blocking their advance and retreat.

Royall led the dovish wing. He demanded that Clay shut his mouth after being quoted in *The New York Times* saying that Moscow could "not drive us out by any action short of war."[54] What was at stake, Royall told him, was "a minor issue": Berlin's currency. In sharp contrast to Clay, who later reflected that there would likely have been no Marshall Plan or NATO if the United States had abandoned Berlin, Royall believed that the United States need not—and indeed, could not—remain in the city. Clay was, he felt, exaggerating the costs of withdrawal to U.S. prestige and influence while underestimating Soviet readiness to use force.

The Joint Chiefs concluded that the "entry of armed American Forces into the Russian zone would in fact be an aggressive act." It was therefore too risky. Some Army officials argued that withdrawal would be necessary to avoid a civilian catastrophe; the only question was how to avoid "the appearance of a rout."[55] U.S. forces were "facing a defeat . . . if the war comes," Leahy said. Yet a retreat, Murphy insisted, "would amount to a public confession of weakness under pressure. It would be the Munich of 1948."[56] (He would sixteen years later say he "should have resigned in public protest against Washington's [feeble] policy." Reliance "exclusively upon the Airlift was a surrender of our hard-won rights in Berlin, a surrender which has plagued us ever since."[57]) Douglas argued that withdrawal "would probably cause failure of the European Recovery Program," if not a complete collapse of confidence in American resolve on the part "of Western Germans and the people of Western Europe" generally.[58]

Marshall wanted to take the issue to the United Nations, but the French pushed back, fearing it would accomplish nothing except provide Truman with a moral basis for war—the effects of which they would bear. The compromise was a simultaneous written protest delivered to the Soviet embassies in the three western capitals on July 6. The Soviet reply came back eight days later.

Once again, Moscow blasted Washington and London for violating their commitments at Yalta and Potsdam: to pacify Germany and to extract reparations for its victims. The Allies were now using currency reform and "dismemberment"—creation of a West German state—to undermine Soviet rights in the country. Berlin, Moscow said, was part of the Soviet zone, and the economic threat to the zone from the B-mark's circulation necessitated the protective measures the western powers were now protesting. "The interests of the Berlin population do not permit the introduction of new currency in the western zones of Germany and special currency in the western sectors of Berlin."

Furthermore, it said, the West's removal of the industrialized Ruhr from four-power control undermined the "demilitarization" and "democratization" of the country. By ignoring their obligations in Germany under earlier agreements, the western powers had forfeited "their right to participation in the administration of Berlin." Moscow therefore not only rejected a lifting of "the measures for the restriction of transport communications between Berlin and the western zones" as a precondition for discussions over Berlin, but insisted that any talks on the city be conducted within the four-power framework. This demand was code for rolling back currency reform and plans for a West German state.

Finally, Moscow said it was willing and able to provide adequate supplies for the entire population of "Greater Berlin" on its own. West Berlin's suffering was the fault of the Allies. Their withdrawal was the surest means of alleviating it.

In the wake of Moscow's defiant response, Marshall told the cabinet confidently that the "tension in Berlin" owed to "Russian desperation in the face of success of [the] ERP."[59] The West was winning. And Clay was as upbeat as ever. "The very violence of the Soviet reaction now," he cabled Army under secretary Draper, "is the proof of the success of our several programs to restore democracy in Europe."[60] His stance is stunning for an American military governor who, until the spring of 1947, had tended to ascribe breakdowns in U.S.-Soviet cooperation not to the triumph of democracy but to failures of unilateralism in Paris and Foggy Bottom, the State Department's new home.

Clay continued to press for ground confrontation, proposing that Brigadier General Arthur Trudeau lead an armored convoy of Allied troops through the Soviet zone and into Berlin. LeMay would then bomb every airfield in East Germany if Trudeau met resistance, which he did not expect. Sokolovsky's troops, however, had been conditioned to believe they were defending "sacred Soviet borders," and would almost certainly have resisted the invaders. Yet when this possibility was put to Clay, he responded by asserting the futility of concessions: the Russians, if they were bent on war, would just pocket them. Nothing, it seemed, could dissuade Clay: both a weak and a bellicose Russia were reasons for confronting it. Bidault condemned his bluster. The British chiefs of staffs rejected his scheme "under any conditions."[61]

Truman was morose. The Soviet response, he reckoned, had been a "total rejection of everything we had asked for."[62] At Bevin's urging, he authorized sending sixty B-29 bombers to Britain, together with a public announcement from the Pentagon. B-29s had bombed Hiroshima and Nagasaki, and he wanted Stalin to take note. "Our only advantage," noted British Air Commodore William Arthur Darville Brook, "is our possession of W.M.D."

Still, Brook wanted this only as a bluff—which it was. These particular B-29s could not carry atomic bombs, though Stalin should not have known this fact—that is, he would not have known except for the fact that Donald Maclean, his super-mole in Washington, told him.[63]

Continuing to take an upbeat tone with the press, Truman lamented to his sister that the situation was "all so futile." Every major poll suggested he was headed for defeat in the November election. And "if I win, I'll probably have a Russian war on my hands."[64]

A TOP SECRET SOVIET INTELLIGENCE REPORT IN JUNE 1948, POSSIBLY WRIT-
ten by Maclean, suggested the Kremlin was anxious to gauge how far Washington
would go to defend its stake in Berlin. Despite French concerns that the U.S. position "seemed dangerous and irresponsible," the report—clearly translated from a
foreign source—said the U.S. military would "resort to force if the Russians at any
time make it impossible for Americans to stay in Berlin." Molotov, who annotated
it, would have noted its observation that Truman had not decided "when and
under what circumstances force would be employed, if it would be employed at
all, to subvert [nonmilitary Soviet] measures."[65] There was thus scope for ratchet-
ing up pressure on the city, short of downing Allied planes.

Determined to escalate the matter to the U.N. if diplomacy failed, Marshall was willing first to try engaging Stalin directly through an oral approach
to Molotov. Bevin thought an oral approach weak, but Marshall insisted it was
the only way to break the logjam. Written communications simply hardened
Russian intransigence over wording.[66] As usual, the American prevailed.

The Allied governments requested a combined ambassadorial-level meeting with Stalin and Molotov on July 30 to discuss Berlin and "its wider implications." Molotov agreed only to meet them serially, hoping, in Smith's estimation,
"to maneuver one or the other" into revealing the price the West would pay to
end the crisis. In his exchange with Smith, he continued to insist that the Allies
could not hope for change in Berlin without engaging on "Germany as a whole."
But he agreed to forward the request for a meeting up to Stalin.[67]

Stalin, thinking the endgame he had envisioned in the spring had begun,
invited the western emissaries to talks on August 2. Smith was accompanied
by French ambassador Yves Chataigneau and British minister Frank Roberts.
At nine that night, early by the Generalissimo's standards, Stalin greeted them
in his office. Highlighting the "unusual" nature of the audience he had granted,
with three Allied representatives present, he set forth his position.

Western rights in Berlin, he said, derived from the city's status as the capital
of a unified Germany. Now, with the Allies setting up their own West German
state, those rights no longer had a "juridical basis." This stance was a dramatic
hardening of the Soviet diplomatic line—denial of all western occupation
rights in the city.

"There would have been no restrictions" in Berlin, he told them pointedly, "had it not been for the London decisions" to divide Germany. "The restrictive measures adopted by the Soviet authorities had been to prevent the invasion of the Soviet zone by the special western currency."

Smith replied that his government would do nothing to prevent the formation of a central German government in the future, should the differences between the two sides be breached. But the United States would not negotiate under duress. As for the currency matter, he proposed that the Allies might withdraw the B-mark from Berlin and begin talks on Germany if the Soviets would lift the blockade.

But Stalin returned again and again to the London Program. "Stop applying the London decisions and withdraw the 'B' mark," he said. Then "there will be no difficulties. It could be done tomorrow. Think about it."

Smith said he would report Stalin's position to his government, but felt "that the implementation of the London decisions had reached a point at which it would be extremely difficult to hold it up."

Around 11 p.m., Stalin proposed resuming talks in the morning. But Smith insisted there was no point. Progress had been "quite inadequate."

Stalin must have known, given Maclean's intimate knowledge of Allied deliberations in Washington, that the West put little stock in the airlift beyond September.[68] Time was on his side. He therefore needed to string the Americans along, to keep them hoping and talking.

Stalin lit a cigarette, smiling.

"Would you like to settle the matter tonight?"

Yes, Smith assured him; he would like nothing better.

Stalin made a new proposal. The B-mark and the blockade could be removed simultaneously. As for the London Program, it could be recorded that its postponement was the Soviet Union's "insistent wish."

Smith was taken aback. Was this a climb-down? He could see no diplomatic meaning in an "insistent wish." It gave the Allies full freedom of maneuver. (He would even suggest that Marshall unilaterally "suspend" parts of the London Program to retain negotiating chits for the future.) The three emissaries agreed to present the proposal to their governments.[69]

Both sides now believed the other was anxious for agreement and looking only to save face. But neither was reading the other accurately. Stalin was ready to roll back the blockade, partially, but not as a prelude to restoring Western powers in the city. He intended to use the Soviet mark to push the Allies out.[70] For its part, the State Department was ready to abandon the B-mark, but would accept nothing less than a full managing stake in a unified currency regime for the city. There was still no locus of interests.

On the ground in Berlin, Clay was horrified that Smith did not see the trap that was being set for him. Having through early 1947 condemned anything that interfered with efforts to bring the Soviets into a partnership for unified German government, Clay now argued against efforts that interfered with progress toward splitting Germany.[71]

Back on July 30, the Soviets had begun using their control over the city's central bank to freeze the accounts of the Magistrat and all western sector enterprises. They were asphyxiating the economy of West Berlin and the powers of the non-Communist government. Municipal officials knew that, with Soviet control over Berlin's money, it was only a matter of time before Moscow and their SED puppets controlled the whole city.[72] "Berlin political leaders [are] frightfully upset at [the] rumor of Soviet currency becoming [the] single currency" in the city, Clay cabled Draper on August 7. "If we are voided of all control, they will be at the mercy of [the] Soviet government."[73]

But Marshall was not as naive as Clay feared. With the B-mark gone, he told Smith, four-power control of the city's currency would be essential and nonnegotiable. Whitehall understood the same.[74]

On August 6, the Allies presented Molotov with a draft communiqué calling for "all restrictions" on transport communications into and out of Berlin to be lifted, specifying conditions under which the Soviet mark would circulate in the city, and stating that four-power talks would aim to resolve wider issues related to Germany. Molotov "immediately opened vigorous attack" on western demands to "control" the currency of the Soviet zone, of which Berlin's economy was an integral part. He further protested that there was "nothing in [the draft] about the insistent desire of Generalissimo Stalin for the postponement of the [London] decisions."

Smith called Molotov's response the "typical Soviet tactic of trying to sell the same horse twice." Still, he assured Marshall there was "no reason to be either depressed or encouraged." "The next meeting," he insisted, "will be more significant."[75] To Bohlen, who had been certain Stalin's "insistent wish" was a ploy to prevent creation of West Germany or pin the Berlin crisis on the Allies, Smith's take must have appeared as dangerous wishful thinking, born of a reluctance to admit he had been snookered.

The British were alarmed. Roberts judged that the Soviets were not optimistic about killing the London Program, but thought they were in a strong position to expel the Allies from Berlin—a good consolation prize. The city's currency, Bevin said, was now "at the heart of our difference with the Russians." Robertson agreed, concluding that "if we withdraw our currency . . . without any agreement on quadripartite control, we shall have lost Berlin and the air-lift will have been in vain."[76]

On August 9, Molotov presented the Allies with his own draft, which seemed to confirm British suspicions. Clay condemned it as "disastrous" and "unthinkable."

Blockade restrictions imposed prior to June 18, the date of the western currency reform, would stay in place—implying that they were defensive in nature and legitimate. Western access rights would not extend beyond those accorded through the "present agreement"—which were nil, in that none were enumerated. Molotov rejected four-power control of Berlin's currency. Power was to lie entirely with the Soviet-established Bank of Emission. A Soviet agency would assume control over the city's exports. This new authority, he argued, was consistent with the Allies having illegally ended quadripartite control over Germany. Finally, Stalin's "insistent wish" was to be clarified; a statement would be issued that the Allies "did not propose for the time being to deal with the question of the formation of a government for Western Germany." This clarification meant that dealing with it would signify a change in the western position, giving Moscow a pretext for retaliation.[77]

On the ground in Berlin, Soviet officials turned up the pressure. They harassed the Magistrat and nullified its powers in the East. Thousands of SED supporters staged violent demonstrations throughout the summer, disrupting the Assembly. Soviet soldiers ran down an American MP in the Western sector before shooting their way out. Rioters beat up reporters from Radio in the American Sector. The CIA concluded that under present conditions the western position in the city was "untenable in the long run."[78]

Further meetings between Smith and Molotov on August 12 and 16 yielded no movement. "All very hard going," Smith said, belying his earlier prediction. Molotov "now appear[ed] to be . . . in no hurry about a settlement," possibly because of "the anticipated effect of winter on our airlift, or hoped for deterioration of economic conditions of the western sectors." His "attitude being quiet and reasonably pleasant," the purpose seemed to be to keep talks going "almost indefinitely" to "prevent us from adopting an alternative course of action." Matters, he told Marshall, were no longer "by any means hopeful."[79]

At a National Security Council meeting on August 19, with Truman presiding, Marshall and Lovett said the Soviets were using power over the city's currency to expand a "physical blockade" into an "economic" and "financial" one. The CIA pondered Stalin's intentions, weighing the costs of compromise against the benefits of ending the "dilemma" in Berlin.[80]

Marshall concluded that "there is nothing to be gained and much to be lost by any further attempt to negotiate with [Molotov]."[81] He decided to make a final appeal to Stalin before escalating to the United Nations—a move supported by Clay, but still opposed by Schuman, who saw it as a prelude to war.[82]

But both sides were feeling time pressure, raising hopes that a deal could still be done. Marshall was concerned about "signs of public restlessness," given that mere technicalities seemed to be preventing agreement. For his part, Stalin was focused on the September 1 start date for the West German Parliamentary Council—staffed by sixty-four elected representatives, under the CDU's Konrad Adenauer as president—to begin drafting a constitution in Bonn.[83] This was his last chance to stop it.

Stalin granted a meeting on the evening of August 23, greeting the western emissaries "quite jovially." Posing once again as the fount of affable reason, he offered broad-brush concessions on the blockade and the currency. He agreed in principle to remove all "recently imposed" communications restrictions on Berlin, no longer just those imposed since June 18. He further agreed that the four-power financial commission would be the "controlling body" for the currency operations of the Soviet bank. It looked like a deal.

Almost. Stalin continued to insist that "something must be said about the

London Conference." He wanted no further movement toward a West German government before a new meeting of the four-power foreign ministers.
He preferred a published statement to this effect, but was willing to consider an
exchange of confidential letters.

After two hours with Stalin, the emissaries spent three more working with
Molotov "as a drafting committee." Other than the ongoing matter of Stalin's
"insistent wish," which the three agreed only to pass on to their governments,
"things went so smoothly," Smith told Marshall, "that I was a little worried. [I]
remembered Stalin's proverb, 'an amiable bear is more dangerous than a hostile
one.'" There was still inordinate detail being left to the military governors in
Berlin to resolve. Would they be able to agree to a plan for simultaneous removal of the blockade and consolidation of the currency on a week's deadline?
It was "an impossible job," Smith feared, but "I don't see how we can spare more
time."[84]

Marshall and Clay expressed alarm that Molotov had refused, for reasons
related to the Soviet "juridical position," to affirm quadripartite control over
Berlin in the draft directive. With what appeared to be a scolding from the secretary, Smith's frustration boiled over.[85] "Quadripartite control does not exist
in Berlin today," he cabled back, and "the Russians have no intention of permitting [its] revival . . . so long as they are unable to achieve quadripartite control
of Germany." Marshall, he believed, needed to accept reality and make up his
mind: either "we simply stay [in Berlin] under present conditions and take the
necessary measures to organize the life of the three western sectors independently" or we accept the blockade's lifting "under circumstances in which we
would not have complete control over the life of our sectors." Trying to have an
independent West Germany and a four-power Berlin was, to his mind, denying
reality. He recommended that the Allies seek concessions from Molotov, with
no expectation of success, and then pass on the directive as is to the military
governors to see if they could make it conform to Washington's demands. If
they failed, Washington could then walk away.[86]

Ominously, Molotov refused to allow any of his or Stalin's oral assurances
into the directive, insisting he would not be drawn into discussing a "new document." He asked repeatedly, however, that Soviet wording on the London
decisions—which the Allies had rejected, and would not agree to in a form

acceptable to Moscow—be included in an immediate communiqué.[87] The reason for the hard line seemed clear. By the time the directive was ready to be issued to the military governors on August 30, the Bonn constitutional convention was two days away. Stalin was about to lose a critical leverage point and, with it, reason to follow through on concessions.

But Stalin had been prepared for this eventuality. He had told Tito deputy Djilas back in February that "the West will make Western Germany their own, and we shall turn Eastern Germany into our own state."[88] The objective was now to secure Berlin as East Germany's undivided capital.

When the military governors gathered at 5 p.m. on August 31, it was the first time they had met in nearly two months. Sokolovsky's demeanor, a concerned Murphy recorded, was "mildly provocative." He seemed imperious, wanting to show his "mastery of the situation." It was not an air he would put on without orders from the top. "I have never felt so discouraged and hopeless," Clay wrote in anticipation of the encounter and the likely fallout.[89]

"Hold on tightly to, and do not make any concessions away from, the decisions agreed upon in Moscow," Molotov had ordered Sokolovsky by Top Secret cable earlier that day. "Keep in mind that the western representatives are particularly striving toward a widening of the authority of the financial commission. This cannot be allowed."[90]

Sokolovsky disavowed knowledge of oral understandings reached with Stalin and Molotov in Moscow. No communications restrictions introduced before June 18, he said, could be lifted.[91] And new ones would now be imposed on air traffic into Berlin, limiting it to support of the occupation forces. Unregulated flights, he explained, undermined operation of the Soviet mark, the city's sole authorized currency. As for the Soviet bank, he insisted the four-power financial commission could have no powers over its operation. Once the Allies withdrew the B-mark, the financial life of the city would pass to Soviet control. The following week, he announced that Soviet aerial military exercises would begin in the corridors over Berlin.[92]

With the airlift now under direct military threat, a furious Clay cabled Draper in Washington on September 3, insisting to know the endgame of U.S. policy. Was the United States determined to remain an occupying power in Berlin? Agreeing to any of Moscow's terms, he was sure, was inconsistent with such an objective. Since the president was still groping for options short of war or withdrawal, Royall could only assure Clay that the administration would not sacrifice its rights for an end to the blockade.[93]

"I am sorry," Murphy cabled Marshall on September 7, the deadline for the governors to complete an agreement, but "we are getting nowhere." The Soviet "attitude is indifferent almost to [the point of being] contemptuous." They "are making only those proposals which would give them complete control so as to make our acceptance impossible." The governors adjourned without agreement on a joint report, or even agreement on a report of their disagreements.

But there were new problems, Murphy explained. Soviet "tactics in Berlin [were] getting rough." On September 6, a 1,500-strong Communist mob blocked the City Assembly from meeting. Three American reporters were beaten up. Under orders from a Soviet officer, uniformed police from the eastern sector arrested dozens of plainclothes officers from the western sector brought in by the deputy mayor to keep order. Murphy feared they were led off "to death or worse."[94]

Over 300,000 Berliners rallied on September 9 in the city's Platz der Republik, near the Brandenburg Gate, to hear Reuter and other city leaders condemn the Soviet blockade. "We cannot be bartered, we cannot be negotiated, we cannot be sold!" Reuter shouted. "[We will] stand together until this fight has been won!" Riots broke out when East Berlin police beat back demonstrators passing through the gate. A Soviet War Memorial flag was burned and police cars overturned. Twelve days later, CDU interim mayor Ferdinand Friedensburg would meet with Major Boris Otschkin, the Soviet chief of the Department of Civil Administration within the city's four-power occupation authority (the Kommandatura), using remarkably bold language to criticize the policies and behavior of the Soviet occupiers:

> The fundamental relationship of the German population to Soviet power
> has been deteriorating. . . . A balancing of the tensions, that have now
> assumed global political extent . . . can only be achieved by improving
> the immediate relations of the German population to the Soviet occupa-
> tion. . . .

The Soviet occupation forces have committed two fundamental errors. . . . The first is that the use of government and administrative forms
that have proven themselves in the Soviet Union is in no way possible in the
same manner towards the German population. [Germans] aspire to make
their political life according to their own democratic forms and to establish
good relations with the Soviet Union in accordance with those forms. However, these efforts stand against the policy of the Soviet military administration. . . . which holds fast to the imposition of other political forms and
restricts the area of German self-government. . . .

The second is that the Soviet occupying power relies . . . on the Communists, to whom they give all possible support. [But] the Communists
constitute a small minority, and will also be a small minority in the future,
having been rejected by the vast majority of the German people. . . .

The intransigence of the Soviet occupying forces has led the German
people to a rigid and often imprudent behavior towards them. [I] deeply regret that after 3 ½ years of Soviet occupation the German and Soviet people
have failed to achieve mutual understanding.[95]

Privately, the city leaders also criticized western diplomacy for being weak.
They struggled to rebuff rumors in the city that the Allies would withdraw the
B-mark as a prelude to withdrawing troops. These rumors were undermining
the currency's value.[96]

"Sokolovsky's position," Marshall concluded, "and with even greater
force the Soviet-inspired disorders designed to overthrow the city Government elected under quadripartite supervision make it plain that the Soviet
Government seeks to nullify our rights in Berlin."[97] Truman assembled his
top military brass on September 13 to review options, including nuclear
strikes.[98]

In Moscow the following day, the Allied emissaries made a final request
for a meeting with the Soviet leader. They were told Stalin was "on vacation."
Molotov received them four days later, but dismissed their complaints that Sokolovsky had not followed the directive. It was they who had distorted it, he
said, by demanding financial commission powers "over the whole activity of
the German Bank" and repudiating an earlier 1945 air corridor accord.[99]

The directive being ambiguous on the commission's powers, the Allies had depended on a measure of Soviet goodwill in hewing to Stalin's oral assurances. Soviet literature, however, had extolled the use of currency manipulation during the Russian Revolution; and Douglas, for one, was not surprised that Stalin wanted to retain that weapon in Berlin. His backtracking on currency cooperation, together with new air traffic restrictions, convinced Marshall the Soviets were yet again negotiating in bad faith.[100] Looking back on events months hence, Foy Kohler, the American chargé in Moscow, would conclude that the Kremlin had fashioned the impasse "to spin out negotiations indefinitely, maintaining [the] blockade meanwhile."[101]

Indeed, Stalin had shifted his chips. Having failed to stop the Bonn constitutional convention, he was now betting the house on the airlift collapsing by winter—and with it the morale of West Berliners. The airlift "had been more successful than we had anticipated," Marshall told the NSC, yet he warned that "in many respects time was [still] on the side of the Soviets." British tonnage had topped out at 1,463 in August, and would fall to 1,259 in September and 1,030 in October as mechanical and logistical problems emerged.[102] But on the American side, even Marshall could not yet see that the Allies were on the verge of a breakthrough. It began quietly in late July, with the appointment of a new airlift commander in the Wiesbaden headquarters.

⁂

MAJOR GENERAL WILLIAM TUNNER WAS NOT YOUR TYPICAL AIR COMmander. He did not share his colleagues' fixation on bombing. A devotee of Frederick Taylor's theories of scientific management, Tunner took an odd interest in the ability of planes to move people and equipment long distances at great speed. He brought in motion-study engineers to analyze the airlift in theory and practice, and ordered what seemed to all involved baffling changes in practice and procedure. They paid off: average daily deliveries rose from 2,226 tons in July to just over 3,800 in August, within reach of Clay's target of 4,500.[103] That month the French also added a new airport in their zone, at Tegel.

By September, the airlift was shuttling in a record 4,593 tons daily, just above Clay's target (though below the 6,000 tons Friedensburg thought necessary). Clay was now arguing that he could best the blockade indefinitely if he could just get some more planes—116 more, to be precise. In Washington, however, it seemed a dangerous gamble to commit more resources. Half the available military air fleet was already devoted to the Berlin mission. Shifting more would degrade the strike force the United States might need to deter or repel a Soviet attack.[104]

Politically, Marshall was being squeezed. To his right, the Joint Chiefs were critical of efforts to contain Russia with relief supplies and diplomacy. To his left, the president was frustrated by failure to nail down what seemed a done deal just a few weeks earlier. Stung by cries of "warmonger" from the Wallace camp,[105] Truman began maneuvering behind Marshall's back to cut a deal with the Soviet leader.

At the urging of political advisers who pointed to rising numbers of voters "fear[ing] the possibility of war,"[106] Truman decided to send a personal envoy to Moscow to meet with Stalin. This would demonstrate to Americans his commitment to securing peace.

Eisenhower—like Marshall, a war hero—was the most prominent name in the mix.[107] But Truman wanted someone he knew, someone who knew him and could speak for him. Someone not like Ike. He insisted on his longtime poker partner and former treasury secretary Fred Vinson. Now Supreme Court chief justice, Vinson had no special knowledge to bring to bear on Berlin, nor experience in Soviet affairs. But Truman hoped he might break down barriers with Stalin, letting him "unburden himself to someone on our side he felt he could trust." The two sides might then "get somewhere."

That a president who prided himself on standing up to the Russian menace should believe that such a complex, dangerous conflict could be treated as a personal misunderstanding reflected, in equal measures, desperation and ignorance of how the Soviet system worked. He had been unchastened by Stalin publishing Smith's private remarks in May. Truman referred to "old Joe" as a "decent fellow," one who was being misled by Molotov and pushed about as "a prisoner of the Politburo." Yet even if it had been true, the idea that it could be overcome by a heart-to-heart with a hard-boiled Kentucky politico seemed far-fetched. Vinson himself was "astonished" at the request, and agreed only with reluctance.

On October 4, Truman finalized the draft of a public address explaining the gravity of the conflict with Russia and his decision to send an envoy to Moscow. Vinson's assignment would not be to "negotiate with respect to the Berlin crisis," but to discuss "the moral relationship" between the two countries. "Premier Stalin," he wrote, had "assured [him] of his desire to talk with Justice Vinson." Truman also implied that the secretary of state had approved the mission.[108] Marshall knew nothing about it.

Lovett was beside himself. He warned the president that his boss, then huddling on the crisis with Bevin and Schuman in Paris, would resign. Truman agreed only to postpone a decision until he returned.

Marshall was now as bullish on Germany and the airlift as he had ever been, and therefore determined to take a firm line with Stalin. A presidential emissary with no knowledge of the recent months of grueling diplomacy was not what he had in mind. "We are on the road to victory," he told Bevin and Schuman. "We have put Western Germany on its feet." As for Berlin, "the air ferry counteracts the blockade very well." It can "take care of the needs of the western sectors . . . for as long as we wish. It is not even [that] expensive."[109]

So when Lovett broke news of the Vinson mission to him on October 5, he was apoplectic. This was, Marshall said, an initiative unique "in the history of diplomatic bungling." But before he could get home to deal with Truman, the story had leaked and broken in the *Chicago Tribune*.

Now having to confront the fallout, Truman regretted the whole idea and was determined to put things right with Marshall. "I won't do it," he told his advisers, even as they insisted that the Vinson mission was still his best chance to stay in office. When Marshall arrived on October 9, the two concocted a story that they had discussed having Vinson carry a message to Stalin "regarding the atomic problem" and the president's "desire to see peace firmly established in the world." But in the end, the statement explained, Truman "decided not to take this step" owing to "the possibilities of misunderstanding."[110]

Though the mission was now scotched, Marshall thought his efforts in Paris badly undermined. Indeed, Bevin and Schuman were now less sure than ever whether Truman wanted to start a war, abandon them to one, or both.

On October 14, State Department Kremlinologist Foy Kohler cabled Marshall from Paris: Stalin, he said, had concluded that there was now "no chance of preventing" the creation of a West German state "by negotiation, even at the price of concessions with respect to Berlin." The only way he saw to "[bring] about the destruction of the London decisions and [disrupt] the ... unity of Western Powers" was, therefore, to undermine their governments. His new strategy was to use "Communist-directed disturbances in France ... to hasten the advent of de Gaulle,"[111] who was himself bitterly opposed to those decisions.

Loyal and discreet, Marshall may or may not have used the word "resign," but, in poor health, he made clear to Truman that he would not remain in his post beyond inauguration day. Expecting Dewey to win the election in any case, he even suggested to John Foster Dulles that, owing to the "emergency character of the world situation," he should replace him immediately following the election. A stunned Dulles reminded Marshall that Truman would still be in office another three months, and that even lame ducks choose their own secretaries of state.[112]

❖

THE CREATION OF THE UNITED NATIONS WAS MEANT TO BE ROOSEVELT'S crowning contribution to the postwar order. It would, he believed, prevent an American retreat into isolationism and turn the Soviets from confrontation to cooperation.

Instead, Marshall was now determined to use it to isolate Moscow on the world stage. In October, he took the blockade to the Security Council under Chapter VII of the U.N. Charter, which covered threats to peace. He set the United States up as prosecutor, targeting its case to the six "neutrals:" Argentina, Belgium, Canada, China, Colombia, and Syria.

Bevin and Schuman signed on only after putting up spirited resistance. The sole purpose they could discern in involving the U.N. was to secure moral sanction to break the blockade with arms, and it was their nations that would bear the brunt of the Soviet response.[113] The Russians, Bevin groused privately, had "played their cards very badly," but this had "forced us into a closer association with the Americans in Germany than we had wished."[114]

Truman, however, who had only just abandoned a peace mission, had made no decision to use force. Some in the administration, like Royall, were still pushing for a face-saving withdrawal from Berlin. Draper called the city "an untenable military outpost." Backtracking from his earlier hard line, Kennan, too, was now concerned over the Allies' "increasingly unfavorable position."[115] He opposed using the U.N. to isolate the Soviets. Rather than mobilize the "smaller nations," he said, it would likely "alarm" and "paralyze" them, undermining "their will to play an active part in the organization." As for "the Russians," if cornered they will just "leave the Organization."[116] Smith, believing the crisis to be a self-inflicted wound, argued that "any U.N. action that enables us to get out of Berlin would be very desirable."[117]

For their part, the Soviets were thrown off guard by the U.N. gambit. To that point, they had had little experience manipulating the Security Council. On September 25, Vyshinsky, in a six-thousand-word speech before the General Assembly, denounced the Western powers and the "instigators of a new war."[118] In a show of sheer comedic paranoia, he backed up his claims of American warmongering by referring to a map allegedly showing "The Third World War, Pacific Theater of Military Operations." The map had been forwarded to him in July by Colonel-General Fyodor Kuznetsov, head of the Main Intelligence Agency (GRU) of the General Staff of the Armed Forces, who said that it had been "created by the American oil company 'ESSO'" and received "from our source in Tokyo." The map was in fact titled "ESSO War Map III, featuring the Pacific Theater;" it was produced during World War II as a customer marketing give-away.[119]

Conscious of the West's built-in voting advantage, and recognizing a show trial when he saw one, Stalin rejected U.N. jurisdiction on the Berlin question. He ordered Vyshinsky to invoke Article 107 of its Charter, which said that "Nothing in the present Charter shall invalidate or preclude action, in relation to any state which during the Second World War has been an enemy of any signatory to the present Charter, taken or authorized as a result of that war by the Governments having responsibility for such action."[120] On this basis, Vyshinsky insisted that German policy could only be discussed within the Council of Foreign Ministers.

By refusing to participate in Security Council debate, however, he gave the three permanent western members free rein to denounce Soviet behavior unrebutted.[121] The result was predictable. On October 5, only Soviet Ukraine joined Vyshinsky in voting against U.N. jurisdiction.

The following week, Vyshsinsky tried to quash the intervention through the Security Council's Argentine president, Juan Atilio Bramuglia. The Peronist is "critical of the capitalist system," Vyshinsky noted approvingly in his diary; "he said [it] had outlived its day." Fawning and apologetic in their secret meetings, Bramuglia had, Vyshinsky told Molotov, "tried to avoid presidency of the Council," and with it responsibility for "the Berlin question, but did not succeed."

On October 11, Bramuglia briefed Vyshinsky, warning him that they were speaking in the strictest privacy. Having conferred with the Allies, he said, the neutrals believed they could take Berlin off the Security Council agenda if the Soviets agreed to a simultaneous lifting of both sides' trade and transport restrictions. The Council of Foreign Ministers could then reconvene to resolve remaining issues related to Berlin and Germany as a whole.

Vyshinsky demurred, demanding that the Allies also complete removal of the B-mark at the same time the restrictions were lifted. Bramuglia warned that the Allies would insist on an end to the blockade *before* the currency transition was complete—not after. If the Soviets wanted their version, what could they offer in exchange? Nothing, Vyshinsky said. The best option was to drop the point. Bramuglia responded that the Allied position was actually closer to the August 30 directive, to which Vyshinsky replied that it could in that case form the basis of the CFM discussion. This proposal served Molotov's aim of elevating the directive—or the Soviet interpretation of it—into a legally binding commitment. Bramuglia liked the idea. Vyshinsky promised an official response within a few days.

After securing approval from Molotov and Stalin, Vyshinsky affirmed his stance, "remind[ing] Bramuglia that the Berlin question was not," in any case, "subject to discussion in the Security Council." It should be removed. Bramuglia returned for clarification the next day: were the Soviets saying the August directive should regulate matters "until" the CFM could meet? This was, he said, how the other neutrals understood it. No, Vyshinsky said. It must govern "within" the CFM. "I thought this was the case," the Argentine responded dejectedly, knowing the Allies would reject it.

Bramuglia, Vyshinsky cabled Molotov on October 15, "expressed regret that he ever fell into this story." The Argentine pledged to "do the utmost for the Berlin question to be decided in the interests of the Soviet Union, seeing as how he is a close friend of the USSR." But "we of course know the worth of Argentine promises." His translator, Yuri Dashkevich, suspected "Bramuglia was acting as a defender of the Anglo-Americans."[122]

Unbeknownst to Vyshinsky, his useful idiot was feeling heat from Washington. The State Department, Acheson revealed years later, was working "to connect the price of Argentine wheat with cooperation on the Berlin matter."[123] On October 25, the neutrals put forward a broad resolution calling for the lifting of all restrictions on traffic and commerce into and out of Berlin, resumption of four-power currency talks, and a reconvening of the Council of Foreign Ministers to resolve other disputed matters in Germany. Marshall had wanted the neutrals simply to condemn the blockade, but the Allies joined in support. The Soviets cast their veto.

Vyshinsky was unconcerned. The French U.N. press department deputy had been passing on encouraging intelligence about airlift challenges from a loose-tongued American delegation contact. "In winter, flights are extremely complex and staff are so exhausted that it requires a great effort to keep the pilots flying," Pravda journalist Georgii Mikhailovich Ratiani recorded; "material parts very quickly wear out. . . . [T]he American army command and the State Department fear that the 'air-bridge' will cease to operate in the very near future."[124] Time, it seemed, was on Moscow's side.

For its part, the State Department suspected that "the Soviets count on the failure of the air lift during the winter months," and "would not lift the blockade until proven wrong."[125] Philip Jessup, the U.S. representative to the U.N. General Assembly, "discounted at 1000 to one [the] probability [of] Soviet desire for [a] real settlement of [the] Berlin situation" at this point.[126] Meaningful diplomacy would have to wait until the Allies could demonstrate mastery of the weather.

The Security Council resolution was, in the end, a minor diplomatic victory for Marshall, helping to show Moscow as intransigent on a matter of global security interest. But there was a cost. The issue would remain on the Council's agenda, and continued efforts by the neutrals to resolve it would clash with events in Berlin—events that were now moving decidedly in Washington's favor.[127]

German children cheering an American airlift plane during the Soviet blockade, Berlin, 1948.

TWELVE

DIVISION

ON NOVEMBER 2, 1948, AMERICAN VOTERS DELIVERED A MONUMENTAL electoral upset. In defiance of the pundits, polls, betting lines (15 to 1 against), and a legendary *Chicago Tribune* headline declaring the reverse, Truman defeated Dewey. The Democrats, furthermore, swept both houses of Congress. Capped off by a relentless six-week whistle-stop national tour, the president, in Marshall's words, had "put over the greatest one-man fight in American history."

The standoff with Russia had played a big part. "The bear got us" in the end, reasoned Dewey aide Elliott Bell. Or at least Truman's handling of it. The Berlin airlift was by now widely seen as a great success. Stalin was on the defensive. And though the president's clumsy peace effort had upset Marshall's delicate diplomacy, even critics such as Walter Lippmann now conceded that it had played well with nervous voters.[1]

Three days after the election, press reports said Truman would reach across the aisle and tap Vandenberg to replace Marshall. The sixty-four-year-old senator had reason to be interested; his party had just lost control of the Senate. But he was determined to stay put. And knowing Truman's propensity to announce-first-and-ask-later, he quashed the idea through friendly Democrats.

By severing ties with Republicans, the senator explained, "I [might] lose my best chance to be helpful in supporting bi-partisan foreign policy." He had, during the campaign, taken exception to Truman's deriding of the "do nothing, good for nothing" 80th Congress. This Congress was, he pointed out, the one that had funded the Truman Doctrine, enacted the Marshall Plan, and laid the groundwork for a North Atlantic security pact. "[I]n all that relates to foreign affairs," he retorted in an October radio address, it was "the best" in the nation's history.[2]

With Vandenberg out, Truman would, at the end of November, quietly offer the post to an astonished but agreeable Acheson.[3] The two men—curiously given their different backgrounds and demeanors—would form a much closer personal bond than Truman and Marshall ever did.

Across the ocean in West Berlin, support for the president was sky-high. Berliners had come to identify American pilots—such as young Lieutenant Gail Halvorsen, "the Candy Bomber" (*der Schokoladen-flieger*), who rained treats on the city's children from the air—with a commitment to preserving their lives and freedoms. In an October survey, 84 percent were confident the Allies would continue adequately supplying the city by air. Ninety-five percent supported their remaining in Berlin.

Overruling concerns about the effect on military preparedness, Truman ordered dozens of new Navy planes to be deployed in the airlift just before the election. And he would approve procurement of twenty-three more planes to replace worn-out C-54s in December. After long deliberations, the Attlee government also agreed to put its aircraft under the control of a Combined Airlift Task Force headed by Tunner.[4] Against this background, Clay ordered a 20 percent increase in Berlin food rations, to 2,000 calories a day. Though far lower than the 3,300 calories the average American was consuming, this was higher than anywhere else in Germany.[5] Meanwhile, Washington even funded cultural initiatives in the besieged western sectors. These included the legendary literary magazine *Der Monat*, founded by American journalist Melvin Lasky. Mixing "anti-Stalinism and esoteric high culture," sixty thousand copies of the first issue arrived from Munich by American bomber in October. It featured original contributions from notables such as Bertrand Russell, Arnold Toynbee, Jean-Paul Sartre, V. S. Pritchett, and Rebecca West.[6]

At the same time, Germans were growing increasingly bitter toward the Soviets. The Red Army had carted off over half Berlin's prewar industrial capacity, more than twice what had been destroyed in the war. Eastern businesses were being pillaged, their bank accounts seized by Soviet authorities. Refugees by the thousands continued to pour into the west each month. Eighty-eight percent of West Berliners said they preferred the privations of life under blockade to Soviet control.[7] And they were about to affirm this conviction in their own historic vote.

On October 8, the City Assembly set December 5 as the date for the election of new legislators. But with the Communist SED set to fare even worse than it had two years earlier, Soviet commandant General Alexander Kotikov imposed impossible conditions for allowing the poll in his sector. The Magistrat and City Assembly therefore voted to proceed in the western sectors alone. Lacking authority but determined to block it, the SED deputy speaker of the Assembly, Ottomar Geschke, called an "extraordinary meeting" for October 30. With only Communists in attendance, the gathering "dismissed" the Magistrat and elected a new one under Fritz Ebert (son of the Weimar Republic's first president).[8] The SED, which now claimed a mandate to rule the entire city, launched a menacing campaign to keep West Berliners from going to the polls. Following orders approved by Stalin and the Soviet Politburo on November 12, the party worked vigorously to "persuade the populations of the western sectors not to participate in elections, to promulgate its platforms, or to disseminate flyers, placards, [or] brochures."[9]

When the NSC met in Washington on November 26, Marshall explained the stakes: proceeding with the election would likely split Berlin for good, while delaying it would be seen as a western "retreat." From Berlin, Murphy cabled an impassioned appeal against delay, insisting it would be a "cowardly surrender" to the SED and the Soviets. Bohlen acknowledged it might give the Security Council time to find "a way out" of the crisis, but "would in effect be confirming the right of the Soviets to act illegally." He insisted the SED coup was a "stroke of luck" that took the millstone of the August 30 directive from Washington's neck and made Moscow responsible for the city's division.

Marshall cabled back his agreement. The consequences of Allied intervention to postpone the election would, he said, be "disastrous." But the Security Council would have to be handled delicately. The neutrals were preparing "currency and trade plans . . . for implementation by a single city administration," which were now "perhaps impossible." They would need to be persuaded that the fault lay with Moscow, which, in blocking the vote in the east, was violating a four-power agreement that city elections be held every two years.

On polling day, voter turnout in the west was, in spite of organized Communist intimidation, a remarkable 86 percent—testimony to the strength of anti-Soviet feeling. The SPD garnered 65 percent of the vote, with the CDU and Free Democrats splitting the remainder. Reuter, a former Communist turned anti-Stalinist, became West Berlin's first mayor. Acknowledging the existential dangers facing the new political entity, however, the SPD agreed to govern with its rivals in a unity coalition. [10]

Though the election affirmed the confidence of Berliners in the airlift, it made the fallout from Marshall's U.N. gambit that much more difficult to manage. Paris and London, still fearful of Russian reprisals, wanted to intensify efforts with the neutrals to secure a currency deal that would end the Berlin standoff. Marshall and Clay, in contrast, were determined to make the new political entity of West Berlin a success—even at the cost of permanent separation from the east. That meant, in the first instance, monetary union with West Germany and an end to U.N. efforts that could only delay it.

❖

"SHE BESTRIDES THE WORLD LIKE A COLOSSUS: NO OTHER POWER AT ANY time in the world's history has possessed so varied or so great an influence on other nations," wrote British historian Robert Payne in 1949. "It is already an axiom that the decisions of the American government affect the lives and livelihood of the remotest people."[11]

This notion owed in no small part to the Marshall Plan. By the end of 1948, nine months after passage of the legislation, it had delivered over $2 billion in assistance ($20.57 billion in today's money). Industrial production in western Europe surpassed prewar levels for the first time. Confidence in recovery was growing. In the donor country itself, a poll at election time found 62 percent

satisfied with the plan's performance, compared to only 14 percent dissatis-
fied.[12] Such public approval was remarkable for an aid initiative.

Truman's inaugural address on January 20, 1949, devoted to foreign policy,
reflected his pride and confidence in the Plan. His breath freezing in the chill
winter air, he blasted communism as a "false philosophy" that "threat[ened]
the efforts of free nations to bring about world recovery and lasting peace." But
the United States would "keep [its] full weight behind the European recovery
program," which he called the "greatest cooperative economic program in history." The ERP would ensure that "the free people of that continent can resume
their rightful place in the forefront of civilization and can contribute once more
to the security and welfare of the world."[13]

Over in Paris, a European partner to the Economic Cooperation Administration, the Organisation for European Economic Co-operation (OEEC),
had been up and running since April 1948. Belgian foreign minister Paul-Henri
Spaak became the first chairman of its council, French economist Robert Mar-
jolin its first secretary general. Ernst van der Beugel, now a Dutch OEEC delegate, credited Hoffman and the Marshall Plan with the impetus behind an
element of recovery that would otherwise have been politically unachievable:
European integration. But there were teething pains. Just as with the Committee of European Economic Cooperation, tasked with formulating the Marshall
aid request the previous summer, the OEEC would struggle with infighting
over the division of aid.

The French chafed under Hoffman's integration drive, although they could
never escape the sense that the alternative was worse. "If we refuse," MRP
(Christian Democrat) politician Jean Letourneau reasoned, "the United States
will bestow this leadership role on Germany within six months." The British, for their part, dragged themselves along for the sake of keeping influence
with Washington, but would never wholly buy into the venture. "We are being
asked," groused one official, "to join the Germans, who started two world wars;
the French, who had in 1940 collapsed in the face of German aggression; the
Italians, who changed sides; and the Low Countries, of whom not much was
known but who seemed to have put up little resistance to Germany." This was
small consolation for loss of an empire.

Hoffman, however, was relentless. "Make no small plans," he told colleagues, "for they have no magic to stir the imagination of men."[14] In December 1948, in a midnight meeting with Sir Stafford Cripps—now Britain's chancellor of the exchequer, and representing the OEEC ministers—Hoffman insisted on showing Congress a 50 percent reduction by volume in intra-European trade barriers by February. At 3 a.m. an "exasperated" Cripps gave his word. "It was done," Hoffman recalled with pride.

Yet Hoffman continued to press, year after year. On October 31, 1949, he would deliver a speech in Paris insisting that the "steady improvement in the conditions of life [requires] nothing less than an integration of the West European economy." A British official complained that it meant remaking Europe in the image of America, "God's own country," yet three days later the OEEC would back the creation of "a single market in Europe." Members would agree to cut quantitative import restrictions in half by year's end, and to collaborate on the creation of a payments union, underwritten with Marshall funds, to eliminate currency barriers to trade.

In January 1950, Hoffman would press further, making up to a quarter of ECA aid dependent on progress in trade liberalization and integration. Cripps decried it as "dollar dictatorship." Even Acheson, ever pragmatic and anxious to sustain solidarity in the face of Soviet threats, opposed such conditionality. But van der Beugel defended Hoffman, noting that "it was again American and not European initiative which pushed Western Europe further on the road to greater cooperation and integration."[15]

Seeing the need for a "Marshall Plan" of his own to showcase Soviet economic leadership in eastern Europe, Stalin decreed one. Launched in January 1949, the Council for Mutual Economic Assistance, often called Comecon, would in practice take the form of Kremlin-dictated bilateral barter arrangements imposed on its captive members: Bulgaria, Czechoslovakia, Hungary, Poland, and Romania. In this regard, it mimicked Nazi trade arrangements.[16] In assigning to each country its own production requirements, it also implemented the very policy that Molotov had claimed, falsely, that Marshall wanted to impose in June 1947. As for the aid element of the Marshall Plan, Comecon operated it in reverse. By the time of Stalin's death in 1953, the Soviet Union would extract as much from its allies in unrequited flows as the United States would confer on its own.[17]

✥

"THE [BERLIN] CRISIS," WROTE *THE NEW REPUBLIC*, "IS CERTAIN TO FIGURE in future textbooks on economics. Seldom before has Gresham's famous law that 'bad money drives out good' had such a proving ground."[18] The Allies, in their earlier determination to leave space for a currency compromise with Moscow, had burdened West Berlin with a currency regime that no competent economist could endorse. East marks, which no one wanted, were accepted for government transactions at par with west marks, which everyone hoarded. Arbitrage incentives driven by perverse price-control, rationing, and tax-accounting regimes worsened shortages. Murphy decried the fact that two thirds of the food provided for Berlin was being paid for in east marks—which was "so much waste paper."[19] And so in early 1949, currency chaos brought the interests of Washington and West Berlin closer together, even as it drove those between Washington and its wartime partners further apart.

Clay wanted to push the east mark out of West Berlin by declaring the West German deutschmark the sole legal tender. The State Department saw diplomatic as well as economic benefits in the move, concluding it would "be viewed as proof of Western . . . determination to remain in Berlin, which might in turn make [the Soviets] reassess the value of the blockade." For Britain, however, this was a step too far. "Bevin," Lovett observed, was "concerned [it] might slam the door on a settlement" with Moscow. Robertson insisted that Germans "would never accept" a divided Germany. Murphy suspected the French did not even want Berlin "tied in politically with the West." He condemned "the British and French attitude" as craven. Washington, Clay concluded, needed to "demand acquiescence in our policy . . . as a condition to our continued financing of the German deficit." And if that didn't do the trick, he suggested, "we have other resources to force the issue."[20]

That a technically simple monetary reform should cause such a rupture in Allied unity might appear strange, but the political significance of the move was considerable. First and foremost, it played to the agenda of West Berlin's new leaders, who were pressing "irrevocably to tie [the] Western sectors" of the city "with the Western zones" of Germany. Reuter wrote an impassioned letter to Clay arguing that with the Russians "no longer execut[ing] any powers" in West

Berlin, "there can no longer be objections, relating to the law of nations, to the inclusion of the three western sectors . . . into the ERP":

> Whilst therefore legal barriers no longer exist, political as well as economic reasons make the inclusion of the western sectors of Berlin into the ERP a matter of utmost importance. Berlin is situated as an outpost of Europe in the struggle against Russian expansionist efforts. Her task has become a European problem. . . . [Inclusion] would mean not only critical economic relief but also a moral support of the population of Berlin and an important demonstration against the Russian plans for strangulation.[21]

But for the French and the British, extending the deutschmark to West Berlin also represented a further unwelcome step in Marshall's radical agenda of binding western Europe together, including as much of Germany as possible.

On January 12, 1949, State Department officials tried to convince their British counterparts to accept January 30 as the date for the currency transition. If the Soviets did not meet requirements for the operation of a single Berlin currency, the east mark would cease to be legal tender in the western sectors. The British refused to go along. State considered banning the east mark unilaterally in the American sector, but ultimately deemed it impractical.

By February 9, however, the British had conceded there was "no hope" the U.N. would resolve the currency standoff in the context of a split city administration. And indeed, the neutrals' "Technical Committee on Berlin Currency and Trade" abandoned its efforts two days later, declaring that "the present positions of the experts of the Four Occupying Powers are so far apart in this matter that further work . . . does not appear useful."[22] So Bevin reversed himself. "The division of Germany, at all events for the present," he concluded, was now "essential for our plans." The Allied-occupied zones needed to be brought within "our Western European system." He proposed March 10 for the currency transition, but refused to join the Americans in telling the French to take it or leave it. If the French left the east mark circulating in their sector it would, he feared, reveal "a split among Western powers" and "damage Anglo-French relations."[23]

On February 16, Clay and Robertson tried to persuade Koenig to join the changeover, but, as expected, he resisted. The matter, he reminded them, was still before the Security Council, and the linkage of "Berlin with [the] Western zones" of Germany was in any case "contrary to his government's policy." On the 19th, Caffery brought the issue to Schuman, who agreed to cooperate only after the Security Council had decided what to do with the neutral committee's forthcoming report.[24]

Acheson, now returned to the front lines as secretary of state, still feared that the resentful neutrals would place some "onus for failure on [the] Western powers."[25] Canadian ambassador to Washington Humphrey Hume Wrong had, after all, asked Bohlen point-blank whether the United States actually wanted a settlement of the Berlin crisis.[26] Acheson did, but, unlike Marshall, never had faith in the U.N.'s ability to assist it. In a blow to the institution in which FDR had lodged such great hopes, he told the House that the U.N. was "utterly worthless to create that environment which we want." Only a "powerful group" of democratic countries, led by the United States, could do this.[27]

Fortunately, Bragmuglia was no longer Security Council president. Cuba's anti-Soviet Alberto Alvarez, who took up the rotating post in March, readily agreed not to publish the neutrals' report as a Council document. When the report was buried instead as a minor press release on March 15, the State Department put out pre-prepared press points blaming the Soviets for the mediation failure.[28]

Five days later, on March 20, the three Allied military governors issued their own release stating that "the East mark shall [henceforth] cease to be legal tender in the Western sectors of Berlin." Reuter was elated. "This step is more important than a whole sheaf of declarations that the Western powers were going to stay here," he proclaimed. "It means the definite recognition that Berlin belongs to the West ideologically and politically."[29] It also split the city economically far more effectively than the blockade, causing a collapse in trade between its eastern and western sectors. West Berlin unemployment soared as its "export" goods became three to six times more expensive in East Berlin, and its firms became uncompetitive against more productive West German counterparts.[30] At that moment, however, the city's leaders were more focused on politics, believing that better economic results would follow in time.

Meeting with Attlee in Berlin before the changeover, Reuter had called for quick recognition of West Berlin as a state (*Länd*) that could be incorporated into the new Federal Republic.[31] Murphy backed his call in cables to Acheson, arguing that West Berliners saw Germany more in an "international frame-work" than West Germans, "who often appear mired in local nationalism." Ber-lin's influence on West Germany would, therefore, be in the direction of State Department thinking.

The French, however, objected to including West Berlin in the new state, fearing that the city's former status as a national capital would help centralize West Germany and make it too powerful. The Soviets condemned the idea as "provocative." Other German political leaders also resisted Reuter's push to bring West Berlin into West Germany too quickly. Mayor Friedensburg acknowledged that there was little hope of reuniting East and West Berlin any-time soon. In spite of "at least 90 percent" of East Berliners thinking exactly as West Berliners, he said, "the 'Trinity' [of] Soviet-style administration, police, and state-owned enterprises formed a very strong framework" for maintain-ing communist control. Still, he opposed treating "a permanent separation be-tween East and West Germany as inevitable," which weighed in favor of keeping West Berlin outside West Germany. Adenauer had political reasons for oppos-ing West Berlin's inclusion. The city was dominated by the SPD, meaning that its incorporation into West Germany would lessen the power of his CDU in the new Bundestag (parliament). In the end, Acheson came down against West Berlin's incorporation "under present air-lift circumstances," arguing that it would strengthen Moscow's case that the Allies had forfeited their rights in the city by abrogating the four-power control agreements.[32]

❖

ALLIED RETALIATION FOR THE BLOCKADE WAS HURTING EASTERN GER-many far worse than Moscow had anticipated. Shortages of coal and steel, a product of the counter-blockade, were acute. The Soviets, too, suffered, as they had been siphoning off food and industrial shipments from western Germany as hidden reparations. This practice was now impossible.[33] Stalin was, further-more, failing to achieve his objectives in either Berlin or western Germany. Mostly mild winter weather meant the airlift could continue indefinitely, ensur-ing the Allies an ongoing propaganda coup. Dean Acheson, a more rigid cold warrior than Marshall, was now heading the State Department. Stalin, faced with the choice of whether to climb down or escalate, characteristically chose both.

On January 30, 1949, in a rare response to an American press query,[34] Stalin said that if the Allies postponed establishment of a West German state pending a meeting of the Council of Foreign Ministers, and lifted their transport and trade restrictions in Germany, the Soviet government saw "no obstacle" to removing its own restrictions.[35] Curiously, he made no mention of withdrawing the B-mark.

Bevin felt sure it was a trap. He thought his reaction confirmed two days later when an SED-organized "German People's Council" issued a statement praising Stalin's call for the Western powers "to *give up* their measures . . . for a [West] German state." The communication was a revival of Stalin's "insistent wish," making clear that his real aim remained abandonment of the London Program.[36] Kohler in Moscow therefore saw no news in Stalin's initiative. The "currency problem and blockade could always have been solved overnight," he cabled Acheson, "if we agreed to make concessions on West Germany satisfactory to Stalin."[37]

But Acheson had no intention of bargaining away West Germany. The London Program, he told the press, remained "necessary." In a cable to Douglas, he said he was willing "to begin discussions with the Soviets for resolution of questions affecting Germany as a whole," but only "once [the] blockade is lifted."[38] Stalin's "insistent wish" remained out of the question.

Nonetheless, Acheson was intrigued that Stalin had delivered his terms publicly without mentioning the currency issue. Was it intentional? Determined neither to negotiate through the press nor to suggest weakness by making official inquiries, Acheson decided on a secret probe. He directed Jessup, recently appointed ambassador-at-large, to approach the Soviet U.N. ambassador, Yakov Malik, ostensibly on his own initiative and out of the spotlight in New York.[39]

On February 15, Jessup contrived to bump into Malik in the U.N. delegates' lounge. Following an exchange of pleasantries and a few "bantering" jokes, Jessup casually began his inquiry. "I wondered," he said, "whether there was anything new in Premier Stalin's reply to the newspaper questions regarding the Berlin question." Malik asked what he meant. Well, Jessup clarified, "Stalin . . . had said nothing about the currency question." Did that have "any special significance?" Malik frowned, shaking his head; he had "no information on that."

Jessup thanked him, adding he "would be glad to have it" if he got any.[40] The back channel was open.

Acheson, however, was not about to reprise the Smith and Vinson fiascoes, in which Truman made himself look feeble through peace overtures. While sending Jessup to New York, Acheson also authorized an expansion of the counter-blockade, banning freight movements across the Allied zones to and from the entire Soviet bloc.[41] Removal of these and other western sanctions would be atop Malik's agenda when he would reemerge in March.

Before he would do so, however, Stalin would reshuffle his diplomatic deck. Having had Molotov's Jewish wife arrested for treason in December, and having compelled him to divorce her, Stalin now, on March 4, sacked him as foreign minister (though he left him deputy prime minister). In Molotov's place, Stalin elevated his deputy, Andrei Vyshinsky—a man known for expressing few thoughts beyond those given him by the *vozhd*. Molotov's demotion must have embarrassed the CIA, which had just tapped him as Stalin's heir apparent.[42] A few weeks later, Stalin would also replace Sokolovsky in Berlin with war hero Marshal Vasily Chuikov. "If anyone attacks us again," Chuikov would say years later, "there will be a new Stalingrad. But this Stalingrad will be far away, somewhere in the West." Meanwhile in Berlin, clear spring skies brought the resumption of regular buzzing maneuvers against U.S. and British transport planes. Stalin showed that he would not shy from a military incident, even in the midst of a diplomatic offensive.[43]

On March 15, Malik invited Jessup to the Soviet U.N. delegation Park Avenue headquarters to hear Moscow's official response. Though his English was fluent, Malik spoke in Russian. Emphasizing the importance of the message, the interpreter himself read the translation from pre-typed English text. Stalin's omission of the German currency matter, Malik said, was "not accidental." It could be discussed among the foreign ministers when they reconvened over the Berlin and German questions.

If true, this statement was a concession. But would the blockade be lifted before such a meeting? Jessup asked. This point was, for Acheson, nonnegotiable.

Malik said he "had no directive on any other point." He could offer only to inquire with Moscow.[44]

Negotiation with Malik, Jessup saw, was to be a classic Soviet diplomatic operation, with the Russian encouraging his counterpart to talk but revealing nothing himself. (A typical Kremlin directive said that "the Soviet expert must not immediately answer the presented questions, but must inform [his counterpart] that answers will be provided after some research."[45]) It would be six more days until he was called back to Malik's office for Moscow's next response. Vyshinsky, Malik told Jessup on March 21, had indicated that "a reciprocal lifting of the restrictions on transportation and trade in Berlin" could take place after a date for a foreign ministers meeting was set but before it actually began. This appeared to be another concession.

But Malik then slipped in Stalin's "insistent wish": Vyshinsky, he said, understood the Allies would also "call off" creation of "the Western German government if there were a CFM" meeting. Jessup cut him off, objecting that he had never suggested such a linkage. He could only say that if a meeting date were set soon it *could*, as a factual matter, be held before such a government were created. He was careful, however, not to suggest that Washington could exercise any power in the matter. Malik, to his surprise, appeared to accept this formulation. Jessup remained wary of a trap.[46]

Malik now wanted assurance that there would be "a full resumption of trade between the zones," meaning elimination of all Allied blockages. Jessup was "careful to dodge this," as American priorities had changed since 1947. Opening up trade with the East had been an objective then, but withholding it was now seen as the more promising way to weaken the Soviet bloc. The severing of trade between East and West Germany had made it impossible for Moscow to fulfill its targets for reparations deliveries from current production. Without trade controls, there was also the likelihood that goods sent to West Germany under the Marshall Plan could end up in Soviet hands. Jessup was, therefore, not authorized to agree to any liberalization that went beyond the status quo ante at the time the blockade was imposed.[47] This was less than Stalin would want as a price for lifting the blockade. But the two agreed to meet again, after the three Allied governments had considered the Soviet position.

Acheson brought Schuman, Bevin, and their advisers together in Washington on April 1 to brief them on the talks and solicit their agreement on an Allied position statement, which Jessup would then present to Malik. The atmosphere was tense. Schuman was skeptical, Bevin scornful. The Briton detested this American habit of using backdoor emissaries, and resented his country being shoved to the margins of European diplomacy. Sir Oliver Franks, now ambassador to Washington, warned that anything resembling an Allied "proposal" risked "expos[ing] ourselves to Soviet propaganda and a swindle." Bevin added that it "might imperil" everything from the creation of West Germany to the Marshall Plan to the solidarity of western Europe and the Atlantic security pact—all of which were arriving at important milestones.[48]

❖

APRIL 3 MARKED THE ONE-YEAR ANNIVERSARY OF THE MARSHALL AID LEGislation. Attlee sent the president a warm message commemorating the event. The $5 billion in assistance ($50 billion in today's money) Congress had thus far authorized had, he said, "given us hope and help when we most needed it. During the last year the whole economic scene in Western Europe has been transformed to a degree which must astonish all of us when we recall the uncertainties and perils of the immediately preceding years." A further $5.43 billion would be authorized by Congress eleven days later.

From England, *Time* offered the stirring story of a Birmingham car plant that had been on the verge of shutting down, with a loss of ten thousand jobs, before Marshall aid began flowing. The firm had been unable to buy carbon black, an essential element for a third of each tire's carcass and tread, owing to the country's paltry dollar reserves, until counterpart funds began financing the imports. "We've never had to worry since," said one of the workers. "Marshall aid saved us from catastrophe."[49]

Meanwhile, backing for the ERP from the most influential American business interests had also grown. The Chamber of Commerce embraced "judicious tariff cuts," arguing that foreign competition would boost domestic productivity. The National Association of Manufacturers urged the country to "recognize its own economic strength and overcome its 'inferiority complex.'" The tariff issue having "shrunk to almost relative insignificance," it called for Washington to "provide the maximum of encouragement to the flow of goods and services as between nations on an honest competitive basis."[50]

Tensions with Moscow, however, had grown over the twelve months. Soviet actions in Berlin, Harriman told Congress, had been a by-product of the

Marshall Plan; the Russians had "perceived [its] immensely constructive po-
tentialities earlier and more fully" than anyone else.[51] Indeed, Stalin was investing ever greater manpower and funds to counter it. Hoffman estimated that
Communist anti–Marshall Plan information officials in Europe outnumbered
his own pro-Marshall staff by 50 to 1. "Run[ning] the ECA without a strong information arm," he concluded, was "as futile as trying to conduct a major business without sales, advertising, and customer-relations departments."

Over the course of 1949, Harriman boosted funds for publications, post-
ers, exhibits, fairs, film documentaries, radio programs, and television shows.[52]
Spending on media publicity would grow from $500,000 in 1948 to about $20
million annually by 1952 ($182 million in today's money).[53] The director of
the State Department's International Broadcasting Division, Charles Taylor,
returned from a European fact-finding trip in January 1949 to file a long confidential report on the need for differentiated programming in the "slave areas"
and the "free areas." He concluded that "the ground is very suitable in Bulgaria
for our propaganda" and that "Czechoslovakia's hatred of Germany and Poland can be exploited as well by the Voice [of America] as it can by Moscow."
France, however, "nationalistic" and "hard-headed," was averse to what its officials called "the 'brutal propaganda' of the United States." In Italy, he reasoned,
"slightly stronger doses of propaganda" were possible.[54]

Secretly, though, the administration was doing far more. Kennan sat on the
advisory committee of a new Office of Policy Coordination. Despite its deliberately dull name, the OPC's mission was anything but: it was the new CIA covert operations arm. Early in the new year, the OPC's new head, Frank Wisner,
approached Hoffman's deputy, Bissell. Wisner, whom Marshall had successfully nominated as its head, knew that the ECA had been receiving 5 percent of
counterpart funds to cover administrative costs. He had come to request some
of these funds for efforts on behalf of the Plan. Given that Harriman had approved, according to Wisner, Bissell agreed.

Though the OPC's budget was less than $5 million at the time, it now began
receiving tens of millions via the ECA. Funding would climb seventeen-fold
before the Marshall Plan wound down in 1952. Staff would grow twenty-fold,
controlling forty-seven overseas stations. Wisner used his new bounty to fund
psychological warfare campaigns through European media, nongovernmental

organizations, and cultural and educational institutions; bribes to labor officials and politicians; and even insurrection efforts in eastern Europe.[55]

In early 1949, Kennan was anxious to show that the Marshall Plan could work without visible muscular interventions, such as military pacts and the division of Germany. Still bitter that Lippmann had portrayed him as the misguided apostle of aggressive and limitless containment, he sought to become the invisible hand behind efforts to head off open militarization. "Operating in a personal capacity," so that the State Department's hand could "be denied by the Secretary," as he explained his work to Lovett, Kennan became an eager and active source of inspiration and guidance for the OPC. Under his stewardship, the Policy Planning Staff would become the effective overseer of all U.S. covert activities.

Secret governments, however, tend to take on a life of their own, resisting the sort of shepherding Kennan tried to provide. The OPC's early Marshall-funded efforts would eventually mushroom to become one of the defining dark features of the Cold War.

Kennan would in consequence come to look back with regret on "all part that I or the [PPS] staff took in any of this."[56] He would, however, primarily blame the Pentagon and its chief, Forrestal, for the OPC's uncontrolled growth. In any event, the effort would, with the coming of the Korean War, become a complement to, and not a substitute for, militarization of the conflict with Moscow.

Well before that, however, the defense establishment's top architect of the Cold War would become a casualty of it.[57] Convinced that the Soviets were driven by a boundless ideological fervor, Forrestal sought every possible means—conventional and covert—to expand America's capacity to fight back. Yet unable to convince the president that foreign aid should not preclude more military spending,[58] and unable to control his own bickering Army, Navy, and Air Force chiefs, Forrestal became consumed by long hours, stress, and outright paranoia. Russians, Zionists, White House aides: all were, he was convinced, stalking and undermining him.

On March 1, Truman demanded his resignation. He replaced him with Louis Johnson, his loyal chief campaign fundraiser.[59] One of Truman's finer qualities was an ability to identify and cultivate subordinates of capacity and judgment, but he failed to display it in this case. Johnson was his worst appointment. Forrestal's

temperamental opposite, he shouted, boasted, and, in the words of one high official, made "two enemies for every dollar he saved." General Bradley would later
say that Truman "replaced one mental case with another."[60]

Forrestal sank into "involutional melancholia," as his April 2 admission
record at Bethesda Naval Hospital would show. Less than two months later,
shortly before 2 a.m. on May 22, a thud was heard below his sixteenth-floor
window. On an asphalt and cinder block ledge three floors above the ground,
his body would be found facedown—a robe sash tied around the neck.

⟡

ARTHUR VANDENBERG WAS THE BRIDGE BETWEEN A DEMOCRATIC WHITE
House and a Republican Congress that made the Marshall Plan possible. When
he rejected the chance to take Marshall's job after Truman's victory in November, he knew this role was still indispensable. A critical task remained, one that
required Senate approval.

Notwithstanding his unwavering support for the Marshall Plan, Vandenberg thought it doubtful that economic stability could take hold in Europe
without American military backing. "I am inclined to think," he wrote in a constituent letter in January 1949, "that 'physical security' is a prerequisite to the
kind of long-range economic planning which Western Europe requires." In this
view, he was at odds with Kennan. To Vandenberg it had been the American
Neutrality Laws of the 1930s, which he had at the time supported, that encouraged Hitler to set off on the path to World War II. The United States now
needed a different peacetime posture. "If an appropriate North Atlantic Pact
is written," he wrote to another constituent, "I think it will exactly reverse this
psychology so far as Mr. Stalin is concerned if, as and when he contemplates
World War Three."[61]

With this conviction, Vandenberg had set out, following passage of the
Marshall legislation, to lay the groundwork for yet more difficult legislation.
On June 11, 1948, by a vote of 64 to 4, the Senate approved Resolution 239,
clearing the way for the country to enter into peacetime collective security arrangements outside the Western Hemisphere. The Vandenberg Resolution, as
it was known, was careful to situate this call within the U.N. Article 51 protections for "collective self-defense" arrangements, but outside the veto Moscow

held on the Security Council. This further embrace of regionalism was yet another blow to FDR's postwar vision, in which universalism would underpin economic and physical security.

The resolution gave the State Department political cover to begin another difficult and painstaking process of reconciling Europe's needs with Congress' tolerance for obligations and costs. Mutual-defense planning among officials from the U.S., Canada, the U.K., France, Belgium (also representing Luxembourg), and the Netherlands began quietly in July 1948 under the aegis of the "Washington Security Talks." Their Top Secret joint memorandum of September 9 stated that whereas the Marshall Plan had dealt a "political setback" to Soviet plans for exploiting the "weakening of the Western European countries" and the "vacuum in Germany," a security pact was important to securing the "confidence . . . essential to full economic recovery."

It recommended a "collective defence arrangement" for the "North Atlantic," which the State Department defined to comprise the signatory countries plus Norway, Denmark, Iceland, Portugal, and perhaps Ireland—"stepping stone countries" important to the defense of western Europe in the event of Soviet attack. The case of Italy would remain controversial, owing to "the military limitations imposed by the Peace Treaty" with the Soviets, geographical difficulties in defending it, and its record of switching sides in two world wars.[62]

By December 1948, the State Department had concluded that "a North Atlantic Security Pact [was] an essential supplement to the Marshall Plan." And "because of the impact of a rearmament program on the European economy," it reasoned, there would have to be "close coordination between the Europeans of the economic aspects of rearmament and ERP." American officials, it said, would also need to collaborate with "the Western Union military staff" to "ensure that the end product is realistic, having in mind European and U.S. resources."[63] The boundaries between Marshall aid and military aid were being erased.

In his January 1949 inaugural address, Truman pledged to buttress the Marshall Plan with "a collective defense arrangement" tying the United States and Canada with western Europe.[64] Vandenberg, however, was unwilling to go as far as Acheson to meet European pleas for guarantees of U.S. military support. Just as he had done with the Marshall legislation, the senator worked to fashion the legislative commitments into a form Congress could digest. In particular, he subjected the North Atlantic Treaty's critical Article 5 collective defense provision[65] to reworking to allow the Europeans to claim an American commitment to defend them in the event of attack and the United States to claim free rein to determine the nature of its response.

In the early months of 1949, the structure of a new North Atlantic Treaty Organization was hammered out with European officials in extreme secrecy, or so they thought. As was so often the case, Maclean's espionage in Washington compromised it. In any case, it officially came to an end on April 4, the day following the ERP's one-year anniversary, when the foreign ministers of ten West European nations and Canada joined Acheson in Washington to sign the historic NATO founding agreement. Vandenberg hailed it as "the greatest war deterrent ever devised."[66]

Beginning on April 27, the Senate Foreign Relations Committee subjected the Treaty to sixteen days of hearings. Though the committee was now under the control of Texas Democrat Tom Connally, Vandenberg once again played a central role in steering Administration witnesses through difficult questioning aimed at assuring senators that the country could not be forced into war or an open-ended aid commitment.

The State Department was convinced aid would be necessary for many years: "It seems clear that the United States must supply much of the military equipment which the countries working for recovery cannot produce themselves," concluded one analysis in February. It decided it would therefore need to seek a substantial $1.13 billion for its allies in 1950 ($11.25 billion in today's money), and undetermined sums thereafter. With the Senate caucus room overflowing its seating capacity of five hundred, including 125 press members, Vandenberg masterfully shepherded Acheson through testimony. "[I]n contemplating future budgets," the senator asked him, was it not true that "the greater the success of the program in increasing pacific and reliable security, the less will be the need—and the need may entirely disappear?"

"That is entirely correct, senator," Acheson dutifully answered.[67]

Lovett, now a former under secretary, argued that "it seemed hardly logical" to undertake the ERP while leaving it unprotected. "All the consequences [it] was designed to avert might [then] be upon us."[68] His successor, James Webb, said the time had come to "get ready for a change-over from dollar diplomacy to one in which greater reliance is placed on security arrangements."[69] As *Time's* Frank McNaughton summarized the administration's argument, "Europe can't fully recover until the sickle is removed from its throat."[70]

By a vote of 82 to 13, the Senate consented to the treaty on July 21, 1949. The president ratified it on the 25th. This marked the first time the country had entered into a peacetime military alliance since the signing of the Constitution. "I don't care whether entangling alliances have been considered worse than original sin since George Washington," pronounced the State Department's Hickerson, one of its driving forces. It was, he believed, a vital response to the threat the country was facing—even if it was, in Acheson's words, a step "completely outside our history."[71] For Truman it would rank, with the Marshall Plan, among his proudest achievements in office.[72] There was an unhappy irony in this pride, in that he had seen the Marshall Plan as a means of avoiding military commitments.

Kennan argued right up to the end that the drive for rearmament in Europe was based on a misconception. Europeans, he insisted, needed "to save themselves from communist pressures [through] economic recovery." A western defense pact would instead lead to a dangerous "militarization of the present dividing-line through Europe."[73] But Acheson rejected these views. "The Pact and the ERP are both essential to the attainment of a peaceful, prosperous, and stable world," according to a March 20 statement from the State Department. "The economic recovery of Europe, the goal of the ERP, will be aided by the sense of increased security which the Pact will promote."[74]

Kennan's formulation ignored the fact that Europeans would not follow the American blueprint for recovery, which was based on economic and political integration, without security guarantees. French prime minister Henri Queuille stressed that France had "taken dangerous steps to bring about a freer and more effective economy in Europe" while adopting "a friendly attitude towards Germany which it had been very difficult to persuade the French people to endorse."[75] NATO—which was, according to its first secretary general, Lord Ismay, founded "to keep the Russians out, the Americans in and the Germans down"—provided a guarantee critical to maintaining French popular support.[76]

As with the Marshall Plan, there was a vital element of psychology in

NATO. It alleviated fears that the United States would once again withdraw into isolation. Still, only two of the fourteen western divisions stationed in Europe were American; Communist forces outnumbered western forces 12 to 1.[77] Washington, of course, had nuclear weapons (though few of them at this stage): "[T]he first priority of the joint defense," General Bradley would tell the House Foreign Affairs Committee in July, "is our ability to deliver the atomic bomb." Yet, in the words of then-State Department official Louis Halle nearly two decades later, in practical fact "its use could hardly [have been] contemplated" by the western European publics—particularly to the extent that they might themselves be affected by it.[78] And most everyone recognized that the U.S. nuclear monopoly would last only a few years, at best.

The Truman administration also aimed, as with the Marshall Plan, to elevate Germany's role over time. "You cannot have any sort of security in western Europe," Acheson would say later that year, "without using German power." The only question was whether it would "be integrated into western European power or grow up to be a power of its own."[79] But this aim was not highlighted during the pact's formation to contain eruptions in Paris.

On the ground in Germany, Clay continued to protest bitterly over French terms for trizonal fusion, particularly unlimited three-power veto rights over German legislation. "What a price to pay for a French zone that cannot sustain itself," he cabled Army assistant secretary Tracy Voorhees on March 19. "[We] obtain a partner who may be essential to our European program but who enters into partnership in Germany for sabotage only."[80] Adenauer, in spite of his determination to develop a constructive rapport with the French, would later tell Acheson privately that the "Americans were the best Europeans."[81]

Certainly, the French price for acquiescence on Germany—the Marshall Plan and NATO—was much steeper than it had been after War World I: the Dawes Plan and Locarno.[82] Yet, in Acheson's words at an April 8 press conference, the combination of "the Marshall Plan and the North Atlantic Pact have tremendously changed the whole attitude of all three [Allied] governments.... It was that background which made it possible in two days to reach complete unanimity on these questions of Germany."

Clay, still afflicted with more than a touch of localitis, was also being shortsighted. Jean Monnet levered American aid and security guarantees to push forward ideas for Franco-German economic fusion that had come to naught when he first unveiled them in the 1920s. Inspired by Monnet, Schuman would in a year's time, May 1950, propose his namesake plan to place the joint output of coal and steel in France and Germany within a supranational structure. This would lead to the creation of the six-member European Coal and Steel Community in 1952. The ECSC would become the building block of Franco-German rapprochement, marked by the return of the Saar Protectorate to Germany in 1957. This rapprochement would in turn be essential to the creation of the European Economic Community in 1958 and, decades later, the European Union.[83]

THE DAY FOLLOWING THE NATO AGREEMENT, APRIL 5, 1949, JESSUP MET with Malik to read him a brief statement affirming Allied willingness to hold a foreign ministers meeting subsequent to the lifting of the blockade. But it also affirmed their unwillingness to delay formation of the Bonn government.[84] The message was clear: if Moscow wanted to talk first, it should talk now. A West German state was weeks, not months, away.

The text was a compromise between Acheson, who wanted to keep the secret talks going to stave off a public proposal from Moscow, and Bevin, who refused to back anything resembling an Allied proposal. The "Stalin-Malik tactics," Bevin said, were "to tear us to pieces" by distorting the Allied position and manipulating world opinion. Twisting Allied aims, Stalin hoped, would halt the creation of West Germany, inhibit "ratification of the Atlantic Pact by continental countries," and "forestall [congressional] appropriation of funds for the Military Assistance Program."[85] These were hard-earned achievements the West could not put at risk.

As usual, Malik had to report to Moscow and await new instructions, which played into Acheson's strategy. Summoning Jessup back on April 11, Malik read him a statement reporting that Vyshinsky understood no West German government would be established before or *during* a CFM meeting. His patience tried, Jessup insisted he had not promised, and could not promise, this would not happen during the conference. Malik tried to wangle some indication it would at least not happen "as a surprise" right after they convened, but Jessup held firm. A commitment was beyond his authority.[86] They broke off again.

Bevin, frustrated, was convinced the Soviets would, irrespective of Jessup's protestations, hold the Allies "morally committed" not to move on Germany while a conference were in session. Acheson, however, remained untroubled, insisting that Soviet desires would not affect "the tempo" of Allied efforts to build West Germany. The two were now deadlocked on tactics, with Acheson wanting Jessup to push for Soviet commitments and Bevin wanting to ignore Malik and push the pace of the Bonn talks.[87]

With the Malik-Jessup channel stalled, Stalin chose, as Acheson expected he would, to go public. On April 26, TASS issued a communiqué summarizing the secret talks. The agency reported that mutual trade and communications restrictions in Berlin could be lifted prior to a meeting of the four foreign ministers if a date for such a meeting could be set.[88] Simultaneous with the TASS publication, new Soviet technology jammed all Russian-language Voice of America programming.[89]

Following a hastily arranged meeting between Jessup and Malik the following day, at which the two sparred over details of the blockade rollbacks and CFM agenda, Jessup emerged onto Park Avenue to face a crush of reporters and flashing cameras. Taking text from his pocket, written by Bohlen in anticipation of the Soviet leaks, he announced that preparations for the creation of the new Federal Republic of Germany would continue uninterrupted. He added, however, that the Allies would continue in their "sincere endeavor" to reach a new four-power agreement[90]—an endeavor Acheson had long since abandoned.

In the coming week, the Soviets would continue to press for delay of the foreign ministers meeting until late June, taking advantage of Jessup's private assurances that no West German state would come to be before it convened. While Bevin fretted about Soviet traps, Acheson remained insouciant. The CFM, for him, had no more significance than he was willing to give it. The Soviets could haggle and harangue. The Allies needed only to bear it and run out the clock.

Acheson prevailed. On May 4, Jessup, together with British ambassador Alexander Cadogan and French ambassador Jean Chauvel, reached an agreement with Malik to end both sides' German trade and communications restrictions[91] on May 12, and to convene a CFM conference in Paris on May 23.[92] They issued a communiqué the following day.[93]

❖

THE AIRLIFT HAD SURVIVED THE WORST NATURE COULD THROW AT IT. Despite snow and high winds, March 1949 saw a record daily average of 6,300 tons—1,500 more than forecast.[94] April's average then climbed to 7,850 tons, with coal deliveries exceeding their target by 50 percent. And to show the world what the Allies were capable of, Tunner organized a herculean twenty-four-hour coal lift, starting at noon on April 15, that delivered 12,941 tons with 1,398 planes, landing nearly one a minute.[95]

On May 11, Acheson gave a press conference hailing the "great morale, great discipline and superb courage" of those who had made the airlift possible. They had carried out an astounding 277,804 relief flights, delivering 2,325,809 tons of food, coal, and other supplies.

It had not, however, "solved the German problem," Acheson stressed. "Whether a solution can be reached depends upon the willingness of the Russians to make or consider proposals which will not retard . . . the great progress which has been made by the Western Powers in their effort to bring as much of Germany as possible into a condition where it can be a peaceful and constructive member of the community of free nations in Europe." That community, he said, was being built around the Marshall Plan. The message was clear: the only acceptable alternative to a West Germany in the ERP was a *united* Germany in the ERP.[96] The United States would never permit the Soviet Union to communize the country, a mirror image of Stalin's determination never to relinquish control in the east.

That night, electricity from Soviet-sector plants began flowing into West Berlin. Just after midnight, a U.S. Army vehicle headed west out of Berlin onto the autobahn in eastern Germany, and a British vehicle headed through the Helmstedt Soviet checkpoint toward Berlin. A passenger train from western Germany entered the Soviet zone, the first in over a year,[97] arriving in Berlin at 5:11 a.m. on May 12.[98] Huge crowds celebrated. The blockade, or at least the most visible manifestations of it, was over. Feeling his job complete, Clay resigned and headed home three days later.

That no Soviet preconditions applied to the blockade's lifting underlined the western triumph. The blockade had ended, Acheson said, because

the Russians themselves decided "it was unsuccessful."[99] This was a vindication of Kennan's position that the Kremlin could "recognize *situations*, if not
arguments."[100] "We are asking ourselves," he wrote in a self-satisfied memo to
Webb, "whether it could be that the fortunes of the cold war have shifted so
dramatically in the past two years that it is now the *Russians* who are trying to
follow, with regard to us, a policy of firmness and patience and unprovocative
containment."[101]

Still, the Soviets maintained whatever barriers they could without triggering an American pullout from the coming CFM conference. "The Soviets,"
Clay's acting successor, James Riddleberger, cabled Acheson on May 19, "have
now returned to their well-known tactics of slanted interpretation. . . . Berlin
remains today in a state of semi-blockade." Clay had foreseen this, having earlier
warned against a premature wind-down of airlift capacity. "The blockade was
broken by airpower," he had cabled Washington on May 1, "and the airpower
should be maintained in full until the Council of Foreign Ministers has completed its deliberations." It would in fact be maintained until September 30.

For their part, the Soviets considered the restrictions justified on two
grounds. First, they had expected the Allies to liberalize trade policy broadly,
which would bring needed goods to the Soviet bloc and permit a revival of
Moscow's reparations policy. The Allies, however, imposed export-licensing
and currency-clearing requirements that, the Soviets insisted, violated commitments they had made in New York. Second, reports from Bonn suggested
formation of a West German government was imminent, which meant that
the CFM conference would not hinder it. They therefore saw no reason to be
more cooperative than was necessary to prevent a withdrawal of Allied concessions.[102]

✣

STALIN HAD LAUNCHED THE BLOCKADE AS LEVERAGE IN GERMANY. YET
it had not rolled back the deutschmark. It had not stopped progress toward a
West German state. It had not stopped creation of a North Atlantic defense
pact. Oddly, the greatest threat to these objectives had come from George
Kennan.

Back in late 1948, with the Allies advancing their plans for a German federal republic and a military alliance, Kennan began raising awkwardly timed questions as to whether these were even sensible constructs. It was, he argued, flawed strategic thinking to freeze the conflict in Europe "with Russian troops 100 miles from Hamburg."[103] East-west confrontation in Berlin could flare at any moment. Furthermore, partitioning Germany was more likely to fuel nationalist passions than it was to assist integration of the western half into Europe. The only way to end the struggle with the Soviets over Germany and, ultimately, to induce them to leave central and eastern Europe was to unify the country and withdraw all occupation forces.

Effectively, Kennan and Clay had swapped positions between 1947 and 1949. Kennan, who had earlier backed German partition, arguing that "the idea of a Germany run jointly with the Russians is a chimera" and that "we have no choice but to lead our section . . . to a form of independence," had now become the leading advocate of German neutrality and unity. A study mission to Germany in March 1949, in which he witnessed firsthand the destruction of the war, convinced him that continued occupation could only lead to a renewed conflagration. Incredibly, the same policies of mutual withdrawal and reunification had been advocated by Lippmann in his 1947 pieces attacking Kennan's "Mr. X" article.[104] For his part, Clay, who had earlier opposed partition and moves to end cooperation with Moscow in Germany, had become the leading advocate of Allied-zone secession and integration with the West.[105] Talks with Kennan in Berlin disturbed him. He feared that Kennan's new position suggested "a lack of determination" in Washington to complete formation of a West German government.[106]

Marshall decided only to hand off "Program A," as Kennan's plan became known, to his successor, Acheson, who had never been part of the London Program planning and had no stake in it. Acheson told aides he "knew little about Germany," and was initially intrigued by Kennan's case.[107] Convinced, like Kennan, that an indefinite occupation of Germany was untenable, he felt it sensible to subject the plan to scrutiny. He thought it might even form the basis of a U.S. proposal within the CFM, if only to smoke the Soviets out and force them to state openly their intentions to dominate Germany. He even wondered aloud how a West German government had become U.S. policy: had it simply been "the brainchild of General Clay"?[108]

For his part, Clay rounded on Program A. It would be "suicidal to our objectives," he said. The Russians would cheat, the French would panic, and the Germans would go communist, militarist, or both. It would also require a root and branch rethinking of the Marshall Plan. "[I]t was very difficult to operate a single economy without a central [West German] government," Clay said of American aims in the country.[109] And withdrawing U.S. forces would be "turning the show over to Russia and the Communists without a struggle."[110] The defense secretary and the Joint Chiefs of Staff united behind him, stressing the dangers of moving American troops three thousand miles westward while Soviet troops moved only a few hundred to the east.[111]

Before Jessup and Bohlen could carry out confidential briefings for the French and British in early May, however, journalist James Reston published a crude version of the leaked plan in *The New York Times*: "United States, British, and French troops now standing between the Soviet Army and Western Europe . . . would be withdrawn" to the area of the North German ports.[112]

Bevin and Schuman were blindsided, thinking they were up against a change in U.S. policy just weeks after the launch of the North Atlantic pact. Acheson tried to assure them the plan was Kennan's alone, and not a "trial balloon" of the U.S. government.[113] And in an off-the-record briefing for American reporters on May 18, 1949, he buried it.

"We will not agree to the withdrawal of occupation troops," he told them. "One would make a . . . grave error to think that any agreement with the Russians on withdrawal would mean anything." Whereas he continued to support the unification of the German people, "or as large a part of them as may prove practicable," his priority was buttressing western Europe against Soviet pressure. Germany was a means to this end. "If a united Germany contributes to that aim, fine; if not, to hell with it."[114]

To Kennan's lament, Acheson was now pushing Kennan's early containment ideas into the realm of offense. Lippmann had been critical of containment on the grounds that it allowed the Soviets to choose the battlefield. Acheson also saw this flaw, and was determined to challenge Moscow on every front—political, economic, and military—after first creating "situations of strength." The United States would, he believed, win the Cold War not through incessant repulsing of Soviet advances but through demonstrations of superior capability and will.

But it was not just the three Allied governments that rejected Kennan's German unity plan. West German leaders themselves would have no truck with it. Both Adenauer and SPD chairman Schumacher insisted that their countrymen, having had "long experience of totalitarian methods," would never accept Russian terms for unification, or even withdrawal of western troops.[115]

The Soviets would continue to champion unification and withdrawal of occupation forces for propaganda purposes, but they, too, rejected Kennan's ideas in practice. "[T]hose who think we should remove our troops," Chuikov told Bohlen after being briefed on the plan, "don't understand [that] the Germans hate us." We must as a matter of national security, he insisted, "maintain our forces in Germany."[116]

The shredding of Program A marked the beginning of the end of Kennan's frontline role in the shaping of postwar Europe. His proposal's morose, rambling defeatism had stood out in sharp contrast to the bold confidence of "Mr. X." Moods colored his analysis, and his current one reflected discomfort with the mainstreaming of his once provocative ideas. Faced with the need for action, as in the Berlin crisis, he tended to brood, seek inspiration in Gibbon, and indulge his distrust of convention—even when that convention was his own creation.[117]

Like Kennan, Acheson had a fine mind, but a practical one, not a ruminative or emotional one. Confronted with a problem, he would insist that "if you can't *do* anything about it, just stop *thinking* about it," recalled his daughter Mary. "Get on with something!"[118] Though Kennan's office continued to adjoin the secretary of state's, he would lose the access he had under Marshall. Acheson dismissed Kremlinologists like Kennan as "dangerous" soothsayers pushing "uncommunicable" guesses that "must be accepted by those who have not the same occult power of divination."[119] He ordered that Policy Planning Staff director memos should go to the assistant secretaries rather than to himself personally. Thus seeing his influence wane toward irrelevance, feeling at times like "a court jester,"[120] Kennan would in December 1949 choose to depart from the think tank he had fathered at State.[121] Under his successor, the less cerebral but more fashionably hawkish Paul Nitze, PPS would be more tank and less think.

❖

THE COUNCIL OF FOREIGN MINISTERS RECONVENED IN PARIS, AFTER AN eighteen-month hiatus, on May 23, 1949. For the Soviets, the talks commenced on the worst possible note.

The Bonn Parliamentary Council approved the new West German constitution—blandly called "the Basic Law" (*Grundgesetz*) to highlight its provisional status while Germany remained divided—on May 8.[122] Accepted by the Allies on May 12 and quickly ratified by the trizonal *Länder*,[123] it now came into force on the same day the four powers began deliberations—deliberations Moscow had demanded to prevent its creation. It was Vyshinsky's first major diplomatic failure.

Still, Adenauer worried. "Let us be under no serious illusions," he told the Bonn Council in his closing speech. "[T]his Paris Conference might have very serious consequences for us.... We do not want conditions in the western zones to converge toward those in the eastern zone as a result of the negotiations."[124]

State Department position papers for the conference stressed that West Germany was "essential to the success of the European Recovery Program," but noted that Moscow aimed to keep the country isolated and prevent "integration of Western Europe under US leadership." [125] For Acheson, however, West Germany was nonnegotiable. "We are making progress . . . with the integration of Germany into a free and democratic Europe," he told Douglas, "and we shall not jeopardize this" in Paris.[126]

With Acheson determined not to make concessions, the conference quickly stalemated when Vyshinsky called for a return to four-power control and a Soviet veto. Acheson dismissed the proposal as "back to Potsdam." The Allies, he said, would never return to a system that had "failed so disastrously." The Soviet zone was in a "state of economic collapse." Shackling West Germany's recovery to the tottering East was, he said, like "asking a paralyzed person who was three-quarters recovered to go back to complete paralysis."

Vyshinsky struggled to break down Acheson's resolute indifference. It was beyond his skills to camouflage Russia's fraying position in Germany. That position had become precarious in December, following the anti-Communist electoral rout in Berlin, and weaker still with the collapse of the blockade. To Acheson's claim that western zone industrial production had reached 90 percent of 1936 levels, Vyshinsky responded that it was now 96.6 percent in the east. The Allied delegates guffawed. "I will certainly see," Bevin said smiling, "that the refugees learned about the paradise which they had left."

If the Allies were going to consider Soviet proposals, Acheson concluded, Vyshinsky needed to make "himself clear on the *substance* of what he wanted" to achieve in Germany. Otherwise "this question of control was an idle discussion."[127] Schuman called it "build[ing a] roof without constructing walls."

Acheson had previewed his Paris strategy in his candid May 18 briefing. If the conference was to be "another [Russian] propaganda episode in the Cold War," he told the reporters, "we too will play that game to the hilt." He would tolerate four weeks at most. "At that point we will pack up our marbles and come home."

The Russians, he said, "called this Conference . . . as a face-saver for the bankruptcy of their policy in Eastern Germany. [But] we have 45 million Germans behind us [who] are not going to let . . . Communist stooges in Eastern Germany dominate them." The United States would "go ahead with the establishment of a Western German government, come hell or high water. Any unification must be on the basis of the Bonn constitution."[128]

The Allies presented this blueprint to Vyshinsky on May 30. It was audacious to the point of provocation, not so much an offer as a surrender demand. They proposed to extend the Bonn constitution country-wide; terminate reparations; establish economic unity on the basis of one currency, free trade, and dissolution of Soviet corporations; and create a new elected German government under four-power supervisory control with majority rule—no Soviet veto.[129]

Acheson braced for Vyshinsky's explosion. But the Russian stayed calm. He merely chided the Allies for "advance agreement" on a plan which "gave [the] impression of *fait accompli*." Though it seemed "hardly [a] suitable document for quadripartite agreement," he said he would study it.[130]

Reading the proposal in Moscow, Stalin, however, was not calm. He was livid. Did Vyshinsky not recognize an insult? Or even a threat? "It looks as if you don't quite understand," Stalin cabled him, "that the three powers' proposal boils down to their intent to merge the eastern zone with the western ones on their own terms. . . . [T]hey want to swallow our zone and to tie us to their chariot in Germany, depriving us . . . of those rights to reparations which we received in Potsdam." It was, he said, "absolutely unacceptable."[131]

Following the lashing from Stalin, Vyshinsky "uncorked his old form." In

Nitze's words, he turned "extreme, assertive, and nasty."[132] He denounced the Allied plan as "undemocratic" and a blatant contravention of Potsdam (which was itself, of course, undemocratic). He called the Bonn constitution a "secret" document "dictated by the West and designed to dismember rather than unite Germany." Majority rule in the Allied Control Council was, he said, itself "dictatorial." The Soviet Union "would never subordinate itself to the rule of the majority."[133] As for reparations, the Allies had no grounds for conflating it with the issue of economic unity. And the proposal to dismantle Soviet companies merely aimed at imposing "American and British monopolistic capitalism" and to "take over all of German industry." This imperialism, he said, was the essence of the Marshall Plan.[134]

Sitting restless hour after hour, day after day, in the "musical comedy setting" of the Hôtel Talleyrand-Périgord's Palais de Marbre Rose, Acheson felt himself driven "to the limits of human endurance" by Vyshinsky's "dialectics." Bevin, for his part, took a more relaxed approach, often napping through them.[135]

In the three weeks that followed, no progress was made on German unity. Only cosmetic wording on future cooperation could be agreed. Intense debate over Austria, however, which was divided into occupation zones like Germany, led to a deal through which the Soviets traded away reparations claims, as well as support for Yugoslav territorial and financial claims, for a lump-sum Austrian payment of $150 million ($1.52 billion in today's money). Remaining details on a peace treaty were to be worked out by deputies, with the aim of reaching agreement by September 1.[136] (It would not come until 1955.[137]) On the most pressing issue, four-power decision making in Berlin, discussions deadlocked.

The Russians persisted in their demands for veto power in the city, saying it was needed to counteract "hostility to the Soviet Union on the part of the Berlin authorities"[138]—a striking admission that the locals despised them. Moscow's stance, Acheson said, "boiled down to a statement that 'the four powers can do what they like in Berlin so long as it is what the USSR wants.' "[139] But the Allies preferred no deal to a new Soviet veto.

Meanwhile, arguments over remaining trade blockages were heated. To keep control over Allied movements in eastern Germany, the Soviets refused entry of western-zone train engineers and crews, demanding a switch at the border to their own trains and crews. They continued to block highway

crossings, impose documentation requirements, ban western-licensed publications, and prohibit exports from Berlin. To Allied protests, the Soviets retorted
that more tonnage was now entering West Berlin than before the blockade. East
Berlin, in contrast, was "receiving nothing but a trickle," which proved that the
Allies "had not really lifted restrictions."[140]

A U.S. intelligence report said that the Soviet blockade "was being raised
largely because of bottle-necks in the Eastern zone economy." The Soviets
needed the Allied restrictions lifted. But once their problems were overcome,
they would reimpose the blockade, "provided Berlin has not entirely fallen by
the autumn."[141] Murphy, a member of the delegation in Paris, revived Clay's
proposal for an armed convoy to challenge any new Soviet obstruction.[142]
Acheson wanted to treat a new Berlin crisis as "close to [an] act of war."[143] Truman said he would, in the event of a new blockade, back "every possible means
of action that would be costly to the Russians."[144]

To Acheson's surprised satisfaction, however, Vyshinsky accepted his proposal of a simple "modus vivendi" on Berlin—a broad agreement just to restore
elements of east-west trade and not to reimpose blockages.[145] The clincher
came at a private dinner talk in which Acheson suggested that "if the goods
coming from the West into East Germany went beyond the Eastern Zone, that
was not a matter which need cause us any difficulty."[146] If the Soviets stole goods
bound for East Germany, Washington would look the other way.

Murphy and Jessup decried a lack of specifics on western access rights in
the city, but Acheson argued that efforts to define them might be worse than
futile. If the United States put specific rights in a draft, and then later agreed to
their removal, the Soviets would interpret this agreement as renunciation.[147] In
any case, given that the blockade had obliterated the rail access the ACC had
defined back in 1945, whether such rights were in writing meant little in practice.[148] The Soviets never saw hard constraints in mere words. A dozen years
later, Stalin's successor would divide Berlin with a wall, triggering a crisis that
would again bring the two sides to the brink of war.[149]

❖

AT 7:30 P.M. ON JUNE 20, HOURS AFTER THE MEETINGS HAD CONCLUDED,
Acheson was giving a press conference when Bohlen slipped him a note.

Vyshinsky wanted to recall the conference communiqué and reconvene. Acheson was astonished.[150]

Bevin, who had already fortified himself with Scotch, met Acheson in the elevator back at the Quai d'Orsay.

"Do you know 'The Red Flag'?" the inexplicably jolly Englishman asked, referring to the old Labour Party anthem.

No, a bemused Acheson said, he didn't.

"Well, you know 'Maryland, My Maryland'?"

"Yes, I know that absolutely," Acheson said. "It is my native song now."

"Well, it's the same tune!" Bevin said. "So when we get out of the lift, you sing 'Maryland, My Maryland,' and I'll sing 'The Red Flag.' " Acheson agreed.

The two exited the elevator, arms around each other. They marched down the hall singing, past a startled French diplomatic corps. As they entered the meeting room, the union man bellowed "raise the scarlet standard high!" And the lawyer: "burst the tyrant's chain!"

Vyshinsky stared, dumbfounded.

"Me and my pal," Bevin explained, "is singing the same tune!"[151]

No response. "Vyshinsky was in trouble," Acheson surmised.

Schuman adviser Alexandre Parodi took the secretary aside. Gromyko, he said, had just savaged Vyshinsky over the phone for his blunders in the agreement on Austria. Called him "a stupid fool" and worse, according to French officials bugging the call.

When the ministers meeting got under way, Vyshinsky explained that the communiqué had to be amended. He needed words affirming the right of Soviet-owned Austrian properties to export profits or other income. He wasn't sure what that meant, though he could get "answers from Moscow."

Vyshinsky "was floundering badly," Acheson observed. After responding archly that this was "the shortest-lived agreement the Soviets had made yet," the American played for time, knowing Bevin would soon have to depart for his train to Calais. When the tipsy foreign secretary rose and made his apologies, Acheson gestured resignedly. Nothing more could be done now, he said to Vyshinsky. "The communiqué has to stand."[152] Thus did the four-power conference, the sixth and final, end in farce.

✥

ACHESON RETURNED TO WASHINGTON ON THE "INDEPENDENCE," THE president's aircraft, to be greeted by a buoyant Truman himself. Both saw the conference as a triumph. The State Department, Acheson recorded, had shown it "could outwork any of them and [knew its] stuff better." And Acheson had not just commanded the effort, as was General Marshall's way; he had been in the trenches, monitoring enemy movements and devising tactical options before directing the assault. This was his department now, and he would inspire loyalty as a different type of leader.

Soviet acceptance of the modus vivendi, Acheson argued, was Stalin's "tacit abandonment" of the position that the Allies had lost their rights in Berlin. There was no need of a larger agreement. The West could now go its own way. The Soviets had "wanted [a] firm grip on East Germany and [a] free opening in [the] West," but "our path in Germany must be pursued."[153] Congress and the press embraced this narrative.

On his departure from Berlin, following the ending of the blockade, General Clay was saluted by eleven thousand U.S. soldiers and dozens of military aircraft—the largest military review the Army ever staged in Germany. Hailed in *The Philadelphia Inquirer* as the "hero of the American resistance to Soviet siege and pressure," and *The New York Times* as "the man who dared to face the showdown and who guided it through to its successful conclusion," he returned home to be honored by the president and Congress and paraded in New York. Declining solicitations to take command of the Japanese occupation from General MacArthur or run for political office, Clay retired from the Army. On his death three decades later, in 1978, he would be buried in the cadet cemetery at West Point. At the foot of his grave, a marble stone from Berlin would be placed, inscribed with the words

WIR DANKEN

DEM BEWAHRER

UNSERER FREITHEIT

We thank the defender of our freedom[154]

On June 5, 1949, the second anniversary of Marshall's Harvard speech, Truman, accompanied by a bevy of West European dignitaries, feted George Marshall as "one of the greatest Americans of all time." Paul Hoffman called him a "military genius" who "knew that freedom could not be maintained by bullets alone." It was, he said, "through the Marshall Plan" that the general "will live forever in the hearts of free men."

"We are winning the 'cold war' through ECA and the North Atlantic Pact," Arthur Vandenberg said. "In my opinion, if it were not for these policies, Soviet Communism would today be in the substantial control of Europe and this would pose the greatest threat to our own national security in the lifetime of the republic."[155] In 1953, Marshall would, in recognition of his efforts to promote European recovery, and in spite of East-West conflict spilling into the Asia-Pacific, receive the Nobel Peace Prize.[156]

❖

ON AUGUST 14, 1949, IN A HISTORIC EVENT STALIN HAD BEEN DETERMINED to prevent, Adenauer's CDU/CSU center-right coalition narrowly outpolled Schumacher's SPD in West Germany's first popular election. Well short of a majority in the new Bundestag, Adenauer refused to accept a grand coalition, thinking it dangerous for both democracy and capitalism in the fledgling state. Determined not to concede the economics ministry to a Socialist, he negotiated a coalition with the free market FDP (Free Democratic Party) and the small agrarian DP (Germany Party). A month later, on September 15, he was elected federal chancellor by the barest majority of 202 to 200 in the Bundestag, naming free marketeer Ludwig Erhard minister of economic affairs and the FDP's Franz Blücher minister for matters of the Marshall Plan. The new seventy-three-year-old leader said his doctor had declared him fit to govern "for at least a year, perhaps for two."[157] He would serve for fourteen years.

Still legally subservient to the supreme authority of the western occupying powers, Adenauer and his top ministers were summoned to receive the "Occupation Statute" from the American, British, and French high commissioners on September 21. Spotlighting their preeminence, the three made their way onto a red carpet. They directed the chancellor-elect to remain just beyond it until André François-Poncet, the French chairman, had proclaimed the statute's entry into force. Adenauer, who considered the ceremony a "disagreeable" rite of passage for his new government, made a show of displeasure by stepping onto the forbidden surface before the proclamation's reading. Pained smiles greeted the act of defiance, a sign that the chancellor would assert his country's democratic legitimacy.[158]

Yet the three need not have worried. Adenauer was committed to Franco-German rapprochement and cementing the Federal Republic of Germany's place in the emerging western alliance. His vision for West Germany was consistent with that embodied in the Marshall Plan, which the country joined through the OEEC. But this conformity also provoked Schumacher to denounce Adenauer as "the chancellor of the Allies."[159]

While McCloy, the new American high commissioner, worried about Adenauer's "age and dictatorial tendencies," he also feared Schumacher's "sensitivity and excitability."[160] Acheson tried to reassure Schumacher, and to contain his nationalist impulse, by stressing that prospects for Germany were vastly better than what they were after World War I. This fact owed to "the new attitude of the U.S.A. to help Europe politically and financially" and "the great change in French sentiment and the willingness of France to cooperate with Germany."[161] The Soviet government, for its part, heaped scorn on the new "marionette 'state.'" It had been formed in violation of Potsdam to act as an "obedient tool of the Western occupation powers for the realization of their aggressive plans in Europe."[162]

Though the 330-member SED-dominated Volksrat (People's Council) in the Soviet zone had adopted its own constitution a year prior, Stalin refrained from authorizing an East German state as long as he could. He hoped the blockade would stop the Allies from dividing the country. That aim now thwarted, the Volksrat proclaimed the birth of the German Democratic Republic (GDR) on October 7, creating a Volkskammer (People's Chamber) and Länderkammer (Chamber of the States) to substitute for democracy by choosing the government's leaders. On October 11, the two chambers unanimously elected longtime Communist stalwart Wilhelm Pieck to the GDR presidency. The following day, former Social Democrat Otto Grotewohl became prime minister after he, together with his proposed cabinet and policy statement, received unanimous votes of confidence from the Volkskammer.

President Harry Truman delivers his famous "Truman Doctrine" address to a joint session of Congress on March 12, 1947, in which he states that U.S. help to "free peoples" fighting "outside pressures . . . should be primarily through economic and financial aid which is essential to economic stability and orderly political processes." Behind him are President Pro Tempore of the Senate Arthur Vandenberg (R-MI) and Speaker of the House Joseph Martin (R-MA).

Secretary of State George Marshall, just arrived from the Moscow Council of Foreign Ministers conference, talks with Under Secretary Dean Acheson at Washington Airport, April 26, 1947.

Secretary of State George Marshall and Senator Arthur Vandenberg (R-MI) confer, February 26, 1948.

Under Secretary of State Robert Lovett and Director of the Policy Planning Staff of the State Department George Kennan, September 6, 1947.

Ambassador to the
U.K. Lewis Douglas
and Under Secretary
of State for Economic
Affairs Will Clayton,
c. October 1, 1947.

State Department
Counselor
Charles Bohlen.

Military Governor for Germany General
Lucius Clay (waving) with political adviser for
Germany Ambassador Robert Murphy.

Secretary of State James Byrnes and Ambassador to the Soviet Union (later special representative in Europe under the Marshall Plan) Averell Harriman leaving the Potsdam conference area, July 19, 1945.

Ambassador to France
Jefferson Caffery, c. 1945.

Ambassador to the Soviet Union
Walter Bedell Smith.

Former Secretary of Commerce and 1948 Progressive Party candidate for president Henry Wallace, an opponent of the Marshall Plan, on his arrival at London Airport, c. 1950.

President Truman, Secretary of State George Marshall, Director of the Economic Co-operation Administration Paul Hoffman, and Secretary of Commerce Averell Harriman discussing the Marshall Plan, November 29, 1948.

Soviet leader Joseph Stalin (right) and Politburo member Andrei Zhdanov, October 11, 1945.

Soviet UN Representative Andrei Vyshinsky (right) and British delegate Hartley Shaw-cross at a United Nations Organization conference held at the Palais de Chaillot, Paris, October 16, 1948.

Soviet Foreign Minister Vyacheslav Molotov arriving in Washington, D.C., March 31, 1945.

Marshal Vasily Sokolovsky, chief of Soviet Military Administration in Germany from 1946 to 1949. (Photo c. 1941.)

Secretary of State George Marshall and British Foreign Minister Ernest Bevin at a United Nations Organization conference held at the Palais de Chaillot, Paris, October 16, 1948.

19

Left: British Foreign Minister Ernest Bevin and French Foreign Minister Georges Bidault at the conference of the new sixteen-nation Committee of European Economic Co-operation, which is to prepare a Marshall Plan aid request, c. July 1947.

Right: Czechoslovak Foreign Minister Jan Masaryk, a supporter of the Marshall Plan who decried Stalin's refusal to allow his country to participate.

Konrad Adenauer, founder and chairman of the Christian Democratic Union and the first chancellor of West Germany.

True power, however, continued to be held by Grotewohl's deputy, Walter Ulbricht. Ulbricht followed Stalin's model, seizing power over the state through the party and not the government. Lacking charm or oratory skills, he was content to control the SED apparatus. In 1946 he had let Pieck and Grotewohl risk their necks in elections, wisely avoiding their public disgrace. Only one opinion, Ulbricht knew, counted: Stalin's. Married to Zhukov's former secretary and speaking fluent Russian, Ulbricht would have three audiences with the *vozhd* in Moscow in 1949–50 before the SED elected him to the post created for him: secretary general.[163] Beyond political domination of East Germany through Ulbricht, Moscow retained legal and economic control through the corporations it had created and the GDR's National Manifesto commitment to discharging reparations claims. Another year would pass before the country would hold its first communist-style public elections, when the SED-controlled National Front list would garner 99.7 percent of the vote.

Following Pieck's and Grotewohl's elections, Stalin sent a letter of congratulations, adding that the German and Soviet peoples together possessed "the greatest potential in Europe for the accomplishment of great acts of world significance." It was further evidence, the U.S. chargé in Moscow, Wally Barbour, cabled Acheson, of the "Kremlin's undeviating view that Germany is key to [the] control and Bolshevization of Europe." The Allied High Commission pronounced the GDR "devoid of any legal basis."[164]

New arenas of confrontation between the Soviet Union and the United States would soon open up around the globe. Stalin had broken the U.S. nuclear monopoly with a test blast on August 29, 1949, three years sooner than most American experts had expected. Future conflicts now threatened to destroy the planet. Yet the world, George Orwell wrote with dark optimism, was probably not headed for imminent annihilation, but rather "an epoch as horribly stable as the slave empires of antiquity." The atomic bomb, he said, had rendered the two hegemons "at once unconquerable and in a permanent state of 'cold war' with their neighbours."[165] Indeed, the boundaries of the conflict in Europe were now set. They would remain so for forty years.

Stalin and Truman play chess over Germany.

THIRTEEN

SUCCESS?

ACCORDING TO LEGEND, THE ELEVENTH-CENTURY ISLAMIC POET MU-
hammad ibn Ammar successfully defended the Kingdom of Seville against the
formidable Christian King Alfonso VI of León and Castile. He did so not on
the battlefield, but in a game of chess. Whether or not historical fact, the story
foreshadows the advent of modern diplomacy, or the idea that nonviolent competition might determine the control of territory and resources.

Though a revolutionary, Joseph Stalin saw himself as an heir to a noble
Russian tradition of imperialist statecraft.[1] He had supreme regard for the po-
tentialities of brute force, yet took pride in his image as a diplomatic virtuoso
who could change the course of events through guile and bluff. Chess books
have reproduced a 1926 match in which he allegedly bested future NKVD chief
Nikolai Yezhov; the match was clearly fabricated, possibly to show him as a
man of strategic vision.[2] Never a serious player himself, Stalin still supported
the game and its Soviet grandmasters as a means of highlighting Soviet intellectual superiority.[3]

George Kennan was also a chess player of no particular note, one who saw himself engaged in a match against the Soviet leader. The doctrine of containment he propounded in 1947 was in fact developed with the image of chess in mind.

Since the Russian threat "is more than a military threat," Kennan said at a War College lecture in October 1947, it could not "be effectively met entirely by military means." It meant "marshal[ing] all the forces at your disposal on the world chessboard . . . in such a way that the Russian sees it is . . . in his interests to do what you want him to do."[4] The Marshall Plan was the centerpiece of Kennan's thinking. Victory would be defined as the revival of a democratic, capitalist western Europe without military confrontation.

Using economic assistance as a vehicle, Kennan intended the Marshall Plan to change the psychology of the beneficiaries. It would convince them that they could regain prosperity and security without resorting to autarky or authoritarianism. It would, Kennan calculated, accomplish this feat partly by forcing Russia to set itself against such assistance and thereby undermine the standing of communism. In chess, such a move is known as a "sham sacrifice": appearing to blunder into loss of a piece to gain tactical advantage.

Unlike Kennan, Benjamin Franklin was an accomplished chess player— one who conducted consequential diplomacy during actual games in Europe. In his essay "On the Morals of Chess," published in 1786, he wrote that the game required *foresight* (seeing the long-term consequences of action), *circumspection* (surveying the landscape and recognizing hidden possibilities), *caution* (avoiding haste or blunder), and *perseverance* (continually looking to improve one's position).[5] So success with the Marshall Plan would require the United States to exhibit such capacity over many years.

It would mean making, in chess terms, controversial "real sacrifices," such as the loss of Poland and Czechoslovakia to the Soviet bloc, to strengthen America's long-term position in the West. Though the Presbyterian-moralist side of Kennan anguished over the loss of these noble nations, the Bismarckian side argued as early as 1944 that a successful American endgame would require conceding pawns in the East early on. He predicted the Prague coup four months before Stalin instigated it, advising no preventive countermeasures.

To Harriman's contention that Washington could not accept "that the Soviet Union has the right to penetrate her immediate neighbors for security,"

Kennan responded that it was not "realistic" to expect Moscow to concede its security belt, given the price it had paid during the war. There was no use in giving Stalin pretexts to challenge America's own Monroe prerogatives in the Western Hemisphere. The object must therefore be to establish "the line beyond which we cannot afford to permit the Russians to exercise unchallenged power," and to be "friendly but firm" in laying it down.[6]

That line was drawn with the Marshall Plan. It was consistent with Kennan's argument, made in a letter to Bohlen at Yalta in 1945, that the United States needed to "divide Europe frankly into spheres of influence—[to] keep ourselves out of the Russian sphere and keep the Russians out of ours."[7] But this division did not mean conceding permanence; it meant waiting patiently for Moscow's defenses to crumble.

⁂

BY 1947, DEAN ACHESON AND WILL CLAYTON CONSIDERED THE FDR VISION of a postwar recovery underpinned by U.N., IMF, and World Bank action "thoroughly discredited." The executive branch, they concluded, would have to "eat practically every word [it] had uttered before Congressional Committees during the past three years."[8] The Marshall Plan took a different approach, aiming to generate a rapid and robust European recovery through unilateral U.S. economic intervention.

By any reasonable standard, such a recovery did occur. Between 1947 and mid-1952, when Marshall aid officially ended, industrial output in the Marshall countries increased by 60 percent. (By way of comparison, the EU-27 industrial output index increased by 15 percent between January 2003 and January 2008, the years preceding the financial crisis.)[9] There were wide variations—growth ranged from 24 percent in Sweden to 241 percent in West Germany—but gains were generally significant and widespread.[10] (Comprehensive macroeconomic and Marshall aid data can be found in Appendix C.)

To what extent, however, was recovery driven by the Marshall Plan itself? Aid may improve a country's standard of living while it is being consumed without improving the country's ability to provide for itself. So what we should ask is whether West European economies actually performed better than they otherwise would have in the absence of Marshall aid.

It is useful first to consider the situation Marshall planners inherited. In 1945, industrial production was a mere 34–46 percent of prewar levels in the Netherlands and France, and 20 percent in Germany and Italy. Only a small portion of the collapse, however, was attributable to bombing and displacement of production facilities. Most of it related to an inability to move raw materials, food, and goods. Damage to transport infrastructure—roads, bridges, rail, and ports—was immense. As such infrastructure underwent repair from mid-1945 to late 1946, recovery was strong.[11] The bitter winter of 1946–47, and the subsequent horrendous harvests, dealt Europe a setback; shortages of food, fuel, and industrial materials reverberated throughout the production chain.[12] This setback was temporary, however. Industrial and agricultural production picked up again by late 1947 and carried over into 1948, when Marshall funding began.

Between 1948 and 1952 (four and a quarter years), the United States transferred $13.2 billion to the sixteen Marshall Plan countries. Accounting for inflation over those years, the total was $14.3 billion (that is, in 1952 dollars). The aid was front-loaded, with 31 percent coming in 1948, 30 percent in 1949, 20 percent in 1950, 12 percent in 1951, and 8 percent in 1952. The largest recipients were the U.K. ($3.2 billion, or $32 billion today), France ($2.7 billion, or $27 billion today), Italy ($1.5 billion, or $15 billion today), and West Germany ($1.4 billion, or $14 billion today). Austria and Norway were the biggest beneficiaries per capita ($130, or $1,300 today). The transfers equaled, on average, 2.6 percent of recipient-country output over the period.

In today's dollars, total Marshall aid was worth $130 billion. But if the United States had run a Marshall Plan of equivalent size as a proportion of GDP (1.1 percent) from 2012 to 2016, this would have amounted to a vastly higher *$800 billion*. The total aid figure is higher still if we account for non-Marshall military and other assistance.[13]

Given that recovery was under way in Europe when Marshall aid started flowing, however, it is challenging to estimate its effects. We know that growth was generally higher in those countries that received more aid, as a percentage of GNP. But to isolate the specific impact of aid on growth, economists have run statistical simulations using historical data, comparing actual growth rates after 1948 with what might have been expected in its absence. The most widely cited estimates suggest that Marshall aid did have a significant positive

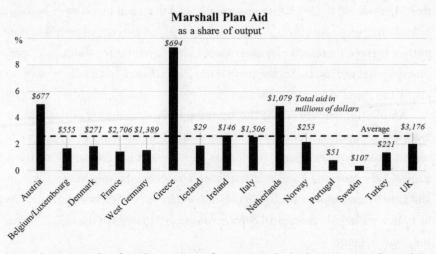

Marshall Plan Aid
as a share of output*

*Gross domestic product for Belgium, Denmark, Greece, Netherlands, Norway, Sweden, and the U.K. Gross national product for Austria, Luxembourg, France, Iceland, Ireland, and Portugal. For West Germany and Turkey, GNP is used to 1949 and GDP thereafter. For Italy, GNP is used to 1951 and GDP thereafter.

Data sources: Bohlin (2010); ECA (1948–1951), *Reports to Congress*, June 1948–June 1951; Mitchell (2007), *Europe*; Mitchell (2007), *Africa, Asia and Oceania*; Mutual Security Agency (1951–1952), *Reports to Congress on the Mutual Security Program*, December 1951 and June 1952; OEEC (1957); Reinhart and Rogoff (2009).

effect—that is, even after controlling for other factors that might have contributed.[14] In France, Germany, Denmark, and the Netherlands, output growth in 1948–49 attributable to the Marshall Plan appears to have been a full 2 to 5 percentage points higher than it would have been in its absence. In Austria, it was 7 percentage points higher.[15]

These growth rates represent remarkable rates of return on U.S. aid—100 percent or more. How might the Marshall Plan have accomplished this, if indeed it did? The primary analyses underlying the congressional case for Marshall aid, such as that carried out by Bissell for the Harriman Report, contended that Europe was experiencing a shortage of working capital that was holding back recovery. They argued that if the dollar gap could be closed, local capital could be liberated for reconstruction.[16] The simulations examined three possible "Keynesian" channels through which this might, in the end, have happened.[17]

One was higher investment, under the logic that the aid supplemented deficient savings in Europe. Broadly, the evidence supports the argument that Marshall aid did stimulate investment, and that such investment boosted growth. But given that the aid amounted to only 2.6 percent of recipient output, on average, increased investment would only account for about half a percentage point of growth. Such growth is not insignificant, but hardly enough to justify the Plan's legendary status.[18]

Another possibility is that the aid reduced constraints on critical noninvestment components of government spending—spending for which private capital could not have been mobilized. This seems plausible, given that war damage was enormous, and that European governments were limited in their ability to finance repairs while meeting immediate social needs. Budget deficits in 1946 were huge—around 10 percent of national income in the U.K., France, Italy, and Belgium.

Yet by the end of that year, nearly six months before Marshall's Harvard speech, the worst of the damage holding back production—damage to electricity and transport—had been repaired, and industrial output (save in Germany) had returned to 1938 levels. Furthermore, recipient-government spending as a share of national income actually *declined*, on average, during the Marshall years. This fact is consistent with State Department pressure for market-led growth, and contrary to GOP fears of Marshall aid financing "socialism."[19] There is, further, no evidence that such spending had a significant impact on growth.[20] In short, the Marshall Plan did not aid recovery by boosting government spending.

A third possibility is that the aid removed constraints on the ability to import. European countries ended the war with meager reserves of dollars and gold, which were by then the only internationally accepted forms of money. Against the background of the 1930s, when two thirds of U.S.-held foreign securities issued in the 1920s went into default, private lending from the United States was not an option this time around. Current account deficits—which were large in Germany, France, the Netherlands, and Austria—could only be sustained with foreign aid. The Marshall Plan provided this.

But how important was the aid? The evidence shows that Marshall countries were able to run larger current account deficits, but the effect is modest—roughly 12 cents larger for each dollar of Marshall aid. This could still be important, however, if the imported materials were bottlenecks for other processes, such as steel production. Coal was one such critical import; without it, Marshall country output might have been as much as 3 percent lower.[21]

Such estimates may overstate the importance of foreign exchange in the Marshall Plan, however. We know, for example, that recipients abjured currency devaluation until 1948–49 (even Keynes had opposed it in Britain), and that this tool was successful in boosting dollar reserves; it could therefore have assisted more if it had been undertaken earlier. Economists such as Gottfried Haberler, Jacob Viner, Fritz Machlup, Friedrich Lutz, and Henry Hazlitt made this argument at the time. Yet American ambivalence about devaluations, driven by traditional concerns not to undermine U.S. trade competitiveness, contributed to delaying these necessary steps.

Altogether, then, the Keynesian-stimulus lens for explaining the apparent economic success of the Marshall Plan is not very useful. Kindleberger, among the more prominent Keynesian implementers of the Marshall Plan at State, became much more circumspect toward the approach in later decades, and would not have been surprised by these results.

"The first use of Keynesian analysis in a major governmental document that I recall is that of the Harriman Report, largely drafted by Richard Bissell," he wrote in 1984. "It was a brilliant use of the links running from investment to national income, both for short-run business cycle analysis and for growth." Yet Kindleberger ultimately "deal[t] a low grade to a Keynesian point of view," at least in explaining the problems of Italy—a major Marshall beneficiary with which he worked. He ultimately concluded that its unemployment problems were structural ("from wrong factor productions") and not cyclical ("from lack of demand"), as American Economic Cooperation Administration economists held.[22]

It is important to recognize, however, that the Marshall Plan's most important early architects and advocates never put their faith in narrow stimulus channels. Such faith came only later, with the arrival of Bissell and the ECA planners. Indeed, the whole exercise of trying to isolate the impact of resource transfers from the United States to explain Europe's recovery is to misapprehend the Plan's motivations. The funds themselves were not originally intended to be more than a pump primer.[23] The Plan's architects, Kennan and Clayton in particular, believed that a multiyear program of assistance was necessary to establish confidence in a long-term American commitment to European recovery and security, to reduce political and social resistance to vital structural policy reforms, and to ease the reintegration of Germany into Europe's economic architecture.[24]

Kennan had argued from the outset that Europe's problems were "psychological," and that the primary stimulative effect of the Marshall Plan would come from beneficiaries seeing that the United States was committed to helping restore them as free and independent nations. Even in Kennan's earliest formulations, immediate aid—to alleviate hardship and remove production bottlenecks—was intended only to "gain time to deal with the long-term problem" of establishing confidence, cooperation, and reform.[25] It meant, as Acheson said in Senate testimony in 1949, that "sickness [could] be better cared for; the aged [were] no longer neglected; there [were] textbooks for the schools; teachers and judges no longer need[ed to] live meanly on the edge of despair; cities [could] be kept clean again; [and] transportation and utilities systems [could] supply the needs of people in carrying on their daily work."[26]

For his part, Clayton argued that, even in the short run, recovery would still have to be driven by structural policy change. On his return from Europe in May 1947, he drew attention to the breakdown in the European division of labor, both within and across countries, occasioned by the war, and the role that national policies were playing in exacerbating the problem. Food shortages in France had been created by government-imposed price rollbacks and controls in a misguided attempt to prevent an inflationary spiral. Farmers hoarded food for themselves and their livestock rather than sell it in the cities, knowing that the proceeds would just get eaten up by soaring prices before they could find consumer goods—which were in short supply for the same reason.

Marshall aid was itself insufficient to make up for food and goods not being produced or sold. Policy change was needed to allow prices of scarce goods to rise, thereby encouraging production. And whereas the policies on which the United States conditioned its aid were not always coherent, public finances and monetary policy shifted in a more prudent direction.[27] Food prices in France and Italy, which had begun their steep rise well before the harsh winter of 1946–47, began declining sharply after announcement of the Marshall Plan. West European inflation in the early post-Marshall period, 1952–58, would fall to levels as low as they would be for the next fifty years.[28] Marshall funds provided a buffer that may have helped market-friendly reforms take hold without being undermined by mass labor and social unrest.

But to what extent were such reforms actually *driven* by Marshall funds? Would different policies have been pursued without them? These would be awkward questions for the American ECA planners, who liked to maintain that their assistance in the design of European policies was just "friendly"—even as they privately cajoled and threatened to get the ones they wanted. American control of so-called counterpart funds provided them the means to influence policy—at least in theory.

✦

AID PROGRAMS INEVITABLY INVOLVE DEGREES OF WASTAGE AND MISAL-location. Hoffman and Bissell took this seriously, and devised market-oriented mechanisms and controls to keep them to a minimum. The first six months were devoted largely to relief efforts, but thereafter the focus shifted to recovery and integration. Kennan had feared that operational control of the Marshall Fund outside the State Department would lead to "confusion, contradiction, and ineffectiveness."[29] Yet in the end, according to the ECA's Robert Oshins, "the major difficulties which were expected . . . never did occur."[30]

The most innovative of the Marshall Plan mechanisms, designed by Bissell, was the use of counterpart funds. Hoffman, who began operating them in September 1948, called them "the single greatest tool we have for recovery." When the press, which was generally laudatory of the Marshall Plan, failed to mention counterpart funds often enough for Hoffman he scolded them. "You mustn't get the idea that you are too perfect," he told the American Society of Newspaper Editors; "you have not explained how counterpart funds are used."[31]

Under the arrangement, a French farmer needing an American harvester would buy it from the French government in francs. The ECA would then pay the American exporter in dollars, while the francs were deposited at the French central bank to fund a recovery program devised in cooperation with the ECA. This structure comprised projects such as mine mechanization, railway electrification, and dam construction, but extended to fiscal and monetary stabilization.

The counterpart funds regime served multiple purposes. The farmer would not be getting a gift, but would be spending his own money on the equipment he needed most. As he would pay in francs, rather than dollars, there would be no negative effect on the French balance of payments. The French government then had the means to finance recovery spending without resorting to inflationary policies, as it had been for so long.

The ECA approved and monitored all expenditures, but Harriman emphasized that "95 percent of the program is European."[32] He neglected to highlight that recipient governments were required to match each dollar of Marshall aid with an equivalent amount in domestic currency, to be used for jointly approved purposes. Each dollar of Marshall aid therefore gave the United States influence over the allocation of two dollars' worth of resources to recovery efforts.[33]

Yet the theory behind counterpart funds was always weak. If a recipient government wanted to spend the local currency it generated by the sale of goods donated from the United States, it could always offset a U.S. blockage of the funds through standard monetary policy operations called "sterilization." Effectively, the central bank could print the equivalent new currency at home and spend it with no inflationary effect. Given that American economists were aware of this at the time,[34] the ECA had to have been as well. Not surprisingly, it used the mechanism sparingly.

In Britain, the Attlee Labour government directed 97 percent of counterpart funds to retiring government debt, thereby depriving the ECA of levers it might, even in principle, have applied to change economic priorities in London. The only areas in which British policy was clearly steered from Washington were trade liberalization (which had been a condition going back to wartime Lend-Lease aid) and European Payments Union membership, both of which London initially resisted.[35] The aid itself, however, amounting to 1.9 percent of GDP from 1948 to 1951, served to prop up a socialist program of nationalization and industrial control with which the Truman administration, not to mention Republican legislators, strongly disagreed. Economists have invoked this factor to help explain why the aid's growth impact appears to have been much poorer in Britain than elsewhere.[36]

Yet in understanding the Marshall Plan, wider American political aims must not be ignored, and indeed cannot be separated from economic ones. "[T]he best way to serve U.S. interests in our relations with the USSR," argued State Department official R. G. Hooker in September 1946, "is to [support] the non-communist left."[37] This dictum was more or less the department's policy toward Britain throughout the Marshall years. "On the ideological level, the election of a socialist-labor government in Britain has strengthened that country's domestic position vis-à-vis Soviet propaganda," reasoned a June 1948 policy statement. "A government of this type is not so vulnerable with its own people as a conservative regime might be to charges of reactionary prejudice against the Soviets, and a socialist flavor to its policies is a good antidote to Communist appeal abroad."[38] The implication was that interference in British domestic economic policy might undermine American political aims, which in turn could stymie economic recovery.

In France and Italy, U.S. influence over policy was even more limited by the priority of keeping the Communists from power. The French and Italian governments, in return for excluding the Communists, had enormous leeway to pursue their own agendas, within broad confines renegotiated continuously with the United States.[39] The contrast between the operation of the Marshall Plan in the two countries illustrates how powerful was the overarching objective of containing the Communists.

❖

AFTER THE WAR, FRANCE AND ITALY HAD A SIMILAR POLITICAL COMPLEXion. Both saw the formation of tripartite coalitions of Christian Democrats on the center-right, Socialists on the center-left, and Communists on the far left. Both countries suffered from high deficits, inflationary pressure, and scarce goods, and focused political energies on keeping peace with Communist-led labor movements. Under pressure from Washington in the spring of 1947, however, both governments expelled the Communists.[40] At this point, their policy paths diverged.

In France, where the left commanded a larger share of the vote, the Socialists became the leading party in the coalition. In Italy, the Christian Democrats assembled a cabinet with no representation from the left. In both cases, the door was left open for future Communist participation, but Stalin slammed it shut. With the creation of the Cominform in September, Moscow ordered the French and Italian Communists to abandon efforts at cooperation with parties supporting the Marshall Plan.

In France, the autumn rise of the Gaullist RPF party—committed to centralization of power, and opposed to American dollar diplomacy—bound the Socialists and Christian Democrats together in a difficult coalition, in opposition to both the Communists and the right. The Socialists dominated, however, and pushed forward with their state-led investment plan. Fiscal and monetary stabilization would take a backseat. Whereas Christian Democrat Georges Bidault remained France's friendly face to the State Department, he was attacked at home, from the left and the right, for being in bed with the "Anglo-Saxons."

In Italy, the economic agenda of the controlling center-right parties was dominated by the free market liberals, led by deputy prime minister, budget minister, Bank of Italy governor, and later president Luigi Einaudi. Einaudi scoffed at the Keynesian American idea that the country's underemployment problems were a symptom of insufficient demand that might be revived with government investment.

Part of the difference between the two national approaches is history. Fears of revived Fascist corporatism, for example, influenced policy in Italy. Another part of the difference relates to a more developed bureaucratic infrastructure for statistics and planning in France. Even if the Italians had had "a Monnet Plan," they would have lacked the capacity to implement one. The result was that the Americans were typically at odds with the French over their neglect of fiscal and monetary stabilization, and with the Italians over excessive zeal in reducing inflation and insufficient commitment to investment planning.[41]

❖

THE MARSHALL PLANNERS SET UP OPERATIONS IN EUROPE IN THE SUMMER of 1948, choosing Paris as their base.[42] This was a time of rapidly rising tensions with Moscow, adding to the premium Washington placed on political stability in France. Trade unions from dockers to postal workers were permeated with Communist moles tasked with disrupting operations and communications related to transatlantic diplomatic and military cooperation. French Communists tarred the country's government as a "second Vichy," operating under the direction of imperialists in Washington. Against this backdrop, Ambassador Caffery was concerned not merely with Schuman's ability to roll back the Communist threat but to survive a preemptive anti-Communist coup led by de Gaulle's intelligence service (which continued on after he left power in January 1946).[43] The general had blasted the provisions of the London Accord on Germany as a prelude to "the formation of a Reich at Frankfurt."[44]

Approving Schuman's program for fiscal and monetary stabilization, Washington released 25 billion francs ($108 million) of Interim Aid counterpart funds in April 1948, mostly for Monnet Plan projects. Undermined in part by Bidault's signature on the London Accord, however, Schuman's government was buffeted by strikes and threats of insurrection. It collapsed on July 19. Fearful of what might replace it, Washington blocked the release of further funds pending the establishment of a new coalition that could show actual progress on stabilization.

Toughness evaporated, however, in September, when Henri Queuille—a soft-spoken, intelligent, but temporizing country doctor—emerged as prime minister. Paris ECA mission chief David Bruce insisted that withholding funds, even if justified on narrow economic grounds, might "boomerang against ERP ultimate goals." He successfully pleaded for their quick release. "The unpleasant fact," Hickerson wrote in October, is "that there is no apparent alternative to our continuing for the present our policy of assisting the French government even though it seems to be losing . . . ground insofar as ECA objectives are concerned."[45] Conditionality was showing its limits. Washington prized a stable, non-Communist, non-Gaullist French government more than it did its own immediate economic objectives.

In January 1949, Paris-based playwright Samuel Beckett finished the script of his now famous *Waiting for Godot*. Throughout that year, ECA Paris would, too, wait impatiently for the man who would never come—the French leader who would bring stabilization. Concerned that Stalin was fomenting Communist violence to trigger a Gaullist coup, or worse, it reluctantly continued releasing aid until Queuille's cabinet fell in October. Bidault's new government returned to the wrangling, however, extracting its re-release. He succeeded not through concessions, but by subtly convincing the ECA that, without the funds, it would resort to even more inflationary financing to sustain investment.

Yet French macroeconomic indicators were improving. The budget deficit fell from 9.7 percent of gross national product in 1948 to 7.3 percent in 1949.[46] Inflation fell from 58.6 percent to 12.7 percent; the current account deficit from 5.7 percent of GNP to 1.8 percent.[47] And whereas the carrot of counterpart funds had not worked as the ECA had hoped, the funds had allowed a succession of moderate governments in France to continue cooperation with the United States on a politically sensitive program of western economic and security integration.

By 1950, the ECA had shifted its focus from badgering Bidault to stabilize the economy to badgering him to publicize the Marshall Plan's success. In line with this lurch, strategy also shifted from threatening to withhold funds to telling Bidault how to use them. Among the more comical propaganda efforts proposed was creating a Marshall Plan Tour de France cycling team and a Tour de France board game, with players advancing over Marshall-funded roads and bridges. These efforts were dismissed by the French cabinet, which argued that they would be mocked by the Communists and do more harm than good if the bike team lost.

ECA efforts to shunt funds from the government's beloved investment initiatives and toward low-cost housing, hospital, and school building, which might give Marshall funding more visible impact, were either refused or only accommodated grudgingly. The government had its own plans for stimulating house construction with private financing, and resented American interference.[48] In May 1950, the ECA conceded defeat. "None of the technicians of the Mission are to insist on having any . . . project undertaken in his way nor is he permitted to employ the threat of withholding counterpart [funds] as a bargaining device," the new directive said. "[A]ttempting to force our views . . . embroils us in French politics" and fails to achieve American aims.[49]

The surprise attack by Communist forces in North Korea on the South in June 1950 triggered fears in Paris that Moscow might initiate similar action in Europe, across the line dividing the Germanies. As French defense expenditures began climbing (they would soar 48 percent in 1951),[50] Washington became concerned inflation would accelerate. The ECA looked again at withholding counterpart funds until Paris came into line on stabilization. In early 1951, however, the ECA-counterpart National Advisory Council[51] concluded that such conditionality was ineffective, and indeed counterproductive. If "the French Treasury is forced to find other means of financing its expenditures, it would undoubtedly resort to additional borrowing from the Bank of France."[52]

In short, Washington failed to buy French compliance with its stabilization demands, in spite of France having secured the second largest share of Marshall aid. It failed not because it had no leverage, but because financial stabilization was not an American priority. Political aims took precedence: in particular, securing French governments committed to resisting Communism.[53]

Queuille stressed to Marshall that he had crushed Communist-led strikes intended to sabotage the ERP. He had cracked down on Communist union racketeering. And he had kept wage increases from running ahead of price rises, even if the latter were higher than Washington wanted. Marshall must not, Queuille implored, lose sight of the big picture. "[I]n this battle between East and West," he said, "France is yet one more time the front-line sentry of civilization."[54]

It was not just the threat of losing Marshall aid that stiffened Queuille's resistance to the Communist Party and its union arm. He knew that any return to tripartism, with the Communists back in government, would mean an end to French influence over the reconstitution of postwar Germany. The United States knew there was no better, more stabilization-friendly French government waiting to emerge. Gaullism or Communism were far more clear-and-present threats to French recovery than elevated deficits and inflation. In the end, then, the Marshall Plan did not institute the sort of robust policy conditionality that Clayton had envisioned in 1947, but, against the much worse Cold War backdrop that prevailed after the Berlin blockade, it did enough to satisfy the changed priorities in both Washington and Paris.

❖

IN ITALY, THE ECA WAS AT WAR WITH ITSELF. ROME MISSION HEAD JAMES Zellerbach, a former paper manufacturing executive from San Francisco, was passionate about redirecting Marshall funds from importing relief supplies, such as wheat and coal, to importing "machinery and equipment to build up Italy's productive system." His policy priorities were lower taxes and interest rates. The ECA and its counterpart National Advisory Council in Washington, however, were focused, as they had been in France, on stabilization—particularly controlling inflation. ECA-Washington was prepared to delay counterpart fund expenditures at the first sign of its rise, and undertook a "campaign of education" to change priorities at the Rome mission.[55]

De Gasperi's government, of its own accord, and before Marshall had even thought of making a speech at Harvard, was also focused on stabilization. Unlike the French, the Italians wanted to spend their counterpart funds slowly to control inflation; they required no arm-twisting from Washington. The result was much more rapid progress in Italy. From 62.1 percent in 1947 (49.2 percent in France) inflation fell to 5.9 percent in 1948 (while rising to 58.6 percent in France); it was down to 1.2 percent by 1949 (against 12.7 percent in France).[56]

Also unlike the French, and to ECA-Rome's constant consternation, the Italians had no interest in investment planning; they wanted to direct the funds to political priorities, such as alleviating unemployment through public works and emigration.[57] Throughout the Marshall years, Italian gross investment (net of inventories) as a proportion of GDP remained below prewar levels, while it rose well above them in France.[58]

In autumn 1948, De Gasperi embraced ECA-Washington, proclaiming his commitment to stabilization. Zellerbach, he understood, could be ignored. He agreed, therefore, only to add some undefined industrial recovery scheme to his priority public works program. Treasury Minister Giuseppe Pella remained determined to rely on private investment, which, he argued, would be stimulated by freeing up funds through cuts in the budget deficit.

The pro-investment faction within the ECA disagreed: more government investment was needed to step in for deficient business confidence. They pleaded for something parallel to France's Monnet Plan: a "national investment budget" that was "not merely the sum of projects which the various agencies" had already devised, but the product of a coherent modernization strategy.[59]

Year after year, ECA stabilizers were at odds with ECA investment enthusiasts. All they could agree on was that De Gasperi and Pella were solidly pro-American and anti-Communist, and therefore merited Washington's support. In Italy, meanwhile, intense factional disagreement on policy within the Christian Democratic party made it impossible for De Gasperi to win approval for the sort of comprehensive investment program Washington wanted. Parliament failed to approve some ECA-approved projects, and approved others the ECA would not approve. The result was slow spending of counterpart funds and increasing American frustration at the disappointing pace of Italian recovery.

The ECA took a new tack in late 1949, threatening to withhold funds for Italian imports unless they included more machinery for industrial modernization. Pella countered that the funds were better spent importing commodities, revenue from the sale of which could be used to relieve unemployment in the south and other depressed regions. The government made only modest, narrow concessions to boost machine tool imports. It never produced an investment program worthy of the name.[60]

In the fall of 1950, new Rome mission chief Leon Dayton created a diplomatic storm by blasting Italian business for profiteering at the expense of underpaid workers. With war in Korea raging, Washington also began pushing Italy in a new direction. "Over-cautious monetary policies," Secretary of State Acheson wrote to the Rome embassy in December, were holding back "both [the] investment program implementation and [an] effective defense production program essential to Italian and Western armament." He criticized Pella for fixating on lira stabilization at the expense of the new American priority of rearmament.[61]

Though European financial stabilization had been a fundamental economic objective of the Marshall Plan, ECA official Harlan Cleveland concluded that, in the case of Italy, stressing it had been a strategic mistake. "Putting equal emphasis on two sides of the scale," stabilization and investment, "is not in practice an impartial attitude when the scale is already tipped by the bias of Italian financial policy in one direction." Given that De Gasperi's government had always been determined to achieve stabilization, he concluded that Washington could only have achieved both objectives by neglecting the first and pushing twice as hard on the second.[62]

❖

BROADLY, IT CANNOT BE SAID THAT THE MARSHALL PLAN SUCCEEDED IN France and Italy by encouraging a policy agenda different from that preferred by their governments. Washington adapted its desires and expectations to a far greater extent than did Paris or Rome.

Without Marshall aid, however, it is far less likely that those governments would have had the necessary popular support, let alone the resources, to pursue those policies. More likely, they would have had different compositions, and therefore different agendas. Communists would likely have remained part of the French and Italian governing coalitions in 1947, although a Gaullist backlash could well have upended Communist participation in France. The

Marshall Plan succeeded in keeping the Communists (and Gaullists) out of government, but that success came at a price: despite the theatrics of negotiation with the ECA, the French and Italian governments did largely as they pleased, at least domestically.

The challenge for France was that it could not resist American policy in Germany. After the launch of the Marshall Plan, France found it increasingly difficult to use its occupation zone as a bargaining chip for economic and security concessions. France not only wanted Marshall aid, but needed it once the United States began shutting off its avenues to extracting reparations, territory, and underpriced commodities from Germany. American power in Germany ultimately obliged Paris to accommodate itself to Washington's western integration agenda.

It is difficult to overstate the singular importance of Germany in the Cold War conflict. In many ways, the conflict was *about* Germany. Kennan understood that West European recovery was essential to the protection of U.S. economic and security interests, and that such recovery was itself dependent on a revival of German industry, most of which was fortuitously based in the western occupation zones. Keeping it beyond Russian control was, therefore, itself essential. The creation of a strong, independent West Germany, integrated into a robust West European economic and North Atlantic security architecture, represented a fundamental departure in policy from the late FDR years, one without which it is difficult now to imagine a peaceful end to the Cold War on American terms.

❖

AS MARSHALL PREPARED TO FLY TO MOSCOW IN MARCH 1947, ELEANOR Roosevelt was organizing a National Conference on the Problem of Germany in New York City, featuring dozens of prominent backers from Henry Morgenthau to Albert Einstein, to protest what was believed to be Marshall's pro-German agenda. The conference urged the secretary of state not to abandon Yalta and Potsdam for the sake of creating a German "buffer state"—one that would, in the words of publishing titan William Ziff, Sr., "inevitably . . . dominate through sheer force of economic power." Instead it called for U.S. endorsement of French claims to the Saar basin[63] and reparations paid "in factories and coal" to build up "non-German European industry."

General Clay took no issue with reparations in principle. Indeed, he dismantled hundreds of German factories deemed surplus because they were not immediately usable (given shortages of fuel, power, and commodities inputs). Across the three Western zones combined, the Allies removed equipment from 706 plants.[64] Germans, for their part, preferred reparations from current production to dismantling.[65] Clay got so angered with "German attacks" over his actions that, in November 1948, he threatened to dismantle twenty plants as "punishment" for each such future attack.[66]

Clay's stance on limiting reparations was based on what a self-sustaining Germany could bear, and not aimed at stymieing Soviet demands. An admirer of FDR's "diplomatic genius" in managing U.S.-Soviet relations, who was on warm personal terms with both Zhukov and Sokolovsky, he had been committed to cooperation with the Soviets in Germany, believing it would create a template for the two countries to work together worldwide.[67] His objection to Morgenthauism was that it was not "a program for German peace." Rather, to him it meant "abandoning [Germany] to chaos."[68] Forced upon a country in which one in three babies was dying within a year, and where coal and other export goods were needed to pay for vital food imports, it meant a deepening humanitarian crisis, threats to basic law and order, and huge additional financial and security burdens on the United States.

By 1948, Germany had emerged from pariah status in the United States to become the fulcrum of the Marshall Plan. During the war, the country expanded its industrial capacity dramatically—an average of 3.36 billion reichsmarks' worth per year ($1.34 billion, or $19.9 billion in today's money) from 1940 to 1945.[69] After the war, the western Allies were surprised to find that, in spite of the enormous damage done to the German housing stock, only about 18 percent of industrial capacity had been destroyed by bombing.[70] Thus, after targeted repairs to bottleneck suppliers and transport infrastructure, Germany emerged from the conflict with considerably greater industrial capacity than that with which it had begun. It therefore had the imminent potential to provide its neighbors with much needed capital goods and industrial commodities—items that the United States could only provide, where it could provide them at all, at greater cost to itself and a dollar-starved Europe. The fact, therefore, that the Truman administration had the means to set policy largely as it wished in western Germany gave it the power to pursue economic statecraft on a grand scale.

On the ground in Germany, one of the earliest significant American efforts to boost output was reconstruction of the rail and transport system in 1947, well before Marshall aid was appropriated.[71] Action of this sort, not to mention the historic airlift in Berlin the following year, disproved Nazi propaganda that defeat would mean the destruction of German industry and mass starvation.[72] It thereby eased acceptance among West Germans of the subsequent division of their country.

The Truman administration was determined that Germany's recovery, and western Europe's, would not be held back by the financial legacy of war. American grants-in-aid to West Germany, which reached a high of 4 percent of GNP in 1950, do not even begin to measure the benefits to the country from Marshall's program.[73] Aid figures ignore the vast and consequential write-off of the country's debt. Germany's total official public debt after the war, 86 percent of which was domestic, amounted to nearly four times the country's 1938 GDP.[74] The United States abolished it through the 1948 currency reform that introduced the deutschmark. (Banks holding the debt received compensating assets to prevent their collapse.) As regards external debt, the 1953 London Agreement reduced the principal and interest on obligations incurred through 1933 (when the country defaulted) and postponed settlement of obligations subsequently created until sometime after a future German unification, when a reparations conference could be held.[75]

During the war, Germany also accumulated large external debts through a European payments clearing system established by the Reichsbank. This mechanism, through which the Nazi regime financed virtually all of its trade deficits with Europe, overvalued the reichsmark as a means of expropriating its neighbors. When calculated at realistic exchange rates, Germany's unsettled external payments obligations amounted to nearly 90 percent of its 1938 GDP by the war's end.

The Truman administration was determined not to repeat the mistakes of the 1924 Dawes Plan, through which the United States effectively financed Germany's external obligations. It cleverly prevented this fate by classifying its aid to Germany as *credits*, rather than grants, and then requiring other Marshall

aid recipients to forgo claims on Germany until the country repaid those credits. Until the United States chose to exercise claims against Germany, which it
had no intention of doing, no one else would be able to. The "value of [our]
claim," Lovett told Marshall in December 1947, was "in treaty negotiations." It
was the "basis for keeping other claims down."[76] Washington forced Germany's
neighbors to choose between Marshall aid and trying to collect on German
debts. They chose the sure thing: U.S. aid.

The United States secured, in return for this aid, only modest influence
over French and Italian economic policy. Yet it was able virtually to dictate policy in Germany. As Clay put it simply, "There was no German government. We
were it. Absolute and sovereign."[77] The United States was therefore far more assertive in imposing its agenda there than elsewhere in Europe. It is notable that
Clay dismissed the first German bizonal economic director, the ever-voluble
Johannes Semler, for the modest crime of publicly condemning American food
aid as *Hühnerfutter*, or "chicken feed."[78] Clay was a dictator. He was a benign
one by any reasonable standard, but a dictator nonetheless—one who was determined to leave his post with Germany committed to capitalism. It was, to
his mind, not just Soviet communism that had to be kept out of Germany, but
British Labour–style democratic socialism.

In his visit to Washington in October 1947, a frustrated SPD leader Kurt
Schumacher demanded to know how America could profess a commitment
to German self-determination while obstructing his party's efforts to advance
"socialization"—state ownership and control of industry.[79] The Truman administration would never find comfort with this question. In April 1948, the State
Department acknowledged internally that, when it came to the issue of socialization, it had "in spite of our handsome statements of policy regarding German
self-determination . . . in practice not arrived at any concrete action."[80]

On the ground in Germany, Clay did his own version of St. Augustine:
"Lord, make me chaste—but not yet." While pledging his commitment to German home rule, he would only permit it after private enterprise and a market
economy seemed assured.

"We do believe that free enterprise has developed a high standard of living
in America," Clay told German trade unionists in September 1947. "However,
we believe in democracy more than we do free enterprise":

We have no desire to impose any particular economic structure upon the German people.... [M]uch has been said about the United States attempting to stop socialization in Germany when it is desired by the German people. That is not our position although we do hope that you will see some of the virtues that result from free enterprise before you make [your decisions].[81]

In practice, Clay used pretexts to block socialization. In 1947 he suspended a Hessian referendum vote in favor of socialization and "co-determination" (union representation on corporate boards), and blocked all subsequent attempts to implement it.[82] "They were foreign to my way of thinking—and to the American way of thinking," Clay commented years later. "I was going to try my best to prove that in encouraging free enterprise we were encouraging a more rapid recovery for Germany." But he denied imposing his ideological views. "I thought it was the job of military government to maintain free enterprise in Germany until the Germans were capable of making that choice for themselves," he said, referring to a future united Germany (or at least the western part of it).[83] This insistence that only the totality of the German people could decide on socialization allowed him to champion self-determination while blocking Länder legislation he didn't like.[84]

Whereas Washington did not try to use its control of Marshall funds to stop socialization in Britain, it did use its funding of food and other British occupation costs to stop socialization in the British zone of Germany. Attlee's Labour government, mainly for ideological reasons, wanted public ownership of coal and heavy industry in the Ruhr.[85] For its part, the Ramadier (and Schuman) government, for far more practical reasons, wanted to shift the locus of such industry to France. Clay was frequently more critical of them than the Soviets. As occupiers, he said, the French "lived in pomp and luxury and . . . took the maximum out of Germany that could be taken."[86] Both the British and French programs in Germany, Clay was convinced, would have set back German industrial recovery.

In April 1947, Clay demanded "assurance from our Government that its desire to make economic fusion [between the American and British zones] work does not make it willing to accept a highly centralized economic control, which will be utilized in the hands of the SPD with the support of the British Military Government, to extend socialist influence."[87] Marshall himself insisted that the United States would "not sit by while the British tried out any ideas which they had of experimenting with socialization of mines."[88]

U.S. aid provided the necessary sweeteners for the two allies to abandon their visions. As Kennan put it in July 1947, the United States offered the French and British "the choice between a rise in German production or no European recovery financed by the US."[89] Or as General Robertson put it for his country, "He who pays the piper calls the tune."[90]

In spring of 1948, Will Clayton returned from Europe with vivid accounts of urban food shortages, which were particularly acute in Germany. The Nazi government had suppressed inflation with price controls, which led industrial output to stagnate and farmers to withhold produce. Firms and individuals resorted to using cigarettes for payment.[91] The Soviets cared about securing German reparations from current production, but little about how the western zones were supposed to produce them without food or economic incentives.

Clay planned the 1948 currency reform that restored such incentives in secret.[92] He had not even discussed the plans with bizonal economics director Ludwig Erhard, who threatened to resign when he discovered them. (Erhard subsequently changed his mind and announced them on radio as his own.)[93] That Clay—who had once been the administration's highest-level advocate of four-power cooperation in Germany—pursued currency reform unilaterally, in spite of bitter Soviet protests, shows that he saw German revival as being far more important to American national interests.

The Marshall Plan aimed at a substitution of German for American capital goods supply in western Europe. It succeeded. It did so on the basis of economic and monetary reforms that the Soviets had not allowed, and would never have allowed, under the four-party control regime. "Time is on our side," Clay argued of his approach in October 1947—ignoring both Germans and Russians who disagreed with him.[94] He was vindicated by the election of Adenauer as West Germany's first chancellor in September 1949. The new leader claimed a popular mandate "against the planned economy."[95]

WITH THE UNITED STATES BLOCKING COLLECTION ON ITS MASSIVE AC-
cumulated debt, the new Federal Republic of Germany faced none of the temp-
tations of post–World War I German governments. Popular pressure to adopt
inflationary monetary policy, radically redistributive fiscal policy, or antiwestern foreign policy was negligible. Washington's treatment of Germany's debt
was thus at the heart of the country's subsequent emergence as a model of macroeconomic orthodoxy and geopolitical conservatism.[96]

The mechanisms imposed by the Truman administration for eliminating
German debt were not incidental to the Marshall Plan; they were integral to
it. They were intended to minimize German and overall European reliance on
American transfer payments by easing the implementation of industrial policies, monetary reforms, and trade regimes that would encourage the most rapid
possible revival of European production. This revival was in turn intended to
buttress democratic government in Europe, keeping communist and other authoritarian political forces at bay—a critical element of the emerging Soviet
containment policy.

"Our basic policy . . . is to push freedom as far east as possible," Acheson
told reporters off the record in May 1949. "If a united Germany contributes to
that aim, fine; if not, to hell with it."[97] In Clay's words, the State Department was
only "interested in Germany's relations with other countries, not in Germany
itself."[98]

Once the United States had unilaterally blocked Germany's debt and reparations, it still had to deal with the problem that its neighbors would not trade
with it other than through barter. No country was willing to run a trade surplus
with Germany, as its exporters would take bottom priority in the long list of
creditors. They would likely never be repaid.

The State Department addressed this problem by mothballing the international monetary system FDR's Treasury had instituted in 1944 at Bretton
Woods and, for the Marshall countries, substituting the European Payments
Union, which operated from 1950 to 1958. The system was multilateral, so participants did not care with whom they traded; exporting to Germany no longer
carried any special credit risks.

At the end of each month, countries' offsetting claims against each other
were canceled out, and remaining surplus or deficit balances consolidated; that

is, no country had any claim on any other—only against the union as a whole. As long as countries' balances, positive or negative, remained within certain quotas, no settlements actually occurred. Once various thresholds were exceeded, however, countries settled in dollars or gold, according to formula. To make the system attractive to both debtors and creditors, the United States subsidized it with $350 million of working capital ($3.5 billion in today's money) through the Marshall Plan. The capital was used to finance debtor deficits by paying out to creditors the difference between the funds the debtors put in and the greater amounts they actually owed. As regards Germany, the EPU, as a closed system, eliminated the country's difficulties importing from its neighbors by making its past debts irrelevant to the conduct of trade. It allowed Germany to reengage with the world commercially, in Clay's words, "unhampered by the curse of past political mistakes."[99]

Since the primary purpose of the system was to encourage intra-European trade, participants were required to end discrimination against imports from all other participants and to cut trade barriers—by 50 percent in December 1949, rising in stages to 90 percent by January 1955.[100] Actual settlement in gold or dollars under the EPU was less than a quarter of what it would have been outside it, which also provided a major stimulus to trade. As a result, trade within Europe expanded robustly under the EPU, from $10 billion in 1950 ($100 billion today) to $23 billion in 1959 ($191 billion today). Intra-European trade grew far more than trade with North America, and far more than could be explained by the much smaller rise in European output.[101] Although West Germany would complain that the system was too debtor-friendly, allowing France and others to avoid settlement in dollars or gold, the alternative would clearly have been much less supportive of the new country's export-led revival.

Creating a regional payments union would seem an archaic way of dealing with trade deficits and a dollar "shortage." Today, countries would simply devalue their currencies, or allow them to depreciate in foreign exchange markets; this would tend to make their goods more competitive internationally and reduce the deficits. Indeed, in August 1949 Britain—virtually dollarless and at odds with Washington over plans for protectionist retreat into the sterling area—reluctantly devalued sterling by 30 percent after its Treasury warned of "another instalment of dollar crisis (even with ERP)."[102] Germany and other nations quickly followed (twenty-three within a week), with the intended effect. Dollar deficits dissipated, and recovery picked up steam. British reserves tripled within two years.[103]

In the context of the early postwar period, however, a time in which most currencies were inconvertible and trade barriers high, global multilateral monetary and trade liberalization, of the sort envisioned at Bretton Woods, was utopian. Within Marshall aid countries, establishing a stable environment in which trust and cooperation could take hold among government, business, and workers was vital to the re-creation of a market economy. Across Marshall countries, U.S. security guarantees and financial support were indispensable to allowing those economies to integrate without engendering unmanageable domestic and foreign conflict.

Much as the State Department had anticipated, American underwriting of the EPU redirected West European imports from the United States to Germany. Western Europe's large dollar deficits between 1945 and 1948 were a reflection of Germany's disappearance as its main capital goods supplier. Massive reconstruction needs had therefore to be filled by the United States. It was an important ambition of the Marshall Plan to eliminate Germany's need for American aid *and* its neighbors' need for dollar imports, simultaneously, by restoring Germany to its traditional export role.

In re-creating a European division of labor, with Germany as an importer of raw materials and exporter of capital goods, the Marshall Plan succeeded in cutting the transatlantic umbilical cord through which western Europe was sucking in unaffordable dollar imports of coal and other industrial supplies. As Europe's dollar balance strengthened under the EPU (doubling between 1950 and 1956), its incentive to discriminate against dollar imports also declined. The higher dollar balance thereby enabled the Marshall countries to begin restoring currency convertibility after the EPU wound down in 1958. The EPU also succeeded in integrating Germany into western Europe even more deeply than the United States had aimed (possibly at a permanent cost to its own export sectors).

Bissell and other Marshall planners saw European integration as only a stepping-stone toward the earlier Bretton Woods vision of a *globally* integrated world. That is, they believed that sometime soon after the Plan was wound down Europe would shed its protectionist trade and currency cocoon and quickly expand trade with the rest of the world. Within Germany, global integration had been economics minister Ludwig Erhard's aim: to "return to the world market." In fact, Germany's intra–western European trade increased more rapidly after 1955 than did its trade with the rest of the world—as did that of all West European countries. Intra-European integration suited Adenauer, whose priority, in contrast to Erhard, was rapprochement with France and its other immediate neighbors.[104] The chancellor was convinced that German integration with western Europe would contribute to the ending of Allied controls over its economy, eventually freeing it to leverage its economic power in the area of foreign affairs.[105]

Two decades after the launch of the Marshall Plan, Kennan concluded that his objections to the creation of the Federal Republic of Germany had been based on "some grievous miscalculations." He had overestimated German hatred toward occupation, division, and Americanization, and underestimated its hatred of Russia and communism. "The political success of the London program and the economic 'miracle' that was shortly to begin in Western Germany," he concluded in retrospect, "stand now in the historical record as authoritative corrections to the extremisms of my outlook in 1949."[106] That "miracle," upon which western Europe's own remarkable recovery was built, may rank as the single most important and consequential economic contribution of the Marshall Plan.

❖

AS WITH ALL LEGENDS, THE MARSHALL PLAN HAS ITS FAIR SHARE OF CONtrarians. On the question of its economic impact, none is more formidable than the late British economic historian Alan Milward. Wielding vast reams of historical facts and figures, typically buried in dense and difficult prose, Milward weaves an elaborate case against the economic relevance of the Marshall Plan. Far from "saving the world," as Kindleberger and others have claimed, Marshall aid was, in Milward's estimation, at best unnecessary. "[T]he postwar European world would have looked much the same without it," he declares with bracing dismissiveness.[107]

As a trenchant skeptic toward Keynesian analyses that suggested large returns to government-directed investment, Milward is naturally unsurprised by the findings of economist Barry Eichengreen and others that offer little empirical support for its importance.[108] He instead argues that Marshall aid allowed governments to operate with greater inflation and balance-of-payments deficits than they should have.[109] The debtor-friendly EPU, a poor alternative to general currency convertibility, in his view, reinforced this.

Milward is further dismissive of the idea, popularized by historians Michael Hogan and Charles Maier, that the Marshall Plan operated through the successful export of New Deal political and social constructs. In particular, Europe's adoption of less conflictual American-style labor-management relations was held to have fueled productivity growth.

This Washington-centric view does indeed seem remote from developments on the ground in Europe—notably in France, where union demands on wages, redistribution, and political representation remained strikingly more hard-edged than in the United States. For its part, the British government consistently pushed back against American efforts to export their industrial management practices. Though "there will undoubtedly be trouble if the Americans think that we are not sufficiently interested in productivity," noted one U.K. Treasury report, their "superficial investigations and ill-considered reports" needed to be resisted: "The relations between workers and employers in this country [are] quite different from that in the United States."[110] In any case, the different uses to which France, Italy, and the U.K. chose to direct Marshall funds (industrial modernization, inflation control, and debt retirement, respectively) demonstrate that they cannot *all* have been pursuing an imported American "model." Whatever that model was, it was not schizophrenic.

Where Milward is on much shakier ground is in arguing that western Europe's hardships were overstated, and that it could have, and would have, gotten onto the same impressive growth trajectory, albeit a few years later, through a combination of toughing-it-out and changing to non-dollar-based suppliers.

Milward insists that lack of food was not a "resource bottleneck." Most Marshall countries, he argued, could have pursued their chosen recovery programs without American aid by maintaining food consumption at 1947 levels. One reason is that they were, he believes, generally consuming much more than government records indicate. Germans, Italians, and Austrians, whose average official rations contained insufficient calories to sustain manual work, had access to a black market that was "as important" for acquiring food as the legal one. That the 1948 German currency reform instantly filled shop windows was evidence of prior hoarding. Change policy and the problem goes away.[111]

This argument is problematic on at least two grounds. First, U.S. officials were aware of the black markets. Department of Agriculture statisticians in fact calculated Germany's food needs under the assumption that the average German had access to 200 calories daily through the black market (an assumption Clay thought reasonable only for those with exceptional means).[112] Second, the State Department was aware of hoarding and its causes. Clayton constantly drew attention to the problem. But he also believed that aid had to accompany policy reform to support basic levels of consumption during the transition.

In Britain, a June 1948 Treasury paper laid out the terrible consequences for food availability if the government were to reject American aid conditions; Milward dismisses it as "alarmist and exaggerated." In France, a January 1948 missive to Washington laid out the costs of the latter failing to continue aid: huge cuts to coal (25 percent), oil (50 percent), and sugar (30 percent) allocations, accompanied by soaring unemployment and a possible Communist takeover. Milward dismisses it similarly: "What else were they likely to say if they wanted the aid?"[113]

Milward's own calculations, however, show that France, even if it had held food consumption at the depressed levels of the summer of 1947, could *not* have paid, two years later, for its dollar-zone finished goods, steel, vehicle, and industrial raw material imports out of export proceeds. These were possible only because of the Marshall Plan. France's industrial modernization program, Milward himself emphasizes, had "widespread national support." Yet it could never have been taken forward without American aid, not even by suppressing food consumption 14 percent below 1949 levels.[114]

So on what can Milward hang his argument that Europe would still have achieved full (but delayed) recovery without the Marshall Plan? First, according to his calculations, some countries—the U.K., Italy, West Germany, Belgium, and Luxembourg—could, unlike France, have successfully followed his budgetary reallocation approach: financing their preferred recovery programs, without aid, at much reduced levels of food consumption.[115] In the case of Italy, at least, however, this conclusion is difficult to accept. The Communists were a powerful political force, and public knowledge was near-universal that no American aid would be forthcoming if they were present in the government. Fear of losing aid clearly had a depressing impact on the Communist Party's electoral performance, and explains its absence from ruling coalitions after 1947. Without the Marshall Plan, therefore, Italian policy would have been very different.

Second, Milward argues that Marshall countries could have shifted their imports to nondollar sources. But which ones? Incredibly, Milward points to "the Federal Republic" of Germany, which was only founded in May 1949. Milward specifically highlights the "Dutch-German economic symbiosis." The Netherlands, like France, also failed his test of whether its recovery program could have been financed without Marshall aid. Yet Milward insists that "the expansion of German trade" after 1947 was "a powerful force for growth in the Dutch economy," as if this somehow negates his test.[116]

There are gaping holes in the argument, however, that German trade could have substituted for Marshall aid. Milward is silent on the mechanism by which a greater "symbiosis" might have been achieved, and how it would have plugged the Dutch government's financing gap. He argues only, first, that the impact of Marshall aid on growth in German national income is unproven, and therefore unimportant in explaining the growth of Dutch-German trade, and, second, that there were forces independent of the Marshall Plan pushing "the integration of the Federal Republic into an expanding intra–West European trade circuit."[117]

But political forces, outside the Marshall Plan, were pushing *against* integration, not for it. France was determined to extract reparations from Germany and to neuter its industrial capacity. It was the United States that made the unilateral decision to reindustrialize Germany, to make French acceptance of this a condition for aid, and to turn the Western-occupied portion of it into an independent state. There is no reason to believe that the United States, had it lacked the motivation to create the Marshall Plan, would still have had the motivation to create West Germany, in defiance of Stalin's threats and pressures. There is further no reason to believe that France and Britain would have entered into any system of economic (let alone security) integration with this new entity. The Marshall Plan not only initiated such integration, but held it together.[118]

Milward's contrarian take has been rightfully influential in rolling back the deference that many had accorded to early eulogistic accounts of the Marshall Plan.[119] Those accounts reflexively ascribed to it all the economic successes that accompanied and followed it. But Milward's case is ultimately uncompelling, relying as it does on the farfetched idea that less food and more Germany could have achieved better results.

❧

SO DID THE MARSHALL PLAN WORK? TO THE EXTENT THAT IT WAS intended to allow the United States to disengage from Europe militarily, the answer is no. The Truman administration was ultimately obliged to conclude, reluctantly, that it had to commit to a military alliance, NATO, to bring its vision to reality. The Marshall Plan and NATO are therefore best understood as two parts of a wider European security policy, which was itself embedded in an emerging Grand Strategy of Soviet containment. But on this level, as a component of a broader strategy, the Marshall Plan did indeed work. A critical insight behind the Marshall Plan was that we could not take a popular commitment to democracy and free enterprise for granted. If people's basic needs for physical and economic security were not met, they were likely to turn to authoritarian alternatives. In the wake of the devastation of WWII, the Marshall Plan and NATO provided western Europe with such security and kept it firmly on the democratic, capitalist path.

And it did so not, as in Soviet propaganda and western revisionist accounts,[120] by forcing American surplus production on them. This would have widened Europe's balance of payments deficit, frustrated Washington's integration aims, and exacerbated shortages at home. Instead, the Truman administration, aided by a striking change in American business lobbying priorities, orchestrated a shift in policy at home away from protectionism and toward encouragement of imports.

Harriman was steadfast in insisting that "the purpose of ECA is to stimulate countries to help themselves," and that, consistent with the ERP legislation, the funds could not be used "to buy surpluses" from "American industry." The National Association of Manufacturers, in turn, warned its own members that "efforts to direct [Marshall] funds to [exporting surpluses] must be firmly resisted." The Chamber of Commerce joined NAM in stating that "US exports [must] be consistent with the ability of our customers abroad to pay for them by their own exports." A State Department directive further stressed that whereas Washington sought "non-discrimination in world trade, it is recognized that during the period in which Germany's balance of payments is in substantial disequilibrium [it] will, like other countries in the Organization for European Economic Cooperation, find it necessary to restrict imports." State insisted, therefore, that the U.S. High Commission in Germany not interfere in trade policy.

Public consciousness of the importance of closing the dollar gap is reflected in the soaring number of newspaper references to the problem between 1947 and 1950.[121] The Marshall Plan helped to close the gap by engineering Germany's revival as western Europe's primary capital goods supplier, replacing the United States. In this effort it was assisted by a relaxation of official resistance to foreign currency devaluation. Washington recognized, for example, that if Germany could not devalue it would simply "revert to [the] tactics of the 1930s" through which it "fostered . . . exports by dumping and other unethical methods."[122] This recognition represented a departure from the mind-set of FDR's Treasury at Bretton Woods, which led it to support U.S. exports by prodding indebted nations to keep their currencies overvalued and to finance trade deficits with more debt—that is, IMF loans.[123] Under the Marshall Plan, greater U.S. openness to imports and a stronger dollar also helped smooth implementation of the GATT and a revival of international trade generally.

The financial assistance aspect of the Marshall Plan also departed from earlier American efforts by abjuring the creation of "unbroken circle[s] of loans to pay back loans,"[124] relying instead on grants-in-aid. The impact of this aid was significant, though far less direct than the U.S. government had intended. It provided a cushion with which recipient governments alleviated the short-term hardships and insecurity that accompanied homegrown economic initiatives— initiatives that American officials often thought insufficient or misguided. But fear of losing aid kept Communist parties out of government, thus satisfying Washington's overriding political and economic imperatives.

There was a geopolitical cost for this success, however. While Eleanor Roosevelt and other liberal American notables saw the Marshall Plan as an enlightened and peaceable alternative to the Truman Doctrine, the Soviets saw it very differently. The Truman Doctrine, notwithstanding its harsh tone, had just restated the existence of an American sphere of influence in the Mediterranean that Stalin had already conceded. The Marshall Plan, in contrast, suggested to him the creation of a permanent American political and military presence in the heart of Europe. This presence would, without determined countermeasures, undermine Soviet control of a buffer region for which the Soviet people had paid dearly in the war.

That Germany, the mortal enemy, would become central to the Marshall Plan made it particularly threatening. To undermine the American plans, Stalin set out to transform western communists into Soviet fifth columns, launched the Cominform, instigated a coup in Prague, and imposed a blockade on Berlin. A July 1947 Central Intelligence Group (CIA predecessor) report to the White House concluded that Marshall's initiative had "intensified Soviet determination to maintain its extraordinary powers of control over [eastern European] countries."[125] These nations would pay a steep price so that democratic capitalism might thrive in the West.

Paris and London, meanwhile, were unwilling to abandon the autarkic thrust of their postwar recovery and development plans without guarantees from Washington that they would be protected against both a revanchist Germany and an increasingly hostile Soviet Union. So whereas the Truman administration had intended the Marshall Plan to ease America's military departure from Europe, it actually served to draw it into an open-ended commitment. Though Stalin saw militarization as endemic to the Plan, NATO was for Truman a regrettable unanticipated cost of implementing it.

At home in the United States, the Marshall Plan became legislation against all odds. By contemporary standards of cross-party cooperation and public support, it was a remarkable triumph. The Republican 80th Congress had been in no mood to devote vast new funds to foreign aid. But the political packaging of the program was masterful. It appealed to internationalists as well as anticommunists. It appealed to those who believed the Morgenthau and Potsdam policies toward Germany were failing. It appealed even to isolationist elements that wanted a "one and done" approach: putting Europe on its feet, and then pushing it out on its own.[126]

Although changing circumstances created the opportunity for radical foreign policy innovations, personalities mattered. Whereas FDR, had he lived to finish his fourth term, would almost surely have adapted his "One World" vision to the reality of clashing U.S. and Soviet interests, it is doubtful he would have empowered capable subordinates the way Truman did. Roosevelt gave the State Department little leeway for independent initiative. The slow-witted Morgenthau and fellow-traveling White at Treasury, who dominated foreign economic policy from 1934 to 1945, were no match for men of judgment and integrity such as Marshall, Acheson, Kennan, Clayton, Bohlen, and Hoffman. Officials on the ground in Europe—notably Clay and Murphy in Berlin, Douglas in London, and Caffery and Harriman in Paris—ensured that the new American strategy was implemented competently and forcefully. It is further questionable whether FDR could have forged the vital political bond with congressional Republicans through its master legislative tactician, Vandenberg. Without it, even the best-laid plan would have remained just that: a plan.

Still, there was a diplomatic cost to be paid for the packaging that got the Marshall Plan through Congress; packaging that elevated anti-Communist rhetoric to a level beyond what Marshall and much of the State Department ever found comfort with. This rhetoric served to help lock the United States onto a course of confrontation with Moscow, and Communist movements generally, by making it necessary to validate the commitment of resources and American prestige the Plan involved.

The question remains whether the Cold War could have been avoided. The Marshall Plan accelerated and intensified it, but the answer is almost surely no: given how the two sides saw their vital interests, the conflict was inevitable. "Soviet domination of the potential power of Eurasia, whether achieved by armed aggression or by political and subversive means," stated U.S. policy paper NSC 20/4, approved by Truman in November 1948, "would be strategically and politically unacceptable to the United States."[127] Mackinder's famous 1904 analysis had suggested that the threat of such domination hinged on Russia concluding an alliance with Germany—an alliance that would therefore itself constitute a mortal threat to the western powers.[128] Moscow, too, of course, had its own red lines on American domination; and in Europe it ran through Germany. Stalin was clear when he told Bulgarian and Yugoslav allies that "All of Germany must be ours. That is, Soviet, Communist."[129] Stalin's actions in Poland and Czechoslovakia show this was not bluster. Germany was the one European power that could destroy his hard-won buffer zone in the East, which itself could only be held together with force or the threat of force.

The blockade crisis highlighted the seriousness with which each side saw its rights and interests in Germany. The Marshall Plan, in accelerating the political division of the country, however, pushed the two sides toward what may have been the only feasible compromise to avert hot war. From this perspective, the Marshall Plan was also conducive to wider European stability.

The Marshall Plan was, of course, only one component of the early American Cold War containment strategy. Yet economic rehabilitation became a primary tool of a so-called strongpoint defense of critical geostrategic regions, in Northeast Asia as well as Europe, aimed at building up energetic, self-confident, independent centers of power capable of resisting Soviet pressure. Just as it had with Germany, the Truman administration concluded that there was less risk to U.S. interests in the rehabilitation of Japan than in negotiating its neutralization with Moscow. "Neutrality is an illusion in the context of East-West tensions," Acheson said in December 1949. "[T]he Soviets would continue to pursue infiltration tactics, permitting them ultimately to turn Japan into an aggressive military threat."[130]

Looking at the distribution of power among U.S. and Soviet allies in Europe and Northeast Asia at the end of the Cold War—considering in particular the rise of West Germany and Japan—it is difficult to conclude that the broad American strategy was not a success. Forty years after Acheson's observation on the need for Washington to have *allies*, rather than trust in neutral zones, its early Cold War alliances were still intact, while Moscow's were in tatters.[131] Henry Cabot Lodge, Jr., had in October 1947 written to Vandenberg, who passed his words on to Marshall, that "the recovery of Western Europe [was] a twenty-five to fifty-year proposition and . . . the aid which we extend now and in the next three or four years will in the long future result in our having strong friends abroad."[132] This insight was keen and important. Containment successfully navigated between appeasement and war for four decades, and the Marshall Plan played a principal role in bonding the West together for the struggle. Many of the institutions we now take for granted as natural elements of the liberal postwar order—in particular, the European Union, NATO, and the World Trade Organization—were forged under U.S. leadership during the early Marshall years.

⁂

BY THE END OF THE COLD WAR, THE MARSHALL PLAN HAD TAKEN ON AN iconic status. "There is hardly a crisis anywhere in the world," observed German economist Werner Abelshauser in 1991, "which in the view of the West ought not be solved by a sort of 'Marshall Plan.' "[133] Even among those who knew little about it, it had become synonymous with noble and intelligent foreign intervention. Indeed it is today axiomatic that when turmoil hits a critical part of the world calls pour forth for "A New Marshall Plan" to alleviate hardship, calm passions, and stir hope. Hillary Clinton invoked it in the context of the Arab Spring.[134] Peer Steinbrueck posed it as the wise alternative to Europe's austerity policies.[135] George Soros pleaded for one to counter Russia in Ukraine.[136] Others have proposed it for Gaza.[137] Greece.[138] North Africa.[139] Even the United States itself.[140] China's foreign investment schemes have been called a "Chinese Marshall Plan."[141] Al Gore wants one for the environment.[142] Others demand one for "global unemployment."[143] Yet the fact that nothing resembling the Marshall Plan ever emerges suggests just how sui generis the conditions surrounding it were.

One of the great challenges in replicating the Marshall Plan, aside from the sums involved, is making conditionality effective—getting beneficial policy reforms in return for aid. Broadly, the more aid involved, the greater the ability of the donor to bring to power, and sustain in power, governments committed to its policy priorities. Beneficiaries, however, can distinguish between donor priorities and mere preferences, and have their own red lines. The Ramadier, Schuman, Queuille, and Bidault governments in postwar France understood that the Americans would not concede on German reindustrialization or exclusion of the Communists from their coalitions. They therefore adapted to them, even taking control of the integration process by way of the Schuman Plan (as Acheson had encouraged Schuman to do).[144] But they understood as well that they were largely free to ignore American demands on domestic economic policy.

As exasperating as this was for U.S. officials at the time, it was of little consequence. France was already a rich country with a market economy and the bureaucratic infrastructure necessary to carry out economic policy. It had done so successfully for generations before the war. Its task was essentially to fix the (many and large) potholes caused by war and occupation. That Paris might prefer asphalt, and Washington concrete, was never going to make the difference between ultimate recovery and stagnation.

Less developed countries, in contrast, tend to be run by governments that lack the capacity and, frequently, the will to deliver public goods. Foreign aid, as Nobel economist Angus Deaton has emphasized, not only fails, all too frequently, to develop such local capacity but to undermine it. Aid can be designed to bypass governments, and to go directly to the population, but disintermediation does nothing to address the problem that effective government is *necessary* for development—something Marshall's State Department took as a given.[145]

It should not be surprising that large-scale American aid has not had transformative effects in more recent post-conflict societies. As of January 2015, U.S. relief and reconstruction aid to Afghanistan totaled $110 billion; to Iraq, $61 billion.[146] The combined nominal total of $171 billion is about $40 billion *more* than the present value of all Marshall aid. But the Afghan and Iraqi governments have faced vastly less favorable circumstances than those of the Marshall countries. They never achieved full control of their territory. Instead, they have been under constant siege from armed domestic and foreign opponents. While the Marshall countries were recovering on their own (weather crises notwithstanding), these economies were collapsing. Their governments were not, like Marshall governments, natural allies of the United States, which has in turn been at odds with alternative neighboring benefactors such as Iran. They further lacked committed, functioning, impartial national bureaucracies capable of implementing major new policies and programs. In short, the foundation that enabled American economic statecraft to be so successful in postwar Europe is lacking.

Historian John Lewis Gaddis has argued that George Kennan's strategy of containment has limited applicability outside a Cold War context.[147] So the strategy of massive conditional foreign aid, itself developed within a containment context, does as well. The United States has not, since the 1940s, been presented with prospective beneficiaries who are of sufficient geostrategic importance to engage legislative and popular support while, at the same time, offering capable government willing and able to implement its agenda over many years.

There is also the challenge that other nations will consider regional economic, political, or security integration initiated by a power like the United States threatening to their own interests. And when the other nation is as large and powerful as Russia, this likelihood raises the prospect of determined interference. Such interference would create dangerous turmoil as NATO and the EU began expanding eastward in the aftermath of the Cold War.

Celebration at the fall of the Berlin Wall, November 9, 1989.

FOURTEEN

ECHOES

ON THE NIGHT OF NOVEMBER 9, 1989, ENORMOUS CROWDS BEGAN SURG-ing toward official crossings on the eastern side of the Berlin Wall. Having received orders not to shoot, twenty-five-year veteran border guard Harald Jäger was running out of options. Bullhorns bellowed warnings that it was not, as a televised statement had said an hour earlier, "possible . . . to go through the border." This failed to deter the throngs.

Jäger improvised a screening process, permitting a few at a time to pass through the Bornholmer Street gate. But this only encouraged them to press harder. With the frenzied crush shouting *"Tor auf!"* ("Open the gate!"), Jäger, fearing for his men's lives, ordered them to do it. As the gates sprang open along the Wall just before midnight, the crowds erupted. Tens of thousands poured into the West. Millions would do so in the coming days.[1]

The division of Berlin was over.

Germany, however, was still two countries. Indeed, the East German government was determined to confront the day's events as a horrid but reversible mistake.[2] Helmut Kohl knew he had to assert his authority before the opportunity was lost.

Anxious to get to Berlin, the West German chancellor faced a hurdle: his planes were barred from flying there under forty-year-old occupation rules. So following a plea to Washington, he boarded a U.S. Air Force transport plane in Hamburg. Arriving in West Berlin shortly before 4:30 p.m. on November 10, he mounted an outdoor stage bathed in bright television lights.

"I would like to call out to everyone in the GDR!" he shouted. "We stand at your side! We are, and will remain, one nation!"[3] It was the opening salvo in a campaign to reunify Germany.

The Cold War, for all the brutal hardship it imposed behind the Iron Curtain, and the nuclear terrors it posed for the world, had stabilized Europe. Once Germany was divided in 1949, both sides acknowledged the political borders between East and West. Changes in the balance of power within Germany have, however, historically had reverberations well beyond it.[4] The year 1989 would prove no exception.

Europe was caught off guard by the collapse of the Wall and Kohl's kinetic response to it. Before the month was out, the chancellor would, with no advance clearing abroad, announce a "Ten Point Program" for unification in the Bundestag. French President François Mitterrand, who had made it a priority to keep in lockstep with his German counterpart, was shocked and offended. Soviet leader Mikhail Gorbachev was furious; he would give Federal Republic foreign minister Hans-Dietrich Genscher a tongue-lashing in Moscow a week later. British prime minister Margaret Thatcher warned Kohl that "reunification [would] open a Pandora's box of border claims right through Central Europe" and "risk[ed] undermining Gorbachev's position," on which the West depended for democratization in the East.

Kohl tried to calm fears the same way Marshall and Adenauer had in the early postwar years: by pledging to embed Germany in European superstructures. "The government of West Germany would now have to agree to practically any French initiative for Europe," Kohl aide Horst Teltschik teasingly told Le Monde on December 1. "If I were French, I would take advantage of that." Mitterrand obliged, much as his political forebears had done in seizing control of European integration from the Americans after the war. As his price for support on German unity, Mitterrand secured from Kohl a public commitment on European monetary union, something the chancellor had been reluctant to provide until after German elections in 1990. "Mitterrand is wise," Kohl observed. He understood how to harness the inevitable to his advantage. Thatcher's stubbornness, in contrast, baffled him. She was, he was sure, isolating herself diplomatically.[5]

He was right. Though just as taken aback by the events of November 9, U.S. president George H. W. Bush offered the chancellor his support. Hours after Kohl's dramatic flight to Berlin on a U.S. military plane, Secretary of State James Baker, speaking on network television, reminded the world that "it has been the policy of the NATO Alliance" as well as "the policy of the United States of America to support reunification for over forty years."[6] This statement hinted at where U.S. policy might be heading. With an end to the Cold War suddenly in sight, the United States had no intention of reviving FDR's plans for an American withdrawal from Europe. It suggested instead that NATO, through which Truman overturned such plans reluctantly, might even expand into the territory of the enemy Warsaw Pact—beginning with East Germany.

An anxious Gorbachev sought to turn the clock back to the years before NATO's founding—to the four-power occupation regime that controlled Germany after the war. Thatcher was sympathetic. Reunification, she said, would cause "all the fixed points in Europe [to] collapse. . . . We must have a structure to stop this happening, and the only one available was the Four Power arrangement."[7]

The United States had been the first power to abandon this arrangement after the war, having concluded that reviving Germany was the highest priority. Now, once again, a U.S. administration was convinced that Germany would convulse, harming American economic and security interests, if its future were held hostage to Moscow's agenda. Bush was persuaded by Kohl's argument that East Germany was headed for political and economic meltdown, and did not want its absorption into the West stalled by Cold War politics.[8] Under pressure from Gorbachev, however, Baker agreed to an ambassador-level meeting on December 11—but, just as in 1948, to "discuss only Berlin."

Held in the same American sector Allied Control Council building used in Berlin at the end of the war, the atmosphere of the gathering was surreal.

"Since we have emerged as the victors of war," proclaimed the Soviet ambassador to East Germany, "we have taken on the responsibility of providing for . . . a peaceful future."[9] Ostrich-like, head buried in the political sands, he could not see what was obvious to his counterparts: that only a bloody Russian military crackdown, comparable to that carried out by the Chinese Communists in Tiananmen Square, could stop Germany unifying.

As with Stalin after the war, Gorbachev wanted to forestall the emergence of a Western-allied Germany, to roll back the American military presence in Europe, and to rebuild the Soviet economy with German compensation. But the Berlin meeting accomplished nothing, other than to anger the excluded West German government. Despite Soviet insistence that the forum be open-ended, Baker promised Kohl its first meeting would be its last. One week later, on December 19, the emboldened chancellor flew to Dresden, his first trip to the GDR since the historic events at the Wall, and spoke before tens of thousands.

"My goal, if this historic hour will allow it," he declared against the symbolic World War II backdrop of a bombed-out church, "is the unity of our country!"

The crowd cheered. "*Einheit! Einheit! Einheit!*" ("Unity!")

Nearby, a nervous but determined thirty-seven-year-old KGB officer observed events. Days before Kohl's arrival, he had been burning mounds of documents in preparation for possible attacks by angry mobs. The volume crippled the KGB's furnace. Years later, Russian journalists would interview the former officer about his work in Germany.

"We were interested in any information about the main opponent," Vladimir Putin explained. "NATO."[10]

❖

ON NOVEMBER 24, A FEW WEEKS BEFORE KOHL'S DRESDEN SPEECH, NIKOLAI Portugalov, acting as a back channel to Soviet Central Committee expert and former ambassador to West Germany Valentin Falin, met privately with Teltschik in Bonn. The Russian gave Teltschik a handwritten document titled "Unofficial Position," positing that the time had come to free East and West Germany from "relics of the past." The document suggested Soviet willingness to accept German unification. But if the Kohl government were preparing to pursue unification, the paper continued, it also needed to prepare for leaving both the European Community (as the EU was then called) and NATO.[11]

Gorbachev had privately accepted that the East German Communists, imploding under the weight of popular revulsion and infighting, were a spent political force, and had begun to reconcile himself to German unification. What he still demanded, however, was assurances that a united Germany would be neutral or nonaligned. Right up to the critical, historic East German elections on March 18, 1990, he would insist publicly that continued German membership of NATO was "absolutely ruled out."

Washington and Bonn, however, refused to contemplate Germany leaving the alliance. Kohl sought the quickest means possible to unify Germany and embed it in NATO. The 1949 West German Basic Law provided a legal vehicle to do so simultaneously. Article 23 allowed for wholesale extension of the Basic Law to other parts of Germany upon their accession. East Germany could effectively be made part of West Germany overnight. Angry Soviet critics denounced the plan as "Anschluss," a western annexation of the east.

Just before leaving for a meeting with Gorbachev off the coast of Malta on December 2–3, Bush consulted with former president Richard Nixon. Nixon thought Ronald Reagan had been misguided in getting too chummy with Gorbachev, given the yawning gap in strategic interests between Washington and Moscow. Gorbachev wanted "the withdrawal of all foreign troops from Western and Eastern Europe," which was unacceptable. Bush should therefore not "negotiate German reunification or the future of NATO." State Department counselor Robert Zoellick advised Baker to seek a "New Atlanticism and a New Europe that reaches farther East."

Such an objective was bound to meet resistance from Gorbachev. Ending the American military presence near Russia's borders had been a strategic priority of Stalin's, and—in spite of *glasnost, perestroika*, and Gorbachev's genuine desire for cooperative relations with the West—little in this regard had changed in forty years.

Yet when Baker met with Gorbachev in Moscow on February 9, 1990, the Soviet leader showed signs of flexibility. Baker told Gorbachev he agreed with the latter's insistence that, following a hypothetical unification of Germany, "any extension of the zone of NATO would be unacceptable." In a letter to

Kohl summarizing the discussion, Baker indicated that Gorbachev was taking the position that Germany could unify but that "NATO's jurisdiction would not shift one inch eastward from its present position." This formulation suggested that Germany might keep its western part in NATO and its eastern part, somehow, outside it. Alarmed by Baker's statement, Bush's National Security Council staff drafted a letter, which the president sent to Kohl, clarifying that the administration would accept only cosmetic restrictions on NATO's ability to operate in the east of the country. Such restrictions would, the NSC hoped, help Gorbachev to save face with his hard-liners without allowing Russia to control the parameters of NATO membership.[12]

State Department Policy Planning adviser Harvey Sicherman argued that if East Germans backed Kohl's center-right "Alliance for Germany" coalition in the March elections, Gorbachev would ultimately have no choice but to accept full German NATO membership.[13] Yet at this point the center-left SPD, which opposed early reunification and NATO membership, was widely expected to prevail. Kohl, however, still had a powerful political weapon to wield in the campaign. In 1949, the western Allies' "currency blockade" in Berlin, declaring the deutschmark the sole legal tender, had split the city even more effectively than the Soviet goods blockade. Now, the West German chancellor would use the deutschmark to force the pace of unification.

"If the *Deutschmark* does not come to us, we will come to the *Deutschmark*!" read protest signs in the East, a month before the vote. Kohl's allies made rapid economic and monetary union a prominent plank in their electoral platform there.[14] This was good politics, practically and electorally. It would staunch the flood of westward migration, while appealing to voters anxious for the same opportunities as Germans in the Federal Republic. Among those campaigning under this banner was a thirty-five-year-old Hamburg-born chemist raised in the East near Berlin. Angela Merkel would later go on to join Kohl's cabinet.

Kohl also thought that quick replacement of the ostmark with the deutschmark was a means to hasten the departure of Soviet troops. Gorbachev was already pulling troops out of eastern Europe, where some were selling weapons on the black market. The chancellor reckoned that the coming of West German money and consumer goods to the East would fuel resentment among ruble-holding Soviet soldiers, increasing the urgency of repatriating them.

What Kohl did not know was that the soldiers had accumulated huge stocks of ostmarks. Their exchange for DM at an overvalued rate would become part of Gorbachev's demands for withdrawing them.

On March 18, turnout for the historic election was staggering: 93 percent. And the results surprised even the ever-confident Kohl. His Alliance for Germany coalition took 48 percent of the vote, with the SPD polling only 21.9 percent. The reformed Communist SED took only 16.4 percent, and the many smaller parties split the remaining 13.7 percent. Political unification was now all but assured.

As a preliminary step, the two governments set July 1 as the date for economic and monetary union. One month after the election, on April 18, Kohl and Mitterrand issued a joint statement calling for a conference to be held in Italy before the end of the year to push forward with European economic and monetary union. A Dublin summit in June would also prepare the way for political union. Much as the Marshall Plan had envisioned in 1947, historic German economic and political reforms were serving as a catalyst for wider European integration.

His leverage collapsing, Gorbachev flailed about for ways to stop or neutralize East Germany's absorption into NATO. In a May interview, he blasted NATO as "an organization designed from the start to be hostile to the Soviet Union." It was "a symbol of the past, a dangerous and confrontational past." He proposed a new pan-European security institution to replace it, a vision Baker complimented dismissively as "an excellent dream, but only a dream." His preferred option rejected, Gorbachev tried to sell him on the idea of a united Germany belonging to both NATO and the Warsaw Pact. Baker called it "schizophrenic." As a last resort, Gorbachev reasoned, if he couldn't beat NATO expansion he would join it. Since the alliance was allegedly no longer directed against the Soviet Union, why not allow his country to become a member as well? Again, Baker demurred, urging that they focus on the immediate issue of Germany's status in NATO.[15]

Desperate to secure concessions for his acquiescence, Gorbachev entered into a summer of difficult negotiations with Kohl. On September 10, they struck a deal acceptable to Washington. Soviet forces would transition out of eastern Germany over a period of up to four years, during which NATO forces would (subject to technical exceptions) stay out. Germany would, in spite of howls from its Finance Ministry, pay Moscow DM 12 billion ($7.43 billion), and lend it another DM 3 billion interest-free, to support the removal of its 400,000 troops.[16]

A few weeks later, on October 3, 1990, Germany became, once again, one country. The Warsaw Pact shrank by one member. NATO moved eastward, filling the gap. Gorbachev worried it would not stop there.

❖

ON THE AFTERNOON OF JUNE 5, 1997, TO WARM APPLAUSE FROM AMIDST A sea of caps and gowns, the secretary of state rose to approach the podium. An immigrant whose family had fled the Czechoslovak Communist coup in 1948, whose father had been a diplomat under foreign minister Jan Masaryk, Madeleine Albright had chosen the time and place for her message carefully. For it was "on this day 50 years ago," she told the young men and women, that George Marshall had addressed the graduating class at Harvard.[17]

Marshall's "words were plain, but his message reached far beyond the audience assembled in this yard." He spoke to "an American people weary of war and wary of new commitments, and to a Europe where life-giving connections between farm and market, enterprise and capital, hope and future had been severed." It was here that he planted the seeds of his plan.

Unlike in Marshall's day, however, Washington was not now offering Europe aid or a path to economic and political integration. This role had been left to a reluctant European Union, itself in part an outgrowth of the Marshall Plan. Instead, it was offering something Marshall had hoped economic assistance could avoid: extending American military commitments.

Albright had come to Harvard to tout NATO enlargement. In one month's time, Poland, the Czech Republic, and Hungary—three former Warsaw Pact members—would be invited to begin accession talks. Numerous others, including former Soviet republics, were also queuing up. Yet "this will not, as some fear," Albright insisted, "create a new source of division within Europe. On the contrary, it is erasing the unfair and unnatural line imposed half a century ago."

Marshall's "vision," she stressed, "was inclusive, leaving the door open to participation by all, including the Soviet Union." This statement was true, though disingenuous. The only part of Marshall's speech that drew interruptive applause was that warning indirectly against Soviet obstruction. Whereas Marshall had indeed left the door to participation open to Moscow, he did so on the basis of George Kennan's assurance that Stalin would slam it shut. The State Department framed the invitation, in Chip Bohlen's words, so to "make it quite impossible for the Soviet Union to accept."[18] Moscow would then bear the blame for dividing Europe. Kennan was right; Stalin took the bait, denouncing the plan and forbidding participation from eastern Europe.

Albright's task was trickier. Russian president Boris Yeltsin hated the new American plan, just as Stalin had hated Marshall's plan. But he also knew Russia was not strong enough, this time around, to stop eastern Europe from joining. And so he insisted, like Gorbachev before him, that if NATO were going to move eastward—which he denounced as "a mistake and a serious one"[19]—Russia, too, must have the right to join.

Washington's new friends in the Visegrád countries (the Czech Republic, Hungary, Poland, and Slovakia), however, not to mention the U.S. Congress, would never abide Russia's inclusion. Eastern Europe had struggled too long, and at too great a cost, to escape Russia's grasp. "To tame the bear, you must put him in a cage and not let him run free in the forest," insisted former Polish president Lech Wałęsa. And so Albright struggled to convey a confusing message: that Russia was a friend, against whom NATO would protect Europe.

❖

IN TRYING TO ASSURE THEIR RUSSIAN COUNTERPARTS THAT NATO WAS not a threat, State Department officials took it for granted that legitimate Russian interests, in an era following *glasnost* and *perestroika*, should not clash with NATO interests. But this view presumed that the problem of the Cold War had been driven by Marx, and not Mackinder. Ideology and not geography.

It was a view George Kennan had sought to dispel half a century ago. "At bottom of [the] Kremlin's neurotic view of world affairs is [a] traditional and instinctive Russian sense of insecurity," he wrote in his Long Telegram. Vast, sparsely populated, and with huge transport challenges, Russia's natural tendency was to fracture. Looking outward, Russia was a "land which had never known a friendly neighbor." Its defining characteristic was indefensibility. No mountain ranges or bodies of water protected its western borders. In consequence, it suffered repeated invasions over centuries. These features encouraged the emergence of a highly centralized and autocratic leadership obsessed with internal and external security. Communists had been just one variety of such leadership, peculiar to the age in which they emerged.

The country's western borders are a particular source of inherent vulnerability. The European landmass up to Russia's borders constitutes a large peninsula surrounded by the Baltic and North Seas to the north, the Atlantic Ocean to the west, and the Black Sea to the south. Russia, in contrast, has few maritime outlets. The Arctic Ocean is remote from its population centers. The country's few ports are largely unusable in the winter. Turkish waters to the south, like Danish waters to the north, can be blocked easily. During the Cold War, Norwegian, British, and Icelandic airbases also hindered Russian access to the sea.

Situated on a vast European plain with few natural barriers against enemies to the west (see Map 5), Russia has never been comfortable within its borders. It had been contained by France and Britain in the latter half of the nineteenth century—in the Balkans, the Middle East, India, and China—well before Kennan made "containment" a household word. Its defensive options being limited, its military doctrine has historically been offensive. It has sought to dominate its neighbors as a means of preventing the borderlands from being used against it by other powers. In the words of Truman State Department official Louis Halle, Russia manifests a "historic impulse to push back" against "the encircling danger" through "the enlargement of its empire."[20] Whereas the West sees Russian fear of invasion as groundless, history has shown Russian leaders that foreign intentions are typically hidden or fluid.[21] There would always be Napoleons and Hitlers. Each age brings new existential threats. After World War II, the threat was, from the Kremlin's perspective, capitalist encirclement led by Washington and its West German puppet regime.

The incorporation of Ukraine and Belarus (1922)[22] and the Baltic countries (1940) into the Soviet Union, and the creation of buffer states further east after the war, bolstered Russian security at the expense of that of the West. Splitting control of Germany created the only stable equilibrium, one that survived four decades. Once Moscow lost control of Berlin in 1989, however, Russia's defensive frontier collapsed, back to borders further east than they had been since the eighteenth century.[23]

No longer able to control his country's rebellious neighbors, Gorbachev presided over the dismantling of the Warsaw Pact's integrated military structure on February 1, 1991. He tried to sustain the grouping as a political entity, yet found no takers. It was dissolved on July 1. He pressed the outgoing members for commitments that they would not join NATO or the EC, but this plea also failed.[24]

Soon after, top members of his government, including Prime Minister Valentin Pavlov and Defense Minister Dimtry Yazov, determined to prevent the dissolution of the Soviet Union itself, decided to take radical action. Yazov, who had virulently opposed East Germany's absorption into NATO, told Bush's national security adviser Brent Scowcroft, on July 31, that "NATO was the threat" which now concerned Russia.[25] On August 19, he and his fellow conspirators detained Gorbachev and took power. But the coup collapsed in three days, dramatically boosting the authority of newly elected Russian president Boris Yeltsin and undermining that of Gorbachev. Ten Soviet republics, including Russia, declared independence in the four months that followed. Subjectless, powerless, Gorbachev resigned on Christmas Day. Before the year was out, the Soviet Union would be no more.

The new democratically elected leaders of eastern Europe saw NATO membership as a vital guarantee against future threats from Russia. "We are all afraid of Russia," Lech Wałęsa told Bush's successor, Bill Clinton, at the White House on May 4, 1993. "If Russia adopts an aggressive foreign policy, that aggression will be directed against Poland and Ukraine."[26] Providing such guarantees was, in turn, valuable to Washington in tamping down a threat perception that, left unchecked, might give rise to authoritarian nationalism in newly democratic states.

Yeltsin's aides, however, were no more accepting of NATO expansion than Yazov had been under Gorbachev. They stressed to the United States that it would be a historic error. Russian defense minister Pavel Grachev warned that his countrymen saw the alliance as a "monster directed against Russia." Deputy Foreign Minister Georgy Mamedov told Deputy Secretary of State Strobe Talbott that "NATO, in Russian, is a four-letter word." Foreign Intelligence Service head Yevgeny Primakov, who would later become foreign minister and prime minister, argued that NATO expansion would necessitate a more robust Russian defense posture and budget. "This is not just a psychological issue for us," he insisted. "It's a security question." Moscow's Council on Foreign and Defense Policy[27] warned that NATO enlargement would make "the Baltic states and Ukraine . . . a zone of intense strategic rivalry."[28] Yeltsin himself said that the United States was "sow[ing the] seeds of distrust." For a Russian leader to "agree to the borders of NATO expanding toward those of Russia," he told Clinton, "would constitute a betrayal of the Russian people."[29]

"Did those who so advocated NATO expansion give any thought to the configuration of political forces in Russia at that time?" Gorbachev asked rhetorically, years after leaving power. "Was the West really blind to the kind of sentiments NATO expansion aroused among influential circles in Russia?" These plans were "seized on by those in favour of confrontation with the West, and [those] intent on using the 'external threat' to their own advantage."[30]

Many American observers had foreseen the problems NATO expansion would create. "The result may stimulate hostile Russian responses," warned historian and political scientist Ronald Steel. "This would be particularly likely if the accommodationist Yeltsin government is succeeded by a more nationalistic and self-confident one."[31]

Russian concerns were authenticated by U.S. ambassador to Moscow Thomas Pickering, who insisted that Russians would, whatever the administration's intentions, interpret NATO expansion as being directed against them. It could, he argued, produce the very Russian actions it was presumably designed to guard against.

"Are we really going to be able to convince the East Europeans that we are protecting them from their historical threats," asked Democratic senator Sam Nunn, "while we convince the Russians that NATO enlargement has nothing to do with Russia as a potential military threat?" Going forward with such a plan, he argued, was likely to produce a more nationalistic and dangerous Russia.

"An expanded NATO that excludes Russia will not serve to contain Russia's retrograde, expansionist tendencies," Talbott warned Secretary of State Warren Christopher. "Quite the contrary, it will further provoke them." He was concerned not only about a Russian backlash but a Ukrainian response to such a backlash. Hard-liners in Kiev, he argued, would insist that being left out of NATO meant they needed a nuclear deterrent.[32]

Bill Clinton, unlike his critics and many of his advisers, was at ease pursuing a major diplomatic and security initiative riddled with contradiction. Sure, countries wanted NATO membership to deter Russia, but both Russia and NATO could change. Russia might someday even join NATO, he told Talbott, notwithstanding that being "blue-sky stuff" at the moment. Truman, he said, never had a "grand strategy" to deal with Stalin. He had "powerful instincts about what had to be done" and "just made it up as [he] went along."[33] Clinton felt he could do the same.

Yet whereas it is true that the Marshall Plan and NATO were not part of Truman's initial blueprint for dealing with Stalin, they were also not improvisations. His State Department recognized how the Soviet Union saw its interests, and what the likely costs of challenging them were. Clinton, in contrast, felt he could have it both ways. He would extend security guarantees to eastern Europe in return for a western orientation while keeping Russia in a state of false consciousness over why the guarantees were needed.

Clinton wanted to endow a "new NATO" with a new raison d'être. His advisers spoke of "squar[ing] the circle" between eastern Europe's security concerns and not alienating Russia. But it is the old, original NATO that brought in the applicants.[34] Whatever an American president might believe, or wish for, NATO was, at its core, an anti-Russian alliance. Clinton did not see, or did not want to see, its expansion as a tool of Kennanite containment. He was committed to encouraging Russia down the path of democratic reform and association with the West.[35] Aspiring members, however, did not hanker to join in "peacekeeping," or "stopping ethnic conflicts beyond the alliance's borders," or battling far-off "new threats."[36] They wanted to come in to keep the Russians out. Most everything else the Americans might want NATO to do was, to them, a cost of joining and not a benefit. President Clinton surely understood this; but *candidate* Clinton also understood that twenty million Americans of East European descent were living in fourteen states accounting for 36 percent of the electoral college. His advisers reminded him.[37]

For their part, congressional Republicans, whose support would be critical to expanding NATO, were unabashed in stating that its logic *was* Russian containment. "The countries of Eastern Europe know only too well what Russia is capable of," said the party's 1994 *Contract with America* election pledge. "Observing its new boundaries . . . goes against [Russia's] centuries old imperial tradition and the belief of many within its military and government."[38] This argument, in contrast to Clinton's narrative, had the advantage of being coherent and historically accurate. Yet given that NATO would, in the coming quarter century, invest little in reinforcing its eastern border, expansion's containment value to the United States may have been outweighed by the provocation costs.

Though U.S. foreign policy is set largely by the executive branch, and not the legislature, the Russians understood that the president and his successors retained the option to use NATO against Russia and its interests. Former State Department official Ron Asmus, an early advocate of NATO expansion, was nonetheless disparaging of Russian officials who rejected uncollateralized American pledges of goodwill toward their country. Such rejection was forthright in the case of Clinton's Partnership for Peace (PfP) initiative, which the president touted as a means to promote cooperation among NATO, eastern Europe, and Russia. Russian Colonel General Leonid Ivashov dismissed it as "a covert program to expand NATO . . . right up to Russia's borders," a reaction Asmus ascribes to his being "notoriously hard line." Yet this fact hardly stands in for showing that Ivashov was wrong. It is, after all, what happened. And State Department planners had been calling for "a phased strategy of [NATO] enlargement" a year before his comments.

Asmus' account, notwithstanding the hopes he and his colleagues had for better U.S.-Russia relations, makes clear that PfP had been sold to the East Europeans as a way station to NATO—a NATO from which Russia would be excluded. "While the Partnership is not NATO membership," Clinton said at a press conference in Prague on January 12, 1994, "neither is it a permanent holding room. It changes the entire dialogue so that now the question is no longer whether NATO will take in new members, but when and how." But once NATO began growing, what sort of dynamic would set in? Each inch of eastward expansion was bound to increase Russian distrust of the West, which would in turn produce more urgency for former Soviet republics further east to join. The only logical end point was Russia's borders.

✜

BORIS YELTSIN, LIKE GORBACHEV BEFORE HIM, WAS BROUGHT DOWN, IN
significant part, by widespread popular and official fears of a security vacuum—
political and economic. Neither leader could halt NATO expansion, but each
battled to keep his country's frontiers from shrinking further. Yeltsin sent the
Russian army into the breakaway republic of Chechnya in 1994. He withdrew
the troops in 1996, only to send them back in again in 1999. His authority fa-
tally weakened, he resigned in December of that year, handing the presidency
to his prime minister.

As prime minister, Vladimir Putin had been riding high in public opinion
polls on the back of his intensified crackdown in Chechnya. The former KGB
officer in East Germany, who had been on the front lines of Moscow's covert
efforts against NATO, would later describe the collapse of the Soviet Union as
the "greatest geopolitical catastrophe of the [twentieth] century."[39] Much of his
long tenure as president would be devoted to, if not restoring the Soviet Union,
restoring elements of its economic space and security frontier in the face of
NATO and EU expansion. His emergence was at least as much a reflection of
Russia's antiwestern turn as it was a cause. As a former intelligence officer, he
had the wherewithal to co-opt and control the new class of business oligarchs
(some of whom came from the intelligence services) and to prevent the old
Soviet empire's constituent parts and satellites from undermining the interests
of the Russian state.[40]

To Putin and the new Russian leadership, the behavior of NATO and its
members in the wake of Albright's speech affirmed what they had believed
since German unification: that NATO would remain a threat to Russian interests, and that whether a country was inside or outside of NATO affected those
interests.

Days after the Czech Republic, Hungary, and Poland joined NATO in
March 1999, the alliance began a three-month bombing campaign against
Serbia—a Slavic Orthodox state like Russia. The attacks appalled ordinary
Russians. Albright had pronounced that NATO was "a defensive alliance that
harbors no territorial ambitions." Yet the attacks were not in defense of a NATO
member, but in support of Muslim separatists in the Serbian province of

Kosovo. NATO had played defense during the Cold War, but had shifted to offense simultaneous with expansion into the former Warsaw Pact. "A dangerous precedent was created," Gorbachev observed, "of military action undertaken against a sovereign country without authorization by the UN Security Council, in violation of the UN Charter and international law."[41] Putin would soon exploit the precedent in carrying out his own liberations.

NATO's actions in the former Yugoslavia—in Bosnia in 1995 as well as in Serbia in 1999—were undertaken with noble aims: to stop the slaughter of innocents. NATO expansion into the former Warsaw Pact, however, added to these attacks a toxic element for U.S.-Russia relations. The new eastern members were not capable of affecting the outcomes, yet as part of the alliance they were now bound to Western policies that challenged Russian interests. As NATO expanded further eastward, nations on Russia's borders would also become tied to such policies. NATO members would moreover take unilateral actions hostile to Russia, actions they would never have taken outside the alliance.

In 2012, Syria shot down a Turkish jet over its territory. An angry president Recep Tayyip Erdoğan insisted that "a short-term border violation [could] never be a pretext for an attack." Yet three years later, Turkey shot down a Russian fighter jet that had crossed into its airspace from Syria, where it was bombing opponents of the Assad regime. Turkey could claim to have acted in self-defense and without territorial ambitions, but it also acted knowing that it could call on NATO protection, under the collective defense principle of Article 5, in the event of Russian military retaliation. "Turkish airspace . . . is NATO airspace," the Turkish Foreign Ministry told Russia after the attack. Russia took notice. "Turkey has not set *itself* up" as the actor, "but the North Atlantic alliance as a whole," observed Prime Minister Dmitry Medvedev. "This is extremely irresponsible."[42]

In a 1997 statement before a NATO gathering in Brussels, Albright argued that the purpose of NATO expansion was "to do for Europe's east what NATO did fifty years ago for Europe's west: to integrate new democracies, eliminate old hatreds, provide confidence in economic recovery, and deter conflict."[43] But this was the purpose of the Marshall Plan, and not NATO. And if the aim were now to repeat such accomplishments in the East, NATO, a military organization built to defend its members against the Soviet Union, was an awkward vehicle to achieve it. It could possibly "deter conflict," but it might also encourage conflict with a distrustful and better-armed Russia.

"If we are talking about the importance of improving the economies and democratization of countries like Hungary and Poland," Senator Paul Wellstone (D-MN) put to Albright at hearings that year, "there is the European Union. I do not know how a military alliance really meets these concerns." Conflating NATO expansion and the Marshall Plan suggested a mismatch between means and ends. Senator Paul Sarbanes (D-MD) added that he could not understand "Albright's suggestion that the 50th anniversary of . . . the Marshall Plan is relevant" to the timing of NATO expansion. "Well," Albright clarified, "we have been celebrating the 50th anniversary of everything."[44]

If historical anniversaries were important for NATO expansion, waiting two years for the eightieth anniversary of the Versailles Treaty would have been more apposite. The treaty heaped humiliations on Germany after World War I, with no clear end in sight, and created the economic and political conditions that led to World War II. Having improbably abandoned communism for democracy and capitalism in a near-bloodless revolution, Russians were, ten years after the fall of the Berlin Wall, feeling similarly humiliated and threatened by an unexpected Western military advance toward their borders.[45]

The European Union, in contrast to NATO, did have the capacity to provide a "Marshall Plan" for the East but was unwilling. The EU's focus was on deepening economic and political integration within its existing boundaries. Membership for former Warsaw Pact nations would not come for another seven years. Richard Holbrooke, the Clinton administration's most aggressive advocate of NATO enlargement, believed that "EU membership was more important" for eastern Europe than NATO membership. But once it became clear to him that it was not going to happen anytime soon, he pronounced it "irresponsible and potentially dangerous to leave these countries outside the 'West.'"[46] He concluded that "NATO enlargement had to fill the void."[47] Or, as Albright put it, "If NATO enlargement can proceed more quickly" than EU enlargement, "why wait until, say, tomato farmers in Central Europe start using the right kinds of pesticides" for EU membership?[48] That it might not be prudent to fill a political and economic void with a military pact did not concern them.

George Marshall and Dean Acheson would never have backed NATO in place of a political and economic strategy. Western European integration was their aim, and the Truman administration only added a military element after the Prague coup showed that Moscow would subvert governments that could not defend themselves. In 1997, however, the Clinton administration insisted that Russia was threatening no one, and did not need to be contained. "This NATO," newly expanded to the East, Albright said, "is not directed against Russia. It is not us versus them or them versus us. We are all on the same side." An influential RAND Corporation study published that same year, coauthored by Asmus, controversially estimated only modest NATO expansion costs on the grounds that the alliance had no enemy; the "premise [was] avoiding confrontation with Russia, not preparing for a new Russian threat."[49]

Many of NATO expansion's most prominent advocates, however, could not abide this thinking. Clinton officials "keep talking about the absence of dividing lines," observed Henry Kissinger at the time. But "with all due respect, this is nonsense. If you have an alliance, you have a dividing line."[50] And Russia was on the other side of the line, just as it was in 1949. The difference was that the Marshall planners and NATO founders acknowledged that a line was being drawn, and were willing to bear the necessary costs to defend it. The Clinton administration, in contrast, was denying the line's existence. The United States could "have [its] cake and eat it too," Holbrooke said. Writing in 1998, he argued that "years from now . . . people will look back at the debate and wonder what all the fuss was about. They will notice that nothing has changed in Russia's relationship with the West."[51]

❖

IN 2000, JUST TWO YEARS LATER, AN OFFICIAL RUSSIAN "FOREIGN POLICY Concept" (FPC) paper approved by President Putin contradicted Holbrooke, declaring that "NATO's present-day political and military guidelines do not coincide with security interests of the Russian Federation and occasionally contradict them." It pointed specifically to NATO's "use-of-force operations outside [of area] without the sanction of the UN Security Council"—a reference to NATO's bombing of Serbia, which began hours after Holbrooke announced that negotiations with its leadership over Kosovo had failed. Such out-of-area action, it must be noted, had always been envisioned by the architects of NATO expansion. In Asmus' words seven years earlier, "NATO must go out of area or out of business"—the presumption being that the latter had to be prevented by finding enemies. The FPC concluded that "Russia retains its negative attitude towards the expansion of NATO."[52]

Asmus' 1997 estimate of NATO expansion costs, based on the belief that Russia would not seriously oppose it, naturally turned out to be way too low. Eleven years later, in 2008, he explained in *Foreign Affairs* that "the West's broader hopes of establishing deeper relations with a more democratic and cooperative Moscow never materialized. . . . Moscow has [instead] become more authoritarian and adversarial." He continued to support NATO expansion to Russia's borders but, retreating from his 1997 paper, now recognized that "antidemocratic forces in Russia"—presumably the Putin government— "will oppose such a move." This conclusion was a tepid acknowledgment that NATO and Russia had indeed become enemies, though he postulated, remarkably, that U.S. policy toward Ukraine would help ameliorate this problem. "Consolidating a pro-Western, democratic Ukraine," he asserted, will "indirectly encourage democratization in Russia." By 2016, that pretense was demolished. RAND published a study that year backing billions of dollars in additional annual NATO spending aimed at "Reinforcing Deterrence on NATO's Eastern Flank"—a direct response to "Russia's . . . aggression against Ukraine."[53] Yet there was no sign that the United States was willing to bear such spending, once again highlighting a critical difference between NATO's founders and its expanders.

But many in the Clinton administration believed that NATO enlargement was necessary less to protect eastern Europe than to promote and entrench democracy there (even in Russia, which would remain outside it).[54] "The deepest aim of NATO enlargement," Russia expert Stephen Sestanovich writes, "may well have been to consolidate the victory of Western ideas."[55] Yet there is no evidence that it did, nor have the mechanics by which it was supposed to accomplish this feat ever been revealed. Remaining outside NATO has had no detrimental effect on democracy or Western ideas in Sweden or Finland. Meanwhile, Turkey, no liberal democracy when it joined NATO in 1952, became less of one under Erdoğan's leadership. Poland regressed under the Law and

Justice (PiS) government after 2015. And membership imposed no constraint on Hungary when its prime minister, Viktor Orbán, declared in 2014 that "the era of liberal democracies is over." Orbán did "not think that [Hungary's] European Union membership," or by extension its NATO membership, "precludes [it] from building an illiberal new state based on national foundations"—which is what he now wished for his country. Moreover, he said, "what is happening right now regarding Russia's relations to the West is really bad for Hungary."[56]

This conclusion is, of course, precisely the one Moscow wanted the Hungarian government to draw. Whereas western supporters of enlargement, like Asmus, argued that Russia had a vested interest in supporting "democratic stability on [its] western border,"[57] Moscow pursued a different strategy: "encouraging authoritarian tendencies or political unreliability in its neighbours." Particularly in Georgia and Ukraine, Moscow's ambition was to keep the regimes "institutionally weak, unpalatable to the West and dependent on Russia."[58]

Whereas Orbán's comments were condemned by many of Hungary's neighbors, Orbán succeeded in clarifying that NATO was a *military* alliance whose political impact was mainly on relations between Russia and the countries that joined, or might wish to join. It was not an organization with either the will or capacity to make or keep countries democratic.

❖

IN 1992, SLAVIC-LANGUAGE-SPEAKING INSURGENTS, SUPPORTED BY RUSsian troops, seized control of the Transnistria region of largely Romanianspeaking Moldova, on the southern border of Ukraine. Though the region's assertion of independence has never been recognized internationally, Russia supports Transnistria economically and maintains an estimated two thousand armed personnel on the ground (including four to five hundred peacekeepers under the 1992 cease-fire agreement).[59]

Since 2008, Russia has created two new "frozen conflicts" in bordering former Soviet republics—Georgia and Ukraine—on the Moldovan model. All three serve an important strategic purpose in keeping NATO and the European Union from expanding further eastward.

Following the so-called Rose Revolution of 2003, the Georgian government of President Mikheil Saakashvili initiated a military modernization program, using American hardware, in conjunction with a campaign for NATO membership. With the aim of demonstrating its commitment and capabilities, Georgia contributed forces and equipment to American-led interventions in Afghanistan and Iraq. This military assistance sent a clear signal to Moscow that it was both aligning its policies with Washington and opening up another front for western forces on Russia's borders.

By 2008, Kremlin officials considered their efforts to dissuade the Georgian government from joining NATO a failure, creating a sense of urgency. Given that the country could call upon Article 5 security guarantees after joining the alliance, the window for low-cost Russian military intervention was closing. In March, the breakaway republics of Abkhazia (largely Russophone) and South Ossetia appealed for Russian recognition of their independence from Georgia, citing the precedent of Kosovo. By August, mounting tensions between Tbilisi and Moscow escalated to war, resulting in a Kremlin-orchestrated standoff marked by ever-growing political, economic, and security ties between Russia and the two effectively autonomous republics. Gorbachev, whose urgings against NATO expansion had been treated as domestic posturing in Washington, backed Russian military action in Georgia.[60]

More recently, Russia followed a similar template in Ukraine. Political crisis in the country erupted in November 2013, after intense pressure from Russia, its main energy provider, persuaded President Viktor Yanukovych to abandon an Association Agreement with the European Union. A struggle between pro-EU forces in the country, mostly in the west, and pro-Russia forces, mostly in the east, led to Yanukovych fleeing the capital in February 2014. Russia denounced his departure as a White House–orchestrated coup, and responded by annexing Crimea in March. Aided by Russian soldiers and matériel, pro-Russian separatist forces in the eastern Donbass region began seizing territory in May. This was a crisis that Kennan had seen coming, having in 1999, at age ninety-five, decried "the thoughtless tossing" of the "un-Ukrainian Crimean peninsula" into Ukraine after the breakup of the Soviet Union.[61]

While the conflicts in Moldova, Georgia, and Ukraine have been attributed to aggressive Kremlin efforts to reestablish elements of the Soviet empire, it is notable that none of the breakaway regions—with the exception of Crimea, which houses the Russian Black Sea Fleet—has been annexed by Russia. The reason is that annexation of pro-Russian territories would have strengthened the pro-Western forces in the remaining parts of each country. Annexation therefore stymies Russia's primary objective, which is keeping the countries beyond the reach of western institutions seen to threaten Russian interests. The presence of frozen conflicts in the three nations effectively blocks them from joining with the West. In the case of NATO, the alliance has always rejected aspirants with unresolved border disputes, internal territorial conflicts, and insufficient military capacity to provide for a credible national defense.

In the cases of Georgia and Ukraine, the timing of the Russian interventions coincided with their achievement of tangible benchmarks on the path to EU and NATO membership. The combined separatist territories, under effective Russian control, now form a valuable protective arc along Russia's western and southwestern border.[62] Just as Stalin strengthened the Soviet Union's buffer zone in response to the Marshall Plan, which he expected Washington to supplement with military force, Putin has strengthened Russia's buffer zone in response to NATO expansion.

❖

IN 2016, ON THE OCCASION OF THE TWENTY-FIFTH ANNIVERSARY OF THE end of the Cold War, the German daily *Bild* interviewed Vladimir Putin. What, he was asked, had gone wrong in relations between Russia and the West?

"Everything," Putin responded. "[T]he Berlin Wall fell, but invisible walls were moved to the East of Europe." Moscow, he insisted, had been promised that "NATO would not expand eastwards," a reference to alleged commitments from then-NATO secretary general Manfred Wörner and U.S. secretary of state James Baker. But NATO and the United States, Putin said, decided that they alone would "sit on the throne in Europe." They went back on their word. "This has led to mutual misunderstandings and assignments of guilt. They are the cause of all crises ever since."

Putin's view was wholly consistent with how Soviet officials perceived the shift in U.S. policy toward Europe back in 1946. Having expected FDR to withdraw American troops within two years after the war's end, they were now convinced Truman wanted "to preserve [U.S.] military potential [in Europe] as a necessary base for carrying out . . . aggressive aims in the future."[63] Putin's perspective was also a pointed challenge to Holbrooke's prediction, eighteen years earlier, that NATO expansion would have no effect on "Russia's relationship with the West." Everyone would "look back . . . and wonder what all the fuss was about."

At the time Putin spoke, Ukraine was the focus of tension between Russia and the West. He justified annexing Crimea by pointing to NATO action the year after Holbrooke's prediction. "Serbia [was] bombarded and attacked with missiles," Putin said. "It was a military intervention of the West and NATO against the then rump Yugoslavia." Why, he asked, "if the Kosovars have the right to self-determination should the people of Crimea not have it?"[64] The implication was that if NATO could go to war to move borders, it was in no position to condemn others for acting in support of the same principle: self-determination. Rather than challenge the American idea of a liberal international order that respected national sovereignty, he exploited an apparent contradiction.

Following the annexation, conflict between Russia and Ukraine over NATO intensified. In November 2014, Putin spokesman Dmitry Peskov told the BBC that Russia wanted "a 100% guarantee that no-one would think about Ukraine joining NATO." Such an expansion was a dangerous "attempt to break the . . . balance of power."[65] One month later, the Ukrainian parliament voted to end the country's nonaligned status, a preliminary step toward joining the alliance. Russian foreign minister Sergei Lavrov condemned the move as "counterproductive," saying it "only worsens confrontation."[66] In June 2016, he clarified that Russia did "not consider the *existence* of NATO a threat," but that "the doctrines of [Russian] security are clearly written, and one of the main threats is the further *expansion* of NATO to the east."[67]

"What do [the Americans] need NATO for?" Putin asked Shimon Peres in a private conversation shortly before the latter's death that year. "The Soviet Union doesn't exist anymore.":

The Warsaw Pact was dismantled. I am ready to be a member of NATO. . . . But why do they need Georgia in NATO? Why do they need Romania in NATO? [If Georgia and Romania] want to go to Europe, [let them] go to Europe. But which army do they want to fight? [The Americans] think I didn't know that Crimea is Russian, and that Khrushchev gave it to Ukraine as a gift? I didn't care, until [the Americans] needed the Ukrainians in NATO. What for? I didn't touch them. They wanted to go to Europe, I said, "Great, go to Europe." But why did [the Americans] need them in NATO?[68]

Kennan, who had died only a decade earlier, age 101, would not have been surprised at the rising tensions. In 1997 he had written an op-ed in *The New York Times* arguing that "expanding NATO would be the most fateful error of American policy in the entire post-cold-war era." Kennan predicted that it would "inflame nationalistic, anti-Western and militaristic tendencies in Russian opinion," "have an adverse effect on the development of Russian democracy," "restore the atmosphere of cold war to East-West relations," and "impel Russian foreign policy in directions decidedly not to our liking."[69]

In figures such as longtime Yeltsin foreign minister Andrei Kozyrev, and economic and political reformers Yegor Gaidar and Anatoly Chubais, Washington had interlocutors in Moscow not unlike Litvinov, Maisky, and Gromyko in the 1940s—figures who viewed cooperation with the West as Russia's most promising course.[70] But NATO expansion undermined their credibility at home. The subsequent two decades would see a different, more nationalist and confrontational, breed of politicians in the Kremlin.

�֎

THE MARSHALL PLAN AIMED AT AIDING AMERICAN MILITARY DISENGAGE-ment from Europe, yet ended up, through NATO, making it both deeper and enduring. That Moscow believed Washington had planned this all along only helped make it so. Stalin's aggressive reaction to the Plan convinced Western leaders that the increased U.S. military commitment he feared had now become vital to their economic and physical security. Given this history, it should not be surprising that EU expansion a half century later also created conflict with Russia.

As with the Marshall Plan and NATO, the EU has for all practical purposes been a body open to all European nations save Russia.[71] The EU began negotiations in 1998, shortly after Albright's Harvard speech, with the ten central and eastern European countries (Czech Republic, Bulgaria, Estonia, Hungary,

Latvia, Lithuania, Poland, Romania, Slovakia, and Slovenia) that would join in 2004 and 2007. Tensions with Russia began rising almost immediately, as they had after Marshall's speech in 1947.

Russia, it was clear, would lose political and economic leverage with countries on its borders that were pooling sovereignty with the EU and its institutions. The Foreign Policy Concept paper approved by Putin in 2000 highlighted a lack of "adequate respect for the interests of the Russian side in the process of the EU expansion." Seeing a connection with the simultaneous enlargement of NATO, the paper further suggested that "the EU's emerging military-political dimension should become an object of particular attention."[72]

In 2000 and 2001, EU-aspirant nations Estonia, Bulgaria, the Czech Republic, and Slovakia imposed visa requirements on Russian visitors. The Russian Foreign Ministry condemned the action, likening it to the erection of a new "Berlin Wall."

Economic restrictions followed travel restrictions, as the EU bound the newcomers to its trade and investment regimes. Rejecting EU arguments that it would benefit from lower average tariffs in the East European accession states, Russia insisted it would face higher ones on its most important exports. It estimated annual export losses from extending the EU common tariff to the ten new eastern member states at €200 million to €300 million.[73] It also criticized new technical-standard barriers and potential anti-dumping levies.

Critical Russian interests, such as energy exports to and through the east, would be infringed further and further through time. The first U.S. liquid natural gas (LNG) tanker to pass through the Baltic Sea, in 2016, would be greeted as a major political event in Europe—"a game changer," according to the EU's energy chief (a Slovak). "U.S. LNG is more than just about gas," said the mayor of the Lithuanian port town that would receive the American ships. "It's about freedom."

As former Soviet satellites and republics shed their dependence on Russia, traditional Kremlin sanctions to discipline their behavior, like trade bans and gas embargoes, would lose their effectiveness. Russia would therefore resort to new and tougher methods—such as covert propaganda campaigns, espionage, cyberwarfare, and political threats—to prevent Western imports from threatening its lucrative monopolies in the East.[74]

Politically, much would change with EU expansion as well, to Russia's detriment. Rotating leadership roles within the EU would frequently place its policies in the hands of hostile states, such as Poland and Latvia. The 2000 FPC had called it an "indispensable condition" of "goodneighborliness and mutual cooperation" between Russia and the Baltic states for there to be "respect for the rights of the Russian–speaking population" within the three neighboring nations.[75] As Russian-speaking communities in such states, often large, became increasingly marginalized, pressure grew in Russia to intervene on their behalf.[76]

Such radical changes in Russia's external environment were bound to have security implications, much as the Marshall Plan had. An isolated Russia would seek to retain and regain influence in its region, while the rest of Europe would insist on upholding its sovereign prerogatives.

"European politicians thought that the creation of the so-called belt of friendly countries on the outer border of the EU would reliably guarantee security," said Russian prime minister Dmitry Medvedev in 2016. "But what were the results of this policy? [A]n exclusion zone with local conflicts and economic trouble on the eastern [and] southern borders."[77]

Much as Moscow sought to undermine "Churchill's reactionary venture" to create "a United States of Europe" in 1947,[78] it today seeks to create an "arc of instability" along its western frontier to subvert EU expansion.[79] Far from welcoming closer ties between its neighbors and the EU, as early expansion advocates argued it should and would, Russia threatened to block Ukrainian access to its market if it went forward with plans to enter a free trade arrangement with the EU.[80] To punish Russia for its military and political intervention in the country, the West hit Russia with economic and financial sanctions.

The EU has rejected Russian criticism of its expansion. European nations, German chancellor Angela Merkel said, denied any obligation to "ask Moscow first" before acting. "That's how it was for 40 years, and I don't want to go back to that."[81] For countries caught between Russia and the EU, the standoff is dangerous. "We don't want somebody over our heads to decide that we will never join," said Georgia's EU ambassador Natalie Sabanadze, "that we will never be part of the Euro-Atlantic community."[82] Here again was the self-perpetuating dialectic of fear and threat, accusation and response, action and reaction, that characterized the early Cold War.[83]

Western political and security interests, as the Marshall planners learned, are difficult to separate. Not surprisingly, elites in Russia, Germany, and the United States have long seen the EU and NATO as two sides of the same coin.[84] This highlights the challenge to the European Union in eastern expansion: the deeper the penetration, the deeper the conflict with Russian interests. If not controlled through negotiation and compromise, conflict spills into the security sphere.

⁂

COMMUNISM IS GONE FROM EUROPE, BUT GEOGRAPHY HAS NOT CHANGED. Russia is, as it has always been, too large and powerful to embed within Western institutions without fundamentally changing them, and too vulnerable to Western encroachment to acquiesce in its own exclusion. Advancing new means of positive engagement will, therefore, require a difficult, perhaps impossible, reimagining of Cold War legacy institutions.

In contrast with the early Cold War period, the post–Cold War period has been marked by the absence of an American Grand Strategy, a calibrated mapping of means to large ends.[85] Over the course of 1946 and 1947, the United States developed a framework of Soviet containment to safeguard its interests without appeasement or war. It then devised the Marshall Plan as the most promising means, given Soviet conventional military superiority in Europe and a large American edge in economic power, to implement it. When France and Britain averred that economic integration made Marshall nations more dependent on each other and less able to defend themselves against hostile action by Russia or Germany, the United States responded with NATO. Together, the Marshall Plan and NATO provided the means to carry out containment.

Yet in the quarter century since the passing of the Soviet Union, Grand Strategy has been set aside in favor of improvisation to pacify competing interests. Democratization has been conflated with security objectives, serving neither. The result is an under-resourced NATO facing growing pressure from an increasingly embittered and authoritarian Russia.[86] "We have signed up to protect a whole series of countries," observed Kennan in 1998, "even though we have neither the resources nor the intention to do so in any serious way."[87] He was right. In consequence, the expansion policy is failing.

The Marshall Plan is remembered as one of the great achievements of American foreign policy not merely because it was visionary but because it worked. It worked because the United States aligned its actions with its interests and capacities in Europe, accepting the reality of a Russian sphere of influence into which it could not penetrate without sacrificing credibility and public support.[88] Great acts of statesmanship are grounded in realism no less than idealism. It is a lesson we need to relearn.

ACKNOWLEDGMENTS

I WAS FORTUNATE TO HAVE HAD SO MUCH ABLE AND ENERGETIC ASSIS-tance in carrying out the research for this book. Andrew Henderson was my research associate here at the Council on Foreign Relations (CFR) for three years, and I could not be more grateful for it. He not only mined U.S. and Ger-man archives and countless books and articles for information, data, and quota-tions (breaking all-time CFR records for inter-library requests), but translated all my German material and acted as chief of staff for the interns and translators. His successor Alex Lloyd George took over in 2016 and skillfully shepherded the book through to production. Talented CFR analyst Emma Smith assisted with data, calculations, and formatting. Semester interns Jason Fauss, Jenny Samuels, Drew Leonard, John Dellamore, Christina Hong, Maxwell Schwartz, Nattakom Shrestha, Caitlin Jokubaitis, Collin Berger, William Bekker, Parul Aggarwal, Rui Yu, Michelle Nedashkovskaya, and Natalie Babjukova identi-fied and reviewed source material, compiled economic and financial data, and checked facts. Michelle later became my translator for most of the huge mass of Russian-language material. Natalie translated segments of Czech books, and Michael Ivkov did the same for Serbian archival material he unearthed in Belgrade. My deepest thanks to all of them.

Special thanks go to historian Svetlana Chervonnaya, who scoured government archives in Moscow and assembled thousands of pages of documents, notes, translations, and detailed commentary. She then critiqued every chapter of this book, including the endnotes. I could not have found a more able, meticulous, and generous Russian collaborator.

I further had the sage guidance of a CFR study group of policy experts and scholars under the chairmanship of former World Bank president Robert Zoellick: Liaquat Ahamed, Graham Allison, David Baldwin, Gary Bass, Willem Buiter, William Drozdiak, Thomas Graham, James Hoge, Reuben Jeffery, Robert Jervis, Stephen Kotkin, Alex Raskolnikov, Nicholas Rostow, Adam Tooze, Lucio Vinhas de Souza, Susan Woodward, and Philip Zelikow. John Lewis Gaddis was also generous with his time, helping me to make sense of George Kennan and to organize my thoughts on the narrative. Two anonymous reviewers commissioned by CFR, and two by Luciana O'Flaherty at Oxford University Press, caught errors and prodded me to sharpen arguments. I am extremely grateful to all of them.

At the end of the process, Ben Loehnen, my brilliant and brutal editor at Simon & Schuster, beat out of me any pretensions that I did not need editing. My agent, Andrew Wylie, was a source of inspiration and keen literary feedback. CFR president Richard Haass and director of studies Jim Lindsay made sure I cut no corners on analysis or clarity. Jonathan Tepperman gave me invaluable advice on sharpening the concluding chapter. Dave Collum proofed the text, including commas and en dashes. I thank them all warmly.

Lastly, I would like to thank the Smith Richardson Foundation for so generously funding the research. I could not have undertaken the copious archival work and translations, in particular, without their support.

Errors and other failings in this, the final product, are of course mine and mine alone.

CAST OF CHARACTERS

Acheson, Dean (1893–1971). American statesman. Under secretary of state, 1945–1947; secretary of state, 1949–1953. A principal architect of the Truman Doctrine and Marshall Plan.

Adenauer, Konrad (1876–1967). German statesman. Founder and chairman of the Christian Democratic Union, 1946–1966; president of the West German Parliamentary Council, 1948–1949; first chancellor of West Germany, 1949–1963.

Alphand, Hervé (1907–1994). French diplomat. Director-general of economic and financial affairs at the French Foreign Ministry, 1944–1950.

Alvarez, Alberto (1905–1985). Cuban diplomat. Foreign minister, 1945–1947. President of the United Nations Security Council during the Berlin blockade crisis, 1949.

Asmus, Ronald (1957–2011). American foreign policy analyst and official. Deputy assistant secretary of state for European affairs, 1997–2000. Strong advocate of NATO expansion after the collapse of the Soviet Union.

Attlee, Clement (1883–1967). British politician. Labour Party leader, 1935–1955; prime minister, 1945–1951.

Auriol, Vincent (1884–1966). French Socialist politician. President, 1947–1954.

Austin, Warren (1877–1962). American politician and diplomat. Senator (R-VT), 1931–1946; ambassador to the United Nations, 1946–1953.

Baker, James, III (1930–). American diplomat. Secretary of state, 1989–1992; White House chief of staff, 1981–1985, 1992–1993.

Barbour, Walworth (1908–1982). American diplomat. Chief, Division of South European Affairs, State Department, 1947–1949; consul in Moscow, 1949–1951.

Barkley, Alben (1877–1956). American politician. Congressman (D-KY), 1913–1927; senator, 1927–1949, 1955–1956; Senate majority leader, 1937–1947; vice president, 1949–1953.

Baruch, Bernard (1870–1965). American financier, philanthropist, and official. Wartime adviser to FDR; U.S. representative to the United Nations Energy Commission, 1946.

Bell, Elliott (1902–1983). American journalist and political operative. Economic adviser to Thomas Dewey; *New York Times* editorial board member, 1941–1942.

Bender, George (1896–1961). American politician. Congressman (R-OH), 1939–1953; senator, 1953–1957. Derided the Marshall Plan as wasteful foreign aid.

Beneš, Edvard (1884–1948). Czechoslovak statesman. President, 1935–1938, 1945–1948. Reestablished the independent state of Czechoslovakia after World War II and led the country until shortly after the February 1948 Communist coup.

Beria, Lavrentiy Pavlovich (1899–1953). Bolshevik revolutionary and Soviet official. People's commissar/minister of internal affairs, 1938–1953. Led the secret police for nearly two decades. Supervised the Soviet atomic bomb project. Arrested and executed after Stalin's death in 1953.

Berman, Jakub (1901–1984). Polish Communist politician with close ties to the Kremlin.

Bevin, Ernest (1881–1951). British trade unionist and statesman. Foreign secretary, 1945–1951. Stalwart anticommunist Labour Party member and leading European advocate of the Marshall Plan and NATO.

Bidault, Georges (1899–1983). French statesman. Foreign minister, 1944–1946, 1947–1948; prime minister, 1946, 1949–1950. A centrist founder of the Christian Democratic MRP party, he was instrumental in launching the Marshall Plan and NATO.

Bilbo, Theodore (1877–1947). American politician. Senator (D-MS), 1935–1947. Faced repeated charges of corruption.

Bissell, Richard, Jr. (1909–1994). American economist and official. Senior executive of the Economic Cooperation Administration, 1948–1952. Wrote the influential bipartisan President's Committee on Foreign Aid (Harriman Committee) report on the Marshall Plan. Later worked for the CIA.

Bloom, Sol (1870–1949). American politician. Congressman (D-NY), 1923–1949; chairman of the House Committee on Foreign Affairs, 1939–1947, 1949.

Blücher, Franz (1896–1959). West German politician. Vice chancellor, 1949–1956; minister for Matters of the Marshall Plan, 1949–1953; minister for Economic Cooperation, 1953–1956. One of the founders of the classical-liberal Free Democratic Party (FDP).

Blum, Léon (1872–1950). French statesman. Prime minister, 1936–1937; presided as president over the all-Socialist caretaker cabinet that installed the Fourth Republic, 1946–1947.

Blunt, Anthony (1907–1983). British art historian and member of the "Cambridge Five" group of double agents who spied for the Soviets.

Bodrov, Mikhail Fedorovich (1903–1988). Soviet diplomat. Chargé in Prague, 1946–1948; ambassador to Bulgaria, 1948–1954.

Bogomolov, Alexander Efremovich (1900–1969). Soviet diplomat. Ambassador to France, 1944–1950.

Bohlen, Charles (1904–1974). American diplomat. State Department counselor, 1947–1949, 1951–1953; ambassador to the Soviet Union, 1953–1957. Soviet specialist and George Marshall's translator in Moscow. Led the drafting of Marshall's June 1947 Harvard speech.

Bonnet, Henri (1888–1978). French diplomat. Ambassador to the United States, 1944–1954.

Bradley, Omar (1893–1981). American military leader. Chief of staff of the Army, 1948–1949; first chairman of the Joint Chiefs of Staff, 1949–1953.

Bramuglia, Juan Atilio (1903–1962). Argentine diplomat. Foreign minister,

1946–1949. President of the United Nations Security Council during the Berlin blockade crisis, 1948.

Bridges, Henry Styles (1898–1961). American politician. Senator (R-NH), 1937–1961. Argued that financial aid to Europe was wasteful and counterproductive.

Brook, William Arthur Darville (1901–1953). British Royal Air Force officer.

Brown, Clarence (1893–1965). American politician. Congressman (R-OH), 1939–1965. Opposed foreign aid in Europe in favor of domestic tax relief.

Brown, Winthrop (1907–1987). American diplomat and official. Chief, Division of Commercial Policy, State Department, 1945–1948; director, Office of International Trade Policy, State Department, 1948–1950. Worked alongside Will Clayton.

Bruce, David (1898–1977). American diplomat. Economic Cooperation Administration mission chief in France, 1948–1949; ambassador to France, 1949–1952.

Bruins, John (1896–1954). American diplomat. Counselor in Prague, 1946–1948.

Brzezinski, Zbigniew (1928–2017). American security expert and official. National security adviser, 1977–1981. Supported NATO expansion in the 1990s.

Bukharin, Nikolai Ivanovich (1888–1938). Russian Bolshevik economist, revolutionary, and Communist Party theoretician. Drafted the Soviet constitution of 1936. Arrested in early 1937; tried and executed in March 1938.

Burgess, Guy (1911–1963). British intelligence officer. Member of the "Cambridge Five" group of double agents who spied for the Soviets.

Byrnes, James (Jimmy) (1882–1972). American diplomat. Secretary of state, 1945–1947. Replaced by George Marshall in January 1947 after relations with Truman grew strained.

Caffery, Jefferson (1886–1974). American diplomat. Ambassador to France, 1944–1949. Played an important role in the diplomacy behind the Marshall Plan's implementation.

Cairncross, Sir Alec (1911–1998). British civil servant. U.K. Treasury economist in Berlin, 1945–1946; director of economics, Organisation for European Economic Co-operation, 1950–1951.

Carter, Marshall (Pat) (1909–1993). American military officer. Top aide to George Marshall.

Catroux, Georges (1877–1969). French general and diplomat. Ambassador to the Soviet Union, 1945–1948.

Celler, Emanuel (1888–1981). American politician. Congressman (D-NY), 1923–1973. Argued that financial aid to Europe promoted socialism.

Chataigneau, Yves (1891–1969). French diplomat. Ambassador to the Soviet Union, 1948–1952.

Chernyshevsky, Nikolai Gavrilovich (1828–1889). Nineteenth-century Russian philosopher, democratic revolutionary, publicist, and writer.

Chiang Kai-shek (1887–1975). Chinese and Taiwanese military leader and statesman. President of China, 1928–1949; president of Taiwan, 1950–1975.

Chuikov, Vasily Ivanovich (1900–1982). Soviet military commander. Succeeded Marshal Sokolovsky as commander in chief of the Group of Soviet forces in Germany, 1949–1953.

Churchill, Sir Winston (1874–1965). British statesman. Prime minister, 1940–1945, 1951–1955; Conservative Party leader, 1940–1955. Led Britain through World War II before losing the premiership to Clement Attlee in 1945. Coined the term "iron curtain" in a 1946 speech that highlighted the division of Europe into Western and Soviet spheres.

Clay, Lucius Dubignon (1897–1978). American general and statesman. Deputy military governor for Germany, 1945–1947; military governor for Germany, 1947–1949. Accomplished military administrator who orchestrated the Berlin airlift.

Clayton, William (1880–1966). American cotton baron and diplomat. Assistant secretary of state for economic affairs, 1944–1946; under secretary of state for economic affairs, 1946–1948. Passionate proponent of free multilateral trade and West European integration. A leading architect of the Marshall Plan.

Clementis, Vladimir (1902–1952). Czechoslovak Communist politician. Deputy prime minister, 1945–1948; foreign minister, 1948–1950. Replaced Jan Masaryk as foreign minister in the aftermath of the February 1948 Communist coup.

Cleveland, Harlan (1918–2008). American diplomat and official. Department chief of the United Nations Relief and Rehabilitation Administration's Italian mission, 1946–1947; department assistant administrator, Far East Program Division, Economic Cooperation Administration, 1949–1951; assistant director, Mutual Security Agency, 1952–1953.

Clifford, Clark (1906–1998). American lawyer and political operative. Assistant naval aide to the president, 1945–1946; naval aide to the president, 1946; special counsel to the president, 1946–1950. Speechwriter and close adviser to Truman.

Clinton, Bill (1946–). American Democratic statesman. President, 1993–2001. Initiated NATO enlargement in the aftermath of the collapse of the Soviet Union.

Clinton, Hillary (1947–). American politician and diplomat. First lady, 1993–2001; senator (D-NY), 2001–2009; secretary of state, 2009–2013.

Cohen, Benjamin (1894–1983). American official. State Department counselor, 1945–1947.

Connally, Tom (1877–1963). American politician. Senator (D-TX), 1929–1953; chairman of the Senate Committee on Foreign Relations, 1941–1947, 1949–1953.

Cortesi, Arnaldo (1897–1966). American *New York Times* reporter stationed in Rome. Won a Pulitzer Prize in 1946.

Cox, Edward Eugene (1880–1952). American politician. Congressman (D-GA), 1925–1952. Argued that Marshall aid without military support would be ineffective.

Cripps, Sir Richard Stafford (1889–1952). British Labour politician. Chancellor of the exchequer, 1947–1950.

Dalton, Lord Edward Hugh (1887–1962). British Labour politician. Chancellor of the exchequer, 1945–1947.

Davies, Joseph (1876–1958). American lawyer and diplomat. Ambassador to the Soviet Union, 1936–1938; special adviser with rank of ambassador, Potsdam Conference, 1945.

Deaton, Sir Angus (1945–). British economist. Won Nobel Prize for Economics in 2015.

De Gasperi, Alcide (1881–1954). Italian statesman. Prime minister, 1945–1953. Pro-American Christian Democrat who oversaw the creation of a new Italian constitution.

de Gaulle, Charles (1890–1970). French military leader and statesman. President, 1958–1969. Led provisional governments during and immediately after World War II before fronting the Rally of the French People (RPF) popular movement in the late 1940s.

Depreux, Édouard (1898–1981). French Socialist politician. Minister of the interior, 1947–1948; education minister, 1948.

Dewey, Thomas (1902–1971). American lawyer and politician. Governor (R-NY), 1943–1955; Republican presidential candidate. Defeated by Truman in the famously close election of 1948.

Djilas, Milovan (1911–1995). Yugoslav politician and writer. Secretary of Yugoslav Communist Party Executive Bureau, 1948–1953.

Dodd, Norris (1879–1968). American official. Under secretary of agriculture, 1946–1948; director-general, Food and Agriculture Organization of the United Nations, 1948–1954.

Douglas, Lewis (1894–1974). American diplomat. Financial adviser to General Clay, 1945; ambassador to the United Kingdom, 1947–1949. A skilled negotiator and polished diplomat, he was one of the Marshall Plan's most important envoys in Europe.

Draper, William Jr. (1894–1974). American military leader and diplomat. Chief, Economics Division, Control Council for Germany, 1945–1946; under secretary of war, 1947; under secretary of the Army, 1947–1949; special representative in Europe, 1952–1953.

Drtina, Prokop (1900–1980). Czechoslovak politician. Justice minister, 1945–1948. Ardent anti-Communist.

Duclos, Jacques (1896–1975). French Communist politician.

Dulles, Allen (1893–1969). American lawyer and intelligence official. President of the Council on Foreign Relations, 1946–1950; director of central intelligence, 1953–1961.

Dulles, John Foster (1888–1959). American politician and diplomat. Senator (R-NY), 1949–1950; secretary of state, 1953–1959. Foreign policy adviser who accompanied George Marshall to conferences in Moscow and London in 1947 and counseled Thomas Dewey during the 1948 presidential campaign.

Dunn, James (1890–1979). American diplomat. Ambassador to Italy, 1946–1952.

Durbrow, Elbridge (1903–1997). American diplomat. Chief, Eastern European Division, State Department, 1944–1946; counselor in Moscow, 1946–1948.

Eady, Sir Wilfred (1890–1962). British diplomat and official. Joint second secretary of the treasury, 1942–1952.

Earle, Edward Mead (1894–1954). American scholar and administrator. Board of

Analysts at the Office of Strategic Services, 1941–1942; special consultant to the commanding general of the American Air Forces, 1942–1945.

Eaton, Charles (1868–1953). American politician. Congressman (R-NJ), 1925–1953; chairman of the House Committee on Foreign Affairs, 1947–1949; chairman of the Select Committee on Foreign Aid, 1947–1948.

Ebert, Friedrich (Fritz) (1894–1979). East German Communist politician. Mayor of East Berlin, 1948–1967. Son of Weimar Republic's first president.

Eccles, Mariner (1890–1977). American banker. Chairman of the Federal Reserve Board, 1934–1948.

Echols, Oliver (1892–1954). American military officer and official. Director, Civil Affairs Division, War Department Special Staff, 1945–1947.

Eden, Sir Robert Anthony (1897–1977). British Conservative statesman. Foreign secretary, 1935–1938, 1940–1945, 1951–1955; prime minister, 1955–1957. Opposed the Morgenthau Plan for deindustrializing postwar Germany.

Eisenhower, Dwight David (1890–1969). American military leader and statesman. Supreme commander of the Allied Expeditionary Force, 1943–1945; chief of staff of the Army, 1945–1948; president, 1953–1961. Led Allied forces in Europe during World War II and was the first military governor of the U.S. zone of occupied Germany.

Elsey, George (1918–2015). American official and presidential aide. Assistant to the special counsel to the president, 1947–1949; administrative assistant to the president, 1949–1951; assistant to the director, Mutual Security Agency, 1951–1953.

Erdoğan, Recep Tayyip (1954–). Turkish politician. Prime minister, 2003–2014; president, 2014– .

Erhard, Ludwig (1897–1977). West German politician. Director of the economic council for the joint Anglo-U.S. zone of occupied Germany, 1948–1949; economics minister, 1949–1963; chancellor, 1963–1966. Free marketeer whose economic reforms were important to West Germany's postwar recovery.

Ethridge, Mark (1896–1981). American diplomat. Delegate to the United Nations Commission of Investigation to study Greek border disputes, 1947; chairman of the U.S. Advisory Commission on Information, 1948–1950.

Feierabend, Ladislav (1891–1969). Czechoslovak politician and writer. Finance minister in the London-based government-in-exile, 1941–1945.

Ferguson, Homer (1889–1982). American politician. Senator (R-MI), 1943–1955. Argued that aid to European governments undermined free enterprise.

Forrestal, James (1892–1949). American official. Secretary of the Navy, 1944–1947; secretary of defense, 1947–1949. One of the most hawkish members of Truman's cabinet.

François-Poncet, André (1887–1978). French diplomat. High commissioner for Germany, 1949–1955.

Franks, Sir Oliver (1905–1992). British diplomat. Chairman of the Committee of European Economic Co-operation, 1947–1948; ambassador to the United States, 1948–1952.

Friedensburg, Ferdinand (1886–1972). German Christian Democratic politician. Interim mayor of Berlin, 1948.

Gaddis, John Lewis (1941–). American Cold War historian and biographer of George Kennan.

Gaidar, Yegor Timurovich (1956–2009). Soviet economist and Russian political and economic reformer.

Ganeval, Jean (1894–1981). French general. Commandant of the French sector of Berlin, 1946–1950.

Genscher, Hans-Dietrich (1927–2016). West German statesman. Chairman of the Free Democratic Party (FDP), 1974–1985; foreign minister, 1974–1992.

Gerashchenko, Vladimir Sergeevich (1905–1995). Soviet finance and banking expert. Assistant chairman of the Board of the State Bank, 1944–1958; head of the Economic Department of the Ministry of Foreign Affairs, 1944–1948.

Geschke, Ottomar (1882–1957). German Communist politician. Deputy speaker of the Berlin City Council, 1946–1948.

Gilbert, Charles (1878–1958). American clergyman. Bishop of the Protestant Episcopal Diocese of New York, 1947–1950.

Gomułka, Władysław (1905–1982). Polish politician. Secretary general of the Communist Party, 1943–1948; first secretary of the Communist Party, 1956–1970.

Gorbachev, Mikhail Sergeevich (1931–). Soviet Communist Party leader and statesman. General secretary of the Communist Party, 1985–1991; last president of the Soviet Union, 1990–1991. Supported closer Russian relations with the West and opposed NATO expansion. Awarded the Nobel Peace Prize in 1990.

Gore, Al (1948–). American Democratic politician. Vice president, 1993–2001. Advocate for action to prevent climate change.

Gottwald, Klement (1896–1953). Czechoslovak Communist politician. Deputy prime minister, 1945–1946; prime minister, 1946–1948; president, 1948–1953. Helped orchestrate the February 1948 Communist coup.

Grachev, Pavel Sergeevich (1948–2012). Soviet military commander and Russian politician. Defense minister, 1992–1996.

Griffis, Stanton (1887–1974). American diplomat. Ambassador to Poland, 1947–1948.

Gromyko, Andrei Andreevich (1909–1989). Soviet diplomat. Ambassador to the United States, 1943–1946; ambassador to the United Nations, 1946–1948; deputy foreign minister, 1946–1949; first deputy foreign minister, 1949–1952.

Grotewohl, Otto (1894–1964). East German Communist politician. Co-chairman of the Communist SED party, 1946–1964; prime minister, 1949–1964.

Haffner, Sebastian (1907–1998). British-German writer and journalist.

Hála, František (1893–1952). Czechoslovak politician. Minister of posts, 1946–1948.

Hall, Alvin (1888–1969). American official. Director, Bureau of Engraving and Printing, 1924–1954.

Halle, Louis, Jr. (1910–1998). American writer and diplomat. Spent many years in the State Department before moving into academia.

Halleck, Charles (1900–1986). American politician. Congressman (R-IN), 1935–1969; House majority leader, 1947–1949, 1953–1955.

Halvorsen, Gail (1920–). American Air Force pilot. Berlin airlift pilot nicknamed the "Candy Bomber."

Harriman, William Averell (1891–1986). American banker, politician, and diplomat. Ambassador to the Soviet Union, 1943–1946; ambassador to the United Kingdom, 1946; secretary of commerce, 1946–1948; special representative in Europe under the Marshall Plan, 1948–1950; special assistant to the president, 1950–1952; director, Mutual Security Agency, 1951–1953. Headed the bipartisan President's Committee on Foreign Aid (Harriman Committee), whose report on the Marshall Plan was instrumental in passing the aid legislation.

Hawkins, Harry (1894–1983). American diplomat. Counselor for economic affairs at the embassy in London, 1944–1947; director, Foreign Service Institute, 1950–1952.

Hay, John (1838–1905). American statesman. Secretary of state, 1898–1905.

Henderson, Loy (1892–1986). American diplomat. Director, Office of Near Eastern and African Affairs, State Department, 1946–1948. Career foreign service officer and Russia specialist.

Herman, Stewart, Jr. (1909–2006). American clergyman. Worked on humanitarian issues with the World Council of Churches in Geneva, 1945–1948.

Herter, Christian (1895–1966). American politician and diplomat. Congressman (R-MA), 1943–1953; governor, 1953–1957; under secretary of state, 1957–1959; secretary of state, 1959–1961. Internationalist who led a congressional research trip to Europe to survey the severity of the continent's postwar economic situation.

Hickerson, John (1898–1989). American official and diplomat. Deputy director, Office of European Affairs, State Department, 1944–1947; director, Office of European Affairs, State Department, 1947–1949; assistant secretary of state, 1949–1953; ambassador to Finland, 1955–1960.

Hinton, Harold (1898–1954). American writer and journalist at *The New York Times*.

Hoffman, Clare (1875–1967). American politician. Congressman (R-MI), 1935–1963.

Hoffman, Paul (1891–1974). American auto executive and official. Director, Economic Cooperation Administration, 1948–1950. Oversaw implementation of the Marshall Plan.

Hogan, Michael (1943–). American historian. Author of *The Marshall Plan: America, Britain, and the Reconstruction of Western Europe, 1947–1952*.

Holbrooke, Richard (1941–2010). American diplomat. Ambassador to Germany, 1993–1994; assistant secretary of state for European and Canadian affairs, 1994–1995; ambassador to the United Nations, 1999–2001. Strong advocate of NATO expansion in the 1990s.

Hoover, Herbert (1874–1964). American Republican statesman. President, 1929–1933. Influential supporter of German reconstruction after World War II.

Hopkins, Harry (1890–1946). American official. Secretary of commerce, 1938–1940. One of FDR's closest aides.

Hottelet, Richard (1917–2014). American journalist and correspondent. Worked with CBS from 1944 to 1985.

Houdek, Vladimir (1912–2006). Czechoslovak diplomat. Ambassador to the United Nations, 1948–1950. Secret conduit between Henry Wallace and Andrei Gromyko in 1948. Defected to the West in 1950.

Hull, Cordell (1871–1955). American politician and diplomat. Congressman (D-TN), 1907–1930; senator, 1931–1933; secretary of state, 1933–1944. Ardent free trader.

Humelsine, Carlisle (1915–1989). American official. State Department executive secretary, 1947–1950; deputy assistant secretary of state for administration, 1950; assistant secretary of state for administration, 1950; deputy under secretary of state for administration, 1950–1953.

Inverchapel, Lord (Sir Archibald Clark Kerr) (1882–1951). British diplomat. Ambassador to the United States, 1946–1948.

Ivashov, Leonid Grigorievich (1943–). Russian official and military historian. Chief, Main Office of International Military Cooperation, Ministry of Defense, 1996–2001.

Jäger, Harald (1943–). East German military officer. Berlin Wall border guard in November 1989.

Jarman, Peterson (1892–1955). American politician. Congressman (D-AL), 1937–1949.

Javits, Jacob (1904–1986). American politician. Congressman (R-NY), 1947–1957; senator, 1957–1981.

Jessup, Philip (1897–1986). American diplomat. Representative to the United Nations General Assembly, 1948–1952; ambassador at large, 1949–1953. Close adviser to Dean Acheson whose backchannel negotiations with Soviet United Nations ambassador Yakov Malik led to the ending of the Berlin blockade.

Johnson, Louis (1891–1966). American official. Assistant secretary of war, 1937–1940; secretary of defense, 1949–1950.

Jones, Joseph, Jr. (1908–1990). American diplomat. Special assistant to the assistant secretary of state for public affairs, 1946–1948; special assistant to the administrator, Economic Cooperation Administration, 1949–1952; special assistant to the U.S. representative in Europe, 1952–1953. Documented the beginnings of the Marshall Plan in his book, *The Fifteen Weeks.*

Judt, Tony (1948–2010). British historian and writer. Author of *Postwar: A History of Europe Since 1945.*

Kardelj, Edvard (1910–1979). Yugoslav Communist revolutionary and politician. Vice president, 1945–1953; foreign minister, 1948–1953.

Kennan, George Frost (1904–2005). American diplomat and intellectual. Counselor in Moscow, 1944–1946; director of policy planning, 1947–1949; ambassador to the Soviet Union, 1952–1953. Expert on the Soviet Union who authored some of the early Cold War's seminal documents. Formulated the policy of Soviet containment. A leading architect of the Marshall Plan.

Khrushchev, Nikita Sergeevich (1894–1971). Soviet Communist Party leader and premier. First secretary of the Communist Party, 1953–1964; chairman of the Council of Ministers, 1958–1964. Succeeded Stalin as leader of the Soviet Union.

Kindleberger, Charles (1910–2003). American economist and official. Chief, Division of German and Austrian Economic Affairs, State Department, 1945–1947; adviser to the European Recovery Program, 1947–1948.

King, William Lyon Mackenzie (1874–1950). Canadian Liberal statesman. Prime minister, 1921–1926, 1926–1930, 1935–1948.

Kissinger, Henry (1923–). American statesman and scholar. National security adviser, 1969–1975; secretary of state, 1973–1977. Received the Nobel Peace Prize in 1973.

Knowland, William (1908–1974). American politician. Senator (R-CA), 1945–1959; Senate majority leader, 1953–1955.

Koenig, Marie-Pierre (1898–1970). French general. Military governor of the French zone of occupied Germany, 1945–1949.

Kohl, Helmut (1930–2017). German statesman. Chairman of the Christian Democratic Union, 1973–1998; chancellor of West Germany, 1982–1990; chancellor of reunified Germany, 1990–1998. Led the drive for rapid German reunification as the Soviet Union collapsed.

Kohler, Foy (1908–1990). American diplomat. Counselor in Moscow, 1948–1949; ambassador to the Soviet Union, 1962–1966.

Kopecký, Václav (1897–1961). Czechoslovak Communist politician. Minister of information, 1945–1953.

Kotikov, Alexander Georgievich (1902–1981). Soviet military commander. Commandant of the Soviet sector of Berlin, 1946–1950.

Kozyrev, Andrei Vladimirovich (1951–). Russian diplomat. Foreign minister, 1990–1996.

Krug, Julius (1907–1970). American official. Secretary of the interior, 1946–1949.

Kuznetsov, Fedor Fedotovich (1904–1979). Soviet military commander. Head of the Intelligence Office, 1943–1945; head of the Main Intelligence Office of the General Staff of the Armed Forces, 1945–1947; assistant chairman of the Committee of Information under the Council of Ministers, 1947–1949.

Ladas, Christos (1891–1948). Greek lawyer and official. Justice minister, 1947–1948. Assassinated by a member of the Greek Communist Party.

La Follette, Robert, Jr. (1895–1953). American Republican and Progressive politician. Senator (WI), 1925–1947; member of the President's Committee on Foreign Aid (Harriman Committee), 1947.

Lasky, Melvin (1920–2004). American journalist. Liberal-left, anti-Communist founder of the German literary journal *Der Monat*.

Lavrov, Sergei Victorivich (1950–). Russian diplomat. Ambassador to the United Nations, 1994–2004; foreign minister, 2004– .

Leahy, William (1875–1959). American naval officer, diplomat, and presidential aide. Ambassador to Vichy France, 1940–1942; chief of staff to FDR, 1942–1945; chief of staff to Truman, 1945–1949.

LeMay, Curtis (1906–1990). American Air Force commander. Chief of staff of the Strategic Air Forces, 1945–1948.

Lenin, Vladimir Ilyich (1870–1924). Russian Communist revolutionary and Soviet leader. Led Bolshevik forces to victory in the Russian Revolution of October 1917 and became the first Soviet head of state.

Letourneau, Jean (1907–1986). French MRP (Christian Democrat) politician. Minister for the associated states, 1950–1953.

Lippmann, Walter (1889–1974). American writer and columnist. Two-time Pulitzer Prize winner noted for his analysis of U.S. foreign policy.

Litvinov, Maxim Maximovich (1876–1951). Russian Communist revolutionary and Soviet diplomat. People's commissar of foreign affairs, 1930–1939; assistant foreign minister, 1940–1946; ambassador to the United States, 1941–1943.

Lodge, Henry Cabot, Jr. (1902–1985). American politician and diplomat. Senator (R-MA), 1937–1944, 1947–1953; ambassador to the United Nations, 1953–1960.

Lomakin, Yakov Mironovich (1904–1958). Soviet economist, journalist, and diplomat. Vice consul in New York, 1941; consul general in San Francisco, 1942–1944; consul general in New York, 1946–1948.

Longo, Luigi (1900–1980). Italian politician. General secretary of the Communist Party, 1964–1972.

Lovett, Robert (1895–1986). American diplomat. Under secretary of state, 1947–1949; deputy secretary of defense, 1950–1951; secretary of defense, 1951–1953. Served as Marshall's deputy in the State and Defense Departments.

Lozovsky, Solomon Abramovich (1878–1952). Russian Communist revolutionary, labor leader, and Soviet diplomat. Assistant foreign minister, 1939–1946. Executed on falsified charges in 1952 with other members of the Soviet Jewish Anti-Fascist Committee.

Lucas, Scott (1892–1968). American politician. Congressman (D-IL), 1935–1939; senator, 1939–1951; Senate majority leader, 1949–1951. Mocked Republican opponents of the Marshall Plan for aligning themselves with the Communist Party.

MacColl, René (1905–1971). British newspaper writer. Washington correspondent for the *Daily Express*.

Mackinder, Sir Halford (1861–1947). British geographer and intellectual. A founder of the discipline of geopolitics.

Maclean, Donald (1913–1983). British diplomat. Member of the "Cambridge Five" group of double agents who spied for the Soviets.

MacVeagh, Lincoln (1890–1972). American diplomat. Ambassador to Greece, 1944–1947.

Maier, Charles (1939–). American historian of the Marshall Plan.

Maisky, Ivan Mikhailovich (1884–1975). Bolshevik revolutionary and Soviet diplomat, historian, and writer. Ambassador to the United Kingdom, 1932–1943; assistant foreign minister, 1943–1946. Arrested in early 1952 and forced to confess to serving as a British spy.

Malenkov, Georgy Maximilianovich (1902–1988). Soviet official. Member of the Politburo, 1946–1957; secretary of the Central Committee of the Communist Party, 1939–1946, 1948–1953; assistant chairman of the Council of Ministers, 1946–1953. Close associate of Stalin.

Malik, Yakov Alexandrovich (1906–1980). Soviet diplomat. Assistant foreign minister, 1947–1953; ambassador to the United Nations, 1948–1952. Engaged in backchannel negotiations with American diplomat Philip Jessup to end the Berlin blockade.

Malone, George (1890–1961). American politician. Senator (R-NV), 1947–1959. Opposed the Marshall Plan on the grounds that it would "finance socialism" in Europe.

Mamedov, Georgy Enverovich (1947–). Russian diplomat. Assistant foreign minister, 1991–2003; ambassador to Canada, 2003–2014.

Mao Tse-tung (1893–1976). Chinese Communist revolutionary and founder of the People's Republic of China.

Marshall, George Catlett (1880–1959). American military leader and statesman. Chief of staff of the Army, 1939–1945; secretary of state, 1947–1949; secretary of defense, 1950–1951. His June 1947 speech at Harvard set the stage for the massive European aid program that would bear his name. Received the Nobel Peace Prize in 1953.

Martin, Joseph (1884–1968). American politician. Congressman (R-MA), 1925–1967; speaker of the house, 1947–1949, 1953–1955. Argued for an American military buildup in the wake of the February 1948 Czechoslovak Communist coup.

Masaryk, Jan (1886–1948). Czechoslovak diplomat. Foreign minister, 1945–1948. Son of the country's post–World War I founder, he sought to preserve his country's independence from the Soviet Union.

Massigli, René (1888–1988). French diplomat. Ambassador to the United Kingdom, 1944–1955.

Matthews, Harrison Freeman (1899–1986). American official and diplomat. Director, Office of European Affairs, State Department, 1944–1947; deputy under secretary of state, 1950–1953.

McClellan, John (1896–1977). American politician. Senator (D-AR), 1943–1977. Argued that senators should not support the Marshall Plan unless they were also prepared to support a military alliance with western Europe.

McCloy, John Jay (1895–1989). American official and diplomat. Assistant secretary of war, 1941–1945; president of the World Bank, 1947–1949; high commissioner for Germany, 1949–1952.

McNaughton, Frank (1906–1978). American writer and journalist. Washington correspondent for *Time*.

Meany, William George (1894–1980). American labor leader. Secretary-treasurer of the American Federation of Labor, 1939–1952; member of the President's Committee on Foreign Aid (Harriman Committee), 1947.

Medvedev, Dmitry Anatolievich (1965–). Russian lawyer and politician. First assistant chairman of the government, 2005–2008; president, 2008–2012; prime minister, 2012– .

Mendès-France, Pierre (1907–1982). French Radical-Socialist diplomat and politician. Prime minister, 1954–1955.

Merkel, Angela (1954–). German stateswoman. Chair of the Christian Democratic Union, 2000– ; chancellor, 2005– .

Merrow, Chester (1906–1974). American politician. Congressman (R-NH), 1943–1963. Argued for building up the U.S. Air Force in 1948 as a response to the growing Soviet threat in western Europe.

Miall, Leonard (1914–2005). British journalist. BBC correspondent in the United States, 1945–1953.

Milward, Alan (1935–2010). British historian. Author of *The Reconstruction of Western Europe, 1945–51*. Argued that Europe could have recovered at least as successfully without the Marshall Plan.

Mitterrand, François (1916–1996). French statesman. First secretary of the Socialist Party, 1971–1981; president, 1981–1995. Pushed for greater European integration after the fall of the Berlin Wall.

Modzelewski, Zygmunt (1900–1954). Polish Communist diplomat. Foreign minister, 1947–1951.

Molotov, Vyacheslav Mikhailovich (1890–1986). Bolshevik revolutionary and Soviet Communist Party, political, and government leader. Chairman of the Council of People's Commissars (head of government), 1930–1941; people's commissar of foreign affairs/foreign minister, 1939–1949, 1953–1956. A doctrinaire Marxist, loyal to Stalin, he was renowned among contemporary statesmen for his stubborn but effective anti-Western diplomacy.

Monnet, Jean (1888–1979). French statesman. President of the High Authority of the European Steel and Coal Community, 1952–1955. Conceived the Monnet

CAST OF CHARACTERS

Plan for French economic recovery and modernization following World War II.

Morgenthau, Henry, Jr. (1891–1967). American official. Treasury secretary, 1934–1945. One of FDR's closest confidants. Lent his name to the Morgenthau Plan, which sought to deindustrialize Germany in the aftermath of World War II.

Mosley, Leonard (1913–1992). British journalist. Correspondent for the *Sunday Times*.

Muggeridge, Malcolm (1903–1990). British journalist. Washington correspondent for *The Daily Telegraph* during the late 1940s.

Mundt, Karl (1900–1974). American politician. Congressman (R-SD), 1939–1948; senator, 1948–1973. Member of the Herter Committee touring Europe to evaluate reconstruction needs in 1947.

Murphy, Robert (1894–1978). American diplomat. Political adviser for Germany, 1945–1949; ambassador to Belgium, 1949–1952. One of General Clay's top advisers in Germany, he favored a confrontational approach toward the Soviet Union.

Nitze, Paul (1907–2004). American official. Deputy director, Office of International Trade Policy, State Department, 1946–1947; deputy assistant secretary of state for economic affairs, 1947–1949; director of policy planning, 1949–1953. Lead statistician and accountant of the "Brown Books," which detailed the needs and finances of countries receiving Marshall aid.

Nixon, Richard (1913–1994). American statesman. Congressman (R-CA), 1947–1950; senator, 1950–1953; vice president, 1953–1961; president, 1969–1974. Member of the Herter Committee touring Europe to evaluate reconstruction needs in 1947.

Nosek, Jindřich (1896–1984). Czechoslovak diplomat. Ambassador to France, 1944–1948.

Nosek, Václav (1893–1955). Czechoslovak Communist politician. Minister of the interior, 1945–1948.

Nourse, Edwin (1883–1974). American scholar and official. Chairman of the Council of Economic Advisers, 1946–1949.

Novikov, Nikolai Vasilievich (1903–1989). Soviet diplomat. Ambassador to the United States, 1946–1947.

Orbán, Viktor (1963–). Hungarian politician. Prime minister, 1998–2002; 2010– .

Otschkin, Boris Romanovich (1921–?). Soviet military officer. Served in Berlin commandant's office from 1945 to 1949.

Parodi, Alexandre (1901–1979). French diplomat. Secretary general of the French Foreign Ministry, 1949–1956.

Patterson, Robert (1891–1952). American judge and official. Secretary of war, 1945–1947.

Patton, George (1885–1945). American military leader. Legendary World War II commander whose pleas to be allowed to press on to Berlin were rejected by General Eisenhower.

Pauley, Edwin (1903–1981). American businessman and political adviser. Personal representative of Truman on the Allied Commission on Reparations, 1945–1947; special adviser to George Marshall, 1947–1948.

Pavlov, Valentin Sergeevich (1937–2003). Soviet politician. Finance minister, 1989–1991; prime minister, 1991. Helped lead failed coup against Gorbachev in August 1991.

Pearson, Drew (1897–1969). American journalist. Author of syndicated newspaper column entitled "Washington Merry-Go-Round," 1932–1969.

Peskov, Dmitry Sergeevich (1967–). Russian official and translator. Press secretary to the prime minister, 2008–2012; presidential press secretary and assistant head of the administration of the president of the Russian Federation, 2012– .

Peterson, Sir Maurice Drummond (1889–1952). British diplomat. Ambassador to the Soviet Union, 1946–1949.

Philby, Harold (Kim) (1912–1988). British intelligence officer. Member of the "Cambridge Five," a ring of British double agents who spied for the Soviets.

Philip, André (1902–1970). French Socialist politician. Finance minister, 1946, 1946–1947.

Pickering, Thomas (1931–). American diplomat. Ambassador to the United Nations, 1989–1992; ambassador to the Russian Federation, 1993–1996.

Pieck, Wilhelm (1876–1960). East German politician. Co-chairman of Communist SED party, 1946–1960; first president of East Germany, 1949–1960.

Primakov, Yevgeny Maximovich (1929–2015). Soviet and Russian politician and diplomat. Head of the Soviet/Russian Foreign Intelligence Service, 1991–1996; foreign minister, 1996–1998; prime minister, 1998–1999.

Putin, Vladimir Vladimirovich (1952–). Russian statesman. Prime minister, 1999,

2008–2012; president, 2000–2008, 2012– . Served as a Soviet KGB officer in East Germany when the Berlin Wall fell. Fierce opponent of NATO expansion.

Queuille, Henri (1884–1970). French Radical-Socialist politician. Prime minister, 1948–1949, 1950, 1951.

Ramadier, Paul (1888–1961). French Socialist politician. Prime minister, 1947.

Ratiani, Georgii Mikhailovich (1917–1978). Soviet journalist, historian, and writer. *Pravda* journalist and editor.

Rayburn, Sam (1882–1961). American politician. Congressman (D-TX), 1913–1961; speaker of the house, 1940–1947, 1949–1953, 1955–1961.

Reagan, Ronald (1911–2004). American statesman. Governor (R-CA), 1967–1975; president, 1981–1989.

Reed, Philip (1899–1989). American businessman. Chairman of General Electric, 1940–1942, 1945–1958.

Reston, James (1909–1995). American *New York Times* reporter for fifty years. Won two Pulitzer Prizes.

Reuter, Ernst (1889–1953). German Social Democratic politician. Mayor of West Berlin, 1948–1953.

Revai, Josef (1898–1959). Hungarian Communist politician. Member of the Politburo, 1945–1952; education minister, 1949–1953.

Riddleberger, James (1904–1982). American diplomat. Chief, Division of Central European Affairs, State Department, 1944–1947; director, Office of Political Affairs, Office of Military Government for Germany-U.S., 1947–1949; acting political adviser to the U.S. military governor and later director, Office of Political Affairs, U.S. High Commissioner for Germany, 1949–1950; political adviser, Economic Cooperation Administration, 1950–1952.

Ripka, Hubert (1895–1958). Czechoslovak politician. Foreign trade minister, 1945–1948. Favored closer economic relations with the West and participation in the Marshall Plan. Fled the country after the February 1948 Communist coup.

Roberts, Sir Frank (1907–1998). British diplomat. Minister in Moscow, 1945–1947; principal private secretary to Bevin, 1947–1949.

Robertson, Sir Brian (1896–1974). British general. Deputy military governor of the British zone of occupied Germany, 1945–1947; military governor and commander in chief, 1947–1949; high commissioner for Germany, 1949–1950.

Roll, Eric (1907–2005). British diplomat. Undersecretary to the treasury,

1948–1949; member of delegation to the Organisation for European Economic Co-operation, 1949.

Roosevelt, Eleanor (1884–1962). American diplomat and wife of FDR. First lady, 1933–1945; delegate to the United Nations General Assembly, 1945–1953.

Roosevelt, Franklin Delano (1882–1945). American Democratic statesman. President, 1933–1945. Led the United States through the Great Depression and World War II. His vision of a postwar world order founded on multilateral institutions and cooperation with the Soviet Union unraveled after his death.

Rostow, Eugene (1913–2002). American scholar and diplomat. Dean of Yale Law School, 1955–1965; under secretary of state, 1966–1969.

Rostow, Walt (1916–2003). American economist and official. Assistant chief, German-Austrian Economic Division, State Department, 1945–1946; assistant to the executive secretary, Economic Community for Europe, 1947–1949.

Royall, Kenneth (1894–1971). American official. Under secretary of war, 1945–1947; secretary of war, 1947; secretary of the Army, 1947–1949. Argued for a withdrawal of Western forces from Berlin during the Soviet blockade.

Saakashvili, Mikheil (1967–). Georgian politician. President, 2004–2007, 2008–2013.

Sabanadze, Natalie (1975–). Georgian diplomat. Ambassador to the European Union, 2013– .

Sazonov, Sergei Dmitrievich (1860–1927). Russian diplomat. Foreign minister, 1910–1916.

Schumacher, Kurt (1895–1952). German politician. Chairman of the Social Democratic Party (SPD), 1946–1952. An anti-Communist Social Democrat, he strongly supported postwar German reunification.

Schuman, Robert (1886–1963). French statesman. Finance minister, 1946; prime minister, 1947–1948; president of the European Parliament, 1958–1960. Staunch advocate of West European integration and multilateral institutions.

Scowcroft, Brent (1925–). American military leader and official. National security adviser, 1975–1977, 1989–1993.

Semenov, Vladimir Semenovich (1874–1960). Soviet official. Military counsel, 1945–1946; political counsel for the Soviet Military Administration in Germany, 1946–1949; political counsel for the Soviet Control Commission in Germany, 1949–1953.

Semler, Johannes (1898–1973). German official. Bizonal economics director in occupied Germany, 1947–1948.

Sforza, Count Carlo (1873–1952). Italian diplomat. Foreign minister, 1920–1921, 1947–1951.

Sicherman, Harvey (1945–2010). American scholar and official. Member of the Policy Planning Staff, 1991–1992.

Široký, Viliam (1902–1971). Czechoslovak Communist politician. Vice premier, 1945–1953; premier, 1953–1963.

Slánský, Rudolf (1901–1952). Czechoslovak Communist politician. Secretary general of the Communist Party, 1945–1951.

Smirnov, Andrei Andreevich (1905–1982). Soviet diplomat. Chief of the III European Department of the People's Commissariat/Ministry of Foreign Affairs, 1943–1949; assistant foreign minister, 1946–1949.

Smith, Frederick (1884–1956). American politician. Congressman (R-OH), 1939–1951. Opposed the Marshall Plan as "outright communism."

Smith, Lawrence (1892–1958). American politician. Congressman (R-WI), 1941–1958. Member of the Herter Committee touring Europe to evaluate reconstruction needs in 1947.

Smith, Walter Bedell (1895–1961). American general and diplomat. Chief of staff to General Eisenhower, 1942–1945; ambassador to the Soviet Union, 1946–1949; director of central intelligence, 1950–1953.

Smutný, Jaromír (1892–1964). Czechoslovak official. Head of the Presidential Office in Exile, 1940–1945; chancellor of the president in Prague, 1945–1948.

Snyder, John (1895–1985). American banker and official. Treasury secretary, 1946–1953.

Sokolovsky, Vasily Danilovich (1897–1968). Soviet military leader. Commander in chief of the Group of Soviet forces in Germany and chief of Soviet Military Administration in Germany, 1946–1949. Represented the Soviet Union in the Allied Control Council.

Soros, George (1930–). Hungarian American investor and philanthropist. Founder of the Open Society Foundations.

Spaak, Paul-Henri (1899–1972). Belgian Socialist statesman. Prime minister, 1938–1939, 1947–1950; foreign minister, 1939–1945, 1954–1957,

Treasury secretary, 1945–1946; chief justice of the Supreme Court, 1946–1953. A close friend of Truman's.

Vursell, Charles (1881–1974). American politician. Congressman (R-IL), 1943–1959. Argued that Marshall aid would be better spent on strengthening the U.S. Air Force.

Vyshinsky, Andrei Januarievich (1883–1954). Soviet lawyer and diplomat. Prosecutor of the Soviet Union, 1935–1939; assistant chairman of the Council of People's Commissars, 1939–1944; assistant people's commissar of foreign affairs/assistant foreign minister, 1940–1949; foreign minister, 1949–1953. Served as Molotov's first deputy for nearly a decade before replacing him in 1949.

Wałęsa, Lech (1943–). Polish trade union leader and statesman. Chairman of Polish trade union Solidarity, 1980–1990; president, 1990–1995.

Wallace, Henry (1888–1965). American politician. Vice president, 1941–1945; secretary of commerce, 1945–1946. A presidential candidate who ran on the Progressive Party ticket in 1948, he condemned the Marshall Plan as belligerent and imperialistic.

Wellstone, Paul (1944–2002). American politician. Senator (D-MN), 1991–2002.

Wherry, Kenneth (1892–1951). American politician. Senator (R-NE), 1943–1951.

White, Harry Dexter (1892–1948). American economist and Treasury official. Sympathetic to the Soviet Union and an admirer of its economic system, he was considered a valuable agent of influence by Soviet intelligence.

White, William (1905–1994). American journalist. Correspondent for *The New York Times*.

Wiley, Alexander (1884–1967). American politician. Senator (R-WI), 1939–1963. Wanted the United States to secure strategic bases or materials in Europe in return for aid.

Wilson, Woodrow (1856–1924). American Democratic statesman. President, 1913–1921. Called for a post–World War I order based on "Fourteen Points," among them self-determination and the elimination of trade barriers.

Wisner, Frank (1909–1965). American official. Deputy assistant secretary of state for the occupied areas, 1947–1948; assistant director for policy coordination at the CIA, 1948–1951.

Wörner, Manfred (1934–1994). German politician and diplomat. Secretary general of NATO, 1988–1994.

Wrong, Humphrey Hume (1894–1954). Canadian diplomat. Ambassador to the United States, 1946–1953.

Yanukovych, Viktor (1950–). Ukrainian politician. Prime minister, 2002–2005, 2006–2007; president, 2010–2014.

Yazov, Dimtry Timofeevich (1924-). Soviet military leader and official. The last defense minister of the Soviet Union, 1984-1991.

Yeltsin, Boris Nickolaevich (1931–2007). Russian statesman. First president of the Russian Federation, 1991–1999. Opposed NATO expansion after the collapse of the Soviet Union.

Yezhov, Nikolai Ivanovich (1895–1940). Soviet Communist Party functionary and official. Secretary of the Central Committee of the Communist Party and chairman of its Commission of Party Control, 1935–1939; people's commissar of internal affairs, 1936–1938. Organizer of mass repressions of 1936–1938. Arrested in 1939 and executed in 1940 on falsified charges of an attempted coup d'état.

Young, Owen (1874–1962). American businessman. Chairman of General Electric, 1922–1939, 1942–1945; member of the President's Committee on Foreign Aid (Harriman Committee), 1947.

Zellerbach, James (18921963). American businessman and diplomat. Economic Cooperation Administration mission chief in Italy, 1948–1950.

Zenkl, Petr (1884–1975). Czechoslovak politician. Chairman of the National Socialist Party, 1945–1948.

Zhdanov, Andrei Alexandrovich (1896–1948). Soviet Communist Party leader and official. Member of the Politburo, 1939–1948; Communist Party Central Committee secretary responsible for ideology and foreign policy, 1934–1948.

Zhukov, Georgy Konstantinovich (1896–1974). Soviet military leader. Assistant supreme commander of the Armed Forces of the Soviet Union, 1942–1945; commander in chief of the Group of Soviet forces in Germany and chief of Soviet Military Administration in Germany, 1945–1946.

Zoellick, Robert (1953–). American diplomat. State Department counselor, 1989–1991; under secretary of state for economic and agricultural affairs, 1991–1992; trade representative, 2001–2005; deputy secretary of state, 2005–2006; president of the World Bank, 2007–2012.

Zorin, Valerian Alexandrovich (1902–1986). Soviet diplomat. Ambassador to Czechoslovakia, 1945–1947; assistant foreign minister, 1947–1955, 1956–1965.

APPENDIX A

(transcript version)

March 12, 1947

MR. PRESIDENT, MR. SPEAKER, MEMBERS OF THE CONGRESS OF THE United States:

The gravity of the situation which confronts the world today necessitates my appearance before a joint session of the Congress. The foreign policy and the national security of this country are involved. One aspect of the present situation, which I present to you at this time for your consideration and decision, concerns Greece and Turkey. The United States has received from the Greek Government an urgent appeal for financial and economic assistance. Preliminary reports from the American Economic Mission now in Greece and reports from the American Ambassador in Greece corroborate the statement of the Greek Government that assistance is imperative if Greece is to survive as a free nation.

I do not believe that the American people and the Congress wish to turn a deaf ear to the appeal of the Greek Government. Greece is not a rich country. Lack of sufficient natural resources has always forced the Greek people to work hard to make both ends meet. Since 1940, this industrious, peace loving country has suffered invasion, four years of cruel enemy occupation, and bitter internal strife.

When forces of liberation entered Greece they found that the retreating Germans had destroyed virtually all the railways, roads, port facilities, communications, and merchant marine. More than a thousand villages had been burned. Eighty-five percent of the children were tubercular. Livestock, poultry, and draft animals had almost disappeared. Inflation had wiped out practically all savings. As a result of these tragic conditions, a militant minority, exploiting human want and misery, was able to create political chaos which, until now, has made economic recovery impossible.

Greece is today without funds to finance the importation of those goods which are essential to bare subsistence. Under these circumstances, the people of Greece cannot make progress in solving their problems of reconstruction. Greece is in desperate need of financial and economic assistance to enable it to resume purchases of food, clothing, fuel, and seeds. These are indispensable for the subsistence of its people and are obtainable only from abroad. Greece must have help to import the goods necessary to restore internal order and security, so essential for economic and political recovery. The Greek Government has also asked for the assistance of experienced American administrators, economists, and technicians to insure that the financial and other aid given to Greece shall be used effectively in creating a stable and self-sustaining economy and in improving its public administration.

The very existence of the Greek state is today threatened by the terrorist activities of several thousand armed men, led by Communists, who defy the government's authority at a number of points, particularly along the northern boundaries. A Commission appointed by the United Nations Security Council is at present investigating disturbed conditions in northern Greece and alleged border violations along the frontiers between Greece on the one hand and Albania, Bulgaria, and Yugoslavia on the other.

Meanwhile, the Greek Government is unable to cope with the situation. The Greek army is small and poorly equipped. It needs supplies and equipment if it is to restore authority of the government throughout Greek territory. Greece must have assistance if it is to become a self-supporting and self-respecting democracy. The United States must supply this assistance. We have already extended to Greece certain types of relief and economic aid. But these are inadequate. There is no other country to which democratic Greece can turn. No other nation is willing and able to provide the necessary support for a democratic Greek government.

The British Government, which has been helping Greece, can give no further financial or economic aid after March 31st. Great Britain finds itself under the necessity of reducing or liquidating its commitments in several parts of the world, including Greece.

We have considered how the United Nations might assist in this crisis. But the situation is an urgent one, requiring immediate action, and the United Nations and its related organizations are not in a position to extend help of the kind that is required.

It is important to note that the Greek Government has asked for our aid in utilizing effectively the financial and other assistance we may give to Greece, and in improving its public administration. It is of the utmost importance that we supervise the use of any funds made available to Greece in such a manner that each dollar spent will count toward making Greece self-supporting, and will help to build an economy in which a healthy democracy can flourish.

No government is perfect. One of the chief virtues of a democracy, however, is that its defects are always visible and under democratic processes can be pointed out and corrected. The Government of Greece is not perfect. Nevertheless it represents eighty-five percent of the members of the Greek Parliament who were chosen in an election last year. Foreign observers, including 692 Americans, considered this election to be a fair expression of the views of the Greek people.

The Greek Government has been operating in an atmosphere of chaos and extremism. It has made mistakes. The extension of aid by this country does not mean that the United States condones everything that the Greek Government has done or will do. We have condemned in the past, and we condemn now, extremist measures of the right or the left. We have in the past advised tolerance, and we advise tolerance now.

Greek's [sic] neighbor, Turkey, also deserves our attention. The future of Turkey, as an independent and economically sound state, is clearly no less important to the freedom-loving peoples of the world than the future of Greece. The circumstances in which Turkey finds itself today are considerably different from those of Greece. Turkey has been spared the disasters that have beset Greece. And during the war, the United States and Great Britain furnished Turkey with material aid.

Nevertheless, Turkey now needs our support. Since the war, Turkey has sought additional financial assistance from Great Britain and the United States for the purpose of effecting that modernization necessary for the maintenance of its national integrity. That integrity is essential to the preservation of order in the Middle East. The British government has informed us that, owing to its own difficulties, it can no longer extend financial or economic aid to Turkey. As in the case of Greece, if Turkey is to have the assistance it needs, the United States must supply it. We are the only country able to provide that help.

I am fully aware of the broad implications involved if the United States extends assistance to Greece and Turkey, and I shall discuss these implications with you at this time. One of the primary objectives of the foreign policy of the United States is the creation of conditions in which we and other nations will be able to work out a way of life free from coercion. This was a fundamental issue in the war with Germany and Japan. Our victory was won over countries which sought to impose their will, and their way of life, upon other nations.

To ensure the peaceful development of nations, free from coercion, the United States has taken a leading part in establishing the United Nations. The United Nations is designed to make possible lasting freedom and independence for all its members. We shall not realize our objectives, however, unless we are willing to help free peoples to maintain their free institutions and their national integrity against aggressive movements that seek to impose upon them totalitarian regimes. This is no more than a frank recognition that totalitarian regimes imposed upon free peoples, by direct or indirect aggression, undermine the foundations of international peace, and hence the security of the United States.

The peoples of a number of countries of the world have recently had totalitarian regimes forced upon them against their will. The Government of the United States has made frequent protests against coercion and intimidation in violation of the Yalta agreement in Poland, Rumania, and Bulgaria. I must also state that in a number of other countries there have been similar developments.

At the present moment in world history nearly every nation must choose between alternative ways of life. The choice is too often not a free one. One way of life is based upon the will of the majority, and is distinguished by free institutions, representative government, free elections, guarantees of individual liberty, freedom of speech and religion, and freedom from political oppression. The second way of life is based upon the will of a minority forcibly imposed upon the majority. It relies upon terror and oppression, a controlled press and radio, fixed elections, and the suppression of personal freedoms.

I believe that it must be the policy of the United States to support free peoples who are resisting attempted subjugation by armed minorities or by outside pressures.

I believe that we must assist free peoples to work out their own destinies in their own way.

I believe that our help should be primarily through economic and financial aid which is essential to economic stability and orderly political processes.

The world is not static, and the status quo is not sacred. But we cannot allow changes in the status quo in violation of the Charter of the United Nations by such methods as coercion, or by such subterfuges as political infiltration. In helping free and independent nations to maintain their freedom, the United States will be giving effect to the principles of the Charter of the United Nations.

It is necessary only to glance at a map to realize that the survival and integrity of the Greek nation are of grave importance in a much wider situation. If Greece should fall under the control of an armed minority, the effect upon its neighbor, Turkey, would be immediate and serious. Confusion and disorder might well spread throughout the entire Middle East. Moreover, the disappearance of Greece as an independent state would have a profound effect upon those countries in Europe whose peoples are struggling against great difficulties to maintain their freedoms and their independence while they repair the damages of war.

It would be an unspeakable tragedy if these countries, which have struggled so long against overwhelming odds, should lose that victory for which they sacrificed so much. Collapse of free institutions and loss of independence would be disastrous not only for them but for the world. Discouragement and possibly failure would quickly be the lot of neighboring peoples striving to maintain their freedom and independence.

Should we fail to aid Greece and Turkey in this fateful hour, the effect will be far reaching to the West as well as to the East.

We must take immediate and resolute action. I therefore ask the Congress to provide authority for assistance to Greece and Turkey in the amount of $400,000,000 for the period ending June 30, 1948. In requesting these funds, I have taken into consideration the maximum amount of relief assistance which would be furnished to Greece out of the $350,000,000 which I recently requested that the Congress authorize for the prevention of starvation and suffering in countries devastated by the war.

In addition to funds, I ask the Congress to authorize the detail of American civilian and military personnel to Greece and Turkey, at the request of those countries, to assist in the tasks of reconstruction, and for the purpose of supervising the use of such financial and material assistance as may be furnished. I recommend that authority also be provided for the instruction and training of selected Greek and Turkish personnel. Finally, I ask that the Congress provide authority which will permit the speediest and most effective use, in terms of needed commodities, supplies, and equipment, of such funds as may be authorized. If further funds, or further authority, should be needed for the purposes indicated in this message, I shall not hesitate to bring the situation before the Congress. On this subject the Executive and Legislative branches of the Government must work together.

This is a serious course upon which we embark. I would not recommend it except that the alternative is much more serious. The United States contributed $341,000,000,000 toward winning World War II. This is an investment in world freedom and world peace. The assistance that I am recommending for Greece and Turkey amounts to little more than 1 tenth of 1 percent of this investment. It is only common sense that we should safeguard this investment and make sure that it was not in vain. The seeds of totalitarian regimes are nurtured by misery and want. They spread and grow in the evil soil of poverty and strife. They reach their full growth when the hope of a people for a better life has died.

We must keep that hope alive.

The free peoples of the world look to us for support in maintaining their freedoms. If we falter in our leadership, we may endanger the peace of the world. And we shall surely endanger the welfare of this nation.

Great responsibilities have been placed upon us by the swift movement of events.

I am confident that the Congress will face these responsibilities squarely.

Source: http://www.americanrhetoric.com/speeches/harrystrumantrumandoctrine.html.

APPENDIX B

(transcript version)

June 5, 1947

MR. PRESIDENT, DR. CONANT, MEMBERS OF THE BOARD OF OVERSEERS, LA-dies and gentlemen, I'm profoundly grateful and touched by the distinction and honor and great compliment accorded me by the authorities of Harvard this morning. I'm overwhelmed, as a matter of fact, and I'm rather fearful of my inability to maintain such a high rating as you've been generous enough to accord to me. In these historic and lovely surroundings, this perfect day, and this very wonderful assembly, it is a tremendously impressive thing to an individual in my position.

I need not tell you gentlemen that the world situation is very serious. That must be apparent to all intelligent people. I think one difficulty is that the problem is one of such enormous complexity that the very mass of facts presented to the public by press and radio make it exceedingly difficult for the man in the street to reach a clear appraisement of the situation. Furthermore, the people of this country are distant from the troubled areas of the earth and it is hard for them to comprehend the plight and consequent reactions of the long-suffering peoples, and the effect of those reactions on their governments in connection with our efforts to promote peace in the world.

In considering the requirements for the rehabilitation of Europe the physical loss of life, the visible destruction of cities, factories, mines and railroads was correctly estimated, but it has become obvious during recent months that this visible destruction was probably less serious than the dislocation of the entire fabric of European economy. For the past ten years conditions have been highly abnormal. The feverish preparation for war and the more feverish maintenance of the war effort engulfed all aspects of national economies. Machinery has fallen into disrepair or is entirely obsolete. Under the arbitrary and destructive Nazi rule, virtually every possible enterprise was geared into the German war machine. Long-standing commercial ties, private institutions, banks, insurance companies and shipping companies disappeared, through loss of capital, absorption through nationalization or by simple destruction. In many countries, confidence in the local currency has been severely shaken. The breakdown of the business structure of Europe during the war was complete. Recovery has been seriously retarded by the fact that two years after the close of hostilities a peace settlement with Germany and Austria has not been agreed upon. But even given a more prompt solution of these difficult problems, the rehabilitation of the economic structure of Europe quite evidently will require a much longer time and greater effort than had been foreseen.

There is a phase of this matter which is both interesting and serious. The farmer has always produced the foodstuffs to exchange with the city dweller for the other necessities of life. This division of labor is the basis of modern civilization. At the present time it is threatened with breakdown. The town and city industries are not producing adequate goods to exchange with the food-producing farmer. Raw materials and fuel are in short supply. Machinery is lacking or worn out. The farmer or the peasant cannot find the goods for sale which he desires to purchase. So the sale of his farm produce for money which he cannot use seems to him an unprofitable transaction. He, therefore, has withdrawn many fields from crop cultivation and is using them for grazing. He feeds more grain to stock and finds for himself and his family an ample supply of food, however short he may be on clothing and the other ordinary gadgets of civilization. Meanwhile people in the cities are short of food and fuel. So the governments are forced to use their foreign money and credits to procure these necessities abroad. This process exhausts funds which are urgently needed for reconstruction. Thus a very serious situation is rapidly developing which bodes no good for the world. The modern system of the division of labor upon which the exchange of products is based is in danger of breaking down.

The truth of the matter is that Europe's requirements for the next three or four years of foreign food and other essential products—principally from America—are so much greater than her present ability to pay that she must have substantial additional help, or face economic, social and political deterioration of a very grave character.

The remedy lies in breaking the vicious circle and restoring the confidence of the European people in the economic future of their own countries and of Europe as a whole. The manufacturer and the farmer throughout wide areas must be able and willing to exchange their products for currencies the continuing value of which is not open to question.

Aside from the demoralizing effect on the world at large and the possibilities of disturbances arising as a result of the desperation of the people concerned, the consequences to the economy of the United States should be apparent to all. It is logical that the United States should do whatever it is able to do to assist in the return of normal economic health in the world, without which there can be no political stability and no assured peace. Our policy is directed not against any country or doctrine but against hunger, poverty, desperation and chaos. Its purpose should be the revival of a working economy in the world so as to permit the emergence of political and social conditions in which free institutions can exist. Such assistance, I am convinced, must not be on a piece-meal basis as various crises develop. Any assistance that this Government may render in the future should provide a cure rather than a mere palliative. Any government that is willing to assist in the task of recovery will find full cooperation, I am sure, on the part of the United States Government. Any government which maneuvers to block the recovery of other countries cannot expect help from us. Furthermore, governments, political parties or groups which seek to perpetuate human misery in order to profit therefrom politically or otherwise will encounter the opposition of the United States.

It is already evident that, before the United States Government can proceed much further in its efforts to alleviate the situation and help start the European world on its way to recovery, there must be some agreement among the countries of Europe as to the requirements of the situation and the part those countries themselves will take in order to give proper effect to whatever action might be undertaken by this Government. It would be neither fitting nor efficacious for this Government to undertake to draw up unilaterally a program designed to place Europe on its feet economically. This is the business of the Europeans. The initiative, I think, must come from Europe. The role of this country should consist of friendly aid in the drafting of a European program and of later support of such a program so far as it may be practical for us to do so. The program should be a joint one, agreed to by a number, if not all European nations.

An essential part of any successful action on the part of the United States is an understanding on the part of the people of America of the character of the problem and the remedies to be applied. Political passion and prejudice should have no part. With foresight, and a willingness on the part of our people to face up to the vast responsibility which history has clearly placed upon our country, the difficulties I have outlined can and will be overcome.

I am sorry that on each occasion I have said something publicly in regard to our international situation; I've been forced by the necessities of the case to enter into rather technical discussions. But to my mind, it is of vast importance that our people reach some general understanding of what the complications really are, rather than react from a passion or a prejudice or an emotion of the moment. As I said more formally a moment ago, we are remote from the scene of these troubles. It is virtually impossible at this distance merely by reading, or listening, or even seeing photographs or motion pictures, to grasp at all the real significance of the situation. And yet the whole world of the future hangs on a proper judgment. It hangs, I think, to a large extent on the realization of the American people, of just what are the various dominant factors. What are the reactions of the people? What are the justifications of those reactions? What are the sufferings? What is needed? What can best be done? What must be done? Thank you very much.

Source: http://marshallfoundation.org/marshall/the-marshall-plan/marshall-plan-speech/.

APPENDIX C

DATA

TABLE 1 MACROECONOMIC INDICATORS FOR MARSHALL AID RECIPIENTS (AND THE UNITED STATES)

Austria

	Real output[1] Annual % change	Inflation Annual % change	Budget deficit as % of GDP	Government debt as % of GDP	Current account as % of GDP
1946	n/a	n/a	n/a	n/a	n/a
1947	10.3	5.6	n/a	n/a	n/a
1948	26.7	14.4	-8.6	35.2	-7.6
1949	19.0	-3.2	-7.2	26.4	-7.8
1950	12.4	-1.1	-7.3	22.1	-4.7
1951	6.8	9.9	-5.5	15.3	-5.1
1952	0.0	0.0	-3.4	13.6	-2.9
1953	4.4	0.0	-0.9	16.6	2.4
1954	10.2	1.0	-0.1	14.3	1.9
1955	11.5	0.0	-0.2	11.9	-3.2

Belgium

	Real output[2] Annual % change	Inflation Annual % change	Budget deficit as % of GDP	Government debt as % of GDP	Current account as % of GDP
1946	n/a	n/a	-19.2	118.3	n/a
1947	n/a	5.6	-14.5	98.6	n/a
1948	35.6	14.4	-2.3	74.2	1.4
1949	5.6	-3.2	-4.4	78.3	0.7
1950	3.1	-1.1	-3.8	73.7	-2.6
1951	5.1	9.9	-1.1	64.5	3.9
1952	4.4	0.0	-2.9	66.3	2.3
1953	1.2	0.0	-4.1	68.5	0.8
1954	4.2	1.0	-4.6	69.9	0.3
1955	4.9	0.0	-2.9	68.6	3.4

Denmark

	Real output[3] Annual % change	Inflation Annual % change	Budget deficit[4] as % of GDP	Government debt as % of GDP	Current account as % of GDP
1946	15.6	-0.6	n/a	10.0	-6.0
1947	5.6	n/a	n/a	71.2	-2.6
1948	3.3	n/a	n/a	56.8	-1.9
1949	4.6	2.5	n/a	51.0	-1.4
1950	7.1	3.7	-2.1	46.3	-3.9
1951	0.6	10.6	-2.2	0.4	1.2
1952	1.6	5.3	-2.6	38.7	0.6
1953	6.0	1.0	-3.1	36.1	0.5
1954	2.9	0.0	-3.2	29.4	-1.9
1955	1.0	5.0	-1.2	29.8	0.7

France

	Real output[1] Annual % change	Inflation Annual % change	Budget deficit as % of GDP	Government debt as % of GDP	Current account as % of GDP
1946	n/a	52.5	n/a	n/a	n/a
1947	n/a	49.2	-8.0	n/a	n/a
1948	7.9	58.6	-9.7	n/a	-5.7
1949	14.3	12.7	-7.3	28.6	-1.8
1950	7.2	9.9	-5.6	27.4	0.7
1951	5.9	16.7	-4.4	22.8	-1.1
1952	3.4	12.1	-6.8	23.5	-0.5
1953	2.5	-2.0	-1.6	25.8	0.2
1954	4.0	0.0	-0.8	24.8	1.0
1955	5.0	1.0	-1.0	23.7	1.3

[1]Gross national product.
[2]Gross domestic product to 1953, then gross national product.
[3]Gross domestic product.
Data sources: Mitchell (2007), *Africa, Asia and Oceania*; Mitchell (2007), *Europe*; Mitchell (2007), *The Americas*; OEEC (1957); Reinhart and Rogoff (2010); United Nations, Statistical Yearbook, various years.

Table 1 continued

West Germany

	Real output[6] Annual % change	Inflation Annual % change	Budget deficit[5] as % of GDP	Government debt as % of GDP	Current account as % of GDP
1946	n/a	10.3	n/a	n/a	n/a
1947	n/a	6.7	n/a	n/a	n/a
1948	18.5	15.0	n/a	n/a	n/a
1949	116382.0	7.6	-3.4	n/a	0.0
1950	19.5	-7.1	-0.2	n/a	0.0
1951	11.5	8.7	-2.5	6.1	0.0
1952	7.9	2.0	-1.7	6.3	0.0
1953	8.1	-2.0	-0.7	7.3	0.0
1954	n/a	0.0	0.7	11.3	0.0
1955	n/a	2.0	1.4	11.1	0.0

Greece

	Real output[4] Annual % change	Inflation Annual % change	Budget deficit[7] as % of GDP	Government debt as % of GDP	Current account as % of GDP
1946	n/a	640.0	n/a	n/a	n/a
1947	31.7	18.9	n/a	n/a	n/a
1948	9.3	43.2	-7.6	n/a	-4.7
1949	n/a	14.3	-10.4	n/a	-0.3
1950	-1.5	8.3	-12.7	11.3	-1.7
1951	10.7	11.5	-11.5	15.0	-1.1
1952	-1.9	5.7	-7.2	18.3	0.1
1953	14.1	8.7	-3.0	15.9	2.8
1954	3.2	16.0	-2.9	13.7	-1.0
1955	13.0	5.2	-3.6	12.2	0.4

Iceland

	Real output Annual % change	Inflation Annual % change	Budget deficit as % of GDP	Government debt as % of GDP	Current account as % of GDP
1946	n/a	n/a	n/a	2.8	n/a
1947	n/a	n/a	n/a	5.8	n/a
1948	n/a	n/a	n/a	9.4	n/a
1949	n/a	n/a	n/a	12.8	n/a
1950	n/a	n/a	n/a	14.6	n/a
1951	n/a	n/a	n/a	14.4	n/a
1952	n/a	n/a	n/a	13.6	n/a
1953	n/a	n/a	n/a	10.7	n/a
1954	n/a	n/a	n/a	9.3	n/a
1955	n/a	n/a	n/a	8.6	n/a

Ireland

	Real output[1] Annual % change	Inflation Annual % change	Budget deficit[5] as % of GDP	Government debt as % of GDP	Current account as % of GDP
1946	n/a	-1.2	n/a	24.5	n/a
1947	n/a	10.2	-1.7	20.6	-9.0
1948	4.8	-1.1	-1.2	21.0	-8.0
1949	4.2	-56.4	-2.0	27.5	-3.7
1950	2.0	1.3	-4.8	37.7	-8.6
1951	2.0	0.0	-4.8	45.6	-16.0
1952	2.3	11.3	-7.7	47.4	-3.6
1953	2.6	10.1	-5.5	49.2	-3.0
1954	1.0	2.0	-6.4	56.0	-2.0
1955	2.0	2.0	-5.1	63.8	-7.0

[4]Gross domestic product.
[5]Fiscal year end March 31.
[6]Gross national product to 1950, then gross domestic product.

Table 1 continued

Italy

	Real output[8] Annual % change	Inflation Annual % change	Budget deficit[7] as % of GDP	Government debt as % of GDP	Current account as % of GDP
1946	-99.8	18.0	-9.6	44.8	-4.8
1947	15.7	62.1	-5.8	25.4	-5.9
1948	6.4	5.9	-7.6	29.5	0.6
1949	7.4	1.2	-5.6	32.1	1.3
1950	6.9	-1.1	-5.0	32.3	1.6
1951	6.4	9.3	-4.9	33.7	0.4
1952	3.9	4.3	-5.9	35.7	-2.0
1953	7.5	2.0	-4.6	36.6	-1.1
1954	4.1	3.0	-2.8	38.4	-0.4
1955	6.7	2.9	-2.8	38.1	-0.3

Netherlands

	Real output[4] Annual % change	Inflation Annual % change	Budget deficit as % of GDP	Government debt as % of GDP	Current account as % of GDP
1946	n/a	7.9	-2.3	223.0	n/a
1947	n/a	6.0	-2.4	214.0	n/a
1948	n/a	3.8	-7.1	175.9	-4.2
1949	4.2	7.9	2.3	162.4	-9.5
1950	6.1	7.3	0.8	141.0	0.4
1951	-2.2	13.6	2.1	114.9	1.8
1952	1.6	0.0	3.0	108.5	9.4
1953	8.7	0.0	0.8	99.3	6.3
1954	5.0	4.0	0.8	91.1	1.0
1955	8.5	1.0	-0.3	87.9	2.6

Norway

	Real output[4] Annual % change	Inflation Annual % change	Budget deficit[7] as % of GDP	Government debt as % of GDP	Current account as % of GDP
1946	10.0	2.5	-3.8	65.0	-4.9
1947	13.9	0.6	-4.7	53.1	-9.6
1948	6.9	-0.6	-0.4	45.5	-4.3
1949	2.5	0.0	-0.7	45.5	-4.1
1950	4.9	5.4	-0.9	31.5	1.5
1951	5.6	15.4	1.6	26.3	2.3
1952	3.5	8.9	2.1	23.8	-0.1
1953	4.2	2.0	1.3	26.0	-4.0
1954	4.9	4.0	-0.5	26.2	-4.8
1955	n/a	1.0	0.8	26.7	-3.7

Portugal

	Real output[1] Annual % change	Inflation Annual % change	Budget deficit as % of GDP	Government debt as % of GDP	Current account as % of GDP
1946	n/a	15.0	n/a	15.6	n/a
1947	n/a	3.0	-2.5	17.6	n/a
1948	3.8	-5.7	-3.2	18.4	-13.1
1949	2.0	1.0	-2.3	19.4	-7.3
1950	9.2	-2.0	-0.4	19.5	n/a
1951	1.3	1.0	0.1	18.2	3.2
1952	-0.2	0.0	0.3	17.5	-0.8
1953	5.7	1.0	0.2	17.3	1.9
1954	6.0	1.0	-0.2	20.3	2.1
1955	1.2	3.0	-0.7	19.7	-0.2

[7]Fiscal year end June 30.

[8]Gross national product to 1951, then gross domestic product.

Table 1 continued

Sweden

	Real output[4] Annual % change	Inflation Annual % change	Budget deficit[7] as % of GDP	Government debt as % of GDP	Current account as % of GDP
1946	4.9	0.7	-0.6	47.2	-0.5
1947	3.5	5.6	-0.9	43.3	-5.8
1948	4.5	1.3	0.3	39.8	-1.5
1949	5.4	1.3	-0.6	39.3	1.5
1950	5.2	1.3	-0.4	36.5	0.5
1951	2.9	16.5	-1.1	30.3	2.2
1952	1.7	7.6	-0.5	27.7	0.3
1953	3.2	1.0	-1.9	27.5	0.8
1954	6.0	1.0	-1.4	28.0	-0.3
1955	3.0	3.0	-1.6	27.8	-0.8

Turkey

	Real output[9] Annual % change	Inflation Annual % change	Budget deficit[10] as % of GDP	Government debt as % of GDP	Current account as % of GDP
1946	n/a	-2.7	n/a	27.2	n/a
1947	n/a	0.9	-0.6	26.9	-0.7
1948	20.9	0.0	-1.1	23.1	-2.1
1949	-10.3	9.3	-0.8	25.6	-1.3
1950	10.0	-3.4	n/a	23.7	0.5
1951	9.1	-1.8	-0.3	24.4	-1.0
1952	8.3	6.3	-1.7	20.8	-2.7
1953	0.0	3.4	-4.3	17.7	-0.9
1954	0.0	8.5	-2.8	14.7	-0.8
1955	0.0	9.7	-2.5	20.5	-1.2

United Kingdom

	Real output[4] Annual % change	Inflation Annual % change	Budget deficit[5] as % of GDP	Government debt as % of GDP	Current account as % of GDP
1946	-0.9	0.0	-235.8	237.1	-0.8
1947	-2.6	0.0	8.1	237.9	-2.4
1948	3.0	8.1	81.7	213.7	0.6
1949	3.2	2.6	-16.6	197.7	0.7
1950	3.7	2.5	-27.3	194.2	2.8
1951	3.6	9.9	27.9	175.2	-3.2
1952	0.0	9.0	-29.1	161.6	1.0
1953	4.6	3.1	-63.4	151.9	1.0
1954	3.8	2.0	-19.9	146.5	0.8
1955	3.2	3.9	-24.7	138.1	-0.9

United States

	Real output[1] Annual % change	Inflation Annual % change	Budget deficit[7] as % of GDP	Government debt as % of GDP	Current account as % of GDP
1946	-11.6	8.6	-1.0	121.3	2.6
1947	-1.1	14.4	-0.7	105.8	3.8
1948	4.2	7.5	0.0	93.8	0.8
1949	-0.5	-1.2	0.1	94.6	0.3
1950	8.7	1.2	0.0	87.6	-0.7
1951	8.1	7.6	0.1	75.2	0.1
1952	4.1	2.2	-0.1	72.3	0.0
1953	4.7	1.1	-0.1	70.1	-0.5
1954	-0.6	0.5	-0.1	71.3	-0.1
1955	7.1	-0.5	0.0	66.2	-0.1

[9]Gross national product to 1949, then gross domestic product.

[10]The data are reported for calendar years up to 1948. The value for 1949 captures a 14-month period from January 1949 to February 1950. From this point onward, each value refers to the 12-month period from March to the following February.

TABLE 2 MARSHALL PLAN PROCUREMENT AUTHORIZATIONS ($ MILLION)

	1948Q2	1948Q3	1948Q4	1949Q1	1949Q2	1949Q3	1949Q4	1950Q1	1950Q2	1950Q3	1950Q4	1951Q1	1951Q2	1951H2	1952H1	Total
Austria	38.6	76.0	97.9	18.6	42.9	54.9	38.9	37.1	37.6	7.9	28.1	35.8	46.4	72.3	43.7	676.7
Belgium/Luxembourg		21.8	117.1	55.9	66.2	105.5	79.3	26.5	17.8	16.0	9.6	14.2	16.6	-0.3	9.3	555.5
Denmark	9.8	33.4	47.9	11.9	23.0	26.9	16.1	20.1	19.7	4.3	14.3	11.9	18.1	8.8	5.2	271.4
France	206.1	267.4	477.5	133.8	228.4	192.4	191.8	141.4	171.3	33.6	89.8	77.9	233.4	49.6	211.8	2706.3
Western Germany	64.2	196.1	139.9	77.8	127.8	91.2	104.8	38.5	55.1	72.1	116.4	105.1	108.3	18.6	73.1	1389.0
of which:																
Bizone	53.1	165.8	118.0	47.6	105.0	77.9										567.4
French Zone	11.1	30.3	21.9	30.2	22.8	13.3										129.6
Greece	32.0	59.3	54.4	29.2	16.8	44.4	36.9	28.2	59.2	8.3	33.5	27.7	85.2	94.9	83.9	693.9
Iceland	2.3		3.1	0.4	2.5	1.1	1.8	-0.2	4.5	0.5	1.4	1.2	5.1	2.7	2.8	29.2
Ireland			51.6	36.2	-2.2	11.6	14.3	6.1	13.0	9.9	2.0	3.6	0.1	0.0	0.0	146.2
Italy	106.6	151.3	236.3	87.9	85.2	111.4	104.7	91.1	83.7	13.4	93.5	48.1	100.8	-2.6	163.0	1474.4
Netherlands	43.0	129.8	198.9	99.7	95.0	77.4	69.6	95.3	64.3	23.4	28.4	25.5	28.4	20.4	79.6	1078.7
Norway	5.8	32.6	29.6	14.4	18.1	28.1	29.1	14.8	23.1	6.8	8.2	8.1	17.9	4.2	12.7	253.5
Portugal								13.1	18.4	2.7	9.7	1.9	4.7	-0.8	0.8	50.5
Sweden	4.0		10.0	29.3	5.9	15.4	13.9	9.8	12.4	1.4	9.5	8.7	2.1	-2.9	-8.5	107.1
Trieste		2.3	3.2	2.8	4.5	3.1	3.3	0.8	3.4	2.5	1.8	-0.2	1.9	-0.5	-1.0	31.9
Turkey			1.7	26.8	5.3	20.3	11.9	16.5	21.0	-0.6	1.9	12.5	35.1	23.7	45.0	221.0
UK	226.1	221.8	645.5	222.1	298.2	283.2	329.5	165.0	170.7	93.4	49.1	-8.1	129.3	39.3	310.8	3175.9
EPU capital fund											350.0					350.0
Total	738.5	1191.8	2114.6	846.8	1017.6	1066.9	1045.9	704.1	775.2	295.6	847.2	373.9	833.4	327.4	1032.3	13211.2
Cumulative total	738.5	1930.3	4044.9	4891.7	5909.3	6976.2	8022.1	8726.2	9501.4	9797.0	10644.2	11018.1	11851.5	12178.9	13211.2	

Note: Switzerland received only an EPU quota.

Data sources: Quarterly reports to Congress of the Economic Cooperation Administration, June 30, 1948, to June 30, 1951 (First Report to Congress of the Economic Cooperation Administration for the Quarter Ended June 30, 1948, to Thirteenth Report to Congress of the Economic Cooperation Administration for the Quarter Ended June 30, 1951). First Report to Congress on the Mutual Security Program, 1951. Second Report to Congress on the Mutual Security Program, 1952.

TABLE 3 MARSHALL PLAN CUMULATIVE COUNTERPART FUND BALANCES ($ MILLION)

	Austria			Belgium/Luxembourg		
	Total Deposits	Authorized releases	Withdrawals	Total Deposits	Authorized releases	Withdrawals
1948Q3	32.9			0.4		
1948Q4	67.5	12.5	12.5	3		
1949Q1	143.8	12.5	12.5	3		
1949Q2	227.9	40	40	2.9		
1949Q3	276.2	109.4	106.8	2.8		
1949Q4	269.4	169	169	2.7		
1950Q1	317.9	187.4	169	2.7		
1950Q2	352.3	189.5	184.2	2.6	2.2	2.1
1950Q3	412.6	250.4	187.8	2.6	2.2	2.1
1950Q4	415.4	277.9	243.3	2.6	2.2	2.1
1951Q1	460	310.6	277.9	2.6	2.2	2.2
1951Q2	543.7	419.6	413.5	2.6	2.2	2.1

	Denmark			France		
	Total Deposits	Authorized releases	Withdrawals	Total Deposits	Authorized releases	Withdrawals
1948Q3	9.2			161.894	17.999	
1948Q4	28.1			367.9	297.5	297.5
1949Q1	32.8	<0.05		540.7	288.7	288.7
1949Q2	51.8	<0.05		738.1	752.9	675
1949Q3	81	<0.05		1152.5	1132.6	1132.6
1949Q4	84	<0.05		1301.9	1238.6	1238.6
1950Q1	107.3	<0.05		1476.9	1353.4	1353.4
1950Q2	125.1	0.1		1613.8	1552.2	1522.2
1950Q3	141	118.8	118.8	1751.7	1665.2	1665.2
1950Q4	151.4	118.8	118.8	1862.2	1756.7	1756.7
1951Q1	167	118.8	118.8	1964.1	1756.3	1765.3
1951Q2	187.1	118.9	118.8	2075	2277.8	2277.8

	West Germany			Greece		
	Total Deposits	Authorized releases	Withdrawals	Total Deposits	Authorized releases	Withdrawals
1948Q3				24.415	81.011	10.049
1948Q4	64			51.5	104.3	28.5
1949Q1	128.7	0.8	0.8	88.4	111.5	63.9
1949Q2	263.3	1.2	1.2	135.9	130	102.9
1949Q3	457.3	152	152	201.6	139.6	118.2
1949Q4	465.9	337.5	172.7	250.9	145.8	129.5
1950Q1	574.4	375.6	373	288.2	219	143.4
1950Q2	707.1	561.1	473	347.7	229	198.1
1950Q3	739.7	645.5	645.5	417.9	256	242.2
1950Q4	812.6	723.2	720.6	498.5	276.1	271.4
1951Q1	886.6	806.7	805.7	552.9	288.2	284.6
1951Q2	980.5	842.5	841.5	625.4	330.4	311.5

Note: no counterpart fund was established in Sweden or Switzerland.
Data sources: ECA (1948–1951), *Reports to Congress*, June 1948–June 1951.

Table 3 continued

	Iceland			Indonesia		
	Total Deposits	Authorized releases	Withdrawals	Total Deposits	Authorized releases	Withdrawals
1948Q3						
1948Q4						
1949Q1						
1949Q2						
1949Q3						
1949Q4	0.9					
1950Q1	1.9					
1950Q2	2.5					
1950Q3	3.9					
1950Q4	6.5			46.3		
1951Q1	8.8			45.9		
1951Q2	11.1	0.9	0.9	47.1		

	Ireland			Italy		
	Total Deposits	Authorized releases	Withdrawals	Total Deposits	Authorized releases	Withdrawals
1948Q3				56.903		
1948Q4				108.9	434.8	
1949Q1				163.9	434.8	
1949Q2				256.5	490.4	
1949Q3				369	186.4	24
1949Q4	3			389.7	190.3	56
1950Q1	3			469.6	206.5	80.1
1950Q2	3			509.8	265.7	150.5
1950Q3	3			579	311.6	265.7
1950Q4	3			634.1	420.5	420.5
1951Q1	6			702.9	457.9	457.9
1951Q2	6.9			783.8	764.7	598.8

	Netherlands			Norway		
	Total Deposits	Authorized releases	Withdrawals	Total Deposits	Authorized releases	Withdrawals
1948Q3	40.181			9.38		
1948Q4	71.1			29.7		
1949Q1	94.7			45	22.2	22.2
1949Q2	168.6	90.5		65.4	42.3	
1949Q3	258.4	90.5	90.5	80.6	73.5	73.5
1949Q4	315.8	90.5	90.5	119.8	73.5	73.5
1950Q1	369.4	162.9	162.9	163.7	73.5	73.5
1950Q2	484.9	162.9	162.9	201.7	73.5	73.5
1950Q3	632.2	178.2	178.2	220.9	73.5	73.5
1950Q4	622.4	244	244	262.6	200.9	200.9
1951Q1	661.8	263.7	263.7	305.1	200.9	200.9
1951Q2	713.4	270.9	270.9	319.7	200.9	200.9

Table 3 continued

	Portugal			Trieste		
	Total Deposits	Authorized releases	Withdrawals	Total Deposits	Authorized releases	Withdrawals
1948Q3				2.7	11.1	
1948Q4				5.6	11.1	3
1949Q1				7.8	12.9	6.8
1949Q2				9.3	12.9	9.3
1949Q3				13.4	12.9	9.8
1949Q4	4.1			14.6	13.9	13.7
1950Q1	4.1			16	15.2	15
1950Q2	4.1			19.8	17.6	17.5
1950Q3	17.6			22.2	18.8	18.3
1950Q4	17.6	7	6.3	23.7	20.4	20.3
1951Q1	17.6	11.5	8.2	26.9	23.2	22.9
1951Q2	17.6	15.4	13.9	29.8	26.4	26.1

	Turkey			UK		
	Total Deposits	Authorized releases	Withdrawals	Total Deposits	Authorized releases	Withdrawals
1948Q3				216.039	201.9	
1948Q4				361.6	330.9	330.9
1949Q1				484.4	435	433.2
1949Q2				628.6	576.1	574.4
1949Q3				805.5	742.3	739.6
1949Q4	8.7			1110.2	786.3	784.4
1950Q1	18.6			1296	787.2	787.2
1950Q2	49.6			1440.4	787.2	787.2
1950Q3	74.2			1574.7	787.2	787.2
1950Q4	71.5	18.7	18.7	1608.8	1532	1532
1951Q1	71.5	32.2	32.2	1667.2	1557.2	1557.2
1951Q2	71.5	34.2	34.2	1756.9	1646.8	1646.8

	Total		
	Total Deposits	Authorized releases	Withdrawals
1948Q3	554.1	312.043	10.0
1948Q4	1158.9	1191.1	672.4
1949Q1	1733.2	1318.4	828.1
1949Q2	2548.3	2136.3	1445.1
1949Q3	3698.3	2639.2	2447
1949Q4	4341.6	3045.4	2727.9
1950Q1	5110	3380.7	3157.5
1950Q2	5864.4	3811	3571.2
1950Q3	6593.2	4307.4	4184.7
1950Q4	7039.2	5598.4	5555.6
1951Q1	7556.9	5838.4	5797.4
1951Q2	8172.1	6951.6	6757.7

APPENDIX D

MAPS

MAP 1

THE GEOSTRATEGIC IMPORTANCE OF RUSSIA

Map of the 'natural seats of power', Halford J. Mackinder (1904) 'The
Geographical Pivot of History', *Geographical Journal*

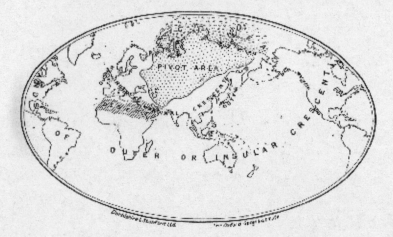

MAP 2

DIVIDED GERMANY AND BERLIN, 1945

APPENDIX D

MAP 3

POLITICAL MAP OF EUROPE, 1943

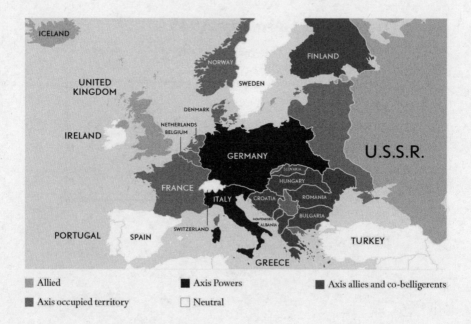

▨ Allied	■ Axis Powers	▨ Axis allies and co-belligerents
■ Axis occupied territory	□ Neutral	

MAP 4

POLITICAL MAP OF EUROPE, 1949

| | Marshall Plan | | NATO | | Marshall Plan & NATO | | Comecon | | Comecon & Cominform |

*Joins NATO in 1955

** Expelled from Cominform in 1948

APPENDIX D

MAP 5

INVERTED VIEW OF RUSSIA'S WESTERN BORDER

RUSSIAN PERSPECTIVE

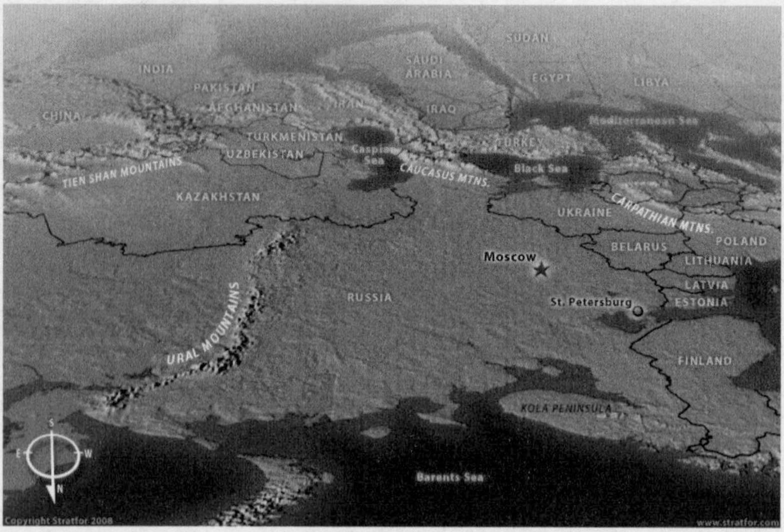

REFERENCES

ARCHIVAL MATERIAL

Archives Nationales, Paris, France.
 Private Archives of M. Georges Bidault
Arhiv Jugoslavije, Belgrade, Serbia.
Arkhiv vneshnei politiki Rossiiskoi Federatsii [AVP RF], Moscow, Russia.
Bundesarchiv, Koblenz, Germany.
Clemson University Library, Clemson, South Carolina.
 James F. Byrnes Papers
George C. Marshall Foundation, Lexington, Virginia.
Harry S. Truman Library and Museum, Independence, Missouri.
 Dean G. Acheson Papers
 Eben A. Ayers Papers
 Will L. Clayton Papers
 George M. Elsey Papers
 Joseph M. Jones Papers
 Charles P. Kindleberger Papers

Frank McNaughton Papers

J. Anthony Panuch Papers

Harry B. Price Papers

Charles W. Thayer Papers

Harry S. Truman Papers

Oral History Interviews

Library of Congress, Washington, DC.

Charles E. Bohlen Papers

Joseph E. Davies Papers

Laurence A. Steinhardt Papers

National Archives and Records Administration, College Park, Maryland.

Record Group 43

Record Group 59

Record Group 226

Record Group 260

Record Group 263

Record Group 335

Record Group 341

Record Group 469

Record Group 519

New York Public Library, New York, New York.

George Kennan Papers

Rossiiskii gosudarstvennyi arkhiv sotsialno-politicheskoi istorii [RGASPI], Moscow, Russia.

Seeley G. Mudd Manuscript Library, Princeton University, Princeton, New Jersey.

James A. Baker III Papers

John Foster Dulles Oral History Collection

George F. Kennan Papers

Sterling Memorial Library, Yale University, New Haven, Connecticut

Dean G. Acheson Papers

United Kingdom National Archives [UKNA], Kew, United Kingdom.

Cabinet Memoranda, 1945–1978

Foreign Office

Treasury Papers

PUBLISHED PRIMARY SOURCES AND DATABASES

Auswärtiges Amt. *Aussenpolitik der Bundesrepublik Deutschland: Dokumente von 1949 bis 1994*. Cologne: Verlag Wissenschaft und Politik, 1995.

Banac, Ivo (ed.). *The Diary of Georgi Dimitrov, 1933–1949*. New Haven: Yale University Press, 2003.

Bland, Larry I. (ed.). *George C. Marshall: Interviews and Reminiscences for Forrest C. Pogue.* Lexington, VA: George C. Marshall Foundation, 1991.

Bland, Larry I., and Mark A. Stoler (eds.). *The Papers of George Catlett Marshall, Vol. VI: "The Whole World Hangs in the Balance."* Baltimore: Johns Hopkins University Press, 2013.

Brookings Institution. *Administration of United States Aid for a European Recovery Program: Report to the Committee on Foreign Relations.* Washington, DC: U.S. Government Printing Office, January 1948.

Carlyle, Margaret (ed.). *Documents on International Affairs, 1947–1948.* London: Oxford University Press, 1952.

Committee of European Economic Co-operation [CEEC]. *General Report, Vol. I.* Paris: Office of Public Affairs, September 1947.

Congressional Quarterly. "Aid to Greece and Turkey." In *CQ Almanac 1947*, third edition. Washington, DC, 1948. http://library.cqpress.com/cqalmanac/cqal47-893-29543-1397927.

Congressional Record. Washington, DC: U.S. Government Printing Office.

Correlates of War Project. "National Material Capabilities dataset (v4.0)." June 2010.

Department of State Bulletin, 1939–1989. Washington, DC: U.S. Government Printing Office.

Economic Cooperation Administration. *Reports to Congress.* Washington, DC: U.S. Government Printing Office, 1948–1951.

Economic Cooperation Administration. *Italy: Country Study.* Washington, DC: U.S. Government Printing Office, 1949.

Food and Agriculture Organization of the United Nations. *World Outlook and State of Food and Agriculture, 1950.* Washington, DC: 1950.

Food and Agriculture Organization of the United Nations. *Food and Agriculture: Review and Outlook, 1952.* Rome: United Nations, 1952.

Foreign Relations of the United States [FRUS]. Washington, DC: U.S. Government Printing Office.

Freedman, Lawrence (ed.). *Europe Transformed: Documents on the End of the Cold War—Key Treaties, Agreements, Statements, and Speeches.* New York: St. Martin's, 1990.

French Yellow Book: Documents of the Conference of Foreign Ministers of France, the United Kingdom, and the U.S.S.R. Held in Paris from the 27th June to the 3rd July, 1947. New York: Hutchinson, 1947.

Government of the Russian Federation. "The Foreign Policy Concept of the Russian Federation, Approved by the President of the Russian Federation, V. Putin, June 28, 2000." 2000.

Government of the Russian Federation. "Munich Security Conference: Dmitry Medvedev's Speech at the Panel Discussion." February 13, 2016. http://government.ru/en/news/21784/.

Government of the Russian Federation. "Dmitry Medvedev's Interview with *Time* Magazine." *Government.ru.* February 15, 2016. http://government.ru/en/news/21790/.

House Committee on Foreign Affairs. *Emergency Foreign Aid: Hearings Before the Committee on Foreign Affairs.* 80th Congress, 1st Session. Washington, DC: U.S. Government Printing Office, 1947.

House Committee on Foreign Affairs. *The Strategy and Tactics of World Communism: Report [of] Subcommittee No. 5, National and International Movements.* Washington, DC: U.S. Government Printing Office, 1948.

House Committee on Foreign Affairs. *United States Foreign Policy for a Post-War Recovery Program: Hearings Before the Committee on Foreign Affairs.* 80th Congress, 1st and 2nd Sessions. Washington, DC: U.S. Government Printing Office, 1948.

House of Commons Debates. Hansard Archives. http://hansard.millbanksystems.com/index.html.

House Select Committee on Foreign Aid. *Final Report on Foreign Aid.* Washington, DC: May 1948.

International Bank for Reconstruction and Development. *Second Annual Report: 1946–1947.* Washington, DC: 1947.

International Monetary Fund. *Annual Report for the Fiscal Year Ending June 30, 1947.* Washington, DC, 1947.

Legislative History of the Assistance to Greece and Turkey, P.L. 80-75. Vols. I and II. 80th Congress, 1st Session. Washington, DC: Covington & Burling, 1947.

Legislative History of the Foreign Aid Act of 1947, P.L. 80-389. Vols. I and II. 80th Congress, 1st Session. Washington, DC: Covington & Burling, 1947.

Legislative History of the Foreign Assistance Act of 1948, P.L. 80-472. 80th Congress, 2nd Session. Washington, DC: Covington & Burling, 1948.

Millis, Walter (ed.). *The Forrestal Diaries.* New York: Viking, 1951.

Mitchell, Brian R. *International Historical Statistics: Africa, Asia and Oceania, 1750–2005.* Sixth edition. New York: Palgrave Macmillan, 2007.

Mitchell, Brian R. *International Historical Statistics: Europe, 1750–2005.* Sixth edition. New York: Palgrave Macmillan, 2007.

Mitchell, Brian R. *International Historical Statistics: The Americas, 1750–2005.* Sixth edition. New York: Palgrave Macmillan, 2007.

Mutual Security Agency. *Reports to Congress on the Mutual Security Program.* Washington, DC: U.S. Government Printing Office, 1951–1952.

Mutual Security Agency. *Second Report to Congress on the Mutual Security Program: Supplement.* Washington, DC: U.S. Government Printing Office, 1952.

Němeček, Jan (ed.). *Československo-sovětské vztahy v diplomatických jednáních, 1939–1945.* Prague: Státní Ústřední Archiv, 1999.

Nicolson, Harold, with Nigel Nicolson (ed.). *Harold Nicolson: Diaries and Letters, 1945–1962.* London: William Collins Sons, 1968.

Norwich, John Julius (ed.). *The Duff Cooper Diaries, 1915–51.* London: Weidenfeld & Nicolson, 2005.

Organisation for European Economic Co-operation [OEEC]. *Statistics of National Product and Expenditure, No. 2, 1938 and 1947 to 1955.* Paris, 1957.

President's Committee on Foreign Aid. *European Recovery and American Aid.* Washington, DC: U.S. Government Printing Office, November 1947.

Public Papers of the Presidents of the United States. Washington, DC: U.S. Government Printing Office.

Reinhart, Carmen M. "Exchange Rates (Official and Parallel)." Data set. http://www.carmenreinhart.com/data/browse-by-topic/.

Rossiiskii faktor v Vostochnoi Evrope 1944–1953. Tom 1, 1944–1948 / Redaktsionnaiia kollegia toma: T. V. Volokitina (otv. redactor), G. P. Murashko, O. V. Naumov, A. F. Noskova, T. V. Tsarevakaiia. Moskva: ROSSPEN, 1999 (*The Soviet Factor in Eastern Europe, 1944–1953, Vol. I, 1944–1948* / The volume's editorial board: T. V. Volokitina [editor in chief], G. P. Murashko, O. V. Naumov, A. F. Noskova, T. V. Tsarevakaiia. Moscow: ROSSPEN, 1999.)

Senate Committee on Foreign Relations. *European Recovery Program: Hearings Before the Committee on Foreign Relations.* 80th Congress, 2nd Session. Washington, DC: U.S. Government Printing Office, 1948.

Senate Committee on Foreign Relations. *Extension of European Recovery: Hearings Before the Committee on Foreign Relations.* 81st Congress, 2nd Session. Washington, DC: U.S. Government Printing Office, 1949.

Senate Committee on Foreign Relations. *Documents on Germany, 1944–1959: Background Documents on Germany, 1944–1959, and a Chronology of Political Developments Affecting Berlin, 1945–1956.* Washington, DC: U.S. Government Printing Office, 1959.

Senate Committee on Foreign Relations. *Legislative Origins of the Truman Doctrine: Hearings Held in Executive Session Before the Committee on Foreign Relations.* 80th Congress, 1st Session. Washington, DC: U.S. Government Printing Office, 1973.

Senate Committee on Foreign Relations. *The Debate on NATO Enlargement: Hearings Before the Committee on Foreign Relations.* 105th Congress, 1st Session. Washington, DC: U.S. Government Printing Office, 1998.

Smith, Jean Edward (ed.). *The Papers of General Lucius D. Clay: Germany 1945–1949.* Two volumes. Bloomington: Indiana University Press, 1974.

Sovetso-amerikanskie otnosheniia 1945–1948. Dokumenty. Moskva: Materik, 2004. (*Soviet-American Relations, 1945–1948. Documents.* Moscow: Materik, 2004.)

SSSR i gernamskii vopros 1941–1949: dokumenty iz arkhiva vneshnei politiki Rossiiskoi Federatsii. T. III: 6 oktiabria 1946 g.–15 ijunia 1948 g. Sost. G. P. Kynin i J. Laufer. Moskva: Mezhdunarodnye otnosheniia, 2003 (*The USSR and the German Question, 1941–1949: The Documents from the Archive of the Foreign Policy of the Russian Federation, Vol. III: October 6 1946–June 15, 1948.* Ed. G. P. Kynin and J. Laufer. Moscow: International Relations, 2003.)

SSSR i gernamskii vopros 1941–1949: dokumenty iz rossiiskikh arkhivov. T. IV: 18 ijunia 1948 g.–5 nojabrja 1949 g. Moskva: Mezhdunarodnye otnosheniia, 2012. (*The USSR and the German Question, 1941–1949: The Documents from the Russian Archives, Vol. IV: June 18, 1948–November 5, 1949.* Moscow: International Relations, 2012.)

State Department. "Austrian State Treaty, 1955." https://2001-2009.state.gov/r/pa/ho/time/lw/107185.htm.

The State Department Policy Planning Staff Papers, 1947–1949. New York: Garland, 1983.

Statistical Office of the United Nations. *Statistical Yearbook.* New York: United Nations.

United Nations Security Council. *Official Records, 3rd Year.* Paris: 1948.

USAID. "U.S. Economic and Miliary Assistance Fiscal Years 1946–2014." *U.S. Overseas Loans and Grants* [Greenbook]. https://eads.usaid.gov/gbk/.

U.S. Atomic Energy Commission. *In the Matter of J. Robert Oppenheimer: Transcript of Hearing Before Personnel Security Board and Texts of Principal Documents and Letters.* Cambridge: MIT Press, 1954 [1970].

Vandenberg, Arthur H., Jr. (ed.). *The Private Papers of Senator Vandenberg.* Boston: Houghton Mifflin, 1952.

Zajavlenie ministrov inostrannykh del SSSR, Albanii, Bolgarii, Chekhoslovakii, Jugoslavii, Pol'shi, Rumynii i Vengrii po povodu reshenij londonskogo soveshchanija o Germanii. Soveshchanie ministrov inostrannykh del vos'mi gosudarstv v Varshave, 23–24 ijunja, 1948 goda. OGIZ-Gospolitizdat, 1948. (*Declaration of the Ministers of Foreign Affairs of the USSR, Albania, Bulgaria, Czechoslovakia, Yugoslavia, Poland, Romania and Hungary on the Decisions of the London Conference on Germany.* The Conference of Foreign Ministers of Eight Nations in Warsaw, June 23–24, 1948. OGIZ-Gospolitizdat, 1948.)

BOOKS AND THESES

Abelshauser, Werner. "American Aid and West German Recovery: A Macroeconomic Perspective." In *The Marshall Plan and Germany: West German Development Within the Framework of the European Recovery Program*, edited by Charles S. Maier, with the assistance of Günter Bischof. New York: Berg, 1991.

Abrams, Bradley F. "The Marshall Plan and Czechoslovak Democracy: Elements of Interdependency." In *The Marshall Plan: Fifty Years After*, edited by Martin A. Schain. London: Palgrave Macmillan, 2001.

Acacia, John. *Clark Clifford: The Wise Man of Washington*. Lexington: University Press of Kentucky, 2009.

Acheson, Dean G. *Present at the Creation: My Years in the State Department*. New York: W. W. Norton, 1969.

Adenauer, Konrad. *Memoirs*. Chicago: Henry Regnery, 1965.

Adibekov, G. M., E. N. Shakhnazarov, K. K. Shirinya. *Orginizatsionnaya Struktura Kominterna. 1919–1943*. Moskva: ROSSPEN, 1997. (*Organization Structure of Comintern, 1919–1943*. Moscow: ROSSPEN, 1997.)

Alliluyeva, Svetlana. *Only One Year*. Translated by Paul Chavchavadze. New York: Harper & Row, 1969.

Annan, Noel. *Changing Enemies: The Defeat and Regeneration of Germany*. Ithaca, NY: Cornell University Press, 1997.

Arkes, Hadley. *Bureaucracy, the Marshall Plan, and the National Interest*. Princeton: Princeton University Press, 1972.

Asmus, Ronald D. *Opening NATO's Door: How the Alliance Remade Itself for a New Era*. New York: Columbia University Press, 2002.

Backer, John H. *Winds of History: The German Years of Lucius Dubignon Clay*. New York: Van Nostrand, 1983.

Bark, Dennis L., and David Gress. *A History of West Germany: From Shadow to Substance, 1945–1963*. Oxford: Blackwell, 1989.

Barnet, Richard. *Alliance*. New York: Simon & Schuster, 1985.

Barney, Timothy. *Mapping the Cold War: Cartography and the Framing of America's International Power*. Chapel Hill: University of North Carolina Press, 2015.

Barysch, Katinka. "EU-Russia Economic Relations." In *Russia and the European Union: Prospects for a New Relationship*, edited by Oksana Antonenko and Kathryn Pinnick. London: Routledge, 2005.

Beevor, Antony, and Artemis Cooper. *Paris After the Liberation: 1944–1949*. New York: Penguin, 1994 [2004].

Behrman, Greg. *The Most Noble Adventure*. New York: Free Press, 2007.

Beisner, Robert L. *Dean Acheson: A Life in the Cold War*. Oxford: Oxford University Press, 2006.

Berger, Helge, and Albrecht Ritschl. "Germany and the Political Economy of the Marshall Plan, 1947–52." In *Europe's Postwar Recovery*, edited by Barry Eichengreen. Cambridge: Cambridge University Press, 1995.

Berkowitz, Morton, P. G. Bock, and Vincent J. Fuccillo. "The Berlin Airlift, 1948." In *The Politics of American Foreign Policy: The Social Context of Decisions*. Englewood Cliffs, NJ: Prentice Hall, 1977.

Beschloss, Michael. *The Conquerors: Roosevelt, Truman and the Destruction of Hitler's Germany, 1941–1945*. New York: Simon & Schuster, 2002.

Bew, John. *Citizen Clem: A Biography of Attlee*. London: Quercus, 2016.

Bidault, Georges. *Resistance: The Political Autobiography of Georges Bidault*. Translated by Marianne Sinclair. New York: Frederick A. Praeger, 1965 [1967].

Bideleux, Robert, and Ian Jeffries. *A History of Eastern Europe: Crisis and Change*. London: Routledge, 1998.

Bidwell, Robin L. *Currency Conversion Tables: A Hundred Years of Change*. London: Rex Collings, 1970.

Bissell, Richard Jr. *Reflections of a Cold Warrior: From Yalta to the Bay of Pigs*. New Haven: Yale University Press, 1996.

Blum, John Morton. *From the Morgenthau Diaries, Vol. III: Years of War, 1941–1945*. Boston: Houghton Mifflin, 1967.

Bohlen, Charles E. *The Transformation of American Foreign Policy*. New York: W. W. Norton, 1969.

———. *Witness to History: 1929–1969*. New York: W. W. Norton, 1973.

Bohlin, Jan. "From Appreciation to Depreciation—The Exchange Rate of the Swedish Krona, 1913–2008." In *Historical Monetary Statistics of Sweden, Vol. I: Exchange Rates, Prices, and Wages, 1277–2008*, edited by Rodney Edvinsson, Tor Jacobson, and Daniel Waldenström. Stockholm: Sveriges Riksbank, 2010.

Boia, Lucian. *Romania: Borderland of Europe*. Translated by James Christian Brown. London: Reaktion, 2001.

Booker, M. Keith. "Stalin, Joseph Vissarionovich (1879–1953)." *Encyclopedia of Literature and Politics, Vol. III: S–Z*. Westport, CT: Greenwood, 2005.

Bordachev, Timofei. "Russia's European Problem: Eastward Enlargement of the EU and Moscow's Policy, 1993–2003." In *Russia and the European Union: Prospects for a New Relationship*, edited by Oksana Antonenko and Kathryn Pinnick. London: Routledge, 2005.

Boterbloem, Kees. *Life and Times of Andrei Zhdanov, 1896–1948*. Montreal: McGill-Queens Press, 2004.

Brookshire, Jerry H. *Clement Attlee*. Manchester: Manchester University Press, 1995.

Brotton, Jerry. *A History of the World in Twelve Maps*. New York: Penguin, 2012.

Brown, William Adams, and Redvers Opie. *American Foreign Assistance*. Washington, DC: The Brookings Institution, 1953.

Buffet, Cyril. *Mourir pour Berlin: la France et l'Allemagne, 1945–1949*. Paris: Armand Colin, 1991.

Bush, George H. W., and Brent Scowcroft. *A World Transformed.* New York: Alfred A. Knopf, 1998.

Butler, L. J. *Britain and Empire: Adjusting to the Post-Imperial World.* London: I. B. Tauris, 2002.

Byrnes, James F. *Speaking Frankly.* New York: Harper & Brothers, 1947.

Buchanan, Patrick J. *A Republic, Not an Empire: Reclaiming America's Destiny.* Washington, DC: Regnery, 1999.

Buchanan, Tom. *Europe's Troubled Peace: 1945 to the Present.* Oxford: John Wiley & Sons, 2006 [2012].

Buchheim, Christoph. "The Establishment of the Bank Deutscher Länder and the West German Currency Reform." In *Fifty Years of the Deutsche Mark,* edited by Deutsche Bundesbank. Oxford: Oxford University Press, 1999.

Buhite, Russell D. *Decision at Yalta: An Appraisal of Summitry Diplomacy.* Wilmington, DE: Scholarly Resources, 1986.

Bullock, Alan. *Ernest Bevin: Foreign Secretary, 1945–1951.* London: Heinemann, 1983.

Burnham, Peter. *The Political Economy of Postwar Reconstruction.* New York: St. Martin's, 1990.

Cairncross, Alec. *The Price of War.* New York: Basil Blackwell, 1986.

Calvocoressi, Peter, assisted by Sheila Harden. *Survey of International Affairs, 1947–1948.* New York: Oxford University Press, 1952.

Campbell, John C. *The U.S. in World Affairs, 1945–1947.* New York: Harper & Brothers (published for the Council on Foreign Relations), 1947.

Carlin, Wendy. "Economic Reconstruction in Western Germany, 1945–55: The Displacement of 'Vegetative Control.'" In *Reconstruction in Post-War Germany: British Occupation Policy and the Western Zones,* edited by Ian D. Turner. New York: St. Martin's, 1989.

Carlisle, Rodney. *Encyclopedia of Intelligence and Counterintelligence.* New York: Routledge; 2015.

Casella, Alessandra, and Barry Eichengreen. "Halting Inflation in Italy and France After the Second World War." In *Monetary Regimes in Transition,* edited by Michael D. Bordo and Forrest Capie. Cambridge: Cambridge University Press, 1993.

Cecil, Robert. *A Divided Life: A Personal Portrait of the Spy Donald Maclean.* New York: William Morrow, 1989.

Chace, James. *Acheson: The Secretary of State Who Created the American World.* New York: Simon & Schuster, 1998.

Cho, Soon Sung. *Korea in World Politics, 1940–1950: An Evaluation of American Responsibility.* Berkeley: University of California Press, 1967.

Chuev, Felix, with Albert Resis (ed.). *Molotov Remembers: Inside Kremlin Politics, Conversations with Felix Chuev.* Chicago: Ivan R. Dee, 1993.

Churchill, Winston S. *The Second World War, Vol. I: The Gathering Storm.* New York: Houghton Mifflin, 1948.

———. *The Second World War, Vol. V: Closing the Ring.* New York: Houghton Mifflin, 1951.

———. *The Second World War, Vol. VI: Triumph and Tragedy.* New York: Houghton Mifflin, 1953.

Clay, Lucius D. *Decision in Germany.* New York: Doubleday, 1950.

Clemens, Diane Shaver. *Yalta.* Oxford: Oxford University Press, 1970.

Conquest, Robert. *The Great Terror.* Paperback edition. New York: Oxford University Press, 1991.

Cook, Bernard. "Organization for European Cooperation (OEEC)." In *Europe Since 1945: An Encyclopedia, Vol. II,* edited by Cook. New York: Garland, 2001.

Crafts, Nicholas. " 'You've Never Had It So Good?': British Economic Policy and Performance, 1945–60." In *Europe's Postwar Recovery,* edited by Barry Eichengreen. Cambridge: Cambridge University Press, 1995.

Cray, Ed. *General of the Army: George C. Marshall, Soldier and Statesman.* New York: W. W. Norton, 1990 [2000].

Crowder, Richard. *Aftermath: The Makers of the Postwar World.* London: I. B. Tauris, 2015.

Dennis, Mike. *The Rise and Fall of the German Democratic Republic, 1945–1990.* Harlow, UK: Pearson Education, 2000.

Di Biagio, Anna. "Establishment of the Cominform." In *The Cominform: Minutes of the Three Conferences 1947/1948/1949.* Milan: Fondazione Feltrinelli, 1994.

Dietrich, John. *The Morgenthau Plan: Soviet Influence on American Postwar Policy.* New York: Algora, 2002.

———. *Conversations with Stalin.* Translated by Michael B. Petrovich. New York: Harcourt Brace, 1962.

Djilas, Milovan. *Vlast.* [*Power.*] London: Nasa Rec, 1983.

Dobney, Frank. *Selected Papers of Will Clayton.* Baltimore: Johns Hopkins University Press, 1971.

Donovan, Robert L. *Conflict and Crisis: The Presidency of Harry S. Truman, 1945–1948.* New York: W. W. Norton, 1977.

Drtina, Prokop. *Ceskoslovensko, Muj Osud.* Prague: Melantrich, 1982.

Duchene, François. *Jean Monnet: The First Statesman of Independence.* New York: W. W. Norton, 1994.

Dunbabin, J. P. D. *The Cold War: The Great Powers and Their Allies.* Abingdon, UK: Routledge, 1994 [2013].

Eden, Anthony. *The Reckoning: The Memoirs of Anthony Eden, Earl of Avon.* New York: Houghton Mifflin, 1965.

Eichengreen, Barry. *Globalizing Capital: A History of the International Monetary System.* Princeton: Princeton University Press, 1996.

Erhard, Ludwig. *Deutschlands Rückkehr zum Weltmarkt.* Düsseldorf: Econ-Verlag GmbH, 1953.

Esposito, Chiarella. *America's Feeble Weapon: Funding the Marshall Plan in France and Italy, 1948–1950.* Westport, CT: Greenwood, 1994.

Etzold, Thomas, and John Lewis Gaddis (eds.). *Containment: Documents on American Policy and Strategy, 1945–1950.* New York: Columbia University Press, 1978.

Feierabend, Ladislav Karel. *Politické Vzpomínky III.* [*Political Memories III.*] Brno, Czech Republic: Atlantis, 1996.

Feigel, Lara. *The Bitter Taste of Victory: Life, Love, and Art in the Ruins of the Reich.* New York: Bloomsbury, 2016.

Fossedal, Gregory A. *Our Finest Hour: Will Clayton, the Marshall Plan, and the Triumph of Democracy.* Stanford, CA: Hoover Institution Press, 1993.

Frank, Mario. *Walter Ulbricht: Eine Deutsche Biographie.* Berlin: 2001.

Furlong, Paul. "The Italian Political System in 2001: Radical Change and Work in Progress." In *The Italian General Election of 2001: Berlusconi's Victory,* edited by James Newell. Manchester: Manchester University Press, 2002.

Fursdon, Edward. *The European Defense Community: A History.* London: Macmillan, 1980.

Gaddis, John Lewis. *Strategies of Containment: A Critical Appraisal of American National Security Policy During the Cold War.* Revised and expanded edition. New York: Oxford University Press, 1982 [2005].

———. *George F. Kennan: An American Life.* New York: Penguin, 2011.

Gallup, George H. (ed.). *The Gallup Poll: Public Opinion, 1935–1971, Vol. I: 1935–1948.* New York: Random House, 1972.

Garvy, George. *Money, Banking, and Credit in Eastern Europe.* New York: Federal Reserve Bank of New York, 1966.

Gerber, David. *Global Competition: Law, Markets, and Globalization.* Oxford: Oxford University Press, 2012.

Gibianski, Leonid. "The 1948 Soviet-Yugoslav Conflict and the Formation of the 'Socialist Camp' Model." In *The Soviet Union in Eastern Europe, 1945–89,* edited by Odd Arne Westad, Sven Holtsmark, and Iver B. Neumann. London: St. Martin's, 1994.

Giersch, Herbert, Karl-Heinz Paqué, and Holger Schmieding. "Openness, Wage Restraint, and Macroeconomic Stability: West Germany's Road to Prosperity, 1948–1959." In *Postwar Economic Reconstruction and Lessons for the East Today,* edited by Rudiger Dornbusch, Wilhelm Nölling, and Richard Layard. Cambridge: MIT Press, 1993.

Gimbel, John. *The American Occupation of Germany: Politics and the Military, 1945–1949.* Stanford, CA: Stanford University Press, 1968.

————. *The Origins of the Marshall Plan.* Stanford, CA: Stanford University Press, 1976.

Gingrich, Newt, Dick Armey, and House Republicans. *Contract with America: The Bold New Plan by Rep. Newt Gingrich, Rep. Dick Armey, and the House Republicans, To Change the Nation.* New York: Times Books and the Republican National Committee, 1994.

Golombek, Harry. *Encyclopedia of Chess.* New York: Crown, 1977 [1997].

Gorbachev, Mikhail. *The New Russia.* Translated by Arch Tait. Cambridge: Polity Press, 2016.

Gordon, Lincoln. "Lessons from the Marshall Plan: Successes and Limits." In *The Marshall Plan: A Retrospective,* edited by Stanley Hoffmann and Charles S. Maier. Boulder, CO: Westview, 1984.

Gore, Al. *An Inconvenient Truth: The Planetary Emergency of Global Warming and What We Can Do About It.* New York: Rodale, 2006.

Grieder, Peter. *The East German Leadership, 1946–73: Conflict and Crisis.* Manchester: Manchester University Press, 2000.

Grob-Fitzgibbon, Benjamin. *Continental Divide: Britain and Europe from the End of Empire to the Rise of Euroscepticism.* Cambridge: Cambridge University Press, 2016.

Gromyko, Andrei. *Memories.* Paperback edition. New York: Doubleday, 1990.

Haas, Lawrence J. *Harry and Arthur: Truman, Vandenberg, and the Partnership That Created the Free World.* Lincoln, NE: Potomac Books, 2016.

Halle, Louis J. *The Cold War As History.* New York: Harper & Row, 1967.

Hanhimäki, Jussi M. *Containing Coexistence: America, Russia, and the "Finnish Solution," 1945–1956.* Kent, OH: Kent State University Press, 1997.

Harbutt, Fraser J. *The Iron Curtain: Churchill, America, and the Origins of the Cold War.* New York: Oxford University Press, 1986.

Harriman, W. Averell, and Elie Abel. *Special Envoy to Churchill and Stalin, 1941–1946.* New York: Random House, 1975.

Harrington, Daniel F. *Berlin on the Brink: The Blockade, the Airlift, and the Early Cold War.* Lexington: University Press of Kentucky, 2012.

Hartmann, Susan M. *Truman and the 80th Congress.* Columbia: University of Missouri Press, 1971.

Haslam, Jonathan. *Russia's Cold War: From the October Revolution to the Fall of the Wall.* New Haven: Yale University Press, 2011.

Hazlitt, Henry. *Will Dollars Save the World?* New York: Appleton-Century, 1947.

Heimann, Mary. *Czechoslovakia: The State That Failed.* New Haven: Yale University Press, 2009.

Heinemann-Grueder, Andreas. "The Soviet Atomic Project and the Shortage of Uranium: Uranium Mining in the GDR and Czechoslovakia After 1945." In *Science and Society: History of the Soviet Atomic Project (40's–50's): Proceedings of the International Symposium.* Vol. 2. Moscow: IZDAT, 1999.

Hertle, Hans-Hermann. *Der Fall der Mauer: Der unbeabsichtigte Selbstauflösing des SED-Staates.* Opladen: Westdeutscher Verlag, 1996.

Hitchcock, William. *France Restored: Cold War Diplomacy and the Quest for Leadership in Europe, 1944–1954.* Chapel Hill: University of North Carolina Press, 1998.

Hodge, Carl Cavanaugh, and Cathal J. Nolan (eds.). *U.S. Presidents and Foreign Policy: 1789 to the Present.* Santa Barbara, CA: ABC-CLIO, 2007.

Hoffmann, Stanley, and Charles S. Maier (eds.). *The Marshall Plan: A Retrospective.* Boulder, CO: Westview, 1984.

Hogan, Michael J. *The Marshall Plan: America, Britain, and the Reconstruction of Western Europe.* Cambridge: Cambridge University Press, 1987.

Holloway, David. *Stalin and the Bomb: The Soviet Union and Atomic Energy, 1939–1956.* New Haven: Yale University Press, 1994.

Howley, Frank. *Berlin Command.* New York: Putnam & Sons, 1950.

Huempfer, Sebastian. "Burden of a Creditor Nation: Business Elites and the Transformation of US Trade Policy, 1917–62." DPhil thesis, Oxford University, 2016.

Irwin, Douglas A., Petros C. Mavroidis, and Alan O. Sykes. *The Genesis of the GATT.* Cambridge: Cambridge University Press, 2008.

Isaacson, Walter, and Evan Thomas. *The Wise Men: Six Friends and the World They Made.* New York: Simon & Schuster, 1986 [2012].

James, Harold. *Europe Reborn: A History, 1914–2000.* New York: Routledge, 2014.

James, Robert Rhodes (ed.). *Winston S. Churchill: His Complete Speeches, Vol. VIII.* New York: Bowker, 1974.

Johnson, Debra, and Paul Robinson. "Editors' Introduction." In *Perspectives on EU-Russia Relations,* edited by Debra Johnson and Paul Robinson. Oxford: Routledge, 2005.

Jones, Joseph M. *The Fifteen Weeks.* New York: Viking, 1955.

Judt, Tony. *Postwar: A History of Europe Since 1945.* New York: Penguin, 2005.

———. *When the Facts Change: Essays 1995–2010.* New York: Penguin, 2015.

Kaplan, Edward S. *American Trade Policy: 1923–1995.* Westport, CT: Greenwood, 1996.

Kaplan, Karel. *The Short March: The Communist Takeover in Czechoslovakia, 1945–1948.* London: C. Hurst, 1987.

Kemp, Walter A. *Nationalism and Communism in Eastern Europe and the Soviet Union: A Basic Contradiction?* New York: St. Martin's, 1999.

Kempe, Frederick. *Berlin 1961: Kennedy, Khrushchev, and the Most Dangerous Place on Earth.* New York: G. P. Putnam's Sons, 2011.

Kennan, George F. *Memoirs, Vol. I: 1925–1950.* Boston: Little, Brown, 1967.

———. *At a Century's Ending: Reflections, 1982–1995.* New York: W. W. Norton, 1996.

Kerr, Sheila. "The Secret Hotline to Moscow." In *Britain and the First Cold War,* edited by Anne Deighton. Houndmills, UK: Macmillan, 1990.

Kershaw, Ian. *To Hell and Back: Europe, 1914–1949.* New York: Viking, 2015.

Kersten, Krystyna. *The Establishment of Communist Rule in Poland, 1943–1948.* Translated by John Micgiel and Michael H. Bernhard. Berkeley: University of California Press, 1991.

Khrushchev, Nikita, with Strobe Talbott (transl., ed.). *Khrushchev Remembers: The Last Testament.* Boston: Little, Brown, 1971.

Kindleberger, Charles P. "The American Origins of the Marshall Plan: A View from the State Department." In *The Marshall Plan: A Retrospective,* edited by Stanley Hoffmann and Charles S. Maier. Boulder, CO: Westview, 1984.

———. "Toward the Marshall Plan: A Memoir of Policy Development in Germany (1945–1947)." In *The Marshall Plan and Germany: Western Development Within the Framework of the European Recovery Program,* edited by Charles S. Maier, with the assistance of Günter Bischof. New York: Berg, 1991.

Kinnard, Douglas. *The Secretary of Defense.* Lexington: University of Kentucky Press, 1980.

Kissinger, Henry. *White House Years.* New York: Simon & Schuster, 1979.

Kolko, Joyce, and Gabriel Kolko. *The Limits of Power: The World and United States Foreign Policy, 1945–1954.* New York: Harper & Row, 1972.

Kornienko, G. M. *Kholodnaya voina. Svidetelstvo ee uchastnika.* Moskva: Olma-Press, 2001. (*The Cold War: Testimony of Its Participant.* Moscow: Olma-Press, 2001.)

Kotkin, Stephen. *Stalin, Vol. I: Paradoxes of Power, 1878–1928.* New York: Penguin, 2014.

Krátký, Karel. "Czechoslovakia, the Soviet Union and the Marshall Plan." In *The Soviet Union in Eastern Europe, 1945–89,* edited by Odd Arne Westad, Sven Holtsmark, and Iver B. Neumann. New York: St. Martin's, 1994.

Krengel, Rolf. *Anlagevermögen, Produktion und Beschäftigung der Industrie im Gebiet der Bundesrepublik von 1924 bis 1956.* Berlin: Duncker & Humblot, 1958.

Kuhns, Woodrow J. *Assessing the Soviet Threat: The Early Cold War Years.* McLean, VA: Center for the Study of Intelligence, 1997.

Laufer, Jochen P. "From Dismantling to Currency Reform: External Origins of the Dictatorship, 1944–1948." In *Dictatorship as Experience: Towards a Socio-Cultural History of the GDR,* edited by Konrad H. Jarausch. Translated by Eve Duffy. New York: Berghahn, 1999.

Laufer, Jochen P., and Georgij Kynin (eds.). *Die UdSSR und die deutsche Frage, 1941–1948. Dokumente aus dem Archiv für Außenpolitik der Russischen Föderation.* Vol. III. Berlin: Dunker & Humblot, 2004.

Leahy, William D. *I Was There.* New York: McGraw-Hill, 1950.

Leffler, Melvyn P. *A Preponderance of Power: National Security, the Truman Administration, and the Cold War.* Stanford, CA: Stanford University Press, 1992.

Leffler, Melvyn P., and David S. Painter (eds.). *Origins of the Cold War: An International History.* New York: Routledge, 1994 [2005].

LeMay, Curtis E., with MacKinlay Kantor. *Mission with LeMay.* Garden City, NY: Doubleday, 1965.

Levering, Ralph B., and Verena Botzenhart-Viehe. "The American Perspective." In *Debating the Origins of the Cold War: American and Russian Perspectives*, edited by Ralph B. Levering, Vladimir O. Pechatnov, Verena Botzenhart-Viehe, and C. Earl Edmondson. Lanham, MD: Rowman & Littlefield, 2001.

Light, Margot. "Russian Political Engagement with the European Union." In *Putin's Russia and the Enlarged Europe,* edited by Roy Allison, Margot Light, and Stephen White. Oxford: Blackwell, 2006.

Lippmann, Walter. *The Cold War: A Study in U.S. Foreign Policy.* New York: Harper & Brothers, 1947.

Lockhart, R. H. Bruce. *Jan Masaryk: A Personal Memoir.* New York: Philosophical Library, 1951.

Loebl, Eugen. *Stalinism in Prague: The Loebl Story.* New York: Grove, 1969.

Lorwin, Val R. *The French Labor Movement.* Cambridge: Harvard University Press, 1954.

Louis, William Roger. *The British Empire in the Middle East, 1945–1951: Arab Nationalism, the United States, and Postwar Imperialism.* Oxford: Clarendon Press, 1984.

Lowe, Keith. *Savage Continent: Europe in the Aftermath of World War II.* New York: St. Martin's, 2012.

Lukes, Igor. *On the Edge of the Cold War: American Diplomats and Spies in Postwar Prague.* Oxford: Oxford University Press, 2012.

Luttwak, Edward N. *The Grand Strategy of the Roman Empire: From the First Century A.D. to the Third.* Baltimore: Johns Hopkins University Press, 1976.

Macintyre, Ben. *A Spy Among Friends.* New York: Crown, 2014.

Mackinder, Halford J. *Democratic Ideals and Reality: A Study in the Politics of Reconstruction.* Washington, DC: Henry Holt, 1919 [1996].

Maier, Charles S. "Introduction: 'Issue then Is Germany and with It the Future of Europe.'" In *The Marshall Plan and Germany: Western Development Within the Framework of the European Recovery Program*, edited by Maier with the assistance of Günter Bischof. New York: Berg, 1991.

Majer, Václav. "Co vim o Marshalloveplanu." In *Politické Vzpomínky III*, by Ladislav Karel Feierabend. Brno, Czech Republic: Atlantis, 1996.

Marer, Paul. "Soviet Economic Policy in Eastern Europe." In *Reorientation and Commercial Relations of the Economies of Eastern Europe*, edited by John P. Hardt. Washington, DC: U.S. Government Printing Office, 1974.

———. "The Political Economy of Soviet Relations with Eastern Europe." In *Soviet Policy in Eastern Europe*, edited by Sarah Meiklejohn Terry. New Haven: Yale University Press, 1984.

Mastny, Vojtech. *The Cold War and Soviet Insecurity: The Stalin Years.* Oxford: Oxford University Press, 1996.

McCullough, David. *Truman.* New York: Simon & Schuster, 1992.

Mee, Charles L., Jr. *Meeting at Potsdam.* New York: M. Evans, 1975.

———. *The Marshall Plan: The Launching of the Pax Americana.* New York: Simon & Schuster, 1984.

Merritt, Anna J., and Richard L. Merritt (eds.). *Public Opinion in Occupied Germany: The OMGUS Surveys, 1945–1949.* Urbana-Champaign: University of Illinois Press, 1970.

Milward, Alan S. *The Reconstruction of Western Europe, 1945–51.* Berkeley: University of California Press, 1984.

———. "The Marshall Plan and German Foreign Trade." In *The Marshall Plan and Germany: West German Development Within the Framework of the European Recovery Program,* edited by Charles S. Maier, with the assistance of Günter Bischof. New York: Berg, 1991.

Milward, Alan S., with George Brennan and Federico Romero. *The European Rescue of the Nation-State.* New York: Routledge, 1992 [2000].

Milward, Alan S. "Europe and the Marshall Plan: 50 Years On." In *The Marshall Plan Today: Model and Metaphor,* edited by John Agnew and J. Nicholas Entrikin. London: Routledge, 2004.

Minford, Patrick. "Reconstruction and the U.K. Postwar Welfare State: False Start and New Beginning." In *Postwar Economic Reconstruction and Lessons for the East Today,* edited by Rudiger Dornbusch, Wilhelm Nölling, and Richard Layard. Cambridge: MIT Press, 1993.

Miscamble, Wilson D. *From Roosevelt to Truman: Potsdam, Hiroshima, and the Cold War.* New York: Cambridge University Press, 2007.

Mommen, André. *Stalin's Economist: The Economic Contributions of Jeno Varga.* New York: Routledge, 2011.

Montanelli, Indro, and Mario Cervi. *L'Italia della repubblica.* Milan: Rizzoli, 1985.

Montefiore, Simon Sebag. *Stalin: The Court of the Red Tsar.* London: Weidenfeld & Nicolson, 2003.

Moorhouse, Roger. *The Devils' Alliance: Hitler's Pact with Stalin, 1939–1941.* New York: Basic Books, 2014.

[Lord] Moran. *Churchill at War, 1940–45.* New York: Carroll & Graf, 2002.

Murphy, Robert D. *Diplomat Among Warriors.* Westport, CT: Greenwood, 1964.

Naimark, Norman M. *The Russians in Germany: A History of the Soviet Zone of Occupation, 1945–1949.* Cambridge: Harvard University Press, 1995.

Nakath, Detlef, Gero Neugebauer, and Gerd-Rüdiger Stephan. *"Im Kreml brennt noch Licht" Spitzenkontakte zwischen SED/PDS und KPdSU 1989–1991.* Berlin: Dietz, 1998.

Narinsky, Mikhail M. "Soviet Foreign Policy and the Origins of the Cold War." In *Soviet Foreign Policy, 1917–1991*, edited by Gabriel Gorodetsky. London: Frank Cass, 1994.

———. "SSSR i plan Marshalla" // *Kholodnaya voina. Novye podkhody. Novye dokumenty*. Moskva: Otvet, 1995. ("The USSR and the Marshall Plan." In *The Cold War. New Approaches. New Documents*. Moscow: Response, 1995.)

———. "The Soviet Union and the Berlin Crisis, 1948–9." In *The Soviet Union and Europe in the Cold War, 1943–53*, edited by Francesca Gori and Silvio Pons. London: Palgrave Macmillan, 1996.

———. "Narastanie konfrontatsii: plan Marshalla, Berlinskii krizis" // *Sovetskoe obshchestvo: vozniknovenie, razvitie, istoricheskii final: V 2 t. T. 2. Apogei i krakh stalinizma*. Pod obshchei redaktsiei Yu.N. Afanasieva. Moskva: Rossiisk. gos. un-t. 1997. S. 54–89. ("Intensification of Confrontation: the Marshall Plan, the Berlin Crisis." In *The Soviet Society: Emergence, Development, Historical End in 2 vols., Vol. 2, The Heyday and the Demise of Stalinism*. Edited by Yu. N. Afanasiev. Moscow: Russian State University, 1997, pp. 54–89.)

———. "The Soviet Union and the Marshall Plan." In *The Failure of Peace in Europe, 1943–48*, edited by Antonio Varsori and Elena Calandri. Palgrave Macmillan, 2002.

National Council of American-Soviet Friendship. "How to End the Cold War and Build the Peace." New York: National Council of American-Soviet Friendship, 1948.

Nedelsky, Nadya. *Defining the Sovereign Community: The Czech and Slovak Republics*. Philadelphia: University of Pennsylvania Press, 2012.

Neiberg, Michael. *Potsdam: The End of World War II and the Remaking of Europe*. New York: Basic Books, 2015.

Nenni, Pietro. *Tempo Di Guerra Fredda: Diari 1943–1956*. Milan: SugarCo., 1981.

Nickolaevsky, B. I. *Tainye stranitsy istorii*. / Red.-sost. Felshtinskii, Yu.G. Moskva: Izdatel'stvo gumanitarnoi literatury, 1995. (*Secret Pages of History*. / Ed. Felshtinsky, Yu.G. Moscow: Humanitarian Literature Publishing House, 1995.)

Nitze, Paul, with Ann M. Smith and Steven L. Rearden. *From Hiroshima to Glasnost: At the Center of Decision—A Memoir*. New York: Grove Weidenfeld, 1989.

Novikov, N. V. *Vospominaniia diplomata*. Moskva: Politizdat, 1989. (*The Memoirs of a Diplomat*. Moscow: Politizdat, 1989.)

Nye, Joseph S., Jr. *Soft Power: The Means to Success in World Politics*. New York: Public Affairs, 2005.

Ocherki istorii rossiiskoi vneshnei razvedki. Tom 5, 1945–1965 gody. Moskva: Mezhdunarodnye otnosheniia, 2003. (*The Essays on the History of Russian Foreign Intelligence, Vol. 5, 1945–1965*. Moscow: International Relations, 2003.)

Payne, Robert. *Report on America*. New York: John Day, 1949.

Pechatnov, Vladimir O. *Stalin, Ruzvelt, Truman: SSSR i SShA v 1940-h gg.* Moskva: TERRA, 2006. (*Stalin, Roosevelt, Truman: USSR and USA in 1940s.* Moscow: TERRA, 2006.)

Pechatnov, Vladimir O. "The Soviet Union and the World, 1944–1953." In *The Cambridge History of the Cold War, Vol. I: Origins,* edited by Melvyn P. Leffler and Odd Arne Westad. Cambridge: Cambridge University Press, 2010.

Pechatnov, Vladimir O., and C. Earl Edmondson. "The Russian Perspective." In *Debating the Origins of the Cold War: American and Russian Perspectives,* edited by Ralph B. Levering, Vladimir O. Pechatnov, Verena Botzenhart-Viehe, and C. Earl Edmondson. Lanham, Maryland: Rowman & Littlefield, 2001.

Petrov, Vladimir. *Money and Conquest: Allied Occupation Currencies in World War II.* Baltimore: Johns Hopkins Press, 1967.

Pisani, Sallie. *The CIA and the Marshall Plan.* Lawrence: University Press of Kansas, 1991.

Plokhy, Serhii M. *Yalta: The Price of Peace.* London: Viking, 2010.

———. *The Last Empire: The Final Days of the Soviet Union.* New York: Basic Books, 2014.

Pogue, Forrest C. *George C. Marshall, Vol. IV: Statesman, 1945–1959.* New York: Viking, 1987.

Price, Harry B. *The Marshall Plan and Its Meaning.* Ithaca, NY: Cornell University Press, 1955.

Pruessen, Ronald W. *John Foster Dulles: The Road to Power.* New York: Free Press, 1982.

Putin, Vladimir, with Nataliya Gevorkyan, Natalya Timakova, and Andrei Kolesnikov. *First Person: An Astonishingly Frank Self-Portrait by Russia's President Vladimir Putin.* Translated by Catherine A. Fitzpatrick. New York: PublicAffairs, 2000.

Rapelli, Paola. *Symbols of Power in Art,* translated by Jay Hyams. Los Angeles: Getty Publications, 2004 [2011].

Raucher, Alan R. *Paul G. Hoffman: Architect of Foreign Aid.* Lexington: University Press of Kentucky, 1986.

Rees, David. *Harry Dexter White: A Study in Paradox.* New York: Coward, McCann & Geoghan, 1973.

Reichlin, Lucrezia. "The Marshall Plan Reconsidered." In *Europe's Postwar Recovery,* edited by Barry Eichengreen. Cambridge: Cambridge University Press, 1995.

Reinhart, Carmen, and Kenneth Rogoff. *This Time It's Different: Eight Centuries of Financial Folly.* Princeton: Princeton University Press, 2009.

Reymen, Dafne C. "The Economic Effects of the Marshall Plan Revisited." In *The Marshall Plan Today: Model and Metaphor,* edited by John Agnew and J. Nicholas Entrikin. London: Routledge, 2004.

Reynolds, David. *From World War to Cold War: Churchill, Roosevelt, and the International History of the 1940s.* Oxford: Oxford University Press, 2006.

Ripka, Hubert. *Czechoslovakia Enslaved: The Story of the Communist Coup d'État.* London: Victor Gollancz, 1950.

Ritchie, Donald A. *Congress and Harry S. Truman: A Conflicted Legacy.* Kirksville, MO: Truman State University Press, 2011.

Ritter, Gerhard A. *Der Preis der deutschen Einheit: Die Wiedervereinigung und die Krise des Sozialstaats.* Munich: Beck, 2006.

Roberts, Andrew. *Masters and Commanders: How Four Titans Won the War in the West, 1941–1945.* New York: HarperCollins, 2009.

Roberts, Geoffrey. *Stalin's Wars: From World War to Cold War, 1939–1953.* New Haven: Yale University Press, 2006.

———. *Molotov: Stalin's Cold Warrior.* Washington, DC: Potomac Books, 2011.

Robertson, Alex J. *The Bleak Midwinter 1947.* Manchester: Manchester University Press, 1987.

Rodden, John. *Repainting the Little Red Schoolhouse: A History of Eastern German Education, 1945–1995.* New York: Oxford University Press, 2002.

Roll, Eric. "The Marshall Plan as Anglo-American Response." In *The Marshall Plan: Fifty Years After,* edited by Martin Shain. New York: Palgrave, 2001.

Roman, Eric. *Austria-Hungary and the Successor States: A Reference Guide from the Renaissance to the Present.* New York: Facts on File, 2003.

Rostow, Walt W. *The Division of Europe After World War II: 1946, Vol. II.* Austin: University of Texas Press, 1981.

Rzheshevskii, Oleg A. *Stalin i Cherchill'.* [*Stalin and Churchill.*] Moscow: Nauka, 2004.

Sarotte, Mary Elise. *1989: The Struggle to Create Post–Cold War Europe.* Princeton: Princeton University Press, 2009.

Sarotte, Mary Elise. *The Collapse: The Accidental Opening of the Berlin Wall.* New York: Basic Books, 2014.

Schäuble, Wolfgang. *Der Vertrag: Wie ich über die deutsche Einheit verhandelte.* Munich: Knaur, 1991.

Schmidt, Dana Adams. *Anatomy of a Satellite.* Boston: Little, Brown, 1952.

Schröder, Hans-Jürgen. "The Economic Reconstruction of West Germany in the Context of International Relations, 1945–1949." In *Great Britain, France, Italy and Germany in a Postwar World, 1945–1950,* edited by Josef Becker and Franz Knipping. New York: de Gruyter, 1986.

Schulze, Hagen. *Germany: A New History.* Translated by Deborah Lucas Schneider. Cambridge: Harvard University Press, 1998.

Schwabe, Klaus. "German Policy Responses to the Marshall Plan." In *The Marshall Plan and Germany: West German Development Within the Framework of the European Recovery Program,* edited by Charles S. Maier, with the assistance of Günter Bischof. New York: Berg, 1991.

Schwartz, Harry. *Russia's Soviet Economy*. Second edition. New York: Prentice Hall, 1954.

Sebestyen, Victor. *1946: The Making of the Modern World*. New York: Pantheon, 2014.

Shenk, David. *The Immortal Game: A History of Chess*. New York: Anchor, 2006.

Sherwood, Robert E. *Roosevelt and Hopkins: An Intimate History*. New York: Enigma, 1948 [2008].

Siklos, Pierre L. *War Finance, Reconstruction, Hyperinflation and Stabilization in Hungary, 1938–48*. Basingstoke, UK: Macmillan, 1991.

Simms, Brendan. *Europe: The Struggle for Supremacy, 1453 to the Present*. New York: Basic Books, 2013.

Singer, J. David, Stuart Bremer, and John Stuckey. "Capability Distribution, Uncertainty, and Major Power War, 1820–1965." In *Peace, War, and Numbers*, edited by Bruce Russett. Beverly Hills, CA: Sage, 1972.

Skidelsky, Robert. *John Maynard Keyes, Vol. III: Fighting for Freedom, 1937–1946*. New York: Viking, 2000.

Smith, Jean Edward. "The View from USFET: General Clay's and Washington's Interpretation of Soviet Intentions in Germany, 1945–1948." In *U.S. Occupation in Europe After World War II*, edited by Hans Schmitt. Lawrence: Regents Press of Kansas, 1978.

———. *Lucius D. Clay: An American Life*. New York: Henry Holt, 1990.

Smith, Walter Bedell. *My Three Years in Moscow*. Philadelphia: Lippincott, 1950.

Soltis, Andy. *Chess Lists*. Second edition. Jefferson, NC: McFarland, 1984 [2002].

Spalding, Elizabeth. *The First Cold Warrior: Harry Truman, Containment, and the Remaking of Liberal Internationalism*. Lexington: University Press of Kentucky, 2006.

Staar, Richard F. *Communist Regimes in Eastern Europe*. Fifth edition. Stanford: Hoover Institution Press, 1971 [1988].

Stalin, I. V. *Sochineniia. Tom 2. [Works, Vol. 2]* Moskva: OGIZ, 1946.

Steel, Ronald. *Walter Lippmann and the American Century*. Boston: Little, Brown, 1980.

Steil, Benn. *The Battle of Bretton Woods: John Maynard Keynes, Harry Dexter White, and the Making of a New World Order*. Princeton: Princeton University Press, 2013.

Stettinius, Edward R., Jr. *Roosevelt and the Russians: The Yalta Conference*. Garden City, NY: Doubleday, 1949.

Stirling, Robin. *The Weather of Britain*. London: Giles de la Mare Publishers, 1997.

Strang, William. *At Home and Abroad*. London: Deutsch, 1956.

Sudoplatov, Pavel, with Anatoli Sudoplatov, Jerrod L. Schecter, and Leona P. Schecter. *Special Tasks: The Memoirs of an Unwanted Witness—A Soviet Spymaster*. Boston: Little, Brown, 1994.

Sutherland, Jon, and Diane Canwell. *Berlin Airlift: The Salvation of a City*. Gretna, LA: Pelican, 2007.

Swain, Nigel. *Hungary: The Rise and Fall of Feasible Socialism*. London: New Left Books, 1992.

Swanson, Roger F. *Canadian-American Summit Diplomacy, 1923–1975*. Kingston, ON, Montreal: McGill-Queen's Press, 1976.

Szabo, Stephen. *The Diplomacy of German Unification*. New York: St. Martin's, 1992.

Talbott, Strobe. *The Russia Hand: A Memoir of Presidential Diplomacy*. New York: Random House, 2002.

Taylor, Frederick. *The Berlin Wall: 13 August 1961–9 November 1989*. London: Bloomsbury, 2006.

Teltschik, Horst. *329 Tage: Innenansichten der Einigung*. Berlin: Siedler, 1991.

Thieme, H. Jörg. "The Central Bank and Money in the GDR." In *Fifty Years of the Deutsche Mark*, edited by Deutsche Bundesbank. Oxford: Oxford University Press, 1999.

Thompson, Nicholas. *The Hawk and the Dove: Paul Nitze, George Kennan, and the History of the Cold War*. New York: Henry Holt, 2009.

Tiersky, Ronald. *French Communism, 1920–1972*. New York: Columbia University Press, 1974.

Toranska, Teresa (ed.). *"Them": Stalin's Polish Puppets*. New York: Harper & Row, 1987.

Trachtenberg, Marc. *A Constructed Peace: The Making of the European Settlement, 1945–1963*. Princeton: Princeton University Press, 1999.

Trohan, Walter. *Political Animals: Memoirs of a Sentimental Cynic*. Garden City, NY: Doubleday, 1975.

Truman, Harry S. *Memoirs, Volume I: Year of Decisions*. Garden City, NY: Doubleday, 1955.

———. *Memoirs, Volume II: Years of Trial and Hope*. Garden City, NY: Doubleday, 1956.

Truman, Margaret. *Harry S. Truman*. New York: William Morrow, 1972.

Tunner, William H. *Over the Hump*. New York: Duell, Sloan & Pearce, 1964.

Unger, Debi, and Irwin Unger, with Stanley Hirshson. *George Marshall: A Biography*. New York: HarperCollins, 2014.

Ungerer, Horst. *A Concise History of European Monetary Integration: From EPU to EMU*. Westport, CT: Quorum, 1997.

Van der Beugel, Ernst Hans. *From Marshall Aid to European Partnership: European Integration as a Concern of American Foreign Policy*. New York: Elsevier, 1966.

Van der Wee, Herman. *Prosperity and Upheaval: The World Economy, 1945–1980*. Berkeley: University of California Press, 1983.

Van Hook, James C. *Rebuilding Germany: The Creation of the Social Market Economy, 1945–1957*. Cambridge: Cambridge University Press, 2004.

Vlavianos, Haris. *Greece, 1941–49: From Resistance to Civil War: The Strategy of the Greek Communist Party*. New York: Macmillan, 1992.

Vyshinsky, Andrei Y. *The U.S.S.R on Guard over the Peace and Security of Nations*. London: Soviet News, 1948.

Wala, Michael. *The Council on Foreign Relations and American Foreign Policy in the Early Cold War*. Providence: Berghahn, 1994.

Warner, Geoffrey. "Ernest Bevin and British Foreign Policy, 1945–1951." In *The Diplomats, 1939–1979*, edited by Gordon A. Craig and Francis L. Loewenheim. Princeton: Princeton University Press, 1994.

Watson, Derek. *Molotov: A Biography*. New York: Palgrave Macmillan, 2005.

Werth, Alexander. *Russia: The Post-War Years*. New York: Taplinger, 1971.

Westad, Odd Arne. "The Cold War and the International History of the Twentieth Century." In *The Cambridge History of the Cold War, Vol. I: Origins*, edited by Melvyn P. Leffler and Odd Arne Westad. Cambridge: Cambridge University Press, 2010.

White, Theodore H. *Fire in the Ashes: Europe in Mid-Century*. New York: William Sloane, 1953.

Wilson, Theodore. *The Marshall Plan: An Atlantic Venture of 1947–1951 and How It Shaped Our World*. New York: Foreign Policy Association, 1977.

Winik, Jay. *1944: FDR and the Year That Changed History*. New York: Simon & Schuster, 2015.

Wohlforth, William C. "How Did the Experts Do?" In *In Uncertain Times: American Foreign Policy After the Berlin Wall and 9/11*, edited by Melvyn P. Leffler and Jeffrey W. Legro. Ithaca, NY: Cornell University Press, 2011.

Wolf, Holger C. "The Lucky Miracle: Germany, 1945–1951." In *Postwar Economic Reconstruction and Lessons for the East Today*, edited by Rudiger Dornbusch, Wilhelm Nölling, and Richard Layard. Cambridge: MIT Press, 1993.

Yergin, Daniel. *Shattered Peace: The Origins of the Cold War and the National Security State*. Boston: Houghton Mifflin, 1977.

Zelikow, Philip, and Condoleezza Rice. *Germany Unified and Europe Transformed: A Study in Statecraft*. Cambridge: Harvard University Press, 1995.

Zubok, Vladimir M. *A Failed Empire: The Soviet Union in the Cold War from Stalin to Gorbachev*. Chapel Hill: University of North Carolina Press, 2007.

Zubok, Vladislav M., and Constantine Pleshakov. *Inside the Kremlin's Cold War: From Stalin to Khruschev*. Cambridge: Harvard University Press, 1996.

Zwass, Adam. *Monetary Cooperation between East and West*. White Plains, NY: International Arts and Sciences Press, 1975.

ARTICLES

Adams, Frank S. "Stassen Plea Wins Legion Convention to Marshall Plan." *New York Times*. September 1, 1947.

Agnew, John. "The Eurozone Crisis and the Marshall Plan Metaphor." *openDemocracy*. August 6, 2012. https://www.opendemocracy.net/john-agnew/eurozone-crisis -and-marshall-plan-metaphor.

Albright, Madeleine. "Why Bigger Is Better." *The Economist*. February 15, 1997.

Albright, Robert C. "House Bill Would Okay Greek-Turk Loan, Grant." *Washington Post*. March 19, 1947.

———. "Junkets Might Alter Next Session's Votes." *Washington Post*. September 7, 1947.

Alsop, Joseph, and Stewart Alsop. "Hoover a Godsend to ERP Foes." *Washington Post*. January 25, 1948.

Asmus, Ronald D. "Europe's Eastern Promise: Rethinking NATO and EU Enlargement." *Foreign Affairs*. January/February 2008.

Asmus, Ronald D., Richard L. Kugler, and F. Stephen Larrabee. "Building a New NATO." *Foreign Affairs*. September/October 1993.

———. "What Will NATO Enlargement Cost?" *Reprints*. Santa Monica, CA: RAND Corporation, 1997. [Originally published in *Survival*, Vol. 38, No. 3 (Autumn 1996): 5–26.]

Asmus, Ronald D., and F. Stephen Larrabee. "NATO and the Have-Nots: Reassurance After Enlargement." *Foreign Affairs*. November/December 1996.

Augusta Chronicle. "Grave Decision." March 13, 1947.

Bacha, Edmar L. "A Three-Gap Model of Foreign Transfers and the GDP Growth Rate in Developing Countries." *Journal of Development Economics*. Vol. 32, No. 2 (April 1990): 279–96.

Barber, Chris. "The Herter Committee: Forging RN's Foreign Policy." April 9, 2014. Nixon Library. https://www.nixonfoundation.org/2014/04/herter-committee-forging-rns-foreign-policy/.

Barnes, Bart. "Financier Robert A. Lovett, 90, Former Secretary of Defense, Dies." *Washington Post*. May 8, 1986.

Barnes, Julian E., and Laurence Norman. "European Union Backs Plan to Expand Military Coordination." *Wall Street Journal*. November 15, 2016.

BBC. "1999: Putin Takes Over as Yeltsin Resigns." *On This Day 1950–2005*. http://news.bbc.co.uk/onthisday/hi/dates/stories/december/31/newsid_4102000/4102107.stm.

BBC. "Ukraine Crisis: Russia Demands Guarantees from Nato." November 18, 2014. http://www.bbc.com/news/world-europe-30107520.

Beevor, Antony. "Eisenhower's Pit Bull." *Wall Street Journal*. October 23, 2010.

Belair, Felix, Jr. "Truman Assumes Lead in Fight on Communism." *New York Times*. March 16, 1947.

———. "Snyder Bars a Cut in Taxes Till Cost of Europe Aid Is Set." *New York Times*. October 30, 1947.

Belair, Felix, Jr. "ERP's Domestic Phases Cause Capital Concern." *New York Times*. November 16, 1947.

———. "Election Year Politics Held a Threat to ERP." *New York Times*. November 23, 1947.

———. "Delay Looms on ERP Action Despite Appeal for Speed." *New York Times*. January 8, 1948.

———. "Draft, Great Costs ERP Alternatives, Say Defense Heads." *New York Times*. January 16, 1948.

———. "Marshall Plan Attacked by Weir." *New York Times*. February 26, 1948.

———. "Way for the ERP Bill Has Now Been Cleared." *New York Times*. February 29, 1948.

———. "Senators Rebuff Taft on ERP Cut." *New York Times*. March 13, 1948.

———. "Martin's Warning: Speaker Tells Majority Steering Group of 'Grave Crisis.'" *New York Times*. March 17, 1948.

———. "Omnibus Bill Carries $5,300,000,000 ERP and Funds for East." *New York Times*. April 1, 1948.

———. "ECA Bill Is Voted; Taft Shifts Plans for 10% Cut in Fund." *New York Times*. April 15, 1949.

Berger, Marilyn. "Former Ambassador Charles E. Bohlen Dies at 69." *Washington Post*. January 2, 1974.

Birnbaum, Michael. "Wary of Russia, Europe Now Tiptoes When It Comes to Expansion." *Washington Post*. May 22, 2015.

Blair, Raymond J. "State Dept. Paper Pictures in Detail Growing Threat of Red Domination," *Washington Post*. September 7, 1947.

Blair, William M. "European Aid Tops Interest in Iowa." *New York Times*. February 16, 1948.

Blome, Nikolaus, Kai Diekmann, and Daniel Biskup. "Putin—The Interview: 'For Me, It Is Not Borders That Matter.'" *Bild*. January 11, 2016.

Bloomberg View. "Arab Spring Needs a Mini–Marshall Plan." January 13, 2013. https://www.bloomberg.com/view/articles/2013-01-13/arab-spring-needs-a-mini-marshall-plan.

Boggs, S. W. "Cartohypnosis." *Scientific Monthly*. Vol. 64, No. 6 (June 1947): 469–76.

Bohemia Band. "Stalin, Czechoslovakia, and the Marshall Plan: New Documentation from the Czechoslovak Archives." Vol. 32, No.1 (1991): 139–44.

Borba [Beograd]. "An Interview with Josip Broz Tito." August 26, 1947.

Bossuat, Gérard. "Le poids de l'aide américaine sur la politique économique et financière de la France en 1948." *Relations internationales*. Vol. 37 (Spring 1984).

Brzezinski, Zbigniew. "A Geostrategy for Eurasia." *Foreign Affairs*. September/October 1997.

Busch, Noel F. "Paul Hoffman." *Life*. April 4, 1949.

Byrnes, Mark S. "'Overruled and Worn Down': Truman Sends an Ambassador to Spain." *Presidential Studies Quarterly*. Vol. 29, No. 2 (June 1999): 263–79.

Callender, Harold. "Paris Parley to Open Today: Molotov and 89 Aides Arrive." *New York Times*. June 27, 1947.

———. "Bid Open to Soviet." *New York Times*. July 4, 1947.

———. "Marshall Gives Pledge to France." *New York Times*. July 24, 1947.

———. "Americans Meet in Paris." *New York Times*. August 13, 1947.

———. "French Heads Fear a General Strike." *New York Times*. November 18, 1947.

———. "Schuman Premier as Paris Assembly Backs Him, 412–184." *New York Times*. November 23, 1947.

———. "E.R.P. Council Asks 50% Cut in Curbs on Mutual Trade." *New York Times*. November 3, 1949.

Cameron, Rob. "Police Close Case on 1948 Death of Jan Masaryk—Murder, Not Suicide." *Radio Prague*. January 6, 2004.

http://www.radio.cz/en/section/curraffrs/police-close-case-on-1948-death-of-jan-masaryk-murder-not-suicide.

Casey, Nicholas, Jay Solomon, and Joshua Mitnick. "Cease-Fire Brokers Grapple with How to Rebuild Gaza." *Wall Street Journal*. July 25, 2014.

Catledge, Turner. "Our Policy Stated: Welles Says Defeat of Hitler Is Greatest Task." *New York Times*. June 24, 1941.

Centre Virtuel de la Connaissance sur l'Europe (CVCE). "From the Schuman Plan to the Paris Treaty, 1950–1952." http://www.cvce.eu/en/unit-content/-/unit/5cc6b004-33b7-4e44-b6db-f5f9e6c01023/678ed16c-b497-41e0-a1b6-d8cb0594f2ef.

Chabris, Christopher. "When Diplomacy Leads to Betrayal." *Wall Street Journal*. February 19, 2016.

Chenery, Hollis B., and Michael Bruno. "Development Alternatives in an Open Economy: The Case of Israel." *Economic Journal*. Vol. 72, No. 285 (March 1962): 79–103.

Chicago Tribune. "Confirm Fifth U.S. Flyer Died in Yugoslavia." August 27, 1946.

Chicago Tribune. "French Strike Spreads; New Cabinet Acts." November 25, 1947.

CNN. "Sec. of State Madeleine Albright Press Conference, March 18, 1997." 1997. http://www.cnn.com/ALLPOLITICS/1997/03/18/fdch.albright/.

Cohen, Roger. "The Case for the Euro: Unshackling Europe to Take on the U.S." *New York Times*. September 18, 1997.

Cormac, John Mac. "Swift Soviet Dash Liberates Prague." *New York Times*. May 10, 1945.

Cortesi, Arnaldo. "Hunt for Plane On." *New York Times*. August 20, 1946.

———. "Communists Urge Italians to Enlist in a Class War." *New York Times*. October 28, 1947.

———. "Rome." *New York Times*. November 16, 1947.

———. "Fear Rises in Italy After Arms Blast." *New York Times*. November 17, 1947.

———. "Sforza Twits Reds Who Deride U.S. Aid." *New York Times*. January 18, 1948.

Crafts, Nicholas. "Saving the Eurozone: Is a 'Real' Marshall Plan the Answer?" *The CAGE-Chatham House Series*. No. 1 (June 2012).

———. "On a 'Real' Marshall Plan for Greece." *The Economist*. July 2, 2012.

Crider, John. "Nonpartisan Vote." *New York Times*. July 14, 1946.

Dales, Douglas. "Harriman: Tenacious, Resolute, Public Spirited." *New York Times*. October 26, 1954.

Daly, KerryLynn. "Supporting Corruption and Dictatorship: U.S. Relations with Spain Under Francisco Franco, 1945–1955." Working paper. Siena College, 2009.

Daniel, Clifton. "Our Ambassador Behind the Iron Curtain." *New York Times*. July 24, 1955.

Danner, Mark. "Marooned in the Cold War: America, the Alliance, and the Quest for a Vanished World." *World Policy Journal*. Vol. 14, No. 3 (Fall 1997): 1–23.

Davis, David. "A 21st-Century Marshall Plan." *Prospect*. June 22, 2011.

Deaton, Angus. "Weak States, Poor Countries." *Project Syndicate*. September 2013 [republished October 12, 2015]. https://www.project-syndicate.org/commentary/economic-development-requires-effective-governments-by-angus-deaton.

DeLong, J. Bradford, and Barry Eichengreen. "The Marshall Plan: History's Most Successful Structural Adjustment Program." *NBER Working Paper Series*. No. 3899 (November 1991).

Dobbs, Michael. "Clinton's NATO Effort Risky; President's Vision Rests on Historic Rationale." *Washington Post*. July 8, 1997.

Drozdiak, William. "The Brussels Wall: Tearing Down the EU-NATO Barrier." *Foreign Affairs*. May/June 2010.

Dulles, John Foster. "Europe Must Federate or Perish." *Vital Speeches of the Day*. Vol. 13, No. 8 (February 1947).

The Economist. "Dollars for Europe?" May 31, 1947.

The Economist. "On the Rocks." February 4, 1948.

Edwards, Willard. "Marshall Plan Debate Roars Toward Close." *Chicago Tribune*. March 26, 1948.

Eichengreen, Barry. "Create a New Marshall Plan for Greece." *Prague Post*. July 20, 2011.

Eichengreen, Barry, and Jorge Braga de Macedo. "The European Payments Union: History and Implications for the Evolution of the International Financial Architecture." OECD Development Centre. March 2001.

Eichengreen, Barry, and Marc Uzan. "The Marshall Plan: Economic Effects and Implications for Eastern Europe and the Former USSR." *Economic Policy*. Vol. 7, No. 14, Eastern Europe (April 1992): 13–75.

Ellman, Michael, and S. Maksudov. "Soviet Deaths in the Great Patriotic War: A Note." *Europe-Asia Studies*. Vol. 46, No. 4 (1994): 671–80.

Emmott, Robin. "Spurred by Trump and Brexit, EU Plans Five-Billion-Euro Defense Fund." Reuters. November 30, 2016.

European Commission. "About the Customs Union." September 19, 2016. http://
    ec.europa.eu/taxation_customs/40customs/customs_general_info/about/index_
    en.htm.

Eurostat. "Industrial Output in the EU and Euro Area: An Analysis of the Industrial Pro-
    duction Index." *Statistics in Focus.* No. 36 (2011).

Fenwick, Charles. "The Ninth International Conference of American States." *American
    Journal of International Law.* Vol. 42, No. 3 (July 1948).

Finkel, Isobel. "Erdogan Warns Russia Against Violating Turkish Airspace." *Bloomberg.*
    January 30, 2016.

Ford, Frederick. "New Marks, Old Mistakes in Berlin." *New Republic.* July 19, 1948.

Fossedal, Gregory, and Bill Mikhail. "A Modest Magician: Will Clayton and the Rebuild-
    ing of Europe." *Foreign Affairs.* May/June 1997.

Foy, Henry. "Poland Reaffirms Its Commitment to Ukraine." *Financial Times.* December
    15, 2015.

Franklin, Benjamin. "The Morals of Chess." *The Columbian Magazine* (December 1786):
    159–61.

Frattini, Franco. "The Arab World Needs a Marshall Plan." *Project Syndicate.* May 26,
    2011.

French Ministry of Foreign Affairs and International Development. "A Tour of the Quai
    d'Orsay." http://www.diplomatie.gouv.fr/en/the-ministry-of-foreign-affairs/a-tour
    -of-the-quai-d-orsay/article/the-main-dining.

Friedman, George. "The Geopolitics of Russia: Permanent Struggle." Stratfor. October
    2008 [April 15, 2012]. https://www.stratfor.com/analysis/geopolitics-russia-per
    manent-struggle.

———. "Russia's Strategy." *This Week in Geopolitics.* December 28, 2015.

———. "Mapping Russia's Strategy." *This Week in Geopolitics.* January 25, 2016.

Friedman, Thomas L. "Foreign Affairs; Now a Word from Mr. X." *New York Times.* May
    2, 1998.

Furman, Bess. "Marshall Urges 'Freedom Gardens.'" *New York Times.* February 3, 1948.

Gaddis, John Lewis. "What Is Grand Strategy?" Karl Von Der Heyden Distinguished
    Lecture, Duke University. February 26, 2009. http://tiss-nc.org/wp-content/up
    loads/2015/01/KEYNOTE.Gaddis50thAniv2009.pdf.

Galeotti, Mark. "Why Did It Take Turkey Just 17 Seconds to Shoot Down Russian Jet?"
    The Guardian. November 26, 2015.

Gallup, George. "French Support Marshall Plan but Some Question Motives." *Washing-
    ton Post.* September 2, 1947.

———. "ERP Recipients Suspect Motives." *Washington Post.* February 8, 1948.

———. "Marshall Plan Holds Support of Voters Familiar with It." *Washington Post.*
    March 3, 1948.

———. "Dutch Favor Marshall Plan but Some Question Motives." *Washington Post.* March 31, 1948.

Gareau, Frederick H. "Morgenthau's Plan for Industrial Disarmament in Germany." *The Western Political Quarterly.* Vol. 14, No. 2 (June 1961): 517–34.

Gobarev, Victor. "Soviet Military Plans and Actions During the First Berlin Crisis, 1948–49." *Journal of Slavic Military Studies.* Vol. 10, No. 2 (September 1997): 1–24.

Gorskii, Vyacheslav. "Problems and Prospects of NATO-Russia Relationship: The Russian Debate." NATO Euro-Atlantic Partnership Council Fellowships Programme. June 2001. http://www.nato.int/acad/fellow/99-01/gorskii.pdf.

Greene, James. "Russian Responses to NATO and EU Enlargement and Outreach." Chatham House. *The Means and Ends of Russian Influence Abroad Series.* June 2012.

Grutzner, Charles. "City Hails Friendship Train." *New York Times.* November 19, 1947.

Guinnane, Timothy. "A Pragmatic Approach to External Debt: The Write-down of Germany's Debts in 1953." *VoxEU.org.* August 13, 2015. http://voxeu.org/article/prag matic-approach-external-debt-write-down-germany-s-debts-1953#fn.

Hachey, Thomas E. (ed.). "American Profiles on Capitol Hill: A Confidential Study for the British Foreign Office in 1943." *The Wisconsin Magazine of History,* Vol. 57, No. 2 (Winter 1973–1974): 141–53.

Harkins, Philip. "Mysterious Mr. X." *New York Herald Tribune Magazine.* January 4, 1948.

Harris, Arthur W. D. "A Special Study of Operation 'Vittles.'" *Aviation Operations.* Vol. 11, No. 5 (April 1949): 1–120.

Harris, Eleanor. "From Polo to Politics." *Washington Post.* July 22, 1956.

Harris, William R. "March Crisis 1948, Act II." *Studies in Intelligence.* Vol. 11 (Spring 1967).

Haslam, Jonathan. "Russia's Seat at the Table: A Place Denied or a Place Delayed?" *International Affairs.* Vol. 74, No. 1 (January 1998): 119–30.

Herring, George C., Jr. "The United States and British Bankruptcy, 1944–1945: Responsibilities Deferred." *Political Science Quarterly.* Vol. 86, No. 2 (June 1971): 260–80.

Hetzel, Robert L. "German Monetary History in the First Half of the Twentieth Century." *Federal Reserve Bank of Richmond Economic Quarterly.* Vol. 88, No. 1 (Winter 2002): 1–35.

Hightower, John M. "Britain Slated to Delay Exit from Greece." *Washington Post.* August 10, 1947.

Hinton, Harold. "Anti-American Campaign Intensified in Europe." *New York Times.* November 19, 1947.

———. "Aid Bill Signed by Truman as Reply to Foes of Liberty." *New York Times.* April 4, 1948.

Hoffman, Paul G. "What ECA Has Accomplished." *Commercial and Financial Chronicle.* April 21, 1949.

Holbrooke, Richard C. "America, A European Power." *Foreign Affairs*. March/April 1995.

Holbrooke, Richard C., and Mark Danner. "Marooned in the Cold War: An Exchange Between Mark Danner and Richard C. Holbrooke." *World Policy Journal*. Vol. 14, No. 4 (Winter 1997/1998): 100–102.

Iber, Patrick. "Literary Magazines for Socialists Funded by the CIA, Ranked." *The Awl*. August 24, 2015. https://theawl.com/literary-magazines-for-socialists-funded -by-the-cia-ranked-93e65a5a710a#.kon2mrmtz.

Inkeles, Alex. "The Soviet Attack on the Voice of America: A Case Study in Propaganda Warfare." *The American Slavic and East European Review*. Vol. 12, No. 3 (October 1953).

International Organization. "Allied Control Councils and Commissions." Vol. 2, No. 1 (February 1948): 146–53.

Izvestia. "Gorbachev Denounced the USA for Support of Georgian Aggression." August 11, 2008.Jones, Eric. "Russia and Frozen Conflicts: Security and Strategy." *Foreign Intrigue*. June 1, 2015. http://foreign-intrigue.com/2015/06/russia-and-frozen -conflicts-security-and-strategy-complete-series/.

Jessup, Philip C. "Park Avenue Diplomacy: Ending the Berlin Blockade." *Political Science Quarterly*. Vol. 87, No. 3 (September 1972): 377–400.

Jordans, Frank. "The Big Story: Merkel Challenger Criticizes Austerity Policies." Associated Press. June 4, 2013.

Kantchev, Georgi. "With U.S. Gas, Europe Seeks Escape from Russia's Energy Grip." *Wall Street Journal*. February 25, 2016.

Kennan, George F. ("X"). "The Sources of Soviet Conduct." *Foreign Affairs*. July 1947.

———. "NATO: A Fateful Error." *New York Times*. February 5, 1997.

Kindleberger, Charles P., and F. Taylor Ostrander. "The 1948 Monetary Reform in Western Germany." Paper prepared for a conference sponsored by the German Historical Institute on "The International Financial System: Past and Present," Princeton University, April 16–17, 1998.

Kruszewski, Charles. "The Pivot of History." *Foreign Affairs*. April 1954.

Kuhn, Ferdinand, Jr. "U.S. to Seek Rare Minerals from Europe." *Washington Post*. November 14, 1947.

———. "ERP Backers Overestimated Public Reaction." *Washington Post*. January 25, 1948.

———. "Senate Unit Backs Marshall Plan Bill." *Washington Post*. February 18, 1948.

———. "Czech, Finn Crises Spur ERP Action in Senate." *Washington Post*. February 29, 1948.

———. "Vandenberg European Aid Plan Triumphs." *Washington Post*. March 9, 1948.

————. "Hoover Urges House to Vote Full ERP Sum." *Washington Post*. March 25, 1948.

————. "American Officials Embarrassed by Moscow Broadcast of 'Acceptance.' " *Washington Post*. May 12, 1948.

Kupchan, Charles A. "Reviving the West: For an Atlantic Union." *Foreign Affairs*. May/ June 1996.

Leffler, Melvin. "The American Conception of National Security and the Beginnings of the Cold War, 1945–48." *American Historical Review*. Vol. 89, No. 2 (April 1984): 346–81.

Le Monde. Editorial. October 17, 1947.

Life. "Big U.S. Loan to Great Britain: Plans Are Made to Lend $4,400,000,000, Cancel Part of Lend-Lease Act Debt." December 24, 1945.

Life. "Italy: An Ancient Citadel of Culture Faces a New Threat." November 24, 1947.

Life. "Trouble: From Paris to Bangkok Men Revolt and Die." December 1, 1947.

Life. "Capital's Busiest Man: ECA's Hoffman Works at Breakfast, Lunch and Dinner." May 10, 1948.

Lippmann, Walter. "A Golden Opportunity." *Washington Post*. March 18, 1947.

————. "Europe Revisited." *New York Times*. November 4, 1947.

————. "The Injection of Party Politics." *Washington Post*. November 20, 1947.

————. "High Stakes at London." *New York Times*. November 24, 1947.

————. "An American Agenda." *New York Times*. December 4, 1947.

————. "After the Truman Doctrine." *New York Times*. January 6, 1948.

————. "The Proposed 'Defense Union.' " *New York Times*. January 22, 1948.

————. "The Issue of Europe." *New York Times*. January 26, 1948.

————. "The Millikin Amendment." *Washington Post*. February 19, 1948.

————. "The Military Phase." *New York Times*. March 15, 1948.

————. "A National Emergency." *New York Times*. March 16, 1948.

————. "Measures for the Crisis." *New York Times*. March 22, 1948.

———— "Strategy Reconsidered." *New York Times*. April 5, 1948.

Lockett, Edward B. "Robert Lovett—Co-Pilot of 'State.' " *New York Times*. August 17, 1947.

Lowe, Christian. "In Ukraine, Poland Comes of Age as an EU Power Broker." Reuters. February 24, 2014.

Lukes, Igor. "The 1948 Coup d'Etat in Prague Through the Eyes of the American Embassy." *Diplomacy & Statecraft*. Vol. 22, No. 3 (September 2011): 431–49.

Lukyanov, Fyodor. "Putin's Foreign Policy: The Request to Restore Russia's Rightful Place." *Foreign Affairs*. May/June 2016.

Lutz, Catherine, and Sujaya Desai. "US Reconstruction Aid for Afghanistan: The Dollars and Sense." Watson Institute for International Studies. January 5, 2015.

Lynch, Frances M. B. "Resolving the Paradox of the Monnet Plan: National and International Planning in French Reconstruction." *The Economic History Review.* Vol. 37, No. 2 (May 1984): 229–43.

MacCormack, John. "U.S. Aid Denounced in Vienna Parade." *New York Times.* May 2, 1948.

Mackinder, Halford J. "The Geographical Pivot of History." *The Geographical Journal.* Vol. 23, No. 4 (April 1904): 421–37.

———. "The Round World and the Winning of the Peace." *Foreign Affairs.* July 1943.

Maiello, Michael. "A Marshall Plan for America." *Forbes.* December 7, 2009.

Maier, Charles S. "The Politics of Productivity: Foundations of American International Economic Policy After World War II." *International Organization.* Vol. 31, No. 4 (Autumn 1977): 607–63.

———. "Europe Needs a German Marshall Plan." *New York Times.* June 9, 2012.

Malling, Jens. "The Value of a Frozen Conflict." *Le Monde Diplomatique.* March 2015.

Mangasarian, Leon. "Putin Emboldened on Instability Arc by EU Defense Divide." *Bloomberg.* May 15, 2014. https://www.bloomberg.com/news/articles/2014-05-14/eu-east-west-defense-divide-emboldens-putin-s-arc-of-inst.

Margh, H. F. "Decision on Czech Loan." *New York Times.* November 1, 1946.

Mayer, Arthur L. "Winter of Discontent." *The New Republic.* March 10, 1947.

McKinnon, Ronald I. "Foreign Exchange Constraints in Economic Development and Efficient Aid Allocation." *Economic Journal.* Vol. 74 (June 1964): 388–409.

McLaughlin, Kathleen. "Berlin Lift Ends in 277,264th Flight." *New York Times.* October 1, 1949.

Menkiszak, Marek. "How Should Europe Respond to Russia? The Polish View." European Council on Foreign Relations. November 18, 2014.

http://www.ecfr.eu/article/commentary_how_should_europe_respond_to_russia_the_polish_view352.

Miall, Leonard. "How the Marshall Plan Started." *The Listener.* May 4, 1961.

Middleton, Drew. "Smith Asks the Russians About It." *New York Times.* March 16, 1947.

———. "Why ERP Is Top Target on the Kremlin's List." *New York Times.* March 28, 1948.

———. "Soviet Proclaims New Berlin Money." *New York Times.* June 23, 1948.

———. "Grave Problem in West Germany Caused by Refugees from the East." *New York Times.* April 7, 1949.

Miller, Christopher. "How Disunity and Instability in Europe Benefits Vladimir Putin." *Mashable.* February 26, 2016. http://mashable.com/2016/02/26/russia-europe-brexit/#8ZYEdG7wkqq8.

Milward, Alan S. "Was the Marshall Plan Necessary?" *Diplomatic History*. Vol. 13, No. 2 (April 1989): 231–52.

Morris, John D. "House Approves Six Billion Slash in Budget, 239–159." *New York Times*. February 21, 1947.

Morrow, Edward A. "Berlin Paper Hints Allies May Leave." *New York Times*. December 20, 1947.

———. "Russians in Berlin Hint They May Try to Push Out Allies." *New York Times*. January 12, 1948.

———. "Communists Halt Berlin Assembly." *New York Times*. June 24, 1948.

———. "75,000 in Berlin Ask Aid of World." *New York Times*. June 25, 1948.

Moscow, Warren. "19,000 at Garden Hear Wallace and Taylor in First Major Rally." *New York Times*. May 12, 1948.

Mount, Ferdinand. "To the End of the Line." *London Review of Books*. Vol. 34, No. 8 (April 26, 2012): 27–28.

Narinsky, Mikhail M. "SSSR i plan Marshala. Po materialam arkhiva Prezidenta RF." *Novaia i Noveishaia Istoriia*, No. 2, 1993, S. 11–19. ("The USSR and the Marshall Plan. On the Materials of the Archive of the President of RF." *Modern and Contemporary History*, No. 2, 1993, pp. 11–19.)

———. "The Soviet Union and the Marshall Plan." *Cold War International History Project Working Paper Series*. No. 7. Washington, DC: Woodrow Wilson International Center for Scholars, March 1994.

———. "Berlinskii krizis 1948–1949 gg." *Vestnik MGIMO Universiteta*, No. 1, 2011, S. 162–72 ("Berlin Crisis of 1948–1949." *The Courier of the MGIMO University*, No. 1, 2011, pp. 162–72.)

National Security Archive. "The Soviet Origins of Helmut Kohl's 10 Points." November 18, 2009. http://nsarchive.gwu.edu/NSAEBB/NSAEBB296/.

New Times. "The Prospects for International Cooperation." No. 20. May 16, 1947.

New York Herald Tribune. "End of the Road." December 16, 1947.

New York Times. "Senators Called to Peace Parley." August 16, 1946.

New York Times. "Assembly in Sofia Has Red Majority." October 29, 1946.

New York Times. "Program Drafted for German Peace." March 7, 1947.

New York Times. "Mr. Truman Goes to Congress." March 12, 1947.

New York Times. "Warning to Russia." March 13, 1947.

New York Times. "The Truman Doctrine." March 16, 1947.

New York Times. "The News of the Week in Review: 'Truman Doctrine.'" March 16, 1947.

New York Times. "Czechs Withdraw Paris Acceptance to Avoid Soviet Ire." July 11, 1947.

New York Times. "French Urge Output Balance." August 15, 1947.

New York Times. "Farm Group Backs Aid-to-Europe Idea." September 2, 1947.

New York Times. "Europe Will Feel Loss." October 15, 1947.

New York Times. "World Bank Loan to Poland Stymied." November 5, 1947.

New York Times. "Support from Mr. Dewey." November 7, 1947.

New York Times. "Foreign Aid Urged on Spiritual Basis." November 19, 1947.

New York Times. "AFL Urges Passage of Marshall Plan." December 6, 1947.

New York Times. "State Dept. to Take Over American Zone by June 30." January 9, 1948.

New York Times. "Would Widen U.S. Plan: Reston Calls for Political Policy in Aid to Europe." February 1, 1948.

New York Times. "Gilbert Says the ERP Needs Christians' Aid." February 9, 1948.

New York Times. "ASPCA Suggests ERP Project for Animals; Society Solicits Funds for Pets Abroad." February 18, 1948.

New York Times. "Attlee Thanks Truman." April 6, 1948.

New York Times. "Our Roving Ambassador Leaving for France." June 2, 1948.

New York Times. "Italian Communists to Fight Marshall Plan, Says Togliatti." June 27, 1948.

New York Times. "Hoffman to Go Abroad." July 13, 1948.

New York Times. "Oil Company Denies Soviet Map Charge." September 26, 1948.

New York Times. "Russian Spurs U.N.: Alleges Forrestal, Other Officials Are Planning Assault on Soviet." September 26, 1948.

New York Times. "The Map That Made Vyshinsky See Red." October 3, 1948.

New York Times. "Victory in Berlin." May 5, 1949.

New York Times. "First Berlin Train from West Sealed." May 12, 1949.

New York Times. "Speeches of Marshall and Truman Stressing Need for Unity." June 6, 1949.

New York Times. "Kennan Maps Rest from U.S. Duties." December 11, 1949.

New York Times. "Statement by Hoffman to the Senate-House Group on Operation of the Marshall Plan." February 22, 1950.

New York Times. "Arthur H. Vandenberg." April 22, 1951.

New York Times. "Diplomacy Easy the Caffery Way." February 20, 1955.

New York Times. "Defense His Specialty: Robert Abercrombie Lovett." February 29, 1960.

New York Times. "Gen. Bedell Smith Is Dead in Capital." August 10, 1961.

New York Times. "William L. Clayton Dead at 86; Once Undersecretary of State: Started as Stenographer." February 9, 1966.

New York Times. "Robert Murphy, Career Diplomat, Dies." January 10, 1978.

New York Times. "Marshall Vasily Chuikov, 82, Dies; Commanded Stalingrad's Defense." March 20, 1982.

New York Times. "Berlin Borderguards Stunned by News." November 10, 1989.

New York Times. "Another Voice on German Role." June 15, 1990.

New York Times Magazine. "Europe: The New Dark Continent." March 18, 1945.

New York Times Magazine. "No.1 Envoy to Europe." September 21, 1947.

Niculae, Vlad, Srijan Kumar, Jordan Boyd-Graber, and Cristian Danescu-Niculescu-Mizil. "Linguistic Harbingers of Betrayal: A Case Study on an Online Strategy Game." *Proceedings of the Association of Computational Linguistics.* June 2015. http://vene.ro/betrayal/niculae15betrayal.pdf.

Norman, Laurence, and Julian E. Barnes. "EU Pushes Deeper Defense Cooperation." *Wall Street Journal.* September 13, 2016.

Nover, Barnet. "It's Up to Us: Investing in World Freedom." *Washington Post.* March 13, 1947.

———. "Marshall vs. Moscow." *Washington Post.* September 28, 1947.

Office of the Historian, U.S. House of Representatives. "Power of the Purse." http://history.house.gov/Institution/Origins-Development/Power-of-the-Purse/.

Office of the Historian, U.S. State Department. "Secretary of State John Hay and the Open Door in China, 1899–1900." https://history.state.gov/milestones/1899-1913/hay-and-china.

Orwell, George. "You and the Atomic Bomb." *Tribune* (London). October 19, 1945.

Oser, Alan S. "Ex-Gov. Averell Harriman, Adviser to 4 Presidents, Dies." *New York Times.* July 27, 1986.

Oweis, Khaled Yacoub. "Mideast Power Brokers Call for 'Marshall Plan' After Unrest." Reuters. October 22, 2011.

Page, Jeremy. "China Sees Itself at Center of New Asian Order." *Wall Street Journal.* November 9, 2014.

Parrish, Scott D. "The Turn Toward Confrontation: The Soviet Reaction to the Marshall Plan, 1947." *Cold War International History Project Working Paper Series.* No. 7. Washington, DC: Woodrow Wilson International Center for Scholars, March 1994.

Pearson, Drew. "The Washington Merry-Go-Round." *Washington Post.* December 6, 1945.

———. "The Washington Merry-Go-Round." *Washington Post.* March 3, 1947.

———. "South Needs 'Marshall Plan.'" *Washington Post.* December 18, 1947.

Pechatnov, Vladimir O. "The Big Three After World War II: New Documents on Soviet Thinking About Post War Relations with the United States and Great Britain." *Cold War International History Project Working Paper Series.* No. 13. Washington, DC: Woodrow Wilson International Center for Scholars, May 1995.

Peel, Quentin. "Germans Revive Greek Marshall Plan Idea." *Financial Times.* February 22, 2012.

Perlmutter, Amos, and Ted Galen Carpenter. "NATO's Expensive Trip East: The Folly of Enlargement." *Foreign Affairs.* January/February 1998.

Phillips, Cabell. "Congressional Tours Big Aid to Marshall Plan." *New York Times.* October 19, 1947.

Pons, Silvio. "Stalin, Togliatti, and the Origins of the Cold War in Europe." *Journal of Cold War Studies.* Vol. 3, No. 2 (Spring 2001): 3–27.

Raack, R. C. "Stalin Plans His Post-War Germany." *Journal of Contemporary History.* Vol. 28, No. 1 (January 1993): 53–73.

Raine, Fernande Scheid. "Stalin and the Creation of the Azerbaijan Democratic Party in Iran, 1945." *Cold War History*, Vol. 2, No. 1 (October 2001): 1–38.

Rapoza, Kenneth. "Russia 'Will Never' Attack a NATO Country, Unless Provoked." *Forbes.* June 6, 2016.

Raymond, Jack. "Taber Opposes Aid to Europe at Once." *New York Times.* October 4, 1947.

———. "German Fate Tied to Marshall Plan." *New York Times.* November 17, 1947.

———. "Clay Declares U.S. Won't Quit Berlin Short of Warfare . . ." *New York Times.* June 25, 1948.

———. "ECA Weighs Aiding German Refugees: Influx of Millions in West Area Creates Extremely Critical Economic Situation." *New York Times.* May 29, 1949.

Raymont, Henry. "Leaders' Papers Reveal a Light Spirit of Yalta." *New York Times.* May 21, 1972.

Reedy, Tom. "Ruthless Stalin Favorite Is New Dictator of East Germany." *Washington Post.* August 27, 1950.

Reinhart, Carmen M., and Kenneth S. Rogoff. "From Financial Crash to Debt Crisis." *NBER Working Paper Series.* No. 15795 (March 2010).

Reston, James. "The No. 1 No. 2 Man in Washington." *New York Times Magazine.* August 25, 1946.

———. "U.S. Weighs Aid to Greece of 350 Millions in 3 Years." *New York Times.* March 1, 1947.

———. "Truman Plans Dual Policy to Meet Russian Expansion." *New York Times.* March 11, 1947.

———. "Bewildered Congress Faces World Leadership Decision." *New York Times.* March 14, 1947.

———. "The Big Question: What Will Our World Role Be?" *New York Times.* March 16, 1947.

———. "U.S. Studies Shift of Help to Europe as a Unit in Crisis." *New York Times.* May 25, 1947.

———. "Comintern Move Held Knell of East-West Unity." *New York Times.* October 7, 1947.

———. "Comintern Move Is Spur to the Marshall Plan." *New York Times.* October 12, 1947.

———. "U.S. Frets Over de Gaulle: Fears a Man on Horseback." *New York Times.* October 21, 1947.

———. "'Freedomtern' Suggested to Rally Democracies." *New York Times*. October 26, 1947.

———. "Antipathy to Aid Fades in Congress." *New York Times*. November 6, 1947.

———. "Democrats Let Vandenberg Carry Load in Aid Debate." *New York Times*. November 25, 1947.

———. "Capital Fears Communists May Ruin Europe Aid Plan." *New York Times*. December 5, 1947.

———. "Actual Studies in Europe Sway Views of Congress." *New York Times*. December 9, 1947.

———. "Congress Now Sees Need to Combat False Reports." *New York Times*. December 11, 1947.

———. "Vandenberg Wants a National Debate on Marshall Plan." December 22, 1947.

———. "ERP Debate Poses a Challenge for America." *New York Times*. January 4, 1948.

———. "Marshall Always Patient, but Adamant on His Plan." *New York Times*. January 9, 1948.

———. "Kremlin, as Usual, Comes to the Rescue of ERP." *New York Times*. January 18, 1948.

———. "Baruch Asserts Revival of Europe Rests on Unity." *New York Times*. January 20, 1948.

———. "U.S. Confronting Problem of Joining Western Bloc." *New York Times*. February 6, 1948.

———. "Moves by Vandenberg Speed Marshall Plan." *New York Times*. February 22, 1948.

———. "Red Threat Spurs Movement for Western Security Pact." *New York Times*. February 27, 1948.

———. "Basic Decision Facing U.S. Foreign Policy." *New York Times*. March 14, 1948.

———. "Crises in Europe Present Moral Problems for U.S." *New York Times*. March 23, 1948.

———. "Economic War Is Feared by the State Department." *New York Times*. March 26, 1948.

———. "Events Spotlight Vandenberg's Dual Role." *New York Times*. March 28, 1948.

———. "ERP Invitation to Spain Poses Diplomats' Dilemma." *New York Times*. March 31, 1948.

———. "Position Clarified: President Acts to Avoid Misconceptions, Denies Hostility to Soviet." *New York Times*. May 12, 1948.

———. "U.S. Plan Weighed: Big 3 Would Withdraw to Ports in the North Under Proposal." *New York Times*. May 12, 1949.

Rettman, Andrew. "Merkel: Russia Cannot Veto EU Expansion." *EUobserver.* November 17, 2014. https://euobserver.com/foreign/126540.

Reynolds, David. "The European Response: Primacy of Politics." *Foreign Affairs*. May/ June 1997.

Reynolds, Genevieve. "Charges Marshall Plan Opponents Follow Red Line." *Washington Post*. January 17, 1948.

Ritschl, Albrecht. "Germany, Greece and the Marshall Plan." *The Economist*. June 15, 2012.

———. "Germany, Greece and the Marshall Plan, Another Riposte." *The Economist*. June 25, 2012.

Roberts, Chalmers M. "Four Presidents Lead Bohlen to Paris Post." *Washington Post*. September 2, 1962.

———. "Robert D. Murphy: Loyal Soldier of the Cold War." *Washington Post*. February 11, 1978.

Roberts, Geoffrey. "Litvinov's Lost Peace, 1941–1946." *Journal of Cold War Studies*. Vol. 4, No. 2 (Spring 2002): 23–54.

Roberts, Gregory. "Moscow and the Marshall Plan." *Europe-Asia Studies*. Vol. 46, No. 8 (1994): 1371–86.

Ross, Albion. "Czech Sees Gains in Marshall Plan." *New York Times*. January 4, 1948.

———. "Czech Socialists Regret Aid Stand." *New York Times*. January 18, 1948.

Samuels, David. "One Last Interview." *Tablet Magazine*. September 29, 2016. http://www.tabletmag.com/jewish-news-and-politics/214621/one-last-interview.

Sanders, Katie. "Did Vladimir Putin Call the Breakup of the USSR 'the Greatest Geopolitical Tragedy of the 20th Century?' " Politifact.com. March 6, 2014. http://www.politifact.com/punditfact/statements/2014/mar/06/john-bolton/did -vladimir-putin-call-breakup-ussr-greatest-geop/.

Sapp, Steven P. "Jefferson Caffery, Cold War Diplomat: American-French Relations, 1944–49," *Louisiana History: The Journal of the Louisiana Historical Association*. Vol. 23, No. 2 (1982).

Sedgwick, A. C. "Athens Bomb Kills Minister; Red Plot on Cabinet Alleged." *New York Times*. May 2, 1948.

Sestanovich, Stephen. "Could It Have Been Otherwise?" *The American Interest*. Vol. 10, No. 5 (April 14, 2015).

Shchetko, Nick, and Alan Cullison. "Ukraine Ends 'Nonaligned' Status, Earning Quick Rebuke from Russia." *Wall Street Journal*. December 23, 2014.

Shlapak, David A., and Michael Johnson. "Reinforcing Deterrence on NATO's Eastern Flank: Wargaming the Defense of the Baltics." *Research Reports*. Santa Monica, CA: RAND Corporation, 2016. http://www.rand.org/content/dam/rand/pubs/re search_reports/RR1200/RR1253/RAND_RR1253.pdf.

Simms, William Phillip. "Truman Doctrine." *Washington Daily News*. March 14, 1947.

Simon, Zoltan. "Orban Says He Seeks to End Liberal Democracy in Hungary." *Bloomberg*.

July 28, 2014. https://www.bloomberg.com/news/articles/2014-07-28/orban-says-he-seeks-to-end-liberal-democracy-in-hungary.

Siracusa, Joseph M. "The Meaning of Tolstoy: Churchill, Stalin, and the Balkans, Moscow, October 1944." *Diplomatic History*. Vol. 3, No. 4 (October 1979): 443–63.

Smith, Jean Edward. "General Clay and the Russians: A Continuation of the Wartime Alliance in Germany, 1945–1948." *Virginia Quarterly*. Vol. 64, No. 1 (Winter 1988): 20–36.

Soros, George. "A Tragic, Historical Mistake by the Germans." *Spiegel Online*. June 26, 2012.

Steel, Ronald. "A Self-Made Man." *New York Review of Books*. August 13, 1992.

———. "Playing Loose with History." *New York Times*. May 26, 1997.

Steil, Benn. "Red White: Why a Founding Father of Postwar Capitalism Spied for the Soviets." *Foreign Affairs*. March/April 2013.

Steinkopf, Alvin J. "Europeans Facing Winter of Hunger." *Washington Post*. September 28, 1947.

Stimson, Henry. "The Challenge to Americans." *Foreign Affairs*. October 1947.

Stivers, William. "The Incomplete Blockade: Soviet Zone Supply of West Berlin, 1948–49." *Diplomatic History*. Vol. 21, No. 4 (Fall 1997): 569–602.

Stokes, Bruce. "Views of NATO and Its Role Are Mixed in U.S.; Other Member Nations." Pew Research Center. March 18, 2016. http://www.pewresearch.org/fact-tank/2016/03/28/views-of-nato-and-its-role-are-mixed-in-u-s-other-member-nations/.

Suddath, Claire. "Why Did World War I Just End?" *Time*. October 4, 2010. http://content.time.com/time/world/article/0,8599,2023140,00.html.

Sulzberger, C. L. "British Declare 'Protocol M' Fake; Red 'Plot' in Ruhr Ruse by German." *New York Times*. April 11, 1948.

Takhnenko, Galina. "Anatomy of a Political Decision: Notes on the Marshall Plan." *International Affairs* [Moscow]. July 1992.

Taylor, A. J. P. "The European Revolution." *The Listener*. November 22, 1945.

Tcherneva, Pavlina. "A Global Marshall Plan for Joblessness?" *New Economic Perspectives*. May 12, 2016. http://neweconomicperspectives.org/2016/05/global-marshall-plan-joblessness.html.

Thompson, Mark. "Soros: Ukraine Needs EU Marshall Plan." *CNNMoney*. March 12, 2014. http://money.cnn.com/2014/03/12/news/economy/ukraine-europe-soros/.

Time. "Cotton's Clayton." August 17, 1936.

Time. "The Year of Decision." January 5, 1948.

Time. "THE CONGRESS: Fateful Calendar." January 12, 1948.

Time. "The Best Bargain the American People Ever Bought." April 11, 1949.

Time. "I Am an Optimist." June 4, 1990.

Tóth, Csaba. "Viktor Orban: 'The Era of Liberal Democracies Is Over.'" *Budapest Beacon.* July 27, 2014. http://budapestbeacon.com/politics/viktor-orban-era-liberal -democracies/10538.

Tower, Samuel A. "Vandenberg Acts to Speed ERP Vote, Sets March 15 Goal." *New York Times.* February 29, 1948.

Troianovski, Anton, and Matthew Karnitsching. "Merkel Rival Kicks Off Campaign, Hits Out at Austerity, Social Issues." *Wall Street Journal.* July 31, 2013.

Trussell, C. P. "Congress Is Solemn; Prepares to Consider Bills After Hearing the President Gravely." *New York Times.* March 13, 1947.

———. "Senate Votes 83–6 for Interim Help to Three Nations." *New York Times.* December 2, 1947.

Ullman, Richard. "The U.S. and the World: An Interview with George Kennan." *New York Review of Books.* August 12, 1999.

Voigt, Karsten. "NATO Enlargement: Sustaining the Momentum." *NATO Review.* Vol. 44, No. 2 (March 1996): 15–19.

Waggoner, Walter H. "Congress Session Meets Opposition." *New York Times.* September 5, 1947.

Wall Street Journal. "The Price of E.R.P." February 3, 1948.

Wall Street Journal. "Devaluation Necessary in Some ERP Countries, Snyder Says: He Rejects a Currency Conference." February 26, 1948.

Wall Street Journal. "Senate Approves Ban on Exports to Russia of Goods Scarce for ERP." March 9, 1948.

Wall Street Journal. "China's Marshall Plan." November 12, 2014.

Walz, Jay. "House Vote Looms This Week on Aid; Revisions Doubted." *New York Times.* March 29, 1948.

Warburg, James P. "Report on Germany." *The New Statesman and Nation.* Vol. 32 (August 10, 1946).

Warren, Lansing. "Ramadier Wins Confidence Vote; Backs Marshall Plan in Entirety." *New York Times.* July 5, 1947.

Warren, Lansing. "Friendship Cargo Hailed by France." *New York Times.* December 18, 1947.

———. "Bidault and Bevin Give Pledge to U.S." *New York Times.* April 6, 1948.

———. "Delay on Germany Explained in Paris." *New York Times.* June 14, 1948.

———. "French Assembly Accepts Accords on West Germany: Gives Approval, 297–289 . . ." *New York Times.* June 17, 1948.

Washington Post. "Civil Administrator." March 31, 1945.

Washington Post. "Yugoslavs Shot Up Plane, Envoy Says." August 19, 1946.

Washington Post. "Roots of the Truman Doctrine." March 16, 1947.

Washington Post. "Ferguson Prefers Loans to Foreign Businesses." September 24, 1947.

Washington Post. "Javits Urges Caution in Marshall Aid Plan." October 5, 1947.

Washington Post. "Dodd Urges Mothers to Aid in Implementing Foreign Policy." October 21, 1947.

Washington Post. "Marshall Plan Rechristened as 'Recovery.'" November 7, 1947.

Washington Post. "Ready for Congress." November 9, 1947.

Washington Post. "Majority Wants U.S. to Stop Shipment of Goods to Russia." December 12, 1947.

Washington Post. "Marshall Plan Called 'World WPA.'" January 11, 1948.

Washington Post. "Russia Warned Bluntly by Bevin That Its Policy Will Lead to War." January 23, 1948.

Washington Post. "Truman Signs Bill to Bolster 'Voice' of U.S." January 28, 1948.

Washington Post. "End Cold War, Wallace Urges U.S., Russia." May 12, 1948.

Washington Post. "Bidault May Quit Post in 6-Power Fight." June 13, 1948.

Washington Post. "Averell Delights Ladies." August 13, 1956.

Washington Post. "Gen. Walter Bedell Smith." August 11, 1961.

White, William S. "Connally Is Cool to Extra Session." *New York Times.* September 24, 1947.

———. "Marshall Plan Faces Under-Cover Opposition." *New York Times.* November 2, 1947.

———. "Stronger 'Voice of America' Is Backed to Counter Soviet." *New York Times.* January 17, 1948.

Whitman, Alden. "Lewis W. Douglas Is Dead." *New York Times.* March 8, 1974.

———. "Paul G. Hoffman Is Dead at 83; Led Marshall Plan and U.N. Aid." *New York Times.* October 9, 1974.

Yacoubian, Mona. "Middle East 'Marshall Plan' Will Sustain Arab Spring." *The Hill (Congress Blog).* January 11, 2012. http://origin-nyi.thehill.com/blogs/congress-blog/foreign-policy/203639-middle-east-marshall-plan-will-sustain-arab-spring.

Zelikow, Philip. "George C. Marshall and the Moscow CFM Meeting of 1947." *Diplomacy & Statecraft.* Vol. 8, No. 2 (July 1997): 97–124.

Zwass, Adam. "Money, Banking, and Credit in the Soviet Union and Eastern Europe." *Eastern European Economics.* Vol. 17, Nos. 1 and 2 (Fall/Winter 1978–1979): 3-233.

SPEECHES AND STATEMENTS

Albright, Madeleine. "Statement." February 18, 1997. http://www.nato.int/cps/en/natohq/opinions_25715.htm?selectedLocale=en.

———. "Harvard University Commencement Address." June 5, 1997. http://gos.sbc.edu/a/albright3.html.

Avalon Project at Yale Law School. "Washington's Farewell Address 1796." Lillian Gold-
    man Law Library. http://avalon.law.yale.edu/18th_century/washing.asp.

British Pathé. "Senator Vandenberg on Marshall Plan (March 1, 1948)." YouTube. Posted
    April 13, 2014. https://www.youtube.com/watch?v=9Z0BxDeKtrQ.

British Pathé. "Vyshinsky at UN (September 18, 1947)." YouTube. Posted April 13, 2014.
    https://www.youtube.com/watch?v=6f7qIPODFfg.

Clinton, Hillary. "Secretary of State Hillary Rodham Clinton's Remarks on Receiving
    the George C. Marshall Foundation Award." June 2, 2011. www.marshallfoundation
    .org/SecretaryClintonremarksJune22011.htm.

Hambro, Carl Joachim. "Presentation Speech." December 10, 1953. Nobelprize.org.
    Nobel Media AB 2014. http://www.nobelprize.org/nobel_prizes/peace/laure
    ates/1953/press.html.

Marshall, George C. "Speech at Princeton University." February 22, 1947. http://mar
    shallfoundation.org/library/digital-archive/6-026-speech-princeton-university
    -february-22-1947/.

———. "The Marshall Plan Speech." June 5, 1947. http://marshallfoundation.org/mar
    shall/the-marshall-plan/marshall-plan-speech/.

———. "Nobel Lecture: Essentials to Peace." December 11, 1953. Nobelprize.org. Nobel
    Media AB 2014. http://www.nobelprize.org/nobel_prizes/peace/laureates/1953/
    marshall-lecture.html.

Nunn, Sam. "The Future of NATO in an Uncertain World." Speech to the SACLANT
    Seminar 95. June 22, 1995. http://www.nato.int/cps/en/natohq/opinions_24781
    .htm?selectedLocale=en.

THULE. "Truman Doctrine—President Truman Speech on March 12, 1947: Giving Aid
    to Greece and Turkey." YouTube. Posted October 23, 2012. https://www.youtube
    .com/watch?v=btCLnh5gCPU.

Vyshinsky, Andrei. "Vyshinsky Speech to U.N. General Assembly." http://astro.temple
    .edu/~rimmerma/vyshinsky_speech_to_un.htm.

NOTES

CHAPTER 1: PROLOGUE

1   Avalon Project: http://avalon.law.yale.edu/18th_century/washing.asp.

2   Sherwood (1948 [2008]:99).

3   Sherwood (1948 [2008]:109).

4   See, for example, Plokhy (2010:17, 30).

5   Eden (1965:513).

6   Plokhy (2010:233–35).

7   Chuev (1993:51).

8   Churchill V (1951:332).

9   Bohlen (1973:200).

10   See, for example, Raymont (May 21, 1972).

11   Plokhy (2010:345); Miscamble (2007:73—74); Harriman and Abel (1975:444).

12   Plokhy (2010:xxiv).

13   Pechatnov (2006:313–19); Pechatnov and Edmondson (2001:101).

14   Neiberg (2015:xiii).

15   FDR in February 1940: "The Soviet Union, as everybody who has the courage to

face the fact knows, is run by a dictatorship as absolute as any other dictatorship in the world. It has allied itself with another dictatorship and it has invaded a neighbor so infinitesimally small that it could do no conceivable harm to the Soviet Union, a neighbor which seeks only to live at peace as a democracy, and a liberal, forward looking democracy at that." See "Address to the Delegates of the American Youth Congress, Washington, DC," February 10, 1940, in *Public Papers of the Presidents: Franklin D. Roosevelt, 1940*.

16   This is Truman's account (Truman I [1955:79–82]). Bohlen's is milder, but it is indisputable from Molotov's own version that the president was undiplomatically harsh. McCullough (1992:376); Bohlen (1973:213); AVP RF, Fond 05, op. 7, P. 2, file 30, pp. 53–55.

17   Isaacson and Thomas (1986 [2012]:256); Catledge (June 24, 1941).

18   Neiberg (2015:59, 103–4).

19   Beschloss (2002:268).

20   Miscamble (2007:184).

21   Mee (1975:262).

22   "Protocol of the Proceedings of the Berlin Conference," No. 1383, August 1, 1945, in *FRUS: The Conference of Berlin (The Potsdam Conference)*, II: 1485–86.

23   Thompson minutes, twelfth plenary meeting, August 1, 1945, in *FRUS: The Conference of Berlin (The Potsdam Conference)*, II: 566–69.

24   Miscamble (2007:209).

25   See Steil (2013) and Steil (March/April 2013).

26   See Steil (2013).

27   Smith (1990:282).

28   Levering and Botzenhart-Viehe (2001:8); Kennan I (1967:57).

29   Pechatnov and Edmondson (2001:105).

30   Pechatnov and Edmondson (2001:107); Dunbabin (1994 [2013]:17); Gromyko (1990:141).

31   Pechnatov and Edmondson (2001:107–10).

32   Orwell (October 19, 1945). See also Westad (2010:3).

33   Acheson (1969:725-26).

34   Bohlen, memorandum, August 30, 1947, in *FRUS, 1947*, I: 763–65.

35   Leffler (April 1984:364).

36   Belair (January 16, 1948).

37   Joseph Davies, diary entry, July 13, 1945, Box 17, Chronological File, Part I, Davies Papers, Library of Congress.

CHAPTER 2: CRISIS

1   Isaacson and Thomas (1986 [2012]:386).

2   Churchill speech (May 14, 1947), quoted in Isaacson and Thomas (1986 [2012]:386).

3   Lowe (2012:xiv, 99); *New York Times Magazine* (March 18, 1945:5).

4   Judt (2005:13, 17).

5   Lowe (2012:50, 147, 150, 204–5, 229, 242–43, 262); Judt (2005:24, 34, 42, 49–50); Kershaw (2015:473–79).

6   Kershaw (2015:470–71, 474).

7   Judt (2005:14–17, 23, 27, 30).

8   Fursdon (1980:20).

9   Isaacson and Thomas (1986 [2012]:288).

10 Lowe (2012:48); Siklos (1991:1); Judt (2005:39); Truman I (1955:102).

11 Judt (2005:86).

12 Lowe (2012:201); Siklos (1991:1); Judt (2005:21).

13 Judt (2005:89).

14 Judt (2005:17).

15 Acheson to Harry Hopkins, memorandum, "The Maintenance of the Civilian Economy of Liberated Areas Is an Essential Instrument of Total War," December 26, 1944, in *FRUS, 1945*, II: 1060.

16 Kennan I (1967:281–82).

17 Swain (1992:35).

18 Taylor (November 22, 1945).

19 Kershaw (2015:488–89, 494, 501–2).

20 *Life* (December 24, 1945:22).

21 Chace (1998:135).

22 Bevin, speech, February 21, 1946, House of Commons Debates, Vol. 419, c. 1365.

23 Brookshire (1995:100).

24 Vlavianos (1992:236).

25 Robertson (1987); Stirling (1997:146–47).

26 Truman II (1956:99–100); Crowder (2015:167); Halle (1967:110–13). The British ended up withdrawing more slowly than originally planned, although by August troop levels were down to six thousand. Source: Hightower (August 10, 1947).

27 Marshall, "Speech at Princeton University," February 22, 1947, in Bland and Stoler VI (2013:47–50). Also available here: http://marshallfoundation.org/library/digital-archive/6-026-speech-princeton-university-february-22-1947/.

28 Raine (October 2001:1).

29 Raine (October 2001:1).

30 From the diary of V. M. Molotov, reception of Turkish ambassador Selim Sarper, June 7, 1945, AVP RF, Fond 06, op. 7, P. 2, file 31, pp. 2–6; Acheson (1969:199–200).

31 Isaacson and Thomas (1986 [2012]:369).

32 Truman II (1956:93); Roberts (2006:309); Halle (1967:99–100). Ertegün died in 1944, not 1946—as claimed in the otherwise useful account of the Iran Crisis in Sebestyen (2014:190–99). His body was not repatriated earlier because of the war.

33 Beisner (2006:38–39).

34 Siracusa (October 1979:449).

35 Beisner (2006:39–43). Acheson, interview by Theodore A. Wilson and Richard D. Mckinzie, June 30, 1971, Oral History Interviews, Truman Library: 2–3; Isaacson and Thomas (1986 [2012]:370–72); McCullough (1992:369).

36 McCullough (1992:540); Donovan (1977:277).

37 Acheson (1969:217–19).

38 Yergin (1977:279); Mark F. Ethridge to Marshall, February 17, 1947, in *FRUS, 1947*, V: 820–21.

39 Isaacson and Thomas (1986 [2012]:389).

40 Isaacson and Thomas (1986 [2012]:233).

41 *Guardian* U.S. correspondent Alistair Cooke claimed the crowd numbered thirty thousand. Beisner (2006:29); Mount (April 26, 2012:27–28); Isaacson and Thomas (1986 [2012]:339).

42 Beisner (2006:29); "Summary of Mr. Acheson's Remarks at the American Platform Guild Conference, State Department, January 3, 1946," Assistant Secretary and Under Secretary of State File, Acheson Papers, Truman Library.

43 Pearson (December 6, 1945).

44 McCullough (1992:490).

45 Reston (August 25, 1946).

46 See, for example, Halle (1967:113–14).

47 Harkins (January 4, 1948).

48 Laura Ruttum, "Finding Aid to the George Kennan Papers: 1856–1987," March 2008, George Kennan Papers, Manuscripts and Archives Division, Humanities and Social Sciences Library, New York Public Library: 8. http://www.nypl.org/sites/default/files/archivalcollections/pdf/kennan.pdf.

49 Thompson (2009:5–11); Kennan to Jeanette Hotchkiss, October 8, 1944, Folder 10: "Hotchkiss, Jeanette (Letters from George), 1919–1945," Box 23, Permanent Correspondence, Correspondence, Kennan Papers, Mudd Library, Princeton University.

50 Isaacson and Thomas (1986 [2012]:229); Oser (July 27, 1986).

51 Isaacson and Thomas (1986 [2012]:373).

52 Kennan to Byrnes ["Long Telegram"], February 22, 1946, in *FRUS, 1946*, VI: 698–708.

53 Gaddis (2011:211); Kennan draft, "The United States and Russia," Winter 1946, in Kennan I (1967:560–65).

54 Acheson (1969:196).

55 Beisner (2006:118); Acheson to John P. Frank, n.d. [1967], Folder 137, Box 11, General Correspondence, Acheson Papers, Sterling Memorial Library, Yale University.

56 Isaacson and Thomas (1986 [2012]:355–56).

57 Kennan ("X") (July 1947).

58 Kissinger (1979:135).

59 Kornienko (2001:60–61).

60 Kennan, "Soviet-American Relations," lecture at the State Department, September 1946, Kennan Papers, Mudd Library, Princeton University (and in National Archives, RG 59).

61 Nye (2005).

62 Kennan to Byrnes ["Long Telegram"], February 22, 1946, in *FRUS, 1946*, VI: 698–708.

63 Between 1946 and 1948, Jones' full title was special assistant to the assistant secretary of state for public affairs. Source: "Biographical Sketch," Jones Papers, Truman Library: https://www.trumanlibrary.org/hstpaper/jonesjm.htm.

64 Bohlen (1973:261).

65 Jones (1955:129–34).

66 Reston (March 1, 1947).

67 Jones (1955:134).

68 Pogue IV (1987:161).

69 Acheson (1969:217–19).

70 Jones (1955:135).

71 McCullough (1992:549).

72 Jones (1955:130).

73 Truman II (1956:103).

74 Jones (1955:139); Crowder (2015:183).

75 Acheson (1969: 219).

76 See, for example, *New York Times* (August 16, 1946).

77 Vandenberg (1952:340).

78 Jones (1955:139–42); Isaacson and Thomas (1986 [2012]:395); Acheson (1969:219); Vandenberg (1952:338–40).

79 Jones (1955:143–44).

80 Jones (1955:143).

81   Jones (1955:145).

82   Reston (March 1, 1947).

83   Jones (1955:145–47); Isaacson and Thomas (1986 [2012]:395).

84   McCullough (1992:545–46).

85   The witness was Katharine Lee Marshall, legislative secretary for the United States section of the Women's International League for Peace and Freedom. Statement Before the House Committee on Foreign Affairs, April 8, 1947, in "Assistance to Greece and Turkey: Hearings Before the House Committee on Foreign Affairs," *Legislative History of the Assistance to Greece and Turkey, P.L. 80-75:* 282.; Jones (1955:159–63); Acheson (1969:3).

86   International Bank for Reconstruction and Development (1947:7).

87   Fossedal (1993:214).

88   Reston (March 11, 1947).

89   Morris (February 21, 1947); Acheson (1969:222).

90   McCullough (1992:545).

91   Byrnes (1947:146); *Washington Post* (August 19, 1946); Acheson to Harold Shantz, August 14, 1946, in *FRUS, 1946*, VI: 921; Acheson to Richard C. Patterson, August 20, 1946, in *FRUS, 1946*, VI: 923; Cortesi (August 20, 1946); Richard C. Patterson to Byrnes, August 20, 1946, in *FRUS, 1946*, VI: 925; *Chicago Tribune* (August 27, 1946); Byrnes to Clayton, August 28, 1946, in *FRUS, 1946*, VI: 930; Acheson to Byrnes, August 29, 1946, in *FRUS, 1946*, VI: 931–32.

92   Mills (1951:210); Beisner (2006:66).

93   Arkes (1972:45–46).

94   Beisner (2006:59); U.S. Atomic Energy Commission (1954 [1970]:41).

95   Kennan to Lovett, August 19, 1947, and Kennan to Forrestal, September 29, 1947, Folder: "Chronological—1947," Box 33, PPS Records, RG 59, National Archives.

96   Acheson (1969:221); Jones (155:167); McCullough (1992:546); Isaacson and Thomas (1986 [2012]:376).

97   McCullough (1992:543–46); Bohlen (1973:261).

98   Isaacson and Thomas (2012 [1986]:397–98).

99   Kruszewski (April 1954:401).

100 Mackinder (1919 [1996]:106).

101 See Brotton (2012:363).

102 Mackinder (July 1943).

103 Boggs (June 1947:472); Barney (2015:93).

104 Kennan, National War College lectures, March 14 and 28, 1947, Folders 30 and 31, Box 298, Unpublished Works, Writings, Kennan Papers, Mudd Library, Princeton University; Gaddis (2011:257); Jones (1955:155).

105 Kennan I (1967:322–23); Gaddis (2011:257).

106 McCullough (1992:549).

107 Truman II (1956:102).

108 McCullough (1992:651).

109 Audio of Truman's address: https://www.youtube.com/watch?v=btCLnh5gCPU (THULE [October 23, 2012]).

110 Crowder (2015:169).

111 See, for example, Beisner (2006:61).

112 Acheson (1969:223).

113 Presidential historian Robert Donovan, quoted in Isaacson and Thomas (1986 [2012]:398).

114 *New York Times* (March 12, 1947).

115 *New York Times* (March 13, 1947).

116 Nover (March 13, 1947).

117 Simms (March 14, 1947). Other notable early uses of the term "Truman Doctrine" in the press are: Reston (March 14, 1947);. Reston (March 16, 1947);. Belair (March 16, 1947); *New York Times* (March 16, 1947), "The News of the Week in Review: 'Truman Doctrine'"; *New York Times* (March 16, 1947), "The Truman Doctrine"; and *Washington Post* (March 16, 1947).

118 *Augusta Chronicle* (Georgia) (March 13, 1947).

119 "The very existence of the Greek state is today threatened by the terrorist activities of several thousand armed men, led by Communists, who defy the government's authority at a number of points, particularly along the northern boundaries."

120 Trussell (March 13, 1947:1).

121 Vandenberg (1952:343–44).

122 "Letter of the USSR Consul General in New York Ya.M. Lomakin to the Assistant Minister of Foreign Affairs of the USSR A.Ya. Vyshinsky on the Truman Doctrine," April 19, 1947, AVP RF, Fond 0129, op. 31, P. 192, file 12, pp. 19–21.

123 Novikov (1989:379); Holloway (1994:254).

124 Judt (2005:127). Judt attributes this to Andrei Zhdanov, but this appears incorrect. The original source is a sixty-five-page memorandum prepared by the Central Committee's Foreign Policy Department in late August or early September 1947, as background for Zhdanov's report to a conference of nine eastern European Communist parties: "International Situation of the Soviet Union," RGASPI, Fond 575, op. 1, file 3, p. 57. I am grateful to Svetlana Chervonnaya for pointing this out.

125 Ivan Maisky, diary, conversation with Harriman, September 12, 1945, AVP RF, Fond 06, op. 7, P. 5, file 51, pp. 69–70 (with a copy sent to Stalin); Plokhy (2010:142).

126 Roberts (Spring 2002:23–54); Plokhy (2010:149).

127 Bidault (1965 [1967]:67).

128 Plokhy (2010:140–42, 147–50, 200, 266, 268–69, 331, 379); Churchill VI (1953:293).

129 Plokhy (2010:200).

130 Pechatnov (May 1995:23); Judt (2005:121).

131 The two Yugoslavs Stalin met with on January 9 were Politburo member Andrija Hebrang and Chief of the Supreme Staff General Arso Jovanović. Source: Georgi Dimitrov, entry of January 10, 1945, in Banac (2003:352–53).

132 Djilas (1962:141).

133 Chuev (1993:76); Pechatnov and Edmondson (2001:119).

134 http://teachingamericanhistory.org/library/document/speech-on-the-truman-doctrine/.

135 Jones (1955:178–80).

136 Isaacson and Thomas (1986 [2012]:408).

137 Lippmann (March 18, 1947).

138 Haas (2016:148); Isaacson and Thomas (1986 [2012]:400–401).

139 The Senate vote was 32–7 among Democrats and 35–16 among Republicans. The House vote was 160–13 among Democrats and 127–94 among Republicans. Source: Congressional Quarterly (1948:270, 274–75).

140 *New York Times* (February 9, 1966).

141 Fossedal (1993); *Time* (August 17, 1936).

142 Clayton, memorandum, March 5, 1947, in Dobney (1971:198–200).

143 Acheson to Robert P. Patterson, March 5, 1947, in *FRUS, 1947,* III: 197.

CHAPTER 3: RUPTURE

1 Isaacson and Thomas (1986 [2012]:403).

2 Cray (1990 [2000]:316–19). On Marshall's roles under FDR, see Roberts (2009).

3 Crowder (2015:161); Marshall, interview by William M. Spencer, July 9, 1947, Six Interviews Collection, Interviews and Reminiscences for Forrest C. Pogue, George C. Marshall Foundation; Marshall, interview by Cols. L. M. Guyer and C. H. Connelly, February 11, 1949, Six Interviews Collection, Interviews and Reminiscences for Forrest C. Pogue, George C. Marshall Foundation.

4 See, for example, Unger and Unger (2014:368–83).

5 Pogue IV (1987:139); McCullough (1992:508).

6 George V. Underwood, Jr., to John E. Hull, "Radio No. MING 99," January 9, 1947, in Bland and Stoler VI (2013:3–4); McCullough (1992:532–33).

7 Cray (1990 [2000]:585–86).

8 Pechatnov and Edmondson (2001:89).

9   Strang (1956:174–75). Molotov could read French well and English and German competently. Chuev (1993:77).

10 Moorhouse (2014:17); Montefiore (2003:206).

11 Byrnes (1947:278–79).

12 Roberts (2011:3–4).

13 Bidault (1965 [1967]:40).

14 Churchill I (1948:330).

15 Novikov (1989).

16 Pogue IV (1987:175).

17 Bidault (1965 [1967]:144); Cray (1990 [2000]:600).

18 Cray (1990 [2000]:600–602).

19 Gimbel (1968:112).

20 Harrington (2012:27). See also Harbutt (1986) and Trachtenberg (1999:vii–viii, 15–55).

21 Reynolds (2006:270). A committee of demographers appointed by Mikhail Gorbachev in 1990 used census and military records to put the number of deaths from the war at approximately 26.6 million; this was out of a prewar population of 196.7 million (13.5 percent). Source: Ellman and Maksudov (1994).

22 Chuev (1993:60).

23 Plokhy (2010:111, 257). Bohlen minutes, "Second Plenary Meeting, February 5, 1945, 4 PM, Livadia Palace," in FRUS: Conferences at Malta and Yalta, III: 621; Churchill I (1948:308); "From Ivan Maisky's Diary," in Rzheshevskii (2004:498).

24 Zubok (2007:14).

25 See the estimates in Kindleberger (1991:77–80) and Maier (1991:18).

26 Reynolds (2006:45).

27 Murphy, memorandum, "Meeting of the Economic Subcommittee," July 20, 1945, in FRUS: The Conference of Berlin (The Potsdam Conference), II: 141–42.

28 Isaacson and Thomas (1986 [2012]:291); Harriman to Stettinius, April 4, 1945, in FRUS, 1945, V: 817–20.

29 Harrington (2012:32).

30 Isaacson and Thomas (1986 [2012]:307). The Soviet understanding was that "the Soviet and American delegations have agreed [that] the total amount of reparations . . . should comprise $20 billion, and that 50 percent of this amount should be due to the USSR": "The Crimean Conference of 1945, 11 Febr. 1945," AVP RF, Fond 06, op. 7a, P. 59, file 32, p. 6.

31 Cairncross (1986:95, 99); Sir Wilfred Eady to Hugh Dalton, July 26, 1945, T23 /263, Treasury Papers, UKNA.

32 Warburg (August 10, 1946:92–93).

33 Gimbel (1976:143-144).

34   Smith (1990:408).

35   Clay to Echols, May 2, 1946, CC4277, in Smith I (1974:203–4); Cairncross (1986:154); Maier (1991:22); Smith (1990:350–51).

36   Cairncross (1986:155).

37   Clay to Echols, July 19, 1946, in Smith I (1974:238–39).

38   Smith to Byrnes, June 21, 1946, in *FRUS, 1946*, VI: 763–65.

39   Clay, press conference, Berlin, May 27, 1946, in Smith I (1974:218–23).

40   Gimbel (1976:127–40) and Smith (1990:350–55) argue passionately that Clay's anger was directed almost entirely at the French, and that anti-Communists in the State Department were at fault for transforming the episode into a Cold War confrontation with the Soviets. Maier (1991:22) disagrees. Clay's correspondence and interviews never point a finger at one to the exclusion of the other.

41   Cable dated June 10, 1946; Rostow II (1981:138–48).

42   Mayer (March 10, 1947:19).

43   Clay to Byrnes, memorandum, "Internationalization of the Ruhr," April 22, 1946, in Smith I (1974:192–201).

44   See, for example, Smith (1990:374).

45   Byrnes, "Stuttgart Address: Restatement of U.S. Policy on Germany," September 6, 1946, in Senate Committee on Foreign Relations (1959:42).

46   Gimbel (1976:161–62).

47   Kennan I (1967:333).

48   Special Report of the Military Governor, "Economic Data on Potsdam Germany," September 1947, Folder: "Economic Data on Potsdam, Germany," Box 12, Military Government of Germany File, Panuch Papers, Truman Library: 13.

49   Byrnes, "Stuttgart Address: Restatement of U.S. Policy on Germany," September 6, 1946, in Senate Committee on Foreign Relations (1959:37).

50   Smith (1990:406).

51   Judt (2005:116).

52   Bidault (1965 [1967]:88).

53   Raack (January 1993:59).

54   "Record of conversation of V. M. Molotov with French Ambassador Georges Catroux," February 19, 1947, AVP RF, Fond 06, op. 9, P. 1, file 20, p. 35.

55   Bidault (1965 [1967]:87).

56   Bohlen (1973:262).

57   Smith (1950:219).

58   Smith (1990:414, 425) is unstinting in the view that Marshall had written off cooperation with Moscow prior to his arrival there, yet his own biography subject, Clay, contradicts it in interviews with him, blaming the Soviets instead: "General Marshall . . . arrived to meet the Russians when they were absolutely unwilling to

negotiate anything. . . . I really believe that after the Moscow conference, General Marshall had no real hope of success" (p. 421).

59 Zelikow (July 1997:107–12); Yergin (1977:296); Acheson, statement before the Senate Committee on Foreign Relations, April 1, 1947, in Senate Committee on Foreign Relations (1973:95).

60 Judt (2005:119).

61 Isaacson and Thomas (1986 [2012]:403). The Soviet record of Stalin's conversation with Marshall is here: AVP RF, Fond 06, op. 9, P. 71, file 1104, pp. 29–39; or RGASPI, Fond 558, op. 11, file 374, pp. 147–58.

62 Nickolaevsky (1995:160–61). It is not clear from police records, however, that Stalin was arrested for these specific crimes—at least not officially. I am grateful to Svetlana Chervonnaya for pointing out the discrepancies in various Soviet accounts.

63 Stalin II (1946:290–367); Booker III (2005:694); Plokhy (2010:56–57); Conquest (1991:6–28). On Stalin's youth and early career, see also the outstanding biography by Kotkin I (2014).

64 Kennan I (1967:279).

65 Bullock (1983:25).

66 Conquest (1991:327); Djilas (1962).

67 Smith to Marshall, March 6, 1948, in *FRUS, 1948*, IV: 818–19.

68 Djilas (1962:69–70).

69 Plokhy (2012:77–79); Eden (1965:595).

70 "Memorandum of Conversation," April 15, 1947, in *FRUS, 1947*, II: 337. The American account of the discussion, which I have quoted from, differs in modest respects from the Soviet one: AVP RF, Fond 06, op. 9, P. 71, file 1104, pp. 29–39.

71 "Memorandum of Conversation," April 15, 1947, in *FRUS, 1947*, II: 337–39.

72 Isaacson and Thomas (1986 [2012]:403).

73 "Memorandum of Conversation," April 15, 1947, in *FRUS, 1947*, II: 339.

74 "Memorandum of Conversation," April 15, 1947, in *FRUS, 1947*, II: 340.

75 Bland and Stoler VI (2013:100).

76 Novikov (1989).

77 "Memorandum of Conversation," April 15, 1947, in *FRUS, 1947*, II: 342.

78 Zubok (2007:66); Zubok and Pleshakov (1996:50); Pechatnov and Edmondson (2001:108–10).

79 Grieder (2000:12); Djilas (1962:139); Pechatnov (2010:103); Pechatnov and Edmondson (2001:109).

80 Zubok (2007:71); Raack (January 1993:58).

81 Plokhy (2010:92–96, 368–69).

82 Frank (2001:241); Taylor (2006); Reedy (August 27, 1950); Rodden (2002:32); Kempe (2011).

83   Macintyre (2014:88–89).

84   Mastny (1996:24).

85   The actual German word is *Sadisten*. Friedensburg, memo, August 20, 1948, Bundesarchiv Koblenz N1114/34.

86   Record of I. V. Stalin's conversation with the leaders of the SED Central Committee, January 31, 1947, RGASPI, Fond 558, op. 11, file 303, pp. 9–11.

87   Pechatnov and Edmondson (2001:120–21).

88   Record of I. V. Stalin's conversation with the leaders of the SED Central Committee, January 31, 1947, RGASPI, Fond 558, op. 11, file 303, pp. 9–11.

89   Pechatnov and Edmondson (2001:120–21).

90   Record of I. V. Stalin's conversation with the leaders of the SED Central Committee, January 31, 1947, RGASPI, Fond 558, op. 11, file 303, pp. 9–11.

91   Steil (2013:265–66, 274–76); Plokhy (2010:98–99); Briefing Book Paper, "The Treatment of Germany," January 12, 1945, in *FRUS: Conferences at Malta and Yalta*, I: 187; Clemens (1970:29–30); Buhite (1986:21–28).

92   Vandenberg (1952:123).

93   Behrman (2007:31–32); Judt (2005:82–83).

94   Gimbel (1968:121–22); Dulles, speech, January 17, 1947, in *Vital Speeches of the Day* (February 1947:234–36); Pogue IV (1987:174).

95   "Memorandum of Conversation," April 15, 1947, in *FRUS, 1947*, II: 341–43.

96   Plokhy (2010:30, 241–51); Bohlen (1973:192); Harriman and Abel (1975:412–13); Leahy (1950:315–16); Stettinius (1949:215); Moran (2002:283).

97   Policy Planning Staff, "Resume of World Situation," PPS/13, November 6, 1947, in *FRUS, 1947*, I: 771.

98   Marshall to U.S. Embassy in London, February 20, 1948, in *FRUS, 1948*, II: 72.

99   Behrman (2007:39–40); Gaddis (2011:264); Cray (1990 [2000]:604–5); "Memorandum of Conversation," April 15, 1947, in *FRUS, 1947*, II: 344; Record of conversation of I. V. Stalin with the U.S. Secretary of State G. C. Marshall, April 15, 1947, AVP RF, Fond 06, op. 9, P. 71, file 1104, pp. 29–39.

100 Niculae, Kumar, Boyd-Graber, and Danescu-Niculescu-Mizil (June 2015). See also Chabris (February 19, 2016).

101 "The worse, the better" referred to the supposed revolutionary benefits of deteriorating social conditions in Russia.

102 Marshall, interview with Harry B. Price, February 18, 1953, Folder: "January–June, 1953," Box 1, Oral History Interview File, Price Papers, Truman Library.

103 Murphy (1964:307).

104 *New York Times* (January 10, 1978); Roberts (February 11, 1978).

CHAPTER 4: PLAN

1   Marshall, interview with Harry B. Price, October 30, 1952, Folder: "August–October, 1952," Box 1, Oral History Interview File, Price Papers, Truman Library.

2   Cray (1990 [2000]:606).

3   Reynolds (2006:281).

4   Halle (1967:134).

5   Marshall, radio address, April 28, 1947, in Bland and Stoler VI (2013:121); Cray (1990 [2000]:606).

6   Italics added. "Report of the Special 'Ad Hoc' Committee of the State-War-Navy Coordinating Committee," April 21, 1947, in *FRUS, 1947*, III: 210–15.

7   Marshall, interview with Forrest Pogue, Tape 19M, November 20, 1956, Interviews and Reminiscences for Forrest C. Pogue, George C. Marshall Foundation: 21–22; Crowder (2015:179).

8   Kennan, interview with Harry B. Price, February 19, 1953, Folder: "January–June, 1953," Box 1, Oral History Interview File, Price Papers, Truman Library; Crowder (2015:178).

9   McCullough (1992:561).

10 Chace (1998:162).

11 Kennan I (1967:327–28); Behrman (2007:56).

12 Kennan (1996:144).

13 Office of the Historian, State Department: https://history.state.gov/milestones /1899-1913/hay-and-china.

14 Isaacson and Thomas (1986 [2012]:234).

15 Gaddis (2011:265).

16 Isaacson and Thomas (1986 [2012]) called Acheson, Bohlen, Harriman, Kennan, Lovett, and McCloy "The Wise Men."

17 Steil (2013:117); Acheson (1969:28).

18 Isaacson and Thomas (1986 [2012]:235).

19 McCullough (1992:561); Steil (2013:272).

20 Isaacson and Thomas (1986 [2012]:236); Steil (2013:266–73).

21 Gimbel (1968:1); Murphy (1964:251).

22 Neiberg (2015:31).

23 Winik (2015:423).

24 See, for example, Beschloss (2002:354); Blum III (1967:463–64); and Steil (2013:266, 274–76).

25 Isaacson and Thomas (1986 [2012]:237–38).

26 Gaddis (1982 [2005]:56–57). See also Luttwak (1976:19, 130–31, 137).

27 Kennan ("X") (July 1947:581). Italics added.

28 Gaddis (1982 [2005]:57, 59); Marshall to Lovett, April 23, 1948, in *FRUS, 1948*, III: 103.

29 Gaddis (1982 [2005]:61–62); Forrestal to Chan Gurney, December 8, 1947, in Millis (1951:350–51).

30 Isaacson and Thomas (1986 [2012]:306, 406, 248).

31 Gaddis (1982 [2005]:58); Marshall to Lovett, April 23, 1948, in *FRUS, 1948*, III: 103. Truman, speech to Inter-American Conference, Rio de Janeiro, September 2, 1947, in *Public Papers of the Presidents: Harry Truman, 1947*: 430; Lovett, memorandum of conversation with Huseyin Ragip Baydur, Turkish Ambassador, July 21, 1948, in *FRUS, 1948*, III: 197.

32 Belair (January 16, 1948).

33 Gaddis (1982 [2005]:58); Forrestal to Chan Gurney, December 8, 1947, in Millis (1951:350–51). Italics added.

34 Undated Truman memorandum, probably early 1949, Folder: "Miscellaneous, 1945–53," Box 131, Bureau of the Budget File, Subject File, President's Secretary's Files, Truman Papers, Truman Library; Gaddis (1982 [2005]:23).

35 Gaddis (1982 [2005]:62).

36 Gaddis (1982 [2005]:66, 69); Acheson to U.S. Embassy in Belgrade, February 25, 1949, in *FRUS, 1949*, V: 873; U.S. chiefs of mission to satellite states, "Conclusions and Recommendations of the London Conference of October 24–26," October 26, 1949, in *FRUS, 1949*, V: 31.

37 Acheson (1969:227).

38 Jones (1955:24).

39 Acheson, speech, "The Requirements of Reconstruction," May 8, 1947, in *Department of State Bulletin, 1947*, XVI: 991–94.

40 Jones (1955:30).

41 Acheson (1969:228).

42 Albright (March 19, 1947:1).

43 Haas (2016:2–6).

44 Vandenberg (1952:10).

45 Vandenberg (1952:10).

46 Haas (2016:27).

47 Haas (2016:4, 46); Vandenberg (1952:165–66).

48 Isaacson and Thomas (1986 [2012]:408); Steel (1980:440–42).

49 Policy Planning Staff, "Top Secret Supplement to the Report of the Policy Planning Staff of July 23, 1947, entitled 'Certain Aspects of the European Recovery Program from the United States Standpoint,'" PPS/4: https://www.state.gov/documents/organization/179131.pdf; Mee (1984:90–91).

50 Nitze (1989:51–52).

51   Acheson (1969:230).

52   Jones (1955:247).

53   Clayton, memorandum, "The European Crisis," May 27, 1947, in *FRUS, 1947*, III: 230–32.

54   Clayton, memorandum, "The European Crisis," May 27, 1947, in *FRUS, 1947*, III: 230–32 (italics in original); Clay memorandum on the Marshall Plan, undated [1947], Folder: "Marshall Plan Memos, 1947," Box 60, General File, Clayton Papers, Truman Library; Acheson (1969:232); Cray (1990[2000]:611); Thompson (2009:73).

55   Truman I (1955:236).

56   Arkes (1972:25–26); Stimson to Truman, "Memorandum for the President," July 16, 1945, in *FRUS: The Conference of Berlin (the Potsdam Conference)*, II: 755–57; Stimson to Truman, memorandum, "The Rehabilitation of Europe as a Whole," undated [likely July 22, 1945], in *FRUS: The Conference of Berlin (the Potsdam Conference)*, II: 808–9.

57   Reston (May 25, 1947).

58   *The Economist* (May 31, 1947).

59   Smith (1990:25).

60   Harold Boeschenstein, onetime War Production Board deputy director and, later, Owens-Corning chairman and CEO, quoted in Smith (1990:581).

61   Paul Cabot, a former deputy director of the War Production Board's conservation division, quoted in Smith (1990:158). See also the comments of Averell Harriman (Smith [1990:4]).

62   Smith (1990:212, 215–16, 219, 396); *Washington Post* (March 31, 1945); Clay (1950:7).

63   Smith (1990:5–6).

64   Smith (1990:233, 238).

65   Clay succeeded General Joseph McNarney on March 15, 1947. McNarney had succeeded Eisenhower as European Theater commander in November 1945, also becoming military governor of Germany and Austria at that time.

66   Gimbel (1968:148–51); Clay to Marshall, "German Economic Recovery," May 2, 1947, in Smith I (1974:346–49).

67   Smith (1990:233).

68   Clay to Oliver Echols and Howard Petersen, "Food Situation in U.S. Zone," March 27, 1946, in Smith I (1974:183–84).

69   Judt (2005:128).

70   Feigel (2016:84–84, 239, 242, 252–64); Annan (1997:xii).

71   Smith (1990:245).

72   Backer (1983:148–49).

73   Smith (1990:290–91, 341–49); Backer (1983:148–49). Smith (1990:278) argues that Clay was "dedicated to FDR's goal of meaningful cooperation with the Soviet Union, and [he] rejected bellicose advice from American diplomats that confrontation was inevitable." But this portrait is belied by Clay's own words in discussion with Smith: "I'm not sure we could ever have made four-power government work over a long period of time. The differences between our systems were just too great" (Smith [1990:261]).

74   Smith (1990:261).

75   Smith (1990:258); Clay (signed Eisenhower) to Joint Chiefs of Staff, FWD 23724, June 6, 1945, in Smith I (1974:18–20).

76   Smith (1990:416).

77   Smith (1990:235).

78   Joint Report of the United States and United Kingdom Military Governors, "The European Recovery Program," September 1948, Folder: "European Recovery Program," Box 12, Military Government of Germany File, Panuch Papers, Truman Library: 2.

79   Acheson (1969:232).

80   Kennan, interview with Harry B. Price, February 19, 1953, Folder: "January–June, 1953," Box 1, Oral History Interview File, Price Papers, Truman Library; Crowder (2015:181).

81   Marshall, interview with Harry B. Price, February 18, 1953, Folder: "January–June, 1953," Box 1, Oral History Interview File, Price Papers, Truman Library.

82   Kennan, interview with Harry B. Price, February 19, 1953, Folder: "January–June, 1953," Box 1, Oral History Interview File, Price Papers, Truman Library.

83   Pogue IV (1987:209–10).

84   Berger (January 2, 1974); Daniel (July 24, 1955); Roberts (September 2, 1962).

85   Jones (1955:254–55); Bohlen (1973:263); Cray (1990 [2000]:612); Behrman (2007:66).

86   Bland (1991:559).

87   Bland (1991:559).

88   Acacia (2009:71).

89   Miall (May 4, 1961); Jones (1955:255–56); Acheson (1969:264); Mee (1984:99–100); Isaacson and Thomas (1986 [2012]:413).

90   The speech was actually delivered after lunch, at a ceremony bestowing honorary degrees, and not at the commencement ceremonies in the morning. Audio can be heard here: http://marshallfoundation.org/marshall/the-marshall-plan/marshall-plan-speech/ ("The Marshall Plan Speech").

91   Acheson (1969:233).

92   Bohlen (1973:265).

93 Reynolds (May/June 1997).

94 Isaacson and Thomas (1986 [2012]:413).

95 Marshall, interview with Harry B. Price, February 18, 1953, Folder: "January–June, 1953," Box 1, Oral History Interview File, Price Papers, Truman Library.

96 Norwich (2005:439).

97 Crowder (2015:190).

98 *New Times* (May 16, 1947:1). See also the account of Stalin's discussions at the Moscow Council of Foreign Ministers meetings with perennial Republican presidential candidate Harold Stassen in Parrish (March 1994:9–11).

99 Parrish (March 1994:12–13).

CHAPTER 5: TRAP

1 Molotov underlined more material than is indicated here; I have abbreviated it. "Russian translation of Marshall's statement at Harvard, June 5," AVP RF, Fond 06, op. 9, P. 18, file 209, pp. 1–5; Parrish (March 1994:14).

2 "Cable of the Soviet Ambassador in the USA N. V. Novikov to the Minister of Foreign Affairs of the USSR V. M. Molotov on the 'Marshall Plan,'" June 9, 1947, AVP RF, Fond 059, op. 18, P. 39, file 250, pp. 207–9, published in *Soviet-American Relations 1945–1948*: 429–30; Leffler and Painter (1994 [2005]:74); Holloway (1994:254); Parrish (March 1994:13).

3 Caffery to Marshall, June 18, 1947, in *FRUS, 1947*, III: 259–60.

4 "On the position of the governments of France, Belgium, Holland, and Luxembourg regarding the 'Marshall Plan,'" AVP RF, Fond 046, op. 7, P. 126, file 48, pp. 2–8.

5 Molotov to Soviet ambassadors in Prague, Warsaw, and Belgrade, telegram, June 22, 1947, AVP RF, Fond 06, op. 9, P. 18, file 214, p. 19. Translation is Narinsky's (March 1994).

6 Parrish (March 1994:19).

7 Extraordinary and Plenipotentiary Ambassador of the Republic of Poland in the USSR M. Nashkovsky to Molotov, Moscow, June 24, 1947, AVP RF, Fond 046, op. 7, P. 126, file 48, p. 20.

8 Behrman (2007:81).

9 Jan Masaryk to M. F. Bodrov, Soviet chargé d'affaires at the Soviet Embassy in Czechoslovakia, Prague, July 1, 1947, AVP RF, Fond 06, op. 9, P. 18, file 212, p. 11.

10 Ripka (1950:52); Heimann (2009:174).

11 Note of the Federal People's Republic of Yugoslavia to the Government of the Soviet Union, June 26, 1947, AVP RF, Fond 06, op. 9, P. 18, file 212, pp. 8–9.

12 *Pravda Ukraine*, June 11, 1947, quoted in Pogue IV (1987:220).

13   *Pravda,* June 17, 1947, quoted in Behrman (2007:80–81).

14   Molotov's draft of the instructions for the Soviet delegation at the Paris Conference, June 24, 1947, RGASPI, Fond 558, op. 11, file 211, pp. 21–23.

15   Parrish (March 1994:20); Novikov to Molotov, June 24, 1947, AVP RF, Fond 059, op. 18, P. 39, file 250, pp. 314–20.

16   Varga earned Stalin's recognition by predicting the economic crisis of 1929, and then its end, but in 1947 fell under suspicion for his 1946 work *The Changes in Capitalist Economy Following World War II,* in which he analyzed Keynesian economics and concluded that government intervention had temporarily mitigated the "contradictions of capitalism." The institute he directed was closed that same year; he was denounced for "ideological mistakes," and then persecuted in the anticosmopolitans campaign. His manuscript criticizing the Soviet economic system, completed shortly before his death in 1964, would not be published until 1989. (I am indebted to Svetlana Chervonnaya for this material.)

17   Evgeny Varga, memorandum, "The Marshall Plan and the Economic Situation of the United States, June 24, 1947," AVP RF, Fond 06, op. 9, P. 18, file 213, pp. 1–5; Narinsky (1994:108–9); Narinsky (March 1994:42–43).

18   Avery F. Peterson, "Memorandum of Conversation: Summary of First Meeting of Under Secretary Clayton and Ambassador with British Cabinet Members," June 24, 1947, in *FRUS, 1947,* III: 269.

19   Caffery to Marshall, June 27, 1947, in *FRUS, 1947,* III: 296; Callender (June 27, 1947); Behrman (2007:84). Some sources suggest Molotov's entourage numbered one hundred or more. See, for example, Watson (2005:230); Mommen (2011:164); Pechatnov and Edmondson (2001:126); and Reynolds (May/June 1997).

20   Judt (2005:88).

21   Molotov's conversation with Bidault, June 26, 1947, AVP RF, Fond 06, op. 9, P. 1, file 22, p. 48.

22   Record of conversation between Molotov and Peterson, June 17, 1947, AVP RF, Fond 06, op. 9, P. 1, file 22, p. 9.

23   Bidault (1965 [1967]:152); Crowder (2015:188).

24   Bidault, statement at first session, June 17, 1947, in *French Yellow Book, 1947:* 25–32.

25   Molotov, statement at the second meeting, June 28, 1947, in *French Yellow Book, 1947:* 38–41.

26   Smith (1990:408–9).

27   Crowder (2015:211).

28   Warner (1994:103–4).

29   Interview with Acheson, Wire IV, July 9, 1953, Folder: "July 8–9, 1953," Box 79, Princeton Seminars File, Acheson Papers, Truman Library: 10–11.

30   See Butler (2002:60).

31   Louis (1984:14); Warner (1994:105).

32   Warner (1994:106).

33   Bevin, speech, November 7, 1945, *House of Commons Debates*, Vol. 415, c. 1342; Warner (1994:106–7).

34   For an excellent contrasting of Bevin and Attlee, see Bew (2016).

35   Warner (1994:107–8).

36   Bevin, statement at the second meeting, June 28, 1947, in *French Yellow Book, 1947*: 45–46.

37   Narinsky (2002:279), citing Arkhiv Prezidenta Rossiiskoi Federatsii, Fond 3, op. 63, file 270, p. 55 (Narinsky saw this file, but it is currently off-limits).

38   Sudoplatov (1994:231).

39   Narinsky (2002:279–80); Narinsky (1993:19); Narinsky (1995:177); Narinsky (1997:54-89), citing as his source Arkhiv Prezidenta Rossiiskoi Federatsii, Fond 03, op. 63, file 270, pp. 59–60—a Politburo Special File that is currently off limits; Sudoplatov (1994:231–32); Plokhy (2010:353). I am indebted to Svetlana Chervonnaya for her explanation of the Kremlin message-delivery and cabling process.

40   G. Arkadiev to Molotov, "Comments on Bevin's proposals," June 30, 1947, AVP RF, Fond 06, op. 9, P. 18, file 213, pp. 13–14; Pechatnov and Edmondson (2001:126–27).

41   Acheson, interview with Harry B. Price on October 20, 1953, reprinted in Price (1955:28).

42   Narinsky (March 1994:46), citing Molotov to Moscow, telegram, June 30, 1947, Arkhiv Prezidenta Rossiiskoi Federatsii, Fond 3, op. 63, file 270, pp. 64–65. Similar translation in *French Yellow Book, 1947*: 49–50.

43   Caffery to Marshall, July 1, 1947, in *FRUS, 1947*, III: 301–2; Mastny in *Bohemia Band* (1991:140).

44   Narinsky (March 1994:47), citing Molotov to Stalin, cipher telegram, July 1, 1947, Arkhiv Prezidenta Rossiiskoi Federatsii, Fond 3, op. 63, file 270, p. 71.

45   Bidault, statement at the fourth meeting, July 1, 1947, in *French Yellow Book, 1947*: 51–52.

46   Narinsky (2002:281); Di Biagio (1994:63, 31).

47   Zubok and Pleshakov (1996:106); Chuev (1993:61).

48   Djilas (1983:126–27).

49   Bullock (1983:422).

50   Molotov, statement at the fifth meeting, July 2, 1947, in *French Yellow Book, 1947*: 58–61.

51   Bidault, statement at the fifth meeting, July 2, 1947, in *French Yellow Book, 1947*: 62–65.

52 Douglas to Marshall, July 3, 1947, in *FRUS, 1947*, III: 306–7.

53 McCullough (1992:565). McCullough provides no source for the quote, though it appears in other secondary sources such as Truman (1972:354).

54 Isaacson and Thomas (1986 [2012]:415).

55 Harriman, interview with Harry B. Price, October 1, 1952, Folder: "August–October, 1952," Box 1, Oral History Interview File, Price Papers, Truman Library.

56 Isaacson and Thomas (1986 [2012]:415).

57 Narinsky (2002:281); Di Biagio (1994:123).

58 Narinsky (1994:109); Fonds 735-4, Carton AP-80, Private Archives of M. Georges Bidault, Archives Nationales: 5–6.

59 Hoffman, interview with Harry B. Price, January 28, 1953, Folder: "January–June, 1953," Box 1, Oral History Interview File, Price Papers, Truman Library.

60 Acheson (1969:646).

61 Hoffmann and Maier (1984:24).

62 Lockett (August 17, 1947); *New York Times* (February 29, 1960); Barnes (May 8, 1986).

63 Joint French-British communiqué, July 3, 1947, in *French Yellow Book, 1947*: 69; Callender (July 4, 1947).

64 Caffery to Marshall, July 3, 1947, in *FRUS, 1947*, III: 308–9.

65 Warren (July 5, 1947).

66 Joseph E. Jacobs to Marshall, July 4, 1947, in *FRUS, 1947*, VI: 688–89; Joseph E. Jacobs to Marshall, July 8, 1947, in *FRUS, 1947*, VI: 695–96; John R. Hodge to Marshall, July 10, 1947, in *FRUS, 1947*, VI: 697–700; *International Organization* (February 1948:152–53); Cho (1967:148).

67 Telegram of the CC [Central Committee] of the VCP (b) [All-Union Communist Party (Bolsheviks)] to Comrades Bierut, Dej, Dimitrov, Gottwald, Kuusinen, and Hoxha, "On the Invitation of European Nations for the Discussion of the Marshall Plan," July 4, 1947, AVP RF, Fond 06, op. 9, P. 20, file 236, pp. 3–4.

68 Cables reprinted in Takhnenko (July 1992:122–24); Roberts (1994); Behrman (2007:92).

69 Telegram of the CC [Central Committee] of the VCP (b) to Comrades Bierut, Tito, Dej, Gottwald, Dimitrov, Rakosi, Kuusinen, and Hoxha, "On the Invitation of European Nations for the Discussion of the Marshall Plan," July 7, 1947, AVP RF, Fond 06, op. 9, P. 20, file 236, p. 5.

70 Mastny in *Bohemia Band* (1991:141); Callender (July 4, 1947).

71 Chuev (1993:61).

72 Pechatnov and Edmondson (2001:127); Parrish (March 1994:27).

73 Campbell (1947:442).

74 Telegram of the CC [Central Committee] to Comrades Bierut, Tito, Dej, Gottwald,

Dimitrov, Rakosi, Kuusinen, and Hoxha, "On the Invitation of European Nations for the Discussion of the Marshall Plan," July 7, 1947, AVP RF, F. 06, op. 9, P. 20, file 236, p. 5.

75 Kavtaradze to Vyshinsky, telegram from Bucharest transmitting the note of the Romanian government for the French and British representatives in response to the invitation to Paris, July 9, 1947, AVP RF, Fond 046, op. 7, P. 126, file 48, pp. 55–57.

76 Pechatnov and Edmondson (2001:128).

77 Letter from Stanoje Simić to Bevin and Bidault, July 9, 1947, Box 1-2, KMJ 1—3e, Arhiv Jugoslavije.

78 *Borba* (August 26, 1947).

79 Mastny in *Bohemia Band* (1991:135); Ripka (1950:53–56).

80 Telegram from Ambassador Plenipotentiary Lebedev in Warsaw to Stalin, Molotov, and others, AVP RF, Fond 06, op. 9, P. 20, file 237, p. 8.

81 Van der Beugel (1966:62).

82 Stanton Griffis to Marshall, July 10, 1947, in *FRUS, 1947*, III: 320–22.

83 Caffery to Marshall, July 11, 1947, in *FRUS, 1947*, III: 328.

84 *New York Times* (November 5, 1947).

85 On those elections, which were reasonably free and fair, see Schmidt (1952:97–98).

86 Krátký (1994:13); Behrman (2007:91–94); Laurence Steinhardt to Clayton, July 7, 1947, in *FRUS, 1947*, III: 313–14.

87 Mastny in *Bohemia Band* (1991:141); Ripka (1950:53); Abrams (2001:97).

88 Narinsky (March 1994:50), citing M. Bodrov to Molotov, telegram, July 9, 1947, Arkhiv Prezidenta Rossiiskoi Federatsii, Fond 3, op. 3, file 270, pp. 183–84; Takhnenko (July 1992:122–24).

89 Yergin (1977:316), Narinsky (March 1994:50), and many others write that the Czechs were "summoned" to discuss the Marshall Plan, but the meeting "had been planned for some time," as Mastny writes in *Bohemia Band* (1991:142). This is confirmed by Ripka (1950:55), who discusses the origins of the meeting.

90 Loebl (1969:38); Laurence Steinhardt to Marshall, July 10, 1947, in *FRUS, 1947*, III: 319–20; Behrman (2007:91–95).

91 Ripka (1950:65–70). The Soviet account of the discussions is not materially different: "Record of Stalin's conversation with Czechoslovak government delegation, July 9, 1947," RGASPI, Fond 558, op. 11, file 393, pp. 101–3.

92 Kaplan (1987:11).

93 *Bohemia Band* (1991:134–37).

94 Ripka (1950:70).

95 Laurence Steinhardt to Marshall, July 10, 1947, in *FRUS, 1947*, III: 319–20; Czech government statement translated by Natalie Babjukova.

96   Ripka (1950:59–62).

97   Abrams (2001:101); Krátký (1994:20).

98   Feierabend (1996:352). Text translation by Natalie Babjukova.

99   Majer (1996:471); Abrams (2001:113); Behrman (2007:91–95).

100   Ripka (1950:63).

101   Lockhart (1951:66).

102   Laurence Steinhardt to Marshall, April 30, 1948, in *FRUS, 1948*, IV: 748.

103   Kemp (1999:98); Kaplan (1987:4).

104   Feierabend (1996:355). Text translation by Natalie Babjukova.

105   Drtina (1982:336, 345–46). Text translation by Natalie Babjukova.

106   Kaplan (1987:70, 73).

107   Smith to Marshall, July 11, 1947, in *FRUS, 1947*, III: 327.

108   Kennan, notes for Marshall, July 21, 1947, in *FRUS, 1947*, III: 335.

CHAPTER 6: UNITY

1   Cook (2001:953–54).

2   See French Ministry of Foreign Affairs and International Development: http://
     www.diplomatie.gouv.fr/en/the-ministry-of-foreign-affairs/a-tour-of-the-quai-d
     -orsay/article/the-main-dining. Rapelli (2004 [2011]:25).

3   Reynolds (May/June 1997).

4   Van der Beugel (1966:70).

5   Crowder (2015:193).

6   *New York Times* (July 11, 1947).

7   Milward (1984:69, 71).

8   Caffery to Marshall, July 11, 1947, in *FRUS, 1947*, II: 983.

9   Kennan, memorandum, July 18, 1947, in *FRUS, 1947*, III: 332.

10   Caffery to Marshall, July 20, 1947, in *FRUS, 1947*, III: 334.

11   Clay to Byrnes, May 11, 1947, Folder 651(2), Byrnes Papers, Clemson University
     Library.

12   Clay, teleconference with Howard Petersen, TT-8362, July 24, 1947, in Smith I
     (1974:387).

13   Bidault, communication, July 17, 1947, in *FRUS, 1947*, II: 992.

14   Smith (1990:435); Clay to Royall, CC-1047, July 28, 1947, in Smith I (1974:391).

15   Wesley C. Haraldson, memorandum of discussions of Clayton, Caffery, Nitze, and
     others in Paris, August 8, 1947, in *FRUS, 1947*, III: 349–50.

16   Milward (1984:97–98).

17   Gallup (September 2, 1947).

18   Wesley C. Haraldson, memorandum, "Paris Discussions on the Marshall Plan, August 4 to August 6, 1947," August 8, 1947, in *FRUS, 1947*, III: 349.

19   *New York Times* (February 20, 1955); Sapp (Spring 1982:181).

20   H. Freeman Matthews to John Hilldring, May 15, 1947, Folder: "Memoranda 1947," Box 10, H. Freeman Matthews Files, RG 59, National Archives.

21   James A. Stillwell to Charles E. Saltzman, "Basic Directive to General Clay," August 25, 1947, 740.00119 Control (Germany)/8-2547, RG 59, National Archives.

22   Bohlen, memorandum, August 30, 1947, in *FRUS, 1947*, I: 763.

23   Gimbel (1976:237–38).

24   Milward (1984:73); Callender (July 24, 1947).

25   Murphy to Marshall, July 25, 1947, in *FRUS, 1947*, II: 1008–9.

26   Smith (1990:438–39).

27   Marshall to Douglas, August 8, 1947, in *FRUS, 1947*, II: 1025.

28   Smith (1990:437–41); Pearson (March 3, 1947); Whitman (March 8, 1974).

29   Milward (1984:74–75); Callender (August 13, 1947); *New York Times* (August 15, 1947).

30   Steil (2013:230, 233).

31   Milward (1984:66–67, 72).

32   Reinhart and Rogoff (2011) put the figure at 49.2 percent. INSEE put it at 59.7 percent.

33   Burnham (1990:102–3); "Summary of Fundamentals of External Financial Policy," T232/199, Treasury Papers, UKNA; "Treasury Note," T232/800, Treasury Papers, UKNA.

34   Second memorandum concerning the final program to be elaborated by the European Economic Co-operation Committee, July 26, 1947, Box 11, General File, Records of Temporary, Committees, Commissions and Boards: Records of the President's Committee on Foreign Aid, Truman Library.

35   Sir David Waley, memorandum, July 29, 1947, T236/794, Treasury Papers, UKNA; Milward (1984:77).

36   Clayton to Lovett, August 1, 1947, in *FRUS, 1947*, III: 342.

37   The issue would come to a head nearly seventy years later in the British "Brexit" referendum.

38   Churchill, speech at Albert Hall, May 14, 1947, in James VIII (1974:7486).

39   Memorandum for the Paris delegation, July 15, 1947, FO 236/782.

40   Marshall to Douglas, September 8, 1947, in *FRUS, 1947*, III: 418–19.

41   Behrman (2007:100); *New York Times Magazine* (September 21, 1947).

42   Behrman (2007:101); Gallup I (1972:661, 666).

43   Behrman (2007:98); Roll (2001:43).

44   Alexander Efremovich Bogomolov was the Soviet ambassador to France from 1944 to 1950.

45   Gerashchenko to Vyshinsky, August 13, 1947, AVP RF, Fond 046, op. 7, P. 126, file 48, p. 145.

46   Clayton via Caffery to Marshall, July 10, 1947, in *FRUS, 1947*, III: 317.

47   Clayton via Caffery to Marshall, July 9, 1947, in *FRUS, 1947*, III: 315–16.

48   Clayton via Caffery to Marshall, July 31, 1947, in *FRUS, 1947*, III: 341.

49   Clayton via Caffery to Marshall, July 29, 1947, in *FRUS, 1947*, III: 340–41.

50   Lovett to Clayton, July 10, 1947, in *FRUS, 1947*, III: 325.

51   Wesley C. Haraldson, memorandum of discussions of Clayton, Caffery, Nitze, and others in Paris, August 8, 1947, in *FRUS, 1947*, III: 349–50.

52   Clayton via Caffery to Marshall, July 29, 1947, in *FRUS, 1947*, III: 340.

53   Marshall to Clayton, August 11, 1947, in *FRUS, 1947*, III: 350.

54   Clayton via Caffery to Lovett and C. Tyler Wood, August 12, 1947, in *FRUS, 1947*, III: 355–56.

55   John D. Hickerson to Marshall, August 11, 1947, in *FRUS, 1947*, III: 351–55.

56   Lovett to Clayton and Caffery, August 14, 1947, in *FRUS, 1947*, III: 356–60.

57   Policy Planning Staff, memorandum, PPS/6, August 14, 1947, in *FRUS, 1947*, III: 360–63; Lynch (May 1984:241).

58   Clayton to Marshall, August 6, 1947, in *FRUS, 1947*, III: 344.

59   Kennan, notes for Marshall, July 21, 1947, in *FRUS, 1947*, III: 336–37. See also Wesley C. Haraldson, memorandum of discussions of Clayton, Caffery, Nitze, and others in Paris, August 8, 1947, in *FRUS, 1947*, III: 350.

60   Wesley C. Haraldson, memorandum of discussions of Clayton, Caffery, Nitze, and others in Paris, August 8, 1947, in *FRUS, 1947*, III: 345–47.

61   Clayton and Caffery to Marshall, August 20, 1947, in *FRUS, 1947*, III: 364.

62   Charles H. Bonesteel III to Lovett, memorandum, "Minutes of Meeting on Marshall 'Plan' 3:00 P.M., August 22, 1947," in *FRUS, 1947*, III: 369–71.

63   Clayton to Clair Wilcox, June 17, 1947, in *FRUS, 1947*, I: 955.

64   Winthrop G. Brown, interview by Richard D. McKinzie, May 25, 1973, Oral History Interviews, Truman Library. Irwin, Mavroidis, and Sykes (2008:90).

65   Lovett to Marshall, August 24, 1947, in *FRUS, 1947*, III: 372–75.

66   Kennan, memorandum, "Situation with Respect to European Recovery Program," September 4, 1947, in *FRUS, 1947*, III: 397.

67   Milward (1992 [2000]:335).

68   Lynch (May 1984:237–40); Hervé Alphand, paper, January 28, 1947, FO371 /64430, Foreign Office, UKNA.

69   Hogan (1987:68–70).

70   Truman (1972:352).

71   Steil (2013:262); Herring (June 1971:271).

72   Clayton to Lovett, August 22, 1947, in *FRUS, 1947*, I: 977–79.

73   Clair Wilcox to Clayton, August 6, 1947, in *FRUS, 1947*, I: 974–77.

74   Lovett to Clayton, August 26, 1947, in *FRUS, 1947*, I: 980–82.

75   Harry C. Hawkins and Winthrop G. Brown, memorandum for Clayton and Douglas, September 24, 1947, in *FRUS, 1947*, I: 996–98.

76   Lovett to Marshall, August 24, 1947, in *FRUS, 1947*, III: 376–77.

77   International Monetary Fund (1947:27).

78   From the diary of M. Cherkasov, First Secretary, Embassy of the USSR in Norway, record of a conversation with the head of the foreign department, "Verdens Gang" newspaper, Hans Engen, July 9, 1947, AVP RF, Fond 046, op. 7, P. 126, file 48, pp. 84–86.

79   Kennan, memorandum, "Situation with Respect to European Recovery Program," September 4, 1947, in *FRUS, 1947*, III: 397.

80   Clayton via Caffery to Marshall and Lovett, August 31, 1947, in *FRUS, 1947*, III: 391–96; Reynolds (May/June 1997).

81   Clayton via Caffery to Marshall and Lovett, August 31, 1947, in *FRUS, 1947*, III: 391–96.

82   Kennan, memorandum, "Situation with Respect to European Recovery Program," September 4, 1947, in *FRUS, 1947*, III: 397–401.

83   Blair (September 7, 1947).

84   Kennan, memorandum, "Situation with Respect to European Recovery Program," September 4, 1947, in *FRUS, 1947*, III: 397–401.

85   Kennan, memorandum, "Situation with Respect to European Recovery Program," September 4, 1947, in *FRUS, 1947*, III: 403–5; Reynolds (May/June 1997).

86   Lovett to Clayton and Caffery, September 7, 1947, in *FRUS, 1947*, III: 417.

87   Marshall to Douglas, September 5, 1947, in *FRUS, 1947*, III: 409.

88   Lovett to U.S. diplomatic representatives accredited to CEEC participant countries, September 7, 1947, in *FRUS, 1947*, III: 413; Lovett to Clayton and Caffery, September 7, 1947, in *FRUS, 1947*, III: 417.

89   Lovett to Truman, September 6, 1947, in *FRUS, 1947*, III: 411; Lovett to Clayton and Caffery, September 7, 1947, in *FRUS, 1947*, III: 417.

90   Hogan (1987:78–79).

91   Douglas to Marshall, September 9, 1947, in *FRUS, 1947*, III: 421; Lovett to Truman, September 6, 1947, in *FRUS, 1947*, III: 420; Clayton, Caffery, and Douglas to Marshall and Lovett, September 11, 1947, *FRUS, 1947*, III: 421–23; Douglas to Marshall, September 12, 1947, in *FRUS, 1947*, III: 428; Milward (1984:87).

92   Clayton, Caffery, and Douglas to Lovett, September 15, 1947, in *FRUS, 1947*, III: 433.

93 "Special Message to the Congress Requesting Extension of the Reciprocal Trade Act," March 1, 1948, in *Public Papers of the Presidents: Harry Truman, 1948*: 169; Irwin, Mavroidis, and Sykes (2008:93). The GATT was intended as a stopgap until the Truman administration could get ratification of the International Trade Organization through Congress; the ITO, however, was never ratified owing to concerns over usurpation of U.S. sovereignty and congressional power. See, for example, Kaplan (1996:52–53) and Gerber (2012:46–47).

94 *New York Times* (October 15, 1947); Fossedal and Mikhail (May/June 1997).

95 Fossedal (1993:258); *Le Monde* (October 17, 1947).

96 Van der Beugel (1966:74).

97 European Commission (September 19, 2016): http://ec.europa.eu/taxation_cus toms/40customs/customs_general_info/about/index_en.htm.

98 Milward (1984:88).

99 CEEC (September 1947:69).

100 Van der Beugel (1966:72).

101 CEEC (September 1947:1–3).

102 Sebastian Haffner in *The Observer* (London), July 17, 1947, quoted in Calvocoressi (1952:105).

103 "Reference" written for Zhdanov in the Foreign Department of the Central Committee, around September 2, 1947, RGASPI, Fond 575, op. 1, file 3, pp. 57, 58, 60, 62.

104 "George Marshall, Secretary of State of USA," September 18, 1947, RGASPI, Fond 575, op. 1, file 35, pp. 103, 103/reverse side.

105 I am indebted to Svetlana Chervonnaya for highlighting this.

106 "References on the USA of the Foreign Department of the Central Committee," September 18, 1947, RGASPI, Fond 575, op. 1, file 35, pp. 28–29.

CHAPTER 7: PERSUASION

1 Beisner (2006:145).

2 Video footage (in Russian): https://www.youtube.com/watch?v=6f7qIPODFfg (British Pathé [April 13, 2014]). Partial text (in English): http://astro.temple .edu/~rimmerma/vyshinsky_speech_to_un.htm ("Vyshinsky Speech to U.N. General Assembly").

3 Smith to Marshall, September 30, 1947, in *FRUS, 1947*, IV: 590–91.

4 Reston (October 26, 1947).

5 The countries participating were Bulgaria, Czechoslovakia, France, Hungary, Italy, Poland, Romania, and the Soviet Union. "Memorandum by A. A. Zhdanov to I. V. Stalin on the anticipated program of the conference of nine Communist parties in Poland," RGASPI, Fond 77, op. 3, file 90.

6 L. Baranov to Zhdanov, untitled instructions for the delegates of VCP (b) at the conference of the Communist parties in Poland, August 15, 1947, RGASPI, Fond 575, op. 1, file 3, pp. 1–3.

7 Zhdanov to Stalin, September 23 and 24, 1947, RGASPI, Fond 77, op. 3, file 92, pp. 16–20; Tiersky (1974:160); Pons (Spring 2001:14).

8 Reston (October 7, 1947).

9 *Life* (November 24, 1947).

10 "References on France of the Foreign Department of the Central Committee," undated, RGASPI Fond 575, op. 1, file. 38, pp. 61–62; Molotov to Sovposol, June 3, 1947, RGASPI, Fond 558, op. 11, file 392, pp. 33–34.

11 Zhdanov to Stalin, September 23, 1947, RGASPI, Fond 77, op. 3, file 92, pp. 6–7; Djilas (1983:134).

12 Zhdanov's texts from the period of the conference, September 24, RGASPI, Fond 77, op. 3, file 92, p. 49; Parrish (March 1994:32–35); Yergin (1977:326); Zubok and Pleshakov (1996:132); Judt (2005:143).

13 Discussion of Zhdanov's report, statements by Duclos and Longo, September 26, 1947, RGASPI, Fond 575, op. 1, file 1, pp. 209–19, 241–44.

14 Judt (2015:71).

15 See, for example, Boterbloem (2004:11).

16 Zubok and Pleshakov (1996:116); Alliluyeva (1969:384).

17 Zhdanov, "On the International Situation," reprinted in House Committee on Foreign Affairs (1948), *Strategy and Tactics of World Communism*.

18 Comintern membership reached seventy-six Communist parties and affiliated groups in 1935, when it met for the last time. Adibekov, Shakhnazarov, and Shirinya (1997).

19 Zhdanov, "On the International Situation," reprinted in House Committee on Foreign Affairs (1948), *Strategy and Tactics of World Communism*.

20 The Bulgarian coalition lasted from September 9, 1944, to October 27, 1946. The four-party "Fatherland Front" coalition was installed in a bloodless coup on September 9, 1944. It included the Communist Bulgarian Workers' Party, the Agrarian Party, the Socialist Party, and the People's Union *Zveno*. ("Current Intelligence Study Number 28," June 29, 1945, Research and Analysis Branch 1930–1946, Office of Strategic Services, RG 226, National Archives.) The Communist Party came to dominate the coalition; it won an absolute majority of seats (277 of 465) in the elections of October 27, 1946. However, it continued to operate through the "Fatherland Front." (*New York Times* [October 29, 1946].)

21 The Czechoslovak coalition lasted from April 5, 1945, to February 20, 1948. Its collapse is described later in the book. Nedelsky (2012:115).

22 The Hungarian coalition lasted from December 22, 1944, to May 15, 1949. A

provisional government formed of five political parties (Communist, Social Democratic, Citizens Democratic, Smallholders, and People's Peasant) was created in December 1944. The coalition continued after the elections of November 1945, in which the Communists received only 17 percent of the vote. The Communists gradually squeezed out their coalition partners one by one (known widely as "salami tactics") until, finally, there was just a single list of candidates issued by the Communist Hungarian's People's Front for Independence for the elections of May 1949. Staar (1971 [1988]:124–25); Roman (2003:613); Hodge and Nolan (2007:428).

23   The Polish coalition government, dominated by the Communist Party in accordance with Stalin's demands at Yalta, was constituted on June 21, 1945. When the Polish Peasant Party was eliminated on February 5, 1947, "the coalition became little more than a façade for Communist power, something even the Communists did not conceal." Kersten (1991:156, 350).

24   The Romanian coalition government lasted from March 6, 1945, to December 30, 1947. Under Soviet influence, Romania formed what appeared to be a "broad coalition government," which included members of the Liberal and National Peasant parties, on March 6, 1945. However, the important government posts were held by Communists. Communists and their allies claimed a big victory in the election of November 1946, which was marked by propaganda and intimidation of the opposition. King Michael attempted to block a total Communist takeover but was forced to abdicate on December 30, 1947. That day, the Romanian People's Republic was declared. Boia (2001:114–15).

25   Kennan I (1967:521).

26   Gomułka's speech in the course of discussion of Zhdanov's report, RGASPI, Fond 575, op. 1, file 1, pp. 244–65; Toranska (1987:282-283); Haslam (2011:89–90).

27   Zubok and Pleshakov (1996:135); Gibianski (1994:41).

28   Yergin (1977:382).

29   Khrushchev (1971:181).

30   Reston (October 12, 1947).

31   Beevor and Cooper (1994 [2004]:292).

32   Central Intelligence Agency to the President, November 7, 1947, Folder: "Memoranda 1945–1948," Box 213, Central Intelligence File, President's Secretary's Files, Truman Papers, Truman Library.

33   Caffery to Marshall, December 5, 1947, in FRUS, 1947, III: 813.

34   Caffery to Marshall, September 30, 1947, in FRUS, 1947, III: 761–62.

35   James C. Dunn to Marshall, September 17, 1947, in FRUS, 1947, III: 974.

36   Caffery to Marshall, Telegram, October 4, 1947, 840.50 Recovery/10-347, RG 59, National Archives.

37 Behrman (2007) claims three million strikers without providing a source. But this number is almost certainly a wild exaggeration, having apparently only come from the CGT confederation of trade unions (Lorwin [1954:124]). An Associated Press report on November 25 said there were an estimated one million strikers at that point (*Chicago Tribune* [November 25, 1947]). Tiersky says that the number "was estimated variously at between one and two million" by the end of November (before the strikes began to subside on December 1). Tiersky (1974:169–70).

38 In the October municipal elections, the RPF received 38 percent of the vote, the Communists 30 percent, and the Socialists 19 percent.

39 Lippmann's *The Cold War* was published on November 12, 1947.

40 Lippmann (November 4, 1947).

41 "Record of the Meeting of Comrade I[osef] V[issarionivich] Stalin with the Secretary of the Central Committee of the French Communist Party [Maurice] Thorez," November 18, 1947, in Levering, Pechatnov, Botzenhart-Viehe, and Edmondson (2001:173–75).

42 A secret State Department report said de Gaulle was propagating "frankly totalitarian concepts," and that "his only firm adherents now are discredited men of the Right." Blair (September 7, 1947); *Life* (December 1, 1947); Reston (October 21, 1947); Beevor and Cooper (1994 [2004]:294–97).

43 Hitchcock (1998:90).

44 Callender (November 23, 1947).

45 Macintyre (2014:111). The OSS was a predecessor to the CIA, which was established through the National Security Act in September 1947.

46 Cortesi (November 17, 1947); Callender (November 18, 1947); Behrman (2007:118–21); Yergin (1977:332).

47 Cortesi (November 16, 1947); Cortesi (October 28, 1947); Cortesi (January 18, 1948).

48 Isaacson and Thomas (1986 [2012]:289).

49 Steil (2013:306–7); Isaacson and Thomas (1986 [2012]:365); Crider (July 14, 1946).

50 Advisory Steering Committee, memorandum, "Immediate Need for Emergency Aid for Europe," September 29, 1947, in *FRUS, 1947*, III: 475.

51 Steinkopf (September 28, 1947).

52 Advisory Steering Committee, memorandum, "Immediate Need for Emergency Aid for Europe," September 29, 1947, in *FRUS, 1947*, III: 476–77.

53 Frank McNaughton to Don Bermingham, October 4, 1947, Folder: "October 1947," Box 14, McNaughton Reports File, McNaughton Papers, Truman Library; Senator Carl A. Hatch to Truman, correspondence, October 16, 1947, Folder: "Economic Cooperation Administration—Special Session of Congress," Box 4, Subject File,

Clifford Papers, Truman Library; Lincoln Gordon, Memorandum for the President, September 20, 1947, Folder: "Economic Cooperation Administration—Special Session of Congress," Box 4, Subject File, Clifford Papers, Truman Library.

54 Raymond (October 4, 1947).

55 *Washington Post* (January 11, 1948).

56 *Washington Post* (October 5, 1947).

57 Waggoner (September 5, 1947).

58 *Washington Post* (September 24, 1947).

59 White (September 24, 1947).

60 Behrman (2007:115); Gallup I (1972:661, 680); Phillips (October 19, 1947).

61 Frank McNaughton to Don Bermingham, October 4, 1947, Folder: "October 1947," Box 14, McNaughton Reports File, McNaughton Papers, Truman Library; Yergin (1977:329).

62 Albright (September 7, 1947).

63 Skidelsky III (2000:432).

64 White (1953:379).

65 Phillips (October 19, 1947); Price (1955:51–55); Behrman (2007:116); Wilson (1977:36).

66 Reston (December 9, 1947).

67 White (November 2, 1947).

68 Price (1955:51–55).

69 House Select Committee on Foreign Aid (May 1948:16–17).

70 In addition to the President's Committee on Foreign Aid (the "Harriman Committee"), there were the Krug and Nourse committees, which reported on October 19 and November 1, respectively. Focusing on the domestic implications of a large-scale foreign aid program, they each broadly concluded that the initiative was manageable.

71 P. Zhuravlev to Gerashchenko, December 6, 1947, AVP RF, Fond 046, op. 7, P. 126, file 48, p. 193.

72 Harris (July 22, 1956).

73 Hachey (Winter 1973–1974:148).

74 Price (1955:45), quoting an unnamed member of the committee's staff.

75 Hogan (1987:101).

76 Wilson (1977:34).

77 Dales (October 26, 1954); *Washington Post* (August 13, 1956).

78 Bissell (1996:37); Behrman (2007:132–33); Pisani (1991:60).

79 President's Committee on Foreign Aid (November 1947:11).

80 Truman, "Special Message to the Congress on the Marshall Plan," December 19, 1947, in *Public Papers of the Presidents: Harry Truman, 1947.*

81 Harold Stein, interview with Harry B. Price, August 7, 1952, Folder: "August–

October, 1952," Box 1, Oral History Interview File, Price Papers, Truman Library. Hogan (1987:100).

82 Hoffman, interview with Harry B. Price, January 28, 1953, Folder: "January–June, 1953," Box 1, Oral History Interview File, Price Papers, Truman Library.

83 Belair (November 16, 1947).

84 Gallup I (1972:683, 691).

85 Lawrence B. Smith, statement, November 14, 1947, in House Committee on Foreign Affairs (1947:231); Price (1955:51–55); Barber (April 9, 2014).

86 Van der Beugel (1966:83).

87 Stimson (October 1947).

88 "Report on the Activities of the Committee for the Marshall Plan to Aid European Recovery," submitted by the Executive Director, April 5, 1948, Folder: "Committee for the Marshall Plan: Correspondence, 1947–1948 [3 of 3]," Box 4, Political and Governmental File, Acheson Papers, Truman Library.

89 Michael Wala provides information on the various study groups that the Council on Foreign Relations convened to discuss the Marshall Plan and related postwar foreign policy initiatives. Wala (1994:159–69).

90 Huempfer (2016).

91 New York Times (December 6, 1947).

92 New York Times (September 2, 1947); Blair (February 16, 1948).

93 Adams (September 1, 1947).

94 New York Times (November 19, 1947).

95 New York Times (February 9, 1948).

96 Washington Post (October 21, 1947).

97 Furman (February 3, 1948).

98 Grutzner (November 19, 1947).

99 Warren (December 18, 1947).

100 Behrman (2007:124–25, 138–39).

101 Pearson (December 18, 1947).

102 New York Times (February 18, 1948).

103 "Provisional Record of Decisions of the Council of Foreign Ministers, Forty-Third Meeting, Moscow, Aviation Industry House, April 24, 4 p.m.," in FRUS, 1947, II: 386–88.

104 Clay (1950:242).

105 Yergin (1977:330–31).

106 Smirnov to Molotov, October 3, 1947, AVP RF, Fond 06, op. 9, P. 45, file 673, pp. 15–23.

107 Molotov to Stalin, November 10, 1947, RGASPI, Fond 558, op. 11, file 107, pp. 119–20.

108 At least this was Churchill's account. See, for example, Roberts (2011:59).

109 Nicolson (1968:115–16).

110 Douglas to Marshall, paraphrasing statement of French ambassador to London René Massigli, February 28, 1948, in *FRUS, 1948,* II: 98.

111 Jacob D. Beam, memorandum of conversation, October 17, 1947, in *FRUS, 1947,* II: 688; Brewster H. Morris, memorandum, undated but transmitted on September 16, 1947, in *FRUS, 1947,* II: 887–89; Harrington (2012:33–34); Naimark (1995:465); Arkes (1972:23).

112 Jacob D. Beam, memorandum of conversation, October 17, 1947, in *FRUS, 1947,* II: 688.

113 Marshall to Lovett, December 11, 1947, in *FRUS, 1947,* II: 765.

114 U.S. Delegation at the CFM to Truman and others, December 12, 1947, in *FRUS, 1947,* II: 766–68; Clay (1950:348).

115 U.S. Delegation at the CFM to Truman and others, December 15, 1947, in *FRUS, 1947,* II: 771.

116 U.S. Delegation at the CFM to Truman and others, December 15, 1947, in *FRUS, 1947,* II: 769–772; Douglas, memorandum of conversation (with Bidault), December 17, 1947, in *FRUS, 1947,* II: 812; British memorandum of conversation (talks between Marshall, Robertson, Clay, and others), undated but sent by Waldemar J. Gallman to John D. Hickerson on December 30, 1947, in *FRUS, 1947,* II: 826; Yergin (1977:332–33); Marshall to Lovett, December 6, 1947, in *FRUS, 1947,* II: 751–53; Marshall to Lovett, December 11, 1947, in *FRUS, 1947,* II: 765; John D. Hickerson—Diplomat, 1965, John Foster Dulles Oral History Collection, Mudd Library, Princeton University; *Time* (January 5, 1948); Arkes (1972:41).

117 *New York Herald Tribune* (December 16, 1947).

118 Clay (1950:348).

119 Smith (1990:416, 419).

120 Clay to Draper, "Government for Germany," CC-2167, November 3, 1947, in Smith I (1974:475–78). Clay would in retirement add, in wholesale contradiction to his views in early 1947, that "the Russians would never agree to elections under the terms and conditions we thought would guarantee free elections. . . . East Germany was obviously a buffer for them." Smith (1990:539).

121 Clay to Draper, CC-2134, October 30, 1947, in Smith I (1974:459).

122 Isaacson and Thomas (1986 [2012]:287); Bohlen (1973:222).

123 Clay to Draper, "London Council of Foreign Ministers," CC-2642, November 20, 1947, in Smith I (1974:501–2). Clay's biographer Jean Edward Smith claims that Clay was "disappointed and distressed at the collapse of the London conference," and that he had remained "deeply committed to German unity" and confident "that Western democracy could be extended to the Soviet zone." Clay, he said, "was virtually alone

in holding to that view in 1947. Washington had changed policy" (1990:450–51). No sources are provided, and indeed none could have been. As Smith himself noted just a few pages earlier, "The fact is, the State Department position had not changed; Clay had, and his tough statement about the Soviets was correctly reported by [CBS' Edward R.] Murrow as a change of direction for Clay" (1990:444–45).

124 Smith (1990:455–60); *New York Times* (January 9, 1948); Smith and Draper, teleconference, TT-9205, March 12, 1948, in Smith II (1974:574–78); Smith and Draper, teleconference, TT-8950, January 9, 1948, in Smith II (1974:529–33).

125 Yergin (1977:330–31)

126 R. H. Hillenkoetter to Truman, March 16, 1948 (referring to CIA memo of December 22, 1947), Folder: "Memoranda 1945–1948," Box 213, Central Intelligence File, President's Secretary's Files, Truman Papers, Truman Library.

127 Marshall to U.S. Embassy in Paris, February 19 and 20, 1948, in *FRUS, 1948*, II: 70–73.

128 Pogue IV (1987:287); Harrington (2012:41).

129 Yergin (1977:335).

130 Harrington (2012:43); Morrow (December 20, 1947) and (January 12, 1948).

131 Raymond (November 17, 1947).

132 Schwabe (1991:228).

133 *Wirtschafts-Zeitung* (Stuttgart), March 26, 1948, in Schwabe (1991:232).

134 Schwabe (1991:225–32).

135 Ulbricht to Suslov, "On Economic Questions," December 12, 1947, RGASPI, Fond 17, op. 128, file 1197, pp. 6-9.

136 Lippmann (January 6, 1948).

137 Lippmann (November 24, 1947).

138 Lippmann (January 22, 1948).

139 Lippmann (December 4, 1947).

140 *New York Times* (February 1, 1948).

141 Reston (December 5, 1947).

142 *Wall Street Journal* (February 3, 1948).

143 Reston (February 27, 1948).

144 Nenni (1981:399–400).

145 Bland and Stoler VI (2013:267).

146 Marshall, statement before the joint meeting of the Senate Foreign Relations Committee and the House Committee on Foreign Affairs, November 10, 1947, 1947—80th Congress, 1st Session Collection, Congressional Testimonies, Marshall Foundation.

147 Marshall, interview with Harry B. Price, February 18, 1953, Folder: "January–June, 1953," Box 1, Oral History Interview File, Price Papers, Truman Library.

148   Truman, "Special Message to the Congress on the First Day of the Special Session," November 17, 1947, in *Public Papers of the Presidents: Harry Truman, 1947.*

149   Truman, "Special Message to the Congress on the Marshall Plan," December 19, 1947, in *Public Papers of the Presidents: Harry Truman, 1947.*

150   *New York Times* (November 7, 1947).

151   *Washington Post* (November 9, 1947).

152   Reston (November 6, 1947).

153   Reston (December 9, 1947).

154   See, for example, *Washington Post* (November 7, 1947).

155   Douglas, statement before the Senate Committee on Foreign Relations, January 12, 1948, in Senate Committee on Foreign Relations (1948:208).

156   Marshall, statement before the Senate Committee on Foreign Relations, January 7, 1948, in House Committee on Foreign Affairs (1948:108), *United States Foreign Policy for a Post-War Recovery Program.*

157   Dulles, statement before the Senate Committee on Foreign Relations, January 20, 1948, in Senate Committee on Foreign Relations (1948:586–88).

158   Douglas, statement before the Senate Committee on Foreign Relations, January 12, 1948, in Senate Committee on Foreign Relations (1948:208, 76).

159   Harriman, quoting President's Committee on Foreign Aid (November 1947:B7), in a statement before the Senate Committee on Foreign Relations, January 12, 1948, in Senate Committee on Foreign Relations (1948:246). See also House Committee on Foreign Affairs (1948:463), *United States Foreign Policy for a Post-War Recovery Program.*

160   Hoffman, statement before the Senate Committee on Foreign Relations, January 23, 1948, in Senate Committee on Foreign Relations (1948:852).

161   Philip D. Reed, statement before the House Committee on Foreign Affairs, in House Committee on Foreign Affairs (1948:578), *United States Foreign Policy for a Post-War Recovery Program.*

162   Henry Wallace, statement before the House Committee on Foreign Affairs, February 20, 1948, in House Committee on Foreign Affairs (1948:1584–99), *United States Foreign Policy for a Post-War Recovery Program.*

163   Reynolds (January 17, 1948).

164   Belair (February 26, 1948).

165   Henry Hazlitt, statement before the Senate Committee on Foreign Relations, January 21, 1948, in Senate Committee on Foreign Relations (1948:687); Hazlitt (1947:18–24); Hogan (1987:95–96); Steil (2013:289).

166   In today's money, the French aid was worth $3.54 billion, the Italian aid $2.45 billion, and the Austrian aid $454 million.

167   Lovett to Marshall, December 4, 1947, in *FRUS, 1947*, III: 482–83.

CHAPTER 8: SAUSAGE

1   Clifford, "Memorandum for the President," November 19, 1947, Folder: "Confidential Memo to the President [Clifford-Rowe Memorandum of November 19, 1947]," Box 22, Political File, Clifford Papers, Truman Library: 6, 14–16, 22–23, 29–30.

2   George Elsey, "Memo Re. Wallace Situation," Folder: "Wallace, Henry [memoranda re foreign policy views, resignation, election of 1948]," Box 19, Subject File, Clifford Papers, Truman Library: 4.

3   Lippmann (November 20, 1947).

4   Clifford, "Memorandum for the President," November 19, 1947, Folder: "Confidential Memo to the President [Clifford-Rowe Memorandum of November 19, 1947]," Box 22, Political File, Clifford Papers, Truman Library; Hartmann (1971:129).

5   Truman, "Special Message to the Congress on the First Day of the Special Session," November 17, 1947, in *Public Papers of the Presidents: Harry Truman, 1947*.

6   Belair (October 30, 1947).

7   Van der Wee (1983:436–49) provides a useful overview of exchange rate management practices, problems, and solutions in the late 1940s and 1950s.

8   Truman, "Special Message to the Congress on the Marshall Plan," December 19, 1947, in *Public Papers of the Presidents: Harry Truman, 1947*.

9   Belair (November 23, 1947).

10 Hartmann (1971:122).

11 *Wall Street Journal* (February 26, 1948).

12 Lippmann (November 20, 1947).

13 Reston (November 25, 1947).

14 *Congressional Record*, 80th Congress, 1st Session, XCIII, 1947: 10980; Trussel (December 2, 1947).

15 *Congressional Record*, 80th Congress, 1st Session, XCIII, 1947: 11307–8.

16 "Conference Report [To accompany S. 1774]," December 13, 1947, in *Legislative History of the Foreign Aid Act of 1947, P.L. 80-389*, II.

17 Senator William Langer (R-ND) requested that the record show that he voted against the bill. *Congressional Record*, 80th Congress, 1st Session, XCIII, 1947: 11354.

18 *Congressional Record*, 80th Congress, 1st Session, XCIII, 1947: 11412–13.

19 Belair (January 8, 1948).

20 Reston (February 22, 1948); Belair (February 29, 1948); Lippmann (February 19, 1948); Kuhn (February 18, 1948).

21 *Time* (January 12, 1948).

22 Behrman (2007:135–37).

23   Kuhn (November 14, 1947).

24   Haas (2016:195).

25   Kuhn (January 25, 1948); Plokhy (2010:107).

26   Reston (January 18, 1948).

27   Huempfer (2016).

28   See, for example, Buchanan (1999).

29   Policy Planning Staff, "Review of Current Trends: U.S. Foreign Policy," PPS/23, February 24, 1948, in *FRUS, 1948*, I: 512.

30   Marshall to Truman, December 21, 1947, 840.50 Recovery/12-147, RG 59, National Archives.

31   Clifford, "Memorandum for the President," November 19, 1947, Folder: "Confidential Memo to the President [Clifford-Rowe Memorandum of November 19, 1947]," Box 22, Political File, Clifford Papers, Truman Library: 36.

32   Reston (January 9, 1948); *Time* (January 5, 1948); Marshall, statements before the Senate Committee on Foreign Relations, January 8, 1948, and the House Committee on Foreign Affairs, January 12, 1948, in House Committee on Foreign Affairs (1948:37, 46), *United States Foreign Policy for a Post-War Recovery Program*.

33   See, for example, the conclusions of a report by the Brookings Institution (January 1948:15–20). Also printed in Senate Committee on Foreign Relations (1948:855–60).

34   *Congressional Record*, 80th Congress, 2nd Session, XCIV, 1948: 1963.

35   Hogan (1987:101–9).

36   Vandenberg (1952:393).

37   Folder: "January, 1948," Box 191, Truman Papers File, Historical File, President's Secretary's Files, Truman Papers, Truman Library.

38   Reston (January 9, 1948).

39   See, for example, Alsop and Alsop (January 25, 1948).

40   *The Economist* (February 4, 1948).

41   Gallup (February 8, 1948).

42   Gallup (March 31, 1948).

43   CEEC Washington Delegation to the State Department, October 27, 1947, in *FRUS, 1947*, III: 455. See also Sir Oliver Franks to Lovett, "Unofficial Aide-Memoire," October 22, 1947, in *FRUS, 1947*, III: 450.

44   Suslov to Stalin, Molotov, Zhdanov, Beria, Mikoyan, and Malenkov, January 26, 1948, RGASPI, Fond 17, op. 128, file 1137, pp. 142–45.

45   Bulletin of International and Domestic Information of the Information Bureau of SVAG #93, August 26, 1947, RGASPI, Fond 17, op. 128, file 369, p. 165.

46   "The Influence of the Decision of the Conference of the Representatives of the Nine Communist Parties on the Growth and Strengthening of Forces of Democracy in

Germany," undated, RGASPI, Fond 575, op. 1, file 53, pp. 68, 70. (CDU = Christian Democratic Union, CSU = Christian Social Union.)

47 Nover (September 28, 1947); Hinton (November 19, 1947); Reston (December 11, 1947); Reston (October 26, 1947); White (January 17, 1948); *Washington Post* (January 28, 1948). On the Soviet response to the VOA, see Inkeles (October 1953:319–20, 332).

48 Haas (2016:206–7).

49 See, for example, Office of the Historian, U.S. House of Representatives: http://history.house.gov/Institution/Origins-Development/Power-of-the-Purse/.

50 Reston (December 22, 1947).

51 Sulzberger (April 11, 1948).

52 Douglas, statement before the Senate Committee on Foreign Relations, January 12, 1948, in Senate Committee on Foreign Relations (1948:76).

53 ERP Summary 7, Senate Foreign Relations Committee Hearing, January 15, 1948, Folder: "European Recovery Program [9 of 9]—Senate Foreign Relations Committee," Box 6, Subject File, Clifford Files, Truman Papers, Truman Library.

54 ERP Summary, House Foreign Affairs Committee, January 20, 1948, Folder: "European Recovery Program [8 of 9]—House Foreign Affairs Committee," Box 6, Subject File, Clifford Files, Truman Papers, Truman Library.

55 ERP Summary 10, Senate Foreign Relations Committee, January 20, 1948, Folder: Folder: "European Recovery Program [9 of 9]—Senate Foreign Relations Committee," Box 6, Subject File, Clifford Files, Truman Papers, Truman Library.

56 Marshall, statement before the House Committee on Foreign Affairs, January 12, 1948, in House Committee on Foreign Affairs (1948), *United States Foreign Policy for a Post-War Recovery Program.*

57 Bernard M. Baruch, statement before the Senate Committee on Foreign Relations, January 19, 1948, in Senate Committee on Foreign Relations (1948:556); Reston (January 20, 1948).

58 Lord Inverchapel (Sir Archibald Clark Kerr) to Marshall, "Summary of a Memorandum Representing Mr. Bevin's Views on the Formation of a Western Union," January 13, 1948, in *FRUS, 1948*, III: 5.

59 *Washington Post* (January 23, 1948); Lippmann (January 26, 1948).

60 Reston (February 6, 1948).

61 Reston (January 18, 1948).

62 Reston (January 4, 1948).

63 Thompson (2009:80-82) Isaacson and Thomas (1986 [2012]:433).

CHAPTER 9: SUBVERSION

1 "Proposal of the IV ED of the MID of the USSR regarding the major direction of the Czechoslovak policy following the February crisis, March 2, 1948," in *The Soviet Factor in Eastern Europe 1944–1953,* I (1999:553–55); Haslam (2011:98–99).

2 Heinemann-Grueder (1999:334, 336); Gottwald to Stalin, November 25, 1947, RGASPI, Fond 558, op. 11, file 393, p. 124; Stalin to Gottwald, November 29, 1947, RGASPI, Fond 558, op. 11, file 393, p. 126.

3 Feierabend (1996:362).

4 Ross (January 18, 1948).

5 Policy Planning Staff, "Résume of World Situation," PPS/13, November 6, 1947, in *FRUS, 1947,* I: 771, 773.

6 Heimann (2009:172); James (2014:283).

7 Charles Yost to Marshall, September 15, 1947, in *FRUS, 1947,* IV: 231.

8 Ripka (1950:210–20).

9 Laurence Steinhardt to Marshall, April 30, 1948, in *FRUS, 1948,* IV: 750; Haslam (2011:99–100); Ripka (1950:222, 227, 231–36); Kaplan (1987:179).

10 Crowder (2015:215).

11 Isaacson and Thomas (1986 [2012]:243); Bohlen (1973:170).

12 Ripka (1950:240–41, 250–51, 265, 267, 278–79, 281, 284–85, 293, 296, 307); Lukes (September 2011:443); Spalding (2006:100).

13 Ripka (1950:7).

14 Laurence Steinhardt to Marshall, April 30, 1948, in *FRUS, 1948,* IV: 747–53; Ripka (1950:299–300).

15 Laurence Steinhardt to Marshall, February 27, 1948, in *FRUS, 1948,* IV: 741–42.

16 Laurence Steinhardt to Marshall, March 10, 1948, in *FRUS, 1948,* IV: 743–44; Laurence Steinhardt to Marshall, April 30, 1948, in *FRUS, 1948,* IV: 751.

17 Cameron (January 6, 2004).

18 Yergin (1977:352).

19 Ripka (1950:313–18).

20 Kennan I (1967:422).

21 Lukes (2012:15).

22 John D. Hickerson to Marshall, memorandum, March 8, 1948, in *FRUS, 1948,* III: 41.

23 Lukes (2012:4, 32); Eugene V. Rostow to Dean Rusk, May 10, 1968, Folder: "6 /1/68," Box 1558, POL—Czech, USSR DEF 4 NATO, Center Foreign Policy Files, RG 59, National Archives. For Dulles' view, see "Notes on the Meeting of the Operations Coordinating Board, Washington, January 5, 1955," in *FRUS, 1955–1957,* XXV: 7.

24   Lukes (2012:8–9); Masaryk, memorandum of conversation with Roosevelt, February 4, 1944, in Němeček (1999:229–30).

25   Lukes (2012:43-45); Eisenhower to U.S. Military Mission, May 6, 1945, FW 860f.01/12-1748, RG 59, National Archives.

26   Cormac (May 10, 1945); Lukes (2012:51).

27   Lukes (2012:106–8); Murphy to Byrnes, August 31, 1945, 860f.01/8-3145, RG 59, National Archives; Laurence Steinhardt to Byrnes, September 4, 1945, in *FRUS, 1945*, IV: 489.

28   Ripka (1950:49); Lukes (2012:108–12, 127–28); Byrnes to Acheson, August 30, 1946, in *FRUS, 1946*, VI: 216–17; Laurence Steinhardt to Byrnes, December 23, 1946, in *FRUS, 1946*, VI: 238–41; Margh (November 1, 1946).

29   John Bruins to Marshall, January 28, 1948, in *FRUS, 1948*, IV: 733.

30   Laurence Steinhardt to Marshall, February 26, 1948, in *FRUS, 1948*, IV: 739.

31   Laurence Steinhardt to Marshall, November 13, 1947, in *FRUS, 1947*, IV: 243.

32   James Riddleberger to Laurence Steinhardt, December 2, 1946, Box 51, 1946, General File, Steinhardt Papers, Library of Congress.

33   Werth (1971:328–29); Ross (January 4, 1948).

34   Marshall to Caffery, February 24, 1948, in *FRUS, 1948*, IV: 735–37.

35   Pechatnov and Edmondson (2001:121).

36   Beisner (2006:167–71); State Department, policy statement, December 1, 1949, in *FRUS, 1949*, V: 443; National Security Council, policy statement, "The Position of the United States with Respect to Scandinavia and Finland," NSC/121, January 8, 1952, in *FRUS, 1952–1954*, VIII: 755.

37   Beisner (2006:167).

CHAPTER 10: PASSAGE

1   Francis Wilcox and Thorsten Kalijarvi, interview with Harry B. Price, August 8, 1952, Folder: "August–December, 1952," Box 1, Oral History Interview File, Price Papers, Truman Library.

2   *New York Times* (April 22, 1951).

3   *Congressional Record*, 80th Congress, 2nd Session, XCIV, 1948: 1915–20. A video clip of the speech is here: https://www.youtube.com/watch?v=9Z0BxDeKtrQ (British Pathé [April 13, 2014]).

4   Gallup (March 3, 1948).

5   Marshall, interviews with Harry B. Price, October 30, 1952 and October 12, 1954, reproduced in Price (1955:65). See also Reston's interesting profile of Vandenberg as a politician: Reston (March 28, 1948).

6   Untitled and undated memo, Folder: "France General," Box 156, Foreign Affairs

File, President's Secretary's Files, Truman Papers, Truman Library; Editorial Note in *FRUS, 1948*, II: 85–86.

7   Douglas to Marshall, March 1, 1948, in *FRUS, 1948*, II: 107. Lovett heartily concurred with Douglas' tactics, authorizing "Douglas to indicate to the French that the United States was unprepared to undertake any commitments as to shipments to the French zone under ERP unless and until we obtain a clear idea as to the French position on German policy, in particular coordination of their zone with Bizonia." Jacob D. Beam, memorandum of telephone conversation, "Telephone Conversation with London regarding German Discussions," March 2, 1948, in *FRUS, 1948*, II: 112.

8   V. Treskov, informational memorandum, "The Foreign Trade of the USA and West European Nations Under the 'Marshall Plan,'" August 7, 1948, AVP RF, Fond 046, op. 8a, P. 74a, file 2, p. 18.

9   Khrushchev (1971:191).

10   Memo recipient was Lieutenant General Stephen J. Chamberlin. See Murphy to Marshall, March 3, 1948, in *FRUS, 1948*, II: 878.

11   Kennan I (1967:400); Gaddis (2011:305).

12   Lippmann (March 15, 1948).

13   See, for example, Hanhimäki (1997).

14   Lippmann (March 16, 1948).

15   Reston (March 14, 1948).

16   Reston (March 26, 1948).

17   *The Essays on the History of Russian Foreign Intelligence*, V: 558–65; British Embassy to State Department, March 11, 1948, in *FRUS, 1948*, III: 46–48; Marshall to Lord Inverchapel (Sir Archibald Clark Kerr), March 12, 1948, in *FRUS, 1948*, III: 48. Kennan I (1967:400–402); Millis (1951:387); Harrington (2012:42–43); Clay to Stephen J. Chamberlin, March 5, 1948, in Smith II (1974:568–69); Smith (1978:75–76); Smith (Winter 1988:34); Smith (1990:467); Isaacson and Thomas (1986 [2012]:440).

18   Interview with Acheson (and Earle), Reel 2, July 2, 1953, Folder: "July 2, 1953 [2 of 2]," Box 79, Princeton Seminars File, Acheson Papers, Truman Library: 17.

19   Kuhn (February 29, 1948).

20   Belair (March 17, 1948).

21   Lippmann (March 22, 1948).

22   Interview with Harriman (and Acheson), Reel 4, Track 2, October 10, 1953, Folder: "October 10–11, 1953," Box 80, Princeton Seminars File, Acheson Papers, Truman Library: 10.

23   Lord Inverchapel (Sir Archibald Clark Kerr) to Marshall, "Summary of a Memorandum Representing Mr. Bevin's Views on the Formation of a Western Union," January 13, 1948, in *FRUS, 1948*, III: 5.

24 Lippmann (April 5, 1948); Lippmann (December 4, 1947).

25 John D. Hickerson to Marshall, memorandum, January 19, 1948, in *FRUS, 1948*, III: 6–7.

26 Josiah Marvel, Jr., to Marshall, March 12, 1948, in *FRUS, 1948*, III: 51.

27 "Paraphrase of a Telegram from Bevin of April 9th Regarding Recent Talks on North Atlantic Security Arrangements," undated, in *FRUS, 1948*, III: 79–80.

28 Marshall to the U.S. Embassy in London, February 28, 1948, in *FRUS, 1948*, II: 101.

29 Douglas to Marshall, March 2, 1948, in *FRUS, 1948*, II: 111.

30 Bidault to Marshall, March 4, 1948, 840.20/3-448, RG 59, National Archives.

31 Lovett, memorandum of conversation with Inverchapel, January 27, 1948, in *FRUS, 1948*, III: 13; John D. Hickerson, memorandum of conversation with Lovett and Inverchapel, February 7, 1948, in *FRUS, 1948*, III: 22; John D. Hickerson to Marshall, memorandum, March 8, 1948, in *FRUS, 1948*, III: 40–41.

32 George H. Butler (PPS), memorandum, "Points for Discussion at S/P Meeting March 19, 3 P.M.," March 19, 1948, in *FRUS, 1948*, III: 59. Italics in original.

33 Minutes of the Second Meeting of the United States–United Kingdom–Canada Security Conversations, March 23, 1948, in *FRUS, 1948*, III: 65.

34 Minutes of the Third Meeting of the United States–United Kingdom–Canada Security Conversations, March 24, 1948, in *FRUS, 1948*, III: 66. Minutes of the Sixth Meeting of the United States–United Kingdom–Canada Security Conversations, April 1, 1948, in *FRUS, 1948*, III: 71–75; Gaddis (2011:307).

35 Semen Kozyrev and Constantine Zinchenko, "Five-nation treaty on the Western Union, signed in Brussels on March 17, 1948 (brief analysis)," March 23, 1948, AVP RF, Fond 07, op. 21, P. 33, file 497, p. 1.

36 "The German question in the relation between the USSR, USA, Britain and France. A survey, Part 3," in *The USSR and the German Question 1941–1949*, III: 661 (citing AVP RF, Fond 048z, op. 11zh, P. 70, file 17, p. 435); Narinsky (1996:63); Smirnov to Molotov, March 12, 1948, in *The USSR and the German Question 1941–1949*, III: 601.

37 Narinsky (2011:164–65); Harrington (2012:43–45); Narinsky (1996:65); Laufer and Kynin III (2004:546); Harris (Spring 1967:12–14) in RG 263, National Archives; Berlin airgram A-247, March 29, 1948, 862.00B/3-2948, RG 59, National Archives; Khrushchev (1971:191).

38 Record of Stalin's conversation with Pieck and Grotewohl, March 26, 1948, RGASPI, Fond 558, op. 11, file 303, p. 34 (the whole record, pp. 24–52); Naimark (1995:307).

39 Narinsky (1996:62), citing Dratvin and Semenov to Molotov and Bulganin, cable, April 17, 1948, Arkhiv Prezidenta Rossiiskoi Federatsii, Fond 3, op. 64, file 789, p. 25.

40   Murphy to Marshall, April 6, 1948, in *FRUS, 1948*, II: 890–91.

41   Narinsky (1996:62), citing Dratvin and Semenov to Molotov and Bulganin, cable, April 17, 1948, Arkhiv Prezidenta Rossiiskoi Federatsii, Fond 3, op. 64, file 789, p. 23.

42   Narinsky (1996:62), citing Dratvin and Semenov to Molotov and Bulganin, cable, April 17, 1948, Arkhiv Prezidenta Rossiiskoi Federatsii, Fond 3, op. 64, file 789, p. 24.

43   Gaddis (2011:310).

44   Gaddis (2011:321); Kennan I (1967:405–8).

45   Kennan, "Comments on the General Trend of U.S. Foreign Policy," August 20, 1948, Folder 53, Box 163, State Department File, Organizations, Kennan Papers, Mudd Library, Princeton University.

46   Kennan, National War College lecture, "Soviet Diplomacy," October 6, 1947, Folder 41, Box 298, Unpublished Works, Writings, Kennan Papers, Mudd Library, Princeton University.

47   Isaacson and Thomas (1986 [2012]:449).

48   Isaacson and Thomas (1986 [2012]:447); Bohlen (1973:267).

49   Middleton (March 28, 1948).

50   Arkes (1972:110–11); *Congressional Record*, 80th Congress, 2nd Session, XCIV, 1948: 2539, 2025, 2038, 2782–83.

51   *Washington Post* (December 12, 1947); Kuhn (March 9, 1948); *Wall Street Journal* (March 9, 1948).

52   Belair (March 13, 1948).

53   Kuhn (March 25, 1948).

54   Central Intelligence Agency, "The Current Situation in Italy," October 10, 1947, Folder: "O.R.E [Office of Reports and Estimates]: 1947: 44–54," Box 216, Central Intelligence Reports File, Intelligence File, President's Secretary's Files, Truman Papers, Truman Library.

55   Truman, "Special Message to the Congress on the Threat to the Freedom of Europe," March 17, 1948, in *Public Papers of the Presidents: Harry Truman, 1948*.

56   Edwards (March 26, 1948).

57   Walz (March 29, 1948).

58   Reston (March 23, 1948).

59   Laurence Steinhardt to Marshall, April 30, 1948, in *FRUS, 1948*, IV: 754.

60   John D. Hickerson to Lovett, March 8, 1948, in *FRUS, 1948*, III: 390–91. Belair (April 1, 1948).

61   Byrnes (June 1999); Daly (2009); Reston (March 31, 1948); Tower (February 29, 1948); *Congressional Record*, 80th Congress, 2nd Session, XCIV, 1948: 4034–36; Howard Piquet, interview with Harry B. Price, February 10, 1953, Folder:

"January–June 1953," Box 1, Oral History Interview File, Price Papers, Truman Library.

62 Hinton (April 4, 1948); Behrman (2007:161); Hoffman, interview with Harry B. Price, January 28, 1953, Folder: "January–June, 1953," Box 1, Oral History Interview File, Price Papers, Truman Library; Willard L. Beaulac to Lovett, April 4, 1948, in *FRUS, 1948,* IX: 31–32; Fenwick (July 1948).

63 *The Economist,* "Unsordid Act," April 10, 1948, quoted in Douglas to Marshall, April 13, 1948, Folder: "Telegrams: London [England]: Winant," Box 166, Foreign Affairs File, Subject File, President's Secretary's Files, Truman Papers, Truman Library.

64 Warren (April 6, 1948).

65 *New York Times* (April 6, 1948).

66 The Socialists and Communists polled 20.7 percent and 18.9 percent respectively in the 1946 election; they ran as a coalition in 1948. Furlong (2002:16).

67 Behrman (2007:164, 175–77); Kennan, interview with Harry B. Price, February 19, 1953, Folder: "January–June, 1953," Box 1, Oral History Interview File, Price Papers, Truman Library.

68 Policy Planning Staff, memorandum, May 4, 1948, in *FRUS, Emergence of the Intelligence Establishment: 1945–1950*: 668–72; Thompson (2009:83–84).

69 Raucher (1986:68); Whitman (October 9, 1974); Busch (April 4, 1949).

70 *Life* (May 10, 1948); Richard W. B. Clarke, interview with Harry B. Price, November 10, 1952, Folder: "November 1–November 10, 1952," Box 1, Oral History Interview File, Price Papers, Truman Library; Hoffman, interview with Philip C. Brooks, October 25, 1964, Oral History Interviews, Truman Library; Behrman (2007:173–74, 177–78, 183).

71 Huempfer (2016).

72 Behrman (2007:174, 184–85, 208); Duchene (1994:171–72); ECA (1948:54), *First Report to Congress.*

73 "*La 5e Colonne américaine en France*" = the American fifth column in France. Price (1955:85); Behrman (2007:188–89, 197); *New York Times* (June 27, 1948); MacCormack (May 2, 1948).

74 Swanson (1976:125).

CHAPTER 11: SHOWDOWN

1 Policy Planning Staff, report, "Review of Current Trends: U.S. Foreign Policy," PPS /23, February 24, 1948, in *FRUS, 1948,* I: 522–23.

2 Marshall (approved by Lovett) to Smith, urgent telegram, undated 1948, Folder: "Russia [7 of 8]," Box 15, Subject File, Clifford Papers, Truman Library.

3   "Molotov's reception of Romanian Ambassador [Iorgu] Iordan, October 3, 1947, 3:00 PM," AVP RF, Fond 06, op. 9, P. 2, file 23, p. 14.

4   *The Essays on the History of Russian Foreign Intelligence*, V: 551–56).

5   *Washington Post* (August 11, 1961); *New York Times* (August 10, 1961); Middleton (March 16, 1947); Beevor (October 23, 2010).

6   Smith to Marshall, telegram, marked with a circled "3," May 10, 1948, Folder: "Russia [7 of 8]," Box 15, Subject File, Clifford Papers, Truman Library. For the Soviet version of the conversations, see Record of conversation with the U.S. Ambassador W. B. Smith on the positions of the US Government on international problems and foreign policy of the USA, May 4, 1948, AVP RF, Fond 06, op. 10, P. 1, file 4, pp. 1–12, and Record of conversation with the U.S. Ambassador W. B. Smith on the state of Soviet-American relations, May 9, 1948, AVP RF, Fond 06, op. 10, P. 1, file 4, pp. 19–29. Kuhn (May 12, 1948).

7   Pechatnov and Edmondson (2001:140).

8   TASS statement, "On Soviet-American Relations," May 11, 1948, *Red Star* 110, RGASPI, Fond 558, op. 11, file 387, pp. 44–45.

9   Reston (May 12, 1948).

10 State Department Weekly Review, Europe and the British Commonwealth: Smith-Molotov Exchange, undated, Folder: "Foreign Relations—Russia (1948)," Box 64, Subject File, Elsey Papers, Truman Library: 3.

11 Douglas to Marshall, transcript of U.K. House of Commons questioning on the Smith-Molotov meeting, May 14, 1948, Folder: "Telegrams: London [England]: Winant," Box 166, Foreign Affairs File, Subject File, President's Secretary's Files, Truman Papers, Truman Library.

12 Gromyko to Molotov, memorandum of meeting with Wallace (with Stalin's notations), April 21, 1948, RGASPI, Fond 558, op. 11, file 387, p. 6;– Pechatnov and Edmondson (2001:85).

13 Gromyko to Molotov, memorandum of meeting with Wallace (with Stalin's notations), April 21, 1948, RGASPI, Fond 558, op. 11, file 387, pp. 5–10; This memo was only made publicly accessible in Moscow in January 2016.

14 These candidates included Truman, Dwight Eisenhower, Harold Stassen, Joseph Martin, and Wallace's soon-to-be running mate, Glen Taylor.

15 Gromyko to Molotov, memorandum of meeting with Wallace (with Stalin's notations), April 21, 1948, RGASPI, Fond 558, op. 11, file 387, pp. 5–10.

16 Gromyko to Molotov, memorandum of meeting with Wallace (with Stalin's notations), April 21, 1948, RGASPI, Fond 558, op. 11, file 387, pp. 5–10; Moscow (May 12, 1948); *Washington Post* (May 12, 1948).

17 National Council of American-Soviet Friendship (1948); Stalin's response to Wallace's letter (with handwritten notations in red pencil), April 27, 1948, RGASPI, Fond 558, op. 11, file 387, pp. 13–21.

18   Durbrow to Marshall, May 18, 1948, in *FRUS, 1948*, IV: 870–71.

19   Gaddis (2011:311–14); Kennan I (1967:346–47); Kennan to Marshall, May 12, 1948, Folder: "USSR 1946–1950," Box 23, PPS Records, RG 59, National Archives; Kennan to Smith, June 18, 1948, Folder 2, Box 140, Miscellaneous Correspondence, Correspondence, Kennan Papers, Mudd Library, Princeton University; Kennan to Lovett, June 9, 1948, Folder: "USSR 1946–1950," Box 23, PPS Records, RG 59, National Archives.

20   Sedgwick (May 2, 1948); Thompson (2009:89).

21   Harrington (2012:181–82); Garvy (1966:9–74); Thieme (1999:576–77); Schwartz (1954:469); Zwass (Fall/Winter 1978–1979: 12, 18–19); Zwass (1975:159).

22   Steil (2013:273–74); Rees (1973:177, 189); Petrov (1967:122–23); Blum III (1967:180–81) Dietrich (2002); Harrington (2012:68–69).

23   "On June 19, 1948, Lucky Strikes reached an all-time high, $2,300 a carton at the official exchange rate." Barnet (1985:40).

24   Frank Wisner to Lovett, March 10, 1948, in *FRUS, 1948*, II: 879–82.

25   Phone cable from the chief commander of SVAG Marshal V. D. Sokolovsky and political adviser of SVAG V. S. Semenov to the Foreign Ministry of the USSR on the meeting of the Control Council, Berlin, March 20, 1948, AVP RF, Fond 06, op. 10, P. 43, file 583, pp. 1–2 (sent to Stalin, Molotov, Beria, Zhdanov, and others); Narinsky (1996:57–75).

26   Narinsky (1996:66); Narinsky (2011:166), citing the resolution of the Council of Ministers of the USSR, "On conducting monetary reform in the Soviet occupation zone of Germany," May 18, 1948, Arkhiv Prezidenta Rossiiskoi Federatsii, Fond 3, op. 64, file 789, pp. 33–35. Italics added.

27   *Washington Post* (June 13, 1948); Warren (June 14, 1948).

28   Smith (1990:486–89); Clay to Draper, June 15, 1948, FMPC-175, in Smith II (1974:678).

29   Warren (June 17, 1948).

30   Feigel (2016:305–6, 319).

31   Editorial Note, "The Establishment of the Berlin Blockade," in *FRUS, 1948*, II: 909.

32   Murphy to Marshall, June 19, 1948, in *FRUS, 1948*, II: 910; Harrington (2012:71–72); Clay to Bradley, CC-4843, June 23, 1948, Folder: "AG 319.1 Transportation Situation Reports, vol. II, 1948," Box 427, OMGUS AGO General Correspondence, RG 260, National Archives; Murphy to Marshall, June 21, 1948, in *FRUS, 1948*, II: 911–12; Narinsky (1996:66).

33   Narinsky (1996:66); "The German question," AVP RF, Fond 048/3, op. 11zh, P.70, file. 17, p. 454.

34   Smith (1990:492); Clay to Royall, CC-4880, June 25, 1948, in Smith II (1974:675–78).

35   Feigel (2016:301, 312); Sutherland and Canwell (2007:37); Narinsky (1996:66–67); Jean Ganeval to Bidault, June 24, 1948, Fonds 457, Carton AP-18, Private Archives of M. Georges Bidault, Archives Nationales; Bidault to Henri Bonnet, June 27, 1948, Fonds 457, Carton AP-18, Private Archives of M. Georges Bidault, Archives Nationales; M. Senin, "Memorandum on the Berlin question, 1950," AVP RF, Fond 082, op. 37, P. 216, file 112, p. 21; Caffery to Marshall, June 24, 1948, in FRUS, 1948, II: 916–17; Hetzel (Winter 2002:27); Buchheim (1999:94); Clay (1950:364); Narinsky (1996:61, 66); Laufer (1999:80–84); Middleton (June 23, 1948); Morrow (June 24, 1948).

36   Feigel (2016:319–20); James Riddleberger to Acheson, March 17, 1949, in FRUS, 1949, III: 693; Smith (1990:529).

37   Recovery in the French zone, where decontrols were delayed, was slower (Giersch, Paqué, and Schmieding [1993:4–5]). Behrman (2007:201–2, 205–6); Smith (1990:483, 523); Clay to Byrnes, September 18, 1948, in Smith II (1974:858–60). Perhaps the best analysis of the currency reform, coauthored by a great economist who was also a Marshall Plan official, is Kindleberger and Ostrander (1998), in Folder: "'The 1948 Monetary Reform in Germany'. . . ," Box 9, Subject File, Kindleberger Papers, Truman Library.

38   Feigel (2016:316); Beevor and Cooper (1994 [2004]:325); Harrington (2012:73–75); Howley (1950:198, 203); Raymond (June 25, 1948); Morrow (June 25, 1948).

39   Declaration of the Ministers of Foreign Affairs of the USSR, Albania, Bulgaria, Czechoslovakia, Yugoslavia, Poland, Romania and Hungary, 1948.

40   Gaddis (2011:328); Kennan to Frank Altschul, July 20, 1948, Folder 2, Box 140, Miscellaneous Correspondence, Correspondence File, Kennan Papers, Mudd Library, Princeton University.

41   Ignatiev's full first name is unknown. See D. Ignatiev, "Background for the 'Marshall Plan' and the revival of the military-industrial potential of West Germany," December 31, 1948, AVP RF, Fond 046, op. 8a, P. 74a, file 2, pp. 143–54.

42   Declaration of the Ministers of Foreign Affairs of the USSR, Albania, Bulgaria, Czechoslovakia, Yugoslavia, Poland, Romania and Hungary, 1948; Mastny (1996:48).

43   Mastny (1996:48); Buffet (1991:190).

44   Harrington (2012:99–100, 268–69).

45   Clay (1950:367).

46   White (1953:145).

47   Gaddis (2011:322); Policy Planning Staff, paper, "The Attitude of This Government Toward Events in Yugoslavia," PPS/35, June 30, 1948, in FRUS, 1948, IV: 1079–81.

48 Harrington (2012:62); Eben A. Ayers, diary, May 17, 1948, Folder: "Jan. 1, 1948–May 31, 1948," Box 20, Ayers Papers, Truman Library.

49 Harrington (2012:85–86, 100–101, 106, 110).

50 Douglas to Marshall, June 26, 1948, in *FRUS, 1948*, II: 924; Harrington (2012:80–81, 95, 103, 112); Paniushkin to Marshall, July 14, 1948, in *FRUS, 1948*, II: 960–64; Ray T. Maddocks to Bradley, June 28, 1948, Folder: "1948—Hot File—P&O 092 TS thru 381 TS," Box 9, General Administrative File, RG 519, National Archives; Harris (April 1949:13–16).

51 Murphy to Marshall, June 26, 1948, in *FRUS, 1948*, II: 919; Harrington (2012:86–88).

52 Clay to Royall and Jacob D. Beam, June 25, 1948, in *FRUS, 1948*, II: 918; Murphy to Marshall, June 26, 1948, in *FRUS, 1948*, II: 920.

53 Harrington (2012:59–60); Berkowitz, Bock, and Fuccillo (1977:45); Teleconference transcript attached to Mayo to Wedemeyer, April 2, 1948, Case 88/26, Sec. 1, P&O 381 TS, Box 102, P&O TS Decimal File, RG 319, National Archives; Douglas to Marshall, April 28, 1948, in *FRUS, 1948*, II: 899–900; Smith (1990:496–97) fails to mention Clay's comment that war appeared "inevitable," but highlights elsewhere that Clay was not averse to embellishing communications to achieve desired effects at given points in time.

54 Raymond (June 25, 1948).

55 Harrington (2012:82, 103); T. S. Timberman to Ray T. Maddocks, June 28, 1948, Case 88/59, and T. S. Timberman to Schuyler, June 30, 1948, Case 88/43, both in Section 2, P&O 381 TS, Box 103, P&O TS Decimal File, RG 319, National Archives.

56 Murphy to Marshall, June 26, 1948, in *FRUS, 1948*, II: 920; Jacob D. Beam, "Memorandum for the Record," June 28, 1948, in *FRUS, 1948*, II: 928.

57 Murphy (1964:317).

58 Douglas to Lovett, July 17, 1948, in *FRUS, 1948*, II: 968–69.

59 "Letter of the Soviet Ambassador in the USA A. S. Paniushkin to the US Secretary of State G. K. Marshall on the violation of the agreed decisions on Germany and Berlin by the western nations, July 14, 1948," AVP RF, Fond 192, op. 15a, P. 150, file 1, pp. 113–20; Leffler (1992:219); Cabinet Meeting Minutes, July 23, 1948, Folder: "July 1948," Box 1, Notes on Cabinet Meetings II, Connelly Papers, Truman Library.

60 Clay to Draper, "Berlin Blockade," CC-5222, July 19, 1948, in Smith II (1974:743–46).

61 Harrington (2012:127–28, 138–39); Clay to Bradley, CC-5118, July 10, 1947, in Smith II (1974:733–35); Gobarev (September 1997:15–17); LeMay (1965:411–12).

62   Harrington (2012:97).

63   Maclean was appointed co-director of a British-American-Canadian atomic power policy office in February 1947, thus greatly increasing his exposure to secret documentation on such issues. *The Essays on the History of Russian Foreign Intelligence*, V: 83; Harrington (2012:81, 119–22).

64   Harrington (2012:150); Truman, "The President's News Conference of July 22, 1948," in *Public Papers of the Presidents: Harry Truman, 1948*: 412; Truman (1974:17).

65   "The Positions of the Official Circles of the USA, England and France in the German Question at the London Conference," June 6–June 29, 1948, AVP RF, Fond 06, op. 10, P. 39, file 525, pp. 4–7. It is unclear the date on which the report went to Molotov, who annotated it in blue pencil, but it may not have been until early July.

66   "Record of Teletype Conference Between the State Department and the Embassy in the United Kingdom," July 22, 1948, in *FRUS, 1948*, II: 979–80.

67   Smith to Marshall, July 31, 1948, in *FRUS, 1948*, II: 996–98; Record of the conversation of the Minister of Foreign Affairs of the USSR V. M. Molotov with the U.S. Ambassador in the USA W. B. Smith on the transportation communication between Berlin and the Western zones, AVP RF, Fond 06, op. 10, P. 64, file 910, pp. 39–42.

68   Cecil (1989:86–87); Kerr (1990).

69   Smith to Marshall, August 3, 1948, in *FRUS, 1948*, II: 999–1006; Smith (1950:245); Harrington (2012:151–53); Narinsky (1996:68); Record of the conversation of I. V. Stalin with the U.S. Ambassador in the USSR W. B. Smith, representative of the UK Foreign Office W. Roberts, and the French Ambassador in the USSR Y. Chataigneau, RGASPI, Fond 558, op. 11, file 382, pp. 58–79.

70   Narinsky (1996:57–75).

71   Smith (1990:515–16).

72   Harrington (2012:153–54); Clay, Royall, Bohlen, and others, teleconference, TT-9890, August 3, 1948, in Smith II (1974:749–51); Clay to Bradley and Royall, August 4, 1948, in *FRUS, 1948*, II: 1011–13.

73   Clay, Draper, and Lawrence Wilkinson, teleconference, TT-1010, August 7, 1948, in Smith II (1974:755–63).

74   Harrington (2012:154); Marshall to Smith, August 3, 1948, in *FRUS, 1948*, II: 1008–9.

75   Smith to Marshall, August 5, 1948, in *FRUS, 1948*, II: 1016–17; Smith to Marshall, August 6, 1948, in *FRUS, 1948*, II: 1018–21; Marshall to Smith, August 10, 1948, in *FRUS, 1948*, II: 1030; Molotov to Stalin, submitting a "detailed record" of his conversation with Smith, Chataigneau, and Roberts, the "draft of a joint comminuqué"

prepared by the ambassadors, and a draft prepared at the Soviet Foreign Ministry, August 7, 1948, AVP RF, Fond 06, op. 10, P. 37, file 496, pp. 1–3.

76 Harrington (2012:155).

77 Murphy to Marshall, August 11, 1948, in *FRUS, 1948*, II: 1031; Harrington (2012:155–56); Smith to Marshall, August 9, 1948, in *FRUS, 1948*, II: 1024–27; Marshall to Smith, August 10, 1948, in *FRUS, 1948*, II: 1028–32; Clay to Draper, August 10, 1948, in Smith II (1974:764).

78 Harrington (2012:74, 158–59); Murphy to Marshall, August 13, 1948, in *FRUS, 1948*, II: 1038–40; Murphy to Marshall, August 27, 1948, 740.00119 Control (Germany)/8-2748, RG 59, National Archives; Clay to Bradley and Draper, CC-5632, August 21, 1948, in Smith II (1974:776); CIA 8-48, August 19, 1948, Folder: "NSC Meeting 18," Box 178, National Security Council—Meetings File, Subject File, President's Secretary's Files, Truman Papers, Truman Library.

79 Smith to Marshall, August 12, 1948, in *FRUS, 1948*, II: 1035–38; Smith to Marshall, August 17, 1948, in *FRUS, 1948*, II: 1042–47; Smith to Marshall, August 17, 1948, in *FRUS, 1948*, II: 1047–49; Record of Molotov's conversations with Smith, Chataigneau, and Roberts, August 12 and 16, 1948, AVP RF, Fond 06, op. 10, P. 37, file 494, pp. 1–28 and 29–61.

80 Harrington (2012:159); R. H. Hillenkoetter to Truman, August 6, 1948, Folder: "Memoranda, 1945–1948," Box 213, Central Intelligence File, President's Secretary's Files, Truman Papers, Truman Library; Memorandum for the President, August 20, 1948, Folder: "Memoranda for the President: Meeting Discussions: 1948," Box 188, National Security Council—Meetings File, Subject File, President's Secretary's Files, Truman Papers, Truman Library.

81 Marshall to Smith, August 17, 1948, in *FRUS, 1948*, II: 1054.

82 For example, Bohlen, memorandum of conversation with Henri Bonnet, August 21, 1948, in *FRUS, 1948*, II: 1060.

83 Smith to Marshall, August 4, 1948, in *FRUS, 1948*, II: 1011; Feigel (2016:331).

84 Smith to Marshall, August 24, 1948, in *FRUS, 1948*, II: 1065–68; Marshall to Smith, August 24, 1948, in *FRUS, 1948*, II: 1077; Record of the conversation of I. V. Stalin with the US ambassador W. B. Smith, the French ambassador in the USSR Y. Chataigneau, and the representative of the UK Foreign Office W. Roberts on the issues of the Berlin crisis, August 23, 1948, RGASPI, Fond 558, op. 11, file 382, pp. 58–79.

85 Smith to Marshall, August 24, 1948, in *FRUS, 1948*, II: 1067–68; Jacob D. Beam, memorandum, August 24, 1948, in *FRUS, 1948*, II: 1071–72; Marshall to Smith, August 24, 1948, in *FRUS, 1948*, II: 1072–74.

86 Smith to Marshall, August 25, 1948, in *FRUS, 1948*, II: 1078–79.

87 Smith to Marshall, August 30, 1948, in *FRUS, 1948*, II: 1093–96.

88   Djilas (1962:153).

89   Murphy to Marshall, August 31, 1948, in *FRUS, 1948*, II: 1099; Harrington (2012:164); Clay to Panuch, August 31, 1948, attached to Panuch to Clay, June 29, 1948, Folder: "Personal Correspondence," Box 13, Military Government of Germany File, Panuch Papers, Truman Library.

90   Molotov's cipher cable to Berlin (with instructions for the forthcoming negotiations of the four commanders in Berlin), August 31, 1948, in *The USSR and the German Question 1941–1949*, IV: 239 (sourced to AVP RF, Fond 059, op. 20, P. 4, file 29, p. 56). Fond 059 holds the cipher cables collection, which is now off-limits.

91   Sokolovsky subsequently offered to remove Berlin communications restrictions imposed after March 30, rather than June 18, but still insisted that agreements in 1945 limited corridor traffic to garrison supply—nothing more.

92   Murphy to Marshall, September 1, 1948, in *FRUS, 1948*, II: 1100–3; Bohlen, memorandum, "Brief for the President," September 2, 1948, in *FRUS, 1948*, II: 1108–9; Clay to the Department of the Army, September 4, 1948, in *FRUS, 1948*, II: 1109–12; Lovett to Paniushkin, September 26, 1948, in *FRUS, 1948*, II: 1187–93; Harrington (2012:165–66); Murphy to Marshall, September 4, 1948, 740.00119 Control (Germany)/9-448, RG 59, National Archives; Clay-Draper correspondence in Smith II (1974:798–826).

93   Harrington (2012:166–67); Clay to Draper, September 3, 1948, in Smith II (1974:814–15); Clay, teleconference with Royall, Draper, and others, TT-1131, September 2, 1948, in Smith II (1974:802).

94   Murphy to Marshall, September 7, 1948, in *FRUS, 1948*, II: 1134; Feigel (2016:320).

95   Friedensburg was deputy mayor of the City Council until August 14, 1948, when he took over from Mayor Louise Schroeder owing to her illness. Ferdinand Friedensburg, memorandum of conversation with Major Otschkin, September 21, 1948, Bundesarchiv Koblenz N1114/34.

96   Feigel (2016:320–21); Harrington (2012:167–68); Murphy to Marshall, September 10, 1948, 862.00/9-1048, RG 59, National Archives; Louis Glaser, "Political Report No. 14," September 11, 1948, Folder: "Political Reports 11–17," Box 903, Public Safety Branch Records, RG 260, National Archives; Louis Glaser, report, September 10, 1948, Folder: "Memos and Reports, Col Glaser," Box 71, Records of the Civil Administration and Political Affairs Branch, RG 260, National Archives.

97   Marshall to Smith, September 10, 1948, in *FRUS, 1948*, II: 1145–46.

98   Harrington (2012:172); Folder: "September, 1948," Box 75, Daily Sheets File, President's Appointment File, President's Secretary's Files, Truman Papers, Truman Library; Forrestal, diary entry, "Meeting—the President," September 13, 1948, in Millis (1951:487).

99   Smith to Marshall, September 14, 1948, in *FRUS, 1948*, II: 1157–60; The Soviet Ministry for Foreign Affairs to the Embassies of the United States, the United Kingdom, and France, September 18, 1948, in *FRUS, 1948*, II: 1162–65; Harrington (2012:173).

100 Jessup to Lovett, October 20, 1948, in *FRUS, 1948*, II: 1228–30; James Riddleberger to Lovett, October 21, 1948, in *FRUS, 1948*, II: 1230–31; Lovett to Caffery, October 22, 1948, in *FRUS, 1948*, II: 1231–33; Douglas to Lovett, October 26, 1948, in *FRUS, 1948*, II: 1234–36.

101 Foy D. Kohler to Acheson, February 2, 1949, in *FRUS, 1949*, III: 667–68.

102 Harrington (2012:170, 175); Memo for the President, September 9, 1948, Folder: "Memoranda for the President: Meeting Discussions: 1948," Box 188, National Security Council—Meetings File, Subject File, President's Secretary's Files, Truman Papers, Truman Library; Smith to Marshall, September 16, 1948, in *FRUS, 1948*, II: 1160–62.

103 Harrington (2012:141–42, 148); Tunner (1964:159–60); Anderson to Symington, August 4, 1948, Sec. 2, Folder: "OPD 381 Berlin (15 Jan 48)," Box 808, TS Decimal File, RG 341, National Archives.

104 "I asked [French] General Ganeval to advocate strongly with his colleagues that everything be undertaken in the near future for an average output of 6000t to arrive daily. This amount is in my opinion necessary for the maintenance of the supply if the Blockade drags on for a longer time." Ferdinand Friedensburg, memorandum, September 13, 1948, Bundesarchiv Koblenz, N1114/34; Harrington (2012:178–79); Royall, Clay, and Draper, teleconference, TT-1271, September 19, 1948, in Smith II (1974:867, 877); T. S. Timberman to Albert C. Wedemeyer, August 23, 1948, Folder: "P&O 092 TS thru 381 TS 1948 Hot File," Box 9, General Administrative File, RG 319, National Archive; Memo for the President, July 23, 1948, Folder: "Memoranda for the President: Meeting Discussions: 1948," Box 188, National Security Council—Meetings File, Subject File, President's Secretary's Files, Truman Papers, Truman Library; Clay to Bradley and LeMay, CC-5895, September 10, 1948, in Smith II (1974:852).

105 Truman II (1956:213).

106 William L. Batt, Jr., to Clifford, memorandum, "Public Opinion on Our Conduct of Foreign Policy," May 8, 1948, Folder: "William L. Batt, Jr., Director of Research, DNC—Misc. Correspondence [1948-49]," Box 21, Political File, Clifford Papers, Truman Library.

107 Eisenhower's name came up as early as July. William L. Batt, Jr., to Clifford, memorandum, July 22, 1948, Folder: "William L. Batt, Jr., Director of Research, DNC—Misc. Correspondence [1948–49]," Box 21, Political File, Clifford Papers, Truman Library.

108   Draft of Truman address on the Vinson mission, October 4, 1948, Folder: "Russia [8 of 8]," Box 16, Subject File, Clifford Papers, Truman Library.

109   Minutes of a meeting of Marshall, Bevin, and Schuman, September 21, 1948, in *FRUS, 1948*, II: 1178.

110   Statement of the President, October 9, 1948, Folder: "OF 198—Berlin Blockade," Box 830, Official File, White House Central Files, Truman Papers, Truman Library; Harrington (2012:190–96); Trohan (1975:239–40); Eben A. Ayers, diary, October 5 and 9, 1948, Folder: "June, 1948–December 31, 1948," Box 20, Diary File, Ayers Papers, Truman Library; Pogue IV (1987:407); Bohlen (1973:269); McCullough (1992:686).

111   Beevor and Cooper (1994 [2004]:327); Foy D. Kohler to Marshall, October 14, 1948, 851.00B/10-1448, RG 59, National Archives.

112   Isaacson and Thomas (1986 [2012]:462); Pruessen (1982:383–88).

113   Ambassador Douglas himself was discomforted, not knowing whether Marshall's aim was seeking a solution or sanction for the use of force. See Jessup, memorandum of conversation, September 27, 1948, in *FRUS, 1948*, II: 1193.

114   Harrington (2012:180).

115   Policy Planning Staff, "Position of the United States with Respect to Germany Following the Breakdown of Moscow Discussions," PPS/42, November 2, 1948, in *FRUS, 1948*, II: 1240–47.

116   Policy Planning Staff, "Résumé of World Situation," PPS/13, November 6, 1947, in *FRUS, 1947*, I: 773.

117   Minutes of the 286th Policy Planning Staff Meeting, September 28, 1948, in *FRUS, 1948*, II: 1196.

118   Vyshinsky, speech to the UN General Assembly, September 25, 1948, printed in Vyshinsky (1948); *New York Times* (September 26, 1948), "Russian Spurs U.N."

119   Kuznetsov to Vyshinsky, July 15, 1948, AVP RF, Fond 07, op. 21d, P. 53, file 21, p. 26; *New York Times* (October 3, 1948); *New York Times* (September 26, 1948), "Oil Company Denies Soviet Map Charge."

120   Instructions to Vyshinsky regarding representation of the USSR at the UN Security Council in the matter of the Berlin issue, October 2–3, 1948, RGASPI, Fond 17, op. 166, file 797.

121   Harrington (2012:189); No. 113 (361st meeting, October 4, 1948) and No. 114 (362nd meeting, October 5, 1948) in UN Security Council (1948); McCullough (1992:685–86).

122   Vyshinsky to Molotov, phone cable, October 6, 1948, RGASPI, Fond 558, op. 11, file 109, p. 98; Vyshinsky to Molotov, ciper cable, October 11, 1948, RGASPI, Fond 558, op. 11, file 109, pp. 110–11; Molotov to Stalin, cipher cable, October 12, 1948, RGASPI, Fond 558, op. 11, file 109, p. 112; Molotov to Vyshinsky,

NOTES TO PAGES 298-302

October 14, 1948, RGASPI, Fond 558, op. 11, file 109; Vyshinsky to Molotov, cipher cable, October 14, 1948, RGASPI, Fond 558, op. 11, file 109, pp. 121–23; Molotov to Stalin, October 15, 1948, RGASPI, Fond 558, op. 11, file 109, p. 124; Stalin to Moscow, CC VCP (b), October 15, 1948, RGASPI, Fond 558, op. 11, file 109, p. 125; Molotov to Stalin, October 15, 1948, RGASPI, Fond 558, op. 11, file 109, p. 130; Stalin to Moscow, October 15, 1948, RGASPI, Fond 558, op. 11, file 109, p. 130; Molotov to CC VCP (b), October 15, 1948, RGASPI, Fond 558, op. 11, file 109, pp. 132–33; From the diary of Vyshinsky, October 21 and 24, 1948, AVP RF, Fond 082, op. 35, P. 165, file 32, pp. 29–35; Lovett to Caffery, October 3, 1948, in *FRUS, 1948*, II: 1210–11; Molotov to Foy D. Kohler, October 3, 1948, in *FRUS, 1948*, II: 1204–5; Bohlen, memorandum of conversation, October 4, 1948, in *FRUS, 1948*, II: 1212; Bohlen to Marshall, October 8, 1948, in *FRUS, 1948*, II: 1215; From the diary of Yu. Dashkevich, November 9, 1948, AVP RF, Fond 082, op. 35, P. 165, file 32, p. 44.

123 Interview with Acheson, Wire II, July 9, 1953, Folder: "July 8–9, 1953," Box 79, Princeton Seminars File, Acheson Papers, Truman Library: 18.

124 From the diary of G. M. Ratiani, recording conversation with U.N. press department deputy Auden, AVP RF, Fond 082, op. 35, P. 165, file 32, p. 46.

125 Jessup to Lovett, October 16, 1948, in *FRUS, 1948*, II: 1227–28.

126 Jessup to Lovett, November 3, 1948, in *FRUS, 1948*, II: 1247.

127 Caffery to Lovett, October 27, 1948, in *FRUS, 1948*, II: 1238; Lovett to Murphy, October 30, 1948, in *FRUS, 1948*, II: 1239; Marshall to Clay, November 18, 1948, in *FRUS, 1948*, II: 1254–55; Lovett to Caffery, November 19, 1948, in *FRUS, 1948*, II: 1255–56; Dulles to Marshall, November 23, 1948, in *FRUS, 1948*, II: 1257–60; Murphy to Marshall, November 24, 1948, in *FRUS, 1948*, II: 1260–62; Murphy to Marshall, November 26, 1948, in *FRUS, 1948*, II: 1268–70; Murphy to Marshall, November 27, 1948, in *FRUS, 1948*, II: 1270–72; Marshall to Jessup and Bohlen, November 28, 1948, in *FRUS, 1948*, II: 1272–74.

CHAPTER 12: DIVISION

1 McCullough (1992:713–14, 717).

2 Haas (2016:250–51).

3 Acheson (1969:249).

4 "U.S. Zone Germans View the Airlift," Report No. 144, October 26, 1948, and "How Berliners Expect and Want the Crisis Settled: With Their Recommendations," Report No. 147, November 17, 1948, in Merritt and Merritt (1970:263–64, 267–68); Lovett to the Embassy in the United Kingdom, December 18, 1948, in *FRUS, 1948*, II: 1281; Harrington (2012:226–27, 244, 249).

5   Smith (1990:524); Howley (1950:230); Haas (2016:166).

6   Feigel (2016:322-24); Iber (August 24, 2015).

7   "Berlin Attitudes on the Air Lift: Further Trends," Report No. 141, October 4, 1948, printed in Merritt and Merritt (1970:261); Raymond (May 29, 1949); Middleton (April 7, 1949).

8   Harrington (2012:202).

9   Decision of the Politburo of the CC VCP (b), Politburo Protocol 66/35, "The question of the SVAG," November 12, 1948, RGASPI, Fond 17, op. 166, file 798, pp. 10-14.

10   Murphy to Marshall (with footnote from Bohlen), November 26, 1948, in *FRUS, 1948*, II: 1268-70; Marshall to Embassy in France, November 28, 1948, in *FRUS, 1948*, II: 1272-74; Harrington (2012:202-3); Memo for the President, November 26, 1948, Folder: "Memoranda for the President: Meeting Discussions: 1948," Box 188, National Security Council—Meetings File, Subject File, President's Secretary's Files, Truman Papers, Truman Library.

11   Payne (1949:3).

12   Gallup I (1972:770-71).

13   McCullough (1992:729-31). The full text of the speech is here: http://www.presidency.ucsb.edu/ws/?pid=13282.

14   Whitman (October 9, 1974).

15   Hoffman, interview with Philip C. Brooks, October 25, 1964, Oral History Interviews, Truman Library: 9-11; Callender (November 3, 1949); Van der Beugel (1966:187); Hogan (1987:302); *New York Times* (February 22, 1950; Beisner (2006:163); Behrman (2007:227, 265-66, 279).

16   Judt (2005:171).

17   Marer (1974:135-63)—see in particular p. 147; Marer (1984:156); Mastny (1996:57-58). On the operation of Comecon broadly, see also Bideleux and Jeffries (1998:534-44).

18   Ford (July 19, 1948).

19   Murphy to Marshall, February 17, 1949, in *FRUS, 1949*, III: 676; Lovett to the Embassy in the United Kingdom, January 12, 1949, in *FRUS, 1949*, III: 652-55.

20   Lovett to the Embassy in France, December 7, 1949, in *FRUS, 1949*, III: 1276-78; Lovett to the Embassy in the United Kingdom, January 12, 1949, in *FRUS, 1949*, III: 652-55; Murphy to Julius C. Holmes, January 13, 1949, in *FRUS, 1949*, III: 656-58; Clay to the Department of the Army, January 15, 1949, in *FRUS, 1949*, III: 659-60.

21   Reuter draft letter to Clay, January 20, 1949, Bundesarchiv Koblenz Z14/22. (It is clear from a nearly identical English-language American aide-memoire that follows in the archive that the letter was sent.)

22 Douglas to Acheson, February 9, 1949, and Editorial Note, both in *FRUS, 1949*, III: 671.

23 Julius C. Holmes to Lovett, January 12, 1949, in *FRUS, 1949*, III: 655; Douglas to Acheson, February 9, 1949, in *FRUS, 1949*, III: 671; Douglas to Acheson, February 14, 1949, in *FRUS, 1949*, III: 672; Harrington (2012:208).

24 Murphy to Acheson, February 17, 1949, in *FRUS, 1949*, III: 676; Caffery to Acheson, February 19, 1949, in *FRUS, 1949*, III: 678.

25 Douglas to Acheson, February 14, 1949, in *FRUS, 1949*, III: 673.

26 This conversation, between Wrong and Bohlen, took place on January 13, 1949. Cited in Douglas to Acheson, February 22, 1949, in *FRUS, 1949*, III: 683–85.

27 Beisner (2006:155).

28 Editorial Note in *FRUS, 1949*, III: 692; Harrington (2012:209); Jessup to Jacob D. Beam, March 14, 1949, 740.00119 Control (Germany)/3-1449, RG 59, National Archives. *Department of State Bulletin, 1949*, XX: 377–79.

29 Backer (1983:268).

30 Stivers (Fall 1997:590–91).

31 Ferdinand Friedensburg, memorandum, "Attlee Visit in Berlin," March 5, 1949, Bundesarchiv Koblenz N1114/34.

32 West Berlin would not become part of the Federal Republic until reunification in 1990. Ferdinand Friedensburg, memorandum, "Attlee Visit in Berlin," March 5, 1949, Bundesarchiv Koblenz N1114/34; Murphy to Acheson, January 26, 1949, in *FRUS, 1949*, III: 188–90; Murphy to Acheson, February 4, 1949, in *FRUS, 1949*, III: 191; Acheson to Murphy, February 7, 1949, in *FRUS, 1949*, III: 192; James Riddleberger to Acheson, February 9, 1949, in *FRUS, 1949*, III: 193–94; Editorial Note in *FRUS, 1949*, III: 194; Murphy to Charles E. Saltzman, February 17, 1949, in *FRUS, 1949*, III: 200; James Riddleberger to Murphy, March 3, 1949, in *FRUS, 1949*, III: 216; "Summary Record of a Meeting of United States Ambassadors at Paris," October 22, 1949, in *FRUS, 1949*, III: 288–89.

33 Harrington (2012:269).

34 The query came from American journalist Joseph Kingsbury-Smith.

35 Harrington (2012:264); Foy D. Kohler to Acheson, January 31, 1949, in *FRUS, 1949*, V: 562–63.

36 Italics added. Harrington (2012:265). German People's Council statement is printed in Carlyle (1952:378–80).

37 Foy D. Kohler to Acheson, February 2, 1949, in *FRUS, 1949*, III: 667–68.

38 Acheson to Douglas, February 25, 1949, in *FRUS, 1949*, III: 688.

39 Acheson (1969:269).

40 Interview with Acheson, Wire II, July 9, 1953, Folder: "July 8–9, 1953," Box 79, Princeton Seminars File, Acheson Papers, Truman Library: 9; Jessup, memorandum of conversation, February 15, 1949, in *FRUS, 1949*, III: 694–95.

41   Harrington (2012:269).

42   Central Intelligence Agency, "The Succession of Power in the USSR," January 13, 1948, Folder: "O.R.E. [Office of Reports and Estimates]: 1948: 6–15," Box 216, Central Intelligence Reports File, Intelligence File, President's Secretary's Files, Truman Papers, Truman Library; Grob-Fitzgibbon (2016:96).

43   *New York Times* (March 20, 1982); Harrington (2012:270, 273).

44   Jessup, memorandum of conversation, March 15, 1949, in *FRUS, 1949*, III: 695–98.

45   See, for example, Instructions for the Soviet financial expert regarding the negotiations in Paris on the Berlin question, Protocol 66/153, December 7, 1948, RGASPI, Fond 17, op. 166, file 798.

46   Jessup, memorandum of conversation, March 21, 1949, in *FRUS, 1949*, III: 700–702.

47   Jessup, memorandum of conversation, March 21, 1949, in *FRUS, 1949*, III: 700–704; "Summary of the Daily Meeting with the Secretary [of State]," March 22, 1949, in *FRUS, 1949*, III: 706–7; Caffery to Acheson, May 12, 1949, in *FRUS, 1949*, III: 752–54; "Record of Teletype Conference Between the Department of the Army and the Office of the United States Military Governor for Germany," May 13, 1949, in *FRUS, 1949*, III: 756–57; Acheson to James Riddleberger, May 17, 1949, in *FRUS, 1949*, III: 775–76.

48   Acheson, memorandum of conversation, April 1, 1949, in *FRUS, 1949*, III: 709–11; Douglas to Acheson, April 25, 1949, in *FRUS, 1949*, III: 731.

49   Attlee to Truman, April 3, 1949, quoted in "Exchange of Letters Between the President and Prime Minister Attlee on the Anniversary of the Signing of the Foreign Assistance Act," April 7, 1949, in *Public Papers of the Presidents: Harry Truman, 1949*; Behrman (2007:248); *Time* (April 11, 1949); Belair (April 15, 1949).

50   Huempfer (2016).

51   Behrman (2007:234); Harriman, statement before the Senate Committee on Foreign Relations, February 8, 1949, in Senate Committee on Foreign Relations (1949:108).

52   Behrman (2007:238–39); ECA (1949:68–71), *Fifth Report to Congress*.

53   Price (1955:245–46).

54   Charles W. Thayer to George V. Allen, Report, undated [1949], Folder: "European Trip, December 1948–January 1949, report to George V. Allen," Box 11, Subject File, Thayer Papers, Truman Library.

55   Behrman (2007:240–42).

56   Gaddis (2011:317–19); Kennan to Lovett, June 30, 1948, in *FRUS, Emergence of the Intelligence Establishment: 1945–1950*: 716; Frank Wisner, memorandum of meeting with Hillenkoetter and Kennan, August 6, 1948, in *FRUS, Emergence of*

the Intelligence Establishment: 1945–1950: 720; Kennan to Lovett, Folder: "Chronological July–December," Box 33, PPS Records, RG 59, National Archives.

57 Steel (August 13, 1992).

58 Truman statement to National Security Council and the Joint Chiefs, Spring 1949, Box 150, President's Security File, Truman Papers.

59 Kinnard (1980:38); Ritchie (2011:188).

60 McCullough (1992:741–42).

61 Haas (2016:257–58); Vandenberg (1952:475–80).

62 "Memorandum of the Fourteenth Meeting of the Working Group Participating in the Washington Exploratory Talks on Security, September 7, 1948," in *FRUS, 1948*, III: 234–35; Memorandum by the Participants in the Washington Security Talks (July 6 to September 9, 1948), "Washington Exploratory Conversations on Security," September 9, 1948, in *FRUS, 1948*, III: 237–45; Lovett to Harriman, December 3, 1948, in *FRUS, 1948*, III: 304; Acheson, "Memorandum of Discussion with the President," March 2, 1949, in *FRUS, 1949*, IV: 142.

63 Lovett to Harriman, December 3, 1948, in *FRUS, 1948*, III: 303, 305.

64 Truman, "Inaugural Address," January 20, 1949, in *Public Papers of the Presidents: Harry Truman, 1949*. Available here: http://www.presidency.ucsb.edu/ws/?pid= 13282.

65 Article 5: "The Parties agree that an armed attack against one or more of them in Europe or North America shall be considered an attack against them all and consequently they agree that, if such an armed attack occurs, each of them, in exercise of the right of individual or collective self-defence recognised by Article 51 of the Charter of the United Nations, will assist the Party or Parties so attacked by taking forthwith, individually and in concert with the other Parties, such action as it deems necessary, including the use of armed force, to restore and maintain the security of the North Atlantic area. Any such armed attack and all measures taken as a result thereof shall immediately be reported to the Security Council. Such measures shall be terminated when the Security Council has taken the measures necessary to restore and maintain international peace and security."

66 Haas (2016:260–64).

67 Frank McNaughton to Don Bermingham, memorandum, Folder: "April 1949," Box 17, McNaughton Reports File, McNaughton Papers, Truman Library: 3; Haas (2016:259–69).

68 Robert T. Elson to Frank McNaughton, teletype with excerpts of Lovett testimony, Folder: "May 1–15, 1949," Box 17, McNaughton Reports File, McNaughton Papers, Truman Library: 2.

69 "Summary of the Daily Meeting with the Secretary [of State]," March 22, 1949, in *FRUS, 1949*, III: 706–7.

70 Frank McNaughton to Don Bermingham, memorandum, Folder: "April 1949," Box 17, McNaughton Reports File, McNaughton Papers, Truman Library: 10.

71 Beisner (2006:129–30).

72 McCullough (1992:735).

73 Policy Planning Staff, "Considerations Affecting the Conclusion of a North Atlantic Security Pact," PPS/43, November 23, 1948, in FRUS, 1948, III: 283–85.

74 "The North Atlantic Pact: Collective Defense and the Preservation of Peace, Security and Freedom in the North Atlantic Community," statement by the State Department, March 20, 1949, in FRUS, 1949, IV: 240.

75 David K. E. Bruce to Webb, September 22, 1949, in FRUS, 1949, III: 452.

76 West Germany would not join NATO until 1955, but the Article 6 provision encompassing attacks against occupation forces covered its territory.

77 Halle (1967:185); Judt (2005:150).

78 Halle (1967:173–74).

79 Simms (2013:410); Leffler (1992:322); "Minutes of the PPS," October 18, 1949, Box 32, PPS Records, RG 59, National Archives.

80 Clay to Voorhees, FMPC 680, March 29, 1949, in Smith II (1974:1063). See also Smith (1990:534–35).

81 "Memorandum of Conversation Prepared in the Office of the United States High Commissioner for Germany," November 13, 1949, in FRUS, 1949, III: 309.

82 The Dawes Plan of 1924 allowed Germany to make reparations payments by borrowing money from American banks. The Locarno Treaties of 1925 involved Germany officially recognizing its new western borders.

83 Reynolds (2006:46). On the founding of the European Coal and Steel Community by France, Germany, Italy, and the three Benelux countries, see Centre Virtuel de la Connaissance sur l'Europe (CVCE): http://www.cvce.eu/en/unit-content/-/unit/5cc6b004-33b7-4e44-b6db-f5f9e6c01023/678ed16c-b497-41e0-a1b6-d8cb0594f2ef.

84 Jessup, memorandum of conversation, April 5, 1949, in FRUS, 1949, III: 712–15; Jessup, statement, April 5, 1949, in FRUS, 1949, III: 716; Acheson, memorandum of conversation, April 1, 1949, in FRUS, 1949, III: 709–12.

85 Jessup, memorandum of conversation, April 20, 1949, in FRUS, 1949, III: 724–28; Douglas to Acheson, April 25, 1949, in FRUS, 1949, III: 730–31.

86 Jessup, memorandum of conversation, April 11, 1949, in FRUS, 1949, III: 717–20; Jessup, memorandum of conversation, April 13, 1949, in FRUS, 1949, III: 722–24.

87 Acheson, memorandum of conversation, April 1, 1949, in FRUS, 1949, III: 710; Jessup, memorandum of conversation, April 20, 1949, in FRUS, 1949, III: 724–28.

88 Editorial Note in FRUS, 1949, III: 731.

89 George V. Allen to Charles Ross, April 27, 1949, Folder: "State Department,

Correspondence, 1948-49 [6 of 6]," Box 40, Correspondence File, State Department File, Confidential File, White House Central Files, Truman Papers, Truman Library.

90 Harrington (2012:272–73); Carlyle (1952:153–54); Bohlen to George V. Allen, April 19, 1949, Folder: "Correspondence A–K," Box 1, Bohlen Papers, RG 59, National Archives; Jessup to Acheson, April 12, 1949, Folder: "Jessup-Malik Conversations . . . ," Box 304, RG 43, National Archives; State Department, "Statement on the Malik-Jessup Talks," April 26, 1949, in Senate Committee on Foreign Relations (1959:57–59); Jessup (September 1972:392).

91 Specifically, those restrictions imposed since March 1, 1948.

92 Paris was designated the host city for the conference in accordance with France's Council on Foreign Ministers rotation rights.

93 Jessup, memorandum of conversation, April 27, 1949, in *FRUS, 1949*, III: 732–35; Jessup, statement, April 27, 1949, in *FRUS, 1949*, III: 735–37; Jessup, memorandum of conversation, April 29, 1949, in *FRUS, 1949*, III: 737–44; Acheson to the Embassy in the United Kingdom, April 30, 1949, in *FRUS, 1949*, III: 744–46; Acheson, memorandum of conversation, May 2, 1949, in *FRUS, 1949*, III: 748–49; Bevin to Acheson, undated [1949], *FRUS, 1949*, III: 749–50; Editorial Note in *FRUS, 1949*, III: 750–51.

94 Sutherland and Canwell (2007:142).

95 Harrington (2012:256–59); Tunner (1964:219–22).

96 Acheson press and radio news conference notes and statements, May 11, 1949, Folder: "January–June 1949," Box 72, Press Conferences File, Secretary of State File, Acheson Papers, Truman Library; Harrington (2012:274).

97 With the Western Allies determined to build up precautionary stocks in Berlin, the airlift continued on until September. Daily tonnage in May and June surpassed 8,000; a daily target of 8,944 was set for July 1949 to June 1950, evidence of plans to sustain the airlift indefinitely. Harrington (2012:255, 257–58, 274); James Riddleberger to Acheson, May 12, 1949, 740.00119 Control (Germany)/5-1249, RG 59, National Archives.

98 *New York Times* (May 12, 1949).

99 Acheson press and radio news conference notes and statements, May 11, 1949, Folder: "January–June 1949," Box 72, Press Conferences File, Secretary of State File, Acheson Papers, Truman Library.

100 Gaddis (2011:326); Kennan, memorandum, "United States Objectives with Respect to Russia," PPS/38, August 18, 1948, in *PPS Papers, 1947–1949*, II: 372–411; *Department of State Bulletin, 1949*, XX: 662.

101 Kennan to Webb, May 26, 1949, Box 163, Foreign Affairs File, President's Secretary's Files, Truman Papers.

102 Clay to Tracy Voorhees, CC-8467, May 1, 1949, in Smith II (1974:1137–38); James Riddleberger to Acheson, May 16, 1949, in *FRUS, 1949*, III: 772–73; Acheson to James Riddleberger, May 17, 1949, in *FRUS, 1949*, III: 773–74; Acheson to James Riddleberger, May 17, 1949, in *FRUS, 1949*, III: 775–76; George P. Hays to the Department of the Army, May 18, 1949, in *FRUS, 1949*, III: 776–79; James Riddleberger to Acheson, May 19, 1949, in *FRUS, 1949*, III: 779–87; McLaughlin (October 1, 1949).

103 Kennan to Marshall and Lovett, memorandum, "Policy Questions Concerning a Possible German Settlement," August 12, 1948, in *FRUS, 1948*, II: 1287–97; Kennan, National War College lecture, "Contemporary Problems of Foreign Policy," September 17, 1948, Folder 12, Box 299, Unpublished Works, Writings, Kennan Papers, Mudd Library, Princeton University.

104 Isaacson and Thomas (1986 [2012]:290, 471); Kennan I (1967:257).

105 Smith (1990:527); Isaacson and Thomas (1986 [2012]:472).

106 James Riddleberger to Acheson, March 26, 1949, in *FRUS, 1949*, III: 231.

107 Beisner (2006:138).

108 Murphy, memorandum of conversation, March 9, 1949, in *FRUS, 1949*, III: 102–5.

109 Smith (1990:538).

110 Smith (1990:536).

111 Louis Johnson to Acheson, May 14, 1949, in *FRUS, 1949*, III: 875–76; Bohlen (1973:285).

112 Reston (May 12, 1949); David K. E. Bruce to Acheson, May 14, 1949, in *FRUS, 1949*, III: 878.

113 Bohlen (1973:285–86).

114 Acheson, off-the-record press conference, Folder: "January–June 1949," Box 72, Press Conferences File, Secretary of State File, Acheson Papers, Truman Library: 2–7.

115 Bevin to Marshall, May 10, 1949, in *FRUS, 1949*, III: 870–72; Kennan to Acheson, May 20, 1949, in *FRUS, 1949*, III: 888–90.

116 Bohlen (1973:285–86); Isaacson and Thomas (1986 [2012]:472).

117 See, for example, Gaddis (2011:336).

118 Gaddis (2011:369–70).

119 Beisner (2006:117).

120 Isaacson and Thomas (1986 [2012]:474); Kennan I (1967:427).

121 *New York Times* (December 11, 1949).

122 Article 23 provided for extension to the eastern provinces upon reunification; this would take on great political significance in 1990.

123 Bavaria did not ratify it but allowed it to come into force.

124 Adenauer, Parliamentary Council Closing Speech, May 20, 1949, Bundesarchiv Koblenz Z12/33.

125 Office of German and Austrian Affairs, paper, "U.S. Position at the Council of Foreign Ministers," May 15, 1949, in *FRUS, 1949*, III: 898–99; Division of Research for Europe, paper, "The Soviet Approach at the Meeting of the C.F.M.," May 17, 1949, in *FRUS, 1949*, III: 909–13.

126 Kennan to Douglas, May 11, 1949, in *FRUS, 1949*, III: 872–73.

127 The United States Delegation at the Council of Foreign Ministers to Truman and Webb, May 24, 1949, in *FRUS, 1949*, III: 917; Interview with Acheson, Wire III, July 16, 1953, Folder: "July 15–16, 1953," Box 79, Princeton Seminars File, Acheson Papers, Truman Library: 7–8 (italics added); The United States Delegation at the Council of Foreign Ministers to Truman and Webb, May 26, 1949, in *FRUS, 1949*, III: 923–24; Acheson, memorandum on CFM, undated [1949], Folder: "Notes for Meetings," Box 78, Princeton Seminars File, Acheson Papers, Truman Library: 6.

128 Acheson, off-the-record press conference, Folder: "January–June 1949," Box 72, Press Conferences File, Secretary of State File, Acheson Papers, Truman Library: 2–5. See also interview with Acheson, Reel 2, July 16, 1953, Folder: "July 15–16, 1953," Box 79, Princeton Seminars File, Acheson Papers, Truman Library: 31.

129 Interview with Acheson, Wire III, July 16, 1953, Folder: "July 15–16, 1953," Box 79, Princeton Seminars File, Acheson Papers, Truman Library: 5–6; Acheson, memorandum on CFM, undated [1949], Folder: "Notes for Meetings," Box 78, Princeton Seminars File, Acheson Papers, Truman Library.

130 The United States Delegation at the Council of Foreign Ministers to Truman and Webb, May 28, 1949, in *FRUS, 1949*, III: 928.

131 Pechatnov and Edmondson (2001:144).

132 Nitze (1989:72).

133 Interview with Acheson, Wire III, July 16, 1953, Folder: "July 15–16, 1953," Box 79, Princeton Seminars File, Acheson Papers, Truman Library: 8; The United States Delegation at the Council of Foreign Ministers to Webb, May 30, 1949, in *FRUS, 1949*, III: 929–30; "United States Delegation Minutes of the 12th Meeting of the Council of Foreign Ministers, Paris, June 4, 1949," in *FRUS, 1949*, III: 954.

134 Interview with Acheson, Wire III, July 16, 1953, Folder: "July 15–16, 1953," Box 79, Princeton Seminars File, Acheson Papers, Truman Library: 8.

135 Acheson, memorandum of conversation, May 30, 1949, in *FRUS, 1949*, III: 935–36.

136 "United States Delegation Minutes of the First Part of the 20th Meeting of the Council of Foreign Ministers, Paris, June 14, 1949," in *FRUS, 1949*, III: 997–99.

137 State Department: https://2001-2009.state.gov/r/pa/ho/time/lw/107185.htm.

138 Status of the CFM, June 7, 1949, Folder: "1949: Paris Conference [May–June]," Box 142, Conferences File, President's Secretary's Files, Truman Papers, Truman Library.

139 Bohlen, memorandum of conversation, June 6, 1949, in *FRUS, 1949*, III: 960–62; Status of the CFM, June 7, 1949, Folder: "1949: Paris Conference [May–June]," Box 142, Conferences File, President's Secretary's Files, Truman Papers, Truman Library.

140 George P. Hays to Joseph O'Hare, May 31, 1949, in *FRUS, 1949*, III: 803–4.

141 George P. Hays to Joseph O'Hare, June 8, 9194, in *FRUS, 1949*, III: 807.

142 Murphy, memorandum, "Comments on JCS Analysis," June 1, 1949, in *FRUS, 1949*, III: 825–26.

143 Acheson to Webb, June 5, 1949, in *FRUS, 1949*, III: 826–27.

144 Webb, memorandum, "Meeting with the President, June 7, 1949," in *FRUS, 1949*, III: 830.

145 "Communiqué of the Sixth Session of the Council of Foreign Ministers," June 20, 1949, in *FRUS, 1949*, III: 1062–65; Interview with Acheson, Wire IV, July 16, 1953, Folder: "July 15–16, 1953," Box 79, Princeton Seminars File, Acheson Papers, Truman Library: 3–1; Acheson to Douglas, May 11, 1949, in *FRUS, 1949*, III: 873.

146 Acheson, memorandum of conversation, June 11, 1949, in *FRUS, 1949*, III: 980.

147 Acheson to Webb, June 14, 1949, in *FRUS, 1949*, III: 995.

148 Harrington (2012:294).

149 See, for example, Kempe (2011).

150 Interview with Acheson, Wire V, July 16, 1953, Folder: "July 15–16, 1953," Box 79, Princeton Seminars File, Acheson Papers, Truman Library: 1.

151 Interview with Acheson, Wire IV, July 16, 1953, Folder: "July 15–16, 1953," Box 79, Princeton Seminars File, Acheson Papers, Truman Library: 11–12. I corrected Acheson's recollection of the verse he sang and guessed the corresponding one in Bevin's tune; I changed "elevator" to "lift" in Bevin's part of the dialogue.

152 Interview with Acheson, Wire V, July 9, 1953, Folder: "July 8–9, 1953," Box 79, Princeton Seminars File, Acheson Papers, Truman Library: 1–3; Bohlen (1973:286); CFM memorandum, undated, Folder: "Notes for Meetings," Box 78, Princeton Seminars File, Acheson Papers, Truman Library; The United States Delegation to the Council of Foreign Ministers to Webb, June 20, 1949, in *FRUS, 1949*, III: 1038–39; Acheson, memorandum on CFM, undated [1949], Folder: "Notes for Meetings," Box 78, Princeton Seminars File, Acheson Papers, Truman Library: 14.

153 Acheson to Webb, June 14, 1949, in *FRUS, 1949*, III: 995; Acheson, memorandum on CFM, undated [1949], Folder: "Notes for Meetings," Box 78, Princeton Seminars File, Acheson Papers, Truman Library: 15. See Beisner (2006:110–11) on Acheson's leadership style.

154 Ivan H. Peterman, *Philadelphia Inquirer*, May 5, 1949, quoted in Department of the Army to Office of Military Government for Germany, May 6, 1949, Folder:

"Annexes," Box 10, Military Government of Germany File, Panuch Papers, Truman Library; *New York Times* (May 5, 1949); Smith (1990:525, 686).

155 Behrman (2007:247, 252); Presidential Address to Be Given in Honor of George C. Marshall by Chiefs of Mission of the Marshall Plan Countries, at the Carlton Hotel, Washington, June 5, 1949, Folder: "1949, June 6, Dinner for George C. Marshall," Box 39, Presidential Speech File, Clifford Papers, Truman Library; Vandenberg (1952:489); Truman, "Address at a Dinner in Honor of George C. Marshall," June 5, 1949, in *Public Papers of the Presidents: Harry Truman, 1949; New York Times* (June 6, 1949).

156 The Nobel Prize presentation speech is here: http://www.nobelprize.org/nobel _prizes/peace/laureates/1953/press.html (Hambro, "Presentation Speech"). Marshall's acceptance speech is here: http://www.nobelprize.org/nobel_prizes/peace /laureates/1953/marshall-lecture.html ("Nobel Lecture: Essentials to Peace").

157 Bark and Gress (1989:244); Editorial Note in *FRUS, 1949*, III: 275.

158 Adenauer (1965:183–84); Schulze (1998:301). The American high commissioner was John J. McCloy; the British high commissioner was former military governor Sir Brian Robertson.

159 Bark and Gress (1989:223).

160 McCloy to Acheson, November 25, 1949, in *FRUS, 1949*, III: 353.

161 "Memorandum of Conversation Prepared in the Office of the United States High Commissioner for Germany," November 13, 1949, in *FRUS, 1949*, III: 313.

162 Alan G. Kirk to Webb, October 1, 1949, in *FRUS, 1949*, III: 276.

163 Reedy (August 27, 1950).

164 Editorial Note in *FRUS, 1949*, III: 531–32; Walworth Barbour to Acheson, October 13, 1949, in *FRUS, 1949*, III: 534; Walworth Barbour to Acheson, October 15, 1949, in *FRUS, 1949*, III: 535–36; Dennis (2000:47, 53).

165 Orwell (October 19, 1945).

CHAPTER 13: SUCCESS?

1 Pechnatov and Edmondson (2001:88).

2 Golombek (1977 [1997]:304); Soltis (1984 [2002]:95–96); Shenk (2006:49, 170).

3 Soltis (1984 [2002]:78, 159, 161, 172, 189).

4 Kennan, National War College lecture, "Soviet Diplomacy," October 6, 1947, Folder 41, Box 298, Unpublished Works, Writings, Kennan Papers, Mudd Library, Princeton University.

5 During chess games with Lady Howe in London in 1774, Franklin negotiated to arrest the slide to war between Britain and the American colonies. Shenk (2006:89, 93–94); Franklin (December 1786).

6 Stimson and McCloy agreed with Kennan that the United States and the Soviet Union should have their respective "orbits," but for the opposite reason: they believed it would facilitate genuine cooperation. Isaacson and Thomas (1986 [2012]:239, 264, 275); Harriman to Cordell Hull, September 20, 1944, in *FRUS: Diplomatic Papers, 1944*, IV: 993.

7 Isaacson and Thomas (1986 [2012]:246); Kennan to Bohlen, February 1945, Folder: "Kennan, George F., letters. 1945," Box 27, Research Material, *Witness to History*, Books, Writings, Speeches and Writings File, Bohlen Papers, Library of Congress.

8 Burnham (1990:83); Washington to Foreign Office, telegram, June 3, 1947, T236 /782, Treasury Papers, UKNA.

9 Eurostat (2011:1).

10 Mutual Security Agency (1952:24), *Supplement*; Brown and Opie (1953:249).

11 Recovery was particularly strong in countries that were not primary theaters in the war (such as the U.K. and much of Scandinavia).

12 Eichengreen and Uzan (April 1992:16–19).

13 Transfers under the Mutual Security Agency—which extended military, economic, and technical assistance through August 1, 1953—boosted the Marshall aid total further. By the end of 1951, U.S. military support funds for western Europe amounted to nearly $5 billion annually—or $46 billion today. See Price (1955:162).

14 Eichengreen and Uzan (April 1992). The authors look at growth out to 1954 to account for lagged effects.

15 Eichengreen and Uzan (April 1992:33–34, 65–69). Reymen (2004) challenges Eichengreen and Uzan's numbers and inferences, but does find broad and significant Marshall effects operating other than through investment, the current account, or government spending.

16 "The decision was made to make our main effort in the ERP one of meeting dollar deficits." ECA Industry Division official Sol Ozer, interview with Roy Foulke, May 12, 1953, Folder: "January–June 1953," Box 1, Oral History Interview File, Price Papers, Truman Library.

17 See, for example, Chenery and Bruno (March 1962), Bacha (April 1990), and McKinnon (June 1964) on mechanisms by which foreign aid can, in principle, increase growth by alleviating fiscal constraints.

18 Eichengreen and Uzan (April 1992:22–26).

19 It can be argued, however, as I explain further on, that the British Labour government would have had a more difficult time financing its nationalization and welfare state agenda without Marshall aid.

20 Eichengreen and Uzan (April 1992:31–32, 65).

21 Eichengreen and Uzan (April 1992:26–31); DeLong and Eichengreen (November 1991).

22 Kindleberger (1984:10–11).

23 See, for example, Berger and Ritschl (1995).

24 The literature offers other explanations, which, in Eichengreen and Uzan's words, may be "of a subtler nature" (April 1992:49–50). One is that Marshall aid moderated conflictual labor relations and paved the path for the famed European "social contract." (See also Maier [Autumn 1977]; Hogan [1987]; and DeLong and Eichengreen [November 1991].) Since this corporatist model is clearly very different from the American, the connection may be more tenuous than subtle.

25 Kennan to Acheson, May 23, 1947, in *FRUS, 1947*, III: 224.

26 "Statement of Secretary Acheson before Senate Foreign Relations Committee concerning ERP," February 8, 1949, Folder: "July–December 1951," Box 73, Press Conferences File, Secretary of State File, Acheson Papers, Truman Library.

27 Reichlin (1995) documents the different ways in which Marshall countries chose to address stabilization challenges. Germany, for example, tackled inflation much more quickly and aggressively than France. Milward (2004) and Esposito (1994) offer more critical takes on the degree to which the United States was able to use counterpart funds to promote financial stabilization. They argue that U.S. influence was highly constrained by the need to keep non-Communists in power in France and Italy.

28 Milward (2004:62); Eichengreen and Uzan (April 1992:37).

29 Policy Planning Staff, report, "Review of Current Trends: U.S. Foreign Policy," PPS /23, February 24, 1948, in *FRUS, 1948*, I: 512.

30 Robert Oshins, interview by Harry B. Price, May 4, 1953, Folder: "January–June, 1953," Box 1, Oral History Interview File, Price Papers, Truman Library.

31 Behrman (2007:232); Hoffman (April 21, 1949).

32 Behrman (2007:199, 209, 249).

33 Eichengreen and Uzan (April 1992:42).

34 Former State Department official Lincoln Gordon (1984:55) recalled Harvard economist Seymour Harris discussing this.

35 ECA (1948–1951), *Reports to Congress*, June 1948–June 1951; Mutual Security Agency (1951); Mitchell (2007), *Europe*; Crafts (1995:261–62); Burnham (1990:106–7).

36 Minford (1993:120). Eichengreen and Uzan (April 1992:34) estimate additional growth of about 1 percentage point for the U.K. in the first year of the Plan. It was two to seven times this for Austria, Belgium, Denmark, France, Germany, Italy, and the Netherlands.

37 Hooker, memorandum, September 20, 1946, 711.61/9-2046, RG 59, National Archives.

38 State Department, policy statement, "Great Britain," June 11, 1948, in *FRUS, 1948,* III: 1092.

39 Casella and Eichengreen's (1993) paper gives the Marshall Plan considerable credit for halting inflation in Italy, but it was published a year before the book-length study of Esposito (1994), which demonstrates convincingly that this priority was home-grown.

40 In early May, De Gasperi suggested to U.S. ambassador James Dunn that it was not wise to form a government without the Communists, but allegedly came away with the clear message that Washington wanted a "purged Cabinet." De Gasperi is reported to have told Communist leader Togliatti: "You have to understand [that] it is a matter of bread," meaning U.S. aid. Casella and Eichengreen (1993:330, 338–39); Montanelli and Cervi (1985:150); James C. Dunn to Marshall, memorandum, "Current Economic and Financial Policies of the Italian Government," May 7, 1947, in *FRUS, 1947,* III: 901; James C. Dunn to Marshall, May 6, 1947, in *FRUS, 1947,* III: 893; Marshall to Embassy in Italy, May 15, 1947, in *FRUS, 1947,* III: 904.

41 Esposito (1994); Kindleberger (1984:11).

42 *New York Times* (June 2, 1948); *New York Times* (July 13, 1948).

43 Carlisle (2015:223).

44 Beevor and Cooper (1994 [2004]:15, 321–24).

45 Beevor and Cooper (1994 [2004]:325); Esposito (1994:46, 50); David K. E. Bruce to Hoffman, September 14, 1948, in *FRUS, 1948,* III: 649.

46 Statistical Office of the United Nations (various years); OEEC (1957); Mitchell (2007), *Europe.*

47 OEEC (1957); Mitchell (2007), *Europe.*

48 Esposito (1994:94–107).

49 Esposito (1994:109).

50 Correlates of War Project (June 2010); Singer, Bremer, and Stuckey (1972).

51 The National Advisory Council was one of two advisory boards set up by the Foreign Assistance Act of 1948 to aid the ECA administrator. It consisted of the secretary of the treasury, the secretary of state, the secretary of commerce, the Fed chairman, the chairman of the Export-Import Bank, and the ECA administrator (as long as the ECA existed). Its purpose was to "coordinate the policies and operations of the representatives of the United States on the [IMF and World Bank boards] and of all agencies of the Government which make or participate in making foreign loans or which engage in foreign financial, exchange or monetary transactions." Source: *Legislative History of the Foreign Assistance Act of 1948, P.L. 80-472.*

52 National Advisory Council Staff Committee to National Advisory Council, "Use

of French Franc Counterpart," January 29, 1951, Box 5, Subject Files, Progr. Div.-Country Desk Section, ECA/OSR, RG 469, National Archives.

53 See, for example, David K. E. Bruce to Dean Acheson, September 1, 1950, in *FRUS, 1950*, III: 1384.

54 Esposito (1994:48–54); Marshall, memorandum of conversation with Queuille and others, November 18, 1948, in *FRUS, 1948*, III: 677–82.

55 Esposito (1994:129); "Meeting for Discussion of the Italian Program, Viminale Palace, Rome," September 11, 1948, Box 40, Country Files, Adm. Serv. Div.-Comm. Rec. Section, ECA/OSR, RG 469, National Archives.

56 Mitchell (2007), *Europe*.

57 ECA (1949).

58 Casella and Eichengreen (1993:339–40).

59 Esposito (1994:133–42); ECA (1949:35).

60 Esposito (1994:172–79).

61 Esposito (1994:190–96); Acheson to U.S. Embassy in Rome, December 2, 1950, in *FRUS, 1950*, III: 1501–2.

62 Esposito (1994:196); Harlan Cleveland to Leon Dayton, October 20, 1950, Box 10, Country Files, Progr. Dev.-Country Desk Section, ECA/OSR, RG 469, National Archives.

63 The Saar only reverted to (West) Germany in 1957.

64 Gareau (June 1961:530).

65 See, for example, Julius C. Holmes to Acheson, September 1, 1949, in *FRUS, 1949*, III: 270.

66 Murphy to Marshall, November 5, 1948, Folder: "Misc. Correspondence, 1948 Campaign [2 of 2]," Box 22, Political File, Clifford Papers, Truman Library.

67 Smith (1990:294); Stuart Symington to Truman, "Interview with General Clay," July 25–30, 1946, Truman Papers, Truman Library.

68 *New York Times* (March 7, 1947); Gimbel (1968:150, 153, 164).

69 Wolf (1993:32); Bidwell (1970:22–24).

70 Krengel (1958).

71 "In response to the crisis [of the winter of 1947, which put strain on the transport system when canals froze], the military authorities directed all efforts to the improvement of transport and by August 1947 the situation was improving. In January 1948, the rail network, rolling stock and waterways were in a satisfactory state—no longer a constraint on the growth of economic activity." Source: Carlin (1989:44).

72 Berger and Ritschl (1995:218–20).

73 OEEC (1957); ECA (1949–1950), *Reports to Congress*, April 1949–December 1950; Mitchell (2007), *Europe*; USAID (undated): https://eads.usaid.gov/gbk/.

74   Statistical Office of the United Nations (1954:477).

75   Berger and Ritschl (1995:221–22); Ritschl (June 15, 2012); Ritschl (June 25, 2012). The London Agreement placed some of Germany's World War I reparations bonds, from the 1920s, on hold—pending future German reunification. In the 1960s and 1970s, when German reunification seemed less likely, the German debt authority purchased the debt back at a significant discount—it traded at 8 percent of face value in the 1970s. This reduced the payments that Germany actually had to incur after reunification. Source: Guinnane (August 13, 2015). Reunification in 1990 revived these debts from the 1920s, and the country began to repay them in 1995. Germany's final payment of $94 million was made on October 3, 2010. Source: Suddath (October 4, 2010).

76   Lovett to Marshall, December 9, 1947, in FRUS, 1947, II: 759; Berger and Ritschl (1995:227); Ritschl (June 15, 2012); Ritschl (June 25, 2012).

77   Smith (1990:230).

78   Smith (1990:453–54). The German word was not quite as pejorative as the official translation, as Semler meant it to refer specifically to American corn—which many Germans disliked.

79   Henry J. Kellermann, memorandum, October 31, 1947, 862.00/10-3147, RG 59, National Archives.

80   Stauffer, memorandum, April 30, 1948, 862.5043/4-3048, RG 59, National Archives.

81   Murphy to State Department, September 16, 1947, 740.00119 Control (Germany)/19-1647, RG 59, National Archives.

82   Gimbel (1968:117).

83   Smith (1990:392–93).

84   Schröder (1986:315).

85   See, for example, Van Hook (2004:69–89).

86   Smith (1990:234).

87   Murphy to H. Freeman Matthews, April 27, 1947, in FRUS, 1947, II: 910; Clay to Daniel Noce, April 29, 1947, in FRUS, 1947, II: 914.

88   Clayton, memorandum of conversation with Marshall, June 20, 1947, in FRUS, 1947, II: 929.

89   Kennan, memorandum, July 18, 1947, in FRUS, 1947, III: 332.

90   Robertson, memorandum, July 5, 1947, FO371/645514, Foreign Office, UKNA.

91   See, for example, Giersch, Paqué, and Schmieding (1993:1–2).

92   Smith (1990:452).

93   Smith (1990:484–85); Backer (1983:227–28).

94   Clay to Draper, October 20, 1947, Box 72, OSA 004 Germany File, RG 335, National Archives.

95   Buchanan (2006 [2012]:57).

96   Berger and Ritschl (1995:221–22). Since German unification in 1990 the planned reparations conference has never been held, and it is widely accepted that the country's war debts have been extinguished.

97   Folder: "January–June 1949," Box 72, Press Conference File, Secretary of State Files, Acheson Papers, Truman Library.

98   Smith (1990:235).

99   Gimbel (1968:152); Clay to Marshall, May 2, 1947, in Smith I (1974:346–49).

100 Price (1955:123); Ungerer (1997:26).

101 Eichengreen and Braga de Macedo (March 2001).

102 Richard Clarke, memorandum, "The Future of Sterling," February 25, 1948, T236 /2398, Treasury Papers, UKNA.

103 Eichengreen (1996:106).

104 Erhard (1953); Milward (1991).

105 Schröder (1986:321).

106 Kennan I (1967:447–48).

107 Milward (April 1989:252).

108 Milward (2004:62–63).

109 This is an argument with which Eichengreen disagrees. See, for example, Eichengreen and Uzan (April 1992).

110 Burnham (1990:99); "American Assistance," July 22, 1948, T232/101, Treasury Papers, UKNA.

111 Milward (2004:69–70).

112 Smith (1990:360).

113 Milward (April 1989:243–44); "Economic Consequences of Receiving No European Recovery Aid," June 23, 1948, Cabinet Paper CP (48) 161, CAB 129/28, UKNA; Bossuat (Spring 1984).

114 French calorie consumption in 1947 was 14.2 percent below 1949 levels. Sources: Food and Agriculture Organization of the United Nations (1950:74) and (1952:19).

115 Milward (1984:105, footnote 20).

116 Milward (April 1989:246).

117 Milward (April 1989:246–47).

118 Note, too, that German raw material imports surged after the outbreak of the Korean War, pushing the country into a balance of payments deficit that its neighbors would never have financed on their own. The Marshall-funded EPU allowed Germany to finance the ramping-up of its export industry, which would come to fulfill the American ambition of supplying western Europe's capital goods needs. See, for example, Giersch, Paqué, and Schmieding (1993:16–18) and Berger and Ritschl (1995:229–40).

119   Price (1955); Jones (1955).

120   See in particular Kolko and Kolko (1972).

121   Huempfer (2016).

122   The State Department chose to err on the side of deutschmark undervaluation, authorizing a greater devaluation than the West German authorities requested. Mc-Cloy to Acheson, September 20, 1949, in *FRUS, 1949*, III: 449; Webb to McCloy, September 21, 1949, in *FRUS, 1949*, III: 450; Bruce to Webb, September 22, 1949, in *FRUS, 1949*, III: 451–52.

123   See Steil (2013).

124   Kolko and Kolko (1972:360).

125   Central Intelligence Group, "Strategy of Soviet Delay in Treaty Ratification," Weekly Summary Excerpt, July 25, 1947, in Kuhns (1997:124); Pechnatov and Edmondson (2001:132–33).

126   See, for example, Gimbel (1968:163–67).

127   National Security Council, report for the president, "Report by the National Security Council on U.S. Objectives with Respect to the USSR to Counter Soviet Threats to U.S. Security," NSC 20/4, November 23, 1948, in *FRUS, 1948*, I: 662–69.

128   Mackinder (April 1904).

129   Grieder (2000:12); Djilas (1962:139); Pechatnov (2010:109).

130   Policy Planning Staff, "Considerations Affecting the Conclusion of a North Atlantic Security Pact," PPS/43, November 23, 1948, in *FRUS, 1948*, III: 287.

131   Gaddis (1982 [2005]:389).

132   Lodge to Vandeberg then Marshall, October 20, 1947, 840.50 Recovery/10-2047, RG 59, National Archives.

133   Abelshauser (1991:367).

134   Hillary Clinton (June 2, 2011): www.marshallfoundation.org/SecretaryClintonremarksJune22011.htm. See also Yacoubian (January 11, 2012); Oweis (October 22, 2011); *Bloomberg View* (January 13, 2013); and Frattini (May 26, 2011).

135   Troianovski and Karnitsching (July 31, 2013) and Jordans (June 4, 2013). See also Maier (June 9, 2012); Soros (June 26, 2012); Crafts (June 2012); and Agnew (August 6, 2012).

136   Thompson (March 12, 2014).

137   Casey, Solomon, and Mitnick (July 25, 2014).

138   Eichengreen (July 20, 2011); Peel (February 22, 2012); Crafts (July 2, 2012).

139   Davis (June 22, 2011).

140   Maiello (December 7, 2009).

141   *Wall Street Journal* (November 12, 2014); Page (November 9, 2014).

142   Gore (2006:11).

143   Tcherneva (May 12, 2016).

144 Judt (2005:156).

145 See, for example, Deaton (September 2013 [October 12, 2015]).

146 Lutz and Desai (January 5, 2015).

147 Gaddis (1982 [2005]:380–85).

CHAPTER 14: ECHOES

1   Sarotte (2009:39–45); Hertle (1996:173–74); "Kontrollen eigelstellt—nicht mehr
    in der Lage.—Punkt," published transcript of an interview with Jäger, in Hertle
    (1996:380–89); *New York Times* (November 10, 1989:A5); Sarotte (2014:139–
    53).

2   Sarotte (2009:63).

3   Zelikow and Rice (1995:103); Sarotte (2009:52–53); "Vor dem Schöneberger
    Rathaus in Berlin am 10. November 1989," in Auswärtiges Amt (1995:618–22).

4   See, for example, Simms (2013).

5   Sarotte (2009:64, 73–77, 79, 82–83); Teltschik (1991:60–61).

6   Sarotte (2009:55); Press reports, Folder 11, Box 108, 8c Monthly Files, Series 8,
    Baker Papers, Mudd Library, Princeton University.

7   Sarotte (2009:80).

8   Sarotte (2009:79).

9   Sarotte (2009:80–81); "Information von Wjatschleslaw Kotschemassow, UdSSR-
    Botschafter in der DDR, an Hans Modrow, DDR-Ministerpräsident, über ein Tref-
    fen mit den Bonner Botschaftern der USA, Großbritanniens und Frankreichs am
    11; Dezember 1989 in Westberlin (Auszüge)," reprinted as Document 10 in Na-
    kath, Neugebauer, and Stephan (1998:93–97).

10 Putin (2000:69); Sarotte (2009:19, 85–86, 93–94, 195).

11 National Security Archive (November 18, 2009); Sarotte (2009:71); Teltschik
    (1991:40–42); "SU und 'deutsche Frage,'" Document 112A, in *Deutsche Einheit
    Sonderedition*: 616–18.

12 Sarotte (2009:77, 107–15, 136–37); "President Gorbachev Interview to Soviet
    and German Journalists," in Freedman (1990:507); "Schreiben des Außenminis-
    ters Baker an Bundeskanzler Kohl, 10. Februar 1990," Document 173, in *Deutsche
    Einheit Sonderedition*: 793–94; "Schreiben des Präsidenten Bush an Bundeskanzler
    Kohl, 9. Februar 1990," reproduced in English as Document 170 in *Deutsche Einheit
    Sonderedition*: 784–85; Zelikow and Rice (1995:183–84).

13 Sarotte (2009:138–40); Harvey Sicherman to Dennis Ross and Robert Zoellick,
    memorandum, March 12, 1990, Folder 14, Box 176, Series 12, Baker Papers, Mudd
    Library, Princeton University.

14 Sarotte (2009:104); Ritter (2006:31); Schäuble (1991:293).

15   Sarotte (2009:142, 147, 159, 164–67); Szabo (1992:93); "Vorlage des Minis-
     terialdirektors Teltschik an Bundeskanzler Kohl," May 8, 1990, Document 270,
     in *Deutsche Einheit Sonderedition*: 1096–98; "Gespräch des Ministerialdirektors
     Teltschik mit Botschafter Karski und dem stellvertretenden Abteilungsleiter
     Sulek, Bonn, 19; März 1990," Document 223, in *Deutsche Einheit Sonheredi-
     tion*: 956n1; "Initiative Kohl-Mitterrand zur Europäischen Union: Botschaft des
     Staatspräsidenten der Französischen Republik, François Mitterrand, und des
     Bundeskanzlers der Bundesrepublik Deutscheland, Helmut Kohl, an den irischen
     Premierminister und amtierenden Präsidenten des Europäischen Rates, Charles
     Haughey, vom 18. April 1990," in Auswärtiges Amt (1995:669–70); *Time* (June
     4, 1990).

16   See Zelikow and Rice (1995:356–63) on the troop deal.

17   Albright (June 5, 1997): http://gos.sbc.edu/a/albright3.html.

18   Steel (1980:442); Bohlen (1969).

19   "The President's News Conference with President Boris Yeltsin of Russia in Hel-
     sinki," March 21, 1997, in *Public Papers of the Presidents: William J. Clinton, 1997*.

20   Halle (1967:132, 136).

21   Friedman (October 2008 [April 15, 2012]). Sestanovich (April 14, 2015) argues
     that NATO was not and is not a military threat to Russia. Unless Article 5 is worth-
     less, however, it is impossible to accept this. Countries that join NATO have at-
     tacked Russian military forces outside Russia and have joined in military actions
     that Russia opposes, all under the protective umbrella of Article 5.

22   More precisely, the Soviet Union incorporated the eastern territories of Ukraine
     and Belorussia in 1922. The western parts would be incorporated in September
     1939. The Republic of Belorussia would change its name to Belarus in 1991.

23   Friedman (January 25, 2016).

24   Asmus (2002:10).

25   Bush and Scowcroft (1998:514); *New York Times* (June 15, 1990); Plokhy
     (2014:25).

26   Asmus (2002:23–24).

27   The Council on Foreign and Defense Policy is a nongovernmental body estab-
     lished by veteran diplomats.

28   Gorskii (June 2001:29); Greene (June 2012).

29   Asmus (2002:115).

30   Gorbachev (2016:307–8).

31   Steel (May 26, 1997).

32   Asmus (2002:45, 122); Nunn (June 22, 1995): http://www.nato.int/cps/en/na
     tohq/opinions_24781.htm?selectedLocale=en.

33   Talbott (2002:132–33).

34   Asmus (2002:35, 43, 66, 70, 74); Clinton, "The President's News Conference with President Boris Yeltsin of Russia in Helsinki," March 21, 1997, in *Public Papers of the Presidents: William J. Clinton*, 1997; Asmus, Kugler, and Larrabee (September/October 1993:35).

35   NATO revised its military strategy in the summer of 1990 and stated that it no longer considered the Soviet Union a threat. (Asmus:2002:5, 26).

36   This is how Asmus (2002:25, 35, 54, 84) characterizes President Clinton's aims in expanding NATO.

37   Haslam (January 1998:124).

38   Gingrich et al. (1994:112–13).

39   BBC (undated); Sanders (March 6, 2014).

40   See, for example, Friedman (December 28, 2015).

41   Gorbachev (2016:309).

42   Finkel (January 30, 2016); Galeotti (November 26, 2015); Government of the Russian Federation (February 15, 2016). Medvedev did not deny the airspace incursion, as earlier Russian commentators had, but said that the Russian plane "might have flown in for a few seconds and immediately left."

43   Albright (February 18, 1997): http://www.nato.int/cps/en/natohq/opinions _25715.htm?selectedLocale=en.

44   Madeleine Albright, statement before the Senate Committee on Foreign Relations, October 7, 1997, in Senate Committee on Foreign Relations (1998:24).

45   See, for example, Dobbs (July 8, 1997).

46   Holbrooke and Danner (Winter 1997/1998). See also Holbrooke (March/April 1995).

47   Cohen (September 18, 1997).

48   Albright (February 15, 1997).

49   Asmus, Kugler, and Larrabee (1997 [Autumn 1996:7]). For an opposing view at the time, see Perlmutter and Carpenter (January/February 1998). CNN (1997).

50   Danner (Fall 1997).

51   Holbrooke and Danner (Winter 1997/1998).

52   Government of the Russian Federation (2000:10); Asmus, Kugler, and Larrabee (September/October 1993:31).

53   Shlapak and Johnson (2016).

54   "[W]hile fostering a cooperative relationship with Russia is desirable, it is important for America to send a clear message about its global priorities. If a choice must be made between a larger Europe-Atlantic system and a better relationship with Russia, the former must rank higher." Brzezinski (September/October 1997). Asmus (January/February 2008:101, 103) argued that NATO acted to "consolidate democratic change" in eastern Europe and "indirectly encourage[d] democratization in Russia."

55   Sestanovich (April 14, 2015).

56   Tóth (July 27, 2014); Simon (July 28, 2014).

57   Asmus (January/February 2008:100).

58   Greene (June 2012:9, 12).

59   Malling (March 2015).

60   Lukyanov (May/June 2016:32); *Izvestia* (August 11, 2008).

61   Ullman (August 12, 1999).

62   Jones (June 1, 2015).

63   Zubok (2007:66); Zubok and Pleshakov (1996:50); Pechatnov and Edmondson (2001:108–10).

64   Blome, Diekmann, and Biskup (January 11, 2016).

65   BBC (November 18, 2014).

66   Shchetko and Cullison (December 23, 2014).

67   Quoted in Rapoza (June 6, 2016). Italics added.

68   The conversation is recounted by Peres in Samuels (September 29, 2016).

69   Kennan (February 5, 1997).

70   Pechatnov and Edmondson (2001:95); Pechatnov (2006:257).

71   See, for example, Light (2006:67–68).

72   Government of the Russian Federation (2000:9–10).

73   Light (2006:51, 63–64); Greene (June 2012); Barysch (2005:118).

74   Kantchev (February 25, 2016).

75   Government of the Russian Federation (2000:10).

76   A Russian official with whom I spoke was highly critical of Polish influence over EU Ukraine policy. See Lowe (February 24, 2014); Foy (December 15, 2015); and Menkiszak (November 18, 2014). Johnson and Robinson (2005:13).

77   Government of the Russian Federation (February 13, 2016).

78   *Pravda*, "On the Forthcoming Conference in Paris," June 25, 1947, RGASPI, Fond 495, op. 261, file 119.

79   Mangasarian (May 15, 2014). See also Miller (February 26, 2016): http://mash able.com/2016/02/26/russia-europe-brexit/#8ZYEdG7wkqq8.

80   Greene (June 2012:18).

81   Rettman (November 17, 2014).

82   Birnbaum (May 22, 2015).

83   Halle (1967:156).

84   For a Russian perspective, see Bordachev (2005:57). For a German perspective, see Voigt (March 1996), who draws "a conceptual linkage between the enlargement of the EU and of NATO." On the American side, Asmus echoed Voigt on "a loose link between the EU and NATO." Asmus and Larrabee (November/December 1996). Kupchan proposed a merger of the EU and NATO into an Atlantic Union (AU).

Kupchan (May/June 1996). For a later American perspective, see Drozdiak (May/June 2010).

EU leaders have also long coveted an independent European defense capacity to supplement NATO. See, for example, Norman and Barnes (September 13, 2016). The initiative received a further boost from the election of Donald Trump as U.S. president in November 2016: see, for example, Barnes and Norman (November 15, 2016); and Emmott (November 30, 2016).

85   See, for example, Gaddis (February 26, 2009:7).

86   See, for example, Shlapak and Johnson (2016), which concludes that "as currently postured, NATO cannot successfully defend the territory of its most exposed members" in the Baltics. As of February 2017, twenty-three of the twenty-eight NATO countries had voted to support Montenegro's accession, which Russia strongly opposes.

87   Kennan, quoted in Friedman (May 2, 1998).

88   Contemporary Western public support for NATO is weak. See, for example, Stokes (March 18, 2016).

ILLUSTRATION CREDITS

p. 234: Bettmann Archive/Getty Images, http://www.gettyimages.co.uk/license/870
261732

p. 246: Courtesy of the George C. Marshall Foundation, Lexington, Virginia

p. 264: Framepool, shot number 658-004-880; http://footage.framepool.com/en
/shot/658004880-berlin-blockade-freedom-rally-dem-deutschen-volke-reichstag

p. 300: Bettmann/Getty Images, http://www.gettyimages.com/license/514880324

p. 338: Solo Syndication, cartoon by Leslie Gilbert Illingworth, ILW1566: *Daily Mail*
02/14/1949, accessible at https://timpanogos.wordpress.com/2012/09/08
/chess-games-of-the-rich-and-famous-truman-vs-stalin-over-berlin/

p. 376: DPA Picture Alliance/Alamy Stock Photo

p. 456: Public Domain

p. 457: W. W. Norton & Company, Inc.

p. 460: Courtesy of Stratfor Worldview, a geopolitical intelligence platform, https://
www.stratfor.com/analysis/geopolitics-russia-permanent-struggle

INSERT 1

1. Courtesy of the George C. Marshall Foundation, Lexington, Virginia
2. Courtesy of the George C. Marshall Foundation, Lexington, Virginia
3. Francis Miller/The LIFE Picture Collection/Getty Images, http://www.getty
images.com/license/50615616
4. Bettmann/Getty Images, http://www.gettyimages.com/license/515241892
5. Keystone-France/Gamma-Keystone/Getty Images, http://www.gettyimages.com
/license/106498810
6. Library of Congress/Corbis Historical Collection/VCG/Getty Images, http://
www.gettyimages.com/license/640462363
7. Hulton Deutsch/Corbis Historical Collection/Getty Images, http://www.getty
images.com/license/613515080
8. Walter Sanders/The LIFE Picture Collection/Getty Images, http://www.getty
images.com/license/53369607
9. Hulton Deutsch/Corbis Historical Collection/Getty Images, http://www.getty
images.com/license/613506876
10. Nat Farbman/The LIFE Picture Collection/Getty Images, http://www.getty
images.com/license/50519421
11. Bettmann/Getty Images, http://www.gettyimages.com/license/515242992

INSERT 2

1. Bettmann/Getty Images, http://www.gettyimages.com/license/514697924

2. Bettmann/Getty Images, http://www.gettyimages.com/license/515301662

3. Bettmann Archive/Getty Images, http://www.gettyimages.com/license/5152 08442

4. Thomas D. McAvoy/The LIFE Picture Collection/Getty Images, http://www.getty images.com/license/50511717

5. Francis Miller/The LIFE Picture Collection/Getty Images, http://www.getty images.com/license/50447180

6. U.S. Embassy, accessible at http://spartacus-educational.com/JFKbohlen1.jpg

7. James Whitmore/The LIFE Picture Collection/Getty Images, http://www.getty images.com/license/50514205

8. U.S. Army Signal Corps, Courtesy of Harry S. Truman Library

9. George Skadding/The LIFE Picture Collection/Getty Images, http://www.getty images.com/license/50493391

10. U.S. Embassy, accessible at https://upload.wikimedia.org/wikipedia/commons /8/83/Ambassador_Walter_Bedell_Smith.jpg

11. J. Wilds/Keystone/Getty Images, http://www.gettyimages.com/license/53023 1441

12. Abbie Rowe, National Park Service. Harry S. Truman Library & Museum

13. Hulton-Deutsch Collection/CORBIS/Corbis/Getty Images, http://www.getty images.com/license/613463476

14. Bert Hardy/Picture Post Collection/Getty Images, http://www.gettyimages.com /license/3435901

15. Marie Hansen/The LIFE Picture Collection/Getty Images, http://www.getty images.com/license/50497147

16. Margaret Bourke-White/The LIFE Picture Collection/Getty Images, http://www .gettyimages.com/license/50875038

17. Bert Hardy/Picture Post Collection/Getty Images, http://www.gettyimages.com /license/3296742

18. Yale Joel/The LIFE Picture Collection/Getty Images, http://www.gettyimages .com/license/53371537

19. Yale Joel/The LIFE Picture Collection/Getty Images, http://www.gettyimages .com/license/53371537

20. Bundesregierung/Rolf Unterberg, photo ID number B 145 Bild-00019708; https://www.bundesarchiv.de/imperia/md/images/abteilungen/abtb/ bildarchiv /galerien/bundeskanzler/b_145_bild-00019708_501x0_0_0.jpg

INDEX

Page numbers in *italics* refer to illustrations.